2021
RUGBY
ALMANACK

2021 RUGBY ALMANACK

Edited by Clive Akers, Adrian Hill
& Campbell Burnes

Cover Photograph
Front: New Zealand Player of the Year, Sam Cane *Getty*

A catalogue record for this book is available from the National Library of New Zealand

A Mower Book
Published in 2021 by Upstart Press Ltd
BDO Tower, Level 6/19 Como Street, Takapuna 0622
Auckland, New Zealand

ISBN 978-1-990003-15-8
© 2021 Text C A Akers, A D Hill and C M Burnes
The moral rights of the authors have been asserted
© 2021 Upstart Press Ltd

All rights reserved No part of this publication may be reproduced or transmitted in any form or by any means, electronic or mechanical, including photocopying, recording, or any information storage and retrieval system, without permission in writing from the publishers

Typesetting and design by CVD Limited (www cvdgraphics nz)
Printed by Printlink Ltd, Wellington

The editors welcome notification of any errors or omissions

Please correspond directly with the editors:

Clive Akers
Opiki
RD4
Palmerston North 4474
Phone: 06 329 1822
email: akers@xtra co nz

Campbell Burnes
2/37 Grotto Street
Onehunga
Auckland 1061
Phone: 021 717 150
email: cmburnes@hotmail com

Adrian Hill
1/212 Grove Road
Hastings 4122
email: adhill@xtra co nz

ACKNOWLEDGEMENTS

The publishers and editors acknowledge the assistance of the New Zealand Rugby Union and appreciate their co-operation and the co-operation of the 26 rugby unions in compiling the *2021 Rugby Almanack*.

KEY

In team record charts

BSC	Bruce Steel Cup
HS	Hanan Shield
RS	Ranfurly Shield
P	Mitre 10 Cup Premiership
C	Mitre 10 Cup Championship
cr	Mitre 10 Cup crossover match
H	Mitre 10 Heartland Championship

In individual appearance charts

15	fullback
14	right wing
13	centre
12	second five-eighth
11	left wing
10	first five-eighth
9	halfback
8	number eight
7	open-side flanker
6	blind-side flanker
5	right lock
4	left lock
3	right (tighthead) prop
2	hooker
1	left (loosehead) prop
*	retired injured or substituted
s	substitute
t	includes penalty try

RUGBY FOUNDATION

WE'RE HERE, BECAUSE ACCIDENTS CAN AND DO HAPPEN

Rugby is a contact sport, as a nation we love it and we play with enthusiasm, passion and pride And whilst no-one ever wants to consider the unimaginable; to permanently lose their mobility due to a rugby accident, sadly, it does occur

The New Zealand Rugby Foundation provides life-long support to catastrophically injured rugby players and their families, financially and emotionally, through all stages of their injury and rehabilitation

We work with New Zealand Rugby (NZR) to communicate the message of safety first, and are strong advocates for safe play

To continue with our life-changing work, we rely on the help and support of our valued members, and the generosity of the public at various fundraising events throughout the year

PATRONS:
Sir Graham Henry
Richie McCaw, ONZ

CONTACTS:
Lisa Kingi-Bon | Chief Executive Officer
lisa@rugbyfoundation nz | 021 212 7399

Ben Sturmfels | Commercial Manager
ben@rugbyfoundation nz | 021 144 1148

www.rugbyfoundation nz

CONTENTS

Editorial 10
Union Directory 12
New Zealand Rugby Union 14
2020 Honours 15
Five Players of the Year 19
Promising Players of the Year 22
New Zealand Representatives 2020 25
All Blacks Management 2020 26
Test Match Records of 2020 New Zealand Representatives 27
Bledisloe Cup and Tri Nations in New Zealand and Australia 2020 28
North Island v South Island. 38
New Zealand Maori v Moana Pasifika 40
Investec Super Rugby 2020 41
      Blues 52
      Chiefs 56
      Hurricanes. 61
      Crusaders 66
      Highlanders. 70
Results From 2020 First-Class Season. 74
National Provincial Championship Winners. 78
Mitre 10 Cup 79
Mitre 10 Heartland Championship 84
   The Unions
    Auckland. 85
    Bay of Plenty 90
    Buller. 96
    Canterbury 99
    Counties Manukau. 104
    Ngati Porou East Coast 109
    Hawke's Bay. 112
    Horowhenua Kapiti 117
    King Country. 120
    Manawatu 123
    Mid Canterbury. 128
    North Harbour 131
    North Otago 136
    Northland 139
    Otago. 144
    Poverty Bay 149
    South Canterbury 152
    Southland 156
    Taranaki. 161
    Tasman 166

    Thames Valley 171
    Waikato 173
    Wairarapa Bush 178
    Wanganui. 181
    Wellington 184
    West Coast. 189
Ranfurly Shield 2020. 190
Happenings. 193
2020 Season's Statistics 199
Current Player Statistics 201
First-Class Statistics 203
Referees. 209
Sevens Rugby 217
Club Finals 232
Secondary Schools Rugby 237
Women's Rugby
    The Almanack New Zealand XV 239
    Player of the Year 241
    Promising Player of the Year 241
    Season in Review 243
    New Zealand Black Ferns 244
    New Zealand Women's Representatives, 1989–2020 247
    Black Ferns Records. 253
    New Zealand Barbarians 257
    Samoa v Tonga. 258
    New Zealand Trial 259
    Results From 2020 First-Class Season in New Zealand 260
    Women's Club Finals. 261
    Farah Palmer Cup 262
        Auckland Storm. 266
        Bay of Plenty Volcanix. 270
        Canterbury. 274
        Counties Manukau Heat. 278
        Hawke's Bay Tui 282
        Manawatu Cyclones 286
        North Harbour Hibiscus. 290
        Northland Kauri. 294
        Otago Spirit 298
        Taranaki Whio 302
        Tasman Mako. 306
        Waikato 310
        Wellington Pride. 314
    Women's First-Class Statistics 318
    Women's Rugby Referees 2020. 322
    Women's Sevens Rugby 325

Chronicle of Events	332
International Results 2020	346
The Foreign Legion	349
Overseas Players in New Zealand First-Class Rugby, 2020	354
New Zealand Origin and First-Class Players Capped Overseas, 2020	356
All Blacks	358
Test Match Record	358
All Blacks Statistics	359
Playing Records of New Zealand Teams	366
Surviving New Zealand Representatives	371
New Zealand Representatives	374
NZR Annual Awards	399
Obituaries	404
Amendments	424

EDITORIAL

The year 2020 will forever be recorded as the year of Covid-19, a flu-like virus, which spread throughout the world and caused the biggest disruption to life on the planet since the Second World War of 1939–45. Countries closed their borders and went into lockdown. The majority of businesses had to cease trading and people were required to stay at home within their own 'bubbles' to prevent further spread, as there was no vaccine for this new virus. There was two-metre social distancing and 14-day quarantines.

When 2020 ended Covid-19 was still thriving in many parts of the world, but in New Zealand there was no community transmission, only imported cases in managed isolation and quarantine facilities. We have been a lot more fortunate than many, many other countries.

Future readers of the *2021 Rugby Almanack* who were not alive in 2020, and therefore with no first-hand experience of it, will be able to get some idea of what the New Zealand public went through by reading our annual *Chronicle of Events* chapter which records it all.

How did it affect rugby in New Zealand in 2020? On the field, Investec Super Rugby was suspended after seven rounds and did not resume; club and school rugby eventually started in June after a three-month delay; the All Blacks' three home July Tests and end-of-year tour to the northern hemisphere were cancelled; The Black Ferns played none of their scheduled eight Tests; the last four tournaments on the 2019/20 World Sevens Series circuit for the men's and women's teams were cancelled, as were the first four tournaments of the 2020/21 series which included the New Zealand leg at Hamilton in February 2021. The sevens teams were also due to appear at the Olympic Games in Tokyo which were postponed to 2021. Also cancelled were the Heartland Championship and the Jock Hobbs Memorial Under 19 competition, as were the regional and national sevens tournaments. The New Zealand Under 20 and Heartland teams did not take the field and the Maori All Blacks did not play international opposition for the first time since 2011. However, they were victorious in a historic exhibition match against a Moana Pasifika side. The Super Rugby clubs cancelled their usual age-grade competitions for their respective provinces. The newly created second-tier national team, styled as *All Blacks XV*, was scheduled to be reintroduced for an end-of-year tour against similar opponents but never happened.

Off the field, at the end of the year New Zealand Rugby (NZR) estimated their loss for the year to be in the tens of millions of dollars. With reserves of close to $93 million at the end of 2019, the national body was in the fortunate position of being able to absorb the loss . . . this year. Nevertheless, NZR, the Super Rugby clubs and the provincial unions reduced staff numbers, players took a percentage wage freeze and many other costs were reduced. It will be interesting to see the financial results declared by the provincial unions in the coming months for 2020, as they had to absorb reduced revenues by reducing costs.

But, better late than never, there was eventually some rugby played. Super Rugby Aotearoa was created for our five clubs in a double round competition in front of very healthy crowds, with a newly created trophy known as Te Kotahi Aotearoa, which translates to Stand As One New Zealand, won by the Crusaders. It was the only rugby being played anywhere in the world at the time. A resuscitation of the inter-island fixture saw the South snatch a win over the North with a try from Crusaders wing Will Jordan after the 80th minute in a game played under Alert Level 2 conditions at Wellington with no crowd in attendance.

In the provincial first-class competitions, the Mitre 10 Cup Premiership and Farah Palmer Cup finals both produced gripping, low-scoring matches of a one-point margin. Tasman successfully defended their crown against Auckland 13–12 in the Premiership and Canterbury made it four consecutive titles in the Farah Palmer Cup with a try after the 80th minute to defeat Waikato 8–7. With a convincing second-half display Hawke's Bay defeated somewhat surprise finalists Northland 36–24 to win the Mitre 10 Cup Championship. Hawke's Bay also completed the season with the Ranfurly Shield which had started in Canterbury, up to Taranaki, down to Otago and up to Hawke's Bay, a journey of some 2200 kilometres for the Log of Wood.

The All Blacks had a new coach in Ian Foster and a new captain in Sam Cane. Six Tests were played for a return of three wins, one draw and two losses. The loss to Argentina in Sydney was a first-ever loss to Argentina, and the manner of it was eerily reminiscent of the All Blacks' defeat to England in 2019's World Cup semi-final. The Black Ferns had two fixtures against a NZ Barbarians side. With the World Cup to be held here in 2021 this was vital match play.

NZR made a momentous decision during the year. A review was undertaken in April into all aspects of New Zealand's current participation in Super Rugby with Argentina, Australia and South Africa. The *Aratipu* report came back in July with a recommendation that New Zealand's best interest would be served if our five clubs were involved in a competition of 8–10 teams with Australia and at least one Pasifika team. NZR immediately announced it would pursue this recommendation, and Super 12/14/15/18/15, a major part of New Zealand rugby since 1996, is now no more.

A decision still to be made is the format of the Mitre 10 Cup in 2021. In November NZR presented a proposal to the Mitre 10 Cup unions of a format change with the 14 unions separated into North Island and South Island pools of seven teams each plus four crossover matches to replace the current Premiership and Championship divisions of seven teams each plus four crossover matches. The new proposal would mean all 14 unions still play a minimum of 10 matches, but all 10 matches would now be for the same one prize with just one set of playoffs and promotion/relegation made obsolete. It had been trialled in this year's Farah Palmer Cup competition and the benefit to NZR would be a substantial saving in travel costs.

The year 2020 was the 150th anniversary of *organised* rugby in New Zealand and passed relatively unnoticed due to Covid-19. On 14 May 1870 Nelson Football Club played Nelson College in the first match in this country played between two constituted organisations (clubs). There may have been a handful of pick-up/scratch/challenge matches around the country prior to 1870, but these ad-hoc matches were played by teams that did not exist before their match or after their match, unlike the two clubs at Nelson on 14 May 1870.

With our current situation of no Covid-19 in the New Zealand community there is optimism of all usual domestic competitions being played in 2021, but the same cannot be said for international interaction with the virus still surging in many parts of the world, despite a vaccine being rolled out. Nevertheless, it is to be hoped our hosting of the Rugby World Cup 2021 and Tokyo's Olympic Games will proceed uninterrupted as the Black Ferns, the All Blacks Sevens and Black Ferns Sevens all have very realistic chances of winning.

The All Blacks have a programme of 14 Tests pencilled in for 2021 with room for two more to be added, while a mini trans-Tasman Super Rugby competition with Australia, after both countries have finished their own competitions, is marked for May and June.

The putting together of the *Rugby Almanack* requires contact with a lot of people for information and confirmation. It just would not happen without the cooperation of NZR, the Super Rugby clubs and the provincial unions as well as our loyal dependable contributors Chris Jansen *(Referees)*, John Lea *(The Foreign Legion)*, Rikki Swannell *(Women's Review)*, Brent Drabble, Lindsay Knight, Geoff Miller, Paul Neazor and Matt Shaw.

Clive Akers, Adrian Hill, Campbell Burnes
January 2021

UNION DIRECTORY

New Zealand Rugby Union
Auckland office:
　3B, 125 The Strand, Parnell, Auckland
　Postal: PO Box 2453, Shortland Street,
　　Auckland 1140
　Telephone: 09 300 4995
Wellington office:
　New Zealand Rugby House, Level 4,
　100 Molesworth Street, Wellington
　Postal: PO Box 2172, Wellington 6140
　Telephone: 04 499 4995
email: info@nzrugby.co.nz
Websites: www.allblacks.com
　www.nzrugby.co.nz

Auckland RU
Office: Eden Park, Walters Rd, Auckland
Postal: PO Box 56-152, Dominion Rd,
Auckland 1446
Telephone: 09 815 4850
Fax: 09 849 5300
email: info@aucklandrugby.co.nz
Website: www.aucklandrugby.co.nz

Bay of Plenty RFU
Office: University of Waikato HP Centre,
　Blake Park, 52 Miro Street, Mt Manganui
Postal: PO Box 4058, Mt Maunganui South 3149
Telephone: 07 574 2037
Fax: 07 574 2046
email: reception@boprugby.co.nz
Website: www.boprugby.co.nz

Buller RFU
Office: Craddock Park, Domett Street, Westport
Postal: PO Box 361, Westport 7866
Telephone: 027 789 8330
email: andrew@bullerrugby.co.nz
Website: www.bullerrugby.co.nz

Canterbury RFU
Office: Rugby Park, Cnr Malvern and Rutland
　Streets, Christchurch
Postal: PO Box 755, Christchurch 8140
Telephone: 03 379 8300
Fax: 03 365 3565
email: info@crfu.co.nz
Website: www.crfu.co.nz

Counties Manukau RFU
Office: Navigation Homes Stadium,
　Stadium Drive, Pukekohe
Postal: PO Box 175, Pukekohe 2340
Telephone: 09 237 0033
Fax: 0800 478429
email: admin@steelers.co.nz
Website: www.steelers.co.nz

Ngati Porou East Coast RFU
Office: Whakarua Park, Ruatoria
Postal: PO Box 106, Ruatoria 4032
Telephone: 06 864 8812
Fax: 06 864 8813
email: admin@npec.co.nz
Website: www.npec.co.nz

Hawke's Bay RFU
Office: 3 Orotu Drive, Poraiti, Napier
Postal: PO Box 201, Napier 4140
Telephone: 06 835 7617
email: admin@hbrugby.co.nz
Website: www.hbmagpies.co.nz

Horowhenua Kapiti RFU
Office: 15-19 Bristol Street, Levin
Postal: PO Box 503, Levin 5540
Telephone: 06 367 8059
email: office@hkrfu.co.nz
Website: www.hkrfu.co.nz

King Country RFU
Office: Cotter St, Te Kuiti
Postal: PO Box 159, Te Kuiti
Telephone: 07 878 7545
email: generalmanager@kingcountryrugby.co.nz

Manawatu RU
Office: Central Energy Trust Arena,
　61 Pascal Street, Palmerston North
Postal: PO Box 1729, Palmerston North 4440
Telephone: 06 357 2633
email: info@manawaturugby.co.nz
Website: www.manawaturugby.co.nz

Mid Canterbury RU
Office: A&P Showgrounds, Brucefield Avenue,
　Ashburton
Postal: PO Box 98, Ashburton 7740
Telephone: 03 308 8718
Fax: 03 308 0103
email: admin@midcanterburyrugby.co.nz
Website: www.midcanterburyrugby.co.nz

North Harbour RU
Office: North Harbour Stadium,
　Stadium Drive, Albany
Postal: PO Box 300 492, Albany 0752
Telephone: 09 447 2100
Fax: 09 447 2101
email: harbour@harbourrugby.co.nz
Website: www.harbourrugby.co.nz

North Otago RFU
Office: Shop 6a, Thames Arcade,
　203 Thames Street, Oamaru
Postal: PO Box 102, Oamaru 9444
Telephone: 03 434 2053　*Fax:* 03 434 2054
email: admin@northotagorugby.co.nz
Website: www.northotagorugby.co.nz

Northland RU
Office: 50 Kioreroa Rd, Whangarei
Postal: PO Box 584, Whangarei 0140
Telephone: 09 438 4743
Fax: 09 438 9185
email: reception@northlandrugby.co.nz
Website: www.taniwha.co.nz

Otago RFU
Office: Forsyth Barr Stadium, Anzac Avenue, Dunedin
Postal: PO Box 691, Dunedin 9054
Telephone: 03 477 0928
email: orfu@orfu.co.nz
Website: www.orfu.co.nz

Poverty Bay RFU
Office: River Oak Mews
74 Grey St, Gisborne
Postal: PO Box 520, Gisborne 4040
Telephone: 06 868 9968
Fax: 06 868 9954
email: karen@povertybayrugby.co.nz
Website: www.povertybayrugby.co.nz

Rugby Southland
Office: Surrey Park, Surrey Park Road, Invercargill
Postal: PO Box 291, Invercargill 9840
Telephone: 03 216 8694
Fax: 03 216 8695
email: reception@rugbysouthland.co.nz
Website: www.rugbysouthland.co.nz

South Canterbury RFU
Office: Alpine Energy Stadium, Church Street, Timaru
Postal: PO Box 787, Timaru 7910
Telephone: 03 688 8653
Fax: 03 688 6179
email: clint@scrfu.co.nz
Website: www.scrfu.co.nz

Taranaki RFU
Office: Pukekura Raceway, Rogan Street, New Plymouth
Postal: PO Box 5004, New Plymouth 4343
Telephone: 06 759 0167
email: mel@trfu.co.nz
Website: www.trfu.co.nz

Tasman RU
Office: Hathaway Terrace, Nelson
Postal: PO Box 7157, Nelson 7042
Telephone: 03 548 7030
email: info@tasmanrugby.co.nz
Website: www.tasmanrugby.co.nz

Thames Valley RFU
Office: 140a Normanby Rd, Paeroa
Postal: PO Box 245, Paeroa 3600
Telephone: 07 862 6352
email: swampfoxes@xtra.co.nz
Website: www.thamesvalleyswampfoxes.co.nz

Waikato RU
Office: FMG Stadium,
128 Seddon Road, Hamilton
Postal: PO Box 9507, Hamilton 3240
Telephone: 07 839 5675
Fax: 07 838 1713
email: admin@mooloo.co.nz
Website: www.mooloo.co.nz

Wairarapa Bush RFU
Office: 149 Dixon St, Masterton
Postal: PO Box 372, Masterton 5840
Telephone: 06 378 8369
email: info@waibush.co.nz
Website: www.waibush.co.nz

Wanganui RFU
Office: 40 Maria Place Extn, Wanganui
Postal: PO Box 4213, Wanganui 4541
Telephone: 06 349 2313
email: info@wanganuirugby.co.nz
Website: www.wanganuirugby.co.nz

Wellington RFU
Office: 191 Thorndon Quay, Wellington
Postal: PO Box 7201, Wellington South 6242
Telephone: 04 389 0020
Fax: 04 389 0889
email: mail@wrfu.co.nz
Website: www.wrfu.co.nz

West Coast RFU
Office: 123 Main South Rd, Greymouth
Postal: PO Box 31, Greymouth 7840
Telephone: 03 768 7822
email: wcrugby@netaccess.co.nz
Website: www.westcoastrfu.co.nz

New Zealand Rugby Museum
326 Main St, Palmerston North
Postal: PO Box 36, Palmerston North 4440
Telephone: 06 358 6947
Fax: 06 358 6947
email: info@rugbymuseum.co.nz
Website: www.rugbymuseum.co.nz

NEW ZEALAND RUGBY UNION

OFFICE BEARERS
2020–2021

Patron
I.A. Kirkpatrick MBE

President
W.M. Osborne (*Tauranga*)

Vice-president
M.G. Spence (*Nelson*)

Chairman
B.G. Impey

Board

Elected members:	B.N. Mackey (*Auckland*), J.S. Mitchell (*Canterbury*), S.R. Nixon (*North Harbour*), Sir Michael Jones KNZM, MNZM (*Auckland*).
Appointed members:	B.T.C. Campbell (*Melbourne*), R.P. Dellabarca (*Auckland*), B.G. Impey (*Auckland*), J.R. Kerr (*Hamilton*).
Maori representative:	Dr F.R. Palmer ONZM (*Manawatu*).

Chief Executive Officer
M.P. Robinson

Life Members
R.A. Guy ONZM; E.J. Tonks CBE*; R.A. Fisher ONZM;
J.A. Sturgeon ONZM, MBE, A.R. Leslie MNZM;
Sir Graham Henry KNZM; R.J. Littlejohn; M.T. Eagle ONZM.
* died during October

NZRU Team Coaches, Selectors

New Zealand:	I.D. Foster (*selector, head coach*), J.C. Plumtree (*selector, forwards coach*), G.E. Feek, S.J. McLeod, B.J. Mooar (*assistants*), G.J. Fox (*selector*).
New Zealand Maori:	C.R. McMillan (*coach*), T.E. Brown (*assistant*), R.Q. Randle (*assistant*).
New Zealand Sevens:	C. Laidlaw (*coach*), L.J. Barry, T. Cama (*assistants*).
New Zealand Women:	G.M. Moore (*coach*), W. Clarke (*assistant*), J. Haggart (*assistant*).
New Zealand Women's Sevens:	A.M. Bunting, C. Sweeney (*co-coaches*), S. Ross (*assistant*).

2020 HONOURS
THE ALMANACK NEW ZEALAND XV

Jordie Barrett
Hurricanes

Will Jordan   Anton Lienert-Brown   Caleb Clarke
Crusaders   *Chiefs*   *Blues*

Jack Goodhue
Crusaders

Richie Mo'unga
Crusaders

Aaron Smith
Highlanderss

Ardie Savea
Hurricanes

Sam Cane (Capt)   Samuel Whitelock   Patrick Tuipulotu   Akira Ioane
Chiefs   *Crusaders*   *Blues*   *Blues*

Nepo Laulala   Dane Coles   Joe Moody
Chiefs   *Hurricanes*   *Crusaders*

Reserves –
Ash Dixon (*Highlanders*), Karl Tu'inukuafe (*Blues*), Ofa Tuungafasi (*Blues*), Scott Barrett (*Crusaders*), Hoskins Sotutu (*Blues*), Folau Fakatava (*Highlanders*), Beauden Barrett (*Blues*), David Havili (*Crusaders*).

COMMENTS

The following comment on leading players is on those who appeared in Super Rugby, being the basis of selection for the All Blacks.

Fullback: Jordie Barrett exhibited top form for the Hurricanes and showed he has the temperament in crucial moments. Where he played for the All Blacks was dictated by where his brother Beauden played, receiving just one opportunity at fullback, but was one of only two players to start all six tests this year.

After last year's successful transition to fullback for the All Blacks there was much interest in which position Beauden Barrett would occupy in 2020. Both the Blues and the All Blacks preferred him at fullback, but his influence on matches was reduced compared to last year, although he had a good game in the All Blacks' win at Sydney against Australia.

Another with something of a subdued season was the Chiefs Damian McKenzie who made a return after missing most of last year with an ACL injury. He started in the opening test at Wellington after Beauden Barrett's late withdrawal, having a mixed game.

David Havili began the season with the Crusaders in superb form when, due to a stomach infection that required surgery, he hardly played again until the Mitre 10 Cup with Tasman where he finished the season as he started. Will Jordan scored eight tries for the Crusaders with his pace and highly effective running from the back. His two tries against Argentina, while individualistic, showed that if the All Blacks' vogue of recent years for a fullback playing on the wing is to be persisted with, he has the best credentials to do so currently.

Wing three-quarters: With Will Jordan our preference on the right wing, Caleb Clarke of the Blues is our automatic selection on the left wing. Despite only scoring four tries, he had an imposing presence with his ability to break tackles and run many metres in a fashion that no other winger did this year.

The Crusaders pairing of Sevu Reece and George Bridge gave good service to their club but Reece found himself overtaken in the All Blacks by the dramatic rise of Caleb Clarke. Bridge started the opening test and suffered a pectoral injury in training before the second test to rule him out of all rugby for at least six months.

Mark Telea (Blues) and Jona Nareki (Highlanders) both looked wings of top quality, heading the try-scoring for their respective teams, Telea being in his second season and Nareki in his first. In his third season Sean Wainui seemed to come of age at this level, proving himself the best of the wings for the Chiefs, scoring five tries.

Kobus van Wyk and Ben Lam missed few try-scoring opportunities for the Hurricanes, scoring 14 tries between them, but both left for overseas after Super Rugby. Salesi Rayasi hardly featured for the club but was such a potent force for Auckland in the Mitre 10 Cup, scoring 14 tries, which was just one short of the Mitre 10 Cup season record.

Centre three-quarter: Our choice Anton Lienert-Brown played more matches for the Chiefs at second five-eighth than at centre, but for the All Blacks he proved to be a consistent performer in this position with excellent defence and strong carries.

Rieko Ioane (Blues) and Braydon Ennor (Crusaders) were both moved into the centre position for their clubs at the beginning of the season, and on occasions looked a real handful for the opposition while still adjusting to the role. Ennor's season ended with injury in the North–South match while Ioane lost the starting position he was given after the opening test.

After a handful of appearances for the Hurricanes in the last couple of seasons, Peter Umaga-Jensen took his chance in the last six weeks of Super Rugby Aotearoa and had an impressive campaign scoring four tries and setting up a couple of others. We suspect this will be a hotly contested position in 2021.

Second five-eighth: Ngani Laumape was the most forceful runner of the candidates in this position, proving almost unstoppable for the Hurricanes against the Blues at Wellington. While the defensive line would be breached there were times, though, when the ball could have been passed instead of going into the next tackle.

After proving his worth at centre in recent seasons for the Crusaders, Jack Goodhue was moved in one place this year and was not as effective in attack with having less room in which to move, but his defence was solid enough. Nevertheless he was the All Blacks selectors' preference, but it looked like he was still adjusting to the position.

TJ Faiane (Blues) and Patelesio Tomkinson (Highlanders) are similar players, and both tried hard and were good link men.

First five-eighth: With his proven ability over recent years with the Crusaders, Richie Mo'unga once again dominated this position in 2020. His ability to influence matches was unrivalled.

There was clear gap back to the next line of players in this position. Josh Ioane was surprisingly tried at second five-eighths with the Highlanders which did not prove fruitful, and it may have been the reason why back at his rightful place at first five-eighth for Otago he was not as successful as last year in the Mitre 10 Cup. Mitchell Hunt had good moments for the Highlanders and is also a handy utility.

Otere Black (Blues) had his best season yet in Super Rugby, proving a lot more authoritative. Between overseas contracts, former All Black Aaron Cruden returned to the Chiefs. Using all his valuable experience, he tried hard to lift a team that struggled, and without him they would have been worse. Kaleb Trask had a good learning experience in his debut season for the Chiefs, while at fullback for Bay of Plenty in the Mitre 10 Cup he was a standout.

Halfback: A disappointment of the season was the loss of form of TJ Perenara. He seemed to be distracted by opposing players at the breakdown and pointing things out to referees, which led to too many moments of indecision.

Brad Weber served the Chiefs well again and was underplayed in the All Blacks while All Blacks incumbent Aaron Smith added to his reputation with consistently fine displays throughout the season. At 32 years old, he seems to be getting better with age, and clearly remains the best halfback in the country.

Finlay Christie finished the season as the Blues starting halfback with some fine displays, proving to be an effective runner. Bryn Hall and Mitchell Drummond were a good pair at the champion Crusaders, almost getting the same game time.

Folau Fakatava, who turned 21 years old in December, hardly featured at the Highlanders behind Aaron Smith, but he was in brilliant form for Hawke's Bay in the Mitre 10 Cup, winning the Duane Monkley medal. Eligible for the All Blacks in 2021, he will be watched with a lot of interest in the new season.

Number eight: With Kieran Read having moved on, as expected Whetukamokamo Douglas filled this position at the Crusaders. A reliable performer in defence, he did not show up on attack to the same extent as others in this position. Pita Gus Sowakula continued from where he left off last year for the Chiefs, proving to be an effective number eight.

An ankle injury for Gareth Evans (Hurricanes) occurred at the same time as Ardie Savea's return to play from his injury sustained at last year's World Cup. Although his club played Savea as a straight replacement for Evans, instead of his usual flanker role, it didn't take long for him to exhibit the high standard of the previous year, but whether he is the best fit to this position long term at international level is debatable.

Hoskins Sotutu (Blues) and Marino Mikaele-Tu'u (Highlanders) both had breakthrough seasons for their clubs. Sotutu gained All Blacks honours and showed enough to suggest the starting test jersey is well within his grasp in 2021.

Flankers: Leaving aside the role as new All Black captain, Sam Cane was under some pressure in the national jersey after his domestic form was questioned, but he responded superbly in all six tests.

Tom Christie stepped up into the Crusaders' first-choice openside flanker role and looked composed in everything he did. Dalton Papali'i displayed his versatility in both flanker roles for the Blues and Dillon Hunt was a strong performer for the Highlanders when James Lentjes' season ended with injury.

After last year's debut season Du Plessis Kirifi made further progress for the Hurricanes. Not selected for the North Island squad, he was something of a surprise addition to the All Blacks Tri Nations squad as temporary injury cover, but he did not play a game.

Shannon Frizell (Highlanders) and Akira Ioane (Blues) were the two leading blindside flanker performers. Frizell earned first chance in the All Blacks, but his effectiveness at international level was variable. Ioane seemed to have matured in his play this year. He had two fine test performances, including being the unlucky player to retire in the first half against Australia at Brisbane due to Tuungafasi's red card.

Cullen Grace had an excellent debut season for the Crusaders, assuming the starting position in just his third game and holding it until injured. His work rate never dropped and he won useful ball in the lineout. Lachlan Boshier had another prominent year for the Chiefs at blindside flanker and continued the form through the Mitre 10 Cup with Taranaki as openside flanker, proving adept at gaining a lot of turnovers at the breakdown.

Injury prevented Luke Jacobson (Chiefs) from playing more than a handful of games, and with the return of All Black Liam Squire from overseas to the Highlanders for 2021, competition for the test team will be even more intense at blindside flanker.

Locks: Sam Whitelock had no challenger for his position in the All Blacks and there was some surprise he was not made All Blacks captain. His partner at test level of many years Brodie Retallick was on a two-year contract with Japanese club Kobelco Steelers and will return to New Zealand rugby in time for the test matches starting in mid-2021.

Patrick Tuipulotu (Blues) was the form lock in Super Rugby while Scott Barrett missed the majority of the Crusaders matches due to injury, and it was only in the final test his fitness and form made him look like the player he was last year.

Twenty-year-old Tupou Vaa'i was not many people's pick as fourth lock for the All Blacks, particularly as the Chiefs tight five never really dominated, but he definitely showed promise in the national jersey and is surely a bright prospect.

The Highlanders pairings of Jack Whetton and Pari Pari Parkinson, Mitchell Dunshea (Crusaders) and James Blackwell (Hurricanes) all continued their development while Scott Scrafton (Hurricanes) probably has his best season in Super Rugby. Veteran Luke Romano did not have much game time for the Crusaders but was great value to Canterbury in the Mitre 10 Cup.

Props: Joe Moody (Crusaders) and Nepo Laulala (Chiefs) were again the best props. In the uninspiring loss to Argentina at Sydney, Moody was one of the few to perform with distinction and Laulala certainly improved things when he came on as a substitute. Both backed it up in the return encounter with Argentina at Newcastle when Laulala started.

At tighthead Ofa Tuungafasi was really to the fore of the Blues' forward efforts in their revival in Super Rugby and at loosehead Karl Tu'inkuafe and Alex Hodgman gave sterling service. Michael Ala'alatoa enhanced his reputation at the Crusaders.

Tyrel Lomax (Hurricanes) is still the best of the younger props and would have found his international selection this year a good learning experience, while in his second season with the Highlanders Ayden Johnstone continued to impress.

Unfortunately Atu Moli Chiefs) had his season end prematurely with illness while Kane Hames' career seems to have ended due to the effects of concussion and he has taken up refereeing.

Hooker: Dane Coles (Hurricanes) reclaimed the premier hooking spot, being back to his running best without neglecting his core duties. Unfortunately, his aggression still gets the better of him on occasions, notably against Argentina at Sydney.

Codie Taylor was one of the Crusaders' best performers but lost his starting place in the national team. With an outstanding season for the Highlanders and then with Hawke's Bay in the Mitre 10 Cup, Ash Dixon ended the year as top try-scorer in first-class rugby, and he is another 32-year-old who seems to be getting better with age.

Asafo Aumua received more game time at the Hurricanes than ever before and just needs to improve consistency while Samisoni Taukei'aho and Brad Slater had a good battle for the position at the Chiefs as did James Parsons and Kurt Eklund at the Blues.

FIVE PLAYERS OF THE YEAR

Lachlan Scott Boshier (*Chiefs/Taranaki*) was considered unlucky not to make the All Blacks in 2020. The flanker's form throughout both versions of Super Rugby had been top class, in particular his arriving at the breakdown with speed and anticipation to secure numerous turnovers, and lineout ball won. The variable performance quality of the Chiefs' tight five, which at times struggled, meant Boshier was not in a dominant forward pack and made his prominent efforts even more meritorious, and rewarded with the Chiefs Players' Player of the Year award.

This form continued for Taranaki in the Mitre 10 Cup, with a noteworthy performance in the successful Ranfurly Shield challenge against Canterbury, and at season's end he won the Taranaki Player of the Year award.

Lachlan Boshier was born at New Plymouth on November 16, 1994. A boarder at New Plymouth Boys' High School, he started 2010 in the schools third XV but was eventually promoted to the First XV where he remained for his last two years 2011–2012, with the captaincy in 2012. He represented Taranaki at Under 16 (2010) and Under 18 (2011–2012) level in this time, and in his final year also gained selection in the Hurricanes Under 18 and New Zealand Secondary Schools teams.

He joined New Plymouth Old Boys club in 2013 and went straight into their senior A team, starting a building apprenticeship the same year. His first-class debut came in 2014 with four matches for the New Zealand Under 20 team followed by his Taranaki debut with one appearance in the province's title-winning ITM Cup Premiership team later that year. He was first called into the Chiefs during 2016 as an injury replacement for Sam Henwood. He made seven appearances that year, and the following year gained a full contract which he has maintained ever since.

Caleb Daniel Clarke (*Blues/Auckland*) had committed himself to the All Blacks Sevens team for the 2019/20 HSBC World Sevens Series and the Olympic Games in Tokyo which was to follow in July. In the normal course of events this would have precluded him from any appearances for the Blues and All Blacks in 2020. The Covid-19 pandemic saw the HSBC World Sevens Series halted in March and the Olympic Games postponed to 2021.

After the country's lockdown, Super Rugby Aotearoa was created and, with no programme for the All Blacks Sevens on the horizon, the 21-year-old left winger was now available for the Blues. In all six matches he showed determination, acceleration, speed, a great sidestep and, with his strong thighs, he proved very difficult to stop on the first tackle for all the other teams.

His selection in the All Blacks squad surprised no one. In his test debut against Australia — the drawn first test at Wellington — he came on as a substitute after 68 minutes and made four runs, beat five tacklers and had many people many wondering if he should start the next test in Auckland. And, start at Auckland he did, after George Bridge suffered an injury at training. At Eden Park he made more runs and beat even more tacklers, receiving a standing ovation as he was subbed off after 67 minutes. The most scintillating break was early in the second half where he ran 50 metres and broke five tackles. The movement ended with Ardie Savea scoring. Rarely has such a beginning to a test career been as noteworthy.

Caleb Clarke was born in Auckland on March 29, 1999. Attending Mount Albert Grammar, he was in the First XV for four years 2013–2016, being part of the 2016 team that won both the Auckland Schools and National Schools titles. There was selection in the NZ Secondary Schools teams of 2015 and 2016.

His first year out of school in 2017 was busy. He made his first-class debut with the NZ Under 20 team that won the world championship, made his first three appearances for Auckland in the Mitre 10 Cup, played for the Auckland team that won the Jock Hobbs Memorial National Under 19 tournament and in November, at the age of 18, signed a full contract with the Blues for Super Rugby.

His father Eroni played 10 tests for the All Blacks 1992-1998.

Ashley Lyonal Dixon (*Highlanders/Hawke's Bay*) had a year to remember.

His 15 tries in 2020 were the most in NZ first-class rugby by any player. He won the Tom French Memorial Cup as Maori Player of the Year, captained Hawke's Bay to the Mitre 10 Cup Championship title and with it promotion to the Premiership for next year, played his 100th Super Rugby match, played his 100th game for Hawke's Bay in the successful Ranfurly Shield challenge against Otago, captained the Maori All Blacks for the fifth consecutive year and passed 250 career first-class games.

Aside from these milestones, he proved himself as one of the most accomplished hookers in the country. For the Highlanders in Super 15 he was used mainly off the bench but in Super Rugby Aotearoa he produced such fine form he reversed the situation and started in all but one game, keeping All Black Liam Coltman on the bench. His co-captaincy with Aaron Smith was also a big influence on the team. It was more of the same for Hawke's Bay in the Mitre 10 Cup. His accuracy at throwing the ball into the lineout was top notch throughout the year.

Ash Dixon was born in Christchurch on September 1, 1988 and educated at Christchurch Boys' High School. He was in the First XV in his final two years — 2005 and 2006, and was captain in 2006. In both years the team won the Sanix Invitational Schools tournament in Japan, the Press Cup for the Crusaders Schools championship, the National Schools championship and defended the Moascar Cup. In the 48 matches played in those two years, the team won 47.

Selection in the NZ Secondary Schools team rounded out 2006, and the following year he joined the Linwood club, playing for the senior team. He was with the 2007 NZ Under19 and 2008 NZ Under 20 teams that each won their respective World Championships and also in 2008 transferred to Hawke's Bay. Two years later there was a shift to Auckland in search of more game time and he earned a full contract with the Blues for 2011 but did not appear for them.

Moving back to Hawke's Bay in 2012, he debuted in Super Rugby for the Hurricanes in 2013 as a wider training group member and played again for them in 2014 on a full contract. He signed with the Highlanders in 2015 and has been co-captain for them since 2018.

Richard Mo'unga (*Crusaders/Canterbury*) produced a number of dominant performances at first five-eighth for the Crusaders as they won Super Rugby Aotearoa with a game to spare. He invariably selected the right option of either taking on the line, releasing the backline outside him, or kicking well out of hand when required. His goalkicking was reliable, too. He finished top points-scorer in Super Rugby Aotearoa with 99, and ended the year with the Super Rugby Player of the Year award.

On attack he certainly changed the course of the Crusaders v Blues match at Christchurch with an outstanding second half, while for the All Blacks he was prominent against Australia at Auckland before producing a man-of-the-match performance against the same opponent in Sydney. He did not shirk any defensive requirement either as his try-saving tackles on Jona Nareki at Dunedin and Marika Koroibete in the second Bledisloe Cup match showed.

Richie Mo'unga was an Almanack Promising Player of the Year for 2013.

Aaron Luke Smith (*Highlanders/Manawatu*) had an outstanding year, the 32-year-old showing no sign of any diminished ability in 2020. In particular, his performance in the Highlanders' comeback against the Chiefs at Hamilton was just inspirational and probably the best halfback display of the year. The chance to play for his province, Manawatu, for the first time since 2011 brought him a lot of personal satisfaction.

While the All Blacks had a mixed year, the instant delivery of pass remained a constant throughout and Smith was one of only a few players not to have a poor game in the loss to Argentina.

Aaron Smith had previously been an Almanack Player of the Year for 2013, 2014 and 2015

PROMISING PLAYERS OF THE YEAR

Qualification for consideration is usually players in their debut season at first-class level or first full season.

Lupeti Chay Fihaki (*Canterbury*) made eight appearances on the right wing for his province and topped their try-scoring list with five in his debut season for Canterbury. But it was his long-range penalty goal in their final match of the season to regain the lead against Auckland with five minutes left that ultimately kept Canterbury in the Premiership for 2021. A miss, and a loss, would have meant relegation for Canterbury. At the end of the year the Crusaders signed him for Super Rugby.

The strongly built 1.93m, 100kg, 19-year-old was born at Auckland on January 3, 2001 and educated at Ellerslie School before enrolling at Sacred Heart College in 2014. For Auckland East, he made the Roller Mills team in 2013, and their Under 14 and Under 16 teams in 2014 and 2015 respectively at either first or second five-eighth. It was in these two positions that he played for the Sacred Heart College First XV in his final two years of 2017 and 2018, and at the end of 2018 he was selected in the NZ Schoolboys team at second five-eighth.

Upon leaving school he was signed by the Crusaders Academy and joined the Christchurch High School Old Boys club in 2019, making his first-class debut with one appearance for the NZ Under 20 team on the wing at the Oceania tournament. Later in the year he was part of the Canterbury team that won the Jock Hobbs Memorial National Under 19 tournament, playing at fullback and kicking four conversions and four penalty goals in their three matches.

All Blacks Josevata Rokocoko and Joeli Vidiri are uncles as is Viliami Fihaki who played for Counties Manukau 2008–2011, North Harbour 2012–2013 and Tonga 2013–2015.

With just 11 first-class games behind him, 20-year-old **Cullen James Grace** (*Canterbury*) made a big impression for the Crusaders in his debut year of Super Rugby.

After appearances as a substitute in their first two games, he became first choice starting blindside flanker for the Crusaders until a broken thumb ended his Super Rugby season. He finished the year by being selected for the All Blacks' Bledisloe Cup and Tri-Nations campaigns and made his test debut off the bench against Australia at Brisbane.

The 1.94m, 107kg loose forward was born at Hawera on December 20, 1999 and educated at Bluestone School in Timaru before starting at Timaru Boys' High School in 2013. He was in the school First XV in his final three years 2015–2017 as a blindside flanker, captaining in his last two years as Timaru Boys' won the Moascar Cup in 2016 for the first time and lost the Crusaders Region Secondary Schools Championship final to Christchurch BHS 18–10 in 2017. Along the way he represented the Crusaders Under 18 team in 2017 and South Canterbury at Under 16 (2015) and Under 18 (2016–17) level.

In his final year he made the NZ Secondary Schools team and won the South Canterbury Young Sportsman of the Year award for the 2017 year. In 2018 he joined Lincoln University and went straight into the senior team which won the Christchurch Metropolitan title, and he captained the Canterbury team at the Jock Hobbs Memorial National Under 19 tournament, appearing for both teams at blindside flanker. He made his first-class debut in 2019 with seven games for the NZ Under 20 team and four for Canterbury, all at lock.

Jacob Wesley John Ratumaitavuki-Kneepkens (*Taranaki*) was a 1.88m, 93 kg 19-year-old wing threequarter who made an impact for his province in the Mitre 10 Cup in his first year at first-class level. In his second match he scored two tries for Taranaki as they won the Ranfurly Shield from Canterbury and finished the season as his union's top try-scorer with eight, which was the third highest tally in the Mitre 10 Cup. At the end of the year, he was signed by the Blues for Super Rugby.

Born at Christchurch on August 3, 2001, he attended Woodleigh Primary School and from there went to Francis Douglas Memorial College in 2013 where he played both rugby and rugby league, making the First XV (first five-eighth) 2017–2019 and the First XIII (fullback) 2017–2018. He signed a three-year academy contract with Sydney league club Parramatta Eels in 2017 but chose to exit the contract in 2018.

There was two years in the NZ Secondary Schools team 2018–2019, Chiefs Under 18 team 2018–2019, Taranaki Sevens at the 2019 nationals, and in October 2019 he signed a two-year contract with the All Blacks Sevens programme. In 2020, his first year out of school, he linked with the Tukapa club.

A brother, Isaac, represented the Fiji Under 20 rugby team in 2019.

In his first full season at Mitre 10 Cup level, 21-year-old **Xavier O'Carroll Roe** (*Waikato*) had an outstanding season for Waikato on their run to a narrow semi-final loss. He appeared in ten of their 11 games. The 1.79m, 85kg halfback's form was rewarded with a two-year contract with the Chiefs in December.

He was born at Hamilton on December 13, 1998 and educated at Hikuai School. In 2011, his only year at Parawai School, he represented Thames Valley at first five-eighth in the Roller Mills tournament. Becoming a boarder at Hamilton Boys High School in 2012, he made the First XV as a halfback in 2015–2016, being part of the team that won the Super 8 title in 2015 and the Chiefs Secondary Schools Competition in 2016. He had represented Waikato at Under 16 level in 2014.

In 2017, he joined the Melville club and was selected in the Waikato team that was runner-up at the Jock Hobbs Memorial National Under 19 tournament. The following year he signed for Taranaki and made his first-class debut with the New Zealand Under 20 side, but appearances for Taranaki in the 2018 and 2019 Mitre 10 Cups were limited to just six matches. With a year still to run on his contract, Xavier secured an early release and returned to Waikato for 2020.

His father Hayden was a flanker with Thames Valley 2009–2010 and its coach 2014–2016, while brother-in-law Richard Judd was a halfback for Thames Valley, Counties Manukau, Bay of Plenty and Hurricanes.

Hooker **Tyrone Te Wehi Jack Thompson** (*Wellington*) caught the eye with a memorable try against Bay of Plenty in just his third match for Wellington in this his debut season at first-class level. The 1.86m 111kg 20-year-old received the ball on halfway from a lineout move and charged down the sideline, evading three tackles, to score. In the very next match against Canterbury, he used his strength to break through two tackles on his way to score from 10 metres out.

Born at Gisborne on May 28, 2000 he started his schooling at the age of five at Rotorua Primary School but later that year the family shifted to Napier where he attended Te Kura Kaupapa Maori O Te Are Hou and Henry Hill schools, followed by Tamatea Intermediate. He entered Napier Boys' High School in 2014 and played for the First XV 2016–2018. In that final year he captained the team to win the Hurricanes Schools Championship and to the National Secondary Schools final where they were runner up to St Peters College. He finished the year in the NZ Secondary Schools team. While at Napier Boys' he represented the Hawke's Bay Under 16 team 2015–2016 and Hurricanes Under 18 in 2018.

Signed by Wellington, he joined the Marist St Pats club in 2019, the club his father Jud had played for. Later in the year he was selected for the Wellington Under 19 team that finished third at the Jock Hobbs Memorial National championship.

Twin brother Leo went through Napier Boys' High School alongside Tyrone, playing at centre in the First XV and captained the 2019 Wellington Under 19 team. In 2020 he joined the Canberra Raiders rugby league club.

NEW ZEALAND REPRESENTATIVES 2020

Of the 36 All Blacks used in the six Test matches of 2020, seven were making their debuts, while Asafo Aumua and Akira Ioane made their Test debuts after appearing in non-Test matches in 2017.

Details of the seven new All Blacks are:

CLARKE, Caleb Daniel *born Auckland, March 29, 1999*
All Blacks #1187
New Zealand Under 20 2017 (8), 2018 (3), Auckland 2017 (3), 2018 (7), 2019 (10), 2020 (2), Blues 2018 (5), 2019 (8), 2020 (6), North Island 2020 (1), New Zealand 2020 (5)

GRACE, Cullen James *born Hawera, December 20, 1999*
All Blacks #1192
New Zealand Under 20 2019 (7), Canterbury 2019 (4), 2020 (5), Crusaders 2020 (8), New Zealand 2020 (1)

HODGMAN, Alexander Thomas O'Connor Atuolo *born Auckland, July 16, 1993*
All Blacks #1190
New Zealand Under 20 2013 (1), Crusader Knights (Development XV) 2013 (2), Canterbury 2014 (9), 2015 (12), 2016 (11), 2017 (13), 2018 (10), Crusaders 2015 (5), 2016 (4), Blues 2017 (5), 2018 (7), 2019 (13), 2020 (8), Auckland 2019 (11), 2020 (2), New Zealand 2020 (4)

JORDAN, William Thomas *born Christchurch, February 24, 1998*
All Blacks #1191
New Zealand Under 20 2017 (7), Tasman 2017 (10), 2018 (11), 2019 (11), 2020 (2), Crusaders 2019 (9), 2020 (10), South Island 2020 (1), New Zealand 2020 (2)

SOTUTU, Hoskins Colin Ryder *born Auckland, July 12, 1998*
All Blacks #1186
New Zealand Under 20 2018 (6), Auckland 2018 (10), 2019 (5), 2020 (2), Blues 2019 (1), 2020 (10), North Island 2020 (1), New Zealand 2020 (5)

UMAGA-JENSEN, Peter Ionatana Jack *born Lower Hutt, December 31, 1997*
All Blacks #1189
New Zealand Under 20 2016 (2), Wellington 2016 (8), 2018 (3), 2019 (11), 2020 (5), Hurricanes 2018 (1), 2019 (4), 2020 (6), North Island 2020 (1), New Zealand 2020 (1)

VAA'I, Tupou Paea'i Okalani *born Auckland, January 27, 2000*
All Blacks #1188
Taranaki 2018 (3), 2019 (6), 2020 (3), New Zealand Under 20 2019 (6), Chiefs 2020 (7), North Island 2020 (1), New Zealand 2020 (4)

ALL BLACKS MANAGEMENT 2020

Head Coach/selector:	Ian Foster
Selector:	Grant Fox
Assistant Coach/Selector (Forwards):	John Plumtree
Assistant Coach (Backs):	Brad Mooar
Assistant Coach (Defence):	Scott McLeod
Assistant Coach (Scrum):	Greg Feek
Manager (Business and Operations):	Darren Shand
Manager (Leadership):	Gilbert Enoka
Strength and Conditioning Coach:	Dr Nic Gill
Assistant Strength and Conditioning Coach:	Kim Simperingham
Performance Analyst:	Jamie Hamilton
Assistant Performance Analyst:	Hayden Chapman
Doctor:	Dr James McGarvey
Physiotherapist:	Peter Gallagher
Manual Therapist:	George Duncan
Nutritionist:	Katrina Darry
Team Services Manager:	Ceilidh Hooper
Media manager:	Joe Locke
Logistics manager:	James Iversen

TEST MATCH RECORDS OF 2020 NEW ZEALAND REPRESENTATIVES
ALL BLACKS CAREER RECORDS TO JANUARY 1, 2021

	Debut	Tests	Starts	Wins	Winning %	Tries	Conversions	Penalty Goals	Dropped Goals	Points
Asafo Aumua	2020	1	–	–	–	–	–	–	–	0
Beauden Barrett	2012	88	58	75	85.2	36	149	55	2	649
Jordie Barrett	2017	23	16	17	73.9	14	11	3	–	101
Scott Barrett	2016	40	20	31	77.5	5	–	–	–	25
George Bridge	2018	10	7	6	60	9	–	–	–	45
Sam Cane	2012	74	54	62	83.7	15	–	–	–	75
Caleb Clarke	2020	5	4	3	60	1	–	–	–	5
Dane Coles	2012	74	53	62	83.7	13	–	–	–	65
Shannon Frizell	2018	13	12	10	76.9	2	–	–	–	10
Jack Goodhue	2018	18	17	11	61.1	3	–	–	–	15
Cullen Grace	2020	1	–	–	–	–	–	–	–	0
Alex Hodgman	2020	4	–	2	50	–	–	–	–	0
Akira Ioane	2020	2	2	1	50	–	–	–	–	0
Rieko Ioane	2016	34	27	25	73.5	26	–	–	–	130
Will Jordan	2020	2	–	1	50	2	–	–	–	10
Nepo Laulala	2015	29	18	24	84.6	–	–	–	–	0
Ngani Laumape	2017	15	7	11	73.3	8	–	–	–	40
Anton Lienert-Brown	2016	49	29	38	77.5	9	–	–	–	45
Tyrel Lomax	2020	6	1	3	50	–	–	–	–	0
Joe Moody	2014	50	43	40	80	5	–	–	–	25
Damian McKenzie	2016	27	17	21	77.7	12	10	–	–	80
Richie Mo'unga	2018	22	15	16	72.7	5	58	13	–	180
Dalton Papali'i	2018	4	1	3	75	–	–	–	–	0
TJ Perenara	2014	69	17	57	82.6	13	–	–	–	65
Sevu Reece	2019	8	8	6	75	4	–	–	–	20
Ardie Savea	2016	49	24	38	77.5	11	–	–	–	55
Aaron Smith	2012	97	89	81	83.5	21	1	–	–	107
Hoskins Sotutu	2020	5	1	3	60	–	–	–	–	0
Codie Taylor	2015	56	29	43	76.7	12	–	–	–	60
Karl Tu'inukuafe	2018	17	8	13	76.4	1	–	–	–	5
Patrick Tuipulotu	2014	35	15	28	80	4	–	–	–	20
Ofa Tuungafasi	2016	39	8	31	79.4	1	–	–	–	5
Peter Umaga-Jensen	2020	1	–	1	100	–	–	–	–	0
Tupou Vaa'i	2020	4	1	1	25	1	–	–	–	5
Brad Weber	2015	7	–	5	71.4	2	–	–	–	10
Sam Whitelock	2010	122	102	103	84.4	6	–	–	–	30

BLEDISLOE CUP AND TRI NATIONS IN NEW ZEALAND AND AUSTRALIA 2020

ALL BLACKS APPEARANCES

	Franchise	Date of Birth	Height	Weight	Tests at 1/1/20
A.J. (Asafo) Aumua	Hurricanes	05-05-97	1.77	108	0
B.J. (Beauden) Barrett	Blues	27-05-91	1.87	91	83
J.M. (Jordie) Barrett	Hurricanes	17-02-97	1.96	101	17
S.K. (Scott) Barrett	Crusaders	20-11-93	1.97	111	36
G.C. (George) Bridge	Crusaders	01-04-95	1.85	96	9
S.J. (Sam) Cane	Chiefs	13-01-92	1.89	106	68
C.D. (Caleb) Clarke	Blues	29-03-99	1.87	103	0
D.S. (Dane) Coles	Hurricanes	10-12-86	1.84	110	69
S.M. (Shannon) Frizell	Highlanders	11-02-94	1.95	108	9
E.J. (Jack) Goodhue	Crusaders	13-06-95	1.87	98	13
C.J. (Cullen) Grace	Crusaders	20-12-99	1.9	106	0
A.T.O.A. (Alex) Hodgman	Blues	16-07-93	1.9	119	0
A.L. (Akira) Ioane	Blues	16-06-95	1.94	113	0
R.E. (Rieko) Ioane	Blues	18-03-97	1.89	103	29
W.T. (Will) Jordan	Crusaders	24-02-98	1.88	91	0
N.E. (Nepo) Laulala	Chiefs	06-11-91	1.84	116	26
K.H. (Ngani) Laumape	Hurricanes	24-04-93	1.77	103	13
A.R. (Anton) Lienert-Brown	Chiefs	15-04-95	1.85	96	43
T.S. (Tyrel) Lomax	Hurricanes	01-06-96	1.92	127	1
D.S. (Damian) McKenzie	Chiefs	20-04-95	1.75	81	23
J.P.T. (Joe) Moody	Crusaders	18-09-88	1.88	120	46
R. (Richie) Mo'unga	Crusaders	25-05-94	1.76	88	17
D.R. (Dalton) Papali'i	Blues	11-10-97	1.9	105	3
T.T.R. (TJ) Perenara	Hurricanes	23-01-92	1.84	90	64
S.L. (Sevu) Reece	Crusaders	13-02-97	1.78	92	7
A.S. (Ardie) Savea	Hurricanes	14-10-93	1.88	100	44
A.L. (Aaron) Smith	Highlanders	21-11-88	1.71	83	92
H.C.R. (Hoskins) Sotutu	Blues	12-07-98	1.92	106	0
C.J.D. (Codie) Taylor	Crusaders	31-03-91	1.83	106	50
G.Z.K. (Karl) Tu'inukuafe	Blues	21-02-93	1.86	135	13
P.T. (Patrick) Tuipulotu	Blues	23-01-93	1.98	120	30
A.O.H.M. (Ofa) Tuungafasi	Blues	19-04-92	1.95	122	35
P.I.J. (Peter) Umaga-Jensen	Hurricanes	31-12-97	1.87	95	0
T.P.O. (Tupou) Vaa'i	Chiefs	27-01-00	1.97	118	0
B.M. (Brad) Weber	Chiefs	17-01-91	1.75	75	5
S.L. (Samuel) Whitelock	Crusaders	12-10-88	2.02	122	117

NB. George Bower, Mitch Dunshea and Du'Plessis Kirifi acted as cover in Australia but did not take the field.

BLEDISLOE CUP AND TRI NATIONS IN NEW ZEALAND AND AUSTRALIA 2020 ALL BLACKS APPEARANCES

2020 ALL BLACKS	Australia I	Australia II	Australia III	Australia IV	Argentina I	Argentina II	TOTALS
B. Barrett	–	15	15	10	15	15	5
McKenzie	15	s	–	s	s	–	4
J. Barrett	14	14	14	15	14	14	6
Jordan	–	–	–	s	–	s	2
Reece	–	–	–	14	–	–	1
Bridge	11	–	–	–	–	–	1
Clarke	s	11	11	–	11	11	5
R. Ioane	13	–	s	11	s	s	5
Umaga-Jensen	–	s	–	–	–	–	1
Goodhue	12	12	12	–	12	12	5
Lienert-Brown	s	13	13	13	13	13	6
Laumape	–	–	s	12	–	–	2
Mo'unga	10	10	10	–	10	10	5
Perenara	s	s	s	9	–	s	5
Smith	9	9	9	–	9	9	5
Weber	–	–	–	s	s	–	2
Sotutu	s	s	8	–	s	s	5
Grace	–	–	–	s	–	–	1
Savea	8	8	–	8	8	8	5
Cane (capt)	7	7	7	7	7	7	6
Papali'i	–	–	s	–	–	–	1
A. Ioane	–	–	–	6	–	6	2
Frizell	6	6	6	–	6	–	4
S. Barrett	–	s	s	4	–	4	4
Tuipulotu	4	4	4	–	4	s	5
Whitelock	5	–	5	5	5	5	5
Vaa'i	s	5	–	s	s	–	4
Laulala	–	s	–	–	s	3	3
Lomax	s	–	s	s	3	s	5
Tuungafasi	3	3	3	3	–	–	4
Moody	1	1	–	–	1	1	4
Tu'inukuafe	s	–	1	1	–	s	4
Hodgman	–	s	s	s	s	–	4
Coles	s	2	2	–	2	2	5
Taylor	2	s	s	2	s	s	6
Aumua	–	–	–	s	–	–	1

INDIVIDUAL SCORING

	Tries	Con	PG	DG	Points
Mo'unga	2	13	4	–	48
J. Barrett	3	2	3	–	28
Cane	2	–	–	–	10
Coles	2	–	–	–	10
R. Ioane	2	–	–	–	10
Jordan	2	–	–	–	10
Savea	2	–	–	–	10
Smith	2	–	–	–	10
Clarke	1	–	–	–	5
Taylor	1	–	–	–	5
Tu'inukuafe	1	–	–	–	5
Tuipulotu	1	–	–	–	5
Vaa'i	1	–	–	–	5
Totals	**22**	**15**	**7**	**0**	**161**
Opposition scored	7	3	12	0	77

BLEDISLOE CUP AND TRI NATIONS IN NEW ZEALAND AND AUSTRALIA

SCORING RECORD 2020 PLAYED 6 WON 3 LOST 2

Date	Opponent	Location	Score	Tries	POINTS FOR 161 Con	PG	POINTS AGAINST 77 DG	Referee
October 11	Australia BC)	Wellington	16–16	J. Barrett, Smith		J. Barrett (2)		P. Williams (New Zealand)
October 18	Australia (BC)	Auckland	27–7	Smith, J. Barrett, Savea, Cane	Mo'unga (2)	Mo'unga		A. Gardner (Australia)
October 31	Australia (BC, TN)	Sydney	43–5	Mo'unga (2), Tu'inukuafe, Coles, R. Ioane, J. Barrett	Mo'unga (5)	Mo'unga		B. O'Keeffe (New Zealand)
November 07	Australia (BC, TN)	Brisbane	22–24	R. Ioane, Taylor, Vaa'i	J. Barrett (2)	J. Barrett		N. Berry (Australia)
November 14	Argentina (TN)	Sydney	15–25	Cane, Clarke	Mo'unga	Mo'unga		A. Gardner (Australia)
November 28	Argentina (TN)	Newcastle	38–0	Jordan (2), Coles, Savea, Tuipulotu	Mo'unga (5)	Mo'unga		N. Berry (Australia)

NEW ZEALAND v AUSTRALIA
Bledisloe Cup

Test #592 Sky Stadium, Wellington October 11, 2020

Drawn 16–16

NEW ZEALAND		AUSTRALIA
Damian McKenzie	15	Tom Banks
Jordie Barrett	14	Filipo Daugunu
Rieko Ioane	13	Hunter Paisami
Jack Goodhue	12	Matt To'omua
George Bridge	11	Marika Koroibete
Richie Mo'unga	10	James O'Connor
Aaron Smith	9	Nic White
Ardie Savea	8	Pete Samu
Sam Cane (capt)	7	Michael Hooper (capt)
Shannon Frizell	6	Harry Wilson
Sam Whitelock	5	Matt Philip
Patrick Tuipulotu	4	Lukhan Salakaia-Loto
Ofa Tuungafasi	3	Taniela Tupou
Codie Taylor	2	Folau Fainga'a
Joe Moody	1	James Slipper
Dane Coles (rep 2, 57m)	16	Jordan Uelese (rep 2, 59m)
Karl Tu'inukuafe (rep 1, 57m)	17	Scott Sio (rep 1, 59m)
Tyrel Lomax (rep 3, 63m)	18	Allan Alaalatoa (rep 3, 51m)
Tupou Vaa'i (rep 4, 75m)	19	Rob Simmons (rep 6, 65m)
Hoskins Sotutu (rep 6, 63m)	20	Rob Valetini
TJ Perenara (rep 9, 68m)	21	Jake Gordon (rep 9, 71m)
Anton Lienert-Brown (rep 13, 56m)	22	Noah Lolesio
Caleb Clarke (rep 15, 68m)	23	Reece Hodge (rep 13, 74m)
Barrett, Smith	Tries	Daugunu, Koroibete
Barrett (2)	Pens	O'Connor (2)

Kickoff: 4pm *Attendance:* 31,020 *Conditions:* Rain, wind

Referee: Paul Williams (New Zealand)
Assistant referees: Ben O'Keeffe (New Zealand), Angus Gardner (Australia)
TMO: Mike Fraser (New Zealand)

Scoring:
First half: 9m Barrett try 5–0, 28m Barrett penalty 8–0, 31m O'Connor penalty 8–3
Second half: 43m Smith try 13–3, 52m Koroibete try 13–8, 62m Daugunu try 13–13, 74m O'Connor penalty 13–16, 78m Barrett penalty 16–16

All Blacks Test debuts: Sotutu (All Black No 1186), Clarke (1187), Vaa'i (1188)
Australia Test debuts: Daugunu, Paisami, Wilson

NEW ZEALAND v AUSTRALIA
Bledisloe Cup

Test #593 Eden Park, Auckland October 18, 2020

New Zealand won 27–7

NEW ZEALAND		AUSTRALIA
Beauden Barrett	15	Tom Banks
Jordie Barrett	14	Filipo Daugunu
Anton Lienert-Brown	13	Hunter Paisami
Jack Goodhue	12	Matt To'omua
Caleb Clarke	11	Marika Koroibete
Richie Mo'unga	10	James O'Connor
Aaron Smith	9	Nic White
Ardie Savea	8	Harry Wilson
Sam Cane (capt)	7	Michael Hooper (capt)
Shannon Frizell	6	Ned Hanigan
Tupou Vaa'i	5	Matt Philip
Patrick Tuipulotu	4	Lukhan Salakaia-Loto
Ofa Tuungafasi	3	Taniela Tupou
Dane Coles	2	Brandon Paenga-Amosa
Joe Moody	1	James Slipper
Codie Taylor (rep 2, 50m)	16	Jordan Uelese (rep 2, 51m)
Alex Hodgman (rep 1, 31m)	17	Scott Sio (rep 1, 54m)
Nepo Laulala (rep 3, 50m)	18	Allan Alaalatoa (rep 3, 40m)
Scott Barrett (rep 5, 52m)	19	Rob Simmons (rep 6, 65m)
Hoskins Sotutu (rep 6, 64m)	20	Liam Wright (rep 8, 51m)
TJ Perenara (rep 9, 55m)	21	Jake Gordon (rep 9, 58m)
Peter Umaga-Jensen (rep 13, 17m temp, and 12, 60m)	22	Jordan Petaia (rep 12, 33m)
Damian McKenzie (rep 11, 67m)	23	Reece Hodge (rep 13, 67m)
Smith, J. Barrett, Savea, Cane	Tries	Koroibete
Mo'unga (2)	Cons	O'Connor
Mo'unga	Pens	O'Connor (2)

Kickoff: 4pm **Attendance:** 46,049 **Conditions:** Fine

Referee: Angus Gardner (Australia)
Assistant referees: Ben O'Keeffe (New Zealand), Paul Williams (New Zealand)
TMO: Mike Fraser (New Zealand)

Scoring:
First half: 18m Mo'unga penalty 3–0, 22m Smith try, Mo'unga conversion 10–0, 29m Koroibete try, O'Connor conversion 10–7
Second half: 4m J. Barrett try 15-7, 48m Savea try 20–7, 55m Cane try, Mo'unga conversion 27–7

All Blacks Test debuts: Umaga-Jensen (All Black No 1189), Hodgman (1190)

The All Blacks extend their unbeaten streak at Eden Park over Australia, dating back to 1986.

NEW ZEALAND v AUSTRALIA
Bledisloe Cup/Tri Nations

Test #594 ANZ Stadium, Sydney October 31, 2020

New Zealand won 43-5

NEW ZEALAND		AUSTRALIA
Beauden Barrett	15	Dane Haylett-Petty
Jordie Barrett	14	Filipo Daugunu
Anton Lienert-Brown	13	Jordan Petaia
Jack Goodhue	12	Irae Simone
Caleb Clarke	11	Marika Koroibete
Richie Mo'unga	10	Noah Lolesio
Aaron Smith	9	Nic White
Hoskins Sotutu	8	Harry Wilson
Sam Cane (capt)	7	Michael Hooper (capt)
Shannon Frizell	6	Ned Hanigan
Sam Whitelock	5	Matt Philip
Patrick Tuipulotu	4	Lukhan Salakaia-Loto
Ofa Tuungafasi	3	Allan Alaalatoa
Dane Coles	2	Brandon Paenga-Amosa
Karl Tu'inukuafe	1	James Slipper
Codie Taylor (rep 2, 44m)	16	Jordan Uelese (rep 2, 59m)
Alex Hodgman (rep 1, 44m)	17	Scott Sio (rep 1, 59m)
Tyrel Lomax (rep 3, 57m)	18	Taniela Tupou (rep 3, 53m)
Scott Barrett (rep 4, 54m)	19	Rob Simmons (rep 4, 44m)
Dalton Papali'i (rep 7, 67m)	20	Fraser McReight (rep 8, 68m)
TJ Perenara (rep 9, 54m)	21	Tate McDermott (rep 9, 59m)
Ngani Laumape (rep 12, 60m)	22	Reece Hodge (rep 10, 67m)
Rieko Ioane (rep 15, 65m)	23	Hunter Paisami (rep 12, 53m)
Mo'unga (2), Tu'inukuafe, Coles, Ioane, J. Barrett	Tries	Lolesio
Mo'unga (5)	Cons	
Mo'unga	Pens	

Kickoff: 7.45pm *Attendance:* 26,000 *Conditions:* Rain

Referee: Ben O'Keeffe (New Zealand)
Assistant referees: Nic Berry (Australia), Paul Williams (New Zealand)
TMO: Angus Gardner (Australia)

Scoring:
First half: 7m Tu'inukuafe try, Mo'unga conversion 7-0, 20m Mo'unga try 12-0, 26m Mo'unga try, conversion 19-0, 30m Coles try, Mo'unga conversion 26-0
Second half: 41m Lolesio try 26-5, 60m Mo'unga penalty 29-5, 71m Ioane try, Mo'unga conversion 36-5, 73m J. Barrett try, Mo'unga conversion 43-5

Yellow cards: Daugunu (4m), J. Barrett (10m), Frizell (80m)
Australia Test debuts: Lolesio, Simone, McDermott, McReight
The All Blacks again retain the Bledisloe Cup, as they have since 2004.
The crowd was reduced due to the need for social distancing.

NEW ZEALAND v AUSTRALIA
Bledisloe Cup/Tri Nations

Test #595 Suncorp Stadium, Brisbane November 7, 2020

Australia won 24–22

NEW ZEALAND		AUSTRALIA
Jordie Barrett	15	Tom Banks
Sevu Reece	14	Tom Wright
Anton Lienert-Brown	13	Jordan Petaia
Ngani Laumape	12	Hunter Paisami
Rieko Ioane	11	Marika Koroibete
Beauden Barrett	10	Reece Hodge
TJ Perenara	9	Nic White
Ardie Savea	8	Harry Wilson
Sam Cane (capt)	7	Michael Hooper (capt)
Akira Ioane	6	Lachlan Swinton
Sam Whitelock	5	Matt Philip
Scott Barrett	4	Rob Simmons
Ofa Tuungafasi	3	Allan Alaalatoa
Codie Taylor	2	Brandon Paenga-Amosa
Karl Tu'inukuafe	1	James Slipper
Asafo Aumua (rep 2, 70m)	16	Folau Fainga'a (rep 2, 65m)
Alex Hodgman (rep 1, 50m)	17	Angus Bell (rep 1, 40m)
Tyrel Lomax (rep 6, 29m)	18	Taniela Tupou (rep 3, 53m)
Tupou Vaa'i (rep 4, 78m)	19	Ned Hanigan (rep 4, 53m)
Cullen Grace (rep 7, 78m)	20	Liam Wright (rep 8, 70m)
Brad Weber (rep 9, 77m)	21	Tate McDermott (rep 9, 68m)
Damian McKenzie (rep 23, 70m)	22	Noah Lolesio (rep 13, 65m)
Will Jordan (rep 12, 65m)	23	Filipo Daugunu (rep 14, 68m)
R. Ioane, Taylor, Vaa'i	Tries	T. Wright, Tupou
J. Barrett (2)	Cons	Hodge
J. Barrett	Pens	Hodge (4)

Kickoff: 7.45pm *Attendance:* 36,626 *Conditions:* Fine, humid

Referee: Nic Berry (Australia)
Assistant referees: Angus Gardner (Australia), Ben O'Keeffe (New Zealand)
TMO: Paul Williams (New Zealand)

Scoring:
First half: 3m T. Wright try 0–5, 9m R. Ioane try 5–5, 21m Hodge penalty 5–8, 33m J. Barrett penalty 8–8
Second half: 49m Hodge penalty 8–11, 51m Taylor try, J. Barrett conversion 15–11, 59m Hodge penalty 15–14, 70m Hodge penalty 15–17, 75m Tupou try, Hodge conversion 15–24, 79m Vaa'i try, J. Barrett conversion 22–24

Red cards: Tuungafasi (23m), Swinton (35m)
Yellow cards: Koroibete (41m), S. Barrett (68m)
All Blacks Test debuts: A. Ioane, Jordan (All Black No 1191), Aumua, Grace (1192)
Australia Test debuts: Wright, Swinton, Bell

NEW ZEALAND v ARGENTINA
Tri Nations

Test #596 Bankwest Stadium, Sydney November 14, 2020

Argentina won 25-15

NEW ZEALAND		ARGENTINA
Beauden Barrett	15	Santiago Carreras
Jordie Barrett	14	Bautista Delguy
Anton Lienert-Brown	13	Matias Orlando
Jack Goodhue	12	Santiago Chocobares
Caleb Clarke	11	Juan Imhoff
Richie Mo'unga	10	Nicolas Sanchez
Aaron Smith	9	Tomas Cubelli
Ardie Savea	8	Rodrigo Bruni
Sam Cane (capt)	7	Marcos Kremer
Shannon Frizell	6	Pablo Matera (capt)
Sam Whitelock	5	Matias Alemanno
Patrick Tuipulotu	4	Guido Petti Pagadizaval
Tyrel Lomax	3	Francisco Gomez Kodela
Dane Coles	2	Julian Montoya
Joe Moody	1	Nahuel Tetaz Chaparro
Codie Taylor (rep 2, 49m)	16	Facundo Bosch (rep 2, 77m)
Alex Hodgman (rep 1, 73m)	17	Mayco Vivas (rep 1, 72m)
Nepo Laulala (rep 3, 58m)	18	Santiago Medrano (rep 3, 72m)
Tupou Vaa'i (rep 4, 70m)	19	Santiago Grondona (rep 8, 54m)
Hoskins Sotutu (rep 6, 50m)	20	Tomas Lezana (rep 5, 73m)
Brad Weber (rep 9, 63m)	21	Gonzalo Bertranou (rep 9, 77m)
Rieko Ioane (rep 13, 32m, temp) (rep 14, 50m)	22	Lucio Cinti Luna
Damian McKenzie (rep 12, 64m)	23	Santiago Cordero (rep 15, 30m, temp)
Cane, Clarke	Tries	Sanchez
Mo'unga	Cons	Sanchez
Mo'unga	Pens	Sanchez (6)

Kickoff: 5.10pm *Attendance:* 9063 *Conditions:* Fine

Referee: Angus Gardner (Australia)
Assistant referees: Nic Berry (Australia), Paul Williams (New Zealand)
TMO: Ben O'Keeffe (New Zealand)

Scoring:
First half: 6m Sanchez penalty 0-3, 12m Mo'unga penalty 3-3, 19m Sanchez try, conversion 3-10, 26m Sanchez penalty 3-13, 33m Sanchez penalty 3-16
Second half: 49m Sanchez penalty 3-19, 53m Cane try, Mo'unga conversion 10-19, 58m Sanchez penalty 10-22, 77m Sanchez penalty 10-25, 82m Clarke try 15-25

Argentina Test debuts: Chocobares, Grondona

This was the Pumas' first victory over the All Blacks in 30 Tests dating back to 1985. It was also their first Test match in 13 months due to the pandemic.
This was the first time since 2011 that the All Blacks have suffered back to back losses.

NEW ZEALAND v ARGENTINA
Tri Nations

Test #597 McDonald Jones Stadium, Newcastle November 28, 2020
New Zealand won 38–0

NEW ZEALAND		ARGENTINA
Beauden Barrett	15	Emiliano Boffelli
Jordie Barrett	14	Santiago Cordero
Anton Lienert-Brown	13	Juan Cruz Mallia
Jack Goodhue	12	Jeronimo de la Fuente
Caleb Clarke	11	Ramiro Moyano
Richie Mo'unga	10	Nicolas Sanchez
Aaron Smith	9	Felipe Ezcurra
Ardie Savea	8	Facundo Isa
Sam Cane (capt)	7	Marcos Kremer
Akira Ioane	6	Pablo Matera (capt)
Sam Whitelock	5	Lucas Paulos
Scott Barrett	4	Guido Petti Pagadizaval
Nepo Laulala	3	Santiago Medrano
Dane Coles	2	Julian Montoya
Joe Moody	1	Mayco Vivas
Codie Taylor (rep 2, 60m)	16	Santiago Socina (rep 2, 67m)
Karl Tu'inukuafe (rep 1, 57m)	17	Nahuel Tetaz Chaparro (rep 1, 56m)
Tyrel Lomax (rep 3, 57m)	18	Lucio Sordoni (rep 3, 56m)
Patrick Tuipulotu (rep 5, 63m)	19	Matias Alemanno (rep 5, 60m)
Hoskins Sotutu (rep 6, 65m)	20	Santiago Grondona (rep 7, 61m)
TJ Perenara (rep 9, 60m)	21	Gonzalo Bertranou (rep 9, 67m)
Rieko Ioane (rep 13, 53m)	22	Santiago Carreras (rep 10, 63m)
Will Jordan (rep 11, 65m)	23	Lucas Mensa (rep 12, 60m)
Jordan (2), Coles, Savea, Tuipulotu	Tries	
Mo'unga (5	Cons	
Mo'unga	Pens	

Kickoff: 7.45pm **Attendance:** 10,107 **Conditions:** Hot

Referee: Nic Berry (Australia)
Assistant referees: Angus Gardner (Australia), Ben O'Keeffe (New Zealand)
TMO: Paul Williams (New Zealand))

Scoring:
First half: 12m Coles try, Mo'unga conversion 7–0, 17m Mo'unga penalty 10–0
Second half: : 51m Savea try, Mo'unga conversion 17–0, 68m Jordan try, Mo'unga conversion 24–0, 70m Jordan try, Mo'unga conversion 31–0, 84m Tuipulotu try, Mo'unga conversion 38–0

Yellow card: Lomax (81)

This win effectively sealed the Tri Nations for the All Blacks with one match of the tournament still to play.

TRI NATIONS 2020

There were several changes to the Rugby Championship before the tournament resorted to the old Tri Nations moniker, running from October 31 to December 5 in Australia.

SANZAAR at first awarded the tournament-hosting rights to New Zealand, before difficulties around quarantine restrictions saw it passed to Australia. A draw was released which did not meet the approval of New Zealand, which wanted its players out of quarantine before Christmas. As it happened, South Africa withdrew on player welfare grounds, claiming its players did not have enough rugby to withstand the rigours of international rugby.

Despite two defeats, New Zealand won the competition, its 17th since 1996, effectively with a week to spare, as Australia and Argentina needed to win their final match by a gargantuan margin of close to 100 points to head the All Blacks on points differential.

Results

October 31	New Zealand	43	Australia	5	Sydney
November 7	Australia	24	New Zealand	22	Brisbane
November 14	Argentina	25	New Zealand	15	Sydney
November 21	Australia	15	Argentina	15	Newcastle
November 28	New Zealand	38	Argentina	0	Newcastle
December 5	Australia	16	Argentina	16	Sydney

Final standings

Team	P	W	D	L	For	Against	Bonus	Total
New Zealand	4	2	–	2	118	54	3	11
Argentina	4	1	2	1	56	84	–	8
Australia	4	1	2	1	60	96	–	8

Scoring distribution

	FOR					AGAINST				
Team	T	C	PG	DG	Pts	T	C	PG	DG	Pts
New Zealand	16	13	4	–	118	4	2	10	–	54
Argentina	2	2	14	–	56	8	7	10	–	84
Australia	4	2	12	–	60	10	8	10	–	96
TOTALS	**22**	**17**	**30**	**0**	**234**	**22**	**17**	**30**	**0**	**234**

NORTH ISLAND V SOUTH ISLAND

The first inter-island match since 2012 was announced on June 26 and set down for August 29 at Eden Park, Auckland. The re-emergence of Covid-19 cases in the Auckland community in August eventually saw the match postponed to September 5 and transferred to Sky Stadium, Wellington, without spectators.

The teams were chosen by the All Blacks selectors and eligibility for each Island was determined by the first province players played their first-class rugby for, which in a number of cases was not the current province they are signed to. (*See Happenings.*)

Two trophies were played for — The Loving Cup and Te Matau a Maui. (*See Happenings.*)

The lead changed hands seven times. The seventh change occurred in the 85th minute when Will Jordan crossed for his second try, which was converted by Jordie Barrett.

Sky Stadium, Wellington   **September 5, 2020**

Won by South Island 38-35

NORTH ISLAND		SOUTH ISLAND
Damian McKenzie	15	Jordie Barrett
Sevu Reece	14	Will Jordan
Rieko Ioane	13	Braydon Ennor
Anton Lienert-Brown	12	Jack Goodhue
Caleb Clarke	11	George Bridge
Beauden Barrett	10	Richie Mo'unga
TJ Perenara	9	Brad Weber
Hoskins Sotutu	8	Tom Sanders
Ardie Savea	7	Tom Christie
Akira Ioane	6	Shannon Frizell
Tupou Vaa'i	5	Mitchell Dunshea
Patrick Tuipulotu (capt)	4	Sam Whitelock (capt)
Ofa Tu'ungafasi	3	Nepo Laulala
Asafo Aumua	2	Codie Taylor
Karl Tu'inukuafe	1	Joe Moody
Ash Dixon (rep 2, 59m)	16	Liam Coltman (rep 2, 50m)
Ayden Johnstone (rep 1, 49m)	17	George Bower (rep 1, 50m)
Angus Ta'avao (rep 3, 49m)	18	Tyrel Lomax (rep 3, 50m)
Scott Scrafton (rep 5, 49m)	19	Manaaki Selby-Rickit (rep 5, 66m)
Dalton Papalii (rep 8, 62m)	20	Dillon Hunt (rep 7, 58m)
Aaron Smith (rep 9, h/t)	21	Finlay Christie (rep 9, 63m)
Peter Umaga-Jensen (rep 14, 62m)	22	Josh Ioane (rep 10, 27m-h/t, 70m)
Mitchell Hunt (rep 10, 59m)	23	Leicester Faingaanku (rep 13, 12m)
Ofa Tu'ungafasi (rep 17, 65m)	3	

R. Ioane (2), McKenzie, Smith, Dixon	Tries	Jordan (2), Laulala, Barrett, Lomax
McKenzie (5)	Conv	Barrett (5)
	Pen	Barrett

Referee: Paul Williams

The selectors named squads of 28 for each Island. North Island squad members who did not gain final selection were Lachlan Boshier, Kurt Eklund, Alex Fidow, Te Toiroa Tahuriorangi and Mark Telea. South Island squad members who did not gain final selection were Mitchell Drummond, Daniel Lienert-Brown, Andrew Makalio, Reed Prinsep, and Patelesio Tomkinson.

Alex Hodgman was an original selection in the South Island squad but withdrew to be replaced by Daniel Lienert-Brown.

Scott Barrett, Sam Cane, Dane Coles, Cullen Grace, David Havili, Ngani Laumape, Pari Pari Parkinson and Quinten Strange were all unavailable for the 28-man squads due to injury.

All Blacks assistant coach John Plumtree was head coach for North Island and All Blacks backs coach Brad Mooar was head coach for South Island.

The All Blacks squad of 35 was named at 11am the following day.

NZ MĀORI v MOANA PASIFIKA

In November, NZR acknowledged further exploration of an additional Super Rugby team in 2022 under the banner of Moana Pasifika. The Moana Pasifika team in this fixture comprised Pacific Islands players, through birth or family lineage, all of whom had appeared in the Mitre 10 Cup this year.

FMG Stadium, Hamilton　　　　　　　　　　　　　　　　　　　**December 5, 2020**

Won by NZ Māori 28–21

NZ MĀORI		MOANA PASIFIKA
Kaleb Trask	15	Stephen Perofeta
Shaun Stevenson	14	Leicester Faingaanuku
Billy Proctor	13	Fetuli Paea
Quinn Tupaea	12	Vince Aso
Sean Wainui	11	Salese Rayasi
Otere Black	10	Josh Ioane
Bryn Hall	9	Folau Fakatava
Liam Messam	8	Pita-Gus Sowakula
Billy Harmon	7	Alamanda Motuga
Whetukamokamo Douglas	6	Marino Mikaele-Tu'u
Manaaki Selby-Rickit	5	Naitoa Ah Kuoi
Isaia Walker-Leawere	4	Gerard Cowley-Tuioti
Josh Hohneck	3	Michael Alaalatoa (capt)
Ash Dixon (capt)	2	Leni Apisai
Pouri Rakete-Stones	1	Daniel Lienert-Brown
Kurt Eklund (rep 2, 69m)	16	Samisoni Taukei'aho (rep 2, 45m)
Ross Wright (rep 1, 65m)	17	Jordan Lay (rep 1, 58m)
Tamaiti Williams (rep 3, 65m)	18	Sione Mafileo (rep 3, 61m)
Ethan Roots (rep 6, 61m)	19	Samipeni Finau (rep 5, 69m)
Mitchell Karpik (rep 7, 61m)	20	Tavake "Nasi" Manu (rep 8, 51m)
Te Toiroa Tahuriorangi (rep 9, 71m)	21	Dwayne Polataivao (rep 9, 74m)
Rameka Poihipi (rep 13, 71m)	22	Asaeli Tikoirotuma (rep 11, 64m)
Mathew Skipwith-Garland (rep 11, 29m)	23	Etene Nanai-Seturo (rep 13, 51m)

Trask, Dixon, Proctor, Karpik	Tries	Motuga, Polataivao
Trask (4)	Conv	Ioane
	Pen	Ioane (3)

Referee: Mike Fraser

Original NZ Māori selections Marcel Renata (starting) and Jonah Lowe (subs bench) subsequently withdrew injured. Pouri Rakete-Stones was promoted from the subs bench to replace Renata and Ross Wright came onto the subs bench. Mathew Skipwith-Garland came on to the subs bench to replace Lowe.

NZ Māori Head Coach: Clayton McMillan

Moana Pasifika Head Coach: Tana Umaga

INVESTEC SUPER RUGBY 2020

ALMANACK SUPER RUGBY NEW ZEALAND XV

Jordie Barrett
Hurricanes

Will Jordan　　　　Anton Lienert-Brown　　　　Caleb Clarke
Crusaders　　　　　*Chiefs*　　　　　　　　　　*Blues*

Jack Goodhue
Crusaders

Richie Mo'unga
Crusaders

Aaron Smith
Highlanderss

Hoskins Sotutu
Blues

Lachie Boshier　　Samuel Whitelock　　Patrick Tuipulotu　　Shannon Frizell
Chiefs　　　　　*Crusaders*　　　　　*Blues*　　　　　　*Highlanders*

Ofa Tuungafasi　　　　Codie Taylor　　　　Joe Moody
Blues　　　　　　　　*Crusaders*　　　　　*Crusaders*

Reserves –
Ash Dixon (*Highlanders*), Tyrel Lomax (*Hurricanes*), Ayden Johnstone (*Highlanders*), Paripari Parkinson (*Highlanders*), Dalton Papali'i (*Blues*), TJ Perenara (*Hurricanes*), David Havili (*Crusaders*), Rieko Ioane (*Blues*).

*Selections were made based on form in both the Super Rugby and Super Rugby Aotearoa competitions.

Super Rugby made its earliest start in 25 seasons, and its earliest finish.

The Blues hosted the Chiefs on January 31 in sweltering summer heat. Seven rounds later, on March 15, the competition was suspended as Covid-19 took hold across the globe. Super Rugby never resumed and no winner was declared by Sanzaar.

Leading the way at the fullstop were the Sharks, who topped the table, ahead of the Brumbies and Crusaders. For once, the log was an accurate reflection of how the competition had panned out to that point.

After a three-month hiatus, a new competition — Super Rugby Aotearoa — kicked off on June 13. It was played before bumper crowds on Saturday nights and Sunday afternoons and the rugby-starved public came out in force until the last weekend, when a resurgence of Covid-19 saw the Highlanders-Hurricanes match played before no spectators and an Eden Park sellout between the Blues and Crusaders cancelled.

The Crusaders were the inaugural champions and this, their 11th championship, might just be their best yet after being shorn of half their starting pack in the off-season.

It was generally accepted that the quality of rugby throughout the 19 matches was not far below Test match intensity and acted as an antidote to some of the hardship many were experiencing throughout the land.

The shape of Super Rugby in 2021, which will kick off the fifth broadcasting deal since the 1996 inception, sees a second Super Rugby Aotearoa, to be followed by a 10-team trans-Tasman Super Rugby competition.

BLUES

The Blues' first playoffs appearance since 2011 remains elusive, but they would surely have qualified had Super Rugby gone the distance and Super Rugby Aotearoa offered semi-finals.

They took their game, after a shaky 1–2 start, to new heights, bringing the consistency to go 9–2 for the rest of the season, spanning two competitions. It was clearly their best campaign since Pat Lam took them to the semi-finals in 2019.

Much of their improvement can be put down to a pack that dominated in most games, led by tighthead prop Ofa Tuungafasi and, by example, skipper Patrick Tuipulotu, who continues to grow in stature.

The tour of South Africa could be seen as a turning point, with the side fashioning contrasting wins over the Bulls and Stormers.

English recruit Joe Marchant offered top value on either the wing or centre, while Rieko Ioane moved in from the wing to find a home in the No 13 jersey.

Mark Telea led all tryscorers with seven and was always dangerous. Caleb Clarke returned from sevens duty for Super Rugby Aotearoa and played his way into the All Blacks.

Stephen Perofeta looked good in either the 10 or 15 jersey in the first half of the season, while Otere Black outdid himself with some mature displays and further accuracy off the tee.

Beauden Barrett took some time to hit his straps at fullback in Super Rugby Aotearoa, but looked more assured at first-five.

At halfback, Sam Nock was effective early and sparky Finlay Christie ended the season as the top No 9. Jonathan Ruru offered good support.

Hoskins Sotutu had a breakout season at No 8, forcing his way into the All Blacks. He pushed Akira Ioane onto the blindside, where the latter was less prominent but more industrious than we have seen since 2018. Veteran Tony Lamborn performed well when called upon, while Dalton Papali'i was consistent in two loose positions. Tom Robinson's season was again cut short by injury just when he was performing well. Tuipulotu manfully carried a heavy workload.

Karl Tu'inukuafe played well pre-Covid, while Alex Hodgman did so in Super Rugby Aotearoa. James Parsons had his injury worries, but Kurt Eklund emerged as the leading hooker, winning seven starts and always offering maximum value off the bench.

It will niggle the Blues that the Crusaders again had the wood on them, twice, but six victories in all over New Zealand opposition told of a franchise that is starting to realise its long-held potential.

The crowds flocked back to Eden Park for Super Rugby Aotearoa, including more than 36,000 who watched the Hurricanes, but a final day sellout against the Crusaders was stymied by another lockdown.

CHIEFS

A season that started so promisingly for the Chiefs ended in crushing disappointment.

After Warren Gatland's charges opened with a 4–2 record pre-Covid, they crashed to a 0–8 winless Super Rugby Aotearoa campaign. They were, however, well in the contest in each defeat, and never lost by more than 13 points.

The outstanding performer was loose forward Lachie Boshier, who tackled his heart out, was accurate at the breakdown, and led the tryscorers with seven. Sam Cane had his injury concerns, while Luke Jacobson was hardly seen due to injury. The Chiefs missed the rugged Canadian Tyler Ardron, who departed for France before the second half of the season. But they missed no one more than lock Brodie Retallick, on sabbatical in Japan. Up stepped Mitch Brown, who again gave yeoman service in the tight, while Tupou Vaa'i, born in the year 2000, slotted into the second row for SRA and did so well he made the All Blacks.

There was another injury crisis in the props, with Atu Moli and Angus Ta'avao absent for much of the season. Aidan Ross was solid at loosehead. Hooker Nathan Harris and lock Laghlan McWhannell weren't sighted after surgery. Samisoni Taukei'aho and Bradley Slater both shared the hooking duties to good effect.

In the backs, Brad Weber was good but not as good as in 2019, while Te Toiroa Tahuriorangi offered valuable support early in the season.

Aaron Cruden played with maturity in the No 10 jersey, raising his Chiefs century. Early calls for his possible elevation to the All Blacks were ill-considered. Kaleb Trask, with an eye to the future, was handed six starts.

Anton Lienert-Brown was the most consistent of the backline, in either midfield position, while centre Quinn Tupaea had some nice moments on attack in his first season at this level. Sean Wainui scored five tries and ran hard on the wing.

Damian McKenzie played well much of the time, goalkicked accurately, and scored 107 points from fullback, but his all-round play was a notch below his brilliance of 2016-18.

In all, the Chiefs used 43 players, an illustration of the struggles they endured with injuries.

HURRICANES

The Hurricanes had a poor start and finish to this elongated season, but there was much good stuff in between.

They did, in fact, reel off five straight victories to be well in contention during Super Rugby Aotearoa until the last two rounds.

After a disrupted off-season in which their head coach John Plumtree was promoted to the All Blacks, meaning assistant Jason Holland stepped up to fill the breach, the Hurricanes were slow out of the blocks, but when they hit their attacking mojo, as against the Sunwolves in Napier, they were hard to contain.

Leading the way were 'hard to stop' wings Kobus van Wyk (8 tries) and Ben Lam (6). But the outstanding player was Jordie Barrett, back in his rightful position of fullback. Though he didn't score a try, he did land some massive long-range kicks and impressed with the sharpness and physicality of his all-round play.

Wes Goosen and Vince Aso both excelled on occasion, but the real comer was centre Peter Umaga-Jensen, whose last four games were so good he cracked the North Island squad. Ngani Laumape was very good, but not as consistently imposing as 2017–19, until he broke his arm.

By Super Rugby Aotearoa, Jackson Garden-Bachop, who enjoyed his best campaign at this level, had usurped Fletcher Smith for the No 10 berth.

Halfback TJ Perenara was again the fulcrum of the attack, and he drew level with Christian Cullen on 56 tries for the franchise. Jamie Booth was a lively back-up.

Gareth Evans was strong at No 8 pre-Covid, but Ardie Savea slotted in at the boot of the scrum for SRA and was almost back to his dynamic best by the end of the competition. Reed Prinsep was his usual consistent, understated self, while Du'Plessis Kirifi continues to grow into a fetcher of top quality. Vaea Fifita's output had fallen far in 2020.

Lock James Blackwell was again the workhorse of the pack, while Scott Scrafton moved up the national rankings with some prime ball-winning displays.

Tyrel Lomax was close to the best Kiwi tighthead prop on show, while hookers Dane Coles and Asafo Aumua played effectively in tandem.

In SRA, the Hurricanes halted the Blues' charge but, more significantly, they lowered the Crusaders in Christchurch, the first time since 2016 the champs had fallen at home in Super Rugby.

CRUSADERS

The Crusaders won a fourth straight title — Super Rugby Aotearoa — and were among the pacesetters pre-Covid, too.

Scott Robertson's charges dropped just two matches, one pre-Covid and one in SRA, proving once again they are the kings of this rugby.

Their backline riches and depth were the envy of all other teams. Will Jordan (8 tries) and Sevu Reece (8) were amongst the tries, with able support from George Bridge (6) and Braydon Ennor (6). Jordan's line-breaking ability was peerless. David Havili showed his versatility and class when available. Jack Goodhue was close to the best back in the entire competition pre-Covid, having moved in one position from centre.

Richie Mo'unga was good value pre-Covid and then simply outstanding in SRA. His heads-up play from a kickoff against the Blues was a season highlight.

Bryn Hall and Mitch Drummond were again an effective 1-2 punch at halfback, though the latter was probably better overall than Hall, even with less starts.

But it was unexpectedly in the pack that the Crusaders won most plaudits. Despite losing Ethan Blackadder for most of the season due to shoulder surgery, less heralded players stepped forward and up. Men like No 8 Whetu Douglas, rookie No 7 Tom Christie, rookie No 6 Cullen Grace and lock Mitch Dunshea all played consistently well. Loose forward Sione Havili offered vital impact off the bench. Sam Whitelock slotted straight back into the second row for SRA and immediately hit the high notes while passing 150 matches for the franchise.

Joe Moody was on top of his game, while Michael Alaalatoa offered tremendous support on the other side of the scrum.

Captain Codie Taylor always maintained the highest standards, as befitting the nation's best rake, while Andrew Makalio chimed in with several aggressive displays as a sub.

The Crusaders were pushed hard in all their SRA matches, but annexed the title with a week to spare. Time and again, as is their wont, they absorbed huge pressure, only to deliver the knockout blow when it counted during the last quarter. They were outmuscled only by the Chiefs in February and the Hurricanes in July, but those were their sole defeats.

The franchise had a new logo, but the flagship team displayed the same winning characteristics that have been the envy of the competition since 1998.

HIGHLANDERS

It all went wrong for the Highlanders pre-Covid, losing their skipper James Lentjes to a bad leg injury and struggling to impose themselves both with and without the ball.

But some soul-searching during lockdown led to a series of resurgent displays during Super Rugby Aotearoa which showcased their time-honoured pride, commitment and innovation.

The 4-9 overall record does not look flash, but when you consider the lack of experience in key areas, it was a fair effort.

Tactically, they didn't do the right things early in the season, the Mitch Hunt-Josh Ioane 10-12 experiment not a success. Hunt played well as such, scoring three tries and topping all scorers with 65, but Ioane looked much better when restored to the No 10 jersey, where he took on the line with aplomb, for the final three games of SRA.

Scott Gregory was up and down in the back three, while Josh McKay at last received his share of opportunities on the wing or at fullback. Michael Collins enjoyed his first 11 outings for his home franchise. Jona Nareki brought the cutting edge on the flanks, scoring five tries. Sio Tomkinson and Rob Thompson never quite found their fluency in midfield.

The standout was halfback Aaron Smith, who hit the 150 for this team, started all 13 games on big minutes and controlled the tempo.

No 8 Marino Mikaele-Tu'u also started all 13 games and came of age at this level, carrying with power and not letting up in his work-rate. Dillon Hunt lifted his game after Lentjes went down, while Shannon Frizell won ball and scored tries in a fine season. Paripari Parkinson and Jack Whetton proved to be the best locks.

Siate Tokolahi and Ayden Johnstone cemented the No 3 and No 1 jerseys respectively.

Ash Dixon and Liam Coltman again shared all the hooking duties, but this season Dixon was clearly the best performer for his leadership, work around the park and four tries, mostly from lineout drives. Coltman's all-round play was not matched by the accuracy of his lineout throwing, whereas Dixon was polished in this set-piece.

The three SRA wins were full of merit, from the moment Bryn Gatland landed a late dropped goal to sink his father's Chiefs 28–27 under the roof to open the new competition in style, to the gutsy effort to down the Chiefs 33–31 in Hamilton, to the five-try 38–21 victory over the Hurricanes in the final round.

Fourth position in SRA, however, is not where this franchise wants to be, and so the contract of head coach Aaron Mauger was not renewed. Tony Brown stepped up, again, as head coach.

SUPER RUGBY STANDINGS

Standings to March 15:

Team	P	W	D	L	F	A	TF	TA	BP	Pts
Sharks	7	6	–	1	213	153	25	19	–	24
Brumbies	6	5	–	1	208	115	31	15	3	23
Crusaders	6	5	–	1	189	105	26	15	3	23
Blues	7	5	–	2	192	134	25	17	2	22
Chiefs	6	4	–	2	194	128	27	18	3	19
Hurricanes	6	4	–	2	168	135	22	17	1	17
Stormers	6	4	–	2	118	94	16	10	1	17
*Jaguares	7	3	1	3	169	135	23	16	3	17
Rebels	6	3	–	3	166	160	23	22	1	13
Reds	7	2	–	5	219	176	32	25	5	13
*Highlanders	6	1	1	4	91	163	11	23	1	7
Bulls	6	1	–	5	115	152	14	20	2	6
Lions	6	1	–	5	109	200	14	27	1	5
Waratahs	6	1	–	5	104	214	15	30	1	5
Sunwolves	6	1	–	5	101	292	15	45	–	4
TOTALS					**2356**	**2356**	**319**	**319**		

*The competition was suspended on March 15 after seven rounds due to the impact of Covid-19 and was never resumed. No winner was declared by SANZAAR.

NB. The Jaguares v Highlanders match in Buenos Aires, scheduled for March 15, was declared a 0–0 draw after being called off by SANZAAR due to uncertainty after the onset of Covid-19.

Points: 4 for a win
2 for a draw
Bonus points were for: a loss by seven points or fewer and/or for scoring three tries more than opponent

PREVIOUS WINNERS

1996	Auckland Blues	2008	Crusaders
1997	Auckland Blues	2009	Bulls
1998	Crusaders	2010	Bulls
1999	Crusaders	2011	Reds
2000	Crusaders	2012	Chiefs
2001	Brumbies	2013	Chiefs
2002	Crusaders	2014	Waratahs
2003	Blues	2015	Highlanders
2004	Brumbies	2016	Hurricanes
2005	Crusaders	2017	Crusaders
2006	Crusaders	2018	Crusaders
2007	Bulls	2019	Crusaders

SUPER RUGBY AOTEAROA FINAL STANDINGS

Standings to March 15:

Team	P	W	D	L	F	A	TF	TA	BP	Pts
*Crusaders	8	6	1	1	219	148	27	13	4	30
*Blues	8	5	1	2	176	149	23	16	2	24
Hurricanes	8	5	–	3	202	213	25	25	1	21
Highlanders	8	3	–	5	197	227	23	30	2	14
Chiefs	8	–	–	8	155	212	14	28	5	5

*Super Rugby Aotearoa kicked off on June 13 involving all five New Zealand franchises. Nineteen of the scheduled 20 matches were played, though there were no playoffs. The August 16 Blues-Crusaders game in Auckland was cancelled as Auckland entered Level 3 lockdown. Both sides were awarded two points for a draw. No crowd was permitted for the August 15 Highlanders-Hurricanes game in Dunedin. The Crusaders had already been crowned the inaugural champions a week earlier, their 11th championship in 25 seasons.

SUPER RUGBY RECORDS

(S12 and S14 records have been rolled forward, they do not include 2020 Super Rugby Aotearoa or Super Rugby AU)

BY THE TEAMS

	BEST IN 2020	**RECORD**
Season totals		
Points	219 Reds	691 Crusaders *2018*
Tries	32 Reds	97 Hurricanes 2017
Conversions	22 Crusaders, Brumbies	75 Crusaders *2018*
Penalty goals	17 Sharks	76 Sharks *2014*
Dropped goals	1 on 4 occasions	11 Bulls *2009*
Match totals		
Points	64 Reds v Sunwolves	96 Crusaders v Waratahs *2002*
Tries	10 Reds v Sunwolves	14 Crusaders v Waratahs *2002*
	10 Hurricanes v Sunwolves	Cheetahs v Sunwolves *2016*
		Lions v Sunwolves 2017
Conversions	7 Reds v Sunwolves	13 Crusaders v Waratahs *2002*
Penalty goals	4 on 3 occasions	9 Hurricanes v Blues *2010*
Dropped goals	1 on 4 occasions	4 Bulls v Crusaders *2009*

BY THE PLAYERS

	BEST IN 2020	**RECORD**
Season totals		
Points	86 C.D. Bosch (Sharks)	263 M. Steyn (Bulls) *2010*
Tries	7 A.J.H. Kellaway (Rebels)	16 M.B. Lam (Hurricanes) *2018*
Match totals		
Points	18 O.W.T.P. Black (Blues v Stormers)	50 G.E. Lawless (Natal v Highlanders) *1997*
Tries	3 J. Montoya (Jaguares v Reds)	4 on 18 occasions
	3 M.E. Telea (Blues v Waratahs)	
	3 J.P. van Wyk (Hurricanes v Sunwolves)	
Conversions	7 J. Campbell (Reds v Sunwolves)	13 A.P. Mehrtens (Crusaders v Waratahs) *2002*
Penalty goals	4 M. Steyn (Bulls v Sharks)	9 E.T. Jantjies (Lions v Cheetahs) *2012*
	4 J.M. Barrett (Hurricanes v Sharks)	
	4 O.W.T.P. Black (Blues v Stormers)	
Dropped goals	1 on 4 occasions	4 M. Steyn (Bulls v Crusaders) *2009*
Career records		
Points	1708 D.W. Carter (Crusaders 2003-15)	
Tries	60 I. Folau (Waratahs 2013-19)	
Games	202 W.W.V. Crockett (Crusaders 2006-18)	

MOST GAMES

Games	Player	Teams
202	W.W.V. Crockett	Crusaders
178	L.J. Messam	Chiefs
177	S.T. Moore	Reds/Brumbies
175	K.F. Mealamu	Blues/Chiefs
174	M.A. Nonu	Hurricanes/Highlanders/Blues
164	G.B. Smith	Brumbies/Reds
162	N.C. Sharpe	Reds/Force
157	T. Mtawarira	Sharks
157	S.U.T. Polota-Nau	Waratahs/Force
157	K.J. Read	Crusaders
156	K.J. Beale	Waratahs/Rebels
156	J.A. Strauss	Cheetahs/Bulls
153	A.M. Ellis	Crusaders
153	O.T. Franks	Crusaders
150	C.R. Flynn	Crusaders
150	R.J. Crotty	Crusaders

MOST POINTS

Points	Player	Team	Games	Tries	Conv	PG	DG
1708	D.W. Carter	Crusaders	141	36	287	307	11
1489	M. Steyn	Bulls	129	14	246	283	26
1238	B.J. Barrett	Hurricanes	125	34	249	187	1
1140	E.T. Jantjies	Lions/Stormers	139	12	270	176	4
1092	B.T. Foley	Waratahs	119	29	244	153	–
1036	S.A. Mortlock	Brumbies	138	56	162	144	–

*The leading points-scorer in Super Rugby Aotearoa 2020 was Richie Mo'unga of the Crusaders (99).

MOST TRIES

Tries	Player	Teams
60	I. Folau	Waratahs
59	D.C. Howlett	Blues/Hurricanes/Highlanders
58	C.S. Ralph	Chiefs/Crusaders
57	J.W.C. Roff	Brumbies
56	C.M. Cullen	Hurricanes
56	M.A. Nonu	Hurricanes/Blues/Highlanders
56	B.G. Habana	Bulls/Stormers
56	S.A. Mortlock	Brumbies
55	T.J. Perenara	Hurricanes
52	S.J. Savea	Hurricanes

*The leading tryscorer in Super Rugby Aotearoa 2020 was Will Jordan of the Crusaders (6).

ALL BLACKS 2020

Winners of the Investec Tri Nations Tournament and Bledisloe Cup

Back row: G. Enoka (*Manager — Leadership*), S. Frizell, S. Barrett, M. Dunshea, T. Vaa'i, S. McLeod (*Asst Coach*), J. McGarvey (*Doctor*). **Fourth row:** K. Simperingham (*Asst S&C Coach*), D. Shand (*Manager — Business & Operations*), J. Iversen (*Logistics Manager*), D. Papali'i, J. Barrett, H. Sorutu, T. Lomax, J. Goodhue, N. Gill (*S&C Coach*), J. Locke (*Media Manager*). **Third row:** H. Chapman (*Asst Performance Analyst*), N. Laumape, A. Hodgman, A. Ioane, P. Tuipulotu, W. Jordan, G. Bridge, B. Weber, C. Hooper (*Team Services Manager*), K. Darry (*Nutritionist*), P. Gallagher (*Physio*). **Second row:** J. Hamilton (*Performance Analyst*), Grant Fox (*Selector*), John Plumtree (*Selector/Asst Coach*), R. Mo'unga, S. Reece, C. Clarke, K. Tu'inukuafe, N. Laulala, D. McKenzie, G. Feek (*Asst Coach*), B. Mooar (*Asst Coach*), G. Duncan (*Muscle Therapist*). **Front row:** A. Lienert-Brown, TJ Perenara, D. Coles, B. Barrett, A. Smith, I. Foster (*Head Coach/Selector*), S. Cane (*Captain*), S. Whitelock, J. Moody, C. Taylor, A. Savea, O. Tuungafasi. **Absent:** A. Aumua, C. Grace, P. Umaga-Jensen.

Photo by Bruce Jarvis Photographic Services Ltd

BLACK FERNS 2020
Downer Series v NZ Barbarians

Back row: J. Haggart (*Asst Coach*), W. Clarke (*Asst Coach*), A. Savage, K. Wills, C. Bremner, P. Tapsell, T. Kalounivale, J. Gavala (*Mental Skills*), J. Tout (*S&C*).
Third row: L. Cournane (*Manager*), K. Simon, L. Connor, A. Itunu, P. Love, R. Demant, C. Tofa, R. Holmes, A. du Plessis, A. Hodge (*Analyst*).
Second row: G. Milne (*Physio*), G. Steinmetz, K. Reynolds, A. Marino-Tauhinu, L. Veainu, Te K. Ngata-Aerengamate, T. Natua, N. Moors, H. Tubic, C. Robins-Reti, M. Keys (*Media Manager*). **Front row:** A-P. Nelson, G. Brooker, C. Alley, G. Moore (*Head Coach*), E. Blackwell (*Captain*), S. Winiata, K. Cocksedge (*Vice-captain*), C. McMenamin.

MĀORI ALL BLACKS 2020
v Moana Pasifika

Back row: A. Thompson (*Media Manager*), J. McLean (*Digital Content*), T. Brown (*Asst Coach*), R. Randle (*Asst Coach*), E. Iupeli (*Logistics*), R. Durie (*Doctor*), M. Sexton (*Campaign Manager*), S. Thomas (*S&C*), A. Letts (*Physio*), J. Ross (*Analyst*). ***Third row:*** J. Hohneck, E. Roots, T. Williams, M. Selby-Rickit, I. Walker-Leaware, S. Stevenson, W. Douglas, M. Skipwith-Garland, R. Prinsep. ***Second row:*** T. Ward (*Manager*), P. Rakete-Stones, B. Harmon, R. Poihipi, M. Karpik, Q. Tupaea, B. Proctor, K. Eklund, J. Lowe, K. Trask. ***Front row:*** B. Hall, M. Renata, O. Black, L. Messam, C. McMillan (*Head Coach*), A. Dixon (*Captain*), L. Crawford (*Kaumatua*), S. Wainui, Te T. Tahuriorangi, R. Wright.

NZ BARBARIANS 2020
Downer Series v Black Ferns

Back row: J. Croker (*Physio*), L. Faleafaga, M. Roos, O. Ward-Duin, C. Nelles, JJ. Taylor, P. Maliepo, R. Todd, K. Wilson (*Mental Skills Coach*). **Third row:** D. Cron (*Analyst*), L.T. Mason (*Manager*), A. Tiplady (*Doctor*), S. Abraham, G. Houpapa-Barrett, A. Rule, M. Lolohea, C. Shepherd (*Asst Coach*). **Second row:** A. Bayler, C. Dallinger, M. Henderson, K. Olsen-Baker, I. Hohaia, R. Kelly, W. Hansen (*Asst Coach*). **Front row:** J. Vaughan, M. Parkes, K. Murray, R. Gibbes (*Head Coach*), A. Bremner (*Captain*), J. Ngan-Woo, K. Moata'ane, M. Tagoai. **Absent:** S. Thompson, C. Mayes.

CRUSADERS

2020 Investec Super Rugby Aotearoa Champions

Back row: E. Blackadder, O. Jager, Q. Strange, M. Dunshea, C. Grace. **Fifth row:** S. Thomas (*Lead Physical Performance*), G. Bridge, E. Roots, W. Jordan, D. McLeod, F. Paea, W. Douglas, T. Sanders, L. Fainga'anuku, P. Bowden (*Analyst*), J. Gardner (*Lead Analyst*), B. McAlister, I. Tu'ungafasi, F. Burke, J. Goodhue, B. Ennor, T. Christie, B. Harmon, J. Roche (*Lead Physio*), N. Tucker (*Physio*), C. Te Haara (*Media Manager*), R. Archibald (*Administrator*), S. Havili, B. Hall, G. Bower, H. Allan, M. Mataele, A. Makalio, V. Le Bas (*PDM*), G. Duder (*Physical Performance*). **Second row:** M. Jones (*Coach*), S. Hansen (*Coach*), J. Ryan (*Coach*), B. Cameron, I. Finau, S. Reece, C. O'Donnell, E. Enari, J. Miles (*Logistics Manager*), S. Fletcher (*Manager*), A. Goodman (*Coach*). **Front row:** R. Mo'unga, J. Moody, S. Whitelock, C. Taylor (*Captain*), S. Robertson (*Head Coach*), S. Barrett (*Captain*), D. Havili (*Vice-captain*), L. Romano, M. Alaalatoa, M. Drummond, M. Swan (*Doctor*), H. Roach. **Absent:** M. Swan (*Doctor*), H. Roach.

Photo by Ken Baker Photography

Photo by Ken Baker Photography

CANTERBURY WOMEN

Winners of the 2020 Farah Palmer Cup

Back row: A. Sisifa, A. Milnes, I. Waterman, C. Nelles, C. Bremrer, N. Poletti, G. Ponsonby, E. Savelio, P. Prendergast. **Third row:** T. Christie (*Asst Coach*), T. Greenslade, L. Jenkins, S. Curtis, G. Steinmetz, A. Matthews M. Lolohea, H. King, A. Rule, S. Donaldson (*S&C Support*), M. Ruscoe (*Asst Coach*), G. Lange (*Analyst*), N. Purdom, M. Puckett, S. O'Cain, G. O'Ro..rke, T. Simpson, S. de Gouw, O. Coady, R. Archibald (*Manager*), J. Croker (*Physio*). **Front row:** W. Hansen (*Asst Coach*), K. Cocksedge, P. Love, L. M<Governe, G. Brooker (*Vice-captain*), A. Bremner (*Captain*), L. Anderson, R. Todd, T. Gapper, B. Baxter (*Head Coach*). **Insets:** A. Lolohea, C. Siataga, T. Aldridge, A. Murphy (*S&C Coach*).

Photo by Evan Barnes Photography

TASMAN MAKO

Winners of the Mitre 10 Cup Premiership

Back row: D. Monaghan *(Asst S&C)*, J. Holden *(S&C)*, D. Poloataivao, B. Stewart, B. Princep, J. Spowart, R. Coxon, S. Matenga, L. Chapman, N. Price *(Analyst)*, K. Harrington *(Physio)*, M. Vercoe *(Manager)*, B. Thornalley *(Asst Manager)*, M. Telea, S. Holani, F. Paea, J. Norris, H. Renton, T. Cirikidaveta, M. Ngakura, I. Ross, C. Suafoa, T. Fox-Matamua, A. Segner, S. Moli, I. Tu'ungafasi, K. Sykes-Martin, S. Christie *(Asst Coach)*, J. Marshall *(Asst Coach)*. **Front row:** A. Goodman *(Head Coach)*, L. Fainga'anuku, I. Salmon, T. Fainga'anuku, Q. MacDonald, A. Ainley, A. Makalio, D. Havili *(Captain)*, M. Hunt, K. Fonotia, A. Nankivell, F. Christie, T. O'Malley, Q. Strange, C. Dermody *(Head Coach)*.

Photo by Corena

HAWKE'S BAY MAGPIES

Winners of the Mitre 10 Cup Championship and Holders of the Ranfurly Shield

Back row: J. Pinfold (*Asst S&C*), B. Jenkinson (*Asst Manager*), T. Jones (*Asst Manager*), F. Deformes (*Scrum Coach*), J. Apikotoa, L. Visinia, D. Flanders, I. Walker-Leaware, E. Martin, N. Waa, O. Sapsford, S. van der Peet (*Analyst*), M. Burgess (*S&C Intern*), L. Stephenson (*Head S&C*), M. Ozich (*Head Coach*), M. Smith (*Manager*), C. McLeod, C. Makene, J. Devery, K. Baker, I. Mapu, S. Funaki, J. Kaifa, A. Tuitavuki, N. Fomai, D. Toala, J. Hintz, L. McCluchie, M. Nicol (*Physio*), J. Syms (*Asst Coach*). **Front row:** F. Fakatava, S. Ili, – Lowe, J. Long, G. Evans, T. Parsons, G. Cridge, A. Dixon (*Captain*), K. Kereru-Symes (*Vice-captain*), B. Evans, M. Mikaele-Tu'u, B. O'Connor, S. Taumalolo, P. Zakete-Stones, M. Emerson. **Absent:** B. Weber, S. McNicol, I. Taylor (*Doctor*).

SUPER RUGBY 2020 RESULTS

Date	Winning team				Venue
January					
31	Chiefs	37	Blues	29	Auckland
31	Brumbies	27	Reds	24	Canberra
31	Sharks	23	Bulls	15	Durban
February					
1	Sunwolves	36	Rebels	27	Fukuoka
1	Crusaders	43	Waratahs	25	Nelson
1	Stormers	27	Hurricanes	0	Cape Town
1	Jaguares	38	Lions	8	Buenos Aires
7	Sharks	42	Highlanders	20	Dunedin
7	Brumbies	39	Rebels	26	Canberra
8	Chiefs	25	Crusaders	15	Hamilton
8	Blues	32	Waratahs	12	Newcastle
8	Lions	27	Reds	20	Johannesburg
8	Stormers	13	Bulls	0	Cape Town
8	Hurricanes	26	Jaguares	23	Buenos Aires
14	Crusaders	25	Blues	8	Auckland
14	Rebels	24	Waratahs	10	Melbourne
15	Chiefs	43	Sunwolves	17	Tokyo
15	Hurricanes	38	Sharks	22	Wellington
15	Highlanders	23	Brumbies	22	Canberra
15	Stormers	33	Lions	30	Johannesburg
15	Jaguares	43	Reds	27	Buenos Aires
21	Crusaders	33	Highlanders	13	Christchurch
22	Sharks	36	Rebels	24	Ballarat
22	Brumbies	26	Chiefs	14	Hamilton
22	Reds	64	Sunwolves	5	Brisbane
22	Stormers	17	Jaguares	7	Cape Town
22	Blues	23	Bulls	21	Pretoria
28	Rebels	28	Highlanders	22	Dunedin
28	Waratahs	29	Lions	17	Sydney
29	Hurricanes	62	Sunwolves	15	Napier
29	Sharks	33	Reds	23	Brisbane
29	Blues	33	Stormers	14	Cape Town
29	Jaguares	39	Bulls	24	Pretoria

March

6	Brumbies	47	Sunwolves	14	Wollongong
6	Crusaders	24	Reds	20	Christchurch
6	Chiefs	51	Waratahs	14	Wollongong
7	Blues	24	Hurricanes	15	Wellington
7	Rebels	37	Lions	17	Melbourne
7	Sharks	33	Jaguares	19	Durban
7	Bulls	38	Highlanders	13	Pretoria
13	Hurricanes	27	Chiefs	24	Hamilton
14	Blues	43	Lions	10	Auckland
14	Crusaders	49	Sunwolves	14	Brisbane
14	Reds	41	Bulls	17	Brisbane
14	Sharks	24	Stormers	14	Durban
14	Jaguares v Highlanders in Buenos Aires was cancelled: 0–0 draw				
15	Brumbies	47	Waratahs	14	Canberra

SUPER RUGBY AOTEAROA 2020 RESULTS

Date	Winning team				Venue
June					
13	Highlanders	28	Chiefs	27	Dunedin
14	Blues	30	Hurricanes	20	Auckland
20	Blues	24	Chiefs	12	Hamilton
21	Crusaders	39	Hurricanes	25	Wellington
27	Blues	27	Highlanders	24	Auckland
28	Crusaders	18	Chiefs	13	Christchurch
July					
4	Crusaders	40	Highlanders	20	Dunedin
5	Hurricanes	25	Chiefs	18	Hamilton
11	Crusaders	26	Blues	15	Christchurch
12	Hurricanes	17	Highlanders	11	Wellington
18	Hurricanes	29	Blues	27	Wellington
19	Highlanders	33	Chiefs	31	Hamilton
25	Hurricanes	34	Crusaders	32	Christchurch
26	Blues	21	Chiefs	17	Auckland
August					
1	Crusaders	32	Chiefs	19	Hamilton
2	Blues	32	Highlanders	21	Dunedin
8	Hurricanes	31	Chiefs	18	Wellington
9	Crusaders	32	Highlanders	22	Christchurch
15	Highlanders	38	Hurricanes	21	Dunedin
16	Blues v Crusaders in Auckland was cancelled: 0–0 draw				

BLUES

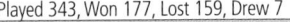

Postal address: Box 77 012 Mt Albert, Auckland 1350
Telephone: (09) 846 5425
Email: info@theblues.co.nz
Home venue: Eden Park, Auckland
Colours: royal and navy blue
Chairman: D.A. (Don) Mackinnon
Chief executive: A.J. (Andrew) Hore

Played 343, Won 177, Lost 159, Drew 7

	Tries	Conv	Pen	DG	Points
For	1092	732	694	12	9048
Against	940	652	761	27	8378

RECORDS — TEAM

Most points in a game	74	v Stormers, 1998
Most points in a season	513	1997
Biggest winning margin	53	60–7 v Hurricanes, 2002
Most tries in a game	11	v Stormers, 1998
Most tries in a season	70	1996

RECORDS — INDIVIDUAL

Most points in a game	29	G.W. Anscombe v Bulls, 2012
Most points in a season	180	A.R. Cashmore, 1998
Most points in a career	619	A.R. Cashmore, 1996-2000
Most tries in a game	4	J. Vidiri v Bulls, 2000
		D.C. Howlett v Hurricanes 2002
		J.M. Muliaina v Bulls, 2002
		R.E. Ioane v Sunwolves, 2019
Most tries in a season	12	D.C. Howlett, 2003
Most tries in a career	55	D.C. Howlett, 1999-2007
Most conversions in a game	7	A.R. Cashmore v Stormers, 1998
		A.R. Cashmore v Bulls, 2000
		C.J. Spencer v Bulls, 2002
Most conversions in a season	34	A.R. Cashmore, 1998
Most conversions in a career	120	C.J. Spencer
Most penalty goals in a game	6	A.R. Cashmore v Chiefs, 1998
		A.R. Cashmore v Hurricanes, 1999
		J.A. Arlidge v Bulls, 2001
		S.A. Brett v Bulls, 2010
		C.M. Noakes v Stormers, 2013
Most penalty goals in a season	34	A.R. Cashmore, 1999
Most penalty goals in a career	114	A.R. Cashmore
Most dropped goals in a game	1	on 12 occasions
Most dropped goals in a season	2	O. Ai'i, 2000
Most dropped goals in a career	3	C.J. Spencer
Most games	164	K.F. Mealamu, 2000-2015

Player	Union	Date of birth	Height	Weight	Blues games	Blues points
B.J. (Beauden) Barrett	Taranaki	27-05-91	1.86	92	7	26
O.W.T.P (Otere) Black	Manawatu	04-05-95	1.85	86	26	166
A.P.E. (Aaron) Carroll	Bay of Plenty	11-10-93	1.93	112	6	-
D.W. (Daniel) Carter	-	05-03-82	1.79	90	-	-
F.T. (Finlay) Christie	Tasman	19-09-95	1.77	84	7	15
C.D. (Caleb) Clarke	Auckland	29-03-99	1.87	103	19	30
G.E. (Gerard) Cowley-Tuioti	North Harbour	16-06-92	1.96	110	52	25
M.D. (Matt) Duffie	North Harbour	16-08-90	1.92	95	55	55
K.A.N. (Kurt) Eklund	Bay of Plenty	05-01-92	1.8	103	13	5
T.J. (Tinoai) Faiane	Auckland	24-10-95	1.84	93	45	20
B.T. (Blake) Gibson	Auckland	19-04-95	1.86	102	50	20
J.K. (Josh) Goodhue	Northland	13-06-95	1.99	115	27	-
J.W. (Jack) Heighton	North Harbour	26-02-99	1.87	90	-	-
A.T.O.A. (Alex) Hodgman	Auckland	16-07-93	1.9	119	33	-
J.S.C. (Jordan) Hyland	Northland	03-10-89	1.88	101	5	10
A.L. (Akira) Ioane	Auckland	16-06-95	1.94	113	74	90
R.E. (Rieko) Ioane	Auckland	18-03-97	1.88	103	60	190
T.A. (Tony) Lamborn	Southland	31-07-91	1.85	107	9	5
E.V. (Ezekiel) Lindenmuth	Counties Manukau	14-07-97	1.87	116	7	-
S.T. (Sione) Mafileo	North Harbour	14-04-93	1.78	128	55	-
J. (Joe) Marchant	Overseas	16-07-96	1.83	95	7	15
E.R. (Emoni) Narawa	Bay of Plenty	13-07-99	1.84	94	7	-
R.F. (Ray) Niuia	Tasman	19-06-91	1.86	120	1	-
S.J. (Sam) Nock	Northland	18-06-96	1.78	85	35	5
J.R. (Jared) Page	North Harbour	22-07-93	1.83	94	-	-
D.R. (Dalton) Papali'i	Counties Manukau	11-10-97	1.9	105	34	40
J.W. (James) Parsons	North Harbour	27-11-86	1.85	108	115	45
S. (Stephen) Perofeta	Taranaki	12-03-97	1.81	85	24	129
J.W.L. (Jacob) Pierce	North Harbour	10-09-97	2.02	112	7	-
H.R.J. (Harry) Plummer	Auckland	19-06-98	1.84	94	30	58
M.T. (Marcel) Renata	Auckland	24-02-94	1.87	121	13	-
W. (Waimana) Riedlinger-Kapa	Auckland	09-02-98	1.96	102	-	-
T.N. (Tom) Robinson	Northland	10-11-94	1.98	110	22	15
J.L. (Jonathan) Ruru	Auckland	02-03-93	1.83	94	35	5
H.C.R (Hoskins) Sotutu	Auckland	12-07-98	1.92	106	11	10
M.E. (Mark) Telea	North Harbour	06-12-96	1.86	94	14	35
T.R. (Tanielu) Tele'a	Auckland	16-06-98	1.87	107	9	20
L.H.V. (Luteru) Tolai	North Harbour	06-01-98	1.81	119	4	-
J.F. (James) Tucker	Waikato	05-08-94	1.97	111	-	-
G.Z.K. (Karl) Tu'inukuafe	North Harbour	21-02-93	1.86	135	19	5
P.T. (Patrick) Tuipulotu (captain)	Auckland	23-01-93	1.98	120	80	55
A.O.H.M. (Ofa) Tuungafasi	Auckland	19-04-92	1.95	129	96	25
J.S. (Joe) Walsh	Southland	23-07-93	1.89	123	1	-

*NB. Page, Heighton, Tele'a, Riedlinger-Kapa and Tucker did not appear in 2020. Carter was a replacement player for Super Rugby Aotearoa, but did not appear.

Original selection Baden Wardlaw (Bay of Plenty) was forced to retire before the season. He was replaced by Carroll.

Manager: Richard Fry
Coach: Leon MacDonald
Assistant coaches: Tom Coventry, Tana Umaga, Daniel Halangahu, Ben Afeaki

BLUES 2020

	Chiefs	Waratahs	Crusaders	Bulls	Stormers	Hurricanes	Lions	Hurricanes	Chiefs	Highlanders	Crusaders	Hurricanes	Chiefs	Highlanders	TOTALS
Duffie	15	15	15	s	s	s	14	s	s	–	s	s	15	15	13
Telea	14	11	11	11	11	11	11	14	14	14	14	11	14	14	14
Narawa	s	s	s	14	–	–	s	–	–	–	–	14	s	–	7
Hyland	–	14	14	–	–	–	–	–	–	–	–	–	–	–	2
Clarke	–	–	–	–	–	–	–	11	11	11	11	–	11	11	6
R. Ioane	11	–	–	–	13	13	13	13	13	13	13	13	13	13	11
Marchant	13	13	13	13	14	14	–	–	–	s	–	–	–	–	7
Faiane	12	12	12	s	12	12	12	12	12	12	s	s	12	12	14
Barrett	–	–	–	–	–	–	–	15	15	15	15	15	10	10	7
Perofeta	10	10	10	15	15	15	15	–	–	–	–	–	–	–	7
Black	–	–	–	10	10	10	10	10	10	10	10	10	s	s	11
Plummer	s	s	s	12	s	s	s	s	s	s	12	12	s	s	14
Ruru	9	9	9	9	s	s	s	–	–	–	s	s	–	–	9
Christie	–	–	–	–	–	–	–	s	s	s	9	9	9	9	7
Nock	s	s	s	s	9	9	9	9	9	9	–	–	s	s	12
A. Ioane	–	s	–	–	–	8	s	–	6	6	6	8	8	8	9
Sotutu	8	8	8	8	8	–	8	8	8	8	8	–	–	–	10
Gibson	s	7	7	–	s	7	7	7	–	–	s	–	7	–	9
Lamborn	7	–	s	7	–	s	–	–	s	s	–	s	s	7	9
Papali'i	6	6	6	s	7	–	6	s	7	7	7	7	6	6	13
Robinson	5	s	s	6	6	6	–	6	–	–	–	–	–	–	7
Carroll	–	–	–	s	s	–	s	–	–	–	s	6	–	s	6
Pierce	–	–	–	5	5	5	5	–	–	–	–	–	–	s	5
Goodhue	s	5	5	–	–	–	–	5	5	5	5	5	s	–	9
Tuipulotu	4	4	4	4	4	4	–	4	4	4	4	4	4	4	13
Cowley-Tuioti	–	–	–	–	–	s	4	s	s	s	–	s	5	5	8
Mafileo	3	3	s	3	3	s	3	–	s	s	s	s	s	s	13
Tuungafasi	s	s	3	s	s	3	–	3	3	3	3	3	3	3	13
Hodgman	1	–	–	–	–	–	–	1	1	1	1	1	s	–	9
Tu'inukuafe	s	1	1	1	1	1	–	–	–	–	s	–	s	1	9
Renata	–	–	–	–	s	–	s	s	s	s	–	s	–	–	6
Lindenmuth	–	s	s	s	–	–	1	s	–	–	–	–	–	–	5
Walsh	–	–	–	–	–	–	s	–	–	–	–	–	–	–	1
Parsons	–	s	2	2	–	s	2	2	2	2	2	–	–	–	9
Eklund	2	2	s	s	2	2	–	s	s	s	s	2	2	2	13
Tolai	–	–	–	–	s	–	s	–	–	–	–	–	s	–	4
Niuia	s	–	–	–	–	*	–	–	–	–	–	–	–	–	1

BLUES INDIVIDUAL SCORING

	Tries	Con	PG	DG	Points
Black	–	17	16	–	82
Telea	7	–	–	–	35
R. Ioane	6	–	–	–	30
Barrett	1	6	2	1	26
Papali'i	5	–	–	–	25
Perofeta	2	4	1	–	21
Christie	3	–	–	–	15
A. Ioane	3	–	–	–	15
Marchant	3	–	–	–	15
Penalty tries	2	–	–	–	14
Clarke	2	–	–	–	10
Faiane	2	–	–	–	10
Sotutu	2	–	–	–	10
Tuipulotu	2	–	–	–	10
Plummer	–	2	2	–	10
Cowley-Tuioti	1	–	–	–	5
Duffie	1	–	–	–	5
Eklund	1	–	–	–	5
Gibson	1	–	–	–	5
Lamborn	1	–	–	–	5
Robinson	1	–	–	–	5
Tu'inukuafe	1	–	–	–	5
Tuungafasi	1	–	–	–	5
Totals	48	29	21	1	368
Opposition scored	33	23	23	1	283

BLUES TEAM RECORD 2020

			Played 14	Won 10	Lost 4	Drew 0	Points for 368		Points against 283
Date	Opponent	Location	Score	Tries	Con	PG	DG		Referee
January 31	Chiefs	Auckland	29–37	R. Ioane (2), Lamborn, Tu'inukuafe	Perofeta (3)	Plummer			A. Gardner (Australia)
February 08	Waratahs	Newcastle	32–12	Telea (3), Gibson, Marchant	Perofeta, Plummer	Perofeta			AJ Jacobs (South Africa)
February 14	Crusaders	Auckland	8–25	Tuipulotu		Plummer			P. Williams
February 22	Bulls	Pretoria	23–21	Robinson, Telea, Perofeta	Black	Black (2)			M. van der Westhuizen (South Africa)
February 29	Stormers	Cape Town	33–14	Marchant (2), Papali'i	Black (3)	Black (4)			J. Peyper (South Africa)
March 07	Hurricanes	Wellington	24–15	A. Ioane, Telea, penalty try	Black (2)	Black			M. Fraser
March 14	Lions	Auckland	43–10	R. Ioane (2), Cowley-Tuioti, Sotutu, Perofeta, penalty try	Black (3), Plummer	Black			M. van der Westhuizen (South Africa)
June 14	Hurricanes	Auckland	30–20	Clarke, Faiane, Papali'i	Black (3)	Black (3)			M. Fraser
June 20	Chiefs	Hamilton	24–12	Sotutu, Telea	Black	Black (2), Barrett	Barrett		B. O'Keeffe
June 27	Highlanders	Auckland	27–24	Papali'i (2), Clarke, R. Ioane	Black (2)	Black			P. Williams
July 11	Crusaders	Christchurch	15–26	Telea, R. Ioane	Black	Black			P. Williams
July 18	Hurricanes	Wellington	27–29	Barrett, Papali'i, A. Ioane, Eklund	Black, Barrett	Black			B. O'Keeffe
July 26	Chiefs	Auckland	21–17	Tuipulotu, Christie, Duffie	Barrett (3)				B. Pickerill
August 02	Highlanders	Dunedin	32–21	Christie (2), Tu'ungafasi, A. Ioane, Faiane	Barrett (2)	Barrett			M. Fraser

CHIEFS

Postal address: Box 4292, Hamilton East 3247
Telephone: (07) 853 0231
Email: admin@chiefs.co.nz
Home venue: FMG Stadium Waikato, Hamilton
Colours: black base with yellow and red, black shorts
Chairwoman: T.M. (Tonia) Cawood
Chief executive: M.J. (Michael) Collins

Played 347, Won 182, Lost 155, Drew 10

	Tries	Conv	Pen	DG	Points
For	1050	762	746	10	9054
Against	961	686	777	26	8592

RECORDS — TEAM

Most points in a game	72	*v Lions, 2010*
Most points in a season	560	*2016*
Biggest winning margin	51	*(61-10) v Sunwolves 2018*
Most tries in a game	9	*v Force, 2007*
	9	*v Blues, 2009*
	9	*v Lions, 2010*
	9	*v Force 2016*
	9	*v Sunwolves 2018*
Most tries in a season	76	*2016*

RECORDS — INDIVIDUAL

Most points in a game	32	*S.R. Donald v Lions, 2010*
Most points in a season	251	*A.W. Cruden, 2012*
Most points in a career	886	*S.R. Donald, 2005-2019*
Most tries in a game	4	*S.W. Sivivatu v Blues, 2009*
	4	*A.T. Tikoirotuma v Blues 2012*
	4	*C.J. Ngatai v Force 2016*
Most tries in a season	12	*R.Q. Randle, 2002*
Most tries in a career	42	*S.W. Sivivatu, 2003-2011*
Most conversions in a game	9	*S.R. Donald v Lions, 2010*
Most conversions in a season	43	*A.W. Cruden, 2012*
	43	*D.S. McKenzie 2016*
Most conversions in a career	151	*S.R. Donald*
Most penalty goals in a game	6	*G.W. Jackson v Reds, 2001*
	6	*S.R. Donald v Crusaders, 2007*
Most penalty goals in a season	50	*A.W. Cruden, 2012*
Most penalty goals in a career	154	*S.R. Donald*
Most dropped goals in a game	1	*on eight occasions*
Most dropped goals in a season	2	*I.D. Foster, 1996*
Most dropped goals in a career	2	*I.D. Foster*
	2	*G.W. Jackson*
Most games	179	*L.J. Messam, 2006-2018*

Investec Super Rugby 2020

Player	Union	Date of birth	Height	Weight	Chiefs games	Chiefs points
N.S. (Naitoa) Ah Kuoi	Wellington	07-10-99	1.96	116	12	-
S. (Solomon) Alaimalo	Waikato	27-12-95	1.95	99	47	90
M.G. (Michael) Allardice	Hawke's Bay	19-10-91	2	115	46	–
T.J. (Tyler) Ardron	Bay of Plenty	16-10-91	1.94	110	30	25
L.S. (Lachlan) Boshier	Taranaki	16-11-94	1.91	106	56	85
M.M. (Mitch) Brown	Taranaki	15-08-93	1.94	110	45	15
S.J. (Sam) Cane (captain)	Bay of Plenty	13-01-92	1.89	105	122	75
R.L. (Rob) Cobb	Waikato	08-04-99	1.89	117	1	-
R.C. (Ryan) Coxon	Tasman	30-09-97	1.83	118	6	-
A.W. (Aaron) Cruden	Overseas	08-01-89	1.78	84	100	721
T.J. (Tiaan) Falcon	Hawke's Bay	19-06-97	1.81	90	4	–
R. (Ross) Geldenhuys	Bay of Plenty	19-04-83	1.89	118	11	-
N.P. (Nathan) Harris	Bay of Plenty	08-03-92	1.86	110	58	35
L.B. (Luke) Jacobson	Waikato	20-04-97	1.91	107	25	25
M.R. (Mitch) Karpik	Bay of Plenty	02-06-95	1.86	103	29	20
N.E. (Nepo) Laulala	Counties Manukau	06-11-91	1.84	116	41	5
O.N.T. (Orbyn) Leger	Counties Manukau	13-03-97	1.84	90	3	-
A.R. (Anton) Lienert-Brown	Waikato	15-04-95	1.87	103	80	55
D.S.K.M. (Donald) Maka	Counties Manukau	29-01-95	1.83	111	1	-
T. (Tumua) Manu	Auckland	18-04-93	1.83	97	20	20
D.S. (Damian) McKenzie	Waikato	20-04-95	1.75	81	84	745
S.J. (Sam) McNicol	Hawke's Bay	06-10-95	1.85	94	18	10
L.E. (Laghlan) McWhannell	Waikato	20-10-98	1.98	114	-	-
L.M. (Lisati) Milo-Harris	Taranaki	05-10-96	1.82	90	5	-
A. (Atu) Moli	Tasman	12-06-95	1.89	125	43	15
K.V. (Kini) Naholo	Taranaki	16-04-99	1.78	92	1	-
E.W.P.S (Etene) Nanai-Seturo	Counties Manukau	20-08-99	1.83	92	14	25
A.P. (Alex) Nankivell	Tasman	25-10-96	1.88	98	31	15
D.M. (Dylan) Nel	Otago	27-11-92	1.85	110	4	-
O.M. (Ollie) Norris	Waikato	11-12-99	1.94	120	4	-
R.G. (Reuben) O'Neill	Taranaki	17-02-95	1.83	117	10	-
S.C. (Simon) Parker	Waikato	06-05-00	1.93	109	1	-
A. (Aidan) Ross	Bay of Plenty	25-10-95	1.89	111	36	5
B.A (Bradley) Slater	Taranaki	23-09-98	1.81	112	15	10
P.G.N (Pita-Gus) Sowakula	Taranaki	10-10-94	1.95	110	28	10
S.T. (Shaun) Stevenson	North Harbour	14-11-96	1.93	95	52	65
B.W.M. (Bailyn) Sullivan	Waikato	03-09-98	1.87	93	4	–
A. (Angus) Ta'avao	Auckland	22-03-90	1.94	124	35	15
H.J.T.T. (Te Toiroa) Tahuriorangi	Bay of Plenty	31-03-95	1.73	84	38	15
S.F. (Samisoni) Taukei'aho	Waikato	08-08-97	1.83	115	36	25
A.J. (Adam) Thomson	Waikato	13-03-82	1.96	110	5	-
K.R. (Kaleb) Trask	Bay of Plenty	27-01-99	1.8	90	9	11
Q.P.C. (Quinn) Tupaea	Waikato	10-05-99	1.86	97	12	5
T.P.O. (Tupou) Vaa'i	Taranaki	27-01-00	1.97	118	7	-
S.T. (Sean) Wainui	Taranaki	23-10-95	1.92	104	38	65
B.M. (Brad) Weber	Hawke's Bay	17-01-91	1.75	75	85	94

NB. Harris, McWhannell and Sullivan did not appear in 2020. Harris underwent shoulder surgery before the season and was replaced by Donald Maka. Other replacements were Cobb, Geldenhuys, Norris, Parker, Thomson and Vaa'i.

Manager: Stew Williams
Coach: Warren Gatland
Assistant coaches: Tabai Matson, Neil Barnes, Nick White, Roger Randle, David Hill

CHIEFS 2020

	Blues	Crusaders	Sunwolves	Brumbies	Waratahs	Hurricanes	Highlanders	Blues	Crusaders	Hurricanes	Highlanders	Blues	Crusaders	Hurricanes	TOTALS
Stevenson	15	–	14	–	14	14	14	14	–	–	–	–	14	14	8
McKenzie	–	15	15	15	–	15	15	15	15	15	15	15	15	15	12
Alaimalo	11	11	11	–	15	11	–	s	–	s	11	11	–	–	9
McNicol	–	–	–	11	–	–	–	–	–	–	–	–	–	–	1
Naholo	–	–	–	–	–	–	–	–	–	–	–	–	–	s	1
Wainui	14	14	–	14	11	–	11	11	14	14	14	14	11	11	12
Nanai-Seturo	–	–	–	–	–	–	s	–	11	11	–	–	–	–	3
Tupaea	13	13	13	s	–	–	13	13	13	12	s	s	s	s	12
Manu	–	–	–	–	13	13	–	–	s	13	–	–	–	–	4
Lienert-Brown	s	12	–	13	12	12	12	12	12	–	13	13	13	13	12
Nankivell	12	s	12	12	s	s	–	–	–	–	12	12	12	12	10
Leger	–	–	s	–	–	–	–	–	–	–	–	–	–	–	1
Trask	10	–	10	s	s	–	10	–	–	–	10	10	s	10	9
Cruden	s	10	–	10	10	10	s	10	10	10	–	s	10	–	11
Falcon	–	–	s	–	–	–	–	–	–	–	–	–	–	–	1
Weber	s	s	9	–	9	9	9	9	9	9	9	9	9	9	13
Tahuriorangi	9	9	s	9	–	–	–	–	–	s	s	–	–	–	6
Milo-Harris	–	–	–	s	s	–	–	s	–	–	–	–	s	s	5
Sowakula	s	s	–	8	8	8	8	8	8	8	8	8	8	8	13
Nel	–	–	8	–	–	–	s	s	–	s	–	–	–	–	4
Cane	8	8	–	7	7	7	–	–	7	7	7	7	7	7	11
Karpik	7	7	–	s	s	s	–	–	s	–	s	s	–	s	9
Boshier	6	6	7	–	6	6	7	7	6	6	6	6	6	–	12
Parker	–	–	–	–	–	–	–	–	–	–	–	–	s	–	1
Jacobson	–	–	–	6	–	–	6	6	–	–	–	–	–	6	4
Thomson	–	–	6	–	–	–	–	s	s	–	s	s	–	–	5
Ardron	4	4	4	–	5	–	–	–	–	–	–	–	–	–	4
Brown	5	5	s	5	–	5	4	–	4	4	5	5	5	5	12
Vaa'i	–	–	–	–	–	–	5	4	–	s	4	4	4	s	7
Allardice	–	–	5	4	4	4	–	–	–	–	–	–	–	–	4
Ah Kuoi	s	s	s	s	s	s	s	5	5	5	–	–	s	4	12
Laulala	3	–	–	–	–	–	3	3	3	3	3	3	3	3	9
Ta'avao	s	–	–	–	–	–	–	–	–	–	–	–	s	s	3
Moli	s	3	3	3	–	s	–	–	–	–	–	–	–	–	5
Geldenhuys	–	s	s	s	3	3	s	s	s	s	s	–	–	–	11
Coxon	–	–	–	–	s	–	s	–	–	–	–	–	–	–	2
Ross	1	1	1	1	1	1	1	1	1	1	1	–	–	–	11
Cobb	–	–	–	–	–	–	–	–	–	–	–	–	–	s	1
Norris	–	s	–	–	–	–	–	–	–	–	–	s	s	1	4
O'Neill	–	–	s	s	s	s	–	s	s	s	s	1	1	–	10
Taukei'aho	2	2	s	s	2	2	2	2	s	s	s	s	s	2	14
Slater	s	s	2	2	–	s	s	s	2	2	2	2	2	s	13
Maka	–	–	–	–	s	–	–	–	–	–	–	–	–	–	1

CHIEFS INDIVIDUAL SCORING

	Tries	Con	PG	DG	Points		Tries	Con	PG	DG	Points
McKenzie	1	18	21	1	107	Penalty try	1	–	–	–	7
Cruden	1	8	5	1	39	Karpik	1	–	–	–	5
Boshier	7	–	–	–	35	Manu	1	–	–	–	5
Alaimalo	5	–	–	–	25	Ross	1	–	–	–	5
Wainui	5	–	–	–	25	Sowakula	1	–	–	–	5
Lienert-Brown	4	–	–	–	20	Tahuriorangi	1	–	–	–	5
Stevenson	3	–	–	–	15	Tupaea	1	–	–	–	5
Weber	3	–	–	–	15						
Trask	1	3	–	–	11	**Totals**	**41**	**29**	**26**	**2**	**349**
Slater	2	–	–	–	10						
Taukei'aho	2	–	–	–	10	*Opposition scored*	*46*	*31*	*14*	*2*	*340*

CHIEFS TEAM RECORD 2020

Played 14   **Won 4**   **Lost 10**   **Drew 0**   **Points for 349**   **Points against 340**

Date	Opponent	Location	Score	Tries	Con	PG	DG	Referee
January 31	Blues	Auckland	37–29	Taukei'aho (2), Ross, Alaimalo, Sowakula	Cruden (3)	Cruden	Cruden	A. Gardner (Australia)
February 08	Crusaders	Hamilton	25–15	Tahuriorangi, Alaimalo, Wainui				B. O'Keeffe
February 15	Sunwolves	Tokyo	43–7	Boshier, Weber, Trask, Alaimalo, Tupaea, Stevenson, McKenzie	Cruden (2)	Cruden (2)		A. Gardner (Australia)
February 22	Brumbies	Hamilton	14–26	Cruden, Lienert-Brown	McKenzie (3), Trask			B. Pickerill
March 06	Waratahs	Wollongong	51–14	Weber (2), Boshier, Wainui, Lienert-Brown, Stevenson, Alaimalo	McKenzie (2)	Cruden (2)		A. Gardner (Australia)
March 13	Hurricanes	Hamilton	24–27	Boshier, Manu, Stevenson	Cruden (3), Trask (2)	McKenzie		J. Peyper (South Africa)
June 13	Highlanders	Dunedin	27–28	Wainui, Lienert-Brown	McKenzie (3)	McKenzie (4)	McKenzie	P. Williams
June 20	Blues	Hamilton	12–24		McKenzie	McKenzie (4)		B. O'Keeffe
June 28	Crusaders	Christchurch	13–18	Wainui		McKenzie (2)		J. Doleman
July 05	Hurricanes	Hamilton	18–25	Boshier, penalty try	McKenzie	McKenzie (2)		B. O'Keeffe
July 19	Highlanders	Hamilton	31–33	Slater (2), Boshier, Lienert-Brown	McKenzie (4)	McKenzie		M. Fraser
July 26	Blues	Auckland	17–21	Boshier, Alaimalo	McKenzie (2)	McKenzie		B. Pickerill
August 01	Crusaders	Hamilton	19–32	Boshier	McKenzie	McKenzie (4)		B. O'Keeffe
August 08	Hurricanes	Wellington	18–31	Wainui, Karpik	McKenzie	McKenzie (2)		J. Doleman

HURRICANES

Postal address: Box 7201, Wellington
Telephone: (04) 389 0020
Email: mail@hurricanes.co.nz
Home venues: SKY Stadium Wellington;
McLean Park, Napier
Colours: yellow and black
Chairman: I. (Iain) Potter
Chief executive: A.D. (Avan) Lee

Played 349, Won 199, Lost 143, Drew 7

	Tries	Conv	Pen	DG	Points
For	1142	805	703	6	9447
Against	936	649	779	25	8400

RECORDS — TEAM

Most points in a game	83	v Sunwolves 2017
Most points in a season	691	2017
Biggest winning margin	66	83-17 v Sunwolves 2017
Most tries in a game	13	v Sunwolves 2017
Most tries in a season	101	2017

RECORDS — INDIVIDUAL

Most points in a game	30	D.E. Holwell v Highlanders, 2001
Most points in a season	223	B.J. Barrett, 2016
Most points in a career	1238	B.J. Barrett, 2011-2019
Most tries in a game	4	M.B. Lam v Rebels, 2018
	4	K.H. Laumape v Blues, 2018
Most tries in a season	16	K.H. Laumape, 2017
	16	M.B. Lam, 2018
Most tries in a career	56	C.M. Cullen, 1996-2003
		T.T.R. Perenara, 2012–2020
Most conversions in a game	9	B.J. Barrett v Rebels, 2012
		O.W. Black v Sunwolves, 2017
Most conversions in a season	50	B.J. Barrett, 2016
Most conversions in a career	249	B.J. Barrett
Most penalty goals in a game	7	J.B. Cameron v Blues, 1996
	7	D.E. Holwell v Highlanders, 2001
Most penalty goals in a season	40	B.J. Barrett, 2014
Most penalty goals in a career	178	B.J. Barrett
Most dropped goals in a game	1	by six players
Most dropped goals in a season	1	by six players
Most dropped goals in a career	1	by six players
Most games	140	T.T.R. Perenara, 2012–2020

Player	Union	Date of birth	Height	Weight	Hurricanes games	Hurricanes points
F.P. (Fraser) Armstrong	Manawatu	18-04-92	1.93	127	31	–
V.T. (Vince) Aso	Wellington	05-01-95	1.86	98	57	115
A.J. (Asafo) Aumua	Wellington	05-05-97	1.77	108	27	15
J.M. (Jordie) Barrett	Taranaki	17-02-97	1.96	96	60	366
J. (James) Blackwell	Wellington	01-04-95	1.9	107	36	5
J.P. (Jamie) Booth	Manawatu	14-01-94	1.71	92	24	15
D.S. (Dane) Coles (co-captain)	Wellington	10-12-86	1.84	110	119	110
G.O. (Gareth) Evans	Hawke's Bay	05-08-91	1.9	107	31	15
A.F. (Alex) Fidow	Wellington	19-08-97	1.87	137	15	5
V.T.L. (Vaea) Fifita	Wellington	17-06-92	1.96	112	68	45
D.J. (Devan) Flanders	Hawke's Bay	20-07-99	1.9	98	11	5
J.K. (Jackson) Garden-Bachop	Wellington	03-10-94	1.83	99	17	39
W.T. (Wes) Goosen	Wellington	20-10-95	1.78	92	50	115
S.C. (Simon) Hickey	Auckland	12-01-94	1.74	85	-	-
D.A. (Du'Plessis) Kirifi	Wellington	03-03-97	1.8	101	29	10
M.B. (Ben) Lam	Wellington	09-06-91	1.94	106	50	160
K.H. (Ngani) Laumape	Manawatu	22-04-93	1.77	103	73	225
K.T.V. (Kane) Le'aupepe	Bay of Plenty	03-12-92	2.01	119	11	10
T.S. (Tyrel) Lomax	Tasman	16-03-96	1.92	127	12	-
J.H. (Jonah) Lowe	Hawke's Bay	09-05-96	1.84	92	4	–
T.T.P. (Tevita) Mafileo	Bay of Plenty	04-02-98	1.87	120	6	-
J.R. (James) Marshall	-	07-12-88	1.83	93	54	87
B. (Ben) May	Hawke's Bay	13-10-82	1.94	119	98	20
L.F. (Liam) Mitchell	Manawatu	10-10-95	1.99	110	16	-
X.J.S (Xavier) Numia	Wellington	29-11-98	1.89	111	11	-
T.T.R. (TJ) Perenara (co-captain)	Wellington	23-01-92	1.84	94	140	282
R.J. (Reed) Prinsep	Canterbury	17-02-93	1.92	108	54	20
B.D. (Billy) Proctor	Wellington	14-05-99	1.87	96	13	5
P.G. (Pouri) Rakete-Stones	Hawke's Bay	17-06-97	1.81	113	8	-
S.I.M (Salesi) Rayasi	Auckland	25-09-96	1.93	105	6	15
J.R. (Ricky) Riccitelli	Taranaki	03-02-95	1.92	110	64	15
A.S. (Ardie) Savea	Wellington	14-10-93	1.88	100	99	105
S.J. (Julian) Savea	-	07-08-90	1.92	108	121	260
S.N. (Scott) Scrafton	Auckland	18-04-93	2	114	13	-
F.H. (Fletcher) Smith	Waikato	01-03-95	1.8	88	13	31
M.V.U. (Murphy) Taramai	North Harbour	17-08-92	1.86	100	1	-
J.A. (Jonathan) Taumateine	Counties Manukau	28-09-96	1.77	82	2	-
C.J. (Chase) Tiatia	Bay of Plenty	14-10-95	1.81	93	16	17
D.S. (Danny) Toala	Hawke's Bay	23-03-99	1.76	95	3	-
P.I.J. (Peter) Umaga-Jensen	Wellington	31-12-97	1.87	95	11	30
J.P. (Kobus) van Wyk	Overseas	22-01-92	1.9	94	8	40
I.E.T. (Isaia) Walker-Leawere	Wellington	16-04-97	1.87	127	25	5

NB. Hickey did not appear, nor did Julian Savea, who was brought in as cover during Super Rugby Aotearoa.

Manager: Tony Ward
Coach: Jason Holland
Assistant coaches: Chris Gibbes, Cory Jane, Dan Cron, Carlos Spencer

HURRICANES 2020

	Stormers	Jaguares	Sharks	Sunwolves	Blues	Chiefs	Blues	Crusaders	Chiefs	Highlanders	Blues	Crusaders	Chiefs	Highlanders	TOTALS
Barrett	15	15	15	–	15	15	–	–	15	15	15	15	15	15	11
Tiatia	–	–	–	15	–	–	15	15	–	–	–	s	–	11	5
Goosen	14	14	14	–	s	s	14	14	s	s	s	14	11	–	12
Lam	11	11	11	11	11	11	11	11	11	11	11	11	–	–	12
Van Wyk	–	–	–	14	14	14	–	s	14	14	14	–	14	–	8
Lowe	–	–	–	–	–	–	–	–	–	–	–	–	s	–	1
Rayasi	–	–	–	–	–	–	–	–	–	–	–	–	–	s	1
Aso	s	s	13	13	13	13	13	13	–	13	–	s	12	14	12
Proctor	13	13	s	–	s	s	s	s	s	s	s	–	s	13	12
Umaga-Jensen	–	–	–	s	–	–	–	–	13	–	13	13	13	12	6
Toala	–	–	–	–	–	–	–	–	–	–	–	–	–	s	1
Laumape	12	12	12	12	12	12	12	12	12	12	12	12	–	–	12
F. Smith	10	s	s	10	10	10	–	–	–	10	–	–	–	–	7
Marshall	–	–	–	s	–	–	–	–	–	–	–	–	–	–	1
Garden-Bachop	s	10	10	–	–	–	10	10	10	–	10	10	10	10	10
Perenara	9	9	9	9	9	9	9	9	9	9	9	9	9	–	13
Booth	s	s	s	–	s	s	s	s	s	s	s	s	s	9	13
Taumateine	–	–	–	s	–	–	–	–	–	–	–	–	–	s	2
Evans	8	8	8	8	8	8	8	s	–	–	–	–	–	–	8
Taramai	–	–	–	–	–	–	–	–	–	s	–	–	–	–	1
Flanders	s	s	s	s	s	6	s	–	–	6	–	s	s	s	11
A. Savea	–	–	–	–	–	–	s	8	8	8	8	8	8	8	8
Prinsep	6	6	–	–	–	–	6	6	6	–	6	6	6	6	9
Kirifi	7	7	7	7	7	7	7	7	7	7	7	7	7	7	14
Fifita	s	s	6	6	6	s	–	5	s	s	s	–	–	–	10
Le'aupepe	–	–	–	–	–	–	–	–	–	–	–	–	s	–	1
Mitchell	–	–	s	–	–	–	–	–	s	–	–	s	–	s	4
Blackwell	4	4	–	4	s	4	4	4	4	4	4	4	4	4	13
Walker-Leawere	–	5	4	5	4	5	s	–	–	–	s	–	–	–	7
Scrafton	5	–	5	5	5	s	5	s	5	5	5	5	5	5	13
Lomax	3	3	3	3	3	–	3	3	3	3	3	–	3	3	12
May	–	–	–	s	–	3	–	s	s	1	–	3	1	1	8
Fidow	–	s	s	s	s	s	s	s	s	s	s	s	–	–	11
Mafileo	s	s	–	–	–	–	s	–	–	–	–	s	s	s	6
Numia	–	–	–	1	1	–	–	–	–	–	–	–	–	–	2
Armstrong	1	1	1	–	–	1	1	1	1	–	1	1	–	–	9
Rakete-Stones	s	–	s	–	s	s	–	–	–	s	s	–	s	s	8
Riccitelli	2	s	–	s	–	–	–	–	s	s	–	s	–	s	7
Coles	–	–	s	–	s	2	2	2	2	–	2	–	2	2	9
Aumua	s	2	2	2	2	s	s	s	–	2	s	2	s	–	12

HURRICANES INDIVIDUAL SCORING

	Tries	Con	PG	DG	Points		Tries	Con	PG	DG	Points
Barrett	–	23	16	–	94	Tiatia	2	1	–	–	12
Van Wyk	8	–	–	–	40	Aso	2	–	–	–	10
Lam	6	–	–	–	30	Evans	1	–	–	–	5
Garden-Bachop	–	2	6	1	25	Fidow	1	–	–	–	5
Coles	4	–	–	–	20	Flanders	1	–	–	–	5
Umaga-Jensen	4	–	–	–	20	Kirifi	1	–	–	–	5
Smith	1	6	–	–	17	Prinsep	1	–	–	–	5
Aumua	3	–	–	–	15	Proctor	1	–	–	–	5
Booth	3	–	–	–	15						
Goosen	3	–	–	–	15	**Totals**	**47**	**33**	**22**	**1**	**370**
Laumape	3	–	–	–	15						
Perenara	2	1	–	–	12	Opposition scored	43*	29	23	–	348

*Includes three penalty tries

HURRICANES TEAM RECORD 2020

Played 14　　Won 9　　Lost 5　　Drew 0　　Points for 370　　Points against 348

Date	Opponent	Location	Score	Tries	Con	PG	DG	Referee
February 01	Stormers	Cape Town	0–27					J. Peyper (South Africa)
February 08	Jaguares	Buenos Aires	26–23	Fidow, Booth	Garden-Bachop, Smith	Barrett (4)		R. Rasivhenge (South Africa)
February 15	Sharks	Wellington	38–22	Lam (2), Laumape, Goosen, Coles	Barrett (5)	Barrett		B. O'Keeffe
February 29	Sunwolves	Napier	62–15	Van Wyk (3), Tiatia (2), Evans, Perenara, Lam, Laumape, Aso	Smith (5), Tiatia			F. Anselmi (Argentina)
March 07	Blues	Wellington	15–24	Lam, van Wyk	Barrett	Barrett		M. Fraser
March 13	Chiefs	Hamilton	27–24	Smith, Lam, Aumua	Barrett (3)	Barrett (2)		J. Peyper (South Africa)
June 14	Blues	Auckland	20–30	Coles, Lam, Booth	Perenara	Garden-Bachop		M. Fraser
June 21	Crusaders	Wellington	25–39	Aumua	Garden-Bachop	Garden-Bachop (5)	Garden-Bachop	B. Pickerill
July 05	Chiefs	Hamilton	25–18	Van Wyk (2), Kirifi	Barrett (2)	Barrett (2)		B. O'Keeffe
July 12	Highlanders	Wellington	17–11	Flanders, Perenara, van Wyk	Barrett			B. Pickerill
July 18	Blues	Wellington	29–27	Laumape, Prinsep, Coles, Aumua	Barrett (3)	Barrett		B. O'Keeffe
July 25	Crusaders	Christchurch	34–32	Goosen (2), Umaga-Jensen	Barrett (2)	Barrett (5)		J. Doleman
August 08	Chiefs	Wellington	31–18	Umaga-Jensen (2), Coles, van Wyk, Proctor	Barrett (3)			J. Doleman
August 15	Highlanders	Dunedin	21–38	Aso, Booth, Umaga-Jensen	Barrett (3)			B. O'Keeffe

CRUSADERS

Postal address: Box 755, Christchurch
Telephone: (03) 379 8300
Email: info@crfu.co.nz
Home venues: Orangetheory Stadium, Christchurch;
Trafalgar Park, Nelson
Colours: red and black
Chairman: G.S. (Grant) Jarrold
Chief executive: C.S. (Colin) Mansbridge

Played 370, Won 260, Lost 102, Drew 8

	Tries	Conv	Pen	DG	Points
For	1303	916	904	46	11,212
Against	858	604	739	29	7804

RECORDS — TEAM

Most points in a game	96	v Waratahs, 2002
Most points in a season	691	2018
Biggest winning margin	77	96–19 v Waratahs, 2002
Most tries in a game	14	v Waratahs, 2002
Most tries in a season	96	2018

RECORDS — INDIVIDUAL

Most points in a game	31	T.J. Taylor v Stormers, 2012
Most points in a season	221	D.W. Carter, 2006
Most points in a career	1708	D.W. Carter, 2003-2015
Most tries in a game	4	C.S. Ralph v Waratahs, 2002
	4	S.D. Maitland v Brumbies, 2011
Most tries in a season	15	R.L. Gear, 2005
	15	G.C. Bridge 2018
	15	S.L. Reece, 2019
Most tries in a career	52	C.S. Ralph, 1999-2008
Most conversions in a game	13	A.P. Mehrtens v Waratahs, 2002
Most conversions in a season	38	D.W. Carter, 2006
	38	R. Mo'unga 2018
Most conversions in a career	287	D.W. Carter
Most penalty goals in a game	8	T.J. Taylor v Stormers, 2012
Most penalty goals in a season	46	C.R. Slade, 2014
Most penalty goals in a career	307	D.W. Carter
Most dropped goals in a game	3	A.P. Mehrtens v Highlanders, 1998
Most dropped goals in a season	4	A.P. Mehrtens, 1998, 1999, 2002
Most dropped goals in a career	17	A.P. Mehrtens
Most games	203	W.W.V. Crockett, 2006-2018

Investec Super Rugby 2020

Player	Union	Date of birth	Height	Weight	Crusaders games	Crusaders points
M.S. (Michael) Alaalatoa	Canterbury	28-08-91	1.9	136	83	25
H.M. (Harry) Allan	Canterbury	07-05-97	1.83	110	12	–
S.K. (Scott) Barrett (captain)	Taranaki	20-11-93	1.98	116	72	65
E.J. (Ethan) Blackadder	Tasman	22-03-95	1.91	107	10	–
G.G. (George) Bower	Otago	28-05-92	1.86	120	23	-
G.C. (George) Bridge	Canterbury	01-04-95	1.85	96	61	165
F.W. (Fergus) Burke	Canterbury	03-09-99	1.89	85	1	9
B.D. (Brett) Cameron	Canterbury	04-10-96	1.71	83	13	19
T.M. (Tom) Christie	Canterbury	04-03-98	1.85	103	11	20
W.H. (Whetu) Douglas	Canterbury	18-04-94	1.9	109	30	25
M.D. (Mitch) Drummond	Canterbury	15-12-94	1.8	86	92	87
M.T.W. (Mitch) Dunshea	Canterbury	18-11-95	1.96	114	22	5
E.C. (Ere) Enari	Canterbury	30-05-97	1.78	84	8	-
B.M. (Braydon) Ennor	Canterbury	16-07-97	1.87	93	35	95
L.O.K.W.P (Leicester) Faingaanuku	Tasman	11-10-99	1.88	103	12	15
K.F. (Inga) Finau	Canterbury	21-08-94	1.77	94	-	-
E.J. (Jack) Goodhue	Northland	13-06-95	1.86	98	57	60
C.J. (Cullen) Grace	Canterbury	20-12-99	1.93	106	8	-
B.D. (Bryn) Hall	North Harbour	03-02-92	1.83	89	64	69
W.K. (Billy) Harmon	Canterbury	23-12-94	1.87	104	12	5
D.K. (David) Havili	Tasman	23-12-94	1.84	95	84	152
S.T. (Sione) Havili	Tasman	25-01-98	1.85	104	9	10
O.G.J.T. (Oli) Jager	Canterbury	05-07-95	1.92	120	27	–
W.T. (Will) Jordan	Tasman	24-02-98	1.88	91	19	80
B.L. (Brodie) McAlister	Canterbury	17-06-97	1.84	109	4	-
D.A.M (Dallas) McLeod	Canterbury	30-04-99	1.88	99	2	-
A. (Andrew) Makalio	Tasman	22-01-92	1.82	122	43	20
M.M.B.T. (Manasa) Mataele	Taranaki	27-11-96	1.85	100	25	80
J.P.T. (Joe) Moody	Canterbury	16-09-88	1.88	120	92	15
R. (Richie) Mo'unga	Canterbury	25-05-94	1.76	86	69	760
F.M.A (Fetuli) Paea	Tasman	16-08-94	1.89	95	4	-
S.L. (Sevu) Reece	Tasman	13-02-97	1.78	92	27	115
H.E. (Hugh) Roach	Tasman	11-09-92	1.78	110	1	-
L. (Luke) Romano	Canterbury	16-02-86	1.59	120	134	50
E.J. (Ethan) Roots	North Harbour	10-11-97	1.88	110	1	-
T.B. (Tom) Sanders	Canterbury	05-02-94	1.91	109	19	5
Q.J. (Quinten) Strange	Tasman	21-08-96	1.99	112	32	10
C.J. (Codie) Taylor (captain)	Canterbury	31-03-91	1.83	111	90	85
I.J. (Isi) Tuungafasi	Northland	10-01-95	1.87	122	10	-
S.L. (Sam) Whitelock	Canterbury	12-10-88	2.03	120	151	40

NB. Allan and Finau did not appear in 2020.

Manager: Shane Fletcher
Coach: Scott Robertson
Assistant coaches: Scott Hansen, Andrew Goodman, Jason Ryan, Mark Jones

CRUSADERS 2020

	Waratahs	Chiefs	Blues	Highlanders	Reds	Sunwolves	Hurricanes	Chiefs	Highlanders	Blues	Hurricanes	Chiefs	Highlanders	TOTALS
D. Havili	15	10	15	15	–	–	s	s	15	15	–	–	–	8
Jordan	14	15	s	–	–	–	15	15	14	s	15	15	15	10
Reece	s	14	14	14	14	14	14	14	s	14	14	14	14	13
Bridge	–	11	11	11	15	15	11	11	–	11	11	11	11	11
Mataele	–	–	–	–	s	s	–	–	–	–	–	–	–	2
Faingaanuku	11	s	–	s	11	11	s	s	11	–	s	s	s	11
Ennor	13	13	13	13	–	13	13	13	13	13	–	–	13	10
McLeod	–	–	–	–	12	12	–	–	–	–	–	–	–	2
Paea	–	–	–	–	–	–	–	–	s	s	13	13	–	4
Goodhue	12	12	12	12	13	–	12	12	12	12	12	12	12	12
Burke	–	–	–	–	–	s	–	–	–	–	–	–	–	1
Mo'unga	10	–	10	10	10	–	10	10	10	10	10	10	10	11
Cameron	s	s	s	s	–	10	–	–	–	–	–	s	s	7
Enari	–	–	–	–	9	s	–	–	s	–	–	–	–	3
Hall	s	s	9	9	–	9	9	9	–	9	9	s	9	11
Drummond	9	9	s	s	s	–	s	s	9	s	s	9	s	12
Douglas	8	8	–	–	–	s	8	8	8	8	8	–	8	9
Christie	7	7	7	7	7	7	–	–	7	7	7	7	7	11
Harmon	–	–	–	–	–	–	7	7	–	–	–	s	–	3
S. Havili	–	–	s	s	s	6	–	–	6	s	s	6	s	9
Sanders	6	6	8	8	8	s	–	–	s	6	6	8	6	11
Roots	–	–	–	s	–	–	–	–	–	–	–	–	–	1
Blackadder	–	–	–	–	–	–	s	s	–	–	–	–	–	2
Barrett	4	4	4	–	4	–	–	–	–	–	–	–	–	4
Grace	s	s	6	6	6	8	6	6	–	–	–	–	–	8
Dunshea	5	5	5	5	5	5	5	5	5	5	5	5	–	12
Strange	–	–	–	–	–	–	–	–	s	s	s	s	5	5
Whitelock	–	–	–	–	–	–	4	4	4	4	4	4	4	7
Romano	s	s	s	4	s	4	s	s	–	–	–	–	s	9
Alaalatoa	s	–	s	3	3	s	3	3	3	3	3	3	3	12
Jager	3	3	3	–	s	3	s	–	s	s	s	s	s	11
Moody	–	1	1	1	1	–	1	1	1	1	–	–	1	10
Bower	1	s	s	s	s	1	s	s	s	s	1	s	s	13
Tuungafasi	s	s	–	s	–	s	–	s	–	–	–	s	–	6
Makalio	2	s	s	s	–	–	–	–	s	s	s	s	s	9
Taylor	s	2	2	2	2	–	2	2	2	2	2	2	2	12
McAlister	–	–	–	–	s	2	s	–	–	–	–	–	–	3
Roach	–	–	–	–	–	s	–	–	–	–	–	–	–	1

CRUSADERS INDIVIDUAL SCORING

	Tries	Con	PG	DG	Points		Tries	Con	PG	DG	Points
Mo'unga	4	21	17	–	113	Cameron	–	5	–	–	10
Jordan	8	–	–	–	40	Burke	1	2	–	–	9
Reece	8	–	–	–	40	Drummond	1	1	–	–	7
D. Havili	1	9	4	–	35	Moody	1	–	–	–	5
Bridge	6	–	–	–	30	Sanders	1	–	–	–	5
Ennor	6	–	–	–	30	Strange	1	–	–	–	5
Christie	4	–	–	–	20	Hall	–	2	–	–	4
Faingaanuku	3	–	–	–	15						
Goodhue	2	–	–	–	10	**Totals**	53	40	21	0	408
S. Havili	2	–	–	–	10						
Romano	2	–	–	–	10	Opposition scored	28	16	26	1	253
Taylor	2	–	–	–	10						

CRUSADERS TEAM RECORD 2019

Played 13 Won 11 Lost 2 Drew 0 Points for 408 Points against 253

Date	Opponent	Location	Score	Tries	Con	PG	DG	Referee
February 01	Waratahs	Nelson	43–25	Ennor (2), Jordan (2), Fainga'anuku, Romano	D. Havili (5)	D. Havili		P. Williams
February 08	Chiefs	Hamilton	15–25	Reece (2)		D. Havili		B. O'Keeffe
February 14	Blues	Auckland	25–8	Mo'unga, Bridge, Goodhue	D. Havili (2)	D. Havili (2)		P. Williams
February 21	Highlanders	Christchurch	33–13	Taylor, Christie, Bridge, Ennor, S. Havili	Hall (2), D. Havili, Drummond			M. Fraser
March 06	Reds	Christchurch	24–20	Moody, Bridge, Fainga'anuku	Mo'unga (3)	Mo'unga		R. Rasivenghe (South Africa)
March 14	Sunwolves	Brisbane	49–14	Reece (2), Romano, S. Havili, Christie, Ennor, Burke	Cameron (5), Burke (2)			B. Pickerill
June 21	Hurricanes	Wellington	39–25	Mo'unga, Reece, Ennor, Goodhue, D. Havili	Mo'unga (4)	Mo'unga (2)		B. Pickerill
June 28	Chiefs	Christchurch	18–13	Jordan (2)	Mo'unga	Mo'unga (2)		J. Doleman
July 04	Highlanders	Dunedin	40–20	Christie (2), Jordan (2), Reece	Mo'unga (3)	Mo'unga (3)		M. Fraser
July 11	Blues	Christchurch	26–15	Drummond, Jordan	Mo'unga (2)	Mo'unga (4)		P. Williams
July 25	Hurricanes	Christchurch	32–34	Mo'unga, Bridge, Reece, Strange	Mo'unga (3)	Mo'unga (2)		J. Doleman
August 01	Chiefs	Hamilton	32–19	Taylor, Sanders, Reece, Jordan, Fainga'anuku	Mo'unga (2)	Mo'unga		B. O'Keeffe
August 09	Highlanders	Christchurch	32–22	Bridge (2), Mo'unga, Ennor	Mo'unga (3)	Mo'unga (2)		P. Williams

HIGHLANDERS

Postal address: Box 6070, Dunedin 9059
Telephone: (03) 479 9280
Email: contactus@highlanders.net.nz
Home venues: Forsyth Barr Stadium, Dunedin;
Colours: blue with gold and maroon
Chairman: D.J. (Doug) Harvie
Chief executive: R.W. (Roger) Clark

Played 332, Won 165, Lost 163, Drew 4

	Tries	Conv	Pen	DG	Points
For	967	673	769	28	8580
Against	1012	730	693	16	8653

RECORDS — TEAM

Most points in a game	65	v Bulls, 1999
Most points in a season	530	2015
Biggest winning margin	49	55-6 v Force, 2017
Most tries in a game	9	v Bulls, 1999
Most tries in a season	64	2017

RECORDS — INDIVIDUAL

Most points in a game	28	B.A. Blair v Sharks, 2005
Most points in a season	191	L.Z. Sopoaga, 2015
Most points in a career	868	L.Z. Sopoaga, 2011-2018
Most tries in a game	3	on 11 occasions
Most tries in a season	13	W.R. Naholo, 2015
Most tries in a career	45	W.R. Naholo, 2015-2019
Most conversions in a game	7	T.E. Brown v Bulls, 1999
Most conversions in a season	41	L.Z. Sopoaga 2018
Most conversions in a career	163	L.Z. Sopoaga
Most penalty goals in a game	8	W.C. Walker v Chiefs, 2003
Most penalty goals in a season	34	T.E. Brown, 2000
Most penalty goals in a career	180	T.E. Brown
Most dropped goals in a game	1	on 28 occasions
Most dropped goals in a season	3	L.Z. Sopoaga, 2015
Most dropped goals in a career	6	T.E. Brown
Most games	153	B.R. Smith, 2009-2019

Investec Super Rugby 2020

Player	Union	Date of birth	Height	Weight	Highlanders games	Highlanders points
T.G. (Teariki) Ben-Nicholas	Wellington	18-07-95	1.95	109	10	5
M.W.V. (Michael) Collins	Otago	03-06-93	1.86	96	11	20
L.J. (Liam) Coltman	Otago	25-01-90	1.85	112	115	35
E.L. (Ethan) de Groot	Southland	22-07-98	1.9	122	2	-
J.M. (Josh) Dickson	Otago	02-01-94	2	109	25	–
A.L. (Ash) Dixon (co-captain)	Hawke's Bay	01-09-88	1.82	105	86	35
L.T. (Tima) Faingaanuku	Tasman	26-04-97	1.88	103	2	-
F.M.L.N. (Folau) Fakatava	Hawke's Bay	16-12-99	1.77	80	5	-
T.H.T. (Tom) Florence	Taranaki	20-05-98	1.9	104	1	-
S.M. (Shannon) Frizell	Tasman	11-02-94	1.95	108	39	75
C.C. (Connor) Garden-Bachop	Wellington	04-02-00	1.89	94	-	-
B.E.C. (Bryn) Gatland	North Harbour	05-10-95	1.78	88	8	9
S.J. (Sam) Gilbert	Canterbury	23-01-99	1.9	95	2	-
S.J. (Scott) Gregory	Northland	07-01-99	1.88	106	5	5
K.W. (Kayne) Hammington	Manawatu	24-09-90	1.7	75	45	20
D. (Dillon) Hunt	North Harbour	23-02-95	1.89	103	44	30
M.J. (Mitch) Hunt	Tasman	19-06-95	1.79	88	13	65
J.R. (Josh) Ioane	Otago	11-07-95	1.76	85	32	179
J.Z.A. (Josh) Iosefa-Scott	Waikato	16-07-96	1.93	133	2	-
R.D. (Ricky) Jackson	Otago	02-08-98	1.8	100	1	-
C.A. (Ayden) Johnstone	Waikato	24-10-96	1.84	120	28	-
Z.R. (Zane) Kapeli	Bay of Plenty	28-09-92	1.89	130	-	-
V.T. (Vilimoni) Koroi	Otago	17-04-98	1.74	91	2	-
K.C.J (Kris) Kuridrani	Counties Manukau	12-12-91	1.9	103	1	-
J.A.R. (James) Lentjes (captain)	Otago	16-01-91	1.88	104	41	25
D.P. (Daniel) Lienert-Brown	Canterbury	09-02-93	1.84	112	84	15
J.A. (Josh) McKay	Canterbury	10-10-97	1.83	92	16	25
M.E.R. (Marino) Mikaele-Tu'u	Hawke's Bay	06-11-97	1.93	114	21	10
N.R. (Nehe) Milner-Skudder	Manawatu	15-12-90	1.8	91	-	-
S.F. (Sione) Misiloi	Otago	03-11-94	1.9	115	-	-
T. (Tevita) Nabura	Counties Manukau	28-06-92	1.92	107	3	–
J.M. (Jona) Nareki	Otago	27-12-97	1.75	83	13	25
C.F. (Conan) O'Donnell	Counties Manukau	23-05-96	1.78	113	2	-
J.W.Z. (Jesse) Parete	Taranaki	20-04-93	1.86	105	9	-
P.P.M. (Paripari) Parkinson	Tasman	12-09-96	2.04	119	17	5
N.G.J. (Ngane) Punivai	Canterbury	30-08-98	1.91	100	5	10
M.W.H. (Manaaki) Selby-Rickit	Southland	05-06-96	2	112	9	-
A.L. (Aaron) Smith (co-captain)	Manawatu	21-11-88	1.71	83	150	145
R. (Rob) Thompson	Manawatu	29-08-91	1.84	103	57	70
J.R. (Jeff) Thwaites	Bay of Plenty	22-11-92	1.9	115	10	-
S.F. (Siate) Tokolahi	Southland	16-03-92	1.84	116	54	15
P.F. (Sio) Tomkinson	Otago	27-05-96	1.82	94	30	50
T.N.M. (Thomas) Umaga-Jensen	Wellington	31-12-97	1.87	95	8	–
T.T. (Tei) Walden	Taranaki	25-05-93	1.82	94	39	50
J.C. (Jack) Whetton	Auckland	24-05-95	1.96	114	13	-

NB. Garden-Bachop did not appear in 2020. He underwent surgery before the season and was replaced by Tima Faingaanuku. Also not appearing were Jackson, Kapeli, Milner-Skudder, Misiloi, Nabura and Umaga-Jensen.
James Lentjes was captain until his season-ending injury, after which Ash Dixon and Aaron Smith were co-captains.

Manager: Paul McLaughlan
Coach: Aaron Mauger
Assistant coaches: Mark Hammett, Tony Brown, Clarke Dermody, Riki Flutey

HIGHLANDERS 2020

	Sharks	Brumbies	Crusaders	Rebels	Bulls	Chiefs	Blues	Crusaders	Hurricanes	Chiefs	Blues	Crusaders	Hurricanes	TOTALS
Koroi	–	–	–	–	–	15	–	s	–	–	–	–	–	2
Gregory	–	–	–	s	–	–	15	–	14	11	11	–	–	5
McKay	15	15	s	14	14	–	–	–	–	14	14	14	14	9
Collins	s	13	15	15	15	–	–	15	15	15	13	13	13	11
Gilbert	–	–	–	–	–	14	14	–	–	–	–	–	–	2
Faingaanuku	14	–	–	–	s	–	–	–	–	–	–	–	–	2
Kuridrani	–	–	14	–	–	–	–	–	–	–	–	–	–	1
Nareki	11	11	11	11	11	11	11	11	11	s	s	11	11	13
Tomkinson	–	14	–	–	–	12	12	12	12	12	12	12	12	9
Punivai	–	–	–	–	13	–	s	14	–	–	–	s	s	5
Thompson	13	–	13	13	–	13	13	13	13	13	–	–	–	8
Walden	–	–	s	s	s	s	–	–	–	–	–	–	–	4
Ioane	12	12	12	12	12	–	–	–	–	s	10	10	10	9
M. Hunt	10	10	10	10	10	10	10	10	10	10	15	15	15	13
Gatland	–	–	–	–	–	s	s	s	s	–	–	–	–	4
A. Smith	9	9	9	9	9	9	9	9	9	9	9	9	9	13
Hammington	s	s	s	–	s	–	–	s	s	–	–	–	–	6
Fakatava	–	–	–	–	–	–	–	–	–	–	s	–	s	2
Ben-Nicholas	s	s	s	6	s	–	s	s	s	–	–	s	s	10
Mikaele-Tu'u	8	8	8	8	8	8	8	8	8	8	8	8	8	13
Lentjes	7	7	7	7	–	–	–	–	–	–	–	–	–	4
D. Hunt	6	s	–	s	7	7	7	7	7	7	7	7	7	12
Frizell	s	6	6	–	6	6	6	6	6	6	6	6	6	12
Florence	–	–	–	–	–	–	–	–	–	–	–	–	s	1
Parete	s	4	4	4	4	–	–	–	s	s	s	s	–	9
Dickson	5	5	5	–	–	5	5	5	–	–	–	–	–	6
Parkinson	4	–	–	–	–	4	4	4	4	4	4	4	4	9
Selby-Rickit	–	–	–	s	5	s	s	–	s	s	s	s	s	9
Whetton	–	s	s	5	s	–	–	s	5	5	5	5	5	10
Thwaites	–	–	–	s	s	s	s	3	s	s	3	s	s	10
Tokolahi	3	3	3	3	3	3	3	s	3	3	s	3	3	13
Johnstone	1	1	1	s	1	1	1	s	1	1	1	1	1	13
O'Donnell	–	s	s	–	–	–	–	–	–	–	–	–	–	2
Lienert-Brown	s	s	s	1	s	s	s	1	s	–	–	s	s	11
Iosefa-Scott	s	–	–	–	–	–	–	–	–	–	–	–	–	1
De Groot	–	–	–	–	–	–	–	–	–	s	s	–	–	2
Coltman	2	2	2	s	2	s	s	2	s	s	s	s	s	13
Dixon	s	s	s	2	s	2	2	s	2	2	2	2	2	13

HIGHLANDERS INDIVIDUAL SCORING

	Tries	Con	PG	DG	Points		Tries	Con	PG	DG	Points
M. Hunt	3	13	8	–	65	Penalty try	1	–	–	–	7
Ioane	1	11	12	–	63	Ben-Nicholas	1	–	–	–	5
Nareki	5	–	–	–	25	Gregory	1	–	–	–	5
Collins	4	–	–	–	20	D. Hunt	1	–	–	–	5
Dixon	4	–	–	–	20	McKay	1	–	–	–	5
Frizell	4	–	–	–	20	Gatland	–	–	–	1	3
Smith	3	–	–	–	15						
Mikaele-Tu'u	2	–	–	–	10	**Totals**	**35**	**24**	**20**	**1**	**288**
Punivai	2	–	–	–	10						
Tomkinson	2	–	–	–	10	Opposition scored	53	37	16	1	390

HIGHLANDERS TEAM RECORD 2019

Played 13 Won 4 Lost 9 Drew 0 Points for 288 Points against 390

Date	Opponent	Location	Score	Tries	Con	PG	DG	Referee
February 07	Sharks	Dunedin	20–42	D. Hunt, Nareki, Collins	M. Hunt	M. Hunt		A. Gardner (Australia)
February 15	Brumbies	Canberra	23–22	Nareki, Ben-Nicholas	Ioane (2)	Ioane (3)		N. Berry (Australia)
February 21	Crusaders	Christchurch	13–33	Nareki, Collins		Ioane		M. Fraser
February 28	Rebels	Dunedin	22–28	Smith, Gregory, McKay	Ioane (2)	Ioane		P. Williams
March 07	Bulls	Pretoria	13–38	Ioane	Ioane	Ioane (2)		AJ Jacobs (South Africa)
June 13	Chiefs	Dunedin	28–27	Dixon, Tomkinson, Mikaele-Tu'u	M. Hunt (2)	M. Hunt (2)	Gatland	P. Williams
June 27	Blues	Auckland	24–27	Dixon, Frizell, M. Hunt	M. Hunt (3)	M. Hunt		P. Williams
July 04	Crusaders	Dunedin	20–40	Frizell, Punivai	M. Hunt (2)	M. Hunt (2)		M. Fraser
July 12	Hurricanes	Wellington	11–17.	Smith		M. Hunt (2)		B. Pickerill
July 19	Chiefs	Hamilton	33–31	Mikaele-Tu'u, Smith, M. Hunt, Tomkinson, Nareki	M. Hunt (4)			M. Fraser
August 02	Blues	Dunedin	21–32	Dixon, Frizell	Ioane	Ioane (3)		M. Fraser
August 09	Crusaders	Christchurch	22–32	Frizell, Nareki, Collins	Ioane (2)	Ioane		P. Williams
August 15	Hurricanes	Dunedin	38–21	Punivai, Dixon, Collins, M. Hunt, penalty try	Ioane (3), M. Hunt	Ioane		B. O'Keeffe

RESULTS FROM 2020 FIRST-CLASS SEASON

Key: S15   SANZAAR Super 15
 SRA Super Rugby Aotearoa
 RS   Ranfurly Shield
 P   Mitre 10 Cup Premiership
 C   Mitre 10 Cup Championship
 cr   Mitre 10 Cup Crossover match between teams from Premiership and Championship divisions.
 sf   Semi-final
 f   Final
 *   not first-class
 aet after extra time

Winning team listed first

JANUARY
Sat-Sun	25-26	*	Round Three 2019-2020 World Rugby Sevens Series				Hamilton, NZ
Fri	31	S15	Chiefs	37	Blues	29	Auckland

FEBRUARY
Sat-Sun	1-2	*	Round Four 2019-2020 World Rugby Sevens Series				Sydney, Australia
Sat	1	S15	Crusaders	43	Waratahs	25	Nelson
	1	S15	Stormers	27	Hurricanes	0	Cape Town
Fri	7	S15	Sharks	42	Highlanders	20	Dunedin
Sat	8	S15	Chiefs	25	Crusaders	15	Hamilton
	8	S15	Blues	32	Waratahs	12	Newcastle
	8	S15	Hurricanes	26	Jaguares	23	Buenos Aires
Fri	14	S15	Crusaders	25	Blues	8	Auckland
Sat	15	S15	Chiefs	43	Sunwolves	17	Tokyo
	15	S15	Hurricanes	38	Sharks	22	Wellington
	15	S15	Highlanders	23	Brumbies	22	Canberra
Fri	21	S15	Crusaders	33	Highlanders	13	Christchurch
Sat	22	S15	Brumbies	26	Chiefs	14	Hamilton
	22	S15	Blues	23	Bulls	21	Pretoria
Fri	28	S15	Rebels	28	Highlanders	22	Dunedin
Sat	29	S15	Hurricanes	62	Sunwolves	15	Napier
	29	S15	Blues	33	Stormers	14	Cape Town
Sat-Sun	29-March 1	*	Round Five 2019-2020 World Rugby Sevens Series				Los Angeles, USA

MARCH
Fri	6	S15	Crusaders	24	Reds	20	Christchurch
	6	S15	Chiefs	51	Waratahs	14	Wollongong
Sat	7	S15	Blues	24	Hurricanes	15	Wellington
	7	S15	Bulls	38	Highlanders	13	Pretoria
Sat-Sun	7-8	*	Round Six 2019-2020 World Rugby Sevens Series				Vancouver, Canada
Fri	13	S15	Hurricanes	27	Chiefs	24	Hamilton
Sat	14	S15	Blues	43	Lions	10	Auckland
	14	S15	Crusaders	49	Sunwolves	14	Brisbane

JUNE
Sat	13	SRA	Highlanders	28	Chiefs	27	Dunedin
Sun	14	SRA	Blues	30	Hurricanes	20	Auckland
Sat	20	SRA	Blues	24	Chiefs	12	Hamilton

Results From 2020 First-Class Season

Day	Date	Comp	Team	Score	Opponent	Score	Venue
Sun	21	SRA	Crusaders	39	Hurricanes	25	Wellington
Sat	27	SRA	Blues	27	Highlanders	24	Auckland
Sun	28	SRA	Crusaders	18	Chiefs	13	Christchurch
JULY							
Sat	4	SRA	Crusaders	40	Highlanders	20	Dunedin
Sun	5	SRA	Hurricanes	25	Chiefs	18	Hamilton
Sat	11	SRA	Crusaders	26	Blues	15	Christchurch
Sun	12	SRA	Hurricanes	17	Highlanders	11	Wellington
Sat	18	SRA	Hurricanes	29	Blues	27	Wellington
Sun	19	SRA	Highlanders	33	Chiefs	31	Hamilton
Sat	25	SRA	Hurricanes	34	Crusaders	32	Christchurch
Sun	26	SRA	Blues	21	Chiefs	17	Auckland
AUGUST							
Sat	1	SRA	Crusaders	32	Chiefs	19	Hamilton
Sun	2	SRA	Blues	32	Highlanders	21	Dunedin
Sat	8	SRA	Hurricanes	31	Chiefs	18	Wellington
Sun	9	SRA	Crusaders	32	Highlanders	22	Christchurch
Sat	15	SRA	Highlanders	38	Hurricanes	21	Dunedin
Fri	28	RS	Canterbury	71	North Otago	7	Christchurch
SEPTEMBER							
Sat	5		South Canterbury	31	Mid Canterbury	31	Timaru
	5		South Island	38	North Island	35	Wellington
Fri	11	P	Canterbury	43	North Harbour	29	Albany
Sat	12		Mid Canterbury	41	Buller	17	Hanmer Springs
	12	P	Waikato	53	Wellington	28	Hamilton
	12		South Canterbury	24	North Otago	7	Oamaru
	12	cr	Auckland	38	Otago	6	Dunedin
	12	cr	Tasman	41	Counties Manukau	24	Pukekohe
Sun	13	C	Northland	43	Manawatu	26	Whangarei
	13	cr	Taranaki	36	Bay of Plenty	29	Inglewood
	13	C	Southland	16	Hawke's Bay	10	Invercargill
Fri	18	cr	Tasman	54	Northland	21	Blenheim
Sat	19	P	Waikato	41	North Harbour	19	Hamilton
	19		Wairarapa Bush	41	Horowhenua Kapiti	8	Levin
	19		Mid Canterbury	30	North Otago	7	Hinds
	19		South Canterbury	78	Buller	10	Timaru
	19		Poverty Bay	34	Ngati Porou East Coast	31	Gisborne
	19	cr RS	Taranaki	23	Canterbury	22	Christchurch
	19	cr	Bay of Plenty	17	Southland	14	Rotorua
Sun	20	C	Hawke's Bay	31	Counties Manukau	17	Napier
	20	C	Otago	36	Manawatu	25	Palmerston North
	20	P	Wellington	39	Auckland	21	Auckland
Fri	25	P	Wellington	32	Bay of Plenty	10	Wellington
Sat	26	P	Tasman	34	Waikato	17	Nelson
	26		Mid Canterbury	35	North Otago	17	Oamaru
	26		South Canterbury	66	Buller	28	Westport
	26		Poverty Bay	42	Ngati Porou East Coast	16	Ruatoria
	26	cr	Southland	11	North Harbour	10	Invercargill
	26		Wairarapa Bush	22	King Country	18	Masterton

	26	cr	Hawke's Bay	20	Canterbury	19	Napier
Sun	27	cr	Auckland	50	Manawatu	12	Auckland
	27	C RS	Otago	30	Taranaki	19	Inglewood
	27	C	Northand	24	Counties Manukau	15	Pukekohe
OCTOBER							
Fri	2	P	Auckland	20	Bay of Plenty	16	Rotorua
Sat	3	C	Counties Manukau	36	Manawatu	30	Pukekohe
	3		Wairarapa Bush	46	Poverty Bay	26	Napier
	3		South Canterbury	37	North Otago	29	Timaru
	3		Wanganui	36	Horowhenua Kapiti	7	Shannon
	3		King Country	34	Ngati Porou East Coast	22	Opotiki
	3	C	Northland	35	Taranaki	25	Whangarei
	3	P	Canterbury	31 aet	Wellington	26 aet	Christchurch
Sun	4	cr	Waikato	10	Southland	9	Invercargill
	4	cr	North Harbour	40	Tasman	24	Albany
	4	C RS	Hawke's Bay	28	Otago	9	Dunedin
Fri	9	cr	Canterbury	34	Manawatu	10	Palmerston North
Sat	10	cr	Auckland	29	Taranaki	28	Inglewood
	10	cr	North Harbour	46	Hawke's Bay	10	Albany
	10		Wairarapa Bush	47	Horowhenua Kapiti	24	Carterton
	10		King Country	16	Wanganui	11	Taumarunui
	10	cr	Otago	35	Wellington	34	Wellington
	10	cr	Waikato	36	Counties Manukau	13	Hamilton
Sun	11	P	Tasman	33	Bay of Plenty	7	Nelson
	11	C	Northland	18	Southland	14	Whangarei
	11		New Zealand	16	Australia	16	Wellington
Fri	16	C RS	Hawke's Bay	33	Northland	17	Napier
Sat	17	cr	Bay of Plenty	53	Manawatu	35	Palmerston North
	17	P	Wellington	25	North Harbour	20	Wellington
	17		Wanganui	29	Wairarapa Bush	8	Wanganui
	17	P	Auckland	31	Tasman	10	Auckland
	17	C	Taranaki	17	Southland	9	Invercargill
Sun	18	P	Waikato	16	Canterbury	15	Christchurch
	18	C	Otago	40	Counties Manukau	22	Dunedin
	18		New Zealand	27	Australia	7	Auckland
Fri	23	C	Otago	30	Northland	7	Dunedin
Sat	24	P	Bay of Plenty	44	Canterbury	8	Tauranga
	24		Wanganui	41	Poverty Bay	38	Napier
	24	C RS	Hawke's Bay	47	Manawatu	12	Napier
	24	P	North Harbour	23	Auckland	22	Albany
Sun	25	cr	Tasman	47	Southland	12	Nelson
	25	cr	Wellington	53	Counties Manukau	20	Pukekohe
	25	cr	Waikato	27	Taranaki	20	Hamilton
Fri	30	cr	Otago	23	Canterbury	16	Christchurch
Sat	31	P	Tasman	19	Wellington	3	Porirua
	31	cr	North Harbour	24	Northland	8	Whangarei
	31	P	Auckland	31	Waikato	10	Auckland
	31	TN	New Zealand	43	Australia	5	Sydney

Results From 2020 First-Class Season

NOVEMBER

Day	Date	Type		Team 1	Score	Team 2	Score	Venue
Sun	1	C		Manawatu	24	Southland	12	Feilding
	1	cr		Bay of Plenty	22	Hawke's Bay	17	Tauranga
	1	C		Counties Manukau	31	Taranaki	27	Inglewood
Fri	6	C		Southland	32	Otago	15	Invercargill
Sat	7	cr		Auckland	24	Northland	20	Auckland
	7	cr		North Harbour	32	Counties Manukau	5	Albany
	7	P		Canterbury	29	Tasman	0	Blenheim
	7	TN		Australia	24	New Zealand	22	Brisbane
Sun	8	cr	RS	Hawke's Bay	34	Wellington	18	Napier
	8	P		Bay of Plenty	33	Waikato	30	Hamilton
	8	C		Taranaki	35	Manawatu	19	Feilding
Fri	13	C		Counties Manukau	25	Southland	17	Pukekohe
Sat	14	cr		Northland	28	Waikato	17	Kaikohe
	14	cr		Wellington	31	Manawatu	5	Wellington
	14	cr		Tasman	26	Otago	20	Dunedin
	14	TN		Argentina	25	New Zealand	15	Sydney
Sun	15	C		Hawke's Bay	34	Taranaki	33	Inglewood
	15	P		Bay of Plenty	37	North Harbour	33	Tauranga
	15	P		Canterbury	34	Auckland	33	Christchurch
Fri	20	C	sf	Northland	32	Otago	19	Dunedin
Sat	21	P	sf	Auckland	23	Waikato	18	Auckland
	21	C	sf	Hawke's Bay	59	Taranaki	23	Napier
	21	P	sf	Tasman	19	Bay of Plenty	10	Nelson
Fri	27	C	f	Hawke's Bay	36	Northland	24	Napier
Sat	28	P	f	Tasman	13	Auckland	12	Auckland
	28	TN		New Zealand	38	Argentina	0	Newcastle

DECEMBER

Day	Date	Type		Team 1	Score	Team 2	Score	Venue
Sat	5			NZ Maori	28	Moana Pasifika	21	Hamilton

147 first-class matches.

NATIONAL PROVINCIAL CHAMPIONSHIP WINNERS

	First Division	Second Division (North)	Second Division (South)
1976	Bay of Plenty	Taranaki	South Canterbury
1977	Canterbury	North Auckland	South Canterbury
1978	Wellington	Bay of Plenty	Marlborough
1979	Counties	Hawke's Bay	Marlborough
1980	Manawatu	Waikato	Mid Canterbury
1981	Wellington	Wairarapa Bush	South Canterbury
1982	Auckland	Taranaki	Southland
1983	Canterbury	Taranaki	Mid Canterbury
1984	Auckland	Taranaki	Southland

	First Division	Second Division	Third Division
1985	Auckland	Taranaki	North Harbour
1986	Wellington	Waikato	South Canterbury
1987	Auckland	North Harbour	Poverty Bay
1988	Auckland	Hawke's Bay	Thames Valley
1989	Auckland	Southland	Wanganui
1990	Auckland	Hawke's Bay	Thames Valley
1991	Otago	King Country	South Canterbury
1992	Waikato	Taranaki	Nelson Bays
1993	Auckland	Counties	Horowhenua
1994	Auckland	Southland	Mid Canterbury
1995	Auckland	Taranaki	Thames Valley
1996	Auckland	Southland	Wanganui
1997	Canterbury	Northland	Marlborough
1998	Otago	Central Vikings	Mid Canterbury
1999	Auckland	Nelson Bays	East Coast
2000	Wellington	Bay of Plenty	East Coast
2001	Canterbury	Hawke's Bay	South Canterbury
2002	Auckland	Hawke's Bay	North Otago
2003	Auckland	Hawke's Bay	Wanganui
2004	Canterbury	Nelson Bays	Poverty Bay
2005	Auckland	Hawke's Bay	Wairarapa Bush

	Air New Zealand Cup	Meads Cup	Lochore Cup
2006	Waikato	Wairarapa Bush	Poverty Bay
2007	Auckland	North Otago	Poverty Bay
2008	Canterbury	Wanganui	Poverty Bay
2009	Canterbury	Wanganui	North Otago

	ITM Cup	Meads Cup	Lochore Cup
2010	Canterbury	North Otago	Wairarapa Bush

	ITM Premiership	ITM Championship	Meads Cup	Lochore Cup
2011	Canterbury	Hawke's Bay	Wanganui	Poverty Bay
2012	Canterbury	Counties Manukau	East Coast	Buller

	ITM Cup		PINK BATTS HEARTLAND CHAMPIONSHIP	
	Premiership	Championship	Meads Cup	Lochore Cup
2013	Canterbury	Tasman	Mid Canterbury	South Canterbury
2014	Taranaki	Manawatu	Mid Canterbury	Wanganui
2015	Canterbury	Hawke's Bay	Wanganui	King Country

	MITRE 10 CUP		MITRE 10 HEARTLAND CHAMPIONSHIP	
	Premiership	Championship	Meads Cup	Lochore Cup
2016	Canterbury	North Harbour	Wanganui	North Otago
2017	Canterbury	Wellington	Wanganui	Mid-Canterbury
2018	Auckland	Waikato	Thames Valley	Horowhenua Kapiti
2019	Tasman	Bay of Plenty	North Otago	South Canterbury
2020	Tasman	Hawke's Bay	NR	NR

MITRE 10 CUP

Going into the final week of the Premiership round robin only one province had secured a semi-final place — top of the table Auckland. Four provinces were in danger of relegation if they lost their last match: Bay of Plenty (4th, 26 points), North Harbour (5th, 25 points), Canterbury (6th, 24 points) and Wellington (7th, 24 points).

In the order of the relegation battle matches played, Wellington defeated Championship side Manawatu, then Bay of Plenty defeated North Harbour. In the final game of round 10, Canterbury had to win against Auckland to stay up, which would see North Harbour relegated. Canterbury won 34–33 with a long range 75th minute penalty goal putting them ahead.

North Harbour's five wins and 27 points are the highest tallies of wins and points achieved by a team to suffer relegation since the Premiership/Championship split started in 2011.

Tasman's 13–12 win over Auckland in the final made Tasman only the third province to win consecutive titles, joining Auckland and Canterbury.

Hawke's Bay won the Championship for the third time to win promotion to the Premiership for 2021, although a proposal is under consideration for the Premiership/Championship divisions to be scrapped and the 14 Unions split into North Island and South Island pools of seven teams each with four crossover matches and crossover playoffs, similar to that used in the Farah Palmer Cup this year.

An innovation in the Mitre 10 Cup this year was the introduction of extra time in the event of scores level after 80 minutes in round robin matches. An extra ten minutes would be played and the "golden point" rule of a score of any kind would end the game immediately in favour of the team who scored. If no score was made in the ten minutes of extra time then the game would be declared a draw. This had been available in Super Rugby Aotearoa this year.

On only one occasion was "golden point" extra time needed and that was the round four clash between Canterbury and Wellington at Christchurch. After 80 minutes the scores were locked at 26–26. After five minutes of extra time Isaia Punivai intercepted to score a try for Canterbury which ended the game immediately 31–26 in the host's favour. The conversion attempt was not required.

The All Blacks were available for the first two rounds but with the country at Covid-19 Alert Level 2, the first two rounds saw restricted crowd levels with spectators required to be in separated 'bubbles' of 100.

But for North Harbour, Auckland and Counties Manukau, their home games in the first two rounds were played with no spectators in attendance. For rounds three and four, separated bubbles of 100 were allowed.

ROUND ROBIN

Each team played all six other teams in their division plus crossover matches against four teams in the other division for a total of ten matches.

	P	W	D	L	B^4	B^7	Pts	T	C	FOR PG	DG	Total	T	C	AGAINST PG	DG	Total
PREMIERSHIP DIVISION																	
Auckland	10	7	0	3	6	2	36	43[1]	32	6	0	299	25	14	15	0	198
Tasman	10	7	0	3	5	0	33	39	30	11	0	288	26	21	10	0	202
Bay of Plenty	10	6	0	4	5	2	31	35[1]	26	13	0	268	37[2]	24	7	0	258
Waikato	10	6	0	4	4	1	29	31[1]	23	17	1	257	31	24	9	0	230
Canterbury	10	5	0	5	5	4	29	34	21	12	1	251	29[1]	16	15	0	224
Wellington	10	5	0	5	7	2	29	40	28	11	0	289	30	19	20	0	248
North Harbour	10	5	0	5	4	3	27	34[1]	25	18	0	276	30	20	12	0	226

B^4 bonus points for four or more tries in a match.
B^7 bonus points for loss by seven or fewer points.
[1] includes one penalty try (7 points)
[2] includes two penalty tries (14 points)

Waikato, Canterbury and Wellington all finished on 29 points. The tiebreaker rule for three teams finishing on the same number of points is: the tied provincial union with the most competition points in that year against the other tied provincial unions shall have the higher position.
Waikato earned 9 points against Canterbury/Wellington, Canterbury earned 6 points against Waikato/Wellington and Wellington earned 3 points against Waikato/Canterbury.

	P	W	D	L	B^4	B^7	Pts	T	C	FOR PG	DG	Total	T	C	AGAINST PG	DG	Total
CHAMPIONSHIP DIVISION																	
Hawke's Bay	10	7	0	3	6	2	36	38[2]	23	8	0	264	27	16	14	0	209
Otago	10	6	0	4	5	1	30	31	19	17	0	244	31[1]	24	13	1	247
Northland	10	5	0	5	3	1	24	29	23	10	0	221	33	26	15	0	262
Taranaki	10	4	0	6	4	4	24	34[1]	20	17	0	263	35[1]	23	14	0	265
Southland	10	3	0	7	1	3	16	17	10	13	0	144	26	18	8	1	193
Counties Manukau	10	3	0	7	2	0	14	26	21	12	0	208	47[2]	31	10	0	331
Manawatu	10	1	0	9	4	1	9	30	15	6	0	198	54	40	9	0	377
TOTALS								461	316	171	2	3470	461	316	171	2	3470

B^4 bonus points for four or more tries in a match.
B^7 bonus points for loss by seven or fewer points.
[1] includes one penalty try (7 points)
[2] includes two penalty tries (14 points)

Northland and Taranaki both finished on 24 points. Northland had the higher rank due to winning their round robin match.

PLAYOFF SUMMARY

In the semi-finals, the top qualifier was home to the fourth-placed qualifier and the second-placed qualifier was home to the third-place qualifier. In the final, the highest qualifier of the two participants played at home.

PREMIERSHIP

Semi-finals: Auckland 23 (3t, c, 2pg) v Waikato 18 (2t, c, 2pg), at Auckland
Tasman 19 (2t, 3pg) v Bay of Plenty 10 (t, c, pg), at Nelson

Final: Tasman 13 (t, c, 2pg) v Auckland 12 (4pg), at Auckland

CHAMPIONSHIP

Semi-finals: Northland 32 (4t, 3c, 2pg) v Otago 19 (3t, 2c), at Dunedin
Hawke's Bay 59 (8t, 8c, pg) v Taranaki 23 (3t, c, 2pg), at Napier

Final: Hawke's Bay 36 (6t, 3c) v Northland 24 (4t, 2c), at Napier

ALMANACK NEW ZEALAND MITRE 10 CUP XV

David Havili
Tasman

Leicester Faingaanuku   Quinn Tupaea   Salesi Rayasi
Tasman   *Waikato*   *Auckland*

Alex Nankivell
Tasman

Bryn Gatland
North Harbour

Folau Fakatava
Hawke's Bay

Tony Lamborn
Southland

Lachie Boshier   Tom Parsons   Luke Romano   Adam Thomson
Taranaki   *Hawke's Bay*   *Canterbury*   *Waikato*

Sione Mafileo   Ash Dixon   Daniel Lienert-Brown
North Harbour   *Hawke's Bay*   *Canterbury*

Reserves: Luteru Tolai (*North Harbour*), Xavier Numia (*Wellington*), Josh Iosefa-Scott (*Wellington*), Josh Goodhue (*Northland*), Devan Flanders (*Hawke's Bay*), Jonathan Ruru (*Auckland*), Kaleb Trask (*Bay of Plenty*), Joe Webber (*Bay of Plenty*) .

RECORDS

BY THE TEAMS

BEST PERFORMANCES 2020 | RECORD 1976–2020
First Division 1976–2005, Air New Zealand Cup 2006–2009, ITM Cup 2010–2015, Mitre 10 Cup 2016-

In a Season

Most points	359	Hawke's Bay	521 Otago, 1998
Most tries	52	Hawke's Bay	74 Wellington, 2017
Most conversions	34	Hawke's Bay	57 Canterbury, 2017
Most penalty goals	19	Waikato / Taranaki	45 Otago, 2012
Most dropped goals	1	Waikato / Canterbury	12 Bay of Plenty, 1985

In a Match

Highest Score	59	Hawke's Bay v Taranaki, November 21	97 Auckland v King Country, 1993
Biggest winning margin	38	Auckland v Manawatu (50–12)	94 Auckland v King Country, 1993 (97–3)
Most tries	8	Tasman v Northland / Auckland v Manawatu / Hawke's Bay v Taranaki, November 21	15 Auckland v King Country, 1993
Most conversions	8	Hawke's Bay v Taranaki, November 21	12 Canterbury v Southland, 2012
Most penalty goals	6	Waikato v Wellington	9 Taranaki v Bay of Plenty, 2011
Most dropped goals	1	Waikato v Southland / Canterbury v Otago	4 Bay of Plenty v Waikato, 1985

BY THE PLAYERS

BEST PERFORMANCES 2020

RECORD 1976–2020
First Division 1976–2005, Air New Zealand Cup 2006–2009, ITM Cup 2010–2015, Mitre 10 Cup 2016-

In a Season

Most points	119	B.E.C. Gatland (North Harbour)	196	T.E. Brown (Otago), 1998
Most tries	14	S.T.M. Rayasi (Auckland)	15	T.J. Wright (Auckland), 1984
				B.J. Laney (Otago), 1998

In a Match

Most points	33	D.S. McKenzie (Waikato) v Wellington	37	B.A. Blair (Canterbury) v Counties Manukau, 1999
Most tries	3	S.L. Reece (Tasman) v Northland	5	T.J. Wright (Auckland) v Manawatu, 1984
		D.K. Havili (Tasman) v Waikato		W.R. Gordon (Waikato) v Southland, 1990
		A. Motuga (Counties Manukau) v Manawatu		C.J. Spencer (Auckland) v Otago, 1996
		J.R. Page (North Harbour) v Hawke's Bay		M.P. Robinson (Taranaki) v Southland, 1997
		S.T.M. Rayasi (Auckland) v Waikato, October 31		J. Maddock (Canterbury) v North Harbour, 2002
		A.L. Dixon (Hawke's Bay) v Taranaki, November 21		S.W. Sivivatu (Waikato) v Auckland, 2004
				T. Li (North Harbour) v Taranaki, 2017
Most conversions	7	L.F. McClutchie (Hawke's Bay) v Taranaki, November 21	12	T.J. Taylor (Canterbury) v Southland, 2012
Most penalty goals	6	D.S. McKenzie (Waikato) v Wellington	9	B.J. Barrett (Taranaki) v Bay of Plenty, 2011
Most dropped goals	1	F.H. Smith (Waikato) v Southland	4	R.J. Preston (Bay of Plenty) v Waikato, 1985
		B.D. Cameron (Canterbury) v Otago		

Leading points-scorers in the Mitre 10 Cup:

B.E.C. Gatland	North Harbour	119
M.J. Hunt	Tasman	97
J.P. Potroz	Taranaki	95
J.K. Garden-Bachop	Wellington	88
J.R. Ioane	Otago	88

Leading try-scorers in the Mitre 10 Cup:

S.M.T. Rayasi	Auckland	14
A.L. Dixon	Hawke's Bay	9
J.W.J. Ratumaitavuki-Kneepkens	Taranaki	8
A.J. Lam	Auckland	7
F.K. Vahaakolo	Otago	7
T.I. Webber	Bay of Plenty	7
L.H.V. Tolai	North Harbour	7

MITRE 10 HEARTLAND CHAMPIONSHIP

The Heartland Championship, scheduled to start on August 22, was not held in 2020, due to the Covid-19 pandemic.

With all rugby suspended in March just before the majority of club competitions were about to start, the 12 Heartland Unions, in agreement with New Zealand Rugby, announced on March 30 that the Heartland Championship would not be held this year primarily as a cost-cutting measure, but with an assurance it would operate in 2021. Clubs and provinces were eventually able to start playing on June 20.

Having to organise their own fixtures, ten of the 12 Heartland Unions played a brief programme of representative matches in September and October, almost all being against neighbouring unions, with numerous old and new trophies being played for. In total, 19 first-class matches were played.

Because of no Heartland Championship, the Unions were able to treat their truncated representative season as a development year and debut a large number of their local players, with no need to bring in any loan players in place of local talent.

Two Unions — Thames Valley and West Coast — chose not to play any representative games.

AUCKLAND

2020 Status: Mitre 10 Cup Premiership
Founded 1883. Original member 1892
President: E. (Eroni) Clarke
Chairman: S.M. (Stuart) Mather
Chief executive officer: J.M. (Jarrod) Bear
Coach: A. (Alama) Ieremia
Assistant coaches: F.I. (Filo) Tiatia, C.E. (Craig) McGrath, D.R. (Daniel) Bowden
Main ground: Eden Park, Auckland
Capacity: 47,000
Colours: Blue and white

RECORDS

Most appearances	192	*'Snow' White, 1950–63*
Most points	2746	*Grant Fox, 1982–93*
Most tries	112	*Terry Wright, 1984–93*
Most points in a season	322	*Grant Fox, 1990*
Most tries in a season	19	*Terry Wright, 1984*
Most conversions in a season	77	*Grant Fox, 1990*
Most penalty goals in a season	48	*Grant Fox, 1989, 1990*
Most dropped goals in a season	8	*Grant Fox, 1990*
Most points in a match	43	*Adrian Cashmore v Mid Canterbury, 1995*
Most tries in a match	8	*John Kirwan v North Otago, 1993*
Most conversions in a match	12	*Grant Fox v Marlborough, 1984*
		Brett Craies v Horowhenua, 1986
		Grant Fox v Nelson Bays, 1991
		Lachie Munro v North Otago, 2008
Most penalty goals in a match	7	*Grant Fox v Canterbury, 1990*
		Grant Fox v Waikato, 1992
Highest team score	139	*v North Otago, 1993*
Record victory (points ahead)	134	*139–5 v North Otago, 1993*
Highest score conceded	59	*v Waikato, 2004*
Record defeat (points behind)	48	*11–59 v Waikato, 2004*

Out of a challenging pre-season, and having to call on 44 players, including 15 debutants, Auckland fashioned a decent Premership campaign, which fell only at the last hurdle to the defending champion.

Much of the rugby played by Alama Ieremia's men was inconsistent, but they were mostly staunch on defence — where coach Craig McGrath can take a bow — aggressive in the forwards and, if all else failed, they could fall back on the most potent strike-force in the Mitre 10 Cup, left wing Salesi Rayasi.

The pre-season was a write-off as the squad could not train properly due to Covid-19 restrictions on gatherings in the Auckland region.

But Auckland was swiftly into its work, annexing the Lin Colling Memorial Trophy in Otago before a strangely flat, insipid display at home against Wellington for the Fred Lucas Memorial Trophy. Then followed four consecutive wins of varying quality, ending with the 31–10 victory over the Mako at Eden Park, easily the best performance of the season, in which the pack stood tall and got physical.

The Battle of the Bridge could have gone either way, and Waikato was dispatched with more ease than in the semi-final. Northland was edged in a truly bizarre game before Canterbury, thanks to a long-range penalty goal by a former First XV player from Auckland, headed the Auks in Christchurch.

Neither the semi-final win over Waikato nor the one-point loss in the final were Auckland's best work, the errors mounting and the tactics questionable.

Yet, for much of the season, there was much productive tactical kicking, either via grubbers or crosskicks, and the set-piece was sound until the playoffs.

Auckland threw open the gates for the decider but, unlike in 2018, could only draw 13,000 on a fine late spring evening in the latest rugby game ever to take place at Eden Park.

Fullback Jordan Trainor looked good before injury, but was usurped by rookie Zarn Sullivan, who went from the third-ranked first five to the top No 15 with some mature displays. He was solid under the high ball, possessed of a howitzer boot and penetrative on attack.

But he was not more penetrative than Rayasi, who threatened the competition season try record of 15, jointly held by Brendan Laney (1998) and Terry Wright (1984). Rayasi built on his six tries in 2019 and crossed for 14 with a compelling mixture of power and pace. He was complemented on the right wing by AJ Lam, scorer of seven tries.

In the midfield, Tumua Manu was mostly good, Tanielu Tele'a was robust after injury, but the backline missed captain TJ Faiane, injured for five of the last six games.

Harry Plummer almost recaptured his 2018 form, and slotted into second five later in games. He goalkicked more accurately and kept the more experienced Simon Hickey on the bench, but Plummer still lacked authority in some of the tight matches.

Halfback Jonathan Ruru was generally outstanding, a precise box kicker and like a fourth loose forward around the rucks.

Auckland had to call on nine loose forwards due to injury and All Blacks' call-ups. Waimana Riedlinger-Kapa was making a good fist of the No 8 berth until he was laid low. Niko Jones made a promising, though quiet, start to his first-class career. Blake Gibson and Adrian Choat, as two fetchers, worked well in tandem, the latter prominent in the win over Tasman.

Locks Jack Whetton and Scott Scrafton both played well when available, with useful back-up from former NZ Under 20s and Canterbury second-rower Hamish Dalzell.

Angus Ta'avao finished the season with the C next to his name, but failed to scrummage with authority in the final, while Marcel Renata was typically industrious and passed the 50-game milestone. James Lay was solid on his return from the UK, while Jarred Adams offered good value in either the No 1 or 17 jerseys.

Hooker Leni Apisai was among the lineout-driven tries, but young rake Soane Vikena was badly injured against Northland.

Higher honours went to:
New Zealand: C. Clarke, A. Hodgman, A. Ioane, R. Ioane, H. Sotutu, P. Tuipulotu, O. Tuungafasi

AUCKLAND REPRESENTATIVES 2020

	Club	Games for Union	Points for Union
Jarred Adams	Suburbs	29	5
Leni Apisai	Ponsonby	22	25
Adrian Choat	Waitemata	22	15
Caleb Clarke	Ponsonby	22	40
Joel Cobb	Ponsonby	4	0
Hamish Dalzell	College Rifles	9	0
TJ Faiane	Pakuranga	46	45
Marco Fepulea'i	Ponsonby	26	5
Inga Finau	Grammar TEC	1	0
Taufa Funaki	Marist	5	0
Blake Gibson	Ponsonby	40	30
Liam Hallam-Eames	Grammar TEC	6	0
Simon Hickey	Grammar TEC	59	447
Alex Hodgman	Suburbs	13	0
Akira Ioane	Ponsonby	50	65
Rieko Ioane	Ponsonby	18	70
Niko Jones	Waitemata	7	0
Felix Kalapu	Grammar TEC	1	0
AJ Lam	Grammar TEC	16	40
James Lay	University	13	0
Tumua Manu	College Rifles	34	50
Fatongia Paea	Pakuranga	1	0
Terrell Peita	Ponsonby	2	5
Harry Plummer	Grammar TEC	35	254
Salesi Rayasi	Marist	31	145
Marcel Renata	University	51	15
Waimana Riedlinger-Kapa	Ponsonby	16	10
Joe Royal	Ponsonby	1	0
Jonathan Ruru	University	34	30
Scott Scrafton	Grammar TEC	39	5
Mike Sosene-Feagai	Marist	23	15
Hoskins Sotutu	Marist	17	10
Zarn Sullivan	College Rifles	9	9
Angus Ta'avao	Eden	45	10
William Talataina	Ponsonby	2	0
Tanielu Tele'a	Marist	20	20
Jordan Trainor	Ponsonby	31	47
Presley Tufuga	Ponsonby	5	5
Patrick Tuipulotu	Ponsonby	23	40
Sione Tuipulotu	Eden	6	5
Danny Tusitala	Ponsonby	17	10
Ofa Tuungafasi	Grammar TEC	43	10
Soane Vikena	Ponsonby	3	0
Jack Whetton	Grammar TEC	44	20

INDIVIDUAL SCORING

	Tries	Con	PG	DG	Points
Plummer	–	25	8	–	74
Rayasi	14	–	–	–	70
Lam	7	–	–	–	35
Hickey	2	8	1	–	29
Apisai	3	–	–	–	15
Manu	3	–	–	–	15
Tele'a	2	–	–	–	10
Sullivan	–	–	3	–	9
Penalty try	1	–	–	–	7
Adams	1	–	–	–	5
Choat	1	–	–	–	5
Clarke	1	–	–	–	5
Gibson	1	–	–	–	5
A. Ioane	1	–	–	–	5
R. Ioane	1	–	–	–	5
Peita	1	–	–	–	5
Renata	1	–	–	–	5
Riedlinger-Kapa	1	–	–	–	5
Ruru	1	–	–	–	5
Trainor	1	–	–	–	5
Tufuga	1	–	–	–	5
S. Tuipulotu	1	–	–	–	5
Whetton	1	–	–	–	5
Totals	**46**	**33**	**12**	**0**	**334**
Opposition scored	28	16	19	0	229

AUCKLAND 2020

Player	Otago	Wellington	Manawatu	Bay of Plenty	Taranaki	Tasman	North Harbour	Waikato	Northland	Canterbury	Waikato (SF)	Tasman (F)	Totals
J.V. Trainor	15	15	15	15	15	–	–	–	–	–	s	s	7
S.T.M. Rayasi	–	–	11	11	11	11	–	11	11	11	11	11	9
J.H.C. Cobb	–	–	–	–	–	–	s	s	s	14	–	–	4
A.J. Lam	14	14	14	14	14	14	14	14	14	–	14	14	11
C.D. Clarke	11	11	–	–	–	–	–	–	–	–	–	–	2
R.E. Ioane	13	13	–	–	–	–	–	–	–	–	–	–	2
T.R. Tele'a	–	–	–	–	s	s	11	–	13	12	12	12	7
T.P. Manu	s	s	13	13	13	13	13	13	–	13	13	13	11
K.F. Finau	–	–	–	–	–	–	12	–	–	–	–	–	1
T.J. Faiane (capt)	12	12	12	12	12	12	–	12	–	–	–	–	7
W. Talataina	–	–	–	–	–	–	–	–	s	s	–	–	2
Z. Sullivan	–	s	s	–	–	15	15	15	15	15	15	15	9
S.C. Hickey	s	–	10	10	s	s	s	s	10	s	s	s	11
H.R.J. Plummer	10	10	s	s	10	10	10	10	12	10	10	10	12
J.L. Ruru	9	9	s	9	s	9	9	9	9	9	9	9	12
D.J.K. Tusitala	s	s	–	–	–	s	s	s	s	s	–	–	6
S.T. Funaki	–	–	9	s	9	–	–	–	–	s	–	s	5
H.C.R. Sotutu	8	8	–	–	–	–	–	–	–	–	–	–	2
P. Tufuga	–	–	–	–	–	–	–	–	6	8	6	s	4
N.A.D. Jones	–	–	–	–	s	s	–	s	7	s	s	7	7
A.J. Choat	7	7	6	6	6	6	6	6	–	–	7	6	10
B.T. Gibson	s	s	7	7	7	7	7	7	–	7	–	–	9
A.L. Ioane	6	6	–	–	–	–	8	–	–	–	–	–	3
W. Riedlinger-Kapa	–	–	8	8	8	8	–	–	–	–	–	–	4
T.M. Peita	–	–	–	–	–	–	–	–	s	6	–	–	2
S. Tuipulotu	–	–	s	s	–	–	–	8	8	–	8	8	6
L.J. Hallam-Eames	s	s	–	–	–	–	s	s	5	s	–	–	6
H. Dalzell	–	–	–	s	s	s	5	5	4	5	5	s	9
J.C. Whetton	5	5	5	5	5	5	–	–	–	–	s	5	8
P.T. Tuipulotu	–	–	s	–	–	–	–	–	–	–	–	–	1
S.N. Scrafton	4	4	4	4	4	4	4	4	–	4	4	4	11
S.A.F.T. Kalapu	–	–	–	–	–	–	–	–	s	–	–	–	1
M.C. Renata	–	–	s	3	3	3	3	3	–	–	s	s	8
A.W.F. Ta'avao-Matau (capt)	s	s	3	–	–	–	–	–	3	3	3	3	7
A.O.H.M. Tuungafasi	3	3	–	–	–	–	–	–	–	–	–	–	2
F.H.I. Paea	–	–	–	–	–	–	–	–	–	s	–	–	1
M.L. Fepulea'i	–	–	–	s	s	s	s	s	s	s	–	–	7
J.M. Lay	–	–	s	s	1	1	1	1	1	s	–	1	9
A.T.O.A. Hodgman	1	1	–	–	–	–	–	–	–	–	–	–	2
J.J. Adams	s	s	1	1	s	s	s	s	s	1	1	s	12
L.C.A. Apisai	2	2	2	2	2	2	2	2	s	–	2	2	11
S.M. Vikena	–	–	–	–	s	–	–	s	2	–	–	–	3
M.A. Sosene-Feagai	s	s	s	s	–	s	s	–	–	2	s	9	9
J.W. Royal	–	–	–	–	–	–	–	–	s	–	–	–	1

AUCKLAND TEAM RECORD 2020

Played 12 Won 8 Lost 4 Points for 334 Points against 229

Date	Opponent	Location	Score	Tries	Con	PG	DG	Referee
September 12	Otago (cr)	Dunedin	38–6	Apisai (2), Lam, R. Ioane, penalty try	Plummer (4)	Plummer		J.D. Munro
September 20	Wellington (P)	Auckland	21–39	Apisai, Ruru, Clarke	Plummer (3)			J.J. Doleman
September 27	Manawatu (cr)	Auckland	50–12	Hickey (2), Lam (2), Riedlinger-Kapa, Rayasi, Gibson, Trainor	Hickey (5)			D.J. Waenga
October 02	Bay of Plenty (P)	Rotorua	20–16	Rayasi (2)	Hickey (2)	Hickey, Plummer		B.D. O'Keeffe
October 10	Taranaki (cr)	Inglewood	29–28	Rayasi (2), Lam (2), Whetton	Plummer, Hickey			J.J. Doleman
October 17	Tasman (P)	Auckland	31–10	Choat, Lam, Renata, Manu, Rayasi	Plummer (3)			B.D. O'Keeffe
October 24	North Harbour (P)	Albany	22–23	Lam, Manu, A. Ioane	Plummer (2)	Plummer		R.P. Kelly
October 31	Waikato (P)	Auckland	31–10	Rayasi (3), S. Tuipulotu	Plummer (4)	Plummer		J.J. Doleman
November 07	Northland (cr)	Auckland	24–20	Rayasi (2), Adams	Plummer (3)	Sullivan		N.P. Briant
November 15	Canterbury (P)	Christchurch	33–34	Rayasi (2), Peita, Tele'a, Tufuga	Plummer (4)			N.P. Briant
November 21	Waikato (P, sf)	Auckland	23–18	Rayasi, Tele'a, Manu	Plummer	Sullivan, Plummer		B.E. Pickerill
November 28	Tasman (P, f)	Auckland	12–13			Plummer (3), Sullivan		

BAY OF PLENTY

2020 Status: Mitre 10 Cup Premiership
Founded 1911. Affiliated 1911
President: K.J. (Kevin) Hennessy
Chairman: P.L. (Paul) Owen
Chief executive officer: M.W. (Mike) Rogers
Coach: C.R. (Clayton) McMillan
Assistant coaches: M.J. (Marty) Bourke, M.P. (Mike) Delany, M.J.K. (Mike) Rogers
Main grounds: Rotorua International Stadium; Tauranga Domain
Capacity: 20,000
Colours: Blue and gold.

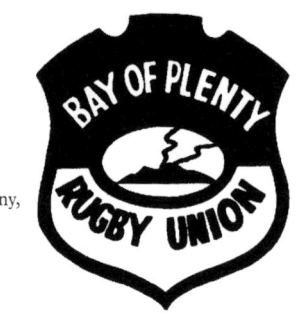

RECORDS

Most appearances	161	*Greg Rowlands, 1969–82*
Most points	1008	*Greg Rowlands, 1969–82*
Most tries	62	*Graeme Moore, 1967–80*
Most points in a season	245	*Andrew Miller, 1996*
Most tries in a season	14	*Damon Kaui, 1995*
Most conversions in a season	53	*Andrew Miller, 1996*
Most penalty goals in a season	48	*Eion Crossan, 1991*
Most dropped goals in a season	13	*Ron Preston, 1985*
Most points in a match	36	*Adrian Cashmore v Thames Valley, 1993*
Most tries in a match	5	*Ian Backhouse v North Otago, 1965*
		Damon Kaui v Thames Valley, 1995
Most conversions in a match	9	*Eion Crossan v Poverty Bay, 1991*
Most penalty goals in a match	6	*Ron Preston v Poverty Bay, 1982*
		Eion Crossan v North Harbour, 1990
		Eion Crossan v Fiji President's XV, 1991
		Eion Crossan v Western Samoa, 1991
		Erin Cossey v Hawke's Bay, 1994
		Andrew Miller v Counties, 1995
		Andrew Miller v King Country, 1996
		Glen Jackson v Northland, 2001
		Glen Jackson v Otago, 2004
		Mike Delany v Waikato, 2009
Highest team score	88	*v East Coast, 1972*
Record victory (points ahead)	79	*88–9 v East Coast, 1972*
		82–3 v Thames Valley, 1995
Highest score conceded	93	*v New Zealand XV, 1993*
Record defeat (points behind)	88	*5–93 v New Zealand XV, 1993*

In the Premiership for the first time since 2013, it was a season that could have gone either way for Bay of Plenty, as going into the final week of the round robin matches they were one of four teams that could either make the semi-finals or be relegated. Fortunately for Bay they won a tight contest with North Harbour which enabled them to finish third, while North Harbour was relegated.

With four defeats in the opening five matches, Bay of Plenty was at the bottom of the Premiership table. Then the second half of the competition saw the upturn in the side's fortune as the Bay found their attacking flair in the trip to Manawatu, scoring seven tries. Canterbury was crushed the following week by a record 44–8 in Tauranga followed by wins against Hawkes Bay, Waikato and North Harbour in closer contests, built on some open running rugby and stern defence.

The result of securing third position was a trip to Nelson for a semi-final clash with defending champions Tasman. However, on the night Tasman proved to be the better team as their kicking game and tight defence nullified the visitors' attacking strengths to eventually win 19–10. Nevertheless, it was a vastly improved performance from Bay of Plenty having been undone in the round robin 7–33 and the side ended with their highest finish since the current format was introduced.

The union was able to assemble a squad of seasoned players for 2020 due to the Covid-19 pandemic which saw several players return from overseas in time for the club season like Joe Tupe (last appearing in 2016), Keepa Mewett, Jordan Lay (both 2017), Zane Kapeli and Kane Leaupepe (both 2018). Regan Ware was available for the season with no NZ Sevens team playing, but the most notable availability was the new All Blacks captain Sam Cane being able to play the first two games before resuming national duties with the All Blacks. Ware and Cane had last played for Bay of Plenty in 2016. New members arriving in the province were Otere Black (Manawatu), Te Toiroa Tahuirorangi (Taranaki), Haereiti Hetet (Waikato), Sam Dickson (NZ Sevens) and Nic Souchon (Canterbury/Otago).

Fullback Kaleb Trask grew in stature this year. His all-round game was outstanding. He scored five tries and his goalkicking was of a high standard. He seems destined for a noteworthy career in the game. Joe Webber played in every game, was very safe under the high ball and several scorching runs saw him notch seven tries. Emoni Narawa and Regan Ware showed glimpses of class and had steady seasons, while Fa'asiu Fuatai suffered a red card against Wellington and unable to displace the incumbents when his suspension ended. Mathew Skipwith-Garland had another good season at centre, his ability to free the ball to his outsides was skilful.

Chase Tiatia was quiet in the first few weeks but led the revival against Manawatu and continued in that vein as he passed 50 games for the union. In his debut year, sevens specialist Scott Curry's versatility saw him cover the midfield off the bench during the first half of the competition and the loose forwards in the second half. Dan Hollinshead again didn't come up to expectations, his goalkicking effort against Wellington being very poor. He then played a limited role off the bench. Otere Black was a revelation at first five-eighth. He ran the team well with his long, raking touch-finders and ability to organise the backline. In addition, he assumed the captaincy against Canterbury and through to the end of the season. Te Toiroa Tahurirorangi was the starting halfback for the first five weeks, but then played second fiddle to Luke Campbell who overcame an early injury to start in the last seven games. Campbell's all-round game was of the highest standard which resulted in a Hurricanes contract for 2021.

After Sam Cane's brief return, Joe Tupe filled the No 8 position as a strong ball carrier until injury ended his season against Manawatu. Sam Dickson took over with a notable presence in his first season. Flanker Joe Johnston came ahead in leaps and bounds to become a regular starter with Mitchell Karpik again playing a leading role after injury hampered him during the early games. Zane Kapeli was an able backup player off the bench. Aaron Carroll was again all vigour and brimstone but suffered a season-ending injury against Tasman in the round robin match.

Of the locks, Stan Van den Hoven was in outstanding form. From the small beginnings of the previous season he grew in stature every game, his lineout work and general play around the field being of the highest quality. Keepa Mewett and Kane Leaupepe were again sound and their experience was valuable in a good forward pack.

Captain Aidan Ross had his season end with injury in the opening game against Taranaki.

Fellow prop Jeff Thwaites had another outstanding season, playing in every game and passed 50 games for the union. Tevita Mafileo, Jordan Lay and Ross Geldenhuys all contributed to a solid front row which was seldom bettered, while newcomer Haereiti Hetet played a small part before being selected for Fiji. Hookers Kurt Eklund and Nathan Vella gave very good performances throughout the season.

From the previous season's team Nathan Harris and Hugh Blake both missed the entire 2020 season injured while Baden Wardlaw had retired due to injury and is now the team's strength and conditioning coach. A number of players who had departed or retired included Jason Robertson (Counties Manukau), Alex Ainley (Tasman), Dennon Robinson-Bartlett (Hawke's Bay), Chris Eves (Manawatu), with Pryor Collier, Joe Ravouvou, Richard Judd, Hoani Matenga, Tom Franklin, Tom McHugh, Abraham Papali'i and Ajay Lafaele-Mua

Higher honours went to:
New Zealand: S. Cane
New Zealand Maori: O. Black, K. Eklund, M. Karpik, M. Skipwith-Garland, T. Tahuriorangi, K. Trask,
New Zealand Sevens: S. Curry, N. McGarvey-Black (before signing for North Harbour), J. Ravouvou, W. Warbrick, R. Ware, J. Webber

BAY OF PLENTY REPRESENTATIVES 2020

	Club	Games for Union	Points for Union
Otere Black	Ruatoki	10	40
Luke Campbell	Te Puke Sports	36	43
Sam Cane	Reporoa	21	25
Aaron Carroll	Mt Maunganui Sports	25	15
Leroy Carter	Tauranga Sports	15	5
Scott Curry	Mt Maunganui Sports	10	5
Sam Dickson	Rangiuru	6	5
Kurt Eklund	Mt Maunganui Sports	21	10
Cole Forbes	Te Puke Sports	5	5
Fa'asiu Fuatai	Rangataua	22	40
Ross Geldenhuys	Rangiuru	29	5
Haereti Hetet	Mt Maunganui Sports	3	0
Dan Hollinshead	Te Puke Sports	45	257
Joe Johnston	Te Puke Sports	11	10
Zane Kapeli	Te Puna	15	0
Mitchell Karpik	Rangataua	35	30
Jordan Lay	Whakarewarewa	17	0
Kane Leaupepe	Te Puke Sports	15	15
Tevita Mafileo	Tauranga Sports	20	5
Keepa Mewett	Tauranga Sports	44	10
Emoni Narawa	Tauranga Sports	21	65
Aidan Ross	Te Puke Sports	37	20
Mathew Skipwith-Garland	Whakarewarewa	28	15
Nic Souchon	Tauranga Sports	3	0
Te Toiroa Tahuriorangi	Rotoiti	9	10
Jeff Thwaites	Te Puna	53	10
Chase Tiatia	Rangataua	57	105
Kaleb Trask	Tauranga Sports	22	132
Joe Tupe	Greerton Marist	40	45
Stan Van Den Hoven	Greerton Marist	10	0
Nathan Vella	Rangataua	18	15
Regan Ware	Rangiuru	19	10
Joe Webber	Rangiuru	26	85

INDIVIDUAL SCORING

	Tries	Con	PG	DG	Points
Kaleb Trask	5	13	7	–	72
Otere Black	–	11	6	–	40
Joe Webber	7	–	–	–	35
Emoni Narawa	3	–	–	–	15
Chase Tiatia	3	–	–	–	15
Dan Hollinshead	1	3	1	–	14
Te Toiroa Tahuriorangi	2	–	–	–	10
Fa'asiu Fuatai	2	–	–	–	10
Nathan Vella	2	–	–	–	10
Joe Johnston	2	–	–	–	10
Penalty Try	1	–	–	–	7
Keepa Mewett	1	–	–	–	5
Leroy Carter	1	–	–	–	5
Regan Ware	1	–	–	–	5
Mathew Skipwith-Garland	1	–	–	–	5
Scott Curry	1	–	–	–	5
Sam Dickson	1	–	–	–	5
Kurt Eklund	1	–	–	–	5
Jeff Thwaites	1	–	–	–	5
Totals	**36**	**27**	**14**	**0**	**278**
Opposition scored	39*	24	10	0	277

* Includes two penalty tries (14 points)

BAY OF PLENTY 2020

	Taranaki	Southland	Wellington	Auckland	Tasman	Manawatu	Canterbury	Hawke's Bay	Waikato	North Harbour	Tasman (sf)	Totals
K.R. Trask	–	–	15	15	15	15	15	15	15	15	15	9
E.R. Narawa	15	–	–	14	14	–	14	14	14	14	14	8
T.J. Webber	14	14	14	s	s	11	11	11	11	11	11	11
F. Fuatai	11	11	11	–	–	–	–	s	–	–	–	4
C.D. Forbes	–	–	s	–	–	s	s	–	–	–	–	3
M.D. Skipwith-Garland	13	s	–	s	–	13	13	13	13	13	13	9
R.E. Ware	s	13	13	13	13	14	–	–	s	s	s	9
C.J. Tiatia	12	12	12	11	11	12	12	12	–	12	12	10
S.B. Curry	–	s	s	12	s	s	s	s	s	s	s	10
D.C. Hollinshead	10	15	10	–	12	s	s	–	12	s	s	9
O.W.T.P. Black	s	10	–	10	10	10	10	10	10	10	10	10
T.T.H. Tahuriorangi	9	9	9	9	9	–	–	s	s	s	s	9
L.A. Campbell	s	s	s	–	–	9	9	9	9	9	9	9
L.B. Carter	–	–	–	s	s	s	s	–	–	–	–	4
S.J. Cane	8	7	–	–	–	–	–	–	–	–	–	2
M.J. Tupe	s	8	8	8	8	8	–	s	–	–	–	7
S.N. Dickson	–	–	–	–	–	s	8	8	8	8	8	6
M.R. Karpik	7	–	–	7	7	–	7	7	7	7	7	8
A.P. Carroll	6	–	6	5	6	–	–	–	–	–	–	4
Z.R. Kapeli	s	6	7	6	–	–	s	s	s	s	s	9
J.F.I. Johnston	–	s	s	s	s	7	6	6	6	6	6	10
T.K.H. Mewett	5	5	5	s	5	5	–	–	5	5	5	9
K.T.V. Leaupepe	4	4	4	4	–	6	5	5	–	–	–	7
S. Van Den Hoven	–	–	s	–	4	4	4	4	4	4	4	8
J.R. Thwaites	3	3	3	3	3	s	3	3	3	3	3	11
A. Ross (capt)	1	–	–	–	–	–	–	–	–	–	–	1
T.T.P. Mafileo	s	1	1	1	s	s	s	s	1	1	1	11
H.B.G. Hetet	s	s	–	s	–	–	–	–	–	–	–	3
R.P. Geldenhuys	–	s	s	s	s	3	s	s	s	s	s	10
J.A. Lay	–	–	s	–	1	1	1	1	s	s	s	8
N.B. Vella	2	s	2	2	2	–	s	–	s	s	s	9
K.A. Eklund	s	2	–	–	s	2	2	2	2	2	2	9
N.P. Souchon	–	–	s	–	s	s	–	–	–	–	–	3

BAY OF PLENTY TEAM RECORD, 2020

Played 11　　Won 6　　Lost 5　　Points for 278　　Points against 277

Date	Opponent	Location	Score	Tries	Con	PG	DG	Referee
September 13	Taranaki (cr)	Inglewood	29–36	Tahuriorangi, Mewett, Narawa, Fuatai	Hollinshead (2), Black	Black		B. O'Keeffe
September 19	Southland (cr)	Rotorua	17–14	Fuatai, Tahuriorangi	Black (2)	Black		D. Waenga
September 25	Wellington (P)	Wellington	10–32	Vella	Hollinshead	Hollinshead		B. Pickerill
October 2	Auckland (P)	Rotorua	16–20	Carter	Black	Black (3)		B. O'Keeffe
October 11	Tasman (P)	Nelson	7–33	Ware	Black			C. Stone
October 17	Manawatu (cr)	Palmerston North	53–35	Webber (2), Trask (2), Tiatia, Skipwith-Garland, Johnston	Black (5), Trask	Black, Trask		J. Bredin
October 24	Canterbury (P)	Tauranga	44–8	Tiatia (2), Penalty Try, Webber, Trask, Curry	Trask (2), Black	Trask (2)		C. Stone
November 1	Hawke's Bay (cr)	Tauranga	22–17	Trask (2), Narawa	Trask (2)	Trask		J. Bredin
November 8	Waikato (P)	Hamilton	33–30	Webber (2), Hollinshead, Dickson, Johnston	Trask (4)			D. Waenga
November 15	North Harbour (P)	Tauranga	37–33	Eklund, Webber, Thwaites, Narawa, Vella	Trask (3)	Trask (2)		R. Kelly
November 21	Tasman (P sf)	Nelson	10–19	Webber	Trask	Trask		R. Kelly

BULLER

2020 Status: Heartland Championship
Founded 1894. Affiliated 1894
Chairman: H.W. (Hugh) McMillan
Rugby Manager: A.C. (Andrew) Duncan
Coach: Justin "Gus" Martyn
Assistant coach: T.J. (Tim) Manawatu
Main ground: Victoria Square, Westport
Capacity: 5000
Colours: Cardinal and blue

RECORDS

Highest attendance	5000	West Coast-Buller v South Africa, 1956
Most appearances	174	L.G. Brownlee, 1999-2018
Most points	575	D.J. Baird, 1981–91
Most tries	44	T.J. Stuart, 1984–99
Most points in a season	147	J.J. Lash, 2017
Most tries in a season	11	I. Ravudra, 2014
Most conversions in a season	32	J.J. Lash, 2016
Most penalty goals in a season	27	D.J. Baird, 1985
Most dropped goals in a season	7	D.J. Baird, 1984
Most points in a match	27	J.J. Lash v West Coast, 2019
Most tries in a match	4	J. Easton v Wellington Colts, 1935
		T.J. Stuart v West Coast, 1992
		M. Taylor v East Coast, 2007
		I. Ravudra v Wairarapa Bush, 2014
		S.T. Sauqaqa v Thames Valley, 2015
Most conversions in a match	7	J.J. Lash v Wairarapa Bush, 2014
		J.J. Lash v East Coast, 2017
		J.J. Lash v Ngati Porou East Coast, 2019
Most penalty goals in a match	6	D.J. Baird v East Coast, 1987
		C.J. Hart v East Coast, 1999
		S.N. Jack, v Wairarapa Bush, 2002
		A.P. Stephens v Horowhenua Kapiti, 2010
Highest team score	67	v East Coast, 2014
Record victory (points ahead)	61	67–6 v East Coast, 2014
Highest score conceded	81	v Wanganui, 1994
Record defeat (points behind)	73	0–73 v Horowhenua Kapiti, 1999

Buller were well beaten in their three matches, being more than 20 points behind at halftime in each of them. The second half effort against Mid Canterbury was Buller's best 40 minutes of the season.

At fullback Alex Paterson stood out as a very dependable last line while Thor Manawatu, who had last represented three years ago, looked a polished halfback and Jesse Pitman-Joass was a confident first five-eighth. In the forward pack lock Petrus "Gabba" de Kock had a tremendous work rate and not far behind him was front rower Anthony Ellis.

Debuts were given to 13 players with flanker Dylan Rusbatch and lock Ben Pratt both having good first seasons, Pratt going on to play all 240 minutes. Alex Lean and Steven Soper had previously represented West Coast and Jesse Pitman-Joass was ex Tasman and West Coast.

With just four senior clubs to pick from player depth is an obvious issue and it is hoped the possible reformation of a senior team from the Reefton club for 2021 will be a step forward in this regard. For the first time since 2007, Buller played no fixture against neighbour West Coast.

BULLER REPRESENTATIVES 2020

	Club	Games for Union	Points for Union		Club	Games for Union	Points for Union
Caleb Aldridge	Westport	3	0	Alex Lean	Westport Old Boys	2	5
Hendrix Babbington-Dougherty	Westport Old Boys	2	0	Thor Manawatu	Westport Old Boys	15	13
Jack Best	Westport	20	15	Michael O'Regan	White Star	3	0
Louis Carmine	White Star	1	0	Kahutia Parata	Westport	24	10
Stephen Crackett	Westport	48	0	Alex Paterson	White Star	12	20
Ben Curnow	Ngakawau-Karamea	3	0	Jesse Pitman-Joass	Westport Old Boys	3	5
Petrus "Gabba" De Kock	White Star	11	20	Ben Pratt	Westport Old Boys	3	0
Anthony Ellis	Ngakawau-Karamea	42	25	Dylan Rusbatch	White Star	3	0
Peter Foote	Westport	8	0	Tokohau Samuels	Westport	17	0
Jesse Forsyth	White Star	3	0	Steven Soper	Wanderers [3]	1	0
Taine Forsyth	White Star	1	0	Iliesa Tora [1]	White Star	55	167
Joel Hands	Westport	8	12	Zach Walsh	Westport	18	5
Mitieli Kaloudigibeci	Westport	45	115	Javorn Walter [2]	Westport	1	0

1 Previously played under the name of Iliesa Ravudra, 2013-2019
2 Player of Origin   3 Tasman RU

INDIVIDUAL SCORING

	Tries	Con	PG	DG	Points
Thor Manawatu	–	5	1	–	13
Petrus De Kock	2	–	–	–	10
Mitieli Kaloudigibeci	2	–	–	–	10
Alex Lean	1	–	–	–	5
Anthony Ellis	1	–	–	–	5
Zach Walsh	1	–	–	–	5
Jesse Pitman-Joass	1	–	–	–	5
Joel Hands	–	1	–	–	2
Totals	**8**	**6**	**1**	**0**	**55**
Opposition scored	29	20	0	0	185

BULLER 2020

	Mid Canterbury	South Canterbury	South Canterbury	Totals
A.M.J. Paterson	15	15	15	3
T.R. Forsyth	–	–	s	1
M. Kaloudigibeci	14	–	s	2
J.W. Forsyth	11	11	11	3
J.G. Hands	s	14	14	3
H.M. Babbington-Dougherty	s	s	–	2
L.J. Carmine	–	s	–	1
A.J. Lean	13	13	–	2
I. Tora	12	12	13	3
T.R. Samuels	s	s	12	3
J.J. Pitman-Joass	10	10	10	3
T.H. Manawatu	9	9	9	3
C.R. Aldridge	s	s	s	3
Z.L. Walsh	8	8	–	2
M.D. O'Regan	s	s	s	3
S.G. Soper	–	–	8	1
K.G. Parata (capt)	7	7	7	3
D.G. Rusbatch	6	6	6	3
J.T. Walter	–	–	s	1
B.R. Pratt	5	5	5	3
P.J. De Kock	4	4	4	3
A.W. Ellis	3	2	2	3
S.R. Crackett	1	1	1	3
J.W. Best	s	3	3	3
B.L. Curnow	s	s	s	3
P.G. Foote	2	s	s	3

BULLER TEAM RECORD, 2020

Date	Opponent	Location	Played 3	Won 0	Lost 3	Points for 55	Points against 185
			Score	Tries	Con	PG DG	Referee
September 12	Mid Canterbury	Hanmer	17–41	Lean, Ellis, Walsh	Manawatu		K. Faagolo
September 19	South Canterbury	Timaru	10–78	Pitman-Joass	Manawatu	Manawatu	J. Henshaw
September 26	South Canterbury	Westport	28–66	De Kock (2), Kaloudigibeci (2)	Manawatu (3), Hands		G. Reilly

CANTERBURY

2020 Status: Mitre 10 Cup Premiership
Founded 1879. Affiliated 1894
President: J.E.A. (Julie) Patterson
Chairman: P.A. (Peter) Winchester
Chief executive officer: T.P. (Tony) Smail
Co-coaches: M.B. (Mark) Brown, R.D. (Reuben) Thorne
Assistant coaches: M.A. (Mark) Jones, G.J. (Grant) Keenan
Main ground: Orangetheory Stadium, Christchurch
Capacity: 20,000
Colours: Red and black

RECORDS

Most appearances	220	*Fergie McCormick, 1958–75*
Most points	1625	*Robbie Deans, 1979–90*
Most tries	93	*Paula Bale, 1989–96*
Most points in a season	279	*Robbie Deans, 1989*
Most tries in a season	24	*Paula Bale, 1989*
Most conversions in a season	52	*Greg Coffey, 1991*
		Ben Blair, 2001
Most penalty goals in a season	50	*Robbie Deans, 1989*
Most dropped goals in a season	10	*Andrew Mehrtens, 1994*
Most points in a match	44	*Jon Preston v West Coast, 1992*
Most tries in a match	7	*Bruce McPhail v Combined Services, 1959*
Most conversions in a match	20	*Jon Preston v West Coast, 1992*
Most penalty goals in a match	7	*Robbie Deans v Counties, 1984*
		Andrew Mehrtens v Fiji, 2003
		Cameron McIntyre v Wellington, 2003
Highest team score	128	*v West Coast, 1992*
Record victory (points ahead)	128	*128–0 v West Coast, 1992*
Highest score conceded	60	*v Wellington, 2017*
Record defeat (points behind)	46	*14–60 v Wellington, 2017*

Who would have picked that it would need the first goal of the season kicked by an unheralded youngster to ensure Canterbury did not finish at the foot of the Premiership table and thus avoid possible relegation?

So it came to pass after one of the more remarkable provincial seasons in living memory.

Wing Chay Fihaki landed a long-range penalty goal to secure the 34-33 win over Auckland in the final regular season match to secure fifth position for Canterbury. It was better than last, but was still the lowest placing by the province since losing the 2006 Air New Zealand quarter-final to Wellington.

In the final analysis, Canterbury lost no less than three games by one point, and dropped three of their four crossover games.

There were 15 rookies used by new co-coaches Reuben Thorne and Mark Brown, which bodes well for 2021 and 2022, but was not enough to consistently impose the red and blacks' game plan in 2020.

After dispatching North Otago to retain the Ranfurly Shield, Canterbury, with its All Blacks in the fold, was too good for North Harbour on opening night to retain the Kevin Gimblett Memorial Trophy.

But then Taranaki divested Canterbury of the Shield, for the second time in three years, while Hawke's Bay won its first match in this fixture since 1982. While a 75m intercept try to Isaiah Punivai sealed the first golden point win over Wellington, the Mooloos won their first game in Christchurch since 2011 and then the Bay of Plenty Steamers demolished Canterbury to the tune of 44–8. It got worse when Otago won in Christchurch for the first time since 2005.

It left red and black fans concerned, but the team rallied to upset Tasman 29-0 and Auckland in the last two rounds. The senior players, in particular, stood up, when it mattered.

Canterbury opted to promote youth rather than make any big signings. Their six All Blacks all turned out to varying degrees. Props Michael Alaalatoa (Manawatu) and Siate Tokolahi (Southland) were the major losses, while several veterans had retired or moved on. Injury ruled loosehead Harry Allan out for the season.

All Blacks Sevens rep Andrew Knewstubb was an interesting newcomer, though Josh McKay was the best fullback. His solo try against the Mako was a season highlight, but he was unable to nail a fulltime Super Rugby contract, which was mystifying.

Fihaki is a midfielder, but found a home on the right wing, where his power and pace yielded a season-high five tries. His crucial goalkick was no surprise to those who had seen him land goals in First XV rugby in Auckland.

Brothers Ngane and Isaiah Punivai both made pleasing progress in the threequarters, and came up with big plays on attack.

Rameka Poihipi was one of three Cantabrians to appear in all 11 games and he impressed with his distribution at second five. Dallas McLeod's season was hit by injury.

Brett Cameron and Ferg Burke shared the No 10 duties to mostly good effect, Cameron landing a rare dropped goal, from 45m, against Otago.

Halfback Mitch Drummond was his usual consistent self.

Canterbury had issues at No 8, where Whetu Douglas was in and out, Cullen Grace was only available for half the games and Tom Sanders was injured for much of the season. It was no surprise that the pack lifted when Sanders was back on deck for the last two games.

Billy Harmon and Tom Christie were two outstanding fetchers, especially working in tandem.

Captain Reed Prinsep continues to be an unsung hero for this side, and he took one for the team by slotting into lock in the last fortnight.

Little was seen of Sam Whitelock, who made his first appearance in 10 years, and Mitch Dunshea, so young Sam Darry delivered on his promise alongside the old warhorse Luke Romano, who led the way against Tasman and Auckland and was adept at pilfering ball and driving in the mauls.

Tamaiti Williams and Oli Jager shared the tighthead propping duties, while Daniel Lienert-Brown was strong in the second half of the season, rarely bettered in the scrums.

Shiloh Klein cemented the No 2 jersey in place of the mostly injured Brodie McAlister.

Higher honours went to:
New Zealand: G. Bridge, C. Grace, J. Moody, R. Mo'unga, C. Taylor, S. Whitelock
New Zealand Maori: W. Douglas, B. Harmon, R. Poihipi, R. Prinsep, T. Williams
New Zealand Sevens: S. Dickson (before signing for Bay of Plenty),
A. Nicole (before signing for Southland)

CANTERBURY REPRESENTATIVES 2020

	Club	Games for Union	Points for Union		Club	Games for Union	Points for Union
Liam Allen	Lincoln University	3	0	Andrew Knewstubb	West Melton	7	10
Cameron Bailey	Christchurch	1	0	Daniel Lienert-Brown	HSOB	46	15
Finlay Brewis	HSOB	7	5	Manasa Mataele	Marist-Albion	5	10
George Bridge	HSOB	31	90	Brodie McAlister	Sydenham	19	15
Fergus Burke	Canterbury University	17	56	Dallas McLeod	Christchurch	15	30
Brett Cameron	Lincoln University	44	354	Josh McKay	Kaiapoi	43	121
Tom Christie	Christchurch	32	15	Scott Mellow	Marist-Albion	5	0
Sam Darry	HSOB	7	15	Joe Moody	Lincoln	34	15
Luke Donaldson	Lincoln University	1	0	Richie Mo'unga	Linwood	51	350
Whetu Douglas	Canterbury University	22	5	Fletcher Newell	Lincoln University	8	0
Mitch Drummond	HSOB	68	114	Rameka Poihipi	Lincoln University	16	15
Mitch Dunshea	Springston	49	35	Lewis Ponini	Lincoln University	2	0
Ere Enari	Lincoln University	40	5	Reed Prinsep	HSOB	67	30
Chay Fihaki	HSOB	8	28	Isaiah Punivai	Burnside	10	20
Bill Fukofuka	Shirley	1	0	Ngane Punivai	Lincoln University	30	20
Zach Gallagher	Burnside	1	0	Luke Romano	Hurunui	60	45
Cullen Grace	Lincoln University	9	15	Tom Sanders	Lincoln University	48	45
Billy Harmon	New Brighton	46	35	Codie Taylor	Sydenham	24	35
Oli Jager	New Brighton	31	10	Sam Whitelock	Lincoln University	21	15
Shiloh Klein	HSOB	13	15	Tamaiti Williams	Burnside	8	5

INDIVIDUAL SCORING

	Tries	Con	PG	DG	Points		Tries	Con	PG	DG	Points
Cameron	–	21	3	1	54	McLeod	2	–	–	–	10
Burke	1	5	7	–	36	Romano	2	–	–	–	10
Fihaki	5	–	1	–	28	Taylor	2	–	–	–	10
I. Punivai	4	–	–	–	20	Brewis	1	–	–	–	5
Darry	3	–	–	–	15	Bridge	1	–	–	–	5
Drummond	3	–	–	–	15	Christie	1	–	–	–	5
Poihipi	3	–	–	–	15	Harmon	1	–	–	–	5
N. Punivai	3	–	–	–	15	Klein	1	–	–	–	5
Mo'unga	1	3	1	–	14	Williams	1	–	–	–	5
Grace	2	–	–	–	10						
Jager	2	–	–	–	10	**Totals**	**45**	**29**	**12**	**1**	**322**
Knewstubb	2	–	–	–	10						
Mataele	2	–	–	–	10	Opposition scored	30*	17	15	0	231
McKay	2	–	–	–	10						

*Includes penalty try

CANTERBURY 2020

	North Otago	North Harbour	Taranaki	Hawke's Bay	Wellington	Manawatu	Waikato	Bay of Plenty	Otago	Tasman	Auckland	Totals
A.S. Knewstubb	15	–	s	15	–	15	15	15	–	s	–	7
J.A. McKay	–	15	15	14	15	s	11	11	15	15	15	10
L.C.V. Fihaki	14	–	–	–	14	14	14	14	14	14	14	8
G.C. Bridge	–	11	11	–	–	–	–	–	–	–	–	2
C.M. Bailey	s	–	–	–	–	–	–	–	–	–	–	1
M.M.B.T. Mataele	11	14	14	11	11	–	–	–	–	–	–	5
I.A. Punivai	13	s	13	s	s	11	s	13	–	s	s	10
N.G.J. Punivai	–	–	–	13	13	13	13	–	11	11	11	7
D.A.M. McLeod	12	13	–	–	–	–	–	s	13	13	13	6
R.H. Poihipi	s	12	12	12	12	12	12	12	12	12	12	11
R. Mo'unga	–	s	10	–	–	–	–	–	–	–	–	2
F.W. Burke	–	–	–	s	10	10	10	10	10	–	–	6
B.D. Cameron	10	10	–	10	s	s	s	s	s	10	10	10
E.C.S. Enari	9	9	–	s	s	9	s	9	–	s	s	9
L.J. Donaldson	s	–	–	–	–	–	–	–	–	–	–	1
M.D. Drummond	–	s	9	9	9	s	9	s	9	9	9	10
W.H. Douglas	–	s	–	8	–	8	8	–	s	s	s	7
C.J. Grace	8	8	8	–	–	s	–	8	–	–	–	5
B.S. Fukofuka	s	–	–	–	–	–	–	–	–	–	–	1
W.K. Harmon	7	7	s	7	s	7	s	s	6	6	6	11
T.M. Christie	–	–	7	s	7	s	7	7	7	7	7	9
R.J. Prinsep (capt)	–	6	6	s	6	6	6	6	8	5	5	10
T.B. Sanders	–	–	–	6	8	–	–	–	–	8	8	4
L.R. Allen	6	–	–	–	–	–	–	–	s	s	–	3
M.T.W. Dunshea	–	s	s	5	5	–	–	4	–	–	–	5
S.L. Whitelock	–	5	5	–	–	–	–	–	–	–	–	2
Z.W. Gallagher	s	–	–	–	–	–	–	–	–	–	–	1
I. Romano	4	4	4	–	4	4	4	5	4	4	4	10
S.G. Darry	5	–	–	4	s	5	5	5	5	–	–	7
O.G.J.T. Jager	–	–	3	3	3	–	–	–	3	3	3	6
T.P.T. Williams	3	s	–	–	3	3	3	3	s	s	–	8
F.D. Newell	s	3	s	s	s	s	s	s	–	–	–	8
S.B. Mellow	s	–	–	s	–	2	s	s	–	–	–	5
L.T. Ponini	–	–	–	–	–	s	s	–	–	–	–	2
D.P. Lienert-Brown	–	–	s	1	–	–	1	1	1	1	1	7
J.P.T. Moody	–	1	1	–	–	–	–	–	–	–	–	2
F.F. Brewis	1	s	–	s	1	1	–	s	–	s	–	7
B.L. McAlister	2	–	–	–	–	–	–	–	2	2	–	3
C.J. Taylor	–	2	2	–	–	–	–	–	–	–	–	2
S.I. Klein	s	s	s	2	2	s	2	2	s	s	2	11

CANTERBURY TEAM RECORD 2020

Played 11 Won 6 Lost 5 Points for 322 Points against 231

Date	Opponent	Location	Score	Tries	Con	PG	DG	Referee
August 28	North Otago (RS)	Christchurch	71–7	Darry (2), Mataele (2), McLeod, Knewstubb, Brewis, I. Punivai, Harmon, Fihaki, Poihipi	Cameron (8)			D.J. Waenga
September 11	North Harbour (P)	Albany	43–29	Taylor (2), Poihipi, Grace, I. Punivai, Bridge	Cameron (4), Mo'unga	Cameron		P.M. Williams
September 19	Taranaki (cr, RS)	Christchurch	22–23	Jager, Mo'unga, Knewstubb	Mo'unga (2)	Mo'unga		B.D. O'Keeffe
September 26	Hawke's Bay (cr)	Napier	19–20	Klein, Darry, McKay	Cameron (2)			C.J. Stone
October 03	Wellington (P)	Christchurch	31–26	Drummond, Christie, I. Punivai, N. Punivai	Burke	Burke (3)		P.M. Williams
October 09	Manawatu (cr)	Palmerston North	34–10	Fihaki (2), Poihipi, Burke, Drummond	Burke (3)	Burke		N.P. Briant
October 17	Waikato (P)	Christchurch	15–16	Romano, Williams	Burke	Burke		C.J. Stone
October 24	Bay of Plenty (P)	Tauranga	8–44	Grace		Burke		C.J. Stone
October 30	Otago (cr)	Christchurch	16–23	Drummond	Cameron	Burke, Cameron	Cameron	B.E. Pickerill
November 07	Tasman (P)	Blenheim	29–0	McKay, Fihaki, N. Punivai, I. Punivai	Cameron (3)	Cameron		M.I. Fraser
November 15	Auckland (P)	Christchurch	34–33	Fihaki, McLeod, N. Punivai, Romano, Jager	Cameron (3)	Fihaki		N.P. Briant

COUNTIES MANUKAU

2020 Status: Mitre 10 Cup Championship
Founded 1926 as South Auckland and affiliated to Auckland.
Granted full union status as South Auckland Counties in 1955.
Name changed to Counties 1956, to Counties Manukau 1996.
President: G.B. (Gary) Wright
Chairman: C.W. (Craig) Carter
General manager: A.B.D. (Aaron) Lawton
Coach: T.R. (Tai) Lavea
Assistant coaches: G.W. (Grant) Henson, S.M. (Mark) Selwyn
Main ground: Navigation Homes Stadium, Pukekohe
Capacity: 18,000
Colours: Red, white and black

RECORDS

Most appearances	201	Alan Dawson, 1976–89
Most points	698	Danny Love, 1993–96
Most tries	58	Alan Dawson, 1976–89
Most points in a season	208	Danny Love, 1995
Most tries in a season	22	Luke Erenavula, 1993
Most conversions in a season	52	Danny Love, 1993
Most penalty goals in a season	47	Stu Hollier, 1989
Most dropped goals in a season	4	Bob Lendrum, 1976
		Joe Harvey, 1983
Most points in a match	37	Jim Graham v East Coast, 1972
Most tries in a match	5	Koiatu Koiatu v King Country, 2004
Most conversions in a match	14	Jim Graham v East Coast, 1972
Most penalty goals in a match	6	Stu Hollier v France, 1989
		Stu Hollier v Thames Valley, 1989
		Danny Love v Manawatu, 1994
		James Semple v Manawatu, 2011
		Baden Kerr v Auckland 2012
Highest team score	108	v Horowhenua, 1994
Record victory (points ahead)	103	103–0 v Poverty Bay, 1993
Highest score conceded	100	v Auckland, 2004
Record defeat (points behind)	85	15–100 v Auckland, 2004

The Counties Manukau Steelers suffered from growing pains in their first season under new head coach Tai Lavea.

They appeared to have the talent to reach the Championship semi-finals but too often clocked off mentally or came up with untimely errors, as has been the case in recent years. Sixth place, though well clear of cell-dwellers Manawatu, was a big disappointment for a proud union that has often punched above its financial weight.

You will struggle to consistently win games when you average 2.6 tries per game and concede 3.31. That their for and against points record was better than in 2019 was solely down to much sharper goalkicking, with 33 successful goals as compared with 19.

A write-off of a month in August due to the Covid-19 restrictions in the wider Auckland region did the Steelers no favours. It was perhaps no surprise that they kicked off the Mitre 10 Cup with three straight, clear, defeats. The home win over the Turbos arrested a 12-match losing streak in Pukekohe, while they were in the contest for the Jonah Lomu Memorial Trophy against Wellington for at least 65 minutes before capitulating.

There was a gutsy win, secured after 87 minutes, in Inglewood against Taranaki. There was some consolation in the 25–17 victory to close the season against Southland, who placed one higher than them.

New signing, lock Lyndon Dunshea from Auckland, did not make it onto the field, but All Blacks Dalton Papali'i and Nepo Laulala were both strong contributors in their two matches each.

Kieran Read made his first-class debut for the Steelers, having signed late from Japan, though the extent of his availability, just five games, should have been communicated better to stakeholders, fans and media.

First fives Baden Kerr (from Japan) and Jason Robertson (Bay of Plenty) were other new signings, as was former Samoa Sevens international Alamanda Motuga.

Some key losses included Sam Henwood and Daymon Leasuasu (Japan) and Kalolo Tuiloma (Northland). There was terrible luck when Tim Metcher and Fotu Lokotui could not get back in the country due to Covid-19, both being foreign passport holders.

Etene Nanai-Seturo, one of eight to play in all 10 games, had his best season yet for the Steelers. In his rightful position at fullback, he scored two tries, set up several others, and was a danger man on the counter. His punting and high ball game still need work, but he was one of the most penetrative backs.

Right wing Kris Kuridrani scored four tries and showed his finishing ability from few opportunities. The experienced threequarters trio of Tevita Nabura, Sione Fifita and Sione Molia all suffered from injury.

Captain Orbyn Leger toiled manfully, enjoying some good moments in the midfield, but he too was not immune to errors.

Kerr performed usefully, but seemed past his best. Robertson took the ball to the line more and kicked 20 of his 22 goals.

Jonathan Taumateine is a skilled halfback who needs to dominate more at this level, while his back-up Cam Roigard showed much promise.

Read played well, though not with All Blacks-like authority, but his best display came in the win over Taranaki. It is to be hoped that Viliami Taulani, who is starting to slowly turn his potential into substance, has learned plenty off him.

Samuel Slade had a fine season, appearing in three positions and showing he was a prime source of lineout ball.

Motuga was also outstanding after replacing Papali'i in the No 7 jersey, scoring a hat-trick against the Turbos and proving an effective fetcher.

Matiaha Martin was one of the best lineout stealers in Mitre 10 Cup, while Potu Leavasa junior showed promise, if not consistency.

The set-piece in general was sometimes unstable, though new hooker Zuriel Togiatama and loosehead prop Ezekiel Lindenmuth both played well for large tracts of the season.

Hooker Shaun Muir, a club stalwart with Bombay, made his debut at the ripe old age of 36.

Higher honours went to:
New Zealand: N. Laulala, D. Papali'i
New Zealand Sevens: S. Molia, E. Nanai-Seturo, A. Rokolisoa

COUNTIES MANUKAU REPRESENTATIVES 2020

	Club	Games for Union	Points for Union		Club	Games for Union	Points for Union
Sue Asomua	Waiuku	13	0	Clinton Malolua	Papakura	8	0
Joseph Casey	Ardmore-Marist	1	0	Matiaha Martin	Bombay	38	5
Pele Cowley	Manurewa	7	5	Sione Molia	Karaka	19	35
Sione Fifita	Pukekohe	22	25	Alamanda Motuga	Ardmore-Marist	8	25
Nikolai Foliaki	Karaka	11	5	Shaun Muir	Bombay	2	0
Latiume Fosita	Ardmore-Marist	14	36	Tevita Nabura	Waiuku	22	25
Kali Hala	Karaka	20	15	Etene Nanai-Seturo	Karaka	17	15
Leigh Hughes	Pukekohe	2	0	Conan O'Donnell	Karaka	19	5
Johnny Kawau	Bombay	27	10	Dalton Papali'i	Patumahoe	2	5
Baden Kerr	Karaka	45	407	Viliame Rarasea	Ardmore-Marist	55	15
Kirisi Kuridrani	Papakura	20	40	Kieran Read	Drury	5	5
Luteru Laulala	Ardmore-Marist	39	74	Jason Robertson	Manurewa	8	57
Nepo Laulala	Ardmore-Marist	3	0	Cameron Roigard	Onewhero	7	5
Potu Leavasa	Manurewa	8	5	Samuel Slade	Pukekohe	16	5
Dylan Leckner	Ardmore-Marist	2	0	Viliami Taulani	Manurewa	18	10
Orbyn Leger	Karaka	36	37	Jonathan Taumateine	Ardmore-Marist	29	15
Ezekiel Lindenmuth	Ardmore-Marist	10	0	Zuriel Togiatama	Ardmore-Marist	10	5
Donald Maka	Onewhero	17	5	Mickey Woolliams	Karaka	11	0

INDIVIDUAL SCORING

	Tries	Con	PG	DG	Points		Tries	Con	PG	DG	Points
Robertson	2	13	7	–	57	Papali'i	1	–	–	–	5
Kerr	–	8	5	–	31	Read	1	–	–	–	5
Motuga	5	–	–	–	25	Roigard	1	–	–	–	5
Kuridrani	4	–	–	–	20	Slade	1	–	–	–	5
Leger	2	–	–	–	10	Taumateine	1	–	–	–	5
Nanai-Seturo	2	–	–	–	10	Togiatama	1	–	–	–	5
Taulani	2	–	–	–	10						
Fosita	1	–	–	–	5	**Totals**	**26**	**21**	**12**	**0**	**208**
Leavasa	1	–	–	–	5						
Molia	1	–	–	–	5	Opposition scored	47*	31	10	0	331

*Includes two penalty tries

COUNTIES MANUKAU 2020

	Tasman	Hawke's Bay	Northland	Manawatu	Waikato	Otago	Wellington	Taranaki	North Harbour	Southland	Totals
E. Nanai-Seturo	15	15	15	15	15	15	11	s	15	15	10
K.C.J. Kuridrani	14	14	14	14	14	14	s	14	14	14	10
S. Fifita	–	–	11	–	11	–	–	11	11	11	5
T. Nabura	–	–	–	11	s	11	14	–	–	–	4
S.L.J. Molia	13	–	–	–	13	13	–	–	13	13	5
K.H.K. Hala	11	11	–	–	–	–	–	s	s	s	5
L.E. Laulala	s	13	s	s	–	s	15	15	s	s	9
N.K. Foliaki	–	–	–	–	–	–	13	13	–	–	2
L. Fosita	–	s	12	12	s	s	12	–	–	–	6
O.N.T. Leger (capt)	12	12	13	13	12	12	–	12	12	12	9
J.R. Robertson	–	s	s	s	10	–	10	10	10	10	8
B.H. Kerr	10	10	10	10	–	10	s	–	–	–	6
P.Z. Cowley	s	s	–	s	–	–	–	–	–	–	3
C.D. Roigard	–	–	s	–	s	s	s	s	s	9	7
J.A. Taumateine	9	9	9	9	9	9	9	9	9	s	10
K.J. Read	8	–	8	–	–	8	8	8	–	–	5
V.T.H. Taulani	s	s	–	–	s	s	s	6	8	8	8
D.R. Papali'i	7	7	–	–	–	–	–	–	–	–	2
A.L. Motuga	–	–	7	7	7	7	7	7	7	7	8
D.J.R. Leckner	–	–	–	s	–	–	–	–	s	–	2
S.V. Slade	6	8	6	8	8	6	6	4	4	6	10
J.D. Kawau	s	6	s	6	6	–	–	s	6	–	7
M. Martin	4	5	4	5	5	5	s	5	5	4	10
P.J. Leavasa	5	s	5	–	4	4	5	s	–	5	8
M.R. Woolliams	s	4	s	4	–	–	4	–	–	–	5
V.L. Rarasea	–	–	–	s	s	s	–	–	s	s	5
S. Asomua	–	–	s	–	s	s	s	3	3	3	7
N.E. Laulala	3	3	–	–	–	–	–	–	–	–	2
L.A. Hughes	–	–	s	–	–	–	–	–	–	–	1
C.M.B. Malolua	s	s	–	–	s	s	s	s	s	s	8
E.V. Lindenmuth	1	1	1	1	1	1	1	1	1	1	10
C.F. O'Donnell	s	s	3	3	3	3	3	s	s	s	10
Z.V.F.B. Togiatama	2	2	2	2	2	s	s	s	s	s	10
J.T.T. Casey	–	–	s	–	–	–	–	–	–	–	1
D.S.K.M. Maka	–	–	–	s	s	2	2	2	2	2	7
S.P. Muir	s	s	–	–	–	–	–	–	–	–	2

COUNTIES MANUKAU TEAM RECORD 2020

Played 10　Won 3　Lost 7　Points for 208　Points against 331

Date	Opponent	Location	Score	Tries	Con	PG	DG	Referee
September 12	Tasman (cr)	Pukekohe	24–41	Leavasa, Papali'i, Taulani	Kerr (3)	Kerr		R.P. Kelly
September 20	Hawke's Bay (C)	Napier	17–31	Kuridrani, Slade	Kerr, Robertson	Kerr		A.W.B. Mabey
September 27	Northland (C)	Pukekohe	15–24	Read, Motuga	Kerr	Kerr		B.D. O'Keeffe
October 03	Manawatu (C)	Pukekohe	36–30	Motuga (3), Leger, Kuridrani	Robertson (3), Kerr	Kerr		M.I. Fraser
October 10	Waikato (cr)	Hamilton	13–36	Nanai-Seturo	Robertson	Robertson (2)		B.E. Pickerill
October 18	Otago (C)	Dunedin	22–40	Motuga, Leger, Taulani	Kerr (2)	Kerr		A.W.B. Mabey
October 25	Wellington (cr)	Pukekohe	20–53	Fosita, Robertson	Robertson (2)	Robertson (2)		D.J. Waenga
November 01	Taranaki (C)	Inglewood	31–27	Robertson, Taumateine, Kuridrani, Nanai-Seturo	Robertson (4)	Robertson		J.D. Munro
November 07	North Harbour (cr)	Albany	5–32	Kuridrani				C.J. Stone
November 13	Southland (C)	Pukekohe	25–17	Molia, Roigard, Togiatama	Robertson (2)	Robertson (2)		M.C.J. Winter

NGATI POROU EAST COAST

2020 Status: Heartland Championship
Founded 1921 as East Coast. Affiliated 1922.
Name changed to Ngati Porou East Coast 2017
President: No appointment
Chairman: C.W. (Campbell) Dewes
Chief executive officer: Cushla Tangaere-Manuel
Coach: H.E. (Hosea) Gear
Assistant coach: M.T.R. (Morgan) Wirepa jnr
Main ground: Whakarua Park, Ruatoria
Capacity: 3000
Colours: Sky blue

RECORDS

Highest attendance	4000	v Poverty Bay (Div 3 final), 1999
Most appearances	113	E.M. Waitoa, 1979–2006
	113	C.F. Harrison, 2003-2017
Most points	406	E.J. Manuel, 1985–98
Most tries	24	J.R. Kururangi, 1979–96
Most points in a season	145	M.R. Flutey, 2000
Most tries in a season	9	S. Vorenasu, 2011
Most conversions in a season	20	M.R. Flutey, 2001
		J.R. Semple, 2012
Most penalty goals in a season	30	M.R. Flutey, 2000
Most dropped goals in a season	3	M.R. Flutey, 2000
Most points in a match	22	V.P. Taingahue v Buller, 1999
Most tries in a match	3	W. Peachy v Bush, 1954
		T.M. Reedy v Horowhenua, 1958
		J.R. Kururangi v West Coast, 1992
		J. Higgins v Poverty Bay, 1993
		M. Vere v Buller, 1999
		T.W. Delamere v Horowhenua Kapiti, 2000
		H.F. Haerewa v Poverty Bay, 2012
		S.P. Destounis, v Poverty Bay, 2016
Most conversions in a match	8	V.P. Taingahue v Buller, 1999
Most penalty goals in a match	7	M.R. Flutey v Nelson Bays, 2001
Highest team score	74	v Buller, 1999
Record victory (points ahead)	69	72–3 v West Coast, 1992
Highest score conceded	116	v North Otago, 2010
Record defeat (points behind)	113	3–116 v North Otago, 2010

Despite losing all three matches Ngati Porou East Coast were always competitive and in each match were able to threaten on attack, having the ability to hold on to the ball for extended periods, which has not always been the case. A win in the opening match against Poverty Bay somehow slipped through their fingers 31-34 after leading 31-19 with 25 minutes left.

Captain and number eight Hone Haerewa was again the team's outstanding player, covering a lot of ground and usually making good progress with ball in hand. Perrin Manuel was a mobile loosehead prop while at tighthead prop Hirini Delamere looked a good find. Loose forward

Moana Mato shone against King Country and 18-year-old debutant lock Kyah Hollis was proving a good lineout source in the same game, until suffering a serious injury just before halftime.

First five-eighth Rapata Haerewa was another prominent debutant in the King Country match. Tawhao Stewart was usually able to provide thrust in the backline and Benny Haerewa was a determined runner on the wing.

Of the 11 debutants, Jorian Tangaere had previously played for Hawke's Bay. The match with King Country was played at Opotiki.

NGATI POROU EAST COAST REPRESENTATIVES 2020

	Club	Games for Union	Points for Union
Hamuera Baker	Waiapu	9	5
Verdon Bartlett	TVC	80	41
Mike Chambers-Raroa	Tokomaru Bay Utd	18	0
Laman Davies	Uawa	21	5
Hirini Delamere	TVC	3	5
Mahue Dewes	University [1]	25	5
Richard Green	Waiapu	9	0
Te Aho Haenga	Tokararangi	1	0
Benny Haerewa	TVC	16	16
Hone Haerewa	Tokararangi	42	39
Rapata Haerewa	Tokararangi	1	2
Kyah Hollis	Tokararangi	1	0
Fabyan Kahaki	Hikurangi	16	0
Perrin Manuel	Waiapu	36	31
Moana Mato	TVC	12	0
Te Aho Morice	Hikurangi	2	0
Tanetoa Parata	Hikurangi	27	5
Trent Proffit	Hikurangi	12	5
Keegan Rowley	TVC	1	0
Pamona Samupo	Tokararangi	24	15
Netani Seruwaqa	Tokomaru Bay Utd	1	0
George Shields	Uawa	2	6
BJ Sidney	Uawa	12	12
Taliq Simeon	TVC	1	0
Tawhao Stewart	TVC	9	15
Frank Taiapa	Hick's Bay	15	0
Jorian Tangaere	Clive [2]	3	0
Hoani Te Moana	TVC	21	0
Tutere Waenga	TVC	3	0
Ricky Waitoa	Tokararangi	33	35
Raniera Whakataka	Uawa	4	0

1 Waikato RU   2 Hawke's Bay RU

INDIVIDUAL SCORING

	Tries	Con	PG	DG	Points
Benny Haerewa	1	1	3	–	16
Perrin Manuel	2	–	–	–	10
Ricky Waitoa	2	–	–	–	10
George Shields	–	–	2	–	6
Hamuera Baker	1	–	–	–	5
Pamona Samupo	1	–	–	–	5
Hone Haerewa	1	–	–	–	5
Tawhao Stewart	1	–	–	–	5
Hirini Delamere	1	–	–	–	5
Rapata Haerewa	–	1	–	–	2
Totals	**10**	**2**	**5**	**0**	**69**
Opposition scored	15*	12	3	0	110

* Includes one penalty try (7 points)

NGATI POROU EAST COAST 2020

	Poverty Bay	Poverty Bay	King Country	Totals
B.J. Sidney	15	15	–	2
T.M.T.I.W. Stewart	14	12	–	2
R.B. Haerewa	11	–	14	2
G. Shields	s	14	–	2
F. Kahaki	–	11	13	2
T. Simeon	–	–	11	1
T.A.M.W. Haenga	–	–	s	1
P. Samupo	13	13	–	2
T.J.H. Waenga	12	10	12	3
V.R.M. Bartlett	10	s	15	3
R. Haerewa	–	–	10	1
H. Baker	9	9	9	3
T.A.M. Morice	s	s	–	2
K. Rowley	–	–	s	1
H. Haerewa (capt)	8	8	8	3
T.C. Proffit	7	s	–	2
R.W. Green	6	6	6	3
S.T. Parata	s	7	–	2
M.H. Mato	s	s	7	3
H.J. Te Moana	5	4	5	3
N. Seruwaqa	4	–	–	1
R.J.S. Waitoa	s	s	s	3
F.C. Taiapa	–	5	s	2
K.J. Hollis	–	–	4	1
H. Delamere	3	s	3	3
P.J. Manuel	1	1	1	3
L.L.A. Davies	s	3	–	2
M.M. Dewes	–	–	s	1
M.R. Chambers-Raroa	–	–	s	1
R.W.M.M. Whakataka	2	2	2	3
J.T. Tangaere	s	s	s	3

NGATI POROU EAST COAST TEAM RECORD, 2020

Played 3 Won 0 Lost 3 Points for 69 Points against 110

Date	Opponent	Location	Score	Tries	Con	PG	DG	Referee
September 19	Poverty Bay	Gisborne	31–34	Baker, Samupo, H. Haerewa, Stewart	B. Haerewa	B. Haerewa (3)		R. Maynard
September 26	Poverty Bay	Ruatoria	16–42	Manuel, Waitoa		Shields (2)		N. Briant
October 3	King Country	Opotiki	22–34	B. Haerewa, Delamere, Manuel, Waitoa	R. Haerewa			S. Fellows

HAWKE'S BAY

2020 Status: Mitre 10 Cup Championship
Founded 1884. Original member 1892
President: N.J. (Neil) Pulford
Chairman: B.J. (Brendon) Mahony
Chief executive officer: J.L. (Jay) Campbell
Coach: M.D. (Mark) Ozich
Assistant coach: J.D. (Josh) Syms
Main ground: McLean Park, Napier
Capacity: 16,500
Colours: Black and white

RECORDS

Most appearances	158	N.W. Thimbleby, 1959–71
Most points	998	J.B. Cunningham, 1990–98
Most tries	73	B.A. Grenside, 1919–31
Most points in a season	237	J.B. Cunningham, 1994
Most tries in a season	18	B.A. Grenside, 1926
		P.J. Cooke, 1986
Most conversions in a season	47	J.B. Cunningham, 1995
Most penalty goals in a season	37	M.W. Berquist, 2009
Most dropped goals in a season	7	B.D.M. Furlong, 1968
		M.K. Sisam, 1979
Most points in a match	36	M.K. Sisam v East Coast, 1979
Most tries in a match	6	R.P. Hunter v East Coast, 1979
Most conversions in a match	13	J.B. Cunningham v Cook Islands, 1995
Most penalty goals in a match	7	J.B. Cunningham v Manawatu, 1993
		J.B. Cunningham v King Country, 1994
		R.G.E. Lewis v North Harbour, 2001
Highest team score	99	v Cook Islands, 1995
		v Mid Canterbury, 2003
Record victory (points ahead)	99	99–0 v Cook Islands, 1995
Highest score conceded	86	v Waikato, 1999
Record defeat (points behind)	86	0–86 v Waikato, 1999

A surprise loss to Southland in the opening game was not representative of what was to follow as the Magpies subsequently clicked into gear to win the Championship and promotion to the Premiership for 2021. Almost all of last year's regulars were available, and with that collective experience Hawke's Bay went one step further than last year.

The Ranfurly Shield was won from Otago and successfully defended three times, Premiership teams Canterbury (for the first time since 1982) and Wellington were defeated in crossover matches and the semi-final and final were both won relatively untroubled. Only two further losses were incurred — to North Harbour when the Magpies rested a number of frontline players and to Bay of Plenty in a match that somehow eluded them despite the majority possession and territory.

NZ Sevens rep Kurt Baker was safe at fullback and a good judge of when to counterattack, no better example than when initiating Neria Fomai's try against Wellington from inside his own 22. Lolagi Visinia and Jonah Lowe were strong running wings with plenty of pace that meant incumbent Mason Emerson hardly featured. Stacey Ili was again an intelligent centre who looked for the gap or passed rather than run into his marker, and made good use of his left boot on occasions.

Coach Mark Ozich alternated between Ollie Sapsford and Danny Toala at second five-eighth. When Sapsford got injured, Ozich surprised by moving Neria Fomai into the position from wing and Fomai played so well he remained there for the rest of the season. Lincoln McClutchie started at first five-eighth but Caleb Makene was preferred for the second half of the campaign, although McClutchie was restored for the final.

There was no doubt this year that Folau Fakatava left the promising tag well behind him and had matured into a fine halfback. The 20-year-old's confidence, speed to the breakdown, accurate passing, a running game for superb tries against Otago and in the semi-final against Taranaki, and defensive kicking and tackling were all displayed and he was a deserving winner of the Duane Monkley medal as Mitre 10 Cup player of the year. He is eligible to represent New Zealand from January 2021.

Hawke's Bay had an abundance of capable loose forwards. Twenty-one-year-old Devan Flanders was another to leave the promising tag well behind him, the impressive No 8 producing consistently high performances. Brendon O'Connor was prominent at the breakdown, unfortunately missing the last three weeks due to concussion. His replacement, Solomone Funaki, performed well in his absence, scoring three tries. Marino Mikaele-Tu'u missed just one game when given a well-deserved rest, while Gareth Evans, who was affected on and off by an ankle injury sustained with the Hurricanes, was used off the bench as cover.

Locks Tom Parsons, Geoff Cridge and Isaia Walker-Leawere were not found wanting, with Parsons again a superb ball winner in the lineout and Walker-Leawere the only forward to play all 12 games. The lineout was statistically the best in the Mitre 10 Cup, successful at 89 per cent of own throws. The front row of Pouri Rakete-Stones, Ash Dixon and tall tighthead prop Joe Apikotoa was rarely troubled in the scrums and all did their work around the field.

Dixon was the team's top try-scorer with nine, the majority coming from Hawke's Bay's potent forward drives from lineouts close to the opposition goal-line, and his effective leadership as captain was visible in every game. Rather appropriately, he played his 100th game for the province in the successful Ranfurly Shield challenge against Otago.

New arrivals with previous provincial experience were NZ Sevens rep Kurt Baker (Manawatu/Taranaki), Lolagi Visinia (Auckland), and Connor McLeod (Otago) who was back in his home province. In addition, Bryn Evans and 'Sona' Taumalolo returned from overseas, both having last played for Hawke's Bay in 2011 and Joe Apikotoa arrived back from Wellington.

The only losses of regular players from last year were Tiaan Falcon and Michael Allardice, both overseas, and Ben May with Taranaki. Brad Weber was only available for two matches due to All Blacks commitments.

Higher honours went to:
New Zealand: B. Weber
New Zealand Maori: A. Dixon, P. Rakete-Stones, I. Walker-Leawere

HAWKE'S BAY REPRESENTATIVES 2020

	Club	Games for Union	Points for Union
Joe Apikotoa	Taradale	21	5
Kurt Baker	Tech OB	12	5
Geoff Cridge	Central HB	49	20
Jacob Devery	Hastings RS	10	0
Ash Dixon	Tech OB	107	125
Mason Emerson	Hastings RS	47	60
Bryn Evans[1]		80	50
Gareth Evans	Havelock North	37	20
Folau Fakatava	Hastings RS	31	40
Devan Flanders	Havelock North	32	35
Neria Fomai	Hastings RS	20	45
Solomone Funaki	MAC	9	15
Joel Hintz	Central HB	18	0
Stacey Ili[1]		33	15
Kianu Kereru-Symes	MAC	27	10
Jason Long	Hastings RS	54	35
Jonah Lowe	Clive	48	102
Caleb Makene	Taradale	22	54
Lincoln McClutchie	MAC	30	106
Connor McLeod	Hastings RS	7	14
Sam McNicol	Napier OB Marist	8	5
Marino Mikaele-Tu'u	Hastings RS	38	45
Brendon O'Connor[1]		53	100
Tom Parsons	Central HB	48	30
Pouri Rakete-Stones	Pirates	42	20
Ollie Sapsford	Taradale	18	5
Alisona "Sona" Taumalolo	Clive	64	90
Danny Toala	Hastings RS	22	63
Anzelo Tuitavuki	Havelock North	1	0
Lolagi Visinia	Clive	11	25
Namatahi Waa	Taradale	12	0
Isaia Walker-Leawere	Clive	22	10
Brad Weber	Napier OB Marist	30	64

1 Arrived from overseas

INDIVIDUAL SCORING

	Tries	Con	PG	DG	Points
Lincoln McClutchie	–	21	5	–	57
Ash Dixon	9	–	–	–	45
Caleb Makene	1	10	3	–	34
Lolagi Visinia	5	–	–	–	25
Devan Flanders	5	–	–	–	25
Neria Fomai	5	–	–	–	25
Jonah Lowe	4	–	–	–	20
Solomone Funaki	3	–	–	–	15
Connor McLeod	1	3	1	–	14
Penalty Try	2	–	–	–	14
Brad Weber	2	–	–	–	10
Folau Fakatava	2	–	–	–	10
Isaia Walker-Leawere	2	–	–	–	10
Marino Mikaele-Tu'u	2	–	–	–	10
Danny Toala	2	–	–	–	10
Jason Long	1	–	–	–	5
Kurt Baker	1	–	–	–	5
Brendon O'Connor	1	–	–	–	5
Stacey Ili	1	–	–	–	5
Tom Parsons	1	–	–	–	5
Pouri Rakete-Stones	1	–	–	–	5
Geoff Cridge	1	–	–	–	5
Totals	**52**	**34**	**9**	**0**	**359**
Opposition scored	34	19	16	0	256

HAWKE'S BAY 2020	Southland	Counties Manukau	Canterbury	Otago	North Harbour	Northland	Manawatu	Bay of Plenty	Wellington	Taranaki	Taranaki (sf)	Northland (f)	Totals
K.T. Baker	15	15	15	15	15	15	s	15	15	15	15	15	12
J.H. Lowe	14	11	11	11	–	–	s	11	11	11	11	11	10
M.R. Emerson	11	–	–	–	11	–	–	–	–	–	–	–	2
L. Visinia	s	14	14	14	–	14	14	14	14	14	14	14	11
A.T.M. Tuitavuki	–	–	–	–	s	–	–	–	–	–	–	–	1
S.I.A. Ili	13	13	13	13	–	13	13	13	13	s	13	13	11
S.J. McNicol	–	–	–	–	13	–	–	–	–	13	–	–	2
O.R. Sapsford	12	12	s	s	12	12	–	–	–	–	s	s	8
D.S. Toala	–	s	12	12	–	s	12	s	s	–	–	–	7
N. Fomai	–	–	–	–	14	11	11	12	12	12	12	12	8
L.F. McClutchie	10	10	10	10	s	10	10	s	s	s	s	10	12
C.L. Makene	s	s	–	s	10	s	15	10	10	10	10	s	11
F.M.N. Fakatava	9	s	9	9	s	9	9	9	9	9	9	9	12
B.M. Weber	s	9	–	–	–	–	–	–	–	–	–	–	2
C.P.A. McLeod	–	–	–	s	9	s	s	s	–	s	s	–	7
D.J. Flanders	8	8	8	8	–	8	8	8	8	8	8	8	11
B.R. O'Connor	7	7	7	7	7	7	7	–	7	–	–	–	8
M.E.R. Mikaele-Tu'u	6	6	6	6	6	6	6	6	6	–	6	6	11
A.S. Funaki	s	s	–	–	s	–	–	s	s	7	7	7	8
G.O. Evans	–	–	s	s	8	s	s	7	–	s	s	s	9
T.I. Parsons	5	5	5	5	–	5	5	s	5	5	5	5	11
G.O. Cridge	4	4	4	4	s	4	4	–	4	6	4	4	11
I.E.T. Walker-Leawere	s	s	s	s	4	s	s	4	s	4	s	s	12
B.R. Evans	–	–	–	–	5	–	–	5	–	s	–	–	3
S.J.L. Apikotoa	3	3	3	3	–	3	3	–	3	3	3	3	10
P.G. Rakete-Stones	1	1	1	1	s	1	1	1	1	s	1	1	12
J.N. Hintz	s	s	–	s	3	s	s	s	–	s	–	–	8
J.B. Long	s	s	s	s	1	s	s	–	–	–	s	s	9
F.K.A. Taumalolo	–	–	–	–	s	–	–	s	s	–	–	–	3
N.T.A. Waa	–	–	–	–	–	–	–	3	s	1	s	s	5
A.L. Dixon (capt.)	2	2	2	2	–	2	2	2	2	s	2	2	11
K.R. Kereru-Symes	s	s	–	s	2	s	s	s	s	2	–	–	9
J.D. Devery	–	–	–	–	s	–	–	–	–	–	s	–	2

K.R. Kereru-Symes captained in matches 5 and 10

HAWKE'S BAY TEAM RECORD, 2020

Played 12　Won 9　Lost 3　Points for 359　Points against 256

Date	Opponent	Location	Score	Tries	Con	PG	DG	Referee
September 13	Southland (C)	Invercargill	10–16	Dixon (2)				J. Doleman
September 20	Counties Manukau (C)	Napier	31–17	Weber (2), Penalty Try, Visinia, Flanders	McClutchie (2)	McClutchie		A. Mabey
September 26	Canterbury (cr)	Napier	20–19	Visinia, Lowe, Long	McClutchie	McClutchie		C. Stone
October 4	Otago (C) (RS)	Dunedin	28–9	Visinia, Fakatava, Walker-Leawere, Baker	McClutchie (2), Makene (2)			C. Stone
October 10	North Harbour (cr)	Albany	10–46	Mikaele-Tu'u	McLeod	McLeod		A. Mabey
October 16	Northland (C) (RS)	Napier	33–15	Fomai, Dixon, Toala, Flanders	McClutchie (2)	McClutchie (3)		B. Pickerill
October 24	Manawatu (C) (RS)	Napier	47–12	Toala, Flanders, Makene, O'Connor, Dixon, Fomai, Walker-Leawere	McClutchie (4), McLeod (2)			N. Briant
November 1	Bay of Plenty (cr)	Tauranga	17–22	Visinia, Lowe, Dixon	Makene			J. Bredin
November 8	Wellington (cr) (RS)	Napier	34–18	Flanders, Mikaele-Tu'u, Ili, Fomai	Makene (3), McClutchie	Makene (2)		R. Kelly
November 15	Taranaki (C)	Inglewood	34–33	Funaki (2), Parsons, Penalty Try, Flanders	Makene (2)	Makene		J. Bredin
November 21	Taranaki (C sf)	Napier	59–23	Dixon (3), Cridge, Funaki, Rakete-Stones, Fakatava, McLeod	McClutchie (7), Makene	McClutchie		N. Briant
November 27	Northland (C f)	Napier	36–24	Lowe (2), Fomai (2), Visinia, Dixon	McClutchie (2), Makene			J. Doleman

HOROWHENUA KAPITI

2020 Status: Heartland Championship
Founded 1893: as Horowhenua. Affiliated 1893.
Name changed to Horowhenua Kapiti 1997.
President: G.B. (Gerald) De Castro
Chairman: John Cribb
Chief executive officer: C.J. (Corey) Kennett
Coach: C.R.K. (Chris) Wilton
Assistant coach: Aleni Feagaiga
Main ground: Levin Park Domain
Capacity: 12,000
Colours: Red, white and blue

RECORDS

Highest attendance	6500	*Hurricanes v Crusaders pre-season, 2014*
Most appearances	153	*P.M. Hirini, 1986–2000*
Most points	431	*C.W. Laursen, 1985–89*
Most tries	70	*D.C. Laursen, 1980–92*
Most points in a season	136	*C.J. Spencer, 1993*
Most tries in a season	13	*D.C. Laursen, 1987*
		C.J. Kennett, 1993
Most conversions in a season	26	*C.J. Spencer, 1993*
		R.F. Aloe, 2008
Most penalty goals in a season	29	*C.W. Laursen, 1987*
Most dropped goals in a season	5	*M. Liddicoat, 1979*
Most points in a match	29	*J.P.M. Hamilton v West Coast, 2010*
		B.C. Laursen v Poverty Bay, 2015
Most tries in a match	5	*D.C. Laursen v West Coast, 1991*
Most conversions in a match	9	*D.P. Nepia v Buller, 1999*
	9	*R.F. Aloe v East Coast, 2008*
Most penalty goals in a match	6	*J. Proctor v Wanganui, 2009*
		J.S. So'oialo v Buller 2017
Highest team score	73	*v Buller, 1999*
		v East Coast, 2008
Record victory (points ahead)	73	*73–0 v Buller, 1999*
Highest score conceded	108	*v Counties, 1994*
Record defeat (points behind)	96	*12–108 v Counties, 1994*

Horowhenua Kapiti lost all three matches played, seeming to fade in their second halves after competitive first halves. Only four tries were scored.

After missing last year due to injury, the return of captain Ryan Shelford was welcomed and together with Sonny Woodmass formed a productive locking partnership. Joel Winterburn had an excellent three games and the versatile David McErlean started each of the three matches in a different front row position.

Jack Tatu-Robertson accounted for almost half his team's points with accurate goalkicking and Sean Pape impressed at first five-eighth.

Vili Tia reappeared after last playing in 2011, as did Alex Brunskill (2015), Teariki Peneha (2015) and Leon Ellison (2018). The Bruce Steel Cup this year was played in a round robin format with Horowhenua Kapiti losing both games.

Higher honours went to:
New Zealand Sevens: A. Knewstubb (before signing for Canterbury)

HOROWHENUA KAPITI REPRESENTATIVES 2020

	Club	Games for Union	Points for Union		Club	Games for Union	Points for Union
Taine Aupouri	Shannon	3	0	Teariki Peneha	Rahui	9	5
Logan Broughton	Shannon	8	5	Ilisoni Rauhihi	Shannon	2	5
Alex Brunskill	Paraparaumu	10	0	Josh Rauhihi	Shannon	1	0
Scott Cameron	Waikanae	53	53	Ryan Shelford	Paraparaumu	91	27
Aaron Campbell	Paraparaumu	1	0	Jack Tatu-Robertson	Rahui	3	19
Konor Coan	Paraparaumu	3	0	Carlos Third	Shannon	1	0
Morehu Connor-Phillips	Rahui	3	0	Vili Tia	Levin COB	7	20
Leon Ellison	Rahui	10	14	Lennix Tovo	Levin COB	2	5
Himiona Henare	Levin COB	20	73	Jordan Tupai-Ui	Levin COB	10	10
Nathan Kendrick	Paraparaumu	27	37	Dallas Wiki	Shannon	3	0
David McErlean	Shannon	49	35	Joel Winterburn	Rahui	23	10
Willie Paia'aua	Levin COB	32	72	Sonny Woodmass	Shannon	9	0
Connor Paki	Foxton	2	0				
Sean Pape	Shannon	4	0				

INDIVIDUAL SCORING

	Tries	Con	PG	DG	Points
Jack Tatu-Robertson	–	2	5	–	19
Ilisoni Rauhihi	1	–	–	–	5
Lennix Tovo	1	–	–	–	5
Himiona Henare	1	–	–	–	5
Logan Broughton	1	–	–	–	5
Totals	**4**	**2**	**5**	**0**	**39**
Opposition scored	18	12	4	0	126

HOROWHENUA KAPITI 2020

	Wairarapa Bush	Wanganui	Wairarapa Bush	Totals
H.T.W.K. Henare	15	15	15	3
M.M. Connor-Phillips	14	14	14	3
I.W. Rauhihi	s	–	11	2
A.S.R. Brunskill	s	s	s	3
W.E. Paia'aua	13	–	–	1
C.C. Third	12	–	–	1
T.K. Aupuori	s	11	13	3
V.N.S. Tia	s	s	s	3
C.L. Paki	–	13	s	2
L.T.P. Tovo	–	s	s	2
S.J. Pape	11	10	10	3
J.T. Tatu-Robertson	10	9	9	3
L.P. Ellison	9	12	–	2
J.T. Rauhihi	–	–	s	1
J.K.M. Winterburn	8	6	6	3
L.P.T. Broughton	s	8	8	3
T.T.W.W. Peneha	7	–	12	2
N.J. Kendrick	–	7	7	2
S.R. Woodmass	5	5	5	3
R.T. Shelford (capt)	4	4	4	3
D.B. Wiki	s	s	s	3
J.L. Tupai-Ui	6	1	1	3
S.A. Cameron	3	–	3	2
A.J.T. Campbell	s	–	–	1
D.J. McErlean	1	3	2	3
K.S. Coan	2	2	s	3

HOROWHENUA KAPITI TEAM RECORD, 2020

Played 3 Won 0 Lost 3 Points for 39 Points against 126

Date	Opponent	Location	Score	Tries	Con	PG	DG	Referee
September 19	Wairarapa Bush	Levin	8–43	I. Rauhihi		Tatu-Robertson		S. Thompson
October 3	Wanganui (BSC)	Shannon	7–36	Tovo	Tatu-Robertson			S. Thompson
October 10	Wairarapa Bush (BSC)	Carterton	24–47	Henare, Broughton	Tatu-Robertson	Tatu-Robertson (4)		A. Payne

KING COUNTRY

2020 Status: Heartland Championship
Founded 1922. Affiliated 1922
President: L.M. (Max) Lamb
Chairman: I.C. (Ivan) Haines to July;
R.J. (Ron) Thomassen from July
General Manager: S.M. (Susan) Youngman to June;
K.P. (Kurt) McQuilkin from August
Coach: I.J. (Isaac) Boss
Assistant coach: T.P. (Daniel) Alofa
Main grounds: Owen Delany Park, Taupo; Rugby Park, Te Kuiti
Capacity: 15,000; 5000
Colours: Gold and maroon

RECORDS

Highest attendance	12,000	*King Country v South Africa, 1994 (Taupo)*
Most appearances	147	*P.L. Mitchell, 1988–2001*
Most points	925	*H.C. Coffin, 1984–95*
Most tries	46	*M.R. Kidd, 1974–84*
Most points in a season	230	*H.C. Coffin, 1992*
Most tries in a season	11	*D.M. Flavell, 1981*
		S.J. Bradley, 1992
Most conversions in a season	40	*H.C. Coffin, 1992*
Most penalty goals in a season	45	*H.C. Coffin, 1992*
Most dropped goals in a season	8	*I.N. Ingham, 1966*
Most points in a match	33	*H.C. Coffin v Poverty Bay, 1992*
Most tries in a match	4	*C.A. Crossman v Auckland XV, 1936*
		J. Haitana & H. Dixon v Thames Valley, 1938
		T. Katene v Golden Bay-Motueka, 1955
		J.A.W. McIlroy v Horowhenua, 1965
		D.W. Koni v Taranaki, 1969
		D.M. Flavell v East Coast, 1979
		N.A. Harrison v East Coast, 1981
		N.A. Harrison v Horowhenua, 1984
		J.W. Wells v East Coast, 1992
Most conversions in a match	10	*H.C. Coffin v Poverty Bay, 1992*
Most penalty goals in a match	7	*L.W.T. Peina v Wanganui, 2000*
Highest team score	99	*v East Coast, 1992*
Record victory (points ahead)	99	*99–0 v East Coast, 1992*
Highest score conceded	97	*v Auckland, 1993*
Record defeat (points behind)	94	*3–97 v Auckland, 1993*

The Rams improved as their three matches went along. They started with a scoreless first half in losing the opening match against Wairarapa Bush and finished with a dominant second half to defeat Wanganui in the final match and probably should have scored more points in doing so.

In a very settled backline newcomer Mohi Roberts was a valuable utility back with an ability to kick goals, Josevata Malimoce was always threatening at centre and Nathaniel Smith was an effective halfback.

The loose forwards Sisa Vosaki and Leveson Gower showed up well and the captain Carl Carmichael played the 100th first-class match of his career (37th for King Country) in the match against Wanganui. His fellow prop Joseva Curuki was a hard man to stop with ball in hand, and Dan Towler, who had last played for King Country in 2011 on loan, had an impressive game against Wanganui.

14 players were given debuts in the three matches with Dion Pye becoming a third generation King Country rep following his grandfather N.W. (Sam) and father Nathan.

The match against Ngati Porou East Coast was played at Opotiki.

KING COUNTRY REPRESENTATIVES 2020

	Club	Games for Union	Points for Union		Club	Games for Union	Points for Union
Josh Balme [1]	Hamilton Marist [2]	9	15	Sam Robinson	Taupo Marist	1	0
Mosese Baravilala	Taumarunui Districts	3	0	Kieron Rollinson	Taupo Sports	18	53
Nick Barnes	Taupo Sports	12	10	Dan Ross	Taumarunui RS	7	5
Carl Carmichael	Taumarunui RS	37	10	Reeve Satherley	Taupo Marist	3	0
Ethan Christensen	Taupo Sports	3	0	Dion Schrieber	Piopio	2	0
Josevata Curuki	Taumarunui Districts	7	10	Bobby Sharpe	Piopio	2	0
Jimmy Davy	Taumarunui RS	2	0	Nathaniel Smith	Taumarunui Districts	8	0
Jesse Douglas	Taupo Sports	7	5	Sam Stewart	Piopio	1	0
Leveson Gower	Taumarunui Districts	2	0	Steve Te Moananui	Waitomo	22	20
Dion Havea	Piopio	1	0	Dan Towler	Taumarunui Districts	6	0
Creedence Lingman	Taupo Sports	1	0	Sam Trangmar	Waitomo	4	0
Josevata Malimoce	Taumarunui Districts	3	5	Stephan Turner	Piopio	26	27
Manawa Owens	Tongariro	8	0	Ratu Vosaki	Taupo Sports	20	15
Joe Perawiti	Waitomo	29	35	Sisa Vosaki	Taupo Sports	16	15
Dion Pye	Waitomo	1	0	Liam Wano	Waitete	2	0
Mohi Roberts	Taupo Marist	3	28				

1 Player of Origin   2 Waikato RU

INDIVIDUAL SCORING

	Tries	Con	PG	DG	Points
Mohi Roberts	1	4	5	–	28
Kieron Rollinson	–	2	2	–	10
Josevata Curuki	2	–	–	–	10
Jesse Douglas	1	–	–	–	5
Nick Barnes	1	–	–	–	5
Josevata Malimoce	1	–	–	–	5
Sisa Vosaki	1	–	–	–	5
Totals	**7**	**6**	**7**	**0**	**68**
Opposition scored	8	3	3	0	55

KING COUNTRY 2020

	Wairarapa Bush	Ngati Porou East Coast	Wanganui	Totals
M.P.T.R. Roberts	15	10	15	3
D.J. Pye	–	15	–	1
R.S. Vosaki	14	11	–	2
S.K. Turner	11	14	14	3
D. Havea	–	s	–	1
J. Malimoce	13	13	13	3
M.R. Baravilala	12	12	11	3
J.R. Douglas	s	–	s	2
D.B. Schrieber	s	–	s	2
J.E. Perawiti	–	s	12	2
K.J. Rollinson	10	s	10	3
N.K. Smith	9	9	9	3
L.W. Wano	s	–	s	2
S.H. Trangmar	8	–	8	2
J.D. Davy	s	–	s	2
C.L.A. Lingman	–	8	–	1
E.L. Christensen	7	–	s	2
L.A. Gower	–	7	7	2
M.K. Owens	s	s	–	2
S.V. Vosaki	6	6	6	3
J.H. Balme	5	5	–	2
R.H. Satherley	4	s	5	3
R.J. Sharpe	–	4	4	2
D.S. Ross	3	–	–	1
C.W. Carmichael (capt)	1	–	1	2
J.V. Curuki	s	1	s	3
S.R.A. Moananui	–	3	–	1
D.S. Towler	–	s	3	2
S.J. Robinson	2	–	–	1
N.G. Barnes	s	2	2	3
S.J. Stewart	–	s	–	1

N.K. Smith captained v Ngati Porou East Coast.

KING COUNTRY TEAM RECORD, 2020

Played 3 Won 2 Lost 1 Points for 68 Points against 55

Date	Opponent	Location	Score	Tries	Con	PG	DG	Referee
September 26	Wairarapa Bush	Masterton	18–22	Roberts, Douglas		Rollinson (2)		A. Payne
October 3	Ngati Porou East Coast	Opotiki	34–22	Barnes, Malimoce, Curuki, S. Vosaki	Roberts (3), Rollinson	Roberts (2)		S. Fellows
October 10	Wanganui	Taumarunui	16–11	Curuki	Roberts	Roberts (3)		C. Cowie

MANAWATU

2020 Status: Mitre 10 Cup Championship
Founded 1886. Original member 1892
President: B.S. (Bruce) Hemara
Chairman: T.J. (Tim) Myers
Chief executive officer: S.M. (Shannon) Paku
Coach: P.C. (Peter) Russell
Assistant coach: A.J. (Aaron) Good, S.B.N. (Shane) Ratima
Main ground: Central Energy Trust Arena; Manfeild Park, Feilding
Capacity: 17,000
Colours: Green and white

MANAWATU RUGBY

RECORDS

Highest attendance	17,100	Manawatu v British & Irish Lions, 2005
Most appearances	145	G.A. Knight, 1975–86
Most points	641	J.J. Holland, 1991–96
Most tries	66	K.W. Granger, 1971–84
Most points in a season	182	J.M. Smith, 1991
Most tries in a season	14	P.L. Alston, 1991
Most conversions in a season	38	D.L. Rollerson, 1981
		J.M. Smith, 1991
Most penalty goals in a season	27	M.C. Finlay, 1984
		A. McMaster, 1987
Most dropped goals in a season	9	J.P.J. Carroll, 1978
Most points in a match	35	J.M. Smith v Horowhenua, 1992
Most tries in a match	5	J.P. Butt v Wanganui, 1944
		N.J. Mears v Horowhenua, 1958
		G.P.D. Henare v Horowhenua, 1987
Most conversions in a match	11	J.M. Smith v Poverty Bay, 1991
Most penalty goals in a match	6	M.R. Love v Waikato, 1983
		M.C. Finlay v Wanganui, 1984
		A. McMaster v Waikato, 1987
		J.J. Holland v Counties, 1994
		I. Thompson v Northland, 2009
Highest team score	94	v Poverty Bay, 1991
Record victory (points ahead)	87	94–7 v Poverty Bay, 1991
Highest score conceded	109	v British & Irish Lions, 2005
Record defeat (points behind)	103	6–109 v British & Irish Lions, 2005

With only one win, over Southland, Manawatu finished bottom of the Mitre 10 Cup table. In the earlier games, lapses in concentration became a habit during the minutes before halftime, or just after halftime, or both, resulting in gifting soft tries to opponents. Performances improved in later games but, generally, the Turbos were outclassed by stronger, faster teams laden with Super experience. All Black Aaron Smith, in his one start for the team, showed his immense experience and scored two tries against Otago.

The backs seldom broke the defensive line but showed glimpses of clever inter-play when this was achieved. The absence of All Black Ngani Laumape, so influential in the previous year's four wins, was very noticeable; so too the departure of Otere Black to Bay of Plenty. Halfback and captain Jamie Booth was again the general until breaking a leg late in the Ranfurly Shield challenge. After a long period recovering from serious injury, Nehe Milner-Skudder returned but was not the brilliant attacker of earlier years. However, he was reliable at fullback, directed the outside backs well and captained the team in the final three games. Te Rangatira Waitokia and Josiah Maraku had few opportunities to show their attacking skills. James Tofa was steady and reliable. More will be seen of newcomers Drew Wild, Stewart Cruden and Bryn Wilson, promising young academy players who didn't disappoint when called in when regulars were injured.

Two contracted locks, Michael FitzGerald and Tom Hughes, missed the season through injury and illness. Liam Mitchell had another grand season and was the main lineout ball-winner. The experienced Crusaders prop Michael Ala'alatoa had his best Turbos season, he being the only forward to start every game. Sam Stewart developed further as a reliable hooker. Chris Eves departed mid-season. Young Shamus Hurley-Langton, from Wellington, established himself as openside flanker while, on the other side, teenager 'TK' Howden rapidly developed as a very energetic and effective loose forward. Injury deprived the Turbos of effective No. 8 Brayden Iose after only three games. Tyler Laubscher took his place and displayed outstanding form as a highly promising loose forward. However, the 19-year-old also suffered injury and the season finished with Kirk Tufuga, the Wairarapa Bush and NZ Universities representative, very capably filling the position. Micaiah Torrance-Read was another newcomer and he made an immediate impression at lock. Other new Turbos to appear with previous first-class experience include Siua Maile (Tonga at 2019 RWC), Nigel Ah Wong (Counties Manukau), Solomona Sakalia (Wellington and Bay of Plenty), Tietie Tuimauga (Wanganui and Wellington) and Sam Liebezeit (West Coast).

The late finish to the championship season, due to the competition being delayed because of the pandemic, meant the stockcar season would commence at Arena before the two last home games. With the possibility of metal objects lying undetected on the playing field, the union was concerned about player safety and chose to play in Feilding. Assisted by the Manawatu District Council, a field was created at Feilding's Manfeild Park, with temporary seating and facilities for the two games.

Higher honours went to:
New Zealand: K.H. Laumape, A.L. Smith

MANAWATU REPRESENTATIVES 2020

	Club	Games for Union	Points for Union
Nigel Ah Wong	OB Marist	7	10
Michael Ala'alatoa	Feilding OB Oroua	46	20
Jamie Booth	University	60	65
Adam Boult	Te Kawau	13	15
Stewart Cruden	College OB	11	15
Griffin Culver	Feilding	7	0
Chris Eves	Bay of Plenty RU	35	20
Johnny Galloway	College OB	16	20
Te Kamaka 'TK' Howden	Feilding	9	0
Tom Hughes	University	12	0
Shamus Hurley-Langton	OB University[1]	9	5
Brayden Iose	Kia Toa	15	10
Tyler Laubscher	University	7	5
Paulo Leleisiuao	Feilding OB Oroua	11	0
Sam Liebezeit	College OB	3	0
Siua Maile	Freyberg OB	9	0
Josiah Maraku	Feilding	16	10
Nehe Milner-Skudder	University	51	35
Liam Mitchell	Te Kawau	34	15
Teofilo Paulo	Kia Toa	9	0
Solomona Sakalia	OB Marist	5	0
Aaron Smith	Feilding	45	55
Kyle Stewart	College OB	8	0
Sam Stewart	Te Kawau	29	15
Gene Syminton	OB Marist	5	0
James Tofa	College OB	27	20
Micaiah Torrance-Read	University	10	5
Newton Tudreu	Kia Toa	40	40
Kirk Tufuga	Eketahuna[2]	4	0
Tietie Tuimauga	Feilding	9	0
Te Rangatira Waitokia	University	24	10
Ben Werthmuller	OB Marist	6	10
Drew Wild	Feilding	11	15
Bryn Wilson	University	7	5
Ben Wyness	Feilding	11	48

1 Wellington RU   2 Wairarapa Bush RU

INDIVIDUAL SCORING

	Tries	Con	PG	DG	Points
Wyness	2	10	6	–	48
Cruden	1	5	–	–	15
S. Stewart	3	–	–	–	15
Tofa	3	–	–	–	15
Wild	3	–	–	–	15
Ah Wong	2	–	–	–	10
Booth	2	–	–	–	10
Maraku	2	–	–	–	10
Mitchell	2	–	–	–	10
Smith	2	–	–	–	10
Waitokia	2	–	–	–	10
Boult	1	–	–	–	5
Galloway	1	–	–	–	5
Hurley-Langton	1	–	–	–	5
Laubscher	1	–	–	–	5
Torrance-Read	1	–	–	–	5
Wilson	1	–	–	–	5
Totals	**30**	**15**	**6**	**0**	**198**
Opposition scored	54	40	9	0	377

MANAWATU 2020	Northland	Otago	Auckland	Counties Manukau	Canterbury	Bay of Plenty	Hawke's Bay	Southland	Taranaki	Wellington	Totals
N.R. Milner-Skudder	15	15	15	15	15	15	15	15	15	15	10
N.W.K. Tudreu	14	s	14	–	–	11	–	–	–	–	4
N.F. Ah Wong	–	–	13	–	14	14	14	14	14	14	7
A.C. Boult	11	11	11	–	11	–	s	–	–	–	5
D. Wild	s	–	–	s	s	s	s	s	s	s	8
Te R.W. Waitokia	–	s	s	14	–	–	11	11	11	11	7
B.B. Werthmuller	–	–	–	11	–	–	–	–	–	–	1
J.M. Maraku	13	13	–	13	13	13	13	13	13	13	9
J. Tofa	12	12	12	12	12	12	12	12	12	12	10
B. Wyness	10	10	s	10	10	s	10	10	10	10	10
S.R. Cruden	s	s	10	s	s	10	–	–	s	s	8
J.P. Booth (Capt)	9	14	9	9	9	9	9	–	–	–	7
A.L. Smith	s	9	–	–	–	–	–	–	–	–	2
B.G. Wilson	–	–	s	–	s	s	s	9	9	9	7
G.J. Culver	–	–	–	–	–	–	–	s	s	s	3
B.D. Iose	8	8	8	–	–	–	–	–	–	–	3
T. Laubscher	s	s	6	8	8	8	–	–	–	–	6
K.M.S. Tufuga	–	–	–	–	–	–	8	8	8	8	4
S.J. Hurley-Langton	–	7	7	7	7	s	7	7	7	7	9
J.B. Galloway	–	–	–	s	s	7	s	s	s	s	7
Te K.D-M. Howden	s	s	s	6	6	–	6	6	6	6	9
L.F. Mitchell	6	6	–	5	5	6	5	4	4	5	9
T.A.M. Paulo	5	5	5	–	5	s	5	5	5	s	9
S.P. Liebezeit	4	–	s	–	–	s	–	–	–	–	3
M.E-L. Torrance-Read	7	4	4	4	4	4	4	s	s	4	10
T.W. Hughes	–	–	–	–	s	–	–	–	–	–	1
M.S. Ala'alatoa	3	3	3	3	3	3	3	3	3	3	10
T.T.J. Tuimauga	1	1	1	1	s	–	s	1	1	1	9
K.L. Stewart	s	s	s	s	–	s	–	s	s	s	8
P. Leleisiuao	s	–	–	–	s	–	s	–	–	–	3
C.I. Eves	–	s	s	1	1	1	–	–	–	–	5
S.L. Sakalia	–	–	–	–	–	s	1	s	s	s	5
S.W. Stewart	?	2	s	2	2	2	2	–	–	–	8
S.P. Maile	s	s	2	s	s	s	s	–	2	2	9
G.W. Syminton	–	–	–	–	–	–	–	s	s	s	3

MANAWATU TEAM RECORD, 2020

Played 10   Won 1   Lost 9   Points for 198   Points against 377

Date	Opponent	Location	Score	Tries	Con	PG	DG	Referee
September 13	Northland (C)	Whangarei	26–43	S. Stewart, Tofa	Wyness (2)	Wyness (4)		B.E. Pickerill
September 20	Otago (C)	Palmerston North	25–36	Smith (2), Booth, Torrance-Read	Cruden	Wyness		R.P. Kelly
September 27	Auckland (cr)	Auckland	12–50	Boult, S. Stewart	Cruden			D.J. Waenga
October 3	Counties Manukau (C)	Pukekohe	30–36	Hurley-Langton, Tofa, S. Stewart, Waitokia, Wild	Wyness	Wyness		M.I. Fraser
October 9	Canterbury (cr	Palmerston North	10–34	Maraku, Wild				N.P. Briant
October 17	Bay of Plenty (cr)	Palmerston North	35–53	Cruden, Laubscher, Booth, Galloway, Wild	Wyness (3), Cruden (2)			J.R. Bredin
October 24	Hawke's Bay (C, RS)	Napier	12–47	Tofa, Wyness	Wyness			N.P. Briant
November 1	Southland (C)	Feilding	24–12	Mitchell, Waitokia, Ah Wong, Wyness	Wyness (2)			N.E.R. Hogan
November 8	Taranaki (C)	Feilding	19–35	Wilson, Mitchell, Ah Wong	Wyness, Cruden			A.W.B. Mabey
November 14	Wellington (cr)	Wellington	5–31	Maraku				B.E. Pickerill

MID CANTERBURY

2020 Status: Heartland Championship
Founded 1904 as Ashburton sub-union affiliated to South Canterbury RU. Name changed to Ashburton County 1905 and affilated to Canterbury RU 1905. Became a full union with affiliation to NZRU 1927. Name changed to Mid Canterbury 1952.
President: M.J. (Mike) Hanham
Chairman: G.P. (Gerard) Rushton
Chief executive officer: I.J. (Ian) Patterson
Coach: D.D. (Dale) Palmer
Assistant coach: J.J. (Jason) Rickard
Main ground: Ashburton Showgrounds
Capacity: 10,000
Colours: Forest green and gold

RECORDS

Highest attendance	8656	Mid Canterbury v British Isles, 1983
Most appearances	158	J.C. Ross, 1970–87
Most points	598	A.H.A. Smith, 1955–68
Most tries	47	G.R. Bryant, 1968–77
Most points in a season	200	S.R. Middleton, 1994
Most tries in a season	13	M.L. Sau, 2017
Most conversions in a season	34	S.R. Middleton, 1994
		J.R. Percival, 2017
Most penalty goals in a season	44	S.R. Middleton, 1994
Most dropped goals in a season	12	M.B. Roulston, 1982
Most points in a match	22	M.C. Williams v East Coast, 2014
Most tries in a match	5	G.R. Bryant v Nelson Bays, 1977
Most conversions in a match	8	S.R. Middleton v West Coast, 1998
Most penalty goals in a match	6	S.R. Middleton v Horowhenua Kapiti, 1998
		D.J. Maw v West Coast, 2007
		M.C. Williams v Wanganui, 2014
Highest team score	90	v West Coast, 1998
Record victory (points ahead)	77	90–13 v West Coast, 1998
Highest score conceded	99	v Hawke's Bay, 2003
Record defeat (points behind)	91	8–99 v Hawke's Bay, 2003

The Hammers showed a lot of improvement on last year's worst ever result in the Heartland Championship. North Otago was defeated twice after a heavy loss to them last year and the 31-31 draw against South Canterbury was the result of a spirited fightback from 9-25 down.

The same backline started in each of the four games with the sole exception of Cameron Butler coming in for Inoke Tonga at fullback for the final match. These starting seven backs of Inoke Tonga, Raitube Vasurakuta, Matthew Holmes, Paovale Sofai, Tait Chisman, Nathan McCloy and Tyler Blackburn developed into a good combination with their regular play and accounted for 12 of the 19 tries scored. McCloy was also an excellent goalkicker and his last minute sideline conversion forced the 31-31 draw against South Canterbury.

Number eight Seta Koroitamana was the standout in the forward pack and lock Irome Dawai and prop Adam Williamson also featured in the forwards' efforts.

For the first time since 2001, Mid Canterbury played no match for the Hanan Shield. Of the 29 players used, 19 were making their debut. Wing Raitube Vasurakuta had played for South Canterbury in 2016.

MID CANTERBURY REPRESENTATIVES 2020

	Club	Games for Union	Points for Union		Club	Games for Union	Points for Union
Hamish Allen	Methven	3	0	Seta Koroitamana	Rakaia	59	163
Harry Ashworth	Rakaia	2	0	Tim Lawn	Methven	4	0
Tyler Blackburn	Methven	37	22	Ashton McArthur	Celtic	3	0
Evan Blyth	Rakaia	3	0	Nathan McCloy	Celtic	13	79
Harvey Blyth	Rakaia	3	2	Lote Nasiga	Celtic	4	0
Callum Burrell	Southern	4	0	Alipeti Polutele	Methven	2	0
Cameron Butler	Celtic	2	0	Lepani Seitava	Rakaia	3	5
Tait Chisman	Methven	4	10	Paovale Sofai	Celtic	4	15
Irome Dawai	Celtic	6	0	Lloyd Stephens	Allenton	2	0
Hamish Finnie	Celtic	9	0	Matthew Stone	Methven	2	0
Luke Gilbert	Methven	3	10	Inoke Tonga	Rakaia	6	5
Hugh Griffiths	Methven	6	0	Elama Touli	Hampstead	3	0
Matthew Groom	Methven	30	15	Raitube Vasurakuta	Rakaia	4	15
Jack Harrex	Celtic	1	0	Adam Williamson	Southern	28	10
Matthew Holmes	Methven	4	0				

INDIVIDUAL SCORING

	Tries	Con	PG	DG	Points
Nathan McCloy	1	8	8	–	45
Paovale Sofai	3	–	–	–	15
Raitube Vasurakuta	3	–	–	–	15
Luke Gilbert	2	–	–	–	10
Adam Williamson	2	–	–	–	10
Seta Koroitamana	2	–	–	–	10
Tait Chisman	2	–	–	–	10
Tyler Blackburn	2	–	–	–	10
Lepani Seitava	1	–	–	–	5
Inoke Tonga	1	–	–	–	5
Harvey Blyth	–	1	–	–	2
Totals	**19**	**9**	**8**	**0**	**137**
Opposition scored	9	6	5	0	72

MID CANTERBURY 2020

	South Canterbury	Buller	North Otago	North Otago	Totals
I.F. Tonga	15	15	15	–	3
H.R. Griffiths	–	s	–	–	1
C.J.R. Butler	–	–	s	15	2
R.M. Vasurakuta	14	14	14	14	4
T.R. Chisman	11	11	11	11	4
T.J. Lawn	s	s	–	s	3
M.B. Holmes	13	13	13	13	4
P. Sofai	12	12	12	12	4
L. Seitava	s	–	s	s	3
N.J. McCloy	10	10	10	10	4
T.A.C. Blackburn	9	9	9	9	4
H. Blyth	–	s	s	s	3
S.S. Koroitamana	8	8	8	8	4
L.M. Gilbert	7	7	–	7	3
H.L.J. Ashworth	–	s	7	–	2
L.L. Nasiga	6	5	6	6	4
E.L. Blyth	–	6	s	s	3
J.D. Harrex	–	s	–	–	1
I. Dawai	5	–	5	5	3
M.J. Stone	4	4	–	–	2
A. Polutele	s	–	4	–	2
A.T. McArthur	s	–	s	s	3
L. Stephens	–	–	s	4	2
H.P. Allen	3	3	s	–	3
A.C.J. Williamson	1	1	3	3	4
M.R. Groom	s	–	–	s	2
H.I. Finnie	–	s	1	1	3
E. Touli	2	s	–	2	3
C. Burrell	s	2	2	s	4

MID CANTERBURY TEAM RECORD, 2020

Date	Opponent	Location	Played 4		Won 3	Drew 1	Lost 0		Points for 137		Points against 72
			Score	Tries			Con	PG	DG		Referee
September 5	South Canterbury	Timaru	31–31	Gilbert, Williamson, Seitava			McCloy (2)	McCloy (4)			J. Rooney
September 12	Buller	Hanmer Springs	41–17	Sofai (2), Gilbert, Koroitamana, Chisman, Blackburn, Vasurakuta			McCloy (3)				K. Faalogo
September 19	North Otago	Hinds	30–7	Vasurakata (2), Sofai, Tonga, Koroitamana			McCloy	McCloy			K. Faalogo
September 26	North Otago	Oamaru	35–17	McCloy, Chisman, Williamson, Blackburn			McCloy (2), H. Blyth	McCloy (3)			D. Winter

NORTH HARBOUR

2020 Status: Mitre 10 Cup Premiership
Founded 1985. Affiliated 1985
President: B.A. (Brett) Norris
Chairman: G.P. (Gerard) van Tilborg
Chief executive: D.B. (David) Gibson
Coach: K.J. (Kieran) Keane
Assistant coaches: S.R.B (Sam) Ward, D.K. (Daniel) Halangahu
Main ground: North Harbour Stadium, Albany
Capacity: 25,000
Colours: White, black and cardinal

RECORDS

Most appearances	145	Ron Williams, 1985–94
		Walter Little, 1987–2000
Most points	1052	Warren Burton, 1990–96
Most tries	63	Richard Kapa, 1985–93
Most points in a season	258	Warren Burton, 1995
Most tries in a season	16	Glenn Davis, 1999
Most conversions in a season	53	Warren Burton, 1991
Most penalty goals in a season	47	Warren Burton, 1995
Most dropped goals in a season	3	Jamie Cameron, 1991
Most points in a match	34	Frano Botica v Queensland Country, 1985
Most tries in a match	5	Glenn Davis v Poverty Bay-East Coast, 1999
		Tevita Li v Taranaki, 2017
Most conversions in a match	10	Frano Botica v Taranaki, 1989
		Jamie Cameron v Marlborough, 1990
		Warren Burton v Wanganui, 1991
Most penalty goals in a match	6	Warren Burton v Counties, 1990
		Warren Burton v Wellington, 1990
		Warren Burton v Otago, 1994
		Warren Burton v Hawke's Bay, 1996
Highest team score	99	v Horowhenua Kapiti, 2008
Record victory (points ahead)	93	99–6 v Horowhenua Kapiti, 2008
Highest score conceded	71	v Auckland, 1995
Record defeat (points behind)	55	10–65 v Canterbury 2002

North Harbour endured an extraordinary season, in many ways.

Tipped by some for relegation, Kieran Keane's charges looked on target for that prediction when dropping their opening three matches, including a crossover loss to Southland. But they rallied strongly, winning five of their last seven off the back of a powerful scrum, deadly lineout drive and the boot and astute generalship of Bryn Gatland.

Along the way, they won the Battle of the Bridge and Lion Red Challenge Trophies against Auckland and Counties Manukau respectively. Still, defeat to Bay of Plenty in a thriller on the last day of the regular season saw Harbour prop up the table. Relegation will depend on whether the format for the 2021 Mitre 10 Cup changes or not.

Nine rookies were assimilated and Harbour did well, as in 2019, to use just 31 players.

The turning point came in rounds 4–5, where Harbour executed two outstanding victories over eventual Premership and Championship winners Tasman and Hawke's Bay. Until the final round, there was a good case to be made that Harbour was the form team of the Mitre 10 Cup, which is why Keane et al will be chastened that five wins could not lift them off the foot of the table.

The only real signing was that of All Blacks Sevens rep Ngarohi McGarvey-Black, who looked good at No 14 until he was injured. Gatland was back from injury that ruled him out in 2019.

The major losses were Matt Duffie and Matt McGahan (Japan), Luatangi Li (Northland) and Mark Telea (Tasman). Wing Osea Qamasea could not get back in the country due to Covid-19 restrictions.

Fullback Shaun Stevenson did not score a try but impressed in almost every game with his penetrative running, especially on the counter. He was one of eight players who started all 10 games. Few other unions could equal that statistic.

Tomas Aoake scored four tries on the left wing, sometimes finishing in spectacular style, as he did against Hawke's Bay, and combining well with Gatland and Bryn Hall on the blindside.

Jared Page was the surprise package. Originally cast as a first five/fullback, he found a home on the right wing, scoring six tries, including a hat-trick against Hawke's Bay.

Centre Asaeli Tikoirotuma did not always start, but still came up with telling plays on defence, including a trysaver on Simon Hickey in the Auckland clash. Loan player Antonio Mikaele-Tu'u was good value. James Little played big minutes and was consistently sound on defence.

Gatland led all scorers in the Mitre 10 Cup (with 119) and impressed with his allround kicking game, slick passing and option-taking. He was well served by Hall, whose blindside probes were a feature of his game. Lewis Gjaltema won his first start at halfback after three seasons, but never seriously threatened Hall.

Murphy Taramai was again industriousness personified at No 8, and he passed the 50-game milestone. Skipper Dillon Hunt, shrugging off a brief bout of concussion, turned out consistently high quality displays, his work-rate and fetching to the fore. Ethan Roots was again consistent, if not as prominent as he was in 2019.

The locking combination of Gerard Cowley-Tuioti and Jacob Pierce was unchanged. The latter, in particular, grew in stature and is finally starting to dominate at this level.

Sione Mafileo, was omnipresent, and proved himself as the best tighthead scrummager in the competition. Nic Mayhew seamlessly slotted into the No 1 jersey in place of All Black Karl Tu'inukuafe, while rookie Teague McElroy made strong advances in his game, mainly off the pine.

James Parsons was rested for the entire Mitre 10 Cup to allow his concussion symptoms to fully clear, so Luteru Tolai took his chance to start every game and score seven tries, mostly on the end of lineout mauls. His understudy Zane Turner, out of club rugby like several others, performed usefully.

Higher honours went to:
New Zealand: K. Tu'inukuafe
New Zealand Maori: B. Hall, E. Roots, S. Stevenson

NORTH HARBOUR REPRESENTATIVES 2020

	Club	Games for Union	Points for Union		Club	Games for Union	Points for Union
Tomas Aoake	East Coast Bays	14	20	Tamarau McGahan	Marist	2	0
Kade Banks	Takapuna	4	0	Ngarohi McGarvey-Black	Marist	3	5
Gerard Cowley-Tuioti	Massey	66	20	Antonio Mikaele-Tu'u	Hastings R and S[1]	7	0
Xavier Cowley-Tuioti	Massey	8	0	Jared Page	East Coast Bays	10	43
Walter Fifita	Massey	3	5	Jacob Pierce	North Shore	27	5
Bryn Gatland	Takapuna	41	447	Ethan Roots	East Coast Bays	20	0
Lewis Gjaltema	East Coast Bays	31	10	Jimmy Roots	East Coast Bays	12	0
Bryn Hall	Northcote	87	89	Tim Sail	Northcote	8	5
Jack Heighton	East Coast Bays	4	0	Shaun Stevenson	Marist	40	68
Dillon Hunt	Marist	25	25	Murphy Taramai	Northcote	51	20
Fine Inisi	Takapuna	8	10	Asaeli Tikoirotuma	Northcote	16	15
Lotu Inisi	Takapuna	11	10	Luteru Tolai	Northcote	26	40
James Little	North Shore	18	25	Karl Tu'inukuafe	Takapuna	29	15
Sione Mafileo	North Shore	63	15	Zane Turner	Silverdale	9	5
Nic Mayhew	Northcote	38	10	Alex Woonton	North Shore	37	0
Teague McElroy	Northcote	10	10				

1 Hawke's Bay

INDIVIDUAL SCORING

	Tries	Con	PG	DG	Points		Tries	Con	PG	DG	Points
Gatland	3	25	18	–	119	F. Inisi	1	–	–	–	5
Tolai	7	–	–	–	35	McGarvey-Black	1	–	–	–	5
Page	6	–	–	–	30	Pierce	1	–	–	–	5
Aoake	4	–	–	–	20	Sail	1	–	–	–	5
Little	2	–	–	–	10	Taramai	1	–	–	–	5
McElroy	2	–	–	–	10	Turner	1	–	–	–	5
Penalty try	1	–	–	–	7						
Fifita	1	–	–	–	5	**Totals**	**34**	**25**	**18**	**0**	**276**
Gjaltema	1	–	–	–	5						
Hunt	1	–	–	–	5	Opposition scored	30	20	12	0	226

NORTH HARBOUR 2020

	Canterbury	Waikato	Southland	Tasman	Hawke's Bay	Wellington	Auckland	Northland	Counties Manukau	Bay of Plenty	Totals
S.T. Stevenson	15	15	15	15	15	15	15	15	15	15	10
K.J. Banks	–	–	s	s	–	–	–	–	s	s	4
N.M. McGarvey-Black	14	14	14	–	–	–	–	–	–	–	3
W.P. Fifita	11	s	11	–	–	–	–	–	–	–	3
T.J. Aoake	s	11	–	11	11	11	11	11	11	11	9
A.T. Tikoirotuma	13	–	13	–	s	13	14	14	–	s	7
A.W. Mikaele-Tu'u	–	–	s	12	12	–	s	12	12	12	7
J.O. Little	12	12	12	13	13	12	13	13	13	13	10
F. Inisi	s	–	–	–	s	s	–	s	s	–	4
J.W. Heighton	–	s	–	–	s	s	12	–	–	–	4
B.E.C. Gatland	10	10	10	10	10	10	10	10	10	10	10
J.R. Page	–	13	–	14	14	14	–	s	14	14	7
B.D. Hall	9	9	–	9	9	9	9	9	9	9	9
L.M. Gjaltema	s	s	9	s	s	s	s	s	s	s	10
L. Inisi	–	s	8	–	–	–	–	–	–	–	2
M.V.U. Taramai	8	8	s	8	8	8	8	8	8	8	10
T. McGahan	s	–	–	s	–	–	–	–	–	–	2
T.J. Sail	–	–	7	7	s	s	s	s	s	s	8
D. Hunt (capt)	7	7	–	–	7	7	7	7	7	7	8
E.J. Roots	6	6	6	6	6	6	6	6	6	6	10
J.W.L. Pierce	5	5	5	5	5	5	5	5	5	5	10
G.E. Cowley-Tuioti	4	4	4	4	4	4	4	4	4	4	10
X. Cowley-Tuioti	–	s	–	s	s	s	–	s	s	s	7
S.T. Mafileo	3	3	3	3	3	3	3	3	3	3	10
A.J.T. Woonton	–	–	–	–	–	–	–	s	s	s	3
J.D. Roots	s	s	s	s	s	s	s	s	s	s	10
T.R.K. McElroy	s	s	s	s	s	s	s	1	1	1	10
G.Z.K. Tu'inukuafe	1	1	–	–	–	–	–	–	–	–	2
N.J. Mayhew	–	–	1	1	1	1	1	–	–	–	5
L.H.V. Tolai	2	2	2	2	2	2	2	2	2	2	10
Z.K. Turner	–	s	s	s	s	s	s	s	s	s	9

NORTH HARBOUR TEAM RECORD 2020

Played 10 Won 5 Lost 5 Points for 276 Points against 226

Date	Opponent	Location	Score	Tries	Con	PG	DG	Referee
September 11	Canterbury (P)	Albany	29–43	McGarvey-Black, Fifita	Gatland (2)	Gatland (5)		P.M. Williams
September 19	Waikato (P)	Hamilton	19–41	Tolai, Pierce, Gjaltema	Gatland (2)			M.I. Fraser
September 26	Southland (cr)	Invercargill	10–11	Sail	Gatland	Gatland		J.D. Munro
October 04	Tasman (P)	Albany	40–24	Page, Tolai, Little, McElroy	Gatland (4)	Gatland (4)		N.P. Briant
October 10	Hawke's Bay (cr)	Albany	46–10	Page (3), Taramai, Gatland, Aoake, Hunt	Gatland (4)	Gatland		A.W.B. Mabey
October 17	Wellington (P)	Wellington	20–25	Gatland, Page, Aoake	Gatland	Gatland		J.J. Doleman
October 24	Auckland (P)	Albany	23–22	Little, Tolai	Gatland (2)	Gatland (3)		R.P. Kelly
October 31	Northland (cr)	Whangarei	24–8	Tolai, Gatland, F. Inisi	Gatland (3)	Gatland		C.J. Stone
November 07	Counties Manukau (cr)	Albany	32–5	Page, Tolai, McElroy, Aoake	Gatland (3)	Gatland (2)		C.J. Stone
November 15	Bay of Plenty (P)	Tauranga	33–37	Tolai (2), Turner, Aoake, penalty try	Gatland (3)			R.P. Kelly

NORTH OTAGO

2020 Status: Heartland Championship
Founded 1904 as sub union affilated to Otago RU.
Became a full union in 1927 with affiliation to NZRU.
President: D.J.L. (David) Douglas
Chairman: W.L. (Warren) Prescott
Chief executive officer: C.S. (Colin) Jackson
Coach: J.A. (Jason) Forrest
Assistant coach: S.M. (Shane) Carter
Main ground: Whitestone Contracting Stadium
Capacity: 7000
Colours: Gold

RECORDS

Highest attendance	6500	North Otago v Marlborough (Div 3 final), 1997
Most appearances	123	M.J. Mavor, 1995–2009
Most points	431	P.M. Ford, 1964–74
Most tries	39	V.T. Fifita, 2000–04
Most points in a season	159	S.M. Porter, 2002
Most tries in a season	15	V.T. Fifita, 2002
Most conversions in a season	42	M. Adair, 2005
Most penalty goals in a season	30	C.J.W. Finch, 1997
		S.M. Porter, 2000
Most dropped goals in a season	4	M.E. Kenworthy, 1986
Most points in a match	28	C.J.W. Finch v Poverty Bay, 1998
		S.M. Porter v Poverty Bay, 2000
Most tries in a match	5	L.M. Herden v East Coast, 2010
Most conversions in a match	9	B. Patston v East Coast, 2010
Most penalty goals in a match	7	C.J.W. Finch v South Canterbury, 1998
Highest team score	116	v East Coast, 2010
Record victory (points ahead)	113	116–3 v East Coast, 2010
Highest score conceded	139	v Auckland, 1993
Record defeat (points behind)	134	5–139 v Auckland, 1993

North Otago used the large number of 41 players for their five matches played, only six of whom appeared in all five matches. Injury was a factor in this but prominent players of last year's Heartland Championship winning side – Lemi Masoe, Michael Williams, Robert Smith, Charles Elton, Ralph Darling, William Kirkwood and Taina Tamou - were only available for the Ranfurly Shield fixture, although Masoe did eventually turn out in the final fixture of the year.

Although all five matches were lost, the return fixture against Mid Canterbury was something of a turning point in the side's play and the more experienced South Canterbury team was run close in the final match.

The experienced Junior Fakatoufifita, Marcus Balchin, Sam Sturgess, Felepi Funaki and Josh Hayward were to the fore in the forward exchanges while young locks Blake Welsh and Oliver Kinzett, along with loose forward Toni Taufa developed well at this level.

In the backline Englishman Josh Phipps, Jacob Day and Tyler Burgess gave a good account of themselves and Samuel Tatupu was a reliable presence at second five-eighth.

Of the 16 debutants Mataitini Feke had played for Tonga Under 20.

NORTH OTAGO REPRESENTATIVES 2020

	Club	Games for Union	Points for Union
Samuela Babiau	Excelsior	2	0
Marcus Balchin	Maheno	15	5
Tyler Burgess	Kurow	10	14
Josh Clark	Maheno	42	5
Tarn Crow	Excelsior	2	0
Ralph Darling	Old Boys	110	101
Jacob Day	Maheno	3	0
Charles Elton	Harbour [2]	11	10
Junior Fakatoufifita	Valley	21	35
Mataitini Feke	Old Boys	1	0
Kelepi Funaki	Old Boys	23	0
Jake Greenslade	Valley	25	15
Josh Hayward	Maheno	12	15
Sione Kavatoe	Old Boys	2	5
Jack Kelly	Kurow	14	10
Oliver Kinzett	Athletic Marist	3	0
William Kirkwood	Green Island [2]	12	0
Melikisua Kolinisau	Valley	45	15
Epineri Logavatu	Athletic Marist	2	0
Lemi Masoe	Old Boys	106	136
Jake Matthews	Valley	4	0
Ben McCarthy [1]	Alhambra Union [2]	1	0
Kayne Middleton	Excelsior	7	0
Antonio Misiloi	Excelsior	5	5
Ben Paton	Valley	3	0
Josh Phipps	Excelsior	4	13
Robert Richardson	Kurow	9	0
Cameron Rowland	Valley	5	0
Tayne Russell	Excelsior	2	0
Robbie Smith	Maheno	51	155
Taine Stirling	Valley	1	0
Sam Sturgess	Valley	35	35
Taina Tamou	Excelsior	19	15
Samuel Tatupu	Maheno	14	10
Toni Taufa	Old Boys	5	0
Bailey Templeton	Kurow	2	0
Kurt Thomas	Kurow	1	0
Mathew Vocea	Valley	38	71
Blake Welsh	Valley	3	0
Jared Whitburn	Athletic Marist	29	11
Michael Williams	Mt Maunganui Sports [3]	8	5

1 Player of Origin 2 Otago RU 3 Bay of Plenty RU

INDIVIDUAL SCORING

	Tries	Con	PG	DG	Points
Josh Hayward	3	-	-	-	15
Josh Phipps	-	5	1	-	13
Jack Kelly	2	-	-	-	10
Tyler Burgess	-	3	1	-	9
Sione Kavatoe	1	-	-	-	5
Antonio Misiloi	1	-	-	-	5
Junior Fakatoufifita	1	-	-	-	5
Sam Tatupu	1	-	-	-	5
Totals	**9**	**8**	**2**	**0**	**67**
Opposition scored	28	18	7	0	197

NORTH OTAGO 2020

	Canterbury	South Canterbury	Mid Canterbury	Mid Canterbury	South Canterbury	Totals
J.W.H. Phipps	15	15	15	15	–	4
S. Kavatoe	14	14	–	–	–	2
M. Vocea	11	11	13	13	13	5
T. Tamou	s	–	–	–	–	1
A.P. Misiloi	s	13	14	14	–	4
J.R. Day	–	–	s	11	11	3
T.G. Russell	–	–	–	s	14	2
L. Masoe	13	–	–	–	15	2
S.T. Tatupu	12	12	12	12	12	5
B.R. Paton	–	s	s	s	–	3
M.D. Williams	10	–	–	–	–	1
K. Middleton	–	10	–	–	–	1
J.R. Matthews	–	s	10	10	9	4
T.M. Stirling	–	–	–	–	s	1
R.L. Smith	9	–	–	–	–	1
B.J. McCarthy	s	–	–	–	–	1
M. Feke	–	9	–	–	–	1
T.C. Crow	–	–	9	9	–	2
T.P. Burgess	–	–	s	s	10	3
J. Fakatoufifita	8	8	8	–	8	4
M.S. Balchin	7	7	7	7	7	5
C.J. Rowland	6	6	6	8	s	5
W.O. Kirkwood	s	–	–	–	–	1
T.O. Taufa	–	s	11	6	6	4
J.A. Clark	5	5	–	–	–	2
C.H. Elton	4	–	–	–	–	1
J.L.R. Hayward	s	s	5	s	4	5
E. Logavatu	–	4	4	–	–	2
J.P. Whitburn	–	s	–	–	–	1
O. Kinzett	–	–	s	4	5	3
B.J. Welsh	–	–	s	5	s	3
K.K. Funaki	3	3	1	1	3	5
R.K. Darling	1	–	–	–	–	1
R. Richardson	s	1	–	s	1	4
S.T. Babiau	–	s	3	–	–	2
B.C. Templeton	–	–	s	–	–	1
M. Kolinisau	–	–	–	3	s	2
S.W. Sturgess (capt)	2	–	–	2	2	3
J.S. Greenslade	s	–	2	s	–	3
J.W. Kelly	s	2	s	s	s	5
K.M. Thomas	–	s	–	–	–	1

C.J. Rowland captained in Sturgess's absence.

NORTH OTAGO TEAM RECORD, 2020

Played 5 Won 0 Lost 5 Points for 67 Points against 197

Date	Opponent	Location	Score	Tries	Con	PG	DG	Referee
August 28	Canterbury (RS)	Christchurch	7–71	Hayward	Phipps			D. Waenga
September 12	South Canterbury (HS)	Oamaru	7–24	Kavatoe	Phipps			C. Kingan
September 19	Mid Canterbury	Hinds	7–30	Misiloi	Phipps			K. Faalogo
September 26	Mid Canterbury	Oamaru	17–35	Hayward, Kelly	Phipps (2)	Phipps		D. Winter
October 3	South Canterbury (HS)	Timaru	29–37	Hayward, Fakatoufifita, Tatapu, Kelly	Burgess (3)	Burgess		C. Paul

NORTHLAND

2020 Status: Mitre 10 Cup Championship
Founded 1920 as North Auckland. Affiliated 1920.
Name changed to Northland 1994
President: S.L. (Sharon) Morgan
Chairman: A.C. (Ajit) Balasingham
Chief executive officer: C.J. (Cameron) Bell
Coach: G.N. (George) Konia
Assistant coaches: C.D. (Cam) Goodhue,
G.C. (Graham) Dewes, T.E. (Tui) Raeli
Main ground: Semenoff Stadium, Whangarei
Capacity: 24,000
Colours: Cambridge blue

RECORDS

Most appearances	165	*Joe Morgan, 1967–81*
Most points	1656	*Warren Johnston, 1986–97*
Most tries	71	*Norman Berryman, 1991–2003*
Most points in a season	283	*David Holwell, 1997*
Most tries in a season	21	*Norman Berryman, 1994*
Most conversions in a season	85	*David Holwell, 1997*
Most penalty goals in a season	34	*Warren Johnston, 1989*
Most dropped goals in a season	10	*Eddie Dunn, 1979*
Most points in a match	38	*David Holwell v Thames Valley, 1997*
Most tries in a match	7	*Norman Berryman v Wairarapa Bush, 1994*
Most conversions in a match	14	*David Holwell v Thames Valley, 1997*
Most penalty goals in a match	6	*Chippie Semenoff v Thames Valley, 1978*
		Warren Johnston v Wairarapa Bush, 1993
		Warren Johnston v France, 1994
		Warren Johnston v Wairarapa Bush, 1995
		Ash Moeke v North Harbour, 2012
		Dan Hawkins v North Harbour, 2014
		Peter Breen v Otago, 2017
Highest team score	113	*v Thames Valley, 1997*
Record victory (points ahead)	99	*113–14 v Thames Valley, 1997*
Highest score conceded	84	*v Otago, 1998*
Record defeat (points behind)	74	*10–84 v Otago, 1998*

Northland made huge strides in 2020, winning four more games than in 2019 and deservedly contesting the Mitre 10 Cup Championship final.

One of those wins was in a crossover fixture against Waikato — the first NPC match staged outside Whangarei. The venue was Lindvart Park in Kaikohe and the Taniwha, with the sun on their backs, gave one of their best displays of the season in upsetting the Mooloos 28–17, even after they had confirmation of a semi-final berth.

With an ounce of self-belief, and luck, they could have scalped another Premiership team, Auckland, at Eden Park, but it was not to be in a bizarre encounter.

Northland started its campaign in fine fettle, racking up four victories from its opening five matches. Tasman in Blenheim offered a reality check, but there was much to like about the way the Taniwha went about their work. They had a stiffer defence, a sound lineout, a solid scrum, an in-form halfback in Sam Nock, and the priceless experience of Rene Ranger, back from injury, at centre.

They did hold a four-game losing streak heading into the Waikato clash, but they righted the ship when it mattered, and then put four tries on Otago under the Forsyth Barr roof in the semifinal. Injuries to Tom Robinson and Nock did not help matters in the final, where the Magpies were too good. But there was a 'never say die' quality to the pack which endeared the Taniwha to rugby fans around the country.

And yet the outlook was not that promising in August. While George Konia led a new coaching staff, Northland appeared to lack depth and it seemed it would battle to make the playoffs. But there were useful signings in props Kalolo Tuiloma (Counties Manukau) and Luatangi Li (North Harbour), while the return of Jack Goodhue (briefly). Johnny Cooper, Jone Macilai and Matt Wright were most welcome.

Key losses were Jack Debreczeni (Japan), Matt Johnson (retired) and Isi Tu'ungafasi (Tasman).

Fullback Matt Wright raised the half-century of matches, one of six Taniwha to do so, and acquitted himself well, even without scoring a try. He was more reliable than Scott Gregory, who continues to confound and delight in equal measure with his mercurial rugby.

Wing Jordan Hyland's campaign was stymied by injury, while Brady Rush, son of All Black Eric, looked a useful prospect on the wing. His immediate future, however, looks to be in sevens.

Tamati Tua had injury issues but combined well with Ranger in midfield. The latter, though prone to errors, can still bust the line, is powerful over the ball, and set up several tries.

Dan Hawkins was the most reliable of the No 10s used, though Cooper displayed a good skillset and accuracy off the tee. His finest hour was against Waikato.

Nock really took command and dominated as one of the best halfbacks in the competition, adding five tries. His absence in the final was a hammer blow.

Sam McNamara did a fine job off the back of the scrum, while he had sterling support in the loose from Kara Pryor and Tom Robinson, both of whom could win the ball aerially or in the collisions. Injury ruled out the promising Saimoni Uluinakauvadra for most of the season.

His compatriot Temo Mayanavanua was solid at lock until called up for Fiji's ill-fated northern tour.

Sam Caird and Josh Goodhue ended up as one of the most effective second-row pairs in the Mitre 10 Cup, the former winning a contract with the NSW Waratahs. Goodhue came up with some big plays at key moments through the season.

In the front-row, Northland was rarely dominated, Li and Coree Te Whata-Colley to the fore. It was pleasing to see the popular Ross Wright hoist his century of games in Cambridge blue.

Hooker Jordan Olsen led by example, latching onto several lineout drives for tries and giving his all around the field.

Higher honours went to:
New Zealand: Jack Goodhue
New Zealand Sevens: S. Gregory
New Zealand Maori: R. Wright

NORTHLAND REPRESENTATIVES 2020

	Club	Games for Union	Points for Union		Club	Games for Union	Points for Union
Paddy-Jo Atkins	Wellsford	22	5	Matt Matich	Western Sharks	44	40
Sam Caird	Old Boys-Marist	21	5	Temo Mayanavanua	Waipu	20	20
Johnny Cooper	Mid Northern	9	28	Sam McNamara	Waipu	25	5
Wiseguy Faiane	Waipu	7	22	Sam Nock	Kerikeri	57	67
Setefano Funaki	Waipu	8	0	Jordan Olsen	Mid Northern	55	30
Kalani Going	Mid Northern	3	0	Kara Pryor	Hora Hora	57	40
Jack Goodhue	Moerewa/United Kawakawa	10	15	Rene Ranger	Wellsford	98	155
Josh Goodhue	Moerewa/United Kawakawa	46	25	Tom Robinson	Kerikeri	23	15
Will Grant	Hora Hora	11	5	Brady Rush	Mid Northern	3	0
Scott Gregory	Hikurangi	32	40	Rob Rush	Mid Northern	5	0
Dan Hawkins	Old Boys-Marist	58	375	Aorangi Stokes	Old Boys-Marist	18	30
Blake Hohaia	Kamo	30	15	Corey Taylor	Kerikeri	2	0
Mason Hohaia	Kamo	1	0	Coree Te Whata-Colley	Western Sharks	22	10
Jordan Hyland	Wellsford	52	65	Ben Tou	Waipu	2	0
Kane Jacobson	Kamo	10	0	Tamati Tua	Hikurangi	34	20
Tyler Kearns	Awanui	7	0	Kalolo Tuiloma	Mid Northern	9	0
Pisi Leilua	Waipu	17	10	Simoni Uluinakauvadra	Waipu	2	0
Harrison Levien	Old Boys-Marist	8	10	Matt Wright	Wellsford	55	96
Luatangi Li	Waipu	11	20	Ross Wright	Wellsford	107	35
Jone Macilai	Awanui	44	75				

INDIVIDUAL SCORING

	Tries	Con	PG	DG	Points		Tries	Con	PG	DG	Points
Hawkins	–	11	8	–	46	Josh Goodhue	1	–	–	–	5
Cooper	–	8	4	–	28	Grant	1	–	–	–	5
Nock	5	–	–	–	25	Leilua	1	–	–	–	5
Olsen	5	–	–	–	25	Levien	1	–	–	–	5
Li	4	–	–	–	20	Matich	1	–	–	–	5
Pryor	4	–	–	–	20	McNamara	1	–	–	–	5
Faiane	–	9	–	–	18	Robinson	1	–	–	–	5
Gregory	3	–	–	–	15	Tua	1	–	–	–	5
Macilai	3	–	–	–	15						
Mayanavanua	2	–	–	–	10	**Totals**	**37**	**28**	**12**	**0**	**277**
Ranger	2	–	–	–	10						
Caird	1	–	–	–	5	Opposition scored	42	31	15	0	317

NORTHLAND 2020

	Manawatu	Tasman	Counties Manukau	Taranaki	Southland	Hawke's Bay	Otago	North Harbour	Auckland	Waikato	Otago (SF)	Hawke's Bay (F)	Totals
S.J. Gregory	15	15	s	11	15	15	15	13	s	s	s	s	12
M.K. Wright	–	–	15	15	–	–	–	15	15	15	15	15	7
J.C. Cooper	–	s	–	s	–	s	s	10	10	s	10	s	9
J.S.C. Hyland	11	14	14	–	–	–	–	–	–	14	14	14	6
J. Macilai	–	–	–	s	14	14	14	–	11	11	11	11	8
B.J.K. Rush	–	–	–	–	–	–	s	14	14	–	–	–	3
P. Leilua	14	11	11	14	11	11	11	11	–	–	–	–	8
K.T. Going	–	–	–	–	s	s	12	–	–	–	–	–	3
T.R. Tua	s	12	12	–	–	–	–	12	12	12	12	12	8
R.M.N. Ranger	13	13	13	13	13	13	13	s	13	13	13	13	12
E.J. Goodhue	12	–	–	–	–	–	–	–	–	–	–	–	1
B.M. Hohaia	–	s	12	12	12	12	–	–	–	–	–	–	5
W.S. Faiane	s	10	s	–	–	–	–	–	s	–	s	–	5
D.C. Hawkins	10	–	10	10	10	10	10	s	–	10	–	10	9
S.J. Nock	9	9	9	9	9	9	s	9	9	9	9	–	11
W.A. Grant	–	–	–	s	–	s	9	s	s	s	s	9	8
C.L. Taylor	–	–	–	–	–	–	–	–	–	–	–	s	1
H.C. Levien	s	s	–	–	–	–	–	–	–	–	–	–	2
K.A. Pryor	7	7	7	7	7	7	7	7	–	7	7	7	11
A.T.H. Stokes	–	–	–	–	–	–	–	–	s	–	–	–	1
M.E.S. Matich	s	s	–	–	8	8	8	8	–	s	s	s	9
K.P. Jacobson	–	–	–	–	–	–	–	–	7	s	s	s	4
S.J. McNamara	8	8	8	8	–	–	–	s	8	8	8	8	9
T.N. Robinson	6	6	6	6	6	6	6	6	–	6	6	6	11
R.H.T. Rush	–	–	–	s	–	s	s	s	6	–	–	–	5
S. Uluinakauvadra	–	–	s	–	–	–	–	–	–	–	–	–	1
S.W. Caird	5	5	s	s	4	5	s	5	5	5	5	5	12
T.S. Mayanavanua	s	s	5	5	5	s	5	–	–	–	–	–	7
S. Funaki	–	–	–	–	s	–	–	–	s	–	–	–	2
J.K. Goodhue	4	4	4	4	–	4	4	4	4	4	4	4	11
T.J. Kearns	3	3	–	–	–	–	s	s	s	s	–	s	7
C.J.W. Te Whata-Colley	s	s	3	3	3	s	s	3	s	3	3	3	12
K.E. Tuiloma	–	–	s	s	s	3	3	–	3	s	s	s	9
B.M.U. Tou	–	s	–	–	–	–	–	2	–	–	–	–	2
L. Li	1	1	1	s	s	s	–	s	1	1	1	1	11
R.G. Wright	s	–	s	1	1	1	1	1	–	s	s	s	10
P-J. Atkins	–	s	s	s	–	s	s	–	–	–	s	–	6
J.D. Olsen (capt)	2	2	2	2	2	2	2	s	2	2	2	2	12
M.J. Hohaia	–	–	–	–	–	–	–	–	s	–	–	–	1

NORTHLAND TEAM RECORD 2020

Played 12　Won 6　Lost 6　Points for 277　Points against 317

Date	Opponent	Location	Score	Tries	Con	PG	DG	Referee
September 13	Manawatu (C)	Whangarei	43–26	Caird, Nock, Pryor, McNamara, Olsen, Ranger	Faiane (4), Hawkins	Hawkins		B.E. Pickerill
September 18	Tasman (cr)	Blenheim	21–54	Pryor (2), Levien	Faiane (3)			P.M. Williams
September 27	Counties Manukau (C)	Pukekohe	24–15	Mayanavanua, Olsen, Leilua	Hawkins (3)	Hawkins		B.D. O'Keeffe
October 03	Taranaki (C)	Whangarei	35–25	Gregory, Josh Goodhue, Macilai, Pryor	Hawkins (3)	Hawkins (3)		A.W.B. Mabey
October 11	Southland (C)	Whangarei	18–14	Mayanavanua, Nock	Hawkins	Hawkins (2)		R.P. Kelly
October 16	Hawke's Bay (C) (RS)	Napier	17–33	Li (2)	Hawkins, Cooper	Hawkins		B.E. Pickerill
October 23	Otago (C)	Dunedin	7–30	Ranger	Hawkins			M.I. Fraser
October 31	North Harbour (cr)	Whangarei	8–24	Gregory		Cooper		C.J. Stone
November 07	Auckland (cr)	Auckland	20–24	Macilai, Nock, Olsen	M. Wright	Cooper		N.P. Briant
November 14	Waikato (cr)	Kaikohe	28–17	Nock, Li, Olsen, Gregory	Cooper (4)			M.I. Fraser
November 21	Otago (C, sf)	Dunedin	32–19	Macilai, Nock, Olsen, Matich	Faiane (2), Cooper	Cooper (2)		M.I. Fraser
November 27	Hawke's Bay (C, f)	Napier	24–36	Li, Grant, Robinson, Tua	Hawkins, Cooper			J.J. Doleman

OTAGO

2020 Status: Mitre 10 Cup Championship
Founded 1881. Affiliated 1895
President: R.D. (Roy) Daniels
Chairman: R.K. (Rowena) Davenport
General manager: R.P. (Richard) Kinley
Coach: T.J.S. (Tom) Donnelly
Assistant coaches: L.W. (Lee) Allan, R.H. (Ryan) Martin
Main ground: Forsyth Barr Stadium, Dunedin
Capacity: 28,000
Colours: Dark blue

RECORDS

Most appearances	170	*Richard Knight, 1981–92*
Most points	1520	*Greg Cooper, 1984–96*
Most tries	73	*Paul Cooke, 1990–96*
Most points in a season	279	*Greg Cooper, 1991*
Most tries in a season	16	*John Timu, 1988*
		John Timu, 1990
		Paul Cooke, 1995
		Brendan Laney, 1998
Most conversions in a season	50	*Greg Cooper, 1989*
Most penalty goals in a season	54	*Greg Cooper, 1989*
Most dropped goals in a season	9	*Lee Smith, 1986*
Most points in a match	39	*Paul Turner v East Coast, 1986*
Most tries in a match	5	*George Owles v South Canterbury, 1920*
		Bill Meates v South Canterbury, 1948
		Bruce Hunter v Marlborough, 1969
		Graham Sims v West Coast, 1972
Most conversions in a match	14	*Paul Turner v East Coast, 1986*
Most penalty goals in a match	7	*Greg Cooper v NZ Combined Services, 1989*
		Greg Cooper v Canterbury, 1991
		Blair Feeney v Wellington, 2002
Highest team score	91	*v East Coast, 1986*
Record victory (points ahead)	85	*88–3 v North Otago, 1983*
Highest score conceded	68	*v Wellington, 2007*
Record defeat (points behind)	61	*7–68 v Wellington, 2007*

The season ended in disappointment for Otago. After their deserved first win since 2005 against Premiership side Canterbury, Otago was top of the Championship table with two round robin matches left. That, unfortunately, was to be as good as it got.

A poor performance against Southland ended in a 15–32 loss followed by a spirited narrow loss to Tasman meant second place and a home semi-final against Northland, whom they had defeated 30–7 in the round robin. But the semi-final was another poor performance and Otago lost 19–32.

In the first half of the season, Otago had recorded excellent victories over Taranaki, to win the Ranfurly Shield, and Premiership team Wellington, where Otago came from 11 points down to win. In between, the Ranfurly Shield was lost to Hawke's Bay after Otago dominated the first half everywhere except the scoreboard. Oddly, Otago had a much better record away (4/5) than they did at home (2/6).

Otago was not short of talent in the backline, all players having good individual moments. Captain Michael Collins was shifted around the backline regularly to fill holes, but nevertheless he still put in consistent displays. NZ Sevens rep Vilimoni Koroi alternated between wing and fullback, and had an excellent game against Taranaki, but his form seemed to fall away in the latter stages of the competition. Freedom Vahaakolo had a very good debut season on the wing and was top try-scorer with seven, including an excellent try against Southland.

Wing Jona Nareki was the outstanding back. His scoring of just one try all season was nowhere near the reward he deserved. He invariably would beat the first tackle and could always find a gap with his foot work and speed, and gave a try to Kayne Hammington between the posts against Tasman when Nareki would have easily scored it himself with no Tasman defender in sight.

Otago missed the services of their most experienced midfielder Patelesio Tomkinson for six weeks due to suspension for a poor tackle that earned a red card in the opening match. First five-eighth Josh Ioane did not always produce the form expected of him but his halfback Kayne Hammington was a reliable performer throughout the season — he had a very good game against Canterbury.

There was nothing wrong with the forwards' efforts in the set pieces. The front row of George Bower, Liam Coltman and Josh Hohneck was one of the best at scrum time. Bower played only half the season before being called into the All Blacks as injury cover, although he never took the field for the national team, and Liam Coltman did not appear after the Canterbury match due to injury. Former All Black Jamie Mackintosh was an able replacement for Bower.

The lineout was, statistically, the second best in the Mitre 10 Cup with Josh Dickson again superb, with good contributions from Will Tucker, Irishman Jack Regan and blindside flanker Charles Elton. Dickson battled injury all year. Otago had a number of proven loose forwards in Dylan Nel, Slade McDowall, Sione Misiloi and Tavake 'Nasi' Manu, but were not always effective collectively.

Regular players who did not appear from the 2019 team were Aki Seiuli, Joe Latta, Louis Conradie, Sekonaia Pole, Joketani Koroi (all overseas), Connor McLeod (Hawke's Bay), while James Lentjes and Kurt Hammer were injured.

New signings with previous first-class experience were All Black Jamie Mackintosh (Southland) and Tavake 'Nasi' Manu (Canterbury), both having returned from overseas while Josh Hohneck also arrived back having last represented the union in 2016. Thomas Umaga-Jensen (Wellington) was another signing but injury kept him out until the final match. Charles Elton represented North Otago last year on loan while Ireland Under 20 rep Jack Regan had made an appearance for Ulster in the Guinness Pro 14. Injuries during the season saw Jono Hickey (Auckland) and Sef Fa'agase (Canterbury and Wellington) brought into the team.

Higher honours went to:
New Zealand Maori: J. Hohneck
New Zealand Sevens: V. Koroi

OTAGO REPRESENTATIVES 2020

	Club	Games for Union	Points for Union		Club	Games for Union	Points for Union
Jonah Aoina	Kaikorai	27	15	Giovanni Leituala	University	1	0
James Arscott	Green Island	8	0	Jamie Mackintosh	Kaikorai	7	0
Henry Bell	University	3	0	Tavake "Nasi" Manu	[2]	8	0
George Bower	Harbour	26	0	Slade McDowall	Kaikorai	35	30
Harrison Boyle	Dunedin	2	0	Sione Misiloi	Harbour	29	0
Michael Collins	Taieri	71	85	Aleki Morris-Lome	Harbour	19	35
Liam Coltman	Alhambra Union	76	30	Jona Nareki	Alhambra Union	40	125
Josh Dickson	University	58	35	Dylan Nel	Green Island	31	25
Charles Elton	Harbour	10	5	Jack Regan	Dunedin	11	5
Sef Fa'agase	Kaikorai	2	0	Yoshihisa "Hisa" Sasagi	Southern	67	0
Samuel Fischli	Taieri	2	0	Mitchell Scott	Taieri	30	50
Kayne Hammington	Zingari Richmond	18	5	Josh Timu	University	18	20
Jono Hickey	Grammar TEC [1]	4	10	Patelesio "Sio" Tomkinson	Harbour	52	84
Josh Hill	University	13	0	Will Tucker	Christchurch [3]	11	0
Josh Hohneck	Eastern	15	5	Thomas Umaga-Jensen	Otago RU	1	0
Josh Ioane	Southern	39	318	Freedom Vahaakalo	Dunedin	10	35
Ricky Jackson	University	16	5	Matt Whaanga	Taieri	17	5
Vilimoni Koroi	Alhambra Union	43	123	Sean Withy	University	4	5

1 Auckland RU   2 Arrived from overseas   3 Canterbury RU

INDIVIDUAL SCORING

	Tries	Con	PG	DG	Points		Tries	Con	PG	DG	Points
Josh Ioane	1	19	15	–	88	Jack Regan	1	–	–	–	5
Freedom Vahaakolo	7	–	–	–	35	Charles Elton	1	–	–	–	5
Vilimoni Koroi	5	–	–	–	25	Josh Hohneck	1	–	–	–	5
Liam Coltman	3	–	–	–	15	Ricky Jackson	1	–	–	–	5
Josh Timu	3	–	–	–	15	Slade McDowall	1	–	–	–	5
Patelesio Tomkinson	3	–	–	–	15	Kayne Hammington	1	–	–	–	5
Josh Dickson	2	–	–	–	10	Jona Nareki	1	–	–	–	5
Jono Hickey	–	2	2	–	10						
Michael Collins	1	–	–	–	5	**Totals**	**34**	**21**	**17**	**0**	**263**
Dylan Nel	1	–	–	–	5						
Sean Withy	1	–	–	–	5	Opposition scored	35*	27	15	1	279

* includes one penalty try (7 points)

OTAGO 2020

	Auckland	Manawatu	Taranaki	Hawke's Bay	Wellington	Counties Manukau	Northland	Canterbury	Southland	Tasman	Northland (sf)	Totals
M.W.V. Collins (capt)	15	13	13	13	15	12	15	s	15	12	15	11
H.J. Boyle	–	–	–	–	–	–	s	–	–	–	–	1
V.T. Koroi	14	15	15	15	14	15	–	15	11	15	14	10
J.M. Nareki	11	11	11	11	11	11	11	11	–	11	11	10
F.K. Vahaakolo	s	14	14	14	s	14	14	14	14	14	–	10
M.J. Scott	–	–	s	s	–	–	–	–	–	–	–	2
J.C. Timu	13	s	–	s	13	13	13	13	13	s	13	10
G.T. Leituala	–	–	–	–	–	–	s	–	–	–	–	1
A.M. Morris-Lome	12	12	12	12	12	–	–	–	s	–	–	6
P.F. Tomkinson	s	–	–	–	–	–	–	12	12	13	12	5
M.A. Whaanga	–	–	–	–	–	s	12	–	s	–	–	3
T.N.M. Umaga-Jensen	–	–	–	–	–	–	–	–	–	–	s	1
J.R. Ioane	10	10	10	10	10	10	–	10	10	10	10	10
K.W. Hammington	9	9	9	9	9	9	9	9	–	9	9	10
J.M. Arscott	s	s	–	s	–	–	s	s	s	s	–	7
J.D. Hickey	–	–	–	–	s	s	10	–	9	–	–	4
D.M. Nel	8	8	8	8	7	7	7	–	8	s	8	10
T.L.L. Manu	s	s	s	–	–	s	s	8	–	8	s	8
S.F. Misiloi	–	–	–	s	8	8	8	s	s	–	–	6
S.R. McDowall	7	7	7	7	–	–	–	7	7	7	7	8
C.H. Elton	6	6	6	6	6	6	6	s	6	6	–	10
S.M. Withy	–	s	–	–	s	s	–	–	–	s	–	4
S.H. Fischli	–	–	–	–	–	–	–	6	–	–	6	2
W.A. Tucker	5	5	5	5	s	s	s	4	5	5	s	11
J.A. Hill	4	s	s	s	–	–	–	–	s	s	–	6
J.A. Regan	s	4	4	4	4	4	4	s	4	4	4	11
J.M. Dickson	–	–	–	–	5	5	5	5	–	–	5	5
J.W. Hohneck	3	3	3	3	3	3	3	3	3	3	3	11
J.T. Aoina	1	s	–	s	–	–	s	s	s	–	–	6
G.G. Bower	s	1	1	1	s	1	–	–	–	–	–	6
Y. Sasagi	s	s	s	s	s	s	s	s	s	s	s	11
J.L. Mackintosh	–	–	–	–	1	s	1	1	1	1	1	7
S.F. Fa'agase	–	–	–	–	–	–	–	–	–	s	s	2
L.J. Coltman	2	2	2	s	2	2	2	2	–	–	–	8
R.D. Jackson	s	s	s	2	s	s	s	s	2	2	2	11
H.D.E. Bell	–	–	–	–	–	–	–	–	s	s	s	3

L.J. Coltman captained v Canterbury

OTAGO TEAM RECORD, 2020

Played 11 Won 6 Lost 5 Points for 263 Points against 279

Date	Opponent	Location	Score	Tries	Con	PG	DG	Referee
September 12	Auckland (cr)	Dunedin	6–38			Ioane (2)		J. Munro
September 20	Manawatu (C)	Palmerston North	36–25	Koroi (2), Coltman, Vahaakolo, Collins	Ioane (4)	Ioane		R. Kelly
September 27	Taranaki (C) (RS)	Inglewood	30–19	Nel, Vahaakolo, Coltman, Ioane	Ioane (2)	Ioane (2)		M. Fraser
October 4	Hawke's Bay (C) (RS)	Dunedin	9–28			Ioane (3)		C. Stone
October 10	Wellington (cr)	Wellington	35–34	Koroi (2), Coltman, Withy, Regan	Ioane (2)	Ioane (2)		A. Gardiner (Australia)
October 18	Counties Manukau (C)	Dunedin	40–22	Timu (2), Dickson (2), Vahaakolo, Elton	Ioane (5)			A. Mabey
October 23	Northland (C)	Dunedin	30–7	Vahaakolo (2), Hohneck, Jackson	Hickey (2)	Hickey (2)		M. Fraser
October 30	Canterbury (cr)	Christchurch	23–16	Tomkinson, Koroi, McDowall	Ioane	Ioane (2)		B. Pickerill
November 6	Southland (C)	Invercargill	15–37	Vahaakolo, Tomkinson	Ioane	Ioane		B. Pickerill
November 14	Tasman (cr)	Dunedin	20–26	Vahaakolo, Hammington	Ioane (2)	Ioane (2)		J. Munro
November 20	Northland (C sf)	Dunedin	19–32	Nareki, Timu, Tomkinson	Ioane (2)			M. Fraser

POVERTY BAY

2020 Status: Heartland Championship
Founded 1890. Affiliated 1893
President: T.J. (Tony) Coutts
Chairman: H.M. (Hayden) Swann
Chief executive officer: J.I. (Josh) Willoughby
Coach: T.J. (Tom) Cairns
Assistant coach: M.N. (Miah) Nikora
Main ground: Rugby Park, Gisborne
Capacity: 18,000
Colour: Scarlet

RECORDS

Highest attendance	15,000	*Poverty Bay-East Coast v British Isles, 1971*
Most appearances	150	*S.T. Ngatu, 2003–2018*
Most points	791	*S.C. Leighton, 2004–12*
Most tries	35	*P.S.R. Ransley, 1961–71*
Most points in a season	144	*S.C. Leighton, 2007*
Most tries in a season	11	*J. Moeke, 1997;*
		J. Stewart, 2010
		J. Stewart, 2011
Most conversions in a season	30	*S.C. Leighton, 2007*
Most penalty goals in a season	27	*D.M. Boyle, 1999*
Most dropped goals in a season	3	*G.B. Ross, 1976; J. Whittle, 1979*
Most points in a match	35	*S.C. Leighton v Thames Valley, 2007*
Most tries in a match	4	*J.L. Penny v Olympians Club, 1953*
		K.A. Twigley v East Coast, 1966
		I.A. Kirkpatrick v East Coast, 1971
		K.D. Ferris v East Coast, 1983
		A.B. Hansen v North Otago, 1987
Most conversions in a match	9	*R.P. Owen v East Coast, 1983*
Most penalty goals in a match	7	*S.P. Parkes v Buller, 2013*
Highest team score	75	*v East Coast, 1980*
Record victory (points ahead)	75	*75–0 v East Coast, 1980*
Highest score conceded	121	*v Waikato, 1998*
Record defeat (points behind)	121	*0–121 v Waikato, 1998*

Poverty Bay had two wins over neighbour Ngati Porou East Coast followed by defeats to Wairarapa Bush and Wanganui. The Jekyll and Hyde nature of the side persisted, coming from 19-31 down to defeat Ngati Porou East Coast 34—31 and lost 38—41 to Wanganui after being 12—41 behind.

Coach Tom Cairns experimented with his lineups in the first three games and put out his best selection in the final match against Wanganui. A total of 13 players were given a debut although this included some with previous first-class experience — William Short (Wanganui), Rawiri Broughton (Horowhenua Kapiti/NZ Defence Force), Jayden Milner (Ngati Porou East Coast) and Louis Devery (Buller).

Andrew Tauatevalu was devastating on attack from fullback and the two wings, Matthew Raleigh and Te Peehi Fairlie, were good finishers when given a chance. The midfield was exposed against Wanganui, it being a shame both Louis Devery and Tane McGuire were absent through injury, having combined well in the previous match against Wairarapa Bush. Kelvin Smith shone against Wanganui in his 50th match.

Flanker Adrian Wyrill led the team well and was again the best forward. He was given good support in the loose from Tamanui Hill. Two debutants who made a favourable impression throughout were prop Atonio Walker-Leawere and lock Fletcher Scammell. Another newcomer, reserve prop Jarryd Broughton, a big man, was a very strong scrummager.

The matches against Wairarapa Bush and Wanganui were both held in Napier, at Park Island and McLean Park respectively. The match against Wanganui was shown live on Sky TV, being the curtain raiser to the Hawke's Bay v Manawatu Ranfurly Shield match.

POVERTY BAY REPRESENTATIVES 2020

	Club	Games for Union	Points for Union		Club	Games for Union	Points for Union
Juston Allen	OB Marist	28	15	Matekaeroa McGuire	HSOB	16	5
William Bollingford	Pirates	11	5	Tane McGuire	Waikohu	17	5
Jarryd Broughton	Waikohu	3	0	Scott McKinley	OB Marist	21	10
Rawiri Broughton	Waikohu	3	0	Jayden Milner	YMP	1	0
Campbell Chrisp	Ngatapa	54	5	Toru Noanoa	Waikohu	25	15
Louis Devery	YMP	1	5	Petelo Palusa	Pirates	2	0
Te Peehi Fairlie	YMP	17	55	Matthew Raleigh	Ngatapa	16	40
Peia Fililava	YMP	2	0	Ethine Reeves	Waikohu	53	134
Tamanui Hill	HSOB	41	40	Fletcher Scammell	HSOB	4	0
Tione Hubbard	Waikohu	2	0	William Short	Ngatapa	3	0
Jesse Kapene	YMP	13	10	Shayde Skudder	YMP	17	0
Kesomi "Nico" Lauti	YMP	3	0	Kelvin Smith	Waikohu	50	113
Jacob Leaf	Pirates	12	0	Andrew Tauatevalu	YMP	28	212
Jack Lewis	Ngatapa	2	0	Rikki Terekia	OB Marist	14	30
Paoraian Manuel-Harman	Tapuae [1]	2	0	Atonio Walker-Leawere	Ngatapa	3	0
Sam McDell	Ngatapa	12	0	Adrian Wyrill	Waikohu	11	20

[1] Hawke's Bay RU

INDIVIDUAL SCORING

	Tries	Con	PG	DG	Points
Kelvin Smith	2	10	–	–	30
Andrew Tauatevalu	3	5	1	–	28
Matthew Raleigh	5	–	–	–	25
Te Peehi Fairlie	3	–	–	–	15
Adrian Wyrill	2	–	–	–	10
Penalty Try	1	–	–	–	7
Jesse Kapene	1	–	–	–	5
William Bolingford	1	–	–	–	5
Scott McKinley	1	–	–	–	5
Louis Devery	1	–	–	–	5
Rikki Terekia	1	–	–	–	5
Totals	**21**	**15**	**1**	**0**	**140**
Opposition scored	18	10	8	0	134

POVERTY BAY 2020

	Ngati Porou East Coast	Ngati Porou East Coast	Wairarapa Bush	Wanganui	Totals
A.H. Tauatevalu	15	15	–	15	3
J.P. Milner	–	s	–	–	1
M.W. Raleigh	14	14	s	13	4
T.P.H.H. Fairlie	11	11	–	11	3
J.O. Lewis	–	–	14	14	2
S. McKinley	–	–	11	–	1
T.R. Hubbard	13	13	–	–	2
J.P. Leaf	12	s	–	12	3
E.S. Reeves	s	–	–	–	1
T.T.R. McGuire	–	12	13	–	2
L.J.S. Devery	–	–	12	–	1
K.M. Smith	10	10	15	10	4
P.W.A. Manuel-Harman	–	s	10	–	2
S.P.T. Fililava	–	–	s	s	2
W.J. Short	9	–	s	s	3
R.S.B. Broughton	–	9	9	9	3
T.G. Hill	8	–	8	8	3
A.E. Wyrill (capt)	7	8	6	7	4
J.J. Kapene	6	6	s	–	3
W.C. Bolingford	s	7	–	6	3
K. Lauti	–	s	7	s	3
F.H. Scammell	5	5	4	4	4
P.T. Palusa	4	s	–	–	2
J.N. Allen	s	4	s	5	4
S.L. McDell	–	–	5	s	2
J. Broughton	3	–	s	s	3
C.P.L. Chrisp	1	s	1	1	4
T.M. Noanoa	s	1	–	–	2
A.J. Walker-Leawere	–	3	3	3	3
R.T. Terekia	2	s	s	2	4
S.P. Skudder	s	2	–	–	2
M.W.E. McGuire	–	–	2	s	2

Played 4	Won 2	Lost 2	Points for 140	Points against 134

Date	Opponent	Location	Score	Tries	Con	PG	DG	Referee
September 19	Ngati Porou East Coast	Gisborne	34–31	Raleigh (2), Fairlie, Wyrill, Tauatevalu	Tauatevalu (3)	Tauatevalu		R. Maynard
September 26	Ngati Porou East Coast	Ruatoria	42–16	Raleigh (2), Kapene, Fairlie, Bolingford, Penalty Try	Smith (4), Tauatevalu			N. Briant
October 3	Wairarapa Bush	Napier	26–46	McKinley, Devery, Smith, Raleigh	Smith (3)			S. Eden-Whaitiri
October 10	Wanganui	Napier	38–41	Tauatevalu (2), Terekia, Fairlie, Wyrill, Smith	Smith (3), Tauatevalu			N. Hogan

POVERTY BAY TEAM RECORD, 2020

SOUTH CANTERBURY

2020 Status: Heartland Championship
Founded 1888. Original member 1892
President: N.F. (Neville) Twaddell
Chairman: G.E. (Grant) Norton
Chief Executive Officer: C.W. (Craig) Calder
Coach: N.G. (Nigel) Walsh
Assistant coaches: S.P. (Shaun) Breen, C.S. (Chris) Gard
Main ground: Alpine Energy Stadium, Timaru
Capacity: 17,000
Colours: Emerald green and black

RECORDS

Highest attendance	17,000	*South Canterbury v France, 1961*
Most appearances	152	*S.J. Todd, 1986–2001*
Most points	1060	*B.J. Fairbrother, 1981–92*
Most tries	60	*S.J. Todd 1986–2001*
Most points in a season	175	*B.J. Fairbrother, 1991*
Most tries in a season	13	*J.S. Ellery, 1960*
		C.J. Dorgan, 1992
		B.J. Laney, 1992
Most conversions in a season	31	*B.J. Fairbrother, 1989*
Most penalty goals in a season	31	*B.J. Fairbrother, 1990*
Most dropped goals in a season	8	*B.J. Fairbrother, 1987*
		B.J. Fairbrother, 1991
Most points in a match	32	*G.I. Dempster v Wairarapa Bush, 1996*
Most tries in a match	4	*G.V. Gerard v Southland, 1926*
		E.W. Ryan v Ashburton County, 1935
		E.W. Ryan v Wellington XV, 1937
		J.M. Cole v North Otago, 1958
		E.C. Smith v Nelson, 1961
		B.J. Matthews v North Otago, 1992
		D.J. Hunter v Poverty Bay, 1993
		I.G. Howden v Marlborough, 1996
		S. Kiole v West Coast, 2002
		E. Tau v Poverty Bay, 2015
Most conversions in a match	8	*B.J. Fairbrother v West Coast, 1989*
		B.J. Fairbrother v North Otago, 1991
		B.J. Fairbrother v North Otago, 1992
		C.S. Gard v North Otago, 1993
		B.J. Laney v North Otago, 1994
		G.I. Dempster v Wairarapa Bush, 1996
Most penalty goals in a match	7	*B.J. Fairbrother v East Coast, 1990*
Highest team score	100	*v Ngati Porou East Coast, 2018*
Record victory (points ahead)	93	*100–7 v Ngati Porou East Coast, 2018*
Highest score conceded	103	*v Canterbury, 2001*
Record defeat (points behind)	103	*0–103 v Canterbury, 2001*

South Canterbury had an unbeaten five-match programme with four wins after a draw in the opening match against Mid Canterbury in which South Canterbury conceded a last-minute converted try. In the two matches against North Otago, the Hanan Shield was won in the first game and successfully defended in the return encounter.

In a big forward pack number eight Siu Kakala was the standout, always impressive with ball in hand, making a number of strong runs, while lock Henry Bryce, who had played just two games in 2017, was a most improved player, getting through plenty of work. Tokomaata Fakatava and the Taelaga brothers were a formidable trio of props.

Hard-running centre Pita Siale always made plenty of metres and the fast wing pair of Kalavini Leatigaga and Clarence Moli finished off the chances given to them. Theo Davidson and Willie Wright remain an excellent halfback pair and first five-eighth Faalele Iosua showed some deft touches.

Ten players were given debuts including "Marco" Mason (Free State Cheetahs), Pita Siale (Tonga Juniors), Taufa Halaafia (Tonga Schools), Pita Halaifonua (Tonga Under 20), Liueli Simote (Tonga A), and Sale Pi'i (North Otago).

SOUTH CANTERBURY REPRESENTATIVES 2020

	Club	Games for Union	Points for Union
Anthony Amato	Waimate	14	20
Henry Bryce	Waimate	7	10
Sireli Buliruarua	Harlequins	10	5
Tim Caird	Waimate	3	0
Theo Davidson	Waimate	46	53
Junior Faavae	Temuka	24	49
Tokomaata Fakatava	Waimate	23	5
Matthew Fetu	Celtic	107	35
Taufa Halaafia	Harlequins	3	0
Pita Halaifonua	Harlequins	5	15
Cameron Hucker	Pleasant Point	8	0
Faalele Iosua	Temuka	6	53
Siu Kakala	Harlequins	14	40
Solomone Lavaka	Temuka	17	20
Kalavini Leatigaga	Temuka	33	146
Frederick "Marco" Mason	Temuka	1	0
Ryan McNab	Mackenzie	5	5
Miles Medlicott	Waimate	62	38
Clarence Moli	Waimate	11	40
Sale Pi'i	Waimate	2	0
Zac Saunders	Celtic	20	55
Salesitangi "Tangi" Savelio	Temuka	4	20
Pita Siale	Temuka	5	15
Liueli Simote	Temuka	4	10
Nick Strachan	Celtic	90	82
Aifala Taelaga	Temuka	8	0
Vaka Taelaga	Temuka	3	0
Jared Trevathan	Mackenzie	61	150
Petero Tuwai	Mackenzie	2	0
James Wilson-Bishop	Pleasant Point	13	5
Willie Wright	Celtic	51	348

INDIVIDUAL SCORING

	Tries	Con	PG	DG	Points
Faalele Iosua	1	11	7	–	48
Willie Wright	2	11	–	–	32
Salesitangi Savelio	4	–	–	–	20
Kalavini Leatigaga	3	–	–	–	15
Junior Faavae	3	–	–	–	15
Clarence Moli	3	–	–	–	15
Pita Siale	3	–	–	–	15
Pita Halaifonua	3	–	–	–	15
Siu Kakala	2	–	–	–	10
Henry Bryce	2	–	–	–	10
Liueli Simote	2	–	–	–	10
Zac Saunders	2	–	–	–	10
Theo Davidson	1	2	–	–	9
James Wilson-Bishop	1	–	–	–	5
Solomone Lavaka	1	–	–	–	5
Jared Trevathan	–	1	–	–	2
Totals	**33**	**25**	**7**	**0**	**236**
Opposition scored	13	10	6	0	103

SOUTH CANTERBURY 2020

	Mid Canterbury	North Otago	Buller	Buller	North Otago	Totals
F.J.M. Mason	15	–	–	–	–	1
L. Simote	–	15	15	15	15	4
S.K. Buliruarua	14	14	–	–	–	2
K.V. Leatigaga	11	–	11	–	11	3
J.L. Wilson-Bishop	–	11	s	11	–	3
C.M. Moli	–	–	14	14	14	3
P.L. Siale	13	13	13	13	13	5
P.R. Tuwai	s	s	–	–	–	2
M.W. Medlicott	12	–	–	–	–	1
Z.C.C. Saunders	s	12	12	–	12	4
F.A. Iosua	10	10	10	10	10	5
J.D. Trevathan	–	s	s	12	s	4
T.R. Davidson	9	9	9	s	9	5
W.A. Wright	s	s	s	9	s	5
S.I.F. Kakala	8	8	s	8	8	5
R.T. McNab	–	s	8	–	s	3
N.J.C. Strachan (capt)	7	7	7	–	–	3
S. Savelio	6	–	6	6	6	4
P.O. Halaifonua	s	6	s	7	7	5
H.J. Bryce	5	5	5	5	5	5
A. Amato	4	4	–	4	s	4
S.B. Pi'i	–	s	–	s	–	2
S.P. Lavaka	–	–	4	s	4	3
A. Taelaga	3	s	3	3	3	5
V. Taelaga	1	1	s	–	–	3
M. Fetu	s	–	–	s	–	2
T. Halaafia	s	–	–	s	s	3
T.M.H.K. Fakatava	–	3	1	1	1	4
J.R. Faavae	2	2	2	2	2	5
T.D. Caird	s	–	s	s	–	3
C.A. Hucker	–	s	–	s	–	2

J.R. Faavae captained in game 4;
T.R. Davidson captained in game 5.

SOUTH CANTERBURY TEAM RECORD, 2020

Played 5 Won 5 Lost 0 Points for 236 Points against 105

Date	Opponent	Location	Score	Tries	Con	PG	DG	Referee
September 5	Mid Canterbury	Timaru	31–31	Leatigaga, Faavae, Kakala	Iosua (2)	Iosua (4)		J. Rooney
September 12	North Otago (HS)	Oamaru	24–7	Bryce, Simote, Saunders	Iosua (3)	Iosua		C. Kingan
September 19	Buller	Timaru	78–10	Moli (3), Savelio (3), Siale (2), Leatigaga (2), Halaifonua, Simote	Wright (7), Davidson (2)			J. Henshaw
September 26	Buller	Westport	66–28	Wright (2), Halaifonua (2), Wilson-Bishop, Iosua, Savelio, Faavae, Siale, Lavaka	Wright (4), Iosua (3), Trevathan			G. Reilly
October 3	North Otago (HS)	Timaru	37–29	Kakala, Bryce, Saunders, Davidson, Faavae	Iosua (3)	Iosua (2)		C. Paul

SOUTHLAND

2020 Status: Mitre 10 Cup Championship
Founded 1887. Affiliated 1894
President: L.M. (Leicester) Rutledge
Chairman: B.J. (Bernie) McKone
General Manager: Brian Hopley (to Jan)
S.R. (Simon) Frisby (interim to April)
Steve Mitchell (from April)
Coach: D.J. (Dale) McLeod
Assistant coaches: D.G. (David) Hall, J.M. (Jason) Kawau
Main ground: Rugby Park Stadium, Invercargill
Capacity: 20,200
Colours: Maroon

RECORDS

Most appearances	139	*Jason Rutledge, 2000–2016*
Most points	976	*Simon Culhane, 1988–98*
Most tries	46	*Bruce Pascoe, 1983–89*
Most points in a season	194	*Simon Culhane, 1994*
Most tries in a season	13	*Simon Forrest, 1992*
Most conversions in a season	38	*Simon Culhane, 1997*
Most penalty goals in a season	41	*Eion Crossan, 1989*
Most dropped goals in a season	10	*Brian McKechnie, 1977*
Most points in a match	37	*Simon Culhane v Manawatu, 1994*
Most tries in a match	5	*Simon Forrest v Poverty Bay, 1992*
Most conversions in a match	11	*Simon Culhane v Malborough, 1997*
Most penalty goals in a match	8	*Simon Culhane v Manawatu, 1994*
Highest team score	92	*v Marlborough, 1997*
Record victory (points ahead)	74	*79–5 v Poverty Bay, 1992*
Highest score conceded	95	*v Waikato, 1998*
Record defeat (points behind)	88	*7–95 v Waikato, 1998*

With three wins Southland had their best year since 2014. The season started with a hard-fought win over eventual Championship winners Hawke's Bay, a last minute penalty goal edged the win over Premiership team North Harbour, and the decisive win over neighbours Otago would have brought a lot of satisfaction.

Five of the seven defeats were by eight points or less. A last-minute dropped goal attempt against Waikato missed, a late penalty against Bay of Plenty was kicked for touch when a successful goal would have forced extra time, and Southland spent the last five minutes of the Northland match in the Northland 22 but just could not cross the try line. While these were close efforts it did highlight Southland's biggest difficulty — their attack. Only 144 points and 17 tries were scored in their 10 games, both tallies by far the lowest in the Mitre 10 Cup, with the backline only able to contribute a meagre six tries to the try total.

There was certainly not much wrong with the defence as the 193 points conceded was the lowest in the Mitre 10 Cup.

Ethan De Groot, Greg Pleasants-Tate and Siate Tokolahi were a strong front row that anchored one of the best scrums in the competition. At the age of 42, hooker Jason Rutledge added four more appearances to his record tally for the province before declaring his unavailability due to work commitments. Mike McKee was a hard-working lock who had a prominent game against Otago and Manaaki Selby-Rickit started the season in excellent form until a knee injury caused him to miss matches. At season's end, Selby-Rickit was in demand from other provinces chasing his services for 2021.

The loose forward trio of Charles Alaimalo, Matthew James and captain Tony Lamborn was a real strength of the side, being very effective at the breakdown. James was a big improver on his debut season of last year while Lamborn was Southland's best player and surely unlucky not to receive a Super Rugby contract.

Logan Crowley was the best of the three halfbacks used, having a standout game against Otago, and Scott Eade was a steady first five-eighths. Ray Nu'u was a forceful runner at second five-eighth but his distribution was variable and Isaac Te Tamaki's try against Northland, to finish off a 75-metre breakout, was superb, but a rare example of the backline completing an attacking opportunity.

Fullback Josh Moorby was a big improver. He seldom made a mistake on defence and always looked likely to spark an attacking threat. It was a shame a fractured left hand ended his season prematurely. Newcomer Tevita Latu looked a good prospect on the wing.

Only 16 of the 36 players used last year reappeared in 2020. Regulars missing were Ben Fotheringham, Jay Renton, Flynn Thomas (all injured), Phil Halder, Marty McKenzie, Brayden Mitchell (all taking a break), Morgan Mitchell (overseas) and Lewis Ormond (returned to Taranaki).

Newcomers with previous first-class experience were Amanaki Nicole (NZ Sevens), Siate Tokolahi (Canterbury), Glenn Preston (North Harbour), Raniera Takarangi (North Harbour/Waikato), Kieran Lee (Thames Valley), Brad Armstrong (King Country) and Matt McKenzie (Taranaki) while Tony Lamborn returned after a year's absence. Jacob Coghlan, who had represented North Otago last year as a loan player, became a third generation Southland rep after his father Kelvin and grandfather Gerald. Sebastian Siataga (Bay of Plenty/Canterbury) and Penikolo Latu (Hawke's Bay/Waikato) were added as injury replacements during the season.

As well, a number of former Southland reps reappeared after a lengthy absence — Talemaitoga Tuapati (2014), Jaye Thompson-Te Muunu (2016), Greg Dyer and Liam Howley (both 2017).

Higher honours went to
New Zealand Maori: M. Selby-Rickit

SOUTHLAND REPRESENTATIVES 2020

	Club	Games for Union	Points for Union		Club	Games for Union	Points for Union
Charles Alaimalo	Woodlands	20	5	Ray Nu'u	Woodlands	25	5
Chris Apoua	Star	24	0	Greg Pleasants-Tate	Star	18	40
Brad Armstrong	Star	1	0	Arese Poliko	Blues	1	0
Jacob Coghlan	Barbarians	3	0	Glenn Preston	Silverdale [6]	7	0
Logan Crowley	Coastal [1]	19	15	Joe Robins	Midlands	1	0
Ethan De Groot	Blues	17	0	Jason Rutledge	Woodlands	143	95
Greg Dyer	Pirates OB	21	37	Manaaki Selby-Rickit	Star	22	20
Scott Eade	Marist	72	299	Sebastian Siataga	New Brighton [5]	5	0
Liam Howley	Woodlands	22	10	Craig Smith	Pirates OB	11	0
Matthew James	Woodlands	19	10	Raniera Takarangi	Marist	4	0
Brad Kooman	Blues	1	0	Raymond Tatafu	Blues	29	0
Tony Lamborn	Havelock North [2]	19	25	Isaac Te Tamaki	Pirates OB	28	40
Penikolo Latu	Tech OB [2]	3	0	Jaye Thompson-Te Muunu	Pirates OB	15	7
Tevita Latu	Marist	6	10	Siate Tokolahi	Southland RU	9	0
Kieran Lee	Woodlands	3	0	Viliami "Lio" Tosi	Marist	7	0
Niko Manaena	Petone [3]	1	0	Talemaitoga Tuapati	Pirates OB	27	15
Michael McKee	[4]	37	5	Nathan Va'atausili	Woodlands	1	0
Matthew McKenzie	Woodlands	1	0	Rory Van Vugt	Barbarians	18	15
Josh Moorby	Woodlands	16	15	Joseph Walsh	Woodlands	44	5
Amanaki Nicole	Sydenham [5]	5	5				

1 Taranaki RU   2 Hawke's Bay RU   3 Wellington RU
4 Arrived from overseas   5 Canterbury RU   6 North Harbour RU

INDIVIDUAL SCORING

	Tries	Con	PG	DG	Points		Tries	Con	PG	DG	Points
Scott Eade	–	8	9	–	43	Isaac Te Tamaki	1	–	–	–	5
Greg Pleasants-Tate	4	–	–	–	20	Logan Crowley	1	–	–	–	5
Tony Lamborn	4	–	–	–	20	Matthew James	1	–	–	–	5
Greg Dyer	–	2	4	–	16						
Tevita Latu	2	–	–	–	10	**Totals**	**17**	**10**	**13**	**0**	**144**
Talemaitoga Tuapati	2	–	–	–	10						
Amanaki Nicole	1	–	–	–	5	Opposition scored	26	18	8	1	193
Rory Van Vugt	1	–	–	–	5						

SOUTHLAND 2020	Hawke's Bay	Bay of Plenty	North Harbour	Waikato	Northland	Taranaki	Tasman	Manawatu	Otago	Counties Manukau	Totals
J.M. Moorby	15	15	15	15	15	15	–	–	–	–	6
M.R. McKenzie	–	–	–	–	–	–	–	15	–	–	1
R.F. Van Vugt	14	14	11	11	s	11	15	–	15	15	9
A.P. Nicole	11	11	14	–	14	–	–	–	–	14	5
T.H.M. Latu	s	–	s	–	–	s	14	–	11	11	6
P.K. Latu	–	–	–	s	11	14	–	–	–	–	3
K.F. Lee	–	–	–	–	–	–	11	11	14	–	3
B.A. Kooman	–	–	–	–	–	–	–	s	–	–	1
I.R. Te Tamaki	13	13	13	14	13	13	13	14	13	13	10
J.B. Thompson-Te Muunu	12	12	–	13	–	–	s	13	s	s	7
R.I. Nu'u	–	s	12	12	12	12	12	12	12	12	9
B. Armstrong	–	–	–	–	–	–	–	s	–	–	1
S.D. Eade	10	10	10	s	10	10	s	10	10	10	10
G.I. Dyer	s	s	s	10	s	s	10	–	s	s	9
L.E. Crowley	9	s	9	s	9	–	s	9	9	9	9
R.R.H. Takaranagi	s	9	–	–	s	9	–	–	–	–	4
L.O. Howley	–	–	s	9	–	s	9	s	s	s	7
T.A. Lamborn (capt)	8	8	8	7	8	8	7	8	8	8	10
A. Poliko	–	–	–	–	–	–	8	–	–	–	1
M.D. James	7	7	7	s	7	7	–	7	7	7	9
C.V. Alaimalo	6	s	6	8	6	6	6	6	6	6	10
G.L. Preston	s	6	s	6	s	s	s	–	–	–	7
J.H. Coghlan	–	–	–	–	–	–	s	–	s	s	3
N.F. Va'atausili	–	–	–	–	–	–	–	s	–	–	1
M.J.F. McKee	5	s	5	–	4	4	–	5	5	5	8
M.W.H. Selby-Rickit	4	5	4	5	5	–	–	–	4	4	7
R.K. Tatafu	s	4	s	4	s	5	5	–	s	s	9
C.W. Smith	–	–	–	s	–	s	4	4	–	–	4
J.D. Robins	–	–	–	–	–	–	–	s	–	–	1
S.F. Tokolahi	3	3	3	3	s	3	–	3	3	3	9
E.L. De Groot	1	s	1	1	s	1	–	1	1	1	9
J.S. Walsh	s	1	s	s	1	s	1	s	s	s	10
C. Apoua	s	s	s	–	3	s	3	s	s	s	9
V.V. Tosi	–	–	–	s	–	–	s	–	–	–	2
N.J.P. Manaena	–	–	–	–	–	–	s	–	–	–	1
G.W. Pleasants-Tate	2	2	2	–	2	2	s	2	2	2	9
J.K. Rutledge	s	s	s	s	–	–	–	–	–	–	4
S.P. Siataga	–	–	–	2	s	s	2	s	–	–	5
T.D. Tuapati	–	–	–	–	–	–	–	–	s	s	2

SOUTHLAND TEAM RECORD, 2020

Played 10   Won 3   Lost 7   Points for 144   Points against 193

Date	Opponent	Location	Score	Tries	Con	PG	DG	Referee
September 13	Hawke's Bay (C)	Invercargill	16–10	Pleasants-Tate (2)		Eade (2)		J. Doleman
September 19	Bay of Plenty (cr)	Rotorua	14–17	Nicole, Pleasants-Tate	Eade (2)			D. Waenga
September 26	North Harbour (cr)	Invercargill	11–10	Van Vugt		Eade, Dyer		J. Munro
October 4	Waikato (cr)	Invercargill	9–10			Dyer (2), Eade		J. Bredin
October 11	Northland (C)	Whangarei	14–18	Lamborn, Te Tamaki	Eade (2)			R. Kelly
October 17	Taranaki (C)	Invercargill	9–17			Eade (3)		J. Munro
October 25	Tasman (cr)	Nelson	10–47	Lamborn	Eade	Dyer		J. Doleman
November 1	Manawatu (C)	Feilding	12–24	Crowley, Pleasants-Tate	Eade			N. Hogan
November 6	Otago (C)	Invercargill	32–15	Lamborn, James, T. Latu, Tuapati	Dyer (2), Eade	Eade (2)		B. Pickerill
November 13	Counties Manukau (C)	Pukekohe	17–25	T. Latu, Lamborn, Tuapati	Eade			M. Winter

TARANAKI

2020 Status: Mitre 10 Cup Championship
Founded 1889. Original member 1892
President: L.R. (Lyal) French-Wright
Chairman: A.S. (Andrew) Thompson
Chief executive officer: L.K. (Laurence) Corlett (from Jan)
Coach: W.T.C. (Willie) Rickards
Assistant coaches: Neil Barnes, T.M. (Tim) Stuck
Main ground: T.E.T. Stadium, Inglewood
Capacity: 3,000
Colours: Amber and black

RECORDS

Most appearances	222	Ian Eliason, 1964–81
Most points	1723	Kieran Crowley, 1980–94
Most tries	64	Kieran Crowley, 1980–94
Most points in a season	233	Jamie Cameron, 1995
Most tries in a season	13	Charlie McAlister, 1985
Most conversions in a season	49	Kieran Crowley, 1983
Most penalty goals in a season	39	Jamie Cameron, 1995
Most dropped goals in a season	11	Ross Brown, 1964
Most points in a match	34	Jamie Cameron v Nelson Bays, 1995
Most tries in a match	5	George Loveridge v Wanganui, 1913
		Dave Vesty v Thames Valley, 1971
		Mark Robinson v Southland, 1997
Most conversions in a match	13	Kieran Crowley v East Coast, 1983
Most penalty goals in a match	9	Beauden Barrett v Bay of Plenty, 2011
Highest team score	104	v Nelson Bays, 1995
Record victory (points ahead)	97	97–0 v East Coast, 1983
Highest score conceded	80	v Otago, 1996
Record defeat (points behind)	60	16–76 v North Harbour, 1989

One of the favourites to return to the Premiership, Taranaki's season had many of the same characteristics as 2019. With the playing roster and talent that the union has at its disposal, it remains a mystery to many as to why Taranaki still finds itself languishing in the middle of the Championship table.

Like last year, there was a lack of accuracy late in games and an inability to convert leads into victories as witnessed against Auckland, Hawkes Bay (round robin), Waikato and Counties Manukau. The only exception to this was the 59–23 blowout in the Championship semi-final to Hawkes Bay, which was Taranaki's heaviest loss in all encounters between these unions.

The absence of key personnel Tei Walden and captain Mitch Brown obviously had an effect, their injuries forcing a rotation of players in key positions. The loss of this duo's on-field leadership was also certainly felt in the loss to Northland.

That said, victories were achieved over Premiership teams Bay of Plenty (where the Chiefs' Centurions Cup and the Peter Burke trophy were both re-captured) and Canterbury in an exhilarating Ranfurly Shield win. The team had a near full complement of their All Blacks available for the Shield game in Christchurch. Beauden Barrett and brother Jordie, who slotted a crucial 50 metre penalty in his first season representing Taranaki, as well as Tupou Vaa'i, were all influential in what was indisputably Taranaki's best performance of the season. However, the celebrations lasted a solitary week, with the Shield quickly returning south to Otago.

In the backs, Jayson Potroz made the fullback jersey his own and proved a reliable goalkicker. He was the team's top points-scorer. Few will forget his thrilling solo scoring spree against Auckland where he appeared to have the ball on a string, scoring 23 points in a little under 20 minutes. Jacob Ratumaitavuki-Kneepkens announced his arrival, scoring two exciting tries on debut in the victorious Ranfurly Shield win against Canterbury. He was the team's top try-scorer with eight tries, showing flair, skill, and plenty of X-factor almost every time he touched the ball.

Lewis Ormond displayed good finishing skills on the wing and linked well with his insides. Daniel Waite, Sean Wainui, Brayton Northcott-Hill and Lukas Halls were all used in the midfield and each of them had their moments. The returning Codey Rei was mostly used as a substitute late in games at wing. Daniel Rona made the most of his opportunities in his three appearances, a feature being a try on debut with his first touch of the ball against Waikato.

After an injury ravaged 2019, Stephen Perofeta's return to form was welcomed. He looked very assured back in his natural position at 10. Whether it was kicking from hand, or bringing his trademark running game, he could be relied upon to ignite his backline with many fine, attacking runs. Lisati Milo-Harris and Warwick Lahmert both shared the halfback duties, with Lahmert's experience called upon more as the season progressed.

Perhaps typical of a Taranaki team, the forward pack brought plenty of work rate and a consistently solid scrum. Seasoned props, Jared Proffit and the veteran Ben May were well supported by Chris Gawler and Reuben O'Neill, who showed great versatility in being able to play on either side of the front row when required. Daniel Brighouse added bulk from the bench and Crusader Faletogoa'i-Malase, who is a product of the union's development programme, appeared to relish his first taste of Mitre 10 Cup rugby in his one and only appearance at prop. It will be interesting to watch his progress. Ricky Riccitelli once again shared the hooking duties with Bradley Slater who continues to develop and impress.

Josh Lord was a mainstay at lock and for such a young player, looks to have a great future ahead of him. He brought a presence and physicality to his game which belies his 19 years of age. Fin Hoeata filled the other locking spot once Vaa'i became unavailable due to All Blacks commitments and the unfortunate injury to Brown struck. When he too succumbed to injury, elder brother Jarrad did not hesitate to swap his coaching bib for a playing jersey, adding three further appearances to his already impressive first-class career tally.

Lachlan Boshier reminded the general populace why he was perhaps the unluckiest player in New Zealand not to be wearing black in 2020. He led the competition turnover count and was a general menace at the breakdown with his durability and extraordinary technique and work rate. He was simply outstanding.

Brother Kaylum Boshier was used at No 8 and lock, bringing abrasiveness and steel to the pack. When Pita Gus Sowakula returned to the team mid-season from injury, his go forward and toughness also helped get the team moving in the right direction with many of his runs coming off the back of the scrum. Tom Florence and Mitchell Crosswell shared the blindside duties — both showing great endeavour and commitment to the jersey, toiling away in the loose and getting through a mountain of defensive work week after week.

Losses from last season included Heiden Bedwell-Curtis and Jesse Parete (both Japan), Leighton Price and Jackson Ormond (both retired), Te Toiroa Tahuriorangi (Bay of Plenty), Scott Mellow (Canterbury), Xavier Roe (Waikato), Matt McKenzie (Southland) and Kyle Stewart (Manawatu).

Off the field, the ongoing structural issues with Yarrow Stadium meant that the union was forced to find a new home ground. TET Stadium in Inglewood was chosen as the union's home for 2020. Its small club ground setting brought a unique community atmosphere and spirit to home matches.

Higher honours went to:
New Zealand: B. Barrett, J. Barrett, S. Barrett, T. Vaa'i
Maori All Blacks: S. Wainui
New Zealand Sevens: K. Baker (before signing for Hawke's Bay).

TARANAKI REPRESENTATIVES 2020

	Club	Games for Union	Points for Union		Club	Games for Union	Points for Union
Beauden Barrett	Coastal	28	191	Brayton Northcott-Hill	New Plymouth OB	16	17
Jordie Barrett	Coastal	2	22	Kylem O'Donnell	Spotswood United	35	15
Kaylum Boshier	New Plymouth OB	20	15	Reuben O'Neill	New Plymouth OB	45	10
Lachlan Boshier	New Plymouth OB	48	50	Lewis Ormond	Southern	11	15
Donald Brighouse	New Plymouth OB	20	5	Stephen Perofeta	Clifton	41	93
Mitchell Brown	Inglewood	42	5	Jayson Potroz	Tukapa	23	127
Mitchell Crosswell	Tukapa	62	30	Jared Proffit	Spotswood United	42	5
Crusader Faletagoa'i-Malase	Inglewood	1	0	Jacob Ratumaitavuki-Kneepkens	Tukapa	11	40
Rhodes Featherstone	Inglewood	1	0	Codey Rei	New Plymouth OB	35	173
Tom Florence	New Plymouth OB	27	10	Ricky Riccitelli	Tukapa	37	30
Chris Gawler	Coastal	27	0	Daniel Rona	Clifton	3	5
Lukas Halls	Tukapa	7	5	Brad Slater	New Plymouth OB	19	10
Fin Hoeata	New Plymouth OB	17	0	Pita-Gus Sowakula	Spotswood United	30	20
Jarrad Hoeata	New Plymouth OB	82	20	Tupou Vaa'i	New Plymouth OB	12	20
Warwick Lahmert	Spotswood United	16	5	Sean Wainui	New Plymouth OB	53	75
Josh Lord	Coastal	14	0	Daniel Waite	New Plymouth OB	21	88
Ben May	Coastal	5	0	Shaan Waite	New Plymouth OB	2	0
Lisati Milo-Harris	Inglewood	18	0	Teihorangi Walden	Spotswood United	23	25

INDIVIDUAL SCORING

	Tries	Con	PG	DG	Points		Tries	Con	PG	DG	Points
Jayson Potroz	3	16	16	–	95	Reuben O'Neill	1	–	–	–	5
Jacob Ratumaitavuki-Kneepkens	8	–	–	–	40	Daniel Rona	1	–	–	–	5
Jordie Barrett	1	4	3	–	22	Mitchell Crosswell	1	–	–	–	5
Tupou Vaa'i	3	–	–	–	15	Sean Wainui	1	–	–	–	5
Stephen Perofeta	3	–	–	–	15	Tom Florence	1	–	–	–	5
Lewis Ormond	3	–	–	–	15	Lukas Halls	1	–	–	–	5
Ricky Riccitelli	2	–	–	–	10	Donald Brighouse	1	–	–	–	5
Kaylum Boshier	2	–	–	–	10						
Brad Slater	2	–	–	–	10	**Totals**	**37**	**21**	**19**	**0**	**286**
Penalty Try	1	–	–	–	7						
Daniel Waite	1	1	–	–	7	Opposition scored	43*	31	15	0	324
Lachlan Boshier	1	–	–	–	5						

* Includes one penalty try (7 points)

TARANAKI 2020	Bay of Plenty	Canterbury	Otago	Northland	Auckland	Southland	Waikato	Counties Manukau	Manawatu	Hawke's Bay	Hawke's Bay (sf)	Opposition Name	Totals
J.M. Barrett	15	15	–	–	–	–	–	–	–	–	–	–	2
J.P. Potroz	s	–	10	15	15	15	15	15	15	15	15	–	10
J.W.J. Ratumaitavuki-Kneepkens	14	14	14	14	14	14	14	14	14	14	14	–	11
L.H. Ormond	11	11	11	11	11	11	s	11	11	11	11	–	11
C.S. Rei	s	–	–	s	s	–	11	s	s	s	s	–	8
S.T. Wainui	13	13	13	13	13	13	13	13	13	12	–	–	10
L.J.M. Halls	–	–	–	s	s	–	–	s	s	13	13	–	6
T.T. Walden	12	12	12	–	–	–	–	–	–	–	–	–	3
D.S. Waite	–	–	s	12	12	12	–	–	12	–	–	–	5
B.K. Northcott-Hill	–	–	s	–	–	–	12	12	–	–	12	–	4
D.K. Rona	–	–	–	–	–	–	s	–	–	s	s	–	3
B.J. Barrett	10	10	–	–	–	–	–	–	–	–	–	–	2
S. Perofeta	–	–	15	10	10	10	10	10	10	10	10	–	9
L.M. Milo-Harris	9	9	9	9	s	s	9	9	9	–	s	–	10
W.H. Lahmert	s	s	–	–	9	9	s	s	s	9	9	–	9
K.F.T.R. O'Donnell	–	–	s	s	–	–	–	–	–	–	–	–	2
S.A. Waite	–	–	–	–	–	–	–	–	–	s	–	–	1
K.L. Boshier	s	8	8	8	4	s	8	8	5	5	–	–	10
P.G.N. Sowakula	–	–	–	s	8	8	–	–	8	8	8	–	6
M.C. Crosswell	8	6	6	s	6	s	6	s	6	s	7	–	11
L.S. Boshier	7	7	7	7	7	7	7	7	7	7	–	–	10
M.M. Brown (capt)	6	–	–	–	s	6	5	6	–	–	5	–	6
T.H.T. Florence	s	s	s	6	–	s	s	s	s	6	6	–	9
R.M. Featherstone	–	–	–	–	–	–	–	–	–	–	s	–	1
T.P.O. Vaa'i	5	5	5	–	–	–	–	–	–	–	–	–	3
J.M.J. Lord	4	4	4	4	s	4	4	4	4	4	–	–	10
F.W.S.P. Hoeata	–	–	s	5	5	5	s	5	–	–	s	–	7
J.M.R.A. Hoeata	–	–	–	–	–	–	–	–	s	s	4	–	3
B. May	3	3	–	3	3	–	–	3	–	–	–	–	5
J.P. Proffit	1	s	1	s	–	1	1	s	1	1	1	–	10
R.G. O'Neill	s	1	3	1	1	3	3	1	s	3	3	–	11
D.I.M. Brighouse	s	s	s	s	s	s	s	s	3	s	s	–	11
C.M. Gawler	–	–	s	–	s	s	s	–	s	–	s	–	6
C.S. Faletagoa'i-Malase	–	–	–	–	–	–	–	–	–	s	–	–	1
J.R. Riccitelli	2	2	s	s	2	2	2	2	s	s	s	–	11
B.A. Slater	s	s	2	2	s	s	s	s	2	2	2	–	11

T.T. Walden captained in matches 2 and 3; L.S. Boshier and S.T. Wainui co-captained in matches 4,5,9,10

TARANAKI TEAM RECORD, 2020

Played 11　　Won 4　　Lost 7　　Points for 286　　Points against 324

Date	Opponent	Location	Score	Tries	Con	PG	DG	Referee
September 13	Bay of Plenty (cr)	Inglewood	36–29	Vaa'i (2), Riccitelli, Penalty Try, J. Barrett	J. Barrett (3)	J. Barrett		B. O'Keeffe
September 19	Canterbury (cr) (RS)	Christchurch	23–22	Ratumaitavuki-Kneepkens (2), Vaa'i	J. Barrett	J. Barrett (2)		B. O'Keeffe
September 27	Otago (C) (RS)	Inglewood	19–30	Perofeta, K. Boshier, L. Boshier	Potroz, D. Waite			M. Fraser
October 3	Northland (C)	Whangarei	25–35	D. Waite, Potroz, Ratumaitavuki-Kneepkens	Potroz (2)	Potroz (2)		A. Mabey
October 10	Auckland (cr)	Inglewood	28–29	Potroz (2), Ratumaitavuki-Kneepkens	Potroz (2)	Potroz (3)		J. Doleman
October 17	Southland (C)	Invercargill	17–9	O'Neill, Ratumaitavuki-Kneepkens	Potroz (2)	Potroz		J. Munro
October 25	Waikato (cr)	Hamilton	20–27	Ratumaitavuki-Kneepkens (2), Rona	Potroz	Potroz		A. Mabey
November 1	Counties Manukau (C)	Inglewood	27–31	Perofeta, Ormond, Crosswell, Wainui	Potroz (2)	Potroz		J. Munro
November 8	Manawatu (C)	Feilding	35–19	Slater (2), Ratumaitavuki-Kneepkens, Ormond	Potroz (3)	Potroz (3)		A. Mabey
November 15	Hawke's Bay (C)	Inglewood	33–34	Ormond, Perofeta, K. Boshier, Florence	Potroz (2)	Potroz (3)		J. Bredin
November 21	Hawke's Bay (C sf)	Napier	23–59	Halls, Riccitelli, Brighouse	Potroz	Potroz (2)		N. Briant

TASMAN

2020 Status: Mitre 10 Cup Premiership
Founded and **affiliated 2005** (December)
President: R.S. (Ramon) Sutherland
Chairman: W.A. (Wayne) Young
Chief executive officer: A.J.F. (Tony) Lewis
Co-coaches: A.D. (Andrew) Goodman, C. (Clarke) Dermody
Assistant coaches: S.A. (Shane) Christie, G.N. (Gray) Cornelius
Main ground: Trafalgar Park, Nelson; Lansdowne Park, Blenheim
Capacity: 18,000
Colours: Navy blue and red

RECORDS

Most appearances	104	*Robbie Malneek, 2006–2017*
Most points	628	*Marty Banks, 2013–2016*
Most tries	25	*Robbie Malneek, 2006–2017*
Most points in a season	173	*Marty Banks, 2014*
Most tries in a season	10	*Peter Playford, 2006*
Most conversions in a season	37	*Marty Banks, 2014*
Most penalty goals in a season	33	*Marty Banks, 2016*
Most dropped goals in a season	1	*by five players*
Most points in a match	28	*Marty Banks v Northland, 2013*
Most tries in a match	4	*Peter Playford v Canada A, 2006*
		Peter Playford v Northland, 2006
Most conversions in a match	7	*Aaron Kimura v Northland, 2006*
		Marty Banks v Manawatu, 2013
Most penalty goals in a match	8	*Tom Marshall v Bay of Plenty, 2010*
Most dropped goals in a match	1	*by five players*
Highest team score	64	*v Waikato, 2013*
		v Manawatu, 2019
Record victory (points ahead)	61	*64-3 v Manawatu, 2019*
Highest score conceded	52	*v Counties Manukau, 2017*
Record defeat (points behind)	42	*7–49 v Auckland, 2007*

The Tasman Mako recorded back-to-back Premiership triumphs — the first province, other than Canterbury, to repeat since Auckland in 2002–03.

But the 2020 victory was achieved in very different style to that of 2019, in which the Mako carried all before them with staunch defence and clinical attack. This time they dropped three matches, badly, and their final winning average was 27–19, down from 37–11.

For all that, the group will be immensely satisfied at going to Eden Park and clinching the final, 13–12 over Auckland, even if the match itself will not live long in the memory.

After a smooth first three outings, the Mako's 15-match win streak came to a crashing halt against North Harbour, before heavy defeats to Auckland and Canterbury raised questions about a potentially soft underbelly. But the Mako rallied, tightened their set-piece and lent on some key players at big moments, such as versatile skipper David Havili, whose first three goals of the season came in the decider, to go with his season-high six tries.

The best displays were the solid home wins against Northland, Waikato and Bay of Plenty. In all, they scored the tryscoring bonus point in five games, down from eight in 2019. While the coaching staff was unchanged, there were some considerable player losses and offshore signings, including Jordan Taufua, Liam Squire and Hugh Roach in the pack.

Loosehead props Wyatt Crockett and Tim Perry hung up the boots. Injuries also prevented Atu Moli, Ethan Blackadder and Paripari Parkinson from taking the field.

The four All Blacks — Shannon Frizell, Will Jordan, Tyrel Lomax and Sevu Reece — played limited but telling roles at the start of the Mitre 10 Cup.

Reece, shifting from Waikato, was one of several big signings. Lock Alex Ainley returned from a season with Bay of Plenty to offer experienced cover at lock, and became the second Mako to raise the century since their 2006 inception. Centre Kieron Fonotia and hooker Quentin MacDonald both returned after several seasons abroad and did solid jobs.

Wing Mark Telea signed from North Harbour and scored two tries in 11 games, but was not as dazzling as he was for the Blues. Prop Isi Tu'ungafasi transferred from Northland and was strong on the loosehead side of the scrum, never more so than in the final, where he got the better of All Black Angus Ta'avao.

Lock Quinten Strange missed the first half of the campaign with injury, which also ruled him out of the All Blacks, but he stood up when it counted in the playoffs.

A feature of the season was that four Mako — Finlay Christie, Mitch Hunt, Alex Nankivell and Andrew Makalio — all passed the 50-game milestone.

Fullback Havili was as reliable as ever, with an eye for a gap or counter-attack opportunity, a big boot and safe under the high ball. He scored a hat-trick against Waikato and played a marvellous captain's knock in the final. Havili is unlucky that New Zealand rugby is flush with top fullbacks or he would surely be in the All Blacks.

Leicester Faingaanuku was the most penetrative back, scored five tries and was one of three to start all 12 games.

Fetuli Paea was again solid at centre, stood out on the final and won a Highlanders contract. Until he broke his hand, Alex Nankivell was probably the best No 12 in the competition, still the glue for this Mako backline. First-five Hunt goalkicked well and proved capable but was not as dominant as in 2019. Christie was again sparky at halfback.

The pack stood up when it mattered, led by industrious loose forward Sione Havili. Former NZ Schools captain Anton Segner was brought on slowly, and he showed promise. Hugh Renton made big strides at No 8 or No 6 in his first full season of provincial rugby after years of injuries.

Te Ahiwaru Cirikidaveta was top value at lock and surprisingly missed a full Super Rugby deal, while former All Black Isaac Ross acted as second-row cover later in the season.

Hookers Andrew Makalio and MacDonald shared seven tries from lineout drives.

Higher honours went to:
New Zealand: S. Frizell, W. Jordan, T. Lomax, S. Reece
New Zealand Sevens: T. Joass, T. Ng Shiu

TASMAN REPRESENTATIVES 2020

	Club	Games for Union	Points for Union
Alex Ainley	Huia	100	45
Louie Chapman	Riwaka	5	0
Finlay Christie	Stoke	53	40
Te Ahiwaru Cirikidaveta	Stoke	22	25
Ryan Coxon	Wanderers	24	0
Leicester Faingaanuku	Nelson	25	60
Tima Faingaanuku	Nelson	42	50
Kieron Fonotia	Marist	72	60
Taina Fox-Matamua	Marist	12	5
Shannon Frizell	Marist	31	40
David Havili	Nelson	64	154
Sione Havili-Talitui	Wanderers	27	40
Mitch Hunt	Stoke	56	439
Will Jordan	Nelson	34	110
Tyrel Lomax	Stoke	32	10
Quentin MacDonald	Central	89	50
Andrew Makalio	Nelson	51	70
Samuel Matenga	Huia	13	0
Sam Moli	Marist	7	5
Alex Nankivell	Stoke	53	50
Mahonri Ngakuru	Wanderers	5	0
Jacob Norris	Marist	13	15
Tim O'Malley	Waitohi	38	87
Fetuli Paea	Waitohi	21	15
Blair Prinsep	Stoke	3	5
Dwayne Polataivao	Wanderers	7	0
Sevu Reece	Waitohi	3	15
Hugh Renton	Awatere	11	0
Isaac Ross	Overseas	7	0
Isaac Salmon	Nelson	29	0
Anton Segner	Nelson	5	0
Braden Stewart	Central	8	0
Quinten Strange	Nelson	43	30
Cameron Suafoa	Nelson	1	0
Kershawl Sykes-Martin	Nelson	3	0
Mark Telea	Central	11	10
Isi Tu'ungafasi	Waitohi	11	0

INDIVIDUAL SCORING

	Tries	Con	PG	DG	Points
Hunt	1	25	14	–	97
D. Havili	6	1	2	–	38
L. Faingaanuku	5	–	–	–	25
Makalio	4	–	–	–	20
S. Havili	3	–	–	–	15
MacDonald	3	–	–	–	15
O'Malley	1	5	–	–	15
Paea	3	–	–	–	15
Reece	3	–	–	–	15
Cirikidaveta	2	–	–	–	10
Nankivell	2	–	–	–	10
Telea	2	–	–	–	10
Christie	1	–	–	–	5
Fox-Matamua	1	–	–	–	5
Frizell	1	–	–	–	5
Jordan	1	–	–	–	5
Norris	1	–	–	–	5
Prinsep	1	–	–	–	5
Strange	1	–	–	–	5
Totals	**42**	**31**	**16**	**0**	**320**
Opposition scored	27	22	15	0	224

TASMAN 2020

	Counties Manukau	Northland	Waikato	North Harbour	Bay of Plenty	Auckland	Southland	Wellington	Canterbury	Otago	Bay of Plenty (SF)	Auckland (F)	Totals
D. K. Havili (capt)	–	12	15	15	15	15	15	15	15	15	15	15	11
W.T. Jordan	15	15	–	–	–	–	–	–	–	–	–	–	2
S.L. Reece	14	14	–	–	–	s	–	–	–	–	–	–	3
M.E. Telea	11	–	14	14	14	14	14	s	14	14	14	14	11
L.T. Faingaanuku	–	s	s	s	s	–	–	14	–	s	–	s	7
L.O.K.W.T. Faingaanuku	13	11	11	11	11	11	11	11	11	11	11	11	12
K.T. Fonotia	–	–	–	–	s	13	s	–	s	s	s	s	7
F.M.A. Paea	s	13	13	13	13	s	13	13	13	13	13	13	12
T.P. O'Malley	s	s	s	s	–	–	s	s	s	12	12	12	10
A.P. Nankivell	12	–	12	12	12	12	12	12	12	–	–	–	8
M.J. Hunt	10	10	10	10	10	10	10	10	10	10	10	10	12
F.T. Christie	9	–	–	9	9	9	9	9	9	9	9	9	10
L.J. Chapman	–	s	s	–	s	s	s	–	–	–	–	–	5
D.E. Polataivao	s	9	9	s	–	–	–	s	s	s	–	–	7
H.T. Renton	8	8	8	8	8	8	6	–	6	6	6	6	11
T.J. Fox-Matamua	–	–	–	–	–	–	8	8	8	8	8	8	6
A. Segner	–	–	–	–	–	–	s	s	–	s	s	s	5
S.T. Havili-Talitui	7	–	7	7	7	7	7	7	7	7	7	7	11
B.J. Stewart	s	s	s	s	s	s	–	–	–	–	–	–	5
J.K. Norris	s	7	6	6	6	6	–	–	–	–	–	–	6
T.A. Cirikidaveta	5	5	5	5	5	5	4	6	s	4	4	4	12
C.J.T.S. Suafoa	–	s	–	–	–	–	–	–	–	–	–	–	1
S.M. Frizell	6	6	–	–	–	–	–	–	–	–	–	–	2
A.N. Ainley	4	–	4	4	4	4	s	4	4	–	–	–	8
I.B. Ross	–	–	–	–	s	s	5	s	s	–	s	s	7
Q.J. Strange	–	–	–	–	–	–	–	5	5	5	5	5	5
M.A. Ngakuru	s	4	s	s	–	–	–	–	–	s	–	–	5
S.I. Matenga	s	–	s	s	3	s	3	–	s	s	3	3	10
T.S. Lomax	3	3	–	–	–	3	–	–	–	–	–	–	3
I.A. Salmon	–	s	3	3	–	–	s	3	3	3	–	s	8
B.E. Prinsep	–	–	–	–	s	–	–	s	–	–	s	–	3
R.C. Coxon	–	–	s	s	s	s	1	s	s	1	1	s	10
I.J. Tu'ungafasi	1	1	1	1	1	1	s	1	1	–	s	1	11
K.J. Sykes-Martin	s	s	–	–	–	–	–	–	s	–	–	–	3
A. Makalio	2	2	2	2	2	2	2	2	2	–	–	2	10
Q.J.R.W.J. MacDonald	s	s	s	s	s	s	–	s	s	s	2	2	11
S. Moli	–	–	–	–	–	–	–	–	–	–	s	s	2

TASMAN TEAM RECORD 2020

Played 12 Won 9 Lost 3 Points for 320 Points against 224

Date	Opponent	Location	Score	Tries	Con	PG	DG	Referee
September 12	Counties Manukau (cr)	Pukekohe	41–24	Makalio (2), Cirikidaveta, Frizell, L. Faingaanuku	Hunt (4), O'Malley	Hunt (2)		R.P. Kelly
September 18	Northland (cr)	Blenheim	54–21	Reece (3), Jordan, Makalio, Paea, Norris, L. Faingaanuku	Hunt (5), O'Malley (2)			P. M. Williams
September 26	Waikato (P)	Nelson	34–17	D. Havili (3), Nankivell, Makalio	Hunt (3)	Hunt		R.P. Kelly
October 03	North Harbour (P)	Albany	24–40	Telea, Christie, D. Havili	Hunt (3)	Hunt		N.P. Briant
October 11	Bay of Plenty (P)	Nelson	33–7	L. Faingaanuku (2), Telea, S. Havili, Prinsep	Hunt (4)			C.J. Stone
October 17	Auckland (P)	Auckland	10–31	Nankivell, MacDonald				B.D. O'Keeffe
October 25	Southland (cr)	Nelson	47–10	D. Havili (2), Paea (2), Fox-Matamua, Hunt, S. Havili	Hunt (4), O'Malley (2)			J.J. Doleman
October 31	Wellington (P)	Porirua	19–3	S. Havili, Cirikidaveta		Hunt (3)		D.J. Waenga
November 07	Canterbury (P)	Blenheim	0–29					M.I. Fraser
November 14	Otago (cr)	Dunedin	26–20	O'Malley, Strange	Hunt (2)	Hunt (4)		J.D. Munro
November 21	Bay of Plenty (P, sf)	Nelson	19–10	MacDonald, L. Faingaanuku		Hunt (3)		R.P. Kelly
November 28	Auckland (P, f)	Auckland	13–12	MacDonald	D. Havili	D. Havili (2)		N.P. Briant

THAMES VALLEY

2020 Status: Heartland Championship
Founded and affiliated 1922
President: K.J. (Kelly) Plummer
Chairman: G.S. (Grant) Dickey
General Manager: Brett Barnham
Coaches: D.P. (David) Harrison and J.R. (Joe) Murray
Assistant coaches: M.J. (Matthew) Rolston
Main ground: Paeroa Domain
Capacity: 3000
Colours: Gold and red

RECORDS

Highest attendance	7000	*Thames Valley v Auckland (Ranfurly Shield), 1989*
Most appearances	143	*B.C. Duggan, 1970–84*
Most points	665	*D.P. Harrison, 2004–15*
Most tries	42	*I.F. Campbell, 1981–94*
Most points in a season	127	*J.R. Reynolds, 2011*
Most tries in a season	14	*I.F. Campbell, 1988*
Most conversions in a season	30	*D.B. McCallum, 1995*
Most penalty goals in a season	25	*J.R. Reynolds, 2011*
Most dropped goals in a season	4	*T.E. Shaw, 1962*
		R.W. Kemp, 1968
Most points in a match	27	*D.B. McCallum v East Coast, 1995*
		M. Griffin v King Country, 2003
Most tries in a match	4	*I.F. Campbell v North Otago, 1990*
		G.A. Ellis v North Otago, 1994
		G.W. McLiver v Marlborough, 1995
Most conversions in a match	8	*G.A. Ellis v West Coast, 1994*
		M.A. Handley v North Otago, 1994
Most penalty goals in a match	7	*D.P. Harrison v Mid Canterbury, 2009*
	7	*J.R. Reynolds v East Coast, 2011*
	7	*R.D. Crosland v Wanganui, 2019*
Highest team score	86	*v North Otago, 1994*
Record victory (points ahead)	79	*86–7 v North Otago, 1994*
Highest score conceded	113	*v Northland, 1997*
Record defeat (points behind)	99	*14–113 v Northland, 1997*

For the first time since 1944 Thames Valley did not field a senior representative team in 2020. With the cancellation of the Heartland Championship the Union decided instead to concentrate resources at the local level.

Affiliation fees were discarded and all clubs and secondary schools were given a substantial grant to help cover their expenses. Although the season was shorter than usual players enjoyed the opportunity to play some rugby and all the respective competitions were hotly contested. Because of attendance restrictions at the time of the finals the TVRFU funded the live streaming of all these club and secondary school games. There was a milestone for the Whangamata Club when it won the senior championship to take out the McClinchy Cup for the first time in its history.

Former assistant coaches of the Swamp Foxes, David Harrison and Joe Murray were promoted to become joint head coaches with Matt Bartleet still on the scene as a resource coach. These positions will carry over to the 2021 season. Late in the season a Thames Valley Under 23 team participated in a competition with Under 20 teams from the Chiefs' Mitre 10 Cup unions. No games were won but it presented an opportunity for up-and-coming Thames Valley players to experience rugby at a higher level.

In February former Thames Valley and New Zealand selector/coach, Ross Cooper was awarded Life Membership of the Thames Valley Rugby Football Union along with former first-class referee and Board Chairman, Graham Hallett.

WAIKATO

2020 Status: Mitre 10 Cup Premiership
Founded 1909 as South Auckland.
Affiliated 1909. Name changed to Waikato 1921
President: D.I. (Duane) Monkley
Chairman: C.J.R. (Colin) Groves
Chief executive officer: B.M. (Blair) Foote
Coach: A.H. (Andrew) Strawbridge
Assistant coaches: R.M. (Rhys) Bayliss, R.A. (Ross) Filipo, N.C. (Nick) White
Main ground: FMG Stadium Waikato, Hamilton
Capacity: 27,000
Colours: Red, yellow and black

RECORDS

Most appearances	148	Ian Foster, 1985–98
		Graham Purvis, 1984–97
Most points	1604	Matthew Cooper, 1990–99
Most tries	70	Bruce Smith, 1979–84
Most points in a season	269	Brett Craies, 1989
Most tries in a season	17	Bruce Smith, 1981
Most conversions in a season	69	Brett Craies, 1989
Most penalty goals in a season	57	Matthew Cooper, 1993
Most dropped goals in a season	10	John Boe, 1981
Most points in a match	35	Bruce Reihana v North Otago, 2000
Most tries in a match	5	Gary Major v East Coast, 1981
		Bruce Smith v Nadi, 1982
		Bruce Smith v South Australia, 1983
		Ian Wilson v South Canterbury, 1984
		Rob Gordon v Southland, 1990
		Roger Randle v Poverty Bay, 1998
		Sitiveni Sivivatu v Auckland, 2004
Most conversions in a match	12	Matthew Cooper v Wairarapa Bush, 1990
		Glen Jackson v West Coast, 2000
Most penalty goals in a match	7	Andrew Strawbridge v Wellington, 1985
		Trent Renata v Bay of Plenty, 2013
Highest team score	121	v Poverty Bay, 1998
Record victory (points ahead)	121	121–0 v Poverty Bay, 1998
Highest score conceded	96	v Harlequins Invitation XV, 1995
Record defeat (points behind)	71	25–96 v Harlequins Invitation XV, 1995

Waikato will be pleased and disappointed in equal measure after a topsy-turvy season in which the Mooloos attained their highest national ranking since contesting the 2011 Premiership final.

Andrew Strawbridge's charges were losing Premiership semi-finalists, the first time they had contested the top tier playoffs since 2011. But they looked a million dollars in the opening two rounds and, in fact, led the Premiership standings on two occasions, chalking up six wins from their first seven matches. However, they limped home with four straight losses to end the season.

Maybe it was the rare presence of Damian McKenzie and Anton Lienert-Brown in the opening salvos, but Waikato looked an immediate Premiership contender with two 40+ wins over Wellington and North Harbour to kick off its campaign. McKenzie scored 49 points in just two games, which remained the team season high, and his 33 against the Lions threatened Bruce Reihana's 20-year-old record for individual points in a game.

But while Waikato chalked up its first win in Christchurch since 2011 and annexed the Ryan Wheeler Memorial Trophy, it was disappointing in the Stan Thomas Memorial clash with Auckland, edged in the Chiefs Country Cup against Bay of Plenty and dropped its final regular season fixture, a crossover match in Kaikohe, to stagger into the semi-finals. And yet, were it not for some untimely errors, Waikato could have upset a misfiring Auckland to reach the decider.

There were some useful gains pre-season: Liam Messam was back from France to finish off his career, while Adam Thomson transferred from Otago. Hooker Steven Misa was back from Australia, and Patrick Osborne arrived from Canterbury. They all boosted the average age of a young squad.

One of the standouts, though, was former NZ Under 20s rep, halfback Xavier Roe, who scored four tries, set up several others, and played his way into a Super Rugby contract.

Losses included Sevu Reece (Tasman) and Api Naikatini (USA), while lock Laghlan McWhannell and prop Ayden Johnstone were injured for the entire season.

McKenzie was the star fullback, but former All Blacks Sevens and Poverty Bay rep Beaudein Waaka, promoted out of Peace Cup rugby, gave sterling service in three positions, including first five, and was handy off the tee.

Osborne played a limited role on the wing, while Gideon Wrampling was a promising, though tryless, newcomer. Liam Coombes-Fabling, one of several debutants, showed a high work-rate, though his impact was blunted in the second half of the season.

Bailyn Sullivan, too, did not cross the whitewash, but showed his versatility in several positions. Centre Quinn Tupaea led all tryscorers with five and enjoyed his third straight productive Mitre 10 Cup.

First-five Fletcher Smith battled injury at times, but showed his class often enough. His omission from any of the five Super Rugby franchises was inexplicable.

Roe established himself as the top No 9, but his understudy Cortez Ratima offered maximum impact off the bench with his sharp running and passing.

Luke Jacobson led from the way in typical fashion and was one of two to start all 11 games. He played a lot at openside, which is not necessarily his best position.

Messam played well at No 8 after a slow start, bruising in the tackle and imposing with the ball. He combined well with Jacobson and the other standout Mooloo, the remarkable 38-year-old Adam Thomson. A lineout target and scorer of three tries, Thomson was fit to rank with the best No 6s in the Mitre 10 Cup.

Hamilton Burr and Samipeni Finau did the job in the second-row, the latter enjoying a breakthrough season for Waikato.

The set-piece in general was occasionally creaky, but the scrum was mostly solid. Josh Iosefa-Scott, another to strangely miss a full Super Rugby deal, and Ollie Norris, were backed up by Sefo Kautai and Rob Cobb.

Hooker Samisoni Taukei'aho's try rate was down – just two in 2020 – but he generally played well around the track

Higher honours went to:
New Zealand: A. Lienert-Brown, D. McKenzie
New Zealand Sevens: T. Mikkelson, D. Collier
New Zealand Maori: L. Messam, F. Smith, Q. Tupaea

WAIKATO REPRESENTATIVES 2020

	Club	Games for Union	Points for Union
Hamilton Burr	Hautapu	18	10
Rob Cobb	Hamilton Old Boys	15	0
Liam Coombes-Fabling	Fraser Tech	11	10
Rhys Dickinson	Fraser Tech	2	0
Greg Dyer	Fraser Tech	2	0
Tolu Fahamokoia	Tawa[1]	2	0
Samipeni Finau	Hamilton Old Boys	16	0
Josh Iosefa-Scott	Melville	41	10
Luke Jacobson	Hautapu	22	10
Mitch Jacobson	Hautapu	51	20
Sefo Kautai	Hamilton Marist	40	5
Matty Lansdown	Fraser Tech	32	49
Anton Lienert-Brown	University	21	20
Sekope Lopeti-Moli	Hautapu	15	5
Damian McKenzie	University	26	300
Liam Messam	Raglan	93	153
Steven Misa	Hamilton Marist	20	15
Hugo Nankivell	Fraser Tech	4	0
Ollie Norris	Hautapu	20	10
Patrick Osborne	Fraser Tech	6	0
Simon Parker	Hautapu	11	10
Cortez Ratima	Otorohanga	10	5
Rivez Reihana	Melville	18	31
Xavier Roe	Hamilton Old Boys	10	20
Louis Rogers	University	12	5
Fletcher Smith	University	30	245
Bailyn Sullivan	Hamilton Marist	35	50
Samisoni Taukei'aho	Fraser Tech	44	100
Valynce Te Whare	Fraser Tech	8	20
James Thompson	Hautapu	13	0
Adam Thomson	Morrinsville Sports	11	15
Quinn Tupaea	Hamilton Old Boys	30	95
Beaudein Waaka	Melville	7	30
Gideon Wrampling	Hamilton Old Boys	8	0

[1] Loaned by Wellington

INDIVIDUAL SCORING

	Tries	Con	PG	DG	Points
McKenzie	2	9	7	–	49
Smith	2	5	4	–	32
Waaka	1	5	5	–	30
Reihana	1	5	4	–	27
Tupaea	5	–	–	–	25
Roe	4	–	–	–	20
Te Whare	3	–	–	–	15
Thomson	3	–	–	–	15
Coombes-Fabling	2	–	–	–	10
L. Jacobson	2	–	–	–	10
Taukei'aho	2	–	–	–	10
Penalty try	1	–	–	–	7
M. Jacobson	1	–	–	–	5
Messam	1	–	–	–	5
Misa	1	–	–	–	5
Norris	1	–	–	–	5
Ratima	1	–	–	–	5
Totals	**33**	**24**	**20**	**0**	**275**
Opposition scored	34	25	11	0	253

WAIKATO 2020	Wellington	North Harbour	Tasman	Southland	Counties Manukau	Canterbury	Taranaki	Auckland	Bay of Plenty	Northland	Auckland (SF)	Totals
D.S. McKenzie	15	15	–	–	–	–	–	–	–	–	–	2
B.R.T. Waaka	–	–	–	–	15	15	15	15	15	10	11	7
R.W.M. Reihana	s	s	s	10	s	10	s	s	10	–	–	9
M.R.T. Lansdown	–	–	–	s	12	–	12	–	–	s	15	5
P.J.J. Osborne	–	–	11	11	11	11	–	–	11	–	s	6
V.C. Te Whare	–	s	s	14	–	–	11	–	–	11	–	5
G.T. Wrampling	s	11	–	–	s	–	s	11	s	14	s	8
L.A. Coombes-Fabling	11	14	15	15	14	14	14	14	14	s	14	11
B.W.M. Sullivan	14	–	14	13	–	12	13	12	12	15	12	9
Q.P.C. Tupaea	13	13	13	–	13	13	–	13	13	13	13	9
L.S. Rogers	–	–	12	12	–	s	–	s	s	12	–	6
A.R. Lienert-Brown	12	12	–	–	–	–	–	–	–	–	–	2
F.H. Smith	10	10	10	s	10	–	10	10	–	–	10	8
R.W. Dickinson	–	–	–	–	–	–	s	–	–	–	s	2
X.O. Roe	9	9	9	s	9	9	–	9	9	9	9	10
C.P. Ratima	s	s	s	9	s	s	9	s	s	s	–	10
L.B. Jacobson (capt)	8	8	7	8	8	8	7	7	7	7	7	11
H.A. Nankivell	–	–	s	–	–	–	s	s	–	–	–	3
M.L. Jacobson	7	7	–	7	7	7	–	–	–	–	–	5
L.J. Messam	–	–	–	s	s	s	8	8	8	8	8	8
S.C. Parker	s	s	8	–	–	–	–	–	–	s	s	5
A.J. Thomson	6	6	6	6	6	6	6	6	6	s	6	11
H.R. Burr	4	4	4	s	4	4	4	4	4	6	4	11
S.U. Finau	5	5	5	5	5	5	5	5	5	5	5	11
J.M.P. Thompson	s	s	s	4	s	s	s	s	s	4	s	11
J.Z.A. Iosefa-Scott	s	3	s	s	3	3	s	3	3	3	s	11
S.S.V. Kautai	3	–	3	3	–	s	3	3	s	s	3	9
R.L. Cobb	s	s	s	1	1	1	s	1	–	s	s	10
O.M. Norris	1	1	1	s	–	s	1	s	1	1	1	10
G.E. Dyer	–	s	–	–	s	–	–	–	–	–	–	2
O.A. Fahamokoia	–	–	–	–	s	–	–	–	s	–	–	2
S.F. Taukei'aho	2	2	2	2	2	2	2	2	s	2	2	11
S. Misa	s	s	s	s	s	s	–	s	2	–	s	9
S. Lopeti-Moli	–	–	–	–	–	–	s	–	–	s	–	2

WAIKATO TEAM RECORD 2020

Played 11 Won 6 Lost 5 Points for 275 Points against 253

Date	Opponent	Location	Score	Tries	Con	PG	DG	Referee
September 12	Wellington (P)	Hamilton	53–28	Roe, Smith, McKenzie, Thomson, L. Jacobson	McKenzie (5)	McKenzie (6)		D.J. Waenga
September 19	North Harbour (P)	Hamilton	41–19	Roe (2), Tupaea, M. Jacobson, McKenzie, Te Whare	McKenzie (4)	McKenzie		M.I. Fraser
September 26	Tasman (P)	Nelson	17–34	Tupaea, Te Whare, Smith	Smith			R.P. Kelly
October 04	Southland (cr)	Invercargill	10–9	Coombes-Fabling	Smith	Smith		J. Bredin
October 10	Counties Manukau (cr)	Hamilton	36–13	Coombes-Fabling, Thomson, Misa, Tupaea, penalty try	Reihana (2), Smith	Smith		B.E. Pickerill
October 18	Canterbury (P)	Christchurch	16–15	Ratima	Reihana	Reihana (3)		C.J. Stone
October 25	Taranaki (cr)	Hamilton	27–20	Waaka, Reihana, Messam	Reihana (2), Smith	Smith (2)		A.W.B. Mabey
October 31	Auckland (P)	Auckland	10–31	Roe	Smith	Reihana		J.J. Doleman
November 08	Bay of Plenty (P)	Hamilton	30–33	Tupaea (2), Norris, Taukei'aho	Waaka (2)	Waaka (2)		D.J. Waenga
November 14	Northland (cr)	Kaikohe	17–28	L. Jacobson, Te Whare	Waaka (2)	Waaka		M.I. Fraser
November 21	Auckland (P, sf)	Auckland	18–23	Taukei'aho, Thomson	Waaka	Waaka (2)		B.E. Pickerill

WAIRARAPA BUSH

2020 Status: Heartland Championship
Founded: Wairarapa 1886 and original member 1892.
Bush 1890 and affiliated 1893. Amalgamated 1971.
President: D.W. (Doug) Bracewell
Chairman: J.N. (Jason) Carruthers
Chief executive officer: A.R. (Tony) Hargood
Coach: J.R. (Joe) Harwood
Assistant coach: Deon van Deventer and Joe Nuku
Main ground: Memorial Park, Masterton
Capacity: 10,000
Colours: Green

RECORDS

Highest attendance	12,000	Wairarapa Bush v British Isles, 1971 and 1983
Most appearances	132	G.K. McGlashan, 1971–83
Most points	561	P. Harding-Rimene, 1999–2008
Most tries	43	M.T. Foster, 1984–92
Most points in a season	166	G.M. Walters, 2012
Most tries in a season	14	S.F. Simanu, 2005
Most conversions in a season	28	M.F.C. Benton, 1987
Most penalty goals in a season	34	G.M. Walters, 2012
Most dropped goals in a season	7	K.W. Carter, 1985
Most points in a match	26	M.J. Berry v South Canterbury, 1995
Most tries in a match	5	S. Malatai v Buller, 2018
Most conversions in a match	11	M.F.C. Benton v Horowhenua, 1987
Most penalty goals in a match	6	J.T. Te Huia v Buller, 2010
		G.M. Walters v South Canterbury, 2012
Highest team score	82	v Horowhenua, 1987
Record victory (points ahead)	73	82–9 v Horowhenua, 1987
Highest score conceded	96	v Canterbury, 2006
Record defeat (points behind)	86	10–96 v Canterbury, 2006

The loss to Wanganui in the final match of the season was a disappointing end to the season after wins in their first four games. In what was a virtual final for the Bruce Steel Cup Wairarapa Bush succumbed 8—29 in coach Joe Harwood's last game. He has retired after four years in charge.

In the competitive forward pack prop Max Tufuga was a strong scrummager and reserve prop Topou Lea'aemanu always provided good impact off the bench in general play and scored three tries. Newcomer Peter Beech won plenty of lineout ball. Number eight Kirk Tufuga captained the team well and after the Wanganui match was called into the Manawatu team for the Mitre 10 Cup.

The best of the backs was Nikora Ewe, a strong running second five-eighth and solid defender. First five-eighth Sam Morison had a good debut season and speedy winger Soli Malatai was always a danger despite only touching down once. The vastly experienced Inia Katia's role was essentially as a second half substitute at halfback and in that position produced a superb display into the strong wind to secure victory against Poverty Bay.

The match against Poverty Bay was played at Park Island, Napier. The Bruce Steel Cup in 2020 was played on a round robin basis among the three competing unions with four points for a win, not on the usual lines of a challenge match.

WAIRARAPA BUSH REPRESENTATIVES 2020

	Club	Games for Union	Points for Union
Joe Beech	Marist	11	5
Peter Beech	Marist	5	0
Nick Birchfield	Eketahuna	5	0
Teihana Brown	Greytown	5	0
Lewis Bush	Greytown	6	15
Leo Eneliko	Marist	4	0
Nikora Ewe	Pioneer	12	25
Sam Gammie	Eketahuna	36	47
Himiona Haira	Pioneer	2	0
Tipene Haira	Martinborough	42	76
Shane Harmon	Pioneer	1	0
Chris Hemi	Greytown	1	5
Nathan Hunt	Martinborough	29	40
Tavita Isaac	Greytown	22	20
Inia Katia	Gladstone	85	65
Topou Lea'aemanu	Carterton	4	15
Soli Malatai	Marist	22	55
Tom McKay	Eketahuna	4	0
Sam Morison	Carterton	4	41
Elijah-James Pakoti	Martinborough	30	5
Cameron Ravenwood	East Coast	5	0
Sam Siaosi	Marist	2	0
Tafa Tafa	Marist	3	5
Joseva Tako	Gladstone	7	10
Terongo Tekii	Carterton	5	0
Lee Thomson	Eketahuna	2	0
Kirk Tufuga	Eketahuna	24	10
Max Tufuga	Eketahuna	23	0
Johan Van Vliet	Eketahuna	44	55

INDIVIDUAL SCORING

	Tries	Con	PG	DG	Points
Sam Morison	–	10	7	–	41
Tavita Isaac	3	–	–	–	15
Lewis Bush	3	–	–	–	15
Topou Lea'aemanu	3	–	–	–	15
Nikora Ewe	3	–	–	–	15
Tipene Haira	–	5	–	–	10
Johan Van Vliet	2	–	–	–	10
Joseva Tako	2	–	–	–	10
Chris Hemi	1	–	–	–	5
Joe Beech	1	–	–	–	5
Soli Malatai	1	–	–	–	5
Kirk Tufuga	1	–	–	–	5
Sam Gammie	1	–	–	–	5
Inia Katia	1	–	–	–	5
Tafa Tafa	1	–	–	–	5
Totals	**23**	**15**	**7**	**0**	**166**
Opposition scored	13	8	8	0	105

WAIRARAPA BUSH 2020

	Horowhenua Kapiti	King Country	Poverty Bay	Horowhenua Kapiti	Wanganui	Totals
T. Tafa	15	–	–	15	15	3
N.J. Birchfield	s	15	15	s	s	5
S.N. Harmon	14	–	–	–	–	1
S. Malatai	11	11	11	11	11	5
I.S.T. Katia	s	14	s	14	s	5
N.S. Hunt	–	–	14	–	14	2
T.W.T.K.H. Brown	13	–	–	13	13	3
L.H. Eneliko	–	s	s	s	s	4
T.T. Haira	10	13	13	–	–	3
N.V. Ewe	12	12	12	12	12	5
S.J. Morison	–	10	10	10	10	4
C.C. Ravenwood	9	9	9	s	9	5
L.J. Thomson	–	s	–	9	–	2
K.M.S. Tufuga (capt)	8	8	8	8	8	5
J.J.A. Van Vliet	7	7	7	7	7	5
J.V. Tako	6	6	6	s	s	5
T.A. Isaac	s	s	s	6	6	5
H. Haira	s	s	2	–	–	2
P.A. Beech	5	5	5	4	4	5
J.G. Beech	4	–	–	–	–	1
T.S. McKay	–	4	4	s	s	4
S.G. Gammie	–	s	1	5	5	4
M.H.P.V. Tufuga	3	1	s	1	1	5
C.T.R. Hemi	1	–	–	–	–	1
L.P. Bush	s	3	3	3	3	5
T.F. Lea'aemanu	–	s	s	s	s	4
E.J. Pakoti	2	2	2	2	2	5
T.T.A. Tekii	s	–	s	s	s	4
S. Siaosi	–	s	s			2

WAIRARAPA BUSH TEAM RECORD, 2020

Played 5 Won 4 Lost 1 Points for 166 Points against 105

Date	Opponent	Location	Score	Tries	Con	PG	DG	Referee
September 19	Horowhenua Kapiti	Levin	43–8	Hemi, J. Beech, Isaac, Malatai, Bush, K. Tufuga, T. Haira (4), Lea'aemanu				S. Thompson
September 26	King Country	Masterton	22–18	Ewe, Var Vliet, Gammie	Morison, T. Haira Morison			A. Payne
October 3	Poverty Bay	Napier	46–26	Ewe (2), Bush, Lea'aemanu, Katia	Morison (5)	Morison (2)		S. Eden-Whaitiri
October 10	Horowhenua Kapiti (BSC)	Carterton	47–24	Tafa, Van Vliet, Bush, Tako, Isaac, Lea'aemanu	Morison (4)	Morison (3)		A. Payne
October 17	Wanganui (BSC)	Wanganui	8–29	Isaac		Morison		B. Lourie

The match at Carterton was played at the Carterton RFC ground.

WANGANUI

2020 Status: Heartland Championship
Founded 1888. Original member 1892
President: T.C. (Tom) Kilgariff
Chairman: J.M. (Jeff) Phillips
Chief executive officer: B.S. (Bridget) Belsham
Coach: J.M. (Jason) Caskey
Assistant coach: J.P. (Jason) Hamlin
Main ground: Cooks Gardens
Capacity: 15,000
Colours: Royal blue, black and white

RECORDS

Highest attendance	6500	*Wanganui v Scotland, 1996*
Most appearances	146	*T.T.T. Olney, 1973–90*
Most points	980	*R.B. Barrell, 1963–77*
Most tries	48	*J.D. Hainsworth, 1984–95*
Most points in a season	184	*G.R.J. Lennox, 1994*
Most tries in a season	14	*H.S. Gordon, 1988*
	14	*P. Fetuia, 2006*
Most conversions in a season	44	*M.K. Davis, 2008*
Most penalty goals in a season	39	*R.B. Barrell, 1975*
Most dropped goals in a season	6	*L.T. Head, 1952*
Most points in a match	32	*K.H. Chase v East Coast, 1989*
Most tries in a match	6	*D.F. Philipson v Taranaki, 1919*
Most conversions in a match	10	*L.K. Harding v West Coast, 1993*
		G.R.J. Lennox v Buller, 1994
Most penalty goals in a match	6	*R.B. Barrell v Manawatu, 1971*
		R.B. Barrell v Taranaki, 1975
		M.K. Davis v East Coast, 2011
Highest team score	81	*v West Coast, 1993*
		v Buller, 1994
Record victory (points ahead)	77	*80–3 v King Country, 2017*
Highest score conceded	88	*v Taranaki, 2000*
Record defeat (points behind)	84	*0–84 v Taranaki, 1995*

With three wins in their four matches Wanganui reclaimed the coveted Bruce Steel Cup which was this year played in a round robin format.

The strength of the team was undoubtedly in its backline. The Fijian trio Vereniki Tikoisolomone, Josaia Bogileka, and Alekesio Vakarorogo (Fiji Sevens rep) were a potent force with their athleticism and speed in any room to manoeuvre in and accounted for half of the team's tries. Fellow countryman Timoci Seruwalu, at second five-eighth, was a strong runner as well. In what may well turn out to be his final year in first-class rugby Craig Clare was still in fine form at the age of 36.

Josh Lane was the pick of the forwards. His lineout play was exceptional and was tireless in general play. Hooker Joe Edwards showed improvement in his second season while the loose forwards Semi Vodesese, Jamie Hughes and the captain Campbell Hart appeared in all four games together.

Debuts were given to eight players, and Cody Hemi and Timoci Seruwalu both returned from Horowhenua Kapiti. The match against Poverty Bay was played at McLean Park in Napier and shown live on Sky TV, being the curtain raiser to the Hawke's Bay v Manawatu Ranfurly Shield match.

WANGANUI REPRESENTATIVES 2020

	Club	Games for Union	Points for Union
Dillon Adrole	Kaierau	3	0
Matthew Ashworth	Kaierau	4	0
Josaia Bogileka	Marist	6	15
Matthew Brown	Taihape	1	0
Craig Clare	Border	31	308
Wiremu Cottrell	Taihape	15	5
Cameron Davies	Kaierau	6	0
Joe Edwards	Kaierau	7	0
Dylan Gallien	Taihape	14	5
Gabriel Hakaraia	Ruapehu	28	15
Campbell Hart	Ruapehu	37	21
Hadlee Hay-Horton	Taihape	4	0
Cody Hemi	Ratana	10	10
Logan Henry	Kaierau	1	0
Jack Hodges	Border	3	5
Lindsay Horrocks	Border	73	87
Jamie Hughes	Ruapehu	42	38
Josh Lane	Kaierau	15	5
Kamipeli Latu	Border	46	25
Bradley O'Leary	Marist	1	0
Cade Robinson	Kaierau	6	5
Ethan Robinson	Kaierau	18	10
Tyler Rogers-Holden	Taihape	20	50
Timoci Seruwalu	Ngamatapouri	13	50
Vereniki Tikoisolomone	Border	13	80
Alekesio Vakarorogo	Border	4	10
Semi Vodesese	Border	4	0
Dane Whale	Taihape	49	135
Jack Yarrall	Marist	13	5

INDIVIDUAL SCORING

	Tries	Con	PG	DG	Points
Craig Clare	3	7	4	–	41
Dane Whale	2	4	1	–	21
Josaia Bogileka	3	–	–	–	15
Vereniki Tikoisolomone	3	–	–	–	15
Alekesio Vakarorogo	2	–	–	–	10
Timoci Seruwalu	1	–	–	–	5
Cade Robinson	1	–	–	–	5
Gabriel Hakaraia	1	–	–	–	5
Totals	**16**	**11**	**5**	**0**	**117**
Opposition scored	9	6	4	0	69

WANGANUI 2020

	Horowhenua Kapiti	King Country	Wairarapa Bush	Poverty Bay	Totals
C.D. Clare	15	15	15	–	3
V.W. Tikoisolomone	14	–	14	14	3
A. Vakarorogo	11	11	s	11	4
D. Adrole	s	s	–	s	3
T.T.H. Rogers-Holden	–	14	11	15	3
L. Henry	–	–	–	s	1
J. Bogileka	13	13	13	13	4
T.S. Seruwalu	12	12	12	12	4
C.T.A.M. Hemi	–	s	s	–	2
D.J. Whale	10	10	10	10	4
C.T. Davies	9	s	s	9	4
L.D. Horrocks	s	9	9	–	3
E.T. Robinson	–	–	–	s	1
S. Vodesese	8	8	8	8	4
B. O'Leary	–	–	–	s	1
J.N. Hughes	7	7	7	7	4
C.J. Hart (capt)	6	6	6	6	4
C. Robinson	s	s	5	–	3
J.I. Hodges	5	–	–	–	1
J.R.C. Lane	4	4	4	4	4
M.T. Ashworth	s	5	s	5	4
M. Brown	–	–	–	s	1
W.H. Cottrell	3	–	1	–	2
K.T. Latu	1	s	3	3	4
G.T.E. Hakaraia	s	3	s	1	4
H. Hay-Horton	s	1	s	s	4
J.T. Edwards	2	2	2	2	4
J.S. Yarrall	s	s	–	–	2
D.R. Gallien	–	–	s	s	2

Played 4 Won 3 Drew 0 Lost 1 Points for 117 Points against 69

WANGANUI TEAM RECORD, 2020

Date	Opponent	Location	Score	Tries	Con	PG	DG	Referee
October 3	Horowhenua Kapiti (BSC)	Shannon	36–7	Clare (2), Whale, Bogileka, Seruwalu	Clare (4)	Clare		S. Thompson
October 10	King Country	Taumarunui	11–16	Whale		Clare (2)		C. Cowie
October 17	Wairarapa Bush (BSC)	Wanganui	29–8	C. Robinson, Tikoisolomone, Clare, Vakarorogo	Clare (3)	Clare		B. Lourie
October 24	Poverty Bay	Napier	41–38	Bogileka (2), Tikoisolomone (2), Vakarorogo, Hakaraia	Whale (4)	Whale		N. Hogan

WELLINGTON

2020 Status: Mitre 10 Cup Premiership
Founded 1879. Original member 1892
President: M.P. (Murray) Blandford
Chairman: I.G. (Iain) Potter
Chief Executive Officer: M.G. (Matt) Evans
Coach: L. (Leo) Crowley
Assistant coaches: T.E. (Tamati) Ellison, D.A.G. (Dion) Waller, G.A. (Greg) Halford
Main ground: Sky Stadium, Wellington
Capacity: 34,500
Colours: Black

RECORDS

Most appearances	173	Graham Williams, 1964–76
Most points	893	Allan Hewson, 1977–86
Most tries	100	Bernie Fraser, 1975–86
Most points in a season	199	John Gallagher, 1987
Most tries in a season	24	Bernie Fraser, 1981
Most conversions in a season	47	Jackson Garden-Bachop, 2017
Most penalty goals in a season	38	Jon Preston, 1994
Most dropped goals in a season	7	John Dougan, 1971
Most points in a match	34	David Holwell v Bay of Plenty, 2002
Most tries in a match	7	Nigel Geany v Wanganui, 1991
Most conversions in a match	14	Peter O'Shaughnessy v Horowhenua, 1988
		Simon Mannix v Rosario, 1995
Most penalty goals in a match	7	Jackson Garden-Bachop v North Harbour, 2016
Highest team score	118	v Rosario, 1995
Record victory (points ahead)	101	118–17 v Rosario, 1995
Highest score conceded	82	v Otago, 1998
Record defeat (points behind)	72	10–82 v Otago, 1998

There were glimpses of very good rugby, and they were in contention for the semi-finals right up until the final day, but in the final analysis, the Wellington Lions will be disappointed with their Mitre 10 Cup Premership campaign.

Even without their four All Blacks, Wellington appeared to have enough talent to challenge, but failed to consistently click under new head coach Leo Crowley.

After suffering a decisive opening round defeat, Wellington gave one of its best displays, knocking off Auckland at Eden Park to retain the Fred Lucas Memorial Trophy, and running away with the Jonah Lomu Memorial Trophy in Pukekohe. Good bonus point wins were gained against Bay of Plenty and Manawatu, and they won a critical victory over North Harbour in the capital. But they dropped the first golden point game in Mitre 10 Cup history, to Canterbury, and lost two crossover games, to Otago, and then in a toothless Ranfurly Shield challenge in Napier.

There was minimal player movement in the off-season. Ben Lam had gone to France, while prop Fraser Armstrong had transferred from Manawatu but was injured. Julian Savea was back in the black jersey after his stint in France.

All Blacks Ardie Savea and TJ Perenara, though not Dane Coles, each made two appearances before national duty called.

Rookie fullback Ruben Love showed some nice touches in his five appearances, while the reliable Trent Renata was the fallback option. Billy Proctor played four games at the back but looked better at centre.

The luckless Connor Garden-Bachop was injured in the first game, after which Wes Goosen tied up the No 14 jersey, scoring thrice and taking his Lions try tally to 27 from 58 games.

Julian Savea ran hard and looked the goods on occasion, showing his versatility by often slotting into the midfield where he was incisive. Pepesana Patafilo was a useful foil in the threequarters.

Vince Aso scored four tries but was not as prominent as he is for the Hurricanes. Peter Umaga-Jensen continued his strong Hurricanes' form before he left for Tri Nations duty with the All Blacks.

Jackson Garden-Bachop again gave fine service in the No 10 jersey, in which he was ever-present. His young understudy, Aidan Morgan, is one for the future.

Kemara Hauiti-Parapara was again the No 1 halfback, but his back-up Connor Collins often gave impetus from the bench, especially against North Harbour, where the Lions may not have won without his contribution.

No 8 Teariki Ben-Nicholas is now a dominant performer at this level, and no one bettered his four tries. Du'Plessis Kirifi was captain in the first six games before he was whisked to Australia on Tri Nations duty. His standards remained high.

Vaea Fifita started all 10 games and looked a very different player from the listless Hurricane of earlier in 2020. He won his ball, galloped around the field and scored three tries, including a brace against the Steelers.

James Blackwell, who was his usual industrious self, skippered the side in the last four games. He formed an effective partnership with Naitoa Ah Kuoi at lock. Taine Plumtree showed enough promise to win a Super Rugby contract.

Alex Fidow was again the main man at tighthead prop, though he doesn't scrummage with the authority of a Sione Mafileo. Xavier Numia returned from injury to be a solid performer on the loosehead.

Asafo Aumua looked set for a big season after the opening two rounds, but was thereafter used as a tackle shield by the All Blacks. The seasoned James O'Reilly admirably filled the starter's role. The rookie of the season for the Lions was reserve hooker Tyrone Thompson, mostly used off the bench. He was vigorous with his carries, and his solo try against the Steamers was something special.

Higher honours went to:
New Zealand: A. Aumua, D. Coles, T. Perenara, A. Savea, P. Umaga-Jensen
New Zealand Maori: B. Proctor

WELLINGTON REPRESENTATIVES 2020

	Club	Games for Union	Points for Union		Club	Games for Union	Points for Union
Naitoa Ah Kuoi	Marist-St Pat's	20	10	Ruben Love	Wainuiomata	5	5
Vince Aso	Paremata-Plimmerton	20	45	Aidan Morgan	Marist-St Pat's	4	4
Asafo Aumua	Avalon	44	95	Xavier Numia	Oriental-Rongotai	27	20
Ben Aumua-Peseta	Tawa	6	0	James O'Reilly	Hutt Old Boys-Marist	45	30
Teariki Ben-Nicholas	Old Boys-University	38	35	Pepesana Patafilo	Tawa	19	20
James Blackwell	Petone	52	35	TJ Perenara	Northern United	19	15
Connor Collins	Hutt Old Boys-Marist	18	0	Taine Plumtree	Old Boys-Unversity	5	0
Caleb Delany	Old Boys-University	6	0	Morgan Poi	Old Boys-University	10	0
Alex Fidow	Oriental-Rongotai	39	80	Billy Proctor	Marist-St Pat's	35	37
Vaea Fifita	Wellington	52	80	Trent Renata	Tawa	33	56
Connor Garden-Bachop	Northern United	6	5	Ardie Savea	Oriental-Rongotai	36	85
Jackson Garden-Bachop	Northern United	74	604	Julian Savea	Oriental-Rongotai	40	85
Wes Goosen	Old Boys-University	58	135	Sam Smith	Wainuiomata	4	5
Kemara Hauiti-Parapara	Tawa	43	35	Josiah Tavita-Metcalfe	Northern United	3	0
Mateaki Kafatolu	Petone	36	15	Tyrone Thompson	Marist-St Pat's	10	10
Bruce Kauika-Petersen	Northern United	1	0	Kaliopasi Uluilakepa	Petone	17	10
Du'Plessis Kirifi	Northern United	33	30	Peter Umaga-Jensen	Wainuiomata	27	35

INDIVIDUAL SCORING

	Tries	Con	PG	DG	Points		Tries	Con	PG	DG	Points
J. Garden-Bachop	1	25	11	–	88	C. Garden-Bachop	1	–	–	–	5
Aso	4	–	–	–	20	Fidow	1	–	–	–	5
Ben-Nicholas	4	–	–	–	20	Hauiti-Parapara	1	–	–	–	5
Fifita	3	–	–	–	15	Love	1	–	–	–	5
Goosen	3	–	–	–	15	Renata	1	–	–	–	5
O'Reilly	3	–	–	–	15	A. Savea	1	–	–	–	5
Proctor	2	1	–	–	12	Smith	1	–	–	–	5
Ah Kuoi	2	–	–	–	10	Uluilakepa	1	–	–	–	5
Numia	2	–	–	–	10	Morgan	–	2	–	–	4
Patafilo	2	–	–	–	10						
J. Savea	2	–	–	–	10	**Totals**	**40**	**28**	**11**	**0**	**289**
Thompson	2	–	–	–	10						
Umaga-Jensen	2	–	–	–	10	Opposition scored	30	19	20	0	248

WELLINGTON 2020

Player	Waikato	Auckland	Bay of Plenty	Canterbury	Otago	North Harbour	Counties Manukau	Tasman	Hawke's Bay	Manawatu	**Totals**
T.W.K. Renata	15	s	s	s	15	–	–	–	s	15	**7**
R. Love	–	–	s	–	–	15	15	15	s	–	**5**
C.C. Garden-Bachop	14	–	–	–	–	–	–	–	–	s	**2**
W.S. Goosen	–	14	14	14	14	14	14	14	14	14	**9**
S.J. Savea	11	–	–	11	11	11	11	11	11	12	**8**
B.D. Proctor	13	15	15	15	13	13	13	13	15	13	**10**
V.T. Aso	12	12	12	12	–	12	12	12	12	s	**9**
P. Patafilo	–	11	11	s	s	s	s	s	13	11	**9**
P.I.J. Umaga-Jensen	s	13	13	13	12	–	–	–	–	–	**5**
A. Morgan	s	–	–	–	s	–	s	s	–	–	**4**
J.K. Garden-Bachop	10	10	10	10	10	10	10	10	10	10	**10**
T.J. Perenara	9	9	–	–	–	–	–	–	–	–	**2**
K.H. Hauiti-Parapara	s	–	9	9	9	9	s	s	9	9	**9**
C.D. Collins	–	s	s	s	s	s	9	9	s	s	**9**
T.G. Ben-Nicholas	s	s	8	8	8	8	8	8	8	8	**10**
A.S. Savea	8	8	–	–	–	–	–	–	–	–	**2**
D.P.A. Kirifi (capt)	7	7	7	7	7	7	–	–	–	–	**6**
S. Smith	–	–	–	–	–	–	s	s	s	s	**4**
M. Kafatolu	–	–	s	s	s	s	7	7	7	7	**8**
V.T.L. Fifita	6	6	6	6	6	6	6	6	6	4	**10**
C. Delany	–	s	s	–	s	s	s	–	–	6	**6**
J. Blackwell (capt)	4	4	4	4	4	4	4	4	4	5	**10**
N.S. Ah Kuoi	5	5	5	5	–	5	5	5	5	s	**9**
T. Plumtree	s	–	–	s	5	–	–	s	s	–	**5**
A.F. Fidow	3	3	–	3	3	s	3	3	3	3	**9**
B. Aumua-Peseta	–	s	s	s	s	3	s	–	–	–	**6**
J. Tavita-Metcalfe	s	–	3	s	–	–	–	–	–	–	**3**
M.P. Poi	s	s	–	–	–	s	s	s	s	–	**6**
X.S. Numia	–	–	s	1	1	1	1	1	1	1	**8**
K. Uluilakepa	1	1	1	–	s	–	–	s	s	s	**7**
B. Kauika-Petersen	–	–	s	–	–	–	–	–	–	–	**1**
T. Thompson	s	s	2	s	s	s	s	s	s	s	**10**
A.J. Aumua	2	2	–	–	–	–	–	–	–	–	**2**
J.P. O'Reilly	–	–	–	2	2	2	2	2	2	2	**7**

WELLINGTON TEAM RECORD 2020

Played 10   Won 5   Lost 5   Points for 289   Points against 248

Date	Opponent	Location	Score	Tries	Con	PG	DG	Referee
September 12	Waikato (P)	Hamilton	28–53	J. Savea, A. Savea, C. Garden-Bachop, Fifita	J. Garden-Bachop (4)			D.J. Waenga
September 20	Auckland (P)	Auckland	39–21	Aso (2), Goosen, Umaga-Jensen, Proctor, Fatafilo	J. Garden-Bachop (3)	J. Garden-Bachop		J.J. Doleman
September 25	Bay of Plenty (P)	Wellington	32–10	Ben-Nicholas (2), Goosen, Thompson, Love	J. Garden-Bachop (2)	J. Garden-Bachop		B.E. Pickerill
October 03	Canterbury (P)	Christchurch	26–31	Aso, Umaga-Jensen, Ah Kuoi, Thompson	J. Garden-Bachop (3)			P.M. Williams
October 10	Otago (cr)	Wellington	34–35	Renata, O'Reilly, Fidow, Hauiti-Parapara	J. Garden-Bachop (4)	J. Garden-Bachop (2)		A. Gardner (Australia)
October 17	North Harbour (P)	Wellington	25–20	Proctor, J. Garden-Bachop, J. Savea	J. Garden-Bachop (2)	J. Garden-Bachop (2)		J.J. Doleman
October 25	Counties Manukau (cr)	Pukekohe	53–20	O'Reilly (2), Fifita (2), Numia, Goosen, Ben-Nicholas	J. Garden-Bachop (4), Morgan (2)	J. Garden-Bachop (2)		D.J. Waenga
October 31	Tasman (P)	Porirua	3–19			J. Garden-Bachop		D.J. Waenga
November 08	Hawke's Bay (RS, cr)	Napier	18–34	Ah Kuoi, Uluilakepa	J. Garden-Bachop	J. Garden-Bachop (2)		R.P. Kelly
November 14	Manawatu (cr)	Wellington	31–5	Numia, Patafilo, Ben-Nicholas, Aso, Smith	J. Garden-Bachop (2), Proctor			B.E. Pickerill

WEST COAST

2020 Status: Heartland Championship
Founded 1890. Affiliated 1893
President: D.P. (David) Walklin
Chairman: M.J. (Mike) Meehan
Chief executive officer: Mike Connors
Coach: No appointment
Assistant coach: No appointment
Main ground: John Sturgeon Park, Greymouth
Capacity: 8000
Colours: Red and white

RECORDS

Highest attendance	10,000	West Coast–Buller v British Isles, 1959
Most appearances	101	M.T. Mudu, 2004–2019
Most points	712	M.A. Foster, 1992–2000
Most tries	27	K.J.J. Beams, 1965–78
Most points in a season	176	M.A. Foster, 1999
Most tries in a season	9	P.A. Teen, 1975
Most conversions in a season	20	M.A. Foster, 1999
Most penalty goals in a season	38	M.A. Foster, 1999
Most dropped goals in a season	9	A.P. O'Regan, 1987
Most points in a match	24	M.A. Foster v Horowhenua Kapiti, 1999
Most tries in a match	4	K. McNee v Buller, 1964
		F.P. O'Donnell v Buller, 1970
		P.A. Teen v Nelson Bays, 1975
		R.J. Stanton v Ngati Porou East Coast, 2018
Most conversions in a match	6	L.T. Martyn v Golden Bay-Motueka, 1933
Most penalty goals in a match	6	P.W. Hutchison v East Coast, 1991
		C.N. Simpson v South Canterbury, 2007
Highest team score	62	v Ngati Porou East Coast, 2018
Record victory (points ahead)	42	45–3 v Golden Bay-Motueka, 1933
Highest score conceded	128	v Canterbury, 1992
Record defeat (points behind)	128	0–128 v Canterbury, 1992

When the club competition finally got under way in July West Coast had pencilled in a home and away series against Buller for the Rundle Cup after the conclusion of the club season. However, with the re-emergence of Covid-19 in the Auckland community in August and the rest of the country put at Level Two restrictions, the club final was postponed for a week and when played there were no spectators allowed.

The planned Rundle Cup series was abandoned and, for the first time since 1918, the union did not field a representative team.

Hokitika club Kiwi won the club championship for the fifth consecutive year, and have now won their last 46 matches, their last defeat being to Blaketown in the opening game of 2017.

RANFURLY SHIELD 2020

In November 2019 Canterbury announced their two defences against Heartland Unions would be against Buller at Westport on July 11 and North Otago at Christchurch on July 17. The matches were postponed due to Covid-19 and when rescheduling was considered there was mutual agreement between Canterbury, Buller and NZR that Buller could postpone their challenge to 2021 as the mandatory challenge. The mandatory challenge is reserved for the Heartland Champion — Meads Cup winner — but as there would be no Heartland Championship this year, Buller could assume that mandatory challenge.

Canterbury's opening defence against North Otago was played at Rugby Park, Christchurch, not Orangetheory Stadium, Christchurch, and in front of no spectators due to Covid-19.

The Shield then changed hands in three successive challenges.

Taranaki led 20–3 after 28 minutes only for Canterbury to fight back and lead for the first time in the match at 22-20. Jordie Barrett then kicked a 48-metre penalty goal in the 74th minute to put Taranaki back in front, 23–22.

With a strong wind behind them, Otago scored two converted tries in the last eight minutes of the first half to open up a 22–5 lead that proved to be too much for Taranaki.

Otago dominated first-half territory and possession but found themselves 6–7 down at halftime against Hawke's Bay who pulled away in the second half. Magpies captain Ash Dixon was playing his 100th match for Hawke's Bay.

Results

Canterbury

701	July 13	v North Otago	Christchurch	won	71–7
702	September 19	v Taranaki	Christchurch	lost	22–23

Taranaki

703	September 27	v Otago	Inglewood	lost	19–30

Otago

704	October 4	v Hawke's Bay	Dunedin	lost	9–28

Hawke's Bay

705	October 16	v Northland	Napier	won	33–17
706	October 24	v Manawatu	Napier	won	47–12
707	November 8	v Wellington	Napier	won	34–18

First and most recent Ranfurly Shield match	Played	Won	Lost	Drawn as holder	Drawn as challenger	Points for	Points against
Auckland (1904–2015)	203	158	39	5	1	5849	2220
Bay of Plenty (1920–2015)	24	2	22	–	–	328	655
Buller (1907–2001)	12	–	11	–	1	36	328
Bush (1927–1968)	7	–	7	–	–	41	285
Canterbury (1904–2020)	199	151	41	6	1	5835	2591
Counties Manukau (1958–2017)	33	7	24	–	2	566	872
East Coast (1953–2013)	7	–	7	–	–	22	430
Golden Bay-Motueka (1958)	1	–	1	–	–	8	56
Hawke's Bay (1905–2020)	100	65[1]	31	3	1	2180	1530
Horowhenua Kapiti (1914–2015)	10	–	10	–	–	92	563
King Country (1922–2016)	20	–	20	–	–	120	664
Manawatu (1914–2020)	40	14	25	–	1	543	812
Manawhenua (1927–1929)	6	3	3	–	–	84	110
Marlborough (1908–2005)	20	7	13	–	–	245	539
Mid Canterbury (1933–2017)	15	–	15	–	–	111	620
Nelson (1924–1959)	2	–	2	–	–	17	66
Nelson Bays (1973–2005)	6	–	6	–	–	46	334
North Harbour (1986–2019)	21	4	17	–	–	487	639
North Otago (1938–2020)	15	–	15	–	–	99	858
Northland (1935–2020)	49	17	31	1	–	732	1086
Otago (1904–2020)	92	44	45	1	2	1505	1368
Poverty Bay (1911–2018)	17	–	17	–	–	78	790
South Auckland (1911)	1	–	1	–	–	5	21
South Canterbury (1920–2006)	26	3	23	–	–	273	821
Southland (1906–2019)	74	30	41	–	3	1099	1439
Taranaki (1906–2020)	103	50	47	3	3	1703	1705
Tasman (2008–2012)	2	–	2	–	–	60	75
Thames Valley (1951–2019)	16	–	16	–	–	97	706
Waikato (1932–2019)	109	67	38	3	1	3173	1713
Wairarapa (1905–1969)	30	12	17	–	1	431	504
Wairarapa Bush (1973–2015)	9	–	9	–	–	67	491
Wanganui (1907–2018)	31	–	30	–	1	239	985
Wellington (1904–2020)	99	50	43	1	5	1563	1377
West Coast (1932–2000)	15	–	15	–	–	107	588

[1] Includes Hawke's Bay's 1927 winning challenge against Wairarapa that was subsequently overturned on protest.

HIGHEST WINNING MARGIN BY A SHIELD HOLDER
134 points   Auckland 139   North Otago 5 at Oamaru 1993

HIGHEST WINNING MARGIN BY A CHALLENGER
45 points   Waikato 52   North Harbour 7 at Albany 2007

INDIVIDUAL PERFORMANCES

Most matches	57	G.J. Fox, Auckland
Most points	932	G.J. Fox, Auckland
Most tries	53	T.J. Wright, Auckland
Most conversions	233	G.J. Fox, Auckland
Most penalty goals	142	G.J. Fox, Auckland
Most dropped goals	14	R.H. Brown, Taranaki; D. Trevathan, Otago
Most goals from a mark	3	J.H. Dufty, Auckland
Most points in a match	40	J.J. Kirwan, Auckland v North Otago, 1993
Most tries in a match	8	J.J. Kirwan, Auckland v North Otago, 1993
Most conversions in a match	12	B.M. Craies, Auckland v Horowhenua, 1986; G.J. Fox, Auckland v Nelson Bays, 1991; G.W. Jackson, Waikato v West Coast, 2000; L.H. Munro, Auckland v North Otago, 2008
Most penalty goals in a match	7	R.M. Deans, Canterbury v Counties, 1984 C.J. McIntyre, Canterbury v Wellington, 2003
Most dropped goals in a match	3	R.H. Brown, Taranaki v Wanganui, 1964; R.H. Brown, Taranaki v North Auckland, 1964; G.P. Coffey, Canterbury v Auckland, 1990; A.P. Mehrtens, Canterbury v Southland, 1995

WINNING CHALLENGES

Canterbury	16		Taranaki	7		Marlborough	1	
Auckland	15[1]		Otago	7		Manawatu	1	
Waikato	11		Northland	4		Bay of Plenty	1	
Wellington	10		Wairarapa	3		North Harbour	1	
Southland	7		South Canterbury	2		Counties Manukau	1	
Hawke's Bay	7[2]		Manawhenua	1				

[1] Auckland were also the first holders, presented the Shield in 1902 by the NZRFU for having the best record that year.
[2] Includes Hawke's Bay's 1927 winning challenge against Wairarapa that was subsequently overturned on protest.

TENURES

Longest tenure	Challenges resisted		Shortest tenure		Days
Auckland	1985–93	61	Hawke's Bay	2013	6
Auckland	1960–63	25	Wellington	1963	7
Canterbury	1982–85	25	Waikato	2007	7
Hawke's Bay	1922–27	24	Otago	2020	7
Auckland	1905–13	23	Taranaki	2020	8
Canterbury	1953–56	23	Otago	2013	9
Canterbury	2000–03	23	Auckland	1972	10
Hawke's Bay	1966–69	21	North Auckland	1960	11
Waikato	1997–00	21			

North Auckland resisted one challenge; the other unions were defeated by the first challenger.

HAPPENINGS

On 23 March, due to the pandemic, NZR announced that, 'Following the New Zealand Government's lifting of the coronavirus alert status to level 3, all rugby in New Zealand will be suspended for the foreseeable future.' One week later the union announced the cancellation of the Heartland Championship, National Under 19 tournament and National Sevens, leaving only the Mitre 10 Cup and Farah Palmer Cup being delayed to a later date. On 8 April the union postponed all community and club rugby. Internationally, the pandemic forced the cancellation of many scheduled events involving New Zealand teams. In addition to the confirmed schedules, the union was also in negotiations making arrangements for other games, particularly for late in the year, but dates and venues had not been finalised.

The All Blacks were to meet Wales at Auckland, 4 July, and at Wellington, 12 July. Also one test against Scotland at Dunedin, 18 July.

The All Blacks Rugby Championship fixtures were set to meet Australia at Melbourne, 8 August; Australia at Wellington, 15 August; Argentina at Hamilton, 29 August; South Africa at Auckland, 5 September; Argentina at Mendoza, 19 September; South Africa at Nelspruit, 26 September.

In November the All Blacks were to meet England at London, 7 November; Wales at Cardiff, 14 November; Scotland at Edinburgh, 21 November.

The All Blacks XV were planning a three-match northern tour during October–November. The All Blacks XV is the latest name given to a national B selection. The only fixture to be confirmed was against Fiji at Vancouver, on 31 October.

The Maori All Blacks were to play two games against Russia in July and, also in July, a New Zealand Under 20 squad to the World Championship in Italy.

The Black Ferns were to meet USA at Dunedin, 18 July; Australia at Melbourne, 8 August; and Australia at Wellington, 15 August. Arrangements had progressed for visits by Canada (one test), England (two tests) and France (two tests). The large eight-test plan was to assist preparations for the 2021 Rugby World Cup.

The All Blacks Sevens and Black Ferns Sevens were to attend the Olympic Games at Tokyo during July–August.

All Blacks Sevens missed the final four rounds of the 2019/20 HSBC series which were cancelled — Hong Kong (3–5 April), Singapore (11–12 April), London (23–24 May), and Paris (30–31 May).

Similarly, the Black Ferns Sevens missed the final three tournaments of the HSBC Sevens Series — Hong Kong (3–5 April), Langford (2–3 May), and Paris (30–31 May). Furthermore, the 2020/21 series did not commence during the year.

• • •

Taranaki had four sets of brothers in its squad, but no more than two sets appeared in any one game. Jordie and Beauden Barrett, along with Kaylum and Lachlan Boshier, were all involved in the first two games. Fin and Jarrad Hoeata and Daniel and Shaan Waite were the other brothers involved during 2020.

• • •

Teague McElroy, a prop for North Harbour in 2020, extends the Barry rugby dynasty to four generations, being a grandson of Kevin Barry (All Black 1962–64). Teague's mother was Kevin's only daughter. Kevin's father, Ned, was an All Black 1932–34, and son Liam (uncle of Teague) an All Black 1993–95. Another of Teague's uncles is Mike Barry who represented North Auckland and North Harbour and is husband of television presenter Hilary.

• • •

Damian and Marty McKenzie are also fourth-generation rugby representatives. Their father, grandfather and great-grandfather all represented Southland. Eric McKenzie was the first, in 1920–21, followed by sons Graeme (1957–61) and Jack (1947–56), grandson Brent (son of Graeme and father of Damian and Marty) 1983–90.

• • •

When Hastings BHS defended the Moascar Cup against Napier BHS in their Super 8 match at Hastings on Saturday, 1 August, the referee was Tipene Cottrell and his Black Ferns wife Krysten was one of the two ARs.

• • •

For the resurrected inter-island match, Ngai Tahu father and son John and David Burke of Tauranga were invited to create a trophy for the occasion. The Te Matau a Maui trophy was designed and carved by the Burkes, being a carved rimu fish hook on a kauri base celebrating the Maori creation story of North Island (Te Ika a Maui) and South Island (Te Waka a Maui).

• • •

Two weeks before the inter-island match was played, the Loving Cup was rediscovered. During 2020 Wellington man Ian St George attempted to track down the whereabouts of the cup and found it was not among the trophy collection held by New Zealand Rugby in its Wellington headquarters. The cup had been presented to the 1924–25 All Blacks at an end-of-tour function at the Hotel Victoria in London on 21 January 1925 to commemorate their unbeaten record. The function was given by Sir James Allen, the NZ High Commissioner to the United Kingdom since 1922. Some 400 to 500 New Zealanders residing in London had contributed to the purchase of the cup and a small replica for each player.
Inscribed on the cup was verse written by William Pember Reeves. Reeves had previously been a New Zealand MP and NZ High Commissioner to the United Kingdom.

> To the shining leaf and the jersey black
> To the journey without defeat
> To the mighty hearts of the striving pack
> And the runners with flying feet
> This loving cup, drink, drink in turn
> While memory stirs each breath
> And lift it high to the silver fern
> And the record that beat the best.

On the team's arrival home, the manager Stan Dean (also the NZRFU chairman at the time) in his tour report to the NZRFU suggested the cup be allocated to the North Island v South Island match, and this was duly done. The publicity given to Ian St George's search for the cup in a story published by *Stuff* in August eventually saw it rediscovered in the last week of August in the bowels of Eden Park's North Stand. How long it had been there and why was unknown. When found, the cup was separate from its base but both were intact, although the sterling silver lid was missing. Plaques recording the winners were on the base up to 1931.

• • •

Eligibility of the North Island and South Island teams was determined on a province-of-origin basis — the province they first played for, not by current province — although for the large majority of players the province they first played for and their current province is the same.

NORTH ISLAND team eligibility

	First province	Current province
Asafo Aumua	Wellington, 2016	Wellington
Beauden Barrett	Taranaki, 2010	Taranaki
Caleb Clarke	Auckland, 2017	Auckland
Ash Dixon	Hawke's Bay, 2008	Hawke's Bay
Mitchell Hunt	Auckland, 2015	Tasman
Akira Ioane	Auckland, 2015	Auckland
Rieko Ioane	Auckland, 2015	Auckland
Ayden Johnstone	Waikato, 2016	Waikato
Anton Lienert-Brown	Waikato, 2014	Waikato
Damian McKenzie	Waikato, 2014	Waikato
Dalton Papali'i	Auckland, 2017	Counties Manukau
TJ Perenara	Wellington, 2010	Wellington
Sevu Reece	Waikato, 2016	Tasman
Ardie Savea	Wellington, 2012	Wellington
Scott Scrafton	Auckland, 2014	Auckland
Aaron Smith	Manawatu, 2008	Manawatu
Hoskins Sotutu	Auckland, 2018	Auckland
Angus Ta'avao	Auckland, 2010	Auckland
Karl Tu'inukuafe	North Harbour, 2015	North Harbour
Ofa Tu'ungafasi	Auckland, 2012	Auckland
Patrick Tuipulotu	Auckland, 2013	Auckland
Peter Umaga-Jensen	Wellington, 2016	Wellington
Tupou Vaa'i	Taranaki, 2018	Taranaki

SOUTH ISLAND team eligibility

	First province	Current province
Jordie Barrett	Canterbury, 2016	Taranaki
George Bower	Otago, 2014	Otago
George Bridge	Canterbury, 2016	Canterbury
Finlay Christie	Tasman, 2016	Tasman
Tom Christie	Canterbury, 2017	Canterbury
Liam Coltman	Otago, 2010	Otago
Mitchell Dunshea	Canterbury, 2015	Canterbury
Braydon Ennor	Canterbury, 2017	Canterbury
Leicester Faingaanuku	Tasman, 2018	Tasman
Shannon Frizell	Tasman, 2016	Tasman
Jack Goodhue	Canterbury, 2014	Northland
Dillon Hunt	Otago, 2015	North Harbour
Josh Ioane	Otago, 2017	Otago
Will Jordan	Tasman, 2017	Tasman
Nepo Laulala	Canterbury, 2011	Counties Manukau
Tyrel Lomax	Tasman, 2017	Tasman
Richie Mo'unga	Canterbury, 2013	Canterbury
Joe Moody	Canterbury, 2011	Canterbury
Tom Sanders	Canterbury, 2014	Canterbury
Manaaki Selby-Rickit	Southland, 2017	Southland
Codie Taylor	Canterbury, 2012	Canterbury
Brad Weber	Otago, 2012	Hawke's Bay
Sam Whitelock	Canterbury, 2008	Canterbury

• • •

With the Ranfurly Shield changing hands three times in 2020, four players were able to play in a winning Ranfurly Shield challenge for the third time in their careers:
Michael Collins when Otago won against Taranaki
Ash Dixon, Brendon O'Connor and Gareth Evans when Hawke's Bay won against Otago.
They join a select band of now 23 players who have appeared in three or more successful winning Ranfurly Shield challenges. In chronological order they are:

4 wins
B.G. Williams — Auckland, 1971, 1972, 1974, 1979

3 wins
A.E. Cooke — Wairarapa 1927, 1928, Wellington 1930
V.L. George — Southland 1929, 1937, 1938
H.L. White — Auckland 1952, 1959, 1960
R.H. Graham — Auckland 1959, 1960, 1965
F.J. Colthurst — Auckland 1959, 1960, North Auckland 1971
D.L. Palmer — Auckland 1971, 1972, 1974
B.R. Johnstone — Auckland 1971, 1974, 1979
A.M. Haden — Auckland 1972, 1979, 1985
M.J.A. Cooper — Waikato 1993, 1996, 1997
I.D. Foster — Waikato 1993, 1996, 1997
S.B. Gordon — Waikato 1993, 1996, 1997
A.R. Cashmore — Auckland 1995, 1996, Bay of Plenty 2004
A.P. Mehrtens — Canterbury 1994, 2000, 2004
C.R. Flynn — Canterbury 2004, 2007, 2009
W.W.V. Crockett — Canterbury 2007, 2009, 2010
T.P. Keats — Canterbury 2007, 2009, Taranaki 2011
A.S. Mathewson — Wellington 2008, Hawke's Bay 2013, Canterbury 2016
T.F.S Bateman — Canterbury 2007, 2009, 2019
M.W.V. Collins — Otago 2013, 2018, 2020
A.L. Dixon — Hawke's Bay 2013, 2014, 2020
G.O. Evans — Otago 2013, Hawke's Bay 2014, 2020
B.R. O'Connor — Hawke's Bay 2013, 2014, 2020

Alby Mathewson has played in winning challenges for three provinces. No other player has played in a winning challenge for more than two provinces.

• • •

Against Auckland, on 10 October, Taranaki's Jayson Potroz scored 23 uninterrupted points within 19 minutes. After one minute, Rayasi (Auckland) scored a try. Potroz was then the sole point-scorer over the next 20 minutes, scoring after 3 minutes (penalty), 9 minutes (try and conversion), 15 minutes (penalty), 18 minutes (penalty) and 22 minutes (try and conversion) to take Taranaki's lead to 23–5. Auckland eventually won 29–28.
At the 1995 Rugby World Cup Simon Culhane scored 24 points in 40 minutes against Japan, but they were not the total points-scored by the All Blacks over that time.

• • •

New Zealand Universities played two non-first class matches in October after their planned biennial April/May tour of Japan was postponed due to Covid-19. Results were as follows:
6 October, at Rugby Park, Christchurch: lost 34–36 to Cantabrians XV
Tries: Graham Urquhart 2, Josh Corrigan 2, Ryan Gordon 1; Cons: Tyrone Elkington-MacDonald 3; Pen: Elkington-MacDonald.
9 October, at Denton Park, Christchurch: defeated Jerry Cross XV (Canterbury Metro) 29–19.
Tries: Isaac Leota, Te Ariki Te Puni, Patrick Thacker, Glen Beardsley; Cons: Elkington-MacDonald 3; Pen: Elkington-MacDonald.
The full squad was: Takaji Young-Yen, Te Ariki Te Puni, Tumama Tu'ulua, Basil Aholelei, Tyrone Elkington-MacDonald (c), George Emosi, Noah Foster (Auckland), Sam Lester, Billy Coman, Ryan Gordon, Isaac Leota, Josh Corrigan (Canterbury), Nick Grogan, Hamish Northcott, Jayden Falcon (Massey), Joel Wisnewski, Jackson Morgan (Victoria), Patrick Thacker, Glen Beardsley, Ryan Barnes (Lincoln), Jack McHugh, Graham Urquhart (Otago), Kalin Felise (NH Marist), Ben Lewis (Napier Pirates).
Management: Jason McLean (head coach), Jack Halpin (assistant coach), Braeden Saul (manager), Lincoln Baltus (doctor), Harley Matthews (physio).

• • •

There was a scoring oddity in each of the three Mitre 10 Cup games played on Sunday, 15 November. To compile 33 points is more often a winning score than a losing score but on this day it was the losing score in each of the three Mitre 10 Cup games.
Bay of Plenty defeated North Harbour 37–33, Canterbury defeated Auckland 34–33, and Hawke's Bay defeated Taranaki 34–33.

• • •

The numbers of players with New Zealand backgrounds in Six Nations squads is on the rise again as the new World Cup preparations cycle gets under way. England has five with varying backgrounds, namely Mako Vunipola, Willi Heinz, Piers Francis, Jacob Umaga and Joe Marchant, returned from the Blues. For Wales, Johnny McNicholl joined Gareth Anscombe and Hadleigh Parkes. James Lowe and Jamison Gibson-Park joined Bundee Aki and Joey Carberry with Ireland. Scotland fielded Blade Thomson, Sean Maitland, Simon Berghan and Blair Cowan, and France used Virimi Vakatawa and Uini Atonio. Monty Ioane recently debuted for Italy, joining Jayden Hayward, Dean Budd and Jimmy Tuivaiti.

• • •

Frank Colthurst (*see* Obituaries) was regarded by the *Almanack* editors as the best-performing hooker of the 1960s. In his debut first-class season, 1959, the editors chose him as a reserve in their Almanack XV. Then followed seven editions in which Colthurst was chosen at hooker in the Almanack XV, 1962, 1963, 1964, 1966, 1968, 1969, 1971. While Frank may have thought the editors were better judges of players than the selectors appointed by the NZRFU, it has remained a mystery why his talents were never recognised by the All Blacks selectors. No non-All Black has ever been in the Almanack XV as frequently as Colthurst.

• • •

The 2020 ASB Rugby Awards moved from the traditional annual function in Auckland to a made-for-TV special on Sky, held on 17 December. The winners are recorded elsewhere in this publication, but we record here the finalists for some of the awards (winner in bold).

- Sky Television Fans Try of the Year — Neria Fomai (Hawke's Bay), **Jack Jones** (Christ's College), Bethel Lutele-Malasia (Boys' High School).
- Charles Monro Rugby Volunteer of the Year — **Jane Chamberlain** (Horowhenua Kapiti), Allen Grainger (Waikato), Scott Kahle (Bay of Plenty).
- New Zealand Rugby Referee of the Year — Mike Fraser, Ben O'Keefe, **Paul Williams**.
- Richard Crawshaw Memorial All Blacks Sevens Player of the Year — Scott Curry, Tim Mikkelson, Ngarohi McGarvey-Black.
- Black Ferns Sevens Player of the Year — Kelly Brazier, **Stacey Fluhler**, Tyla Nathan-Wong.
- Duane Monkley Medal (Mitre 10 Cup Player of the Year) — **Folau Fakatava** (Hawke's Bay), Salesi Rayasi (Auckland), Kaleb Trask (Bay of Plenty).
- Fiao'o Faamausili Medal (Farah Palmer Cup Player of the Year) — Chelsea Alley (Waikato), **Kendra Cocksedge** (Canterbury), Stacey Fluhler (Waikato).
- Investec Super Rugby Player of the Year — Jordie Barrett (Hurricanes), **Richie Mo'unga** (Crusaders), Aaron Smith (Highlanders), Patrick Tuipulotu (Blues).
- Tom French Memorial Maori Player of the Year — **Ash Dixon** (Hawke's Bay), Stacey Fluhler (Waikato), Aaron Smith (Manawatu).
- ASB National Coach of the Year — Andrew Goodman and Clarke Dermody (Tasman), Mark Ozich (Hawke's Bay), **Scott Robertson** (Crusaders), James Semple (Waikat FPC).
- ASB New Zealand Coach of the Year — **Allan Bunting and Cory Sweeney** (Black Ferns Sevens), Ian Foster (All Blacks), Clark Laidlaw (All Blacks Sevens), Glenn Moore (Black Ferns), Clayton McMillan (Maori All Blacks).
- Black Ferns Player of the Year — **Chelsea Alley**, Kendra Cocksedge, Kennedy Simon.
- All Blacks Player of the Year — **Sam Cane**, Dane Coles, Aaron Smith.
- adidas National Team of the Year — Crusaders, Hawke's Bay, Canterbury (FPC), **Tasman**.
- adidas New Zealand Team of the Year — All Blacks, All Blacks Sevens, Black Ferns, **Black Ferns Sevens**, Maori All Blacks.

2020 SEASON'S STATISTICS

LEADING SCORERS IN ALL FIRST-CLASS MATCHES IN NEW ZEALAND AND FOR NEW ZEALAND TEAMS OVERSEAS

(Record: 519, G.J. Fox, 1989 in 32 games, 2 Tries, 122 Con, 88 PG, 1 DG)

	Teams	M	Tries	Con	PG	DG	Total
R. Mo'unga	Crusaders/South Island/Canterbury/New Zealand	19	7	37	22	0	175
D.S. McKenzie	Chiefs/North Island/Waikato/New Zealand	19	4	32	28	1	171
J.M. Barrett	Hurricanes/South Island/Taranaki/New Zealand	20	5	34	23	0	162
M.J. Hunt	Highlanders/North Island/Tasman	26	4	38	22	0	162
J.R. Ioane	Highlanders/South Island/Otago/Moana Pasifika	21	2	31	30	0	162
O.W.T.P. Black	Blues/Bay of Plenty/NZ Maori	22	0	28	22	0	122
B.E.C. Gatland	Highlanders/North Harbour	14	3	25	18	1	122
J.K. Garden-Bachop	Hurricanes/Wellington	20	1	27	17	1	113
K.R. Trask	Chiefs/Bay of Plenty/NZ Maori	19	7	20	7	0	96
J.P. Potroz	Taranaki	10	3	16	16	0	95

LEADING TRY-SCORERS

(Record: 36, J.J. Kirwan, 1987 in 32 games)

Tries	Games		Teams
15	26	A.L. Dixon	Highlanders/North Island/Hawke's Bay/NZ Maori
14	11	S.T.M. Rayasi	Hurricanes/Auckland/Moana Pasifika
13	15	W.T. Jordan	Crusaders/South Island/Tasman/New Zealand
11	18	S.L. Reece	Crusaders/North Island/Tasman/New Zealand
11	19	R.E. Ioane	Blues/North Island/Auckland/New Zealand
9	25	M.E. Telea	Blues/Tasman
8	8	J.P. Van Wyk	Hurricanes
8	22	L.S. Boshier	Chiefs/Taranaki
8	11	J.W.J. Ratumaitavuki-Kneepkens	Taranaki
8	25	L.O.K.W.T. Faingaanuku	Crusaders/South Island/Tasman/Moana Pasifika

THREE (or more) TRIES IN A MATCH
(Record: 8, T.R. Heeps, New Zealand v Northern NSW, 1962;
J.J. Kirwan, Auckland v North Otago, 1993)

3	M.E. Telea	Blues v Waratahs
3	J.P. Van Wyk	Hurricanes v Sunwolves
3	S.L. Reece	Tasman v Northland
3	C.M. Moli	South Canterbury v Buller, Sept 19
3	T. Savelio	South Canterbury v Buller, Sept 19
3	D.K. Havili	Tasman v Waikato
3	A.L. Motuga	Counties Manukau v Manawatu
3	J.R. Page	North Harbour v Hawke's Bay
3	S.T.M. Rayasi	Auckland v Waikato
3	A.L. Dixon	Hawke's Bay v Taranaki, Nov 21

21 (or more) POINTS IN A MATCH
(Record: 45, S.D. Culhane, New Zealand v Japan, 1995, 1 try, 20 conversions)

33	D.S. McKenzie	Waikato v Wellington, 1t, 5c, 6pg
23	J.P. Potroz	Taranaki v Auckland, 2t, 2c, 3pg
23	R. Mo'unga	New Zealand v Australia, Sydney, 2t, 5c, 1pg
21	C.D. Clare	Wanganui v Horowhenua Kapiti, 2t, 4c, 1pg

SIX (or more) CONVERSIONS IN A MATCH
(Record: 20, J.P. Preston, Canterbury v West Coast, 1992;
S.D. Culhane, New Zealand v Japan, 1995)

8	B.D. Cameron	Canterbury v North Otago
7	W.A. Wright	South Canterbury v Buller, Sept 19
7	L.F. McClutchie	Hawke's Bay v Taranaki, Nov 21

SIX (or more) PENALTY GOALS IN A MATCH
(Record: 9, A.P. Mehrtens, New Zealand v Australia, at Auckland, 1999;
A.P. Mehrtens, New Zealand v France, at Paris, 2000;
B.J. Barrett, Taranaki v Bay of Plenty, 2011)

6	D.S. McKenzie	Waikato v Wellington

TWO (or more) DROPPED GOALS IN A MATCH
(Record: 5, M.K. Sisam, Hawke's Bay v East Coast, 1979)

No player drop kicked more than one goal in a match in 2020

SCORED IN ALL FOUR WAYS
No player scored all four ways in a match in 2020

CURRENT PLAYER STATISTICS

CAREER RECORDS OF PLAYERS APPEARING IN NEW ZEALAND FIRST-CLASS RUGBY 2020

125 GAMES OF FIRST-CLASS RUGBY

K.J. Read	341	A.O.H.M. Tu'ungafasi	189	P.T. Tuipulotu	148
L.J. Messam	336			D.S. McKenzie	147
A.L. Smith	301	A.W.F. Ta'avao-Matau	184	A.L. Ioane	146
S.L. Whitelock	300			T.W. Renata	143
D.S. Coles	268	A.J. Thomson	183	S.K. Barrett	140
B.J. Barrett	257	J.P.T. Moody	182	D.P. Lienert-Brown	136
B. May	256	C.J.D. Taylor	182	V.T.L. Fifita	132
A.L. Dixon	254	B.M. Weber	170	M.S. Ala'alatoa	131
T.T.R. Perenara	238	M.D. Drummond	168	A.T. Tikoirotuma	131
J.L. Mackintosh	236	J.M.R.A. Hoeata	167	M.J. Hunt	130
L. Romano	229	T.L. Manu	166	R. Thompson	130
J.W. Parsons	227	C.I. Eves	164	V.T. Aso	129
S.J. Cane	224	A.R. Lienert-Brown	162	O.W. Black	129
A.W. Cruden	212	A.N. Ainley	156	R.J. Prinsep	129
L.J. Coltman	206	D.K. Havili	156	R.K. Darling	128
J.K. Rutledge	205	S.F. Tokolahi	156	R.G. Wright	127
B.D. Hall	199	N.E. Laulala	153	B.R. O'Connor	126
A.S. Savea	196	R. Mo'unga	153	J.R. Riccitelli	126
		G.O. Evans	149	K.W. Hammington	125

500 POINTS IN FIRST-CLASS RUGBY

B.J. Barrett	2139	J.M. Barrett	706	F.H. Smith	616
R. Mo'unga	1351	J.K. Garden-Bachop	667	C.D. Clare	546
D.S. McKenzie	1180			J.R. Ioane	529
O.W. Black	815	T.W. Renata	658	B.E.C. Gatland	518
M.J. Hunt	719				

50 TRIES IN FIRST-CLASS RUGBY

R.E. Ioane	81	K.H. Laumape	69	M.B. Lam	57
B.J. Barrett	80	G.C. Bridge	64	S.L. Reece	55
L.J. Messam	77	K.J. Read	63	W.T. Jordan	51
T.T.R. Perenara	76	A.L. Smith	63	A.J. Thomson	50

100 GAMES FOR A TEAM

Player	Games	Team	Player	Games	Team
Liam Messam	179	Chiefs	Julian Savea	121	Hurricanes
Kieran Read	157	Crusaders	Dane Coles	119	Hurricanes
Samuel Whitelock	151	Crusaders	James Parsons	115	Blues
Aaron Smith	150	Highlanders	Liam Coltman	115	Highlanders
Jason Rutledge	143	Southland	Ralph Darling	110	North Otago
TJ Perenara	140	Hurricanes	Matthew Fetu	107	SthCanterbury
Luke Romano	134	Crusaders	Ash Dixon	107	Hawke's Bay
Kieran Read	128	New Zealand	Ross Wright	107	Northland
Beauden Barrett	125	Hurricanes	Lemi Masoe	106	North Otago
Jamie Mackintosh	123	Southland	James Parsons	106	North Harbour
Sam Whitelock	122	New Zealand	Aaron Cruden	100	Chiefs
Sam Cane	122	Chiefs			

400 POINTS FOR A TEAM

Player	Points	Team	Player	Points	Team
Richie Mo'unga	760	Crusaders	Bryn Gatland	447	North Harbour
Damian McKenzie	745	Chiefs	Simon Hickey	447	Auckland
Aaron Cruden	721	Chiefs	Mitch Hunt	439	Tasman
Jackson Garden-Bachop	604	Wellington	Baden Kerr	407	Counties Manukau

25 TRIES FOR A TEAM

Player	Tries	Team	Player	Tries	Team
TJ Perenara	56	Hurricanes	Liam Messam	30	Waikato
Ngani Laumape	45	Hurricanes	Salesi Rayasi	29	Auckland
Rieko Ioane	38	Blues	Aaron Smith	29	Highlanders
Beauden Barrett	36	New Zealand	Wes Goosen	27	Wellington
George Bridge	33	Crusaders	Rieko Ioane	26	New Zealand
Iliesa Tora	33	Buller	Ash Dixon	25	Hawke's Bay
Liam Messam	32	Chiefs	Lemi Masoe	25	North Otago
Seta Koroitamana	32	Mid Canterbury	Jona Nareki	25	Otago
			Sevu Reece	25	Waikato

FIRST-CLASS STATISTICS

to January 1, 2021

250 GAMES OF FIRST-CLASS RUGBY

K.F. Mealamu	384	2000-15	A.P. Mehrtens	282	1993-2005
W.W.V. Crockett	375	2005-19	R.S. Crotty	279	2008-19
C.E. Meads	361	1955-74	A.J. Wyllie	279	1964-80
S.B.T. Fitzpatrick	348	1983-97	C.J. Spencer	277	1992-2005
M.A. Nonu	344	2002-19	A.M. Stone	275	1980-94
K.J. Read	341	2005-20	J.A. Collins	275	1994-2010
L.J. Messam	336	2003-20	M.J.A. Cooper	270	1985-99
R.H. McCaw	334	2000-15	D.E. Holwell	270	1995–2010
T.D. Woodcock	330	2000-15	J.M. Muliaina	270	1999-2014
J.F. Umaga	329	1994-2011	B.G. Williams	269	1968-84
A.M. Haden	328	1971-86	K.R. Tremain	268	1957-72
Q.J. Cowan	326	2000-16	J.J. Kirwan	268	1983-94
R.W. Loe	321	1980-97	D.S. Coles	268	2007-20
G.W. Whetton	314	1979-95	A.M. Ellis	267	2004-16
Z.V. Brooke	311	1985-97	L.R. MacDonald	266	1994-2009
A.K. Hore	311	1999-2016	C.G. Smith	266	2003-15
W.F. McCormick	310	1958-78	C.C. King	265	2002-18
C.S. Ralph	306	1996-2008	G.L. Slater	263	1991-2005
G.J. Fox	303	1982-95	R.D. Thorne	263	1996-2011
A.L. Smith	301	2008-20	H.T.P. Elliot	261	2005-17
A.D. Oliver	300	1993-2007	K.J. Crowley	260	1980-94
S.L. Whitelock	300	2008-20	T.J. Blackadder	260	1990-2001
N.J. Hewitt	296	1988-2001	C.H. Hoeft	260	1993-2005
J. Kaino	296	2003-18	I.A. Eliason	259	1964-82
S.C. McDowell	294	1982-98	C.S. Jane	259	2003-17
R.M. Brooke	292	1987-2001	E. Clarke	258	1990-2005
C.R. Flynn	289	2001-17	S.J. Bachop	257	1986-99
D.W. Carter	287	2002-15	B.J. Barrett	257	2010-20
I.D. Jones	286	1988-2000	B. May	256	2004-20
O.T. Franks	286	2007-19	G.A. Knight	255	1972-86
I.A. Kirkpatrick	286	1966-79	G.M. Somerville	255	1997-2008
W.K. Little	285	1988-2000	A.L. Dixon	254	2008-20
J.W. Marshall	284	1992-2005	I.J. Clarke	252	1951-63
P.A.T. Weepu	284	2003-17	S.M. Going	252	1962-80
B.R. Smith	284	2007-19	B.J. Robertson	250	1971-84

1000 POINTS IN FIRST-CLASS RUGBY

	Career	Games	Tries	Con	PG	DG/Mark	Points
G.J. Fox	1982–95	303	29	901	683	47	4112
D.W. Carter	2002–2015	287	78	649	646	19	3683
A.P. Mehrtens	1993–2005	282	40	556	571	55	3190
M.J.A. Cooper	1985–99	270	78	475	420	2	2573
K.J. Crowley	1980–94	260	87	375	376	9	2265
G.J.L Cooper	1984–96	188	60	384	385	14	2210
D.E. Holwell	1995–2010	270	39	451	366	2	2201
W.B. Johnston	1986–2001	220	29	420	396	5	2177
B.J. Barrett	2010-20	257	80	436	285	4	2139
R.M. Deans	1979–90	187	45	390	370	1	2073
W.F. McCormick	1958–78	310	57	457	314	9	2065
T.E. Brown	1995–2011	211	29	345	373	14	1996
A.R. Cashmore	1992–2005	187	64	356	294	2	1920
C.J. Spencer	1992–2005	277	101	335	221	12	1872
D.B. Clarke	1951–64	226	22	366	320	28/3	1851
S.R. Donald	2001-19	243	68	337	274	2	1842
S.D. Culhane	1988–99	155	20	291	313	19	1672
J.B. Cunningham	1990–98	136	52	316	226	1	1569
B.A. Blair	1999–2006	149	59	302	221	–	1562
L.Z. Sopoaga	2010-18	171	26	295	265	5	1530
A.W. Cruden	2008–17	201	33	245	267	2	1462
G.W. Jackson	1996–2004	175	41	267	215	8	1408
D.W. Hill	1997–2006	177	30	279	230	1	1401
R. Mo'unga	2013–2020	153	46	343	145	–	1351
A.R. Hewson	1973–88	154	19	247	229	17	1308
J.P. Preston	1987–98	175	21	244	230	–	1276
M. Williment	1958–68	121	17	296	188	16	1255
F.M. Botica	1985–2001	150	37	263	176	7	1224
L.W. Mains	1967–76	142	13	212	228	13	1194
D.S. McKenzie	2014-20	147	48	224	162	2	1180
E.J. Crossan	1987–96	91	29	191	219	–	1158
G.D. Rowlands	1969–82	179	42	198	185	15	1151
C.L. McAlister	2002–11	151	19	204	207	1	1127
I.T. West	2012–18	139	27	223	179	2	1124
J.W. Wilson	1992–2002	233	151	76	68	4	1123
W.J. Burton	1990–96	93	11	217	199	5	1099
J.A. Gopperth	2002–09	126	27	228	167	2	1098
J.A. Gallagher	1984–90	139	67	196	144	1	1095
B.J.W. Fairbrother	1981–92	118	20	132	183	61	1076
R.B. Barrell	1963–79	147	20	125	225	10	1030
D.P. Lilley	1993–2003	162	41	139	176	6	1029
G.W. Anscombe	2010–14	83	27	163	182	1	1010

100 TRIES IN FIRST-CLASS RUGBY

	Games	Tries		Games	Tries
J.J. Kirwan	268	199	S.W. Sivivatu	187	116
T.J. Wright	217	177	I.A. Kirkpatrick	286	114
D.C. Howlett	240	173	N.R. Berryman	190	114
B.G. Fraser	200	171	J. Vidiri	153	114
C.M. Cullen	233	164	C.I. Green	162	111
Z.V. Brooke	311	161	J.T. Rokocoko	214	111
J.F. Umaga	329	156	H.E. Gear	228	111
J.W. Wilson	233	151	G.B. Batty	142	109
R.A. Jarden	134	145	B.R. Ford	196	109
R.Q. Randle	189	141	E. Clarke	258	109
B.G. Williams	269	137	J.K.R. Timu	182	108
K.R. Tremain	268	136	R.L. Gear	197	108
P.J. Cooke	195	133	T.W. Mitchell	155	106
C.S. Ralph	306	133	S.S. Wilson	202	106
J.T. Lomu	203	126	A.R. Sutherland	211	103
M. Clamp	139	123	E.J. Rush	205	103
S.J. Savea	212	121	B.W. Smith	147	102
M.A. Nonu	344	120	R.M. Smith	152	102
A.E. Cooke	131	119	C.J. Spencer	277	101

MOST DROPPED GOALS IN FIRST-CLASS RUGBY

B.J.W. Fairbrother	61	M.A. Herewini	47	P.M. Martin	34
A.P. Mehrtens	55	R.J. Preston	39	B.J. McKechnie	33
M.B. Roulston	50	J.W. Boe	37	E.J. Dunn	31
G.J. Fox	47	R.H. Brown	35	D. Trevathan	31

MOST POINTS IN A FIRST-CLASS MATCH

	Match	Tries	Con	PG	DG	Total
S.D. Culhane	New Zealand v Japan, 1995	1	20	–	–	45
J.P. Preston	Canterbury v West Coast, 1992	1	20	–	–	44
R.M. Deans	New Zealand v South Australia, 1984	3	14	1	–	43
A.R. Cashmore	Auckland v Mid Canterbury, 1995	5	9	–	–	43
J.F. Karam	New Zealand v South Australia, 1974	2	15	1	–	41
J.J. Kirwan	Auckland v North Otago, 1993	8	–	–	–	40
P.W. Turner	Otago v East Coast, 1986	2	14	1	–	39
J.W. Wilson	New Zealand Colts v Thames Valley, 1993	4	5	3	–	39
D.J. Kellett	Western Samoa v Marlborough, 1993	3	12	–	–	39
R.A. Jarden	New Zealand v Central West (Aust), 1951	6	10	–	–	38
D.E. Holwell	Northland v Thames Valley, 1997	2	14	–	–	38
B.A. Blair	New Zealand v Ireland A, 2001	3	4	5	–	38
R.J. du Preez	Sharks v Blues 2018	1	6	7	–	38
J.L. Graham	Counties v East Coast, 1972	–	14	3	–	37
S.D. Culhane	Southland v Manawatu, 1994	1	1	8	2	37
J.B. Cunningham	Central Vikings v South Canterbury, 1997	3	11	–	–	37
B.A. Blair	Canterbury v Counties Manukau, 1999	3	11	–	–	37

100 GAMES FOR TWO TEAMS

Colin Meads	King Country 139	New Zealand 133	1955-74
Bruce Robertson	Counties 123	New Zealand 102	1971-84
Bryan Williams	Auckland 130	New Zealand 113	1968-84
Andy Haden	Auckland 157	New Zealand 117	1971-86
Gary Whetton	Auckland 178	New Zealand 101	1979-95
Zinzan Brooke	Auckland 140	New Zealand 100	1985-97
Sean Fitzpatrick	Auckland 153	New Zealand 128	1983-97
Tana Umaga	Wellington 100	Hurricanes 122	1994-2011
Dan Carter	Crusaders 141	New Zealand 112	2002-15
Keven Mealamu	Blues 164	New Zealand 133	2000-15
Richie McCaw	Crusaders 145	New Zealand 149	2000-15
Tony Woodcock	Blues 137	New Zealand 118	2000-15
Jimmy Cowan	Southland 111	Highlanders 108	2000-16
Owen Franks	Crusaders 153	New Zealand 108	2007-19
Ma'a Nonu	Hurricanes 126	New Zealand 104	2002-19
Kieran Read	Crusaders 157	New Zealand 128	2005-19
James Parsons	North Harbour 106	Blues 115	2007-20
Sam Whitelock	Crusaders 151	New Zealand 122	2008-20

150 GAMES FOR A TEAM

I.A. Eliason	Taranaki	222	1964-81
W.F. McCormick	Canterbury	220	1959-75
W.W.V. Crockett	Crusaders	203	2006-18
A.J. Dawson	Counties	201	1976-89
K.J. Crowley	Taranaki	199	1980-94
H.L. White	Auckland	192	1950-63
G.J. Fox	Auckland	189	1982-93
A.I. Wyllie	Canterbury	187	1964-79
A.W. Slater	Taranaki	180	1989-2001
J.N. Coe	Counties Manukau	179	1986-99
L.J. Messam	Chiefs	179	2006-18
G.W. Whetton	Auckland	178	1980-92
R.S. Sutherland	Marlborough	177	1958-74
G.L. Slater	Taranaki	174	1991-2005
L.G. Brownlee	Buller	174	1999-2018
G.C. Williams	Wellington	173	1964-76
R.C. Ketels	Counties	171	1974-87
R.J. Knight	Otago	170	1982-92
K.E. Barrett	Taranaki	167	1986-99
L.J. Davis	Canterbury	166	1964-77
J.E. Morgan	North Auckland	165	1967-81
K.F. Mealamu	Blues	164	2000-15
D.E. Latta	Otago	162	1986-96
G.D. Rowlands	Bay of Plenty	161	1969-82
W.B. Johnston	North Auckland	161	1986-97
P.L. Phillips	Marlborough	160	1980-97

N.W. Thimbleby	Hawke's Bay	158	1959-71
J.C. Ross	Mid Canterbury	158	1970-87
A.M. Haden	Auckland	157	1971-86
K.J. Read	Crusaders	157	2007-19
D.R. Mohi	Bay of Plenty	156	1961-77
K.C. Bloxham	Otago	155	1974-86
P.J. Beveridge	Buller	155	1993-2018
T.J. Stuart	Buller	154	1984-99
A.M. Ellis	Crusaders	154	2006-16
J.E. Spiers	Counties	153	1970-82
S.B.T. Fitzpatrick	Auckland	153	1984-97
P.M. Hirini	Horowhenua	153	1986-2000
O.T. Franks	Crusaders	153	2009-19
B.R. Smith	Highlanders	153	2009-19
L.J. Hughes	Counties	152	1968-81
R.J. Preston	Bay of Plenty	152	1980-91
G.C. Frew	Mid Canterbury	152	1979-94
F.W. Marfell	Marlborough	152	1982-95
S.J. Todd	South Canterbury	152	1986-2001
R.S. Crotty	Crusaders	152	2009-19
C.R. Flynn	Crusaders	151	2002-14
S.L. Whitelock	Crusaders	151	2010-20
A.J. Whetton	Auckland	150	1981-92
E. Clarke	Auckland	150	1991-2002
S.T. Ngatu	Poverty Bay	150	2003-18

1000 POINTS FOR A TEAM

			Games	Tries	Con	PG	DG	Total
G.J. Fox	Auckland	1982-93	189	25	613	441	31	2746
K.J. Crowley	Taranaki	1980-94	199	64	291	286	5	1723
D.W. Carter	Crusaders	2003-15	141	36	287	307	11	1708
W.B. Johnston	North Auckland	1986-97	161	21	320	303	4	1656
R.M. Deans	Canterbury	1979-90	146	34	299	296	1	1625
M.J.A. Cooper	Waikato	1990-99	124	38	331	252	1	1604
D.W. Carter	New Zealand	2003-15	112	29	293	281	8	1598
G.J.L. Cooper	Otago	1984-96	121	36	261	280	3	1520
W.F. McCormick	Canterbury	1959-75	220	38	269	204	7	1294
B.J. Barrett	Hurricanes	2011-19	125	34	249	189	1	1238
G.J. Fox	New Zealand	1984-93	78	2	225	192	1	1067
B.J.W. Fairbrother	South Canterbury	1981-92	115	20	130	180	60	1060
A.P. Mehrtens	Canterbury	1993-2005	108	15	204	163	28	1056
W.J. Burton	North Harbour	1990-96	88	11	210	188	5	1052
G.D. Rowlands	Bay of Plenty	1969-82	161	38	166	164	15	1008

70 TRIES FOR A TEAM

		Games	Tries	
T.J. Wright	Auckland	135	112	1984-93
J.J. Kirwan	Auckland	141	104	1983-94
B.G. Fraser	Wellington	121	100	1975-86
Z.V. Brooke	Auckland	140	94	1986-97
P. Bale	Canterbury	102	93	1989-96
R.M. Smith	Canterbury	134	92	1949-60
B.R. Ford	Marlborough	145	81	1972-83
B.A. Grenside	Hawke's Bay	87	73	1918-31
P.J. Cooke	Otago	107	73	1990-96
J.C. Stringfellow	Wairarapa	109	72	1925-35
M. Clamp	Wellington	87	72	1980-88
E. Clarke	Auckland	150	72	1991-2002
P.L. Phillips	Marlborough	160	71	1980-97
N.R. Berryman	Northland	107	71	1991-2003
R.A. Jarden	Wellington	61	70	1949-56
B.W. Smith	Waikato	83	70	1979-84
D.C. Laursen	Horowhenua	121	70	1980-92
P.M. Hirini	Horowhenua	153	70	1986-2000

REFEREES
by Chris Jansen

2020 NEW ZEALAND RUGBY NATIONAL REFEREES SQUAD

	Union	Squad Debut	Tests	SR	P	HC	FPC	Sevens	Nat[1]	Prov[2]	RS[3]	Total
J.R. Bredin	Otago	2019	–	–	4	5	4	–	–	–	–	13
N.P. Briant	Bay of Plenty	2009	8	58	66	11	2	27	15	1	12	188
J.J. Doleman	Auckland	2014	–	4	28	18	2	29	7	–	1	89
M.I. Fraser	Wellington	2007	8	67	67	17	2	5	18	1	9	185
N.E.R. Hogan	Hawke's Bay	2017	–	–	8	9	6	3	1	1	–	28
R.P. Kelly	Taranaki	2009	–	–	58	15	1	66	4	3	4	147
A.W.B. Mabey	Auckland	2014	–	–	30	20	1	–	2	–	1	53
J.D. Munro	Canterbury	2011	–	–	15	14	3	3	1	–	1	36
Dr. B.D. O'Keeffe	Horowhenua-Kapiti	2012	23	54	48	6	1	1	1	7	7	141
B.E. Pickerill	North Harbour	2012	5	31	46	8	1	3	10	–	4	104
C.J. Stone	Taranaki	2012	–	–	24	22	2	2	–	1	1	51
D.J. Waenga	Hawke's Bay	2018	–	–	12	2	2	1	3	–	1	20
M.C.J. Winter	Waikato	2015	–	–	10	21	7	6	1	–	–	45
P.M. Williams	Taranaki	2014	17	35	32	7	–	3	7	2	4	103

SR Super Rugby
P Mitre 10 Cup (total includes former ITM Cup fixtures)
HC Heartland Championship
FPC Farah Palmer Cup
[1]NZR appointment — international tour, Ranfurly Shield (non-Mitre 10 Cup), national trial, and women's international.
[2]interprovincial (non-Mitre 10 Cup, non-Heartland Championship, non-Ranfurly Shield)
[3]Ranfurly Shield — also included within N1 or Nat (if a non-Mitre 10 Cup match)
[4]Men refereeing FPC fixtures are credited with a first-class appointment.

REFEREE APPOINTMENTS 2020

Jono Bredin

September	6	FPC	North Harbour v Bay of Plenty	Albany
	19	FPC	Wellington v Hawke's Bay	Petone
	26	FPC	Tasman v Otago	Nelson
October	4	P	Southland v Waikato	Invercargill
	17	P	Manawatu v Bay of Plenty	Palmerston North
November	1	P	Bay of Plenty v Hawke's Bay	Tauranga
	15	P	Taranaki v Hawke's Bay	Inglewood

Nick Briant

September	26		East Coast v Poverty Bay	Ruatoria
October	4	P	North Harbour v Tasman	Albany
	9	P	Manawatu v Canterbury	Palmerston North
	24	P/RS	Hawke's Bay v Manawatu	Napier
November	7	P	Auckland v Northland	Auckland
	15	P	Canterbury v Auckland	Christchurch
	21	P s-f	Hawke's Bay v Taranaki	Napier
	28	P p-f	Auckland v Tasman	Auckland

Chris Cowie (King Country)

October	10		King Country v Wanganui	Taumaranui

James Doleman

January	26/27		New Zealand World Rugby Sevens	Hamilton
February	2/3		Australia World Rugby Sevens	Sydney
March	7	SR	Rebels v Lions	Melbourne
June	28	SR	Crusaders v Chiefs	Christchurch
July	25	SR	Crusaders v Hurricanes	Christchurch
August	8	SR	Hurricanes v Chiefs	Wellington
September	13	P	Southland v Hawke's Bay	Invercargill
	20	P	Auckland v Wellington	Auckland
October	10	P	Taranaki v Auckland	Inglewood
	17	P	Wellington v North Harbour	Wellington
	25	P	Tasman v Southland	Hamilton
	31	P	Auckland v Waikato	Auckland
November	14	P	Wellington v Manawatu	Wellington
	27	P c-f	Hawke's Bay v Northland	Napier

Sheldon Eden-Whaitiri (Hawke's Bay)

October	3		Poverty Bay v Wairarapa Bush	Napier

Kalifa Faalogo (Mid Canterbury)

September	12		Mid Canterbury v Buller	Hanmer Springs
	19		Mid Canterbury v North Otago	Hinds

Sam Fellows (Bay of Plenty)

October	3		East Coast v King Country	Opotiki

Mike Fraser

February	21	SR	Crusaders v Highlanders	Christchurch
March	7	SR	Hurricanes v Blues	Wellington
	14	SR	Reds v Bulls	Brisbane
June	14	SR	Blues v Hurricanes	Auckland
July	4	SR	Highlanders v Crusaders	Dunedin
	19	SR	Chiefs v Highlanders	Hamilton
August	2	SR	Highlanders vs Blues	Dunedin
September	19	P	Waikato v North Harbour	Hamilton
	27	P/RS	Taranaki v Otago	Inglewood
October	3	P	Counties Manukau v Manawatu	Pukekohe
	23	P	Otago v Northland	Dunedin
November	7	P	Tasman v Canterbury	Nelson
	14	P	Northland v Waikato	Kaikohe
	20	P s-f	Otago v Northland	Dunedin
December	5		NZ Maori v Moana Pasifika	Hamilton

Josh Henshaw (South Canterbury)

September	19		South Canterbury v Buller	Timaru

Nick Hogan

September	20	FPC	Manawatu v Tasman	Palmerston North
	27	FPC	Counties Manukau v Northland	Pukekohe
October	24		Poverty Bay v Wanganui	Napier
November	1	P	Manawatu v Southland	Feilding
	14		NZ Black Ferns v NZ Barbarians	Auckland

Richard Kelly

January	26/27		New Zealand World Rugby Sevens	Hamilton
February	2/3		Australia World Rugby Sevens	Sydney
September	12	P	Counties Manukau v Tasman	Pukekohe
	20	P	Manawatu v Otago	Palmerston North
	26	P	Tasman v Waikato	Nelson
October	11	P	Northland v Southland	Whangarei
	24	P	North Harbour v Auckland	Albany
November	8	P/RS	Hawke's Bay v Wellington	Napier
	15	P	Bay of Plenty v North Harbour	Tauranga
	21	P s-f	Tasman v Bay of Plenty	Nelson

Craig Kingan (North Otago)

September	12	North Otago v South Canterbury	Oamaru

Ben Lourie (Wanganui)

October	17	Wanganui v Wairarapa Bush	Wanganui

Angus Mabey

September	20	P	Hawke's Bay v Counties Manukau	Napier
October	3	P	Northland v Taranaki	Whangarei
	11	P	North Harbour v Hawke's Bay	Albany
	18	P	Otago v Counties Manukau	Dunedin
	25	P	Waikato v Taranaki	Hamilton
November	8	P	Manawatu v Taranaki	Feilding

Royce Maynard (Poverty Bay)

September	19	Poverty Bay v East Coast	Gisborne

James Munro

September	13	P	Otago v Auckland	Dunedin
	26	P	Southland v North Harbour	Invercargill
October	17	P	Southland v Taranaki	Invercargill
November	1	P	Taranaki v Counties Manukau	Inglewood
	14	P	Otago v Tasman	Dunedin

Ben O'Keeffe

February	1	SR	Sunwolves v Rebels	Fukuoka
	8	SR	Chiefs v Crusaders	Hamilton
	15	SR	Hurricanes v Sharks	Wellington
	22	6N	Italy v Scotland	Rome
	29	SR	Bulls v Jaguares	Pretoria
March	7	6N	England v Wales	London
June	20	SR	Chiefs v Blues	Hamilton
July	5	SR	Chiefs v Hurricanes	Hamilton
	18	SR	Hurricanes v Blues	Wellington
August	1	SR	Chiefs v Crusaders	Hamilton
	16	SR	Highlanders v Hurricanes	Dunedin
September	13	P	Taranaki v Bay of Plenty	Inglewood
	19	P/RS	Canterbury v Taranaki	Christchurch
	27	P	Counties Manukau v Northland	Pukekohe
October	2	P	Bay of Plenty v Auckland	Rotorua
	17	P	Auckland v Tasman	Auckland
	31	3N	Australia v New Zealand	Sydney

Chris Paul (South Canterbury)
October	3		South Canterbury v North Otago	Timaru

Alistair Payne (Wairarapa Bush)
September	26		Wairarapa Bush v King Country	Masterton
October	10		Wairarapa Bush v Horowhenua Kapiti	Masterton

Brendon Pickerill
February	22	SR	Chiefs v Brumbies	Hamilton
	29	SR	Reds v Sharks	Brisbane
March	14	SR	Crusaders v Sunwolves	Brisbane
June	21	SR	Hurricanes v Crusaders	Wellington
July	12	SR	Hurricanes v Highlanders	Wellington
	26	SR	Blues v Chiefs	Auckland
September	13	P	Northland v Manawatu	Whangarei
	25	P	Wellington v Bay of Plenty	Wellington
October	10	P	Waikato v Counties Manukau	Hamilton
	16	P/RS	Hawke's Bay v Northland	Napier
	30	P	Canterbury v Otago	Christchurch
November	6	P	Southland v Otago	Invercargill
	14	P	Wellington v Manawatu	Wellington
	21	P s-f	Auckland v Waikato	Auckland

Gary Reilly (Tasman)
September	26		Buller v South Canterbury	Westport

Josh Rooney (South Canterbury)
September	5		South Canterbury v Mid Canterbury	Timaru

Cameron Stone
September	26	P	Hawke's Bay v Canterbury	Napier
October	4	P/RS	Otago v Hawke's Bay	Dunedin
	11	P	Tasman v Bay of Plenty	Nelson
	18	P	Canterbury v Waikato	Christchurch
	24	P	Bay of Plenty v Canterbury	Tauranga
	31	P	Northland v North Harbour	Whangarei
November	7	P	North Harbour v Counties Manukau	Albany

Sam Thompson (Horowhenua Kapiti)
September	19		Horowhenua Kapiti v Wairarapa Bush	Levin
October	3		Horowhenua Kapiti v Wanganui	Shannon

Daniel Waenga
March	6	PC	Fiji Warriors v Samoa A	Suva
	10	PC	Fiji Warriors v Tonga A	Suva
August	28	RS	Canterbury v North Otago	Christchurch
September	12	P	Waikato v Wellington	Hamilton
	19	P	Bay of Plenty v Southland	Rotorua
	27	P	Auckland v Manawatu	Auckland
October	25	P	Counties Manukau v Wellington	Pukekohe
	31	P	Wellington v Tasman	Wellington
November	8	P	Waikato v Bay of Plenty	Hamilton

Referees

David Winter (North Otago)

September	26		North Otago v Mid Canterbury	Oamaru

Michael Winter

September	5	FPC	Counties Manukau v North Harbour	Pukekohe
	13	FPC	Northland v Auckland	Whangarei
	20	FPC	Auckland v Counties Manukau	Auckland
	25	FPC	Wellington v Manawatu	Wellington
October	3	FPC	Auckland v Bay of Plenty	Auckland
November	13	P	Counties Manukau v Southland	Pukekohe

Paul Williams

February	1	SR	Crusaders v Waratahs	Nelson
	14	SR	Blues v Crusaders	Auckland
	28	SR	Highlanders v Rebels	Dunedin
March	8	6N	Scotland v France	Edinburgh
June	13	SR	Highlanders v Chiefs	Dunedin
	27	SR	Blues v Highlanders	Auckland
July	11	SR	Crusaders v Blues	Christchurch
August	9	SR	Crusaders v Highlanders	Christchurch
September	5		North v South	Wellington
	11	P	North Harbour v Canterbury	Albany
	18	P	Tasman v Northland	Blenheim
October	3	P	Canterbury v Wellington	Christchurch
	11	BC	New Zealand v Australia	Wellington
November	21	3N	Argentina v Australia	Newcastle

BC   Bledisloe Cup
SR   Super Rugby
PC   World Rugby Pacific Challenge
6N   Six Nations
3N   Tri Nations 2020

One overseas referee controlled one Mitre 10 Cup fixture:
Angus Gardner (Australia) Oct 10: Wellington v Otago,

INTERNATIONAL ASSISTANT REFEREES AND
TELEVISION MATCH OFFICIALS

Mike Fraser
February	1	6N	Wales v Italy	Cardiff
	8	6N	Ireland v Wales	Dublin
October	11	BC	New Zealand v Australia (TMO)	Wellington
	18	BC	New Zealand v Australia (TMO)	Auckland

Glenn Newman
February	1	6N	Ireland v Scotland (TMO)	Dublin
	8	6N	Ireland v Wales (TMO)	Dublin

Dr Ben O'Keeffe
October	11	BC	New Zealand v Australia	Wellington
	18	BC	New Zealand v Australia	Auckland
November	7	3N	Australia v New Zealand	Brisbane
	14	3N	New Zealand v Argentina (TMO)	Sydney
	21	3N	Argentina vs Australia	Newcastle
	28	3N	Argentina v New Zealand	Newcastle

Brendon Pickerill
February	2	6N	France v England	Paris
	9	6N	France v Italy	Paris

Paul Williams
March	14	6N	France v Ireland	Paris
October	18	BC	New Zealand v Australia	Auckland
	31	3N	Australia v New Zealand	Sydney
November	7	3N	Australia v New Zealand (TMO)	Brisbane
	14	3N	New Zealand v Argentina	Sydney
	28	3N	Argentina v New Zealand (TMO)	Newcastle

(TMO) Television Match Official
BC   Bledisloe Cup
6N   Six Nations
3N   Tri Nations 2020

2020 INTERNATIONAL REFEREES

Dr B.D. O'Keeffe   2016: Samoa v Georgia, Japan v Scotland, Scotland v Argentina; 2017: Italy v France, South Africa v France, South Africa v Australia, Ireland v South Africa, England v Australia; 2018: Wales v France, South Africa v England, South Africa v Argentina, Wales v Australia, Ireland v USA; 2019: Ireland v France, Australia v Argentina, Fiji v Tonga, England vs Italy, Australia v Fiji (RWC), France v USA (RWC), Japan v Scotland (RWC), 2020: Italy v Scotland, England v Wales, Australia v New Zealand,

P.M. Williams   2016: Romania v USA; 2017: Italy v Scotland, Fiji v Italy, Samoa vs Fiji (RWCQ), Ireland v Fiji; 2018: Australia v Ireland, England v Japan, Scotland v Argentina; 2019: England v Scotland, South Africa v Australia, Australia v Samoa, England v Tonga (RWC), Georgia v Fiji (RWC), Argentina v USA (RWC), 2020: Scotland v France, New Zealand v Australia, Argentina v Australia,

MOST INTERNATIONAL APPOINTMENTS BY REFEREES
to 06 December, 2020

N. Owens	Wales	2003–2020	100	D.T.M. McHugh	Ireland	1994–2004	29
W. Barnes	England	2006–2020	93	A.R. Gardner	Australia	2011–2020	28
J.I. Kaplan	South Africa	1996–2013	70	L.W. Pearce	England	2013–2020	28
R. Poite	France	2006–2020	70	D.A. Pearson	England	2003–2012	28
C.P. Joubert	South Africa	2003–2016	69	W.J. Erickson	Australia	1994–2002	27
A.C.P. Rolland	Ireland	2001–2014	66	S.M. Lawrence	South Africa	2000–2011	27
S.R. Walsh	New Zealand/ Australia	1998–2014	60	A.J. Watson	South Africa	1996–2004	27
				D.J. Bishop	New Zealand	1986–1995	26
J. Garces	France	2010–2019	56	B. Gabbei	Germany	1993–2006	26
J.D. Peyper	South Africa	2011–2020	51	M. Raynal	France	2009–2020	26
C.R. White	England	1998–2009	51	S.M. Young	Australia	1994–2006	26
P. Gauzere	France	2010–2020	49	K.V.J. Fitzgerald	Australia	1985–1991	25
S.J. Dickinson	Australia	1997–2011	47	M. Jonker	South Africa	2005–2014	25
P.G. Honiss	New Zealand	1997–2008	46	B.J. Lawrence	New Zealand	2005–2011	25
G.J. Clancy	Ireland	2006–2016	45	C. Norling	Wales	1978–1991	25
D.A. Lewis	Ireland	1998–2010	45	J.P. Doyle	England	2009–2017	24
W.D. Bevan	Wales	1985–2000	44	C.J. Hawke	New Zealand	1990–2001	24
J.M. Fleming	Scotland	1985–2001	41	K.M. Deaker	New Zealand	2001–2008	23
A.J. Spreadbury	England	1990–2008	41	K.D. Kelleher	Ireland	1959–1971	23
E.F. Morrison	England	1991–2001	38	Dr. B.D. O'Keeffe	New Zealand	2016–2020	23
P.D. O'Brien	New Zealand	1994–2005	37	D.G. Walters	Wales	1959–1966	23
J. Jutge	France	1996–2007	35	J. Dume	France	1993–2003	22
G.W. Jackson	New Zealand	2012–2019	32	M. Joseph	Wales	1966–1977	22
A.J. Cole	Australia	1997–2005	31	C.J. Pollock	New Zealand	2005–2015	22
J.G.A. Lacey	Ireland	2010–2018	31	R.C. Williams	Ireland	1957–1964	21
P.L. Marshall	Australia	1993–2003	30				

INTERNATIONAL REFEREES
to 1 January, 2021

Bishop, D.J. (Southland) 1986–95	26	McKenzie, E. (Wairarapa) 1921	1
Bray, L.E. (Wellington) 2001–08	9	McKenzie, H.J. (Wairarapa) 1936	1
Briant, N.P. (Bay of Plenty) 2014–18	8	McLachlan, L.L. (Otago) 1989–94	7
Brown, K.W. (Southland) 2008–11	8	McMullen, R.F. (Auckland) 1973	1
Campbell, A. (Auckland) 1908	2	Matheson, A.M. (Taranaki) 1946	1
Dainty, C.J. (Wellington) 1982–86	2	Millar, D.H. (Otago) 1965–78	8
Deaker, K.M. (Hawke's Bay) 2001–08	23	Moffit, J. (Wellington) 1936	1
Doocey, T.F. (Canterbury) 1976–83	3	Munro, V.G. (Canterbury) 2009–10	2
Downes, A.D. (Otago) 1913	1	Murphy, J.P. (North Auckland) 1959–69	13
Duffy, B.W. (Taranaki) 1977	1	Neilson, A.E. (Wellington) 1921	2
Duncan, J. (Otago) 1908	1	Nicholson, G.W. (Auckland) 1913	1
Evans, F.T. (Canterbury) 1904	1	O'Brien, P.D. (Southland) 1994–2005	37
Farquahar, A.B. (Auckland) 1961–64	6	O'Keeffe, Dr B.D. (Wellington) 2016–19	23
Fleury, A.L. (Otago) 1959	1	Parkinson, F.G.M. (Manawatu) 1955–56	3
Fong, A.S. (West Coast) 1946–50	2	Pickerill, B.E. (North Harbour) 2017–19	5
Forsyth, R.A. (Taranaki) 1958	1	Pollock, C.J. (Hawke's Bay) 2005–15	22
Francis, R.C. (Wairarapa Bush) 1984–86	10	Pring, J.P.G. (Auckland) 1966–72	8
Fraser, M.I. (Wellington) 2013–19	8	Robson, C.F. (Waikato) 1963	1
Fright, W.A. (Canterbury) 1956	2	Simpson, J.L. (Wellington) 1913	1
Frood, J. (Otago) 1952	1	Skeen, B.D. (Auckland) 2008–09	2
Garrard, W.G. (Canterbury) 1899	1	Sullivan, G. (Taranaki) 1950	1
Gillies, C.R. (Waikato) 1958–59	4	Sutherland, F.E. (Auckland) 1930	1
Griffiths, A.A. (Waikato) 1952	1	Taylor, A.R. (Canterbury) 1965–72	3
Harrison, G.L. (Wellington) 1979–83	4	Thompson, M.W. (Auckland) 1983	2
Hawke, C.J. (South Canterbury) 1990–2001	24	Tindill, E.W.T. (Wellington) 1950–55	3
Hill, E.D. (Auckland) 1949	1	Wahlstrom, G.K. (Auckland) 1994–97	6
Hollander, S. (Canterbury) 1930–31	4	Walsh, L. (Canterbury) 1949	1
Honiss, P.G. (Canterbury & Waikato) 1997–2008	46	Walsh, S. (Wellington) 1994–97	5
Jackson, G.W. (Bay of Plenty) 2012–19	32	Walsh, S.R. (North Harbour) 1998–2008	33
King, J.S. (Wellington) 1937	2	White, J.M (Auckland) 2013	2
Lawrence, B.J. (Bay of Plenty) 2005–11	25	Williams, J. (Otago) 1905	1
Lawrence, K.H. (Bay of Plenty) 1985–91	13	Williams, P.M. (Taranaki) 2016–19	17
Macassey, L.E. (Otago) 1937	1	Williamson G.L. (Wellington) 2010–13	2
McAuley, C.J. (Otago) 1962	1	Wise, G.J. (Hawke's Bay) 2004	1
McDavitt, P.A. (Wellington) 1972–77	5	Wolstenholme, B. (Poverty Bay) 1955	1

100 AND MORE FIRST-CLASS MATCHES
to 1 January, 2021

P.D. O'Brien	1988-2005	230	Dr. B.D. O'Keeffe	2012-2020	141
P.G. Honiss	1992-2008	227	G.K. Wahlstrom	1985-2002	132
S.R. Walsh	1994-2008	214	G.L. Williamson	2003-2014	117
B.J. Lawrence	1997-2012	205	Dr. J.M. White	2000-2013	116
C.J. Pollock	2000-2016	204	D.J. Bishop	1976-1995	114
G.W. Jackson	2010-2019	196	G.J. Wise	1996-2007	114
N.P. Briant	2009-2020	188	K.W. Brown	1999-2012	112
M.I. Fraser	2007-2020	185	B.E. Pickerill	2012–2020	104
C.J. Hawke	1983-2001	183	S. Walsh	1980-2000	103
K.M. Deaker	1996-2008	181	P.M. Williams	2013–2020	103
R.P. Kelly	2009-2020	147	K.H. Lawrence	1971-1992	100
L.E. Bray	1991-2008	144			

SEVENS RUGBY
NEW ZEALAND SEVENS SQUADS 2020

The Covid-19 pandemic forced an early conclusion to the scheduled 10 tournaments for the 2019/20 HSBC Sevens Series and also the postponement of the 2020 Tokyo Olympics and the annual National Sevens.

The All Blacks Sevens squad, having finished second at Dubai and winning at Cape Town in December 2019, commenced the New Year with a strong points lead. This lead was extended with winning in front of a home crowd at Hamilton in January. A week later Fiji defeated New Zealand in pool play but had the satisfaction of defeating host team Australia in the play-off for fifth place. A third place at Los Angeles and winning at Vancouver in March gave the All Blacks Sevens a total of 115 series points, 11 ahead of South Africa, when World Rugby abandoned future events and terminated the series declaring New Zealand the winners, its first series win since 2013/14. Scott Curry was included in the HSBC Dream Team.

Name	Province	New Zealand	Australia	USA	Canada	TOTALS
Kurt Baker	Taranaki	*	*	–	–	2
Caleb Clarke	Auckland	–	*	*	*	3
Dylan Collier	Waikato	*	*	–	–	2
Scott Curry	Bay of Plenty	*	*	–	–	2
Sam Dickson	Canterbury	*	*	*	*	4
Andrew Knewstubb	Horowhenua Kapiti	–	–	*	*	2
Vilimoni Koroi	Otago	*	*	–	*	3
Ngarohi McGarvey-Black	Bay of Plenty	*	*	*	–	3
Tim Mikkelson	Waikato	*	*	*	*	4
Sione Molia	Counties Manukau	*	*	*	*	4
Etene Nanai-Seturo	Counties Manukau	*	*	*	*	4
Tone Ng Shiu	Tasman	*	s	*	*	4
Amanaki Nicole	Canterbury	–	–	*	*	2
Joe Ravouvou	Bay of Plenty	–	–	*	*	2
Salesi Rayasi	Auckland	–	*	–	–	1
Akuila Rokolisoa	Counties Manukau	–	–	*	*	2
William Warbrick	Bay of Plenty	–	–	*	*	2
Regan Ware	Bay of Plenty	*	*	–	–	2
Joe Webber	Bay of Plenty	*	–	–	–	1

s reserve replacing injured Baker on second day.

Captaincy was shared with Curry and Mikkelson (New Zealand, Australia) and Mikkelson and Molia (USA, Canada).

Coach: Clark Laidlaw (*Taranaki*)
Assistant coach: Tomasi Cama (*Manawatu*) at NZ and Australia;
  Liam Barry (*North Harbour*) at USA and Canada.
Manager: Ross Everiss (*Bay of Plenty*)
Physiotherapist: Damian Banks (*Bay of Plenty*) at NZ, Australia
  Kate Niederer (*Bay of Plenty*) at USA, Canada.

INDIVIDUAL SCORING

	Tries	Con	Points		Tries	Con	Points
Mikkelson	13	1	67	Collier	3	–	15
Koroi	5	18	61	Molia	3	–	15
McGarvey-Black	4	16	52	Rayasi	3	–	15
Clarke	10	–	50	Baker	2	1	12
Ravouvou	8	–	40	Ng Shiu	2	–	10
Knewstubb	3	11	37	Nicole	1	–	5
Ware	7	–	35	Warbrick	1	–	5
Rokolisoa	4	7	34	Webber	1	–	5
Curry	6	1	32				
Dickson	6	–	30	**TOTALS**	**87**	**55**	**545**
Nanai-Seturo	5	–	25				
				Opposition scored 221 points			

Final points for 2019/20 World Rugby Sevens Series: New Zealand 115, South Africa 104, Fiji 83, Australia 81, England 77, France 74, USA 72, Canada 57, Argentina 56, Ireland 49, Scotland 37, Kenya 35, Samoa 33, Spain 33, Wales 13, Japan 10, Korea 1. The series was held over six tournaments between December 2019 and March 2020.

Previous winners: New Zealand 2000, 2001, 2002, 2003, 2004, 2005, 2007, 2008, 2011, 2012, 2013, 2014; Fiji 2006, 2015, 2016, 2019; South Africa 2009, 2017, 2018; Samoa 2010.

World Rugby Sevens Series Cup championship titles (1999 to 1 January 2021): New Zealand 56, Fiji 42, South Africa 30, England 19, Samoa 10, Australia 7, United States 3, Argentina 2, Scotland 2, France 1, Kenya 1, Canada 1.

NEW ZEALAND AT HSBC NEW ZEALAND SEVENS
Waikato Stadium, Hamilton — January 25/26, 2020

Date	Opponent	Result	Tries	Conversions
Jan 25	Wales	won 47–0	Mikkelson (2), Ware, Webber, Curry, Baker, Koroi	McGarvey-Black (5), Koroi
Jan 25	USA	won 26–5	Curry, Baker, Mikkelson, Dickson	McGarvey-Black (2), Baker
Jan 26	Scotland	won 38–12	Mikkelson (2), Ng Shiu, Collier, Curry, Koroi	Koroi (3), McGarvey-Black
Jan 26	Australia (Cup semi-final)	won 17–14	McGarvey-Black, Ware, Collier	McGarvey-Black
Jan 26	France (Cup final)	won 27–5	Curry (3), Ware (2)	McGarvey-Black

NEW ZEALAND AT HSBC AUSTRALIA SEVENS
Bankwest Stadium, Sydney — February 1/2, 2020

Date	Opponent	Result	Tries	Conversions
Feb 1	Wales	won 54–5	Clarke (2), Rayasi (2), Mikkelson, Dickson, Nanai-Seturo, Ware	Koroi (6), McGarvey-Black
Feb 1	Fiji	lost 5–26	Ware	
Feb 2	Kenya	won 19–5	Rayasi, Mikkelson, Dickson	Curry, McGarvey-Black
Feb 2	Australia (for 5th place)	won 24–7	Molia, Ware, Collier, Clarke	McGarvey-Black (2)

Fiji defeated South Africa 12–10 in the Cup final

NEW ZEALAND AT HSBC USA SEVENS
Dignity Health Sports Park, Carson, Los Angeles — Feb 29/Mar 1, 2020

Date	Opponent	Result	Tries	Conversions
Feb 29	Wales	won 42–7	Nanai-Seturo, Mikkelson, Clarke, Warbrick, McGarvey-Black, Dickson	Rokolisoa (4), Mikkelson, Knewstubb
Feb 29	Spain	won 21–7	Ravouvou, Mikkelson, Rokolisoa	Knewstubb (2), Rokolisoa
Feb 29	England	won 21–17	McGarvey-Black, Knewstubb, Nanai-Seturo	Knewstubb (2), McGarvey-Black
Mar 1	France (Cup q-final)	won 29–14	Ravouvou (2), Molia, McGarvey-Black, Clarke	Knewstubb (2)
Mar 1	South Africa (Cup semi-final)	lost 0–17		
Mar 1	Australia (for 3rd)	won 21–19	Nanai-Seturo, Rokolisoa, Mikkelson	Knewstubb, Rokolisoa, McGarvey-Black

South Africa defeated Fiji 29–24 in the Cup final

NEW ZEALAND AT HSBC CANADA SEVENS
BC Place Stadium, Vancouver — March 7/8, 2020

Date	Opponent	Result	Tries	Conversions
Mar 7	Kenya	won 29–0	Koroi (2), Ravouvou, Ng Shiu, Clarke	Koroi (2)
Mar 7	Spain	won 31–0	Knewstubb, Mikkelson, Dickson, Clarke, Ravouvou	Koroi (3)
Mar 7	Ireland	won 33–24	Rokolisoa (2), Clarke, Koroi, Nicole	Knewstubb (2), Rokolisoa, Koroi
Mar 8	Fiji (Cup q-final)	won 17–5	Mikkelson, Molia, Ravouvou	Koroi
Mar 8	South Africa (Cup semi-final)	won 27–15	Clarke (2), Mikkelson, Nanai-Seturo, Dickson	Knewstubb
Mar 8	Australia (Cup final)	won 17–14	Ravouvou (2), Knewstubb	Koroi

PLAYING RECORD OF NEW ZEALAND SEVENS TEAMS

	Tournaments			Games				Points	
	Attended	Won	Runner-up	Played	Won	Draw	Lost	For	Against
1973	1	–	–	3	2	–	1	58	50
1983	1	–	–	5	4	–	1	114	4
1984	1	–	1	5	4	–	1	74	40
1985	1	–	–	4	3	–	1	88	18
1986	3	3	–	16	15	–	1	414	72
1987	2	1	1	11	10	–	1	284	66
1988	2	1	1	11	10	–	1	274	37
1989	2	2	–	11	11	–	–	316	71
1990	1	–	1	5	4	–	1	134	44
1991	1	–	1	5	4	–	1	150	18
1992	1	–	1	5	4	–	1	130	34
1993	3	–	–	17	12	–	5	420	175
1994	2	1	–	10	9	–	1	361	89
1995	5	2	1	22	19	–	3	681	182
1996	5	3	2	29	27	–	2	1263	236
1997	4	1	1	21	18	–	3	670	287
1998	11	6	2	59	54	–	5	2134	473
1999	10	7	2	54	49	1	4	1574	426
2000	10	6	3	59	55	–	4	2048	354
2001	10	7	1	60	56	–	4	2042	330
2002	13	8	2	75	68	1	6	2377	565
2003	7	1	3	40	34	–	6	1285	411
2004	8	3	2	46	39	–	7	1396	395
2005	8	3	1	48	41	–	7	1509	441
2006	9	2	1	48	36	2	10	1380	551
2007	8	4	–	44	40	–	4	1391	355
2008	8	4	2	47	43	–	4	1350	367
2009	9	2	2	49	37	–	12	1262	514
2010	9	2	2	51	43	1	7	1531	541
2011	9	4	1	50	43	–	7	1479	519
2012	9	3	4	54	46	–	8	1375	556
2013	10	3	4	60	52	–	8	1651	584
2014	10	4	3	60	50	–	10	1645	511
2015	8	1	3	47	33	1	13	1039	692
2016	11	3	1	64	45	3	16	1357	860
2017	11	1	2	64	48	–	16	1396	802
2018	13	3	1	73	52	–	21	1746	887
2019	10	2	2	60	47	-	13	1594	730
2020	4	2	–	21	19	–	2	545	221
TOTALS	**250**	**95**	**54**	**1413**	**1186**	**9**	**218**	**40537**	**13508**

SEVENS RECORDS
to January 1, 2021

BY NEW ZEALAND TEAMS

Most successive wins	47	2007–08
Most successive tournament wins	7	2007–08
Most successive appearances in finals	12	1986–92

Tournament records
Most points	463	Portugal, 1996
Most tries	69	Portugal, 1996
Most conversions	59	Portugal, 1996

Match records
Highest team score	94	v Moldova, Portugal, 1996
Record victory (*points ahead*)	94	94–0, v Moldova, 1996
Highest score conceded	61	v Fiji, Japan, 1996
Record defeat (*points behind*)	56	5–61, v Fiji, Japan, 1996
Most tries	14	v Moldova, Portugal, 1996
Most conversions	12	v Moldova, Portugal, 1996
		v Hungary, Portugal, 1996

BY THE PLAYERS

Career records
Attended most tournaments	98	T.J. Mikkelson
Most points	2122	T. Cama
Most tries	246	T.J. Mikkelson

Tournament records
Most points	136	C.M. Cullen, Hong Kong, 1996
Most tries	20	B.R.M. Fleming, Portugal, 1996
Most conversions	28	D.A. Smith, Portugal, 1996

Match records
Most points	37	C.M. Cullen, v Sri Lanka, Hong Kong, 1996
Most tries	7	C.M. Cullen, v Sri Lanka, Hong Kong, 1996
Most conversions	9	T.J. Wright, v Korea, Sydney, 1989
		M. Ashford, v Sri Lanka, Dubai, 2001

NEW ZEALAND SEVENS REPRESENTATIVES, 1973–2020

	Tournaments		Tournaments
Ahki, P.J. (*North Harbour*) 2013–14–16	7	Cama, T. (*Manawatu*) 2005–07–08–09–10–11–12–13–14	63
Ai'i, O. (*Auckland*) 1999–00–01–02–04–05	25	Camburn, M. (*North Harbour*) 2005	3
Alley, G. (*North Harbour*) 1992–93	2	Cashmore, A.R. (*Auckland*) 1995	4
Andrews, L.S. (*Otago*) 1999	2	Christie, S.A. (*Tasman*) 2011	2
Anesi, S.R. (*Waikato*) 2004–06	7	Clamp, M. (*Wellington*) 1984–85–86	4
Arnold, T.C. (*Bay of Plenty*) 2009–10–11–12	19	Clarke, C.D. (*Auckland*) 2018–20	5
Ashford, M.R. (*Auckland*) 2001–05	10	Clarke, E. (*Auckland*) 1993	1
Atiga, B.A.C. (*Auckland*) 2007	1	Clutterbuck, M.J. (*Bay of Plenty*) 2014	1
Austin, H.S.E. (*Taranaki*) 1999	1	Cocker, E. (*Otago*) 2005–06–07 (*Auckland*) 2008–09	28
Auva'a, O.J. (*Auckland*) 2006–09	5	Collier, D.J. (*Waikato*) 2015–16–17–18–19–20	42
Bachop, G.T.M. (*Canterbury*) 1990–91–92–94	5	Colling, G.L. (*Otago*) 1973	1
Baker, K.T. (*Manawatu*) 2008–09–17–18–19 (*Taranaki*) 2010–12–13–14–16–20	47	Collins, N.I. (*Bay of Plenty*) 2001–02	6
Bale, P. (*Canterbury*) 1990–92–93	3	Crowley, A.E. (*Taranaki*) 1987–88–89–91	6
Barrett, B.J. (*Taranaki*) 2010	2	Cullen, C.M. (*Manawatu*) 1995–96 (*Wellington*) 1998–00	7
Batty, G.B. (*Wellington*) 1973	1	Curry, S.B. (*Manawatu*) 2010–12–13 (*Bay of Plenty*) 2011–14–15–16–17–18–19–20	59
Baxter, C.N.O. (*Bay of Plenty*) 2003–06–07	9	Curtis, A.A.D. (*Wellington*) 2013–14–15 (*Manawatu*) 2017	19
Berryman, N.R. (*Northland*) 1997	1		
Blackadder, T.J. (*Canterbury*) 1993	2		
Blackie, J.M. (*Otago*) 2002–03–04–05–06	12	Dagg, I.J.A. (*Hawke's Bay*) 2007–08	6
Blowers, A.F. (*Auckland*) 1995	3	Daniel, B.W. (*Bay of Plenty*) 1997	2
Blythe, T.G. (*Waikato*) 1999 (*Bay of Plenty*) 2001	3	Dauwai, A. (*Thames Valley*) 2006	2
Booth, J.P. (*Manawatu*) 2017	2	Dawson, A.J. (*Counties*) 1983–85	2
Botica, F.M. (*North Harbour*) 1985–86–87–88	8	De Goldi, C.D. (*Bay of Plenty*) 1998–99–00 (*Auckland*) 2001–02–03–04	41
Bourke, C.R. (*Hawke's Bay*) 2004	3	Dickson, S.N. (*Canterbury*) 2012–13–14–15–16–17–18–19–20	59
Brooke, Z.V. (*Auckland*) 1986–87–88–89–90	10	Donald, A.J. (*Wanganui*) 1983	1
Brooke-Cowden, M. (*Auckland*) 1986–87	5	Duggan, R.J.L. (*Waikato*) 1997	1
Bruning, K.T. (*Waikato*) 1994 (*Nelson Bays*) 1995	3	Ellis, M.C.G. (*Otago*) 1993	1
Bryant, R.J. (*Taranaki*) 1997	1	Ellison, T.E. (*Wellington*) 2005–06	5
Bunce, F.E. (*North Harbour*) 1993	2	Ensor A.C. (*Otago*) 2014	1
Bunce; J.F. (*Manawatu*) 2015 (*Waikato*) 2018	4	Erenavula, L. (*Counties*) 1994	2
Bunting, A.M. (*Bay of Plenty*) 2002–03	6	Evans, N.J. (*North Harbour*) 2002	8
		Faddes, M.A. (*Otago*) 2013	3
		Fainga'anuku, L.T. (*Tasman*) 2018	1

	Tournaments
Farani, D. (*Wellington*) 1997	1
Flavell, T.V. (*North Harbour*) 1998	2
Fleming, B.R.M.	
(*Bay of Plenty*) 1995	
(*Canterbury*) 1996–97–98	
(*Wellington*) 1998–99–00–01–02	
(*Otago*) 2003–04	35
Foote, B.M. (*Waikato*) 1997	
(*North Harbour*) 1998	3
Forbes, D.J. (*Auckland*) 2006–07	
(*Counties Manukau*) 2008–09–10–	
11–12–13–14–15–16–17	94
Forster, S.T. (*Otago*) 1993	2
Fry, R.J. (*Auckland*) 1983–84	2
Fuatai, F. (*Otago*) 2017	2
Gallagher, J.A. (*Wellington*) 1989–90	3
Gear, R.L. (*Auckland*) 1998–99–01	9
Gear, H.E. (*North Harbour*) 2003	
(*Wellington*) 2010–12	4
Going, S.J.	
(*Northland*) 1999–00–01–02–03	29
Goodhue, E.J. (*Northland*) 2015	2
Granger, K.W. (*Manawatu*) 1983	1
Grant, P.W. (*Otago*) 2008–09–10	15
Green, C.I. (*Canterbury*) 1986	2
Gregory, S.J. (*Northland*) 2018–19	8
Grice, R.J.L. (*Waikato*) 2011	3
Guildford, Z.R. (*Hawke's Bay*) 2010	1
Haami, B.D. (*Taranaki*) 2000	2
Halai, F. (*Waikato*) 2010–11–12	15
Hales, D.A. (*Canterbury*) 1973	1
Hamilton, L.G. (*North Harbour*) 2009	1
Hamilton, A.R.	
(*Hawke's Bay*) 1994–95–96	5
Haugh, T.C. (*Otago*) 2018	2
Heem, B.I. (*Auckland*) 2010–11–12	
(*Tasman*) 2013–14	22
Hoeata, J.M.R.A. (*Taranaki*) 2006	2
Holmes, B. (*North Auckland*) 1973	1
Hona, J. (*Bay of Plenty*) 2005	4
Houston, J.D.W. (*Canterbury*) 2017	1
Howarth, S.P. (*Auckland*) 1991	1
Hudson, C. (*Canterbury*) 1999–00	6
Hunt, N. (*Wellington*) 2005–06–07–08	
(*Bay of Plenty*) 2009	28

	Tournaments
Ieremia, A. (*Wellington*) 1997	1
Ioane, A. (*Counties Manukau*) 1997	2
Ioane, A.L. (*Auckland*) 2014–16	11
Ioane, R.E. (*Auckland*) 2015–16	11
Ioasa, T.S.J.	
(*Hawke's Bay*) 2001–04–05–06–07–08	
(*Wellington*) 2002–03	48
Iopu, I.P. (*Auckland*) 2012	
(*Taranaki*) 2016–17	9
Izatt, C.S. (*Manawatu*) 1999	2
Jackman, M.B. (*HB/Cant*) 2012–13	
–14	10
Jane, C.S. (*Wellington*) 2006	5
Joass, T.J. (*Tasman*) 2017	
(*Tas/BOP*) 2018–19	17
John, O.W. (*Counties Manukau*) 1996	2
Jones, M.T.	
(*Bay of Plenty*) 1993–94–95–96–97	11
Kaino, J. (*Auckland*) 2005	2
Kaka, G.G. (*Hawke's Bay*)	
2013–14–15–16	33
Kamana, T.J.K.J. (*Waikato*) 2007	2
Karauna, D.T. (*Waikato*) 1996–97–	
98–00–01–02–03	35
Kepu, S.K.M. (*Auckland*) 2001	1
Keresoma, M.M. (*Auckland*) 2012–13	3
Khan, R.N. (*Auckland*) 2013–16–17–18	12
King, P.S.V.	
(*Bay of Plenty*) 2006–07–08–09–10	
(*North Harbour*) 2011–12	33
Kinikinilau, R.U.	
(*Wellington*) 2002–03–04–05–06	
(*Waikato*) 2007	13
Kiri Kiri, A.I. (*Manawatu*) 2015–16	4
Kirk, D.E. (*Otago*) 1984	
(*Auckland*) 1985–86	5
Kirwan, J.J. (*Auckland*)	
1984–85–86–88	5
Knewstubb, A.S. (*Tasman*) 2017	
(*Tas/Horo Kap*) 2018	
(*Horowhenua Kapiti*) 2019–20	29
Koloto, E.T. (*Manawatu*) 1987	2
Konia, G.N. (*Hawke's Bay*) 1997	1
Koonwaiyou, A. (*Auckland*) 2002	1
Koroi, V.T. (*Otago*) 2017–18–19–20	23
Lahmert, W.H. (*Taranaki*) 2012–13	5

Tournaments

Lam, M.B. (*Auckland*) 2012–13–14–16	15
Lam, P.R. (*Auckland*) 1989–90–91–92–93	7
Latimer, T.D. (*Bay of Plenty*) 2004–05–06	15
Lawrence, Z.W. (*North Harbour*) 2005–06–07 (*Bay of Plenty*) 2008–09–10	35
Lee, F.A. (*Counties Manukau*) 2010	4
Leo'o, J.J. (*Canterbury*) 2000–01	8
Lewis, A.J. (*Otago*) 1984	1
Lindsay, A.C. (*Canterbury*) 1983–84	2
Llewellyn, R.A.M. (*Canterbury*) 2012	1
Lomu, J.T. (*Counties Manukau*) 1994–95–96–98–99 (*Wellington*) 2000–01	13
Lynn, K.G. (*Southland*) 2008	2
McMaster, A. (*Manawatu*) 1987	2
McPhee, J.B. (*North Harbour*) 2010	2
McQuoid, G.A. (*Bay of Plenty*) 2004	3
MacDonald, L.T.J. (*Bay of Plenty*) 2005–09	3
McGarvey-Black, N.M. (*Bay of Plenty*) 2018–19–20	13
McKenzie, M.R. (*Southland*) 2014	2
Mafi, L.O. (*Manawatu*) 2003 (*Taranaki*) 2004–05	8
Maher, J.T. (*Counties Manukau*) 2006	2
Maidens, T.K. (*Hawke's Bay*) 1995	1
Malo, J.R. (*Waikato*) 2012	1
Marshall, J.R. (*Tasman*) 2011	2
Martin, E.M. (*Waikato*) 1996	1
Martin, R.E. (*Bay of Plenty*) 2001–02	11
Martine, H.R.I. (*King Country*) 2000	1
Masirewa, L.R. (*Waikato*) 2012–13 (*Bay of Plenty*) 2018	12
Masirewa, W. (*Counties Manukau*) 1996–97–98	10
Masoe, M.C. (*Taranaki*) 2001–02–04	22
Messam, L.J. (*Bay of Plenty*) 2002 (*Waikato*) 2003–04–05–06–10–16	26
Mikkelson, T.J. (*Waikato*) 2007–08–09–10–11–12–13–14–15–16–17–18–19–20	98
Miller, A.J. (*Bay of Plenty*) 1997	1
Mills, J.G. (*Auckland*) 1984	1
Milne, B.W.T. (*Southland*) 2002	2
Molia, S.L.J. (*Counties Manukau*) 2016–17–18–19–20	41
Monaghan, A.C. (*Northland*) 1998–00	18
Muliaina, J.M. (*Auckland*) 1999–00–01–02	11
Munro, L.H. (*Auckland*) 2006	4
Murray, C.D. (*Counties*) 1994	1
Naholo, W.R. (*Taranaki*) 2012–13–14	8
Nanai-Seturo, E.W.P.S. (*Counties Manukau*) 2018–20	12
Nanai-Williams, T.T. (*Counties Manukau*) 2008–09	7
Naoupu, G.E. (*Canterbury*) 2005	3
Nareki, J.M. (*Otago*) 2018–19	14
Nepia, D.S.M. (*Bay of Plenty*) 2000–01	5
Newby, C.A. (*Bay of Plenty*) 1999 (*North Harbour*) 1999–00–01–02	13
Ng Shiu, I.J.S. (*Tasman*) 2017–18–19–20	29
Ngaluafe, N.S.J. (*Southland*) 2016	1
Nicole, A.P. (*Canterbury*) 2018–19–20	9
Nonoa, S.I. (*Waikato*) 1998	1
Nonu, M.A. (*Wellington*) 2004	2
Nowell, B.C. (*Canterbury*) 2000	2
O'Donnell, D.P.T. (*Waikato*) 2010–11–14–15	12
O'Donnell, K.F.T. (*Taranaki*) 2011–12	5
Ormsby, K.M.T. (*Counties Manukau*) 2000	1
Ormond, J.T. (*Taranaki*) 2010–11	3
Ormond, L.H. (*Taranaki*) 2015–16–17	12
Osborne, G.M. (*Nth Harbour*) 1992–93–94–96–97	6
Paramore, J. (*Counties*) 1993	2
Parkinson, D.T. (*Auckland*) 1998–99 (*Otago*) 2001 (*North Harbour*) 2003	15
Parkinson, M.T. (*North Harbour*) 1999–2003–04 (*Bay of Plenty*) 2005	14

	Tournaments		Tournaments
Peacocke, G.M.		**Rickards, W.T.C.**	
(*North Harbour*) 1996–97	3	(*Southland*) 2006–07–08–09	8
Pearson, M.B. (*Wellington*) 2015	1	**Robertson, G.A.** (*Waikato*) 2011	3
Pedersen, H.L. (*Otago*) 2005	2	**Rokocoko, J.T.** (*Auckland*) 2002–05	8
Pelenise, A.		**Rokolisoa, A.T.**	
(*Canterbury*) 2005–06–07	13	(*Counties Manukau*) 2018–19–20	14
Phillips, C.M.			
(*North Auckland*) 1986	3	**Ropiha, B.J.** (*Hawke's Bay*) 2016	1
Philpott, S. (*Canterbury*) 1988	2	**Ruddell, N.K.** (*North Auckland*) 1986	1
Pierce, M.S.L.		**Ruru, J.L.** (*Otago*) 2016	2
(*North Harbour*) 1989–91–92–93–95	6	**Rush, E.J.** (*Auckland*) 1988–89–90–91	
Piutau, S.T. (*Auckland*) 2011–12	8	(*North Harbour*) 1992–93–94–95–	
Popoali'i, B. (*Wellington*) 2009		96–97–98–99–00–01–02–03–04	62
(*Otago*) 2011	8		
Puletua, J.R. (*Auckland*) 2009	1	**Samuels, T.D.G.** (*Hawke's Bay*) 2017	1
Pulu, A.W.		**Savea, A.S.** (*Wellington*) 2012–16	8
(*Counties Manukau*) 2015–16	7	**Savea, S.J.** (*Wellington*) 2008–09	7
Putt, K.B. (*Waikato*) 1987–89	2	**Savou, T.H.** (*Manawatu*) 1998	1
		Schmidt-Uili, P.T. (*Manawatu*) 1998	2
Qio, J. (*NZ Fijians*)[1] 1999	1	**Schrijvers, D.J.** (*Wellington*) 2018	1
		Schuster, N.J.	
Raikabula, L.		(*Wellington*) 1986–88–89–90	6
(*Wellington*) 2006–11–12–13–14–15		**Scown, A.I.** (*Taranaki*) 1973	1
(*Hawke's Bay*) 2007		**Scrimgeour, O.J.**	
(*Manawatu*) 2008–09–10	70	(*Bay of Plenty*) 1995–96	
Raikuna, D.A. (*Counties Manukau*) 2011		(*Waikato*) 1995–96–97–98–99	22
(*North Harbour*) 2013–14	12	**Senio, K.** (*Auckland*) 2001	2
Raki, L.E. (*Counties Manukau*) 1985–87	3	**Seymour, D.J.**	
Ralph, C.S.		(*Canterbury*) 1988–89–90–91–	
(*Bay of Plenty*) 1996–97–98		92–93–99–00–02	
(*Canterbury*) 2000	7	(*Hawke's Bay*) 1994–95–96	
Ranby, R.M. (*Waikato*) 2005	2	(*Wellington*) 1997–98–99	35
Randle, R.Q.		**Shelford, W.T.**	
(*Hawke's Bay*) 1995–96–97–98		(*North Harbour*) 1985–86–87	5
(*Waikato*) 2000–01–02	10	**Simonsson, B.G.** (*Bay of Plenty*) 2017–18	3
Ranger, R.M.N.		**Skudder, G.R.** (*Waikato*) 1973	1
(*Northland*) 2006–07–08	8	**Smith, B.R.** (*Otago*) 2010	1
Ravouvou, J. (*Auckland*) 2017–18–19		**Smith, B.W.** (*Waikato*) 1983	1
(*Bay of Plenty*) 2020	24	**Smith, David** (*Auckland*) 2008	1
Rayasi, P. (*Wellington*) 1993	1	**Smith, D.A.** (*Canterbury*) 1996	3
Rayasi, S.T.M. (*Auckland*) 2018–19–20	7	**Smith, W.R.** (*Canterbury*)	
Reid, H.B. (*Otago*) 2001		1984–85–86	4
(*North Harbour*) 2002–03–04		**Smylie, C.B.** (*North Harbour*) 2002	2
(*Bay of Plenty*) 2005–06	28	**Soakai, A.** (*Otago*) 2006–07	9
Reid, H.R. (*Bay of Plenty*) 1983	1	**So'oialo, R.** (*Wellington*) 2000–01–02	6
Reihana, B.T. (*Waikato*) 1998–02	2	**Souness, B.J.** (*Taranaki*) 2009–10–11	17
Rich, G.J.W. (*Auckland*) 1983–84–85	3	**Spooner-Neera, T.A.** (*Hawke's Bay*) 2013	4

Tournaments

Stanaway, T.Z.B.P. (*Bay of Plenty*) 2015–16–17–18 — 9
Stanley, J.T. (*Auckland*) 1983 — 1
Steinmetz, P.C. (*Wellington*) 1999 — 3
Stephens, T.P.O.T.R. (*Tasman*) 2019 — 1
Stevens, I.N. (*Wellington*) 1973 — 1
Stowers, S.L. (*Auckland*) 2004
  (*Counties Manukau*) 2009–10–12–13–14–15–16–17 — 42
Sutherland, A.R.
  (*Marlborough*) 1973 — 1
Sweeney, D.W.H. (*Waikato*) 2006 — 6

Tagaloa, T.D.L. (*Wellington*) 1991 — 1
Tairea, F.T. (*Auckland*) 2009 — 1
Tamani, G.B. (*Japan*)[1] 1997 — 1
Tanivula, I. (*Auckland*) 2002 — 2
Taramai, M.V.U. (*Wellington*) 2014–15 — 4
Taufahema, T. (*Auckland*) 1998 — 5
Tauiwi, J.J.
  (*Bay of Plenty*) 1994–95–96–97 — 14
Te Aute, I.N. (*Bay of Plenty*) 2016 — 1
Te Nana, K.S.
  (*Wellington*) 1996–97–98–99
  (*North Harbour*) 1999–00–01–02–03 — 42
Te Tamaki, I.R. (*Waikato*) 2015–16–17–18 — 15
Thomas, J.T. (*Waikato*) 1998 — 1
Thomson, A.J. (*Otago*) 2007 — 4
Thomson, N.J. (*Canterbury*) 2006–07 — 6
Thorpe, A.J. (*Canterbury*) 1984 — 1
Tiatia, J.A.
  (*Canterbury*) 2000–01–02–03–04 — 21
Tietjens, G.F. (*Waikato*) 1983 — 1
Tilsley, G. (*Wellington*) 2011
  (*Manawatu*) 2014 — 6
Timu, J.K.R. (*Otago*) 1993 — 2
Tipoki, T.R. (*Auckland*) 1997–98
  (*North Harbour*) 1998–99–02 — 10
Toeava, I. (*Auckland*) 2005 — 3
Tokula, S. (*Waikato*) 2009–10 — 12
Tololima-Auva'a, O.J. *see* **Auva'a, O.J.** (*Auckland*) 2006
Tuatagaloa, B. (*Wellington*) 2012
  (*Canterbury*) 2013 — 9
Tuhakaraina, M.
  (*Bay of Plenty*) 1999–00 — 2

Tui'avii, D. (*Wellington*) 1993 — 1
Tuilevu, A. (*Waikato*) 1997–98 — 5
Tuitavake, A.S.
  (*North Harbour*) 2002–03–04 — 20
Tuitavake, N.H.
  (*North Harbour*) 2008–09–10 — 12
Tulou, A. (*Wellington*) 2008 — 1
Tuoro, C.K.
  (*Counties Manukau*) 2008–09 — 10
Tupuola, T. (*Wellington*) 2010 — 2
Umaga-Marshall, T.P.
  (*Wellington*) 2006–09 — 4

Vaka, S.T.
  (*Counties Manukau*) 2014–15 — 4
Valence, A.
  (*Auckland*) 1998–99–00–01–02–05–06
  (*Hawke's Bay*) 2003–04 — 67
van Lieshout, J.J.A.
  (*Counties Manukau*) 2016 — 2
Verran, J.A. (*Canterbury*) 2012 — 1
Vidiri, J.
  (*Counties Manukau*) 1995–96–98
  (*Auckland*) 2000 — 6
Visinia, L. (*Auckland*) 2012 — 2
Vito, V.V.J. (*Wellington*) 2007–08–09 — 8

Waaka, B.R.T. (*Taranaki*) 2015–16–17 — 14
Waldrom, S.L. (*Wellington*) 2002
  (*Taranaki*) 2007–10 — 5
Walker, N.A.
  (*Bay of Plenty*) 2002–03–04 — 15
Waqaseduadua, V.M.
  (*North Harbour*) 2005–09 — 4
Warbrick, W.J.P. (*Bay of Plenty*) 2019–20 — 3
Ware, R.E. (*Waikato*) 2015–16
  (*Bay of Plenty*) 2017–18–19–20 — 39
Webb, G.A. (*Otago*) 2003 — 1
Webber, T.J. (*Waikato*) 2011–12–13–14–15–16–17–18–19–20 — 41
Whitelock, A.J. (*Canterbury*) 2014 — 2
Williams, S.
  (*Counties Manukau*) 2016 — 7
Williams-Spiers, G.D.
  (*Auckland*) 2012 — 1
Wilson, B.A. (*North Harbour*) 2005 — 1

---

[1]Tournament reserve players called upon when injuries prevented New Zealand from having fit reserves for the final.

Wilson, J.C. (*Bay of Plenty*) 1999–00
  (*Auckland*) 2001–02
  (*Wellington*) 2003–04–05   32
Wilson, J.H. (*Bay of Plenty*) 2012   3
Wolfe, T.W.N. (*Taranaki*) 1993   1
Woods, P.G.A. (*Bay of Plenty*) 1993
  (*Nth Harbour*) 1994–95–96–97–98   15
Wotherspoon, K.J.
  (*Hawke's Bay*) 1996   1
Wright, T.J.
  (*Auckland*) 1986–87–88–89–90–
  91–92   11
Wulf, R.N.
  (*North Harbour*) 2004–05–06   7
Wyllie, A.J. (*Canterbury*) 1973   1

Yates, S.P. (*Canterbury*) 2007–08   12

NEW ZEALAND INTERNATIONAL SEVENS
FMG Waikato Stadium, Hamilton   January 25/26, 2020

POOL PLAY
A   USA 24 Scotland 7; New Zealand 47 Wales 0; Scotland 24 Wales 19;
    New Zealand 26 USA 5; USA 42 Wales 0; New Zealand 38 Scotland 12.
B   England 24 Kenya 19; South Africa 31 Japan 5; Kenya 12 Japan 12;
    England 21 South Africa 19; England 26 Japan 7; Kenya 36 South Africa 14.
C   Canada 26 Ireland 21; France 21 Spain 17; Ireland 28 Spain 17;
    France 12 Canada 12; Canada 21 Spain 14; France 17 Ireland 7.
D   Australia 38 Argentina 7; Fiji 19 Samoa 12; Argentina 40 Samoa 7;
    Fiji 19 Australia 12; Australia 33 Samoa 19; Argentina 26 Fiji 10.

Play-off for 15th place	Samoa 21 Wales 7
Play-off for 13th place	Spain 19 Japan 15
Play-off for 11th place	Scotland 24 Ireland 19
Play-off for 9th place	Fiji 12 South Africa 5
Play-off for 7th place	Argentina 19 Kenya 17
Play-off for 5th place	Canada 28 USA 7
Play-off for Bronze	Australia 33 England 21

CUP CHAMPIONSHIP
Semi-finals   *France 10 England 5; New Zealand 17 Australia 14*
Final   *New Zealand 27 France 5.*

Tournament referees: James Doleman (*New Zealand*), Craig Evans (*Wales*), Francisco Gonzalez (*Uruguay*), Richard Kelly (*New Zealand*), Damon Murphy (*Australia*), Tevita Rokovereni (*Fiji*), Jeremy Rozier (*France*), Damian Schneider (*Argentina*), Jordan Way (*Australia*).

New Zealand International Sevens Tournaments

	Cup final	Plate winner	Bowl winner	Shield winner
2000	Fiji 24, New Zealand 14	Canada	France	
2001	Australia 19, Fiji 17	Samoa	South Africa	Japan
2002	South Africa 17, Samoa 14	Argentina	France	Cook Is
2003	New Zealand 38, England 26	Samoa	Canada	Tonga
2004	New Zealand 33, Fiji 15	Tonga	Argentina	USA
2005	New Zealand 31, Argentina 7	Australia	Kenya	Niue
2006	Fiji 27, South Africa 22	England	Scotland	Tonga
2007	Samoa 17, Fiji 14	England	Argentina	Portugal
2008	New Zealand 22, Samoa 7	South Africa	England	USA
2009	England 19, New Zealand 17	South Africa	Cook Is	Scotland
2010	Fiji 19, Samoa 14	Australia	Wales	USA
2011	New Zealand 29, England 14	Fiji	Kenya	USA
2012	New Zealand 24, Fiji 7	South Africa	Kenya	Scotland
2013	England 24, Kenya 19	Australia	Canada	Wales
2014	New Zealand 21, South Africa 0	Australia	Kenya	USA
2015	New Zealand 27, England 21	Fiji	France	Canada
2016	New Zealand 24, South Africa 21	Australia	Samoa	France

	Cup final	Challenge Trophy winner
2017	South Africa 26, Fiji 5	Kenya
2018	Fiji 24, South Africa 17	USA
2019	Fiji 38, USA 0	England
2020	New Zealand 27, France 5	

NATIONAL SEVENS
TOURNAMENT TROPHY WINNERS

	Venue	Cup	Plate	Bowl	Shield
1975	Auckland	Marlborough			
1976	Christchurch	Marlborough			
1977	Blenheim	Manawatu			
1978	Hamilton	Manawatu			
1979	Palmerston Nth	Manawatu			
1980	Palmerston Nth	Auckland			
1981	Palmerston Nth	Taranaki			
1982	Feilding	Taranaki			
1983	Feilding	Auckland			
1984	Feilding	Auckland			
1985	Feilding	Counties			
1986	Feilding	Nth Harbour			
1987	Christchurch	Nth Harbour	Canterbury	Horowhenua	
1988	Pukekohe	Auckland	Manawatu	Wai Bush	
1989	Palmerston Nth	Auckland	Taranaki	Wanganui	Hawke's Bay
1990	Palmerston Nth	Canterbury	Bay of Plenty	Wanganui	Manawatu B
1991	Palmerston Nth	Auckland	Counties	Canterbury	East Coast
1992	Palmerston Nth	Nth Harbour	Counties	Auckland	Manawatu B
1993	Palmerston Nth	Canterbury	Nth Harbour	Taranaki	King Country
1994	Palmerston Nth	Counties	Nth Harbour	Canterbury	Manawatu B
1995	Palmerston Nth	Counties	Wellington	King Country	Manawatu B
1996	(Mar) Palm Nth	Waikato	C'nties M'kau	Wai Bush	Poverty Bay
1996	(Nov) Palm Nth	Waikato	Wellington	Wai Bush	Wanganui
1997	Rotorua	Waikato	Auckland	Otago	Wai Bush
1998	Rotorua	Waikato	Canterbury	Wai Bush	Otago
1999	Palmerston Nth	Nth Harbour	Canterbury	King Country	Nelson Bays
2000	Palmerston Nth	Nth Harbour	Wanganui	Nelson Bays	Southland
2001	Palmerston Nth	Nth Harbour	C'nties M'kau	Manawatu	West Coast
2002	Palmerston Nth	Wellington	Waikato	Marlborough	West Coast
2004	Queenstown	Nth Harbour	Auckland	Canterbury	Manawatu
2005	Queenstown	Auckland	Wellington	Otago	Manawatu
2006	Queenstown	Auckland	Bay of Plenty	Southland	Cantabrians
2007	Queenstown	Auckland	C'nties M'kau	Wellington	Northland

	Venue	Cup	Plate	Bowl	Shield
2008	Queenstown	Auckland	Manawatu	Wellington	Tasman
2009	Queenstown	Nth Harbour	Wellington	Otago	Southland
2010	Queenstown	Waikato	Nth Harbour	Horo' Kapiti	Tasman
2011	Queenstown	Auckland	Nth Harbour	Manawatu	Canterbury
2012	Queenstown	Auckland	Taranaki	Tasman	Bay of Plenty
2013	Queenstown	Taranaki	Auckland	Hawke's Bay	C'nties M'kau
2014	Rotorua	Wellington	Manawatu	Nth Harbour	Waikato
2015	Rotorua	Waikato	Taranaki	NthHarbour	Canterbury
2016	Rotorua	C'nties M'kau	Auckland	Northland	Wanganui
2017	Rotorua	C'nties M'kau	Auckland	Bay of Plenty	Otago
2018					
(Jan)	Rotorua	Waikato	Bay of Plenty	C'nties M'kau	Northland
(Dec)	Tauranga	Tasman	Taranaki	Auckland	Manawatu
2019	Tauranga	Waikato	Tasman	C'nties M'kau	Manawatu
2020	Cancelled due to Covid-19				

CLUB FINALS
Results of the 2020 senior club finals.

Covid-19 severely disrupted all club competitions. Almost all club competitions were set to start on March 21 but four days beforehand their starts were postponed, initially until April 18. Starts were eventually made from June 20 and competitions were invariably rescheduled for just one complete round instead of two. With the re-emergence of Covid-19 in the greater Auckland community in August, all club matches after August 11 outside of Auckland could continue but with no spectators or with limited spectators well-spaced apart. However, the North Harbour, Auckland and Counties Manukau unions had to cease playing immediately. The three unions were eventually allowed to resume their competitions after September 23 but all three had chosen to abandon their competitions without a winner before that date.

Auckland – Gallaher Shield:

On September 7 the Adult Rugby Committee chose to abandon the remainder of the club season with no winner declared.

Bay of Plenty – Baywide Premier Trophy:

Western Bay sub union — Charles Hardy Memorial Cup
August 22: Tauranga Sports 32 v Te Puna 26
Both teams contested last year's Baywide final. Halftime 15–7. Tauranga had only 13 men for the last five minutes, conceding one try during it.

Eastern Bay sub union — Eastern Bay SU Premier Cup
August 29: Opotiki 13 Te Teko 12
Halftime 6–12. A converted try in the 63rd minute to Opotiki were the only points of the second half.

Central Bay sub union — Rotorua SU Banner
September 5: Whakarewarewa 38 Ngongotaha 9
Halftime 18–6. Five tries to nil. Ngongotaha were promoted to the final just four days before the match after Rotoiti were found to have played ineligible players in two round robin matches they won and were stripped of eight points.

Buller – Senior Shield:

August 22: Westport 25 v Westport OB 13
Postponed from the 15th. Halftime 11–8.

Canterbury

Metropolitan — Canstaff Trophy (new).
September 13: Lincoln University 30 v Marist Albion 29
Halftime 13–15. A try with five minutes left enabled Marist Albion to retake the lead 29–23. With a minute left Lincoln University scored a converted try to win 30–29.

Ellesmere sub union – Coleman Shield:
September 12: Southbridge 40 v Waihora 32
Halftime 22–24. Waihora scored a try in the final minute to narrow the gap.

Club Finals

North Canterbury sub union – Hunnibel Memorial Trophy:
August 15: Glenmark-Cheviot 32 v Kaiapoi 24
Repeat finalists. Halftime 10–17. A try with six minutes left took Glenmark-Cheviot out to 32–24.

Counties Manukau – McNamara Cup:
On September 14 the Club Council delegates abandoned the remainder of the club season with no winner declared.

Ngati Porou East Coast – Rangiora Keelan Memorial Shield:
August 29: Tokararangi 13 v Tihirau Victory Club 12
Halftime 3–5. Against 14 men (yellow card) Tokararangi scored a converted try with 12 minutes left to lead 13–12.

Hawke's Bay – Maddison Trophy Cup:
August 29: Hastings RS 22 v Taradale 16
Halftime 10–10. Hastings RS won their first title since 1999.

Horowhenua Kapiti – Ramsbotham Cup:
August 15: Rahui 26 v Shannon 25
Halftime 20–10. Shannon scored three tries to two but Hamish Buick kicked a 75th minute penalty goal to put Rahui 26–25 in front.

King Country – Meads Shield:
September 5: Taumarunui Districts 27 v Taupo Sports 20
Halftime 15–13. The lead changed hands five times and there was no scoring in the last 23 minutes.

Manawatu – Hankins Shield:
August 14: Feilding 27 v Massey University 24
Repeat finalists. Halftime 14–7. University scored four tries to two and the match finished with a University player tackled into touch three metres from the goal-line after two handy shots from penalties were, instead, tap-kicked in the lead up.

Mid Canterbury – Watters Cup:
August 1: Methven 22 v Rakaia 9
Repeat finalists. Halftime 9–6, all penalty goals. The match was stopped for 15 minutes in the second half (at 17–6) due to a player suffering a broken leg which required the arrival of an ambulance onto the field.

Northland
Northland Premiership – Joe Morgan Memorial Trophy:
August 22: Waipu 18 a.e.t. v Mid Northern 15 a.e.t.
Halftime 5–8. 80 minutes 15–15. A Ben Mathers penalty goal was the only score in extra time.

Bay of Islands sub union – Championship Shield:
August 22: Otiria 31 v Taiamai Ohaeawai 26
Halftime 10–21. Otiria retook the lead with six minutes left and defended in their own 22 for the remainder to win their first title since 1961.

Mangonui sub union – Bell Shield:
August 22: Te Rarawa 22 v Awanui 19
The match doubled as the North Zone Championship final. Halftime 12–0. A last minute penalty goal put Te Rarawa in front again and ended the game, in their 100th Centenary year.

North Harbour – A.S.B. Cup:
On September 14 the Council of Clubs abandoned the remainder of the club season with no winner declared.

North Otago – Citizen's Shield:
August 22: Valley 22 v Maheno 19
Halftime 14–19. With the brisk wind at their backs Valley scored a penalty goal and try in the first seven minutes of the second half to complete the scoring and win.

Otago
Metropolitan – Speight's Championship Shield:
September 19: Taieri 40 v University 26
Repeat finalists. Taieri scored five tries in leading 33–0 after 28 minutes.

Central Region – Super Liquor Trophy:
August 22: Cromwell 32 v Arrowtown 20.
Repeat finalists. Halftime 10–3, Cromwell led throughout the match.

Southern Region – Speight's Cup:
August 15: West Taieri 24 v Clutha Valley 22.
Halftime 14–8. Clutha Valley scored a converted try to close to two points with just a minute left to play. West Taieri's debut year in the Southern Region competition having previously played in the Metropolitan competition.

Poverty Bay – Lee Brothers Shield:
September 5: Waikohu 27 v YMP 20.
Halftime 10–10. Waikohu scored the first points of the second half — a converted try — and stayed ahead. YMP runners-up for third year in a row.

Southland – Galbraith Shield:
August 15: Woodlands 83 v Star 31
Woodlands scored the first of their 13 tries after just 55 seconds, straight from the kickoff. Halftime 47–12.

South Canterbury – Hamersley Cup:
August 29: Temuka 20 v Waimate 18

Taranaki – McMasters Shield:
August 15: Tukapa 33 v Inglewood United 29
Halftime 14–12. Inglewood scored a 78th minute try against 14 men (yellow card) to close to 33–29 but Tukapa repulsed one final attack.

Tasman:
Marlborough sub union – Champion of Champions Trophy:
August 29: Central 31 v Waitohi 10
Repeat finalists. Halftime 12–3, Central pulled away to 31–3.

Nelson Bays sub union – Strange Memorial Cup + Centennial Cup:
August 29: Marist 34 v Waimea OB 32
Repeat finalists. Halftime 23–6. A last-minute Waimea OB penalty attempt to win fell short.

Thames Valley – McClinchy Cup:
August 22: Whangamata 21 v COBRAS 15
Halftime 14–3. Whangamata won their first ever title. COBRAS scored their final try with one minute left.

Waikato – Breweries Shield:
August 22: Hautapu 37 v Otorohanga 33
Halftime 20–7. Down 20–28 Hautapu scored three tries for a 37–28 lead until Otorohanga scored with two minutes left.

Wanganui – President's Rosebowl:
September 19: Border 22 v Taihape 19
Repeat finalists. Halftime 16–12. Taihape scored three tries to one. Border led all the way, and were twice down to 14 men in the second half, including the last nine minutes.

Wairarapa Bush – Tui Cup:
September 5: Marist 39 v Greytown 37
Halftime 12–27. With 80 minutes gone, James Goodger kicked a penalty goal with the last kick of the game to give Marist the win in their 75th Jubilee Year.

Wellington – Jubilee Cup:
September 26: Old Boys University 22 v Northern United 14
Halftime 17–3. OBU scored three tries to one, with Northern scoring theirs with five minutes left.

West Coast – Taylorville Wallsend Trophy:
August 22: Kiwi 33 v Wests 19.
Postponed from August 15. Kiwi led 33–5 after 44 minutes, and have now won their last 46 matches. First all-Hokitika final since 1990 and Wests first final.

Most consecutive championships:
14 Star (Southland) 1890-1903
10 Athletic (North Otago) 1906-1915; Celtic (South Canterbury) 2009-2018
8 Star (Southland) 1919-1926; Westport (Buller) 1963-1970; Invercargill (Southland) 1987-1994; Ponsonby (Auckland) 2004-2011

Most consecutive Sub Union championships:
13 Mahia (Wairoa) 1981-1993
11 Dannevirke O.B. (Dannevirke) 1946-1955, (Central HB-Dannevirke) 1956

SECONDARY SCHOOLS RUGBY

SCHOOLS RUGBY REVIEW
The First XV season was a stop-start affair due to Covid-19.

No play was possible until late June, but championships were decided in all the major competitions except the Auckland and North Harbour 1A. They could not be completed due to the tight lockdown restrictions on numbers at gatherings in the wider Auckland region through August and September.

Hastings BHS, the national Top 4 champion from 2019, was denied a shot at the April Sanix tournament in Japan, which was cancelled.

The Top 4 tournament was cancelled for the first time since its 1982 inception, and the NZ Schools and NZ Barbarians Schools could not assemble for their usual tri or quad tournament with Australia and a Pacific Island nation due to Covid-19 border restrictions.

Furthermore, the NZ Barbarians Area Schools, for those in more remote, far-flung areas, were not able to assemble in 2020.

The 15s season culminated in October when those attending the NZ Barbarians Under 18 camp split into two teams — Andy Haden XV versus Alan Whetton XV — for a match in Hamilton. Whetton was the current President of the NZ Barbarians club while the late Haden was a stalwart of the Baabaas club.

Out of that match, two paper teams were chosen. This was the first time since 1977, the year before its inception, that NZ Schools had not played a fixture.

The schools sevens season was highlighted by two December tournaments, both held in Auckland. The 35th edition of the Condors Sevens went off without a hitch, though the World Schools Sevens Aotearoa, which normally includes 32 teams from around the Asia-Pacific region, was down to 16 due to border restrictions, and featured only NZ-based schools players.

The paper 2020 national schools teams were:

NEW ZEALAND SCHOOLS 2020
Ajay Faleafaga (*St Peter's College, Auckland*), Allan Craig (*St Kentigern College*), Blake Makiri (*St Peter's, Cambridge*), Che Clarke (*King's College*), Fabian Holland (*Christchurch BHS*), Fehi Fineanganofo (*Auckland Grammar*), Fletcher Anderson (*Christ's College*), George Methven (*St Bede's College*), Hanz Leota (*Scots College*), Harry Godfrey (*Whanganui Collegiate*), Havila Molia (*St Paul's Collegiate*), Isa Saumaki (*St Andrew's College*), James Mullan (*Rangiora High School*), Jamie Hannah (*Christchurch BHS*), Joel Parry (*St Andrew's College*), Luron Iosefa (*King's College*), Mason Tupaea (*Hamilton BHS*), Monu Moli (*Marlborough BC*), Noah Hotham (*Hamilton BHS*), Oliver Foote (*Hamilton BHS*), Riley Higgins (*St Patrick's College, Silverstream*), Rohan Wingham (*King's High School*), Siale Lauaki (*St Patrick's College, Town*), Caleb Tangitau (*Westlake BHS*), Torian Barnes (*St Andrew's College*), Will Bason (*St Kentigern College*)

NEW ZEALAND BARBARIANS SCHOOLS
Adam Lennox (*Whanganui Collegiate*), Bradley Crichton (*St Pat's Town*), Chicago Doyle (*King's College*), Christian Stenhouse (*St Pat's Town*), Dayton Iobu (*King's College*), Dominic Ropeti (*Scots*), Elyjah Crosswell (*Palmerston North BHS*), Fiti Sa (*Christ's*), Harris McRobbie (*Rangiora HS*), Jadin Kingi (*Sacred Heart College*), Jayden Stok (*Napier BHS*), Jeremiah Asi (*St Peter's, Auckland*), Jone Rova (*New Plymouth BHS*), Lucas Payne (*Dargaville College*), Mini Toga (*St Andrew's*), Ollie Curtis (*Christchurch BHS*), Ollie Haig (*Otago BHS*), Owen Wright (*Aotea College*), Quinlan Tupou (*St Peter's, Cambridge*), Steve Salelea (*King's HS*), Taha Kemara (*Hamilton BHS*), Te Rama Reuben (*St Kentigern*), Tony Tafa (*Kelston BHS*), Wallace Sititi (*De La Salle College*)

MOASCAR CUP

In 2020, there were three different holders of the coveted and iconic Moascar Cup, the Ranfurly Shield equivalent of First XV rugby.

Rotorua BHS holds the silverware going into the 2021 season.

The Moascar stayed in the Super 8. Hastings BHS started the season with the trophy after clinching it from King's College in the 2019 national Top 4 final. But the Hawke's Bay school was divested of the Moascar on August 1 by local rival Napier BHS, which prevailed 15–10. This was Napier's first run with the Moascar since 2003.

It was to be, however, a short-lived tenure of three weeks. After beating Tauranga BC 22–10, Napier BHS was edged 25–22 by the hungry Rotorua BHS under the coaching of Ngarimu Simpkins. Rotorua, in turn, beat Palmerston North BHS 22–20 and Hastings BHS 24–14 in two tight cup defences.

OTHER HIGHLIGHTS

- Hamilton BHS won a remarkable 13th Super 8 in 15 seasons, beating arch-rival Rotorua BHS 26-13 in the final; second Luke Ale, with a double, and halfback Noah Hotham were the standouts
- The Central North Island final ended in a 36-all stalemate between two Waikato schools, St Paul's Collegiate and St Peter's (Cambridge), at the neutral venue of Taupo's Owen Delany Park; St Paul's thus take a share of its sixth title in seven seasons
- Otago BHS won the ODT Cup, beating King's High School 33–19 in the final, Cameron Millar scoring 23 points for the victors
- St Andrew's College (STAC) won its first ever UC Championship/Press Cup championship, defeating perennial First XV heavyweight Christchurch BHS 35–26 after trailing 20–0 after just 15 minutes
- Scots College won a second straight Wellington Premiership, and fourth in all, edging St Patrick's Silverstream 24–21
- Napier BHS won the 117th Polson Banner clash, 50–21 over Palmerston North BHS, at McLean Park
- The powerful Christchurch GHS outfit won the UC Cup, crushing Avonside GHS 81–5
- The best match of the season, arguably, was Christ's College's 28–27 win over Christchurch BHS in the 137th clash between the two schools since 1892; the try of the year, as voted at the NZR awards, went to Christ's replacement prop Jack Jones, who crossed in brilliant fashion from 30m out to seal this famous victory
- Auckland Grammar won the time-honoured clash with King's College, 34–32, after trailing 24–17 at the break
- Hamilton BHS won a record-extending sixth straight Condors Sevens crown (and record eighth in all), defeating Kelston BHS 14–10 in the boys' Cup final in Auckland, thanks to a solo try to Ollie Foote
- In the girls' Cup final at the Condors, Howick College won its first title, beating Manukura 12–5 in the decider
- The World Schools Sevens saw braces to Kaipo Olsen-Baker and Jorja Miller help the NZ Condors blank the NZ Fiji Barbarians 44–0 in the girls' Cup final, while in the boys' Cup final, NZ Condors beat Tongan Barbarians 21–14 in a tight encounter for their third straight title, Cooper Flanders scoring the winning try off a sharp Riley Higgins break.

WOMEN'S RUGBY
THE ALMANACK NEW ZEALAND XV

Renee Holmes
Waikato

Ruby Tui   Theresa Fitzpatrick   Stacey Fluhler
Counties Manukau   *Auckland*   *Waikato*

Chelsea Alley
Waikato

Hazel Tubic
Counties Manukau

Kendra Cocksedge
Canterbury

Kaipo Olsen-Baker
Manawatu

Kennedy Simon   Cindy Nelles   Chelsea Bremner   Alana Bremner (capt)
Waikato   *Canterbury*   *Canterbur*   *Canterbury*

Toka Natua   Rebecca Todd   Krystal Murray
Waikato   *Canterbury*   *Northland*

Reserves –

Luka Connor (*Bay of Plenty*), Phillipa Love (*Canterbury*), Aleisha-Pearl Nelson (*Auckland*), Charmaine McMenamin (*Auckland*), Aroha Savage (*Northland*), Arihiana Marino-Tauhinu (*Counties Manukau*), Amy du Plessis (*Otago*), Grace Brooker (*Canterbury*).

COMMENTS

The Farah Palmer Cup produced many outstanding individual performances and the quality and general standard of play continues to strengthen, this being assisted by the availability of the contracted sevens players. It was unfortunate the pandemic prevented the Black Ferns from any international fixtures but the end-of-season pair of games between the Black Ferns and New Zealand Barbarians showcased the best performers of the provincial competition.

Fullback: Renee Holmes (*Waikato*) stood out with her enterprising play and was rewarded with national selection. Patricia Maliepo (*Auckland*) showed her versatility in this position after being at first five-eighth in 2019. Grace Steinmetz (*Canterbury*) impressed either at fullback or wing. The evergreen Selica Winiata (*Manawatu*) remains a dangerous attacker 20 years after her debut.

Wing: Ruby Tui (*Counties Manukau*) and Stacey Fluhler (*Waikato*), stars of the Sevens circuit, were outstanding while several others also impressed with their speed including Cheyelle Robins-Reti (*Waikato*), Lyric Faleafaga (*Wellington*), Martha Lolohea (*Canterbury*), Lanulangi Veainu (*Counties Manukau*), Crystal Mayes (*Manawatu*), Natahlia Moors (*Auckland*) and Ayesha Leti-I'iga (*Wellington*). Unfortunately, injury prevented sevens star Michaela Blyde (*Bay of Plenty*) from showing her speed and class in the domestic season.

Centre: The qualities of Theresa Fitzpatrick (*Auckland*) is often underestimated, a reliable centre who reads play very well. Grace Brooker (*Canterbury*), Amy du Plessis (*Otago*), Janna Vaughan (*Manawatu*) and Monica Tagoai (*Wellington*) were also prominent. Northland benefited from the powerful Portia Woodman and Waikato appreciated the availability of the experienced former Black Fern Carla Hohepa.

Second five-eighth: The Waikato captain Chelsea Alley was again in fine form. Olivia McGoverne (*Canterbury*) made a successful move from fullback to become more involved in a solid backline. Ruahei Demant (*Auckland*) and Kilisitina Moata'ane (*Otago*) served their teams well. The young Sylvia Brunt (*Auckland*) shows promise.

First five-eighth: The experience of Hazel Tubic (*Counties Manukau*) was clearly displayed while Rosie Kelly (*Otago*) and young Carys Dallinger (*Manawatu*) attracted attention. Gayle Broughton (*Taranaki*) gave valuable leadership to her team.

Halfback: Kendra Cocksedge (*Canterbury*) remains the first-choice halfback with Arihiana Marino-Tauhinu (*Counties Manukau*) a quality deputy. Ariana Bayler (*Waikato*) and Tyler Nathan-Wong (*Northland*) were assets to their teams as was Emma Jensen (*Hawke's Bay*) who extended her remarkably long first-class career. Iritana Hohaia (*Taranaki*) is a younger player to impress.

No. 8: There was very little between Charmaine McMenamin (*Auckland*), Aroha Savage (*Northland*), Kennedy Simon (*Waikato*), Morgan Henderson (*Otago*) and Pia Tapsell (*North Harbour and Bay of Plenty*) but we were very impressed with the advances made by Manawatu schoolgirl Kaipo Olsen-Baker.

Flanker: Kennedy Simon (*Waikato*) played in this position for the Black Ferns and Canterbury captain Alana Bremner made a strong statement for 2021 Black Ferns selection by leading the Barbarians in two strong performances against the national side. Marcelle Parkes (*Wellington*) and the Bay of Plenty pair of Lesley Elder and Kendra Reynolds, were effective for their teams. Injury denied Manawatu the services of Black Ferns Sevens captain Sarah Hirini.

Lock: Eloise Blackwell and promising young Maia Roos provided Auckland with excellent lineout options. However, it was the Canterbury pairing of Chelsea Bremner and Canadian international Cindy Nelles whose efforts for the champion Farah Palmer Cup team could not be ignored. Kelsie Wills (*Bay of Plenty*) and Joanah Ngan-Woo (*Wellington*) were prominent, the latter particularly so in the Barbarians jersey.

Prop: There was little between Aleisha Nelson (*Auckland*), Toka Natua (*Waikato*), Phillipa Love (*Canterbury*), Aldora Itunu (*Auckland*) and Cristo Tofa (*Auckland*), all Black Ferns and effective scrummagers. However, it was the set-piece strength and general play of Northland and Barbarians prop Krystal Murray that greatly impressed us, she being a performer of international standard. We chose Murray to partner Natua in our front row. There were also commendable efforts from Amy Rule (*Canterbury*), Tanya Kalounivale (*Waikato*) and the North Harbour pair Olivia Ward-Duin and Jay Jay Taylor.

Hooker: Rebecca Todd (*Canterbury*) is our choice with Te Kura Ngata-Aerengamate (*Northland*), Luka Connor (*Bay of Plenty*), Grace Houpapa-Barrett (*Waikato*) and Forne Burkin (*Hawke's Bay*) enjoying fine seasons. Saphire Abraham (*Auckland*) continues to develop.

PLAYER OF THE YEAR

Stacey Jamie Aroha Kirsten Fluhler (nee Waaka) *(Waikato)* enjoyed an outstanding year, firstly with the Black Ferns Sevens for which she scored 31 tries in the five tournaments of the 2019/20 series — the most by any player — and was included in the HSBC Dream Team. Late in December 2019, soon after arriving home from the Dubai and Cape Town rounds, Waaka married Ricky Fluhler prior to preparing for the New Zealand Sevens at Hamilton in January. Later in the year, after an absence of three years, she made a welcome return to the Waikato squad for the Farah Palmer Cup, scoring eight tries, extending her record to 31 tries in 26 games for Waikato. Fluhler's electrifying runs lit up games and her beaming smiles showed that she is enjoying the sport.

Born at Papakura on November 3, 1995, Stacey Waaka was educated at Taneatua School 2005–08 and Whakatane High School 2009–13. She commenced her rugby career at high school in 2011. Talented in many sports, she was involved in netball, touch, hockey and athletics. Moving to attend university in Hamilton, she represented Waikato and New Zealand at touch.

In 2014, Waaka made her Farah Palmer Cup debut for Waikato and the following year the first of 16 tests for the Black Ferns and was a member of the 2017 Rugby World Cup winning squad. First appearing for the Black Ferns Sevens in 2016, Waaka was a member of the gold medal-winning teams at the 2018 Commonwealth Games and Rugby World Cup event in San Francisco. After 19 tournaments she has now scored 58 tries.

The Waaka family have excelled in sport with two older brothers also achieving in both rugby and touch. Beaudein represented NZ Schools, Poverty Bay, Taranaki, Waikato (2020) and All Blacks Sevens while also representing Bay of Plenty and New Zealand at touch. Bronson represented NZ Universities at rugby and Bay of Plenty, Waikato and NZ Maori at touch. Their father, Simon, represented Thames Valley in 1981 and, a decade later when in Australia, appeared for Victoria against the touring 1992 All Blacks. On Tracey's mother's side, All Black Arthur Stone and Kiwis league internationals Phillip and Robert Orchard are also related.

PROMISING PLAYER OF THE YEAR

Kaipo Teaiki Olsen-Baker *(Manawatu)* showed promise in the 2019 championship and this extended into 2020 with several very impressive performances for the Cyclones. She attended the Hurricanes Under-18 camp and late in the year she was chosen for the NZ Barbarians team where the 18-year-old Manukura schoolgirl opposed the Black Ferns who had two other Gisborne-bred players in their side, Charmaine McMenamin and Renee Holmes. Olsen-Baker has the potential to follow in their footsteps. After being winless during 2019, the Cyclones were semi-finalists in the 2020 Farah Palmer Cup and Olsen-Baker's workrate and effectiveness as a No 8 forward were large factors in the team's success and she was chosen as the Cyclones player of the year. Her year finished when she captained Manukura at the Condor Sevens in Auckland. Manukura compiled 175 points during their four pool games without conceding a point, defeating Feilding HS 24–5 in a quarter-final, Christchurch GHS 24–9 in a semi-final, before losing the cup final 12–5 to Howick College.

Kaipo Olsen-Baker was born at Gisborne on May 7, 2002 and first played rugby while at Awapuni School. Moving on to Gisborne GHS, she was in Poverty Bay age-grade teams, including an unbeaten Under-18 Sevens team in 2016. In addition to rugby, she participated at squash, netball, basketball, softball, soccer. She was a NZ Under-14 basketball representative in 2015.

In 2019 Olsen-Baker moved south to Palmerston North to attend Manukura. The form of the 17-year-old schoolgirl playing for Manukura and for the Feilding Old Boys Oroua club soon caught the eye of Cyclones coach Fusi Feaunati, who recognised the potential in the energetic athlete. Brought into the squad, she played at No 8 in the last three games during which the Cyclones conceded an average of 40 points per game. Despite the heavy defeats, Olsen-Baker's form impressed as a player of the future. She also excelled for her school's sevens team, Manukura winning the Condor Sevens plate final.

With each game during 2020 Olsen-Baker became more effective, a strong tackler and using her strength when carrying the ball forward. At 1.71m and 90kg, she is still developing physically and is a quick learner. Her aerobic fitness, instinctiveness, determination and courage mark her as an athlete possessing the vital attributes necessary for international rugby.

SEASON IN REVIEW
By Rikki Swannell

Few teams felt the impact of the Covid upheaval more than the Black Ferns. Slated to play an unprecedented eight tests in 2020, seven of them at home, their entire international calendar was wiped out and left them with a limited build-up less than a year out from the World Cup.

In some quarters the decision to cancel matches against USA, Australia, England and France was deemed hasty, but in reality there was little other option. It's easy to forget that not every country makes the investment in the women's game that New Zealand and England do, and every penny and resource spent on women's rugby is still done so judiciously. We got back to 'normal' fairly quickly but the Northern Hemisphere countries only returned to training in bubbles in September and Australia had no programme running. In effect, there was no one for the Black Ferns to play.

But while they didn't get any test matches, the Black Ferns were able to play the best of the rest in New Zealand. After a Possibles versus Possibles trial, they played two matches against a New Zealand Barbarians side which featured a handful of capped players, a host of Farah Palmer Cup standouts and Canterbury's impressive Canadian international Cindy Nelles. The Black Ferns were pushed hard in both matches, which were played with intensity and at pace.

Ten players made debuts for the Black Ferns across the two matches, with Otago midfielder Amy du Plessis in particular, making the most of her opportunities. The return of Counties veteran Hazel Tubic to the national team for the first time since 2017 will add depth at first-five and it surely can't be long until the prodigious talent of Patricia Maliepo also joins those ranks. The 17-year-old looked assured playing the first match at fullback for the Baabaas but was a constant threat when she moved to first-five in the second match.

The likely addition of a handful of Black Ferns Sevens players to the World Cup squad gives coach Glenn Moore an undeniable depth of talent to choose from next year. Those Sevens players will have about six weeks between the Tokyo Olympics and the start of the World Cup.

The Olympic Games were the biggest global sporting casualty of Covid, and while it halted the Black Ferns progress towards their major goal of Olympic gold, they had enough time to wrap up another World Series title, albeit in a truncated season. After finishing third in the first tournament of the season (October 2019) in Glendale, New Zealand went on to win the next four events in Dubai, Cape Town, Hamilton and Sydney. The win in Hamilton was a highlight for both the teams and a large number of supporters in the crowd to see the first full women's tournament played in New Zealand. With the final three tournaments cancelled, the Black Ferns were deemed series winners.

The undoubted star of the season was Stacey Fluhler. With a whopping 31 tries in five tournaments, Fluhler, previously an unsung hero of the team, well and truly stepped out of the shadow of fellow fliers Portia Woodman and Michaela Blyde. Notable too was Tyla Nathan-Wong becoming just the second woman behind Canada's Ghislaine Landry to score 1000 series points, while Ruby Tui was named alongside Fluhler and Nathan-Wong in the season Dream Team.

The silver lining of the abrupt end to the World Sevens Series meant the bulk of the squad were able to play in the Farah Palmer Cup. They, along with a full contingent of Black Ferns XVs players elevated the competition to new heights. Although the North-South pools did bring about some significant mismatches, the overall standard of play among the top teams was exceptional and the final between Canterbury and Waikato was one of the tensest and most dramatic matches seen in years. Of course, the more things change, the more they stay the same and Canterbury found a way to win their fourth straight title.

Given all that has come to pass this year, the fact a full Farah Palmer Cup was played, the Black Ferns were able to assemble and the women's sevens programme got back to full capacity is significant. While Covid could have been a ready-made excuse to pull back, it seems there is genuine awareness of the value and importance of the women's game, and while the level of financial and resource commitment can always be greater, the future is getting brighter off the field and starting to match the quality and improvement on it.

NEW ZEALAND BLACK FERNS

In March, 31 players were given Black Ferns contracts to prepare for a programme of eight tests, seven being in New Zealand. Unfortunately, the pandemic gave the union no option but to cancel all international fixtures. There was some consolation with two games being arranged in November against a New Zealand Barbarians selection consisting of players on the fringe of selection, some having Black Ferns contracts. In effect, the Barbarians were a B team with several enhancing their chances of Black Ferns selection to prepare for the 2021 World Cup. Contracted sevens players were not considered for selection.

NEW ZEALAND, 2020

	Union	Date of Birth	Height	Weight	Tests at 1/1/21
C.H. (Chelsea) Alley	Waikato	7/11/92	1.78	81	24
E.S. (Eloise) Blackwell (capt)	Auckland	28/12/90	1.82	89	43
C.J. (Chelsea) Bremner	Canterbury	11/4/95	1.81	88	0
G.E. (Grace) Brooker	Canterbury	20/6/99	1.73	75	1
K.M. (Kendra) Cocksedge (vice-capt)	Canterbury	1/7/88	1.57	61	53
L.H.J. (Luka) Connor	Bay of Plenty	24/9/96	1.71	95	4
D.R. (Ruahei) Demant	Auckland	21/4/95	1.69	81	11
A. (Amy) du Plessis	Otago	7/7/99	1.69	73	0
R.M.M. (Renee) Holmes	Waikato	21/12/99	1.68	70	0
A.T. (Aldora) Itunu	Auckland	28/6/91	1.78	110	20
T.J.M. (Tanya) Kalounivale	Waikato	20/1/99	1.78	129	0
P.E.A. (Phillipa) Love	Canterbury	8/4/90	1.73	90	11
C.J. (Charmaine) McMenamin	Auckland	13/5/90	1.73	84	25
A.A.H. (Arihiana) Marino-Tauhinu	Counties Manukau	29/3/92	1.61	74	6
I.M.P. (Ilisapeti) Molia	Counties Manukau	16/8/01	1.78	94	0
D.B. (Natahlia) Moors	Auckland	7/12/95	1.63	73	?
T.I.Te O. (Toka) Natua	Waikato	22/11/91	1.70	101	22
A.P. (Aleisha) Nelson	Auckland	2/3/90	1.82	104	35
T.R. (Te Kura) Ngata-Aerengamate	Northland	21/10/91	1.64	96	29
K.L. (Kendra) Reynolds	Bay of Plenty	25/1/93	1.63	77	0
C.R.A. (Cheyelle) Robins-Reti	Waikato	9/3/97	1.63	64	0
A. (Aroha) Savage	Northland	11/3/90	1.73	83	33
K.W. (Kennedy) Simon	Waikato	1/10/96	1.72	80	4
G.L. (Grace) Steinmetz	Canterbury	16/1/98	1.68	71	0
P.H. (Pia) Tapsell	Bay of Plenty	2/8/98	1.78	86	6
L.C.S. (Cristo) Tofa	Auckland	11/12/87	1.69	105	2
H.S. (Hazel) Tubic	Counties Manukau	31/12/90	1.65	69	11
L.L. (Lanulangi) Veainu	Counties Manukau	3/11/93	1.69	72	0
K.P. (Kelsie) Wills	Bay of Plenty	8/1/93	1.84	81	0
S.C. (Selica) Winiata	Manawatu	14/11/86	1.55	58	40

Not considered due to injury: L. Elder (Bay of Plenty), J. Patea-Fereti (Wellington), Carla Hohepa (Waikato), F. Burkin (Hawke's Bay), R. Wickliffe (Bay of Plenty) and A. Leti-I'iga (Wellington). After initial selection, Molia withdrew with injury and was replaced by Moors who was originally selected in the NZ Barbarians squad.

Coach: Glenn Moore
Manager: Lauren Cournane
Doctor: Dr Steve Smith
Mental skills coach: Jhan Gavala
Assistant coaches: Wesley Clarke, John Haggart
Physiotherapist: Georgia Milne
Strength & conditioning coach: Jamie Tout
Analyst: Arran Hodge

NEW ZEALAND v NEW ZEALAND BARBARIANS

The Trusts Arena, Waitakere, Auckland   November 14, 2020

New Zealand won 34–15

NEW ZEALAND		*NZ BARBARIANS*
Selica Winiata	15	Patricia Maliepo
Cheyelle Robins-Reti	14	Lyric Faleafaga
Grace Brooker	13	Janna Vaughan
Chelsea Alley	12	Kilisitina Moata'ane
Langi Veainu	11	Martha Lolohea
Hazel Tubic	10	Carys Dallinger
Kendra Cocksedge	9	Ariana Bayler
Aroha Savage	8	Kaipo Olsen-Baker
Kennedy Simon	7	Marcelle Parkes
Charmaine McMenamin	6	Alana Bremner (capt)
Kelsi Wills	5	Cindy Nelles
Eloise Blackwell (capt)	4	Joanah Ngan-Woo
Aleisha Nelson	3	Amy Rule
Luka Connor	2	Saphire Abraham
Toka Natua	1	Krystal Murray
Cristo Tofa (rep 1, 66m)	16	Rebecca Todd (rep 2, 40m)
Te Kura Ngata-Aerengamate (rep 2, 67m)	17	Jay Jay Taylor (rep 1, 54m)
Aldora Itunu (rep 3, 66m)	18	Olivia Ward-Duin (rep 3, 59m)
Chelsea Bremner (rep 5, 61m)	19	Maia Roos (rep 8, 59m)
Kendra Reynolds (rep 8, 68m)	20	Morgan Henderson (rep 14, 65m)
Arihiana Marino-Tauhinu (rep 9, 64m)	21	Iritana Hohaia (rep 9, 45m)
Ruahei Demant (rep 15, 51m)	22	Grace Houpapa-Barrett (rep 6, 76m)
Amy du Plessis (rep 11, 61m)	23	Rosie Kelly (rep 10, 52m)
Veainu (2), Cocksedge, Wills, Robins-Reti, Brooker	Tries	Murray, Faleafaga
Cocksedge, Tubic	Cons	Maliepo
	Pens	Maliepo

Kickoff: 4.35pm   **Attendance:** 3000   **Conditions:** Fine

Referee: Nick Hogan
Assistant referees: Lauren Jenner, Maggie Cogger-Orr
TMO: Lee Jeffrey

Halftime: New Zealand 20 – NZ Barbarians 8

Black Ferns debuts: Robins-Reti (Black Fern No 215), Veainu (216), Wills (217), C. Bremner (218), du Plessis (219), Reynolds (220)

NEW ZEALAND v NEW ZEALAND BARBARIANS

Trafalgar Park, Nelson
November 21, 2020

New Zealand won 19–17

NEW ZEALAND		NZ BARBARIANS
Renee Holmes	15	Carys Dallinger
Grace Steinmetz	14	Lyric Faleafaga
Amy du Plessis	13	Janna Vaughan
Chelsea Alley	12	Kilisitina Moata'ane
Langi Veainu	11	Crystal Mayes
Ruahei Demant	10	Patricia Maliepo
Kendra Cocksedge	9	Ariana Bayler
Charmaine McMenamin	8	Cindy Nelles
Kennedy Simon	7	Marcelle Parkes
Pia Tapsell	6	Alana Bremner (capt)
Chelsea Bremner	5	Maia Roos
Eloise Blackwell (capt)	4	Joanah Ngan-Woo
Aleisha Nelson	3	Amy Rule
Te Kura Ngata-Aerengamate	2	Rebecca Todd
Phillipa Love	1	Krystal Murray
Luka Connor (rep 2, 67m)	16	Saphire Abraham (rep 4, 65m)
Toka Natua (rep 1, 59m)	17	Jay Jay Taylor (rep 1, 43m)
Aldora Itunu (rep 3, 65m)	18	Olivia Ward-Duin (rep 3, 79m)
Kelsie Wills (rep 5, 57m)	19	Kaipo Olsen-Baker (rep 5, 48m)
Aroha Savage (rep 6, 48m)	20	Morgan Henderson (rep 7, 40m)
Arihiana Marino-Tauhinu (rep 9, 68m)	21	Iritana Hohaia (rep 9, 48m)
Hazel Tubic (rep 12, 68m)	22	Shyanne Thompson (rep 11, 62m)
Natahlia Moors (rep 11, 65m)	23	Rosie Kelly (rep 15, 74m)
Love (2), Ngata-Aerengamate Cocksedge (2)	Tries	A. Bremner, Rule
	Cons	Maliepo (2)
	Pens	Maliepo

Kickoff: 4.35pm *Conditions:* Fine

Referee: Rebecca Mahoney
Assistant referees: Lauren Jenner, Maggie Cogger-Orr
TMO: Lee Jeffrey

Halftime: New Zealand 19 NZ Barbarians 14

Black Ferns debuts: Holmes (Black Fern No 221), Steinmetz (222)

NEW ZEALAND WOMEN'S REPRESENTATIVES, 1989–2020

Name	B&D	Representative Team	Internationals Games	Points
Aiatu, Muteremoana S.	1981–	(Wellington) 2011	1	–
Alley, Chelsea H.	1992–	(Waikato) 2013–14–17–18–19–20; (North Harbour) 2015–16	24	27
Andrew, Shannon R.	1972–	(Auckland) 1996	2	–
Aniseko, Fa'anati	1989–	(Auckland) 2007	2	5
Apiata, Jacquileen W.	1966–	(Canterbury) 1989–90–91–92–93–94–95	5	–
Atkins, Leanne T.	1976–	(Northland) 1994	–	–
Baker, Lise		(Wellington) 1990	–	–
Baker, Miriama	1962–	(Auckland) 1989–91	–	–
Baker, Shakira J.	1992–	(Wellington) 2011; (Manawatu) 2012–14	13	40
Ballinger, Shona	1970–	(Wellington) 1990–91	–	–
Barclay, F.J. see King, F.J.				
Berry, Zoey P.	1987–	(Canterbury) 2012	1	–
Blackledge, V.E. see Grant, V.E.				
Blackwell, Eloise S.	1990–	(Auckland) 2011–12–13–14–15–16–17–18–19–20	43	50
Blyde, Cherrie		(Taranaki) 1992	–	–
Borthwick, Nicole M.	1980–	(Auckland) 2005	2	7
Bosman (nee Ngatai), Melodie, 2010. see Ngatai, M.M.				
Brazier, Kelly A.	1989–	(Otago) 2009–10–12–13–14–16; (Canterbury) 2011; (Bay of Plenty) 2017–19	40	190
Bremner, Chelsea J.	1995–	(Canterbury) 2020	–	–
Brett, Lesley	1968–	(Canterbury) 1990–91	3	12
Brooker, Grace E.	1999–	(Canterbury) 2019–20	1	–
Broughton, Florence		(Wellington) 1990	–	–
Burkin, Forne K.	1998–	(Canterbury) 2019	2	–
Canterbury, Marina R.	1984–	(Hawke's Bay) 2005	5	10
Chase, Debbie P.M.	1966–	(Canterbury) 1990–91–93	3	12
Chittock, Barbara J.	1985–	(Canterbury) 2009	–	–
Coady, Olivia R.	1990–	(Canterbury) 2008–09	4	5
Cobley, Rhonda J.	1971–	(Canterbury) 1992–94	–	–
Cocksedge, Kendra M.	1988–	(Canterbury) 2007–08–09–10–11–12–13–14–15–16–17–18–19–20	53	342
Codling, Monalisa M.	1977–	(Otago) 1998; (Auckland) 1999–02–03–04–05–06–07–08–10	30	25
Connor, Luka H.J.	1996–	(Bay of Plenty) 2019–20	4	–
Cootes, Vanessa	1969–	(Waikato) 1995–96–97–98–00–01–02	16	215
Cottrell, Krysten J.	1992–	(Hawke's Bay) 2018–19	8	–
Crossman, Lydia J.	1986–	(Hawke's Bay) 2011; (Auckland) 2012	5	–
Cunningham, Vicky		(Auckland) 1997	1	–
Davie, Mary		(Canterbury) 1992–93	–	–
Dawson, Susan	1971–	(Northland) 1999–00–02	4	5
de Jong, Catherine L.	1984–	(Otago) 2005	1	–
Demant, D. Ruahei	1995–	(Auckland) 2018–19–20	11	14
Demant, Kiritapu W.	1996–	(Auckland) 2015	2	–
du Plessis, Amy	1999–	(Otago) 2020	–	–

Name	B&D	Representative Team	Internationals Games	Points
Edwards (nee Shelford), Exia T.	1975–	(Bay of Plenty) 1998–99–00–01–02–03–04–05–06	27	90
Edwards, Maree	1975–	(Otago) 1998–00; (Canterbury) 2003	4	5
Edwards, Tangaloa		(Auckland) 1989	–	–
Elder (nee Ketu), Lesley T.	1987–	(Waikato) 2015–17; (Bay of Plenty) 2018–19	18	10
Ellis, Judith M.	1966–	(Canterbury) 1993–94–95	1	–
Engebretsen, Lauren J.	1983–	(Waikato) 2004	3	–
Epiha, Eva A.	1974–	(Auckland) 1994	–	–
Everitt, Rawinia P.	1986–	(Auckland) 2011–12; (Counties Manukau) 2013–14–16–17	21	25
Ewe, Donna	1964–	(Auckland) 1990–91	3	–
Faamausili, Fiao'o	1980–	(Auckland) 2002–03–05–06–07–08–09–10–11–12–13–14–15–16–17–18	57	85
Fa'aope, Lili		(Canterbury) 1989–90	–	–
Faneva, Karli J.K.	1998–	(Bay of Plenty) 2019	2	–
Farr, Amy M.	1982–	(Wellington) 2007	1	–
Fereti (nee Patea), Jackie S. see Patea, J.S.				
	1966–	(Canterbury) 1989–90–91	3	–
Fitzpatrick, Theresa M.	1995–	(Auckland) 2017–18–19	11	15
Ford, Amanda	1970–	(Canterbury) 1989–90–91	1	4
Ford, Deborah	1965–	(Canterbury) 1989–90–91	–	–
Frost, Seuga	1966–	(Canterbury) 1990–91	–	–
Garden, Susan	1961–2008	(Canterbury) 1989–90–91; (Otago) 1992	–	–
Gavet, Sandra	1961–	(Auckland) 1990–92	–	–
Goss, Sarah L.	1992–	(Manawatu) 2016–17	10	5
Grant (nee Blackledge), Victoria E.	1982–	(Auckland) 2006–07–08–09–10–11; (Waikato) 2013	17	35
Gray, Isabel	1974–	(Wellington) 1999–02–05	5	5
Gubb (nee Halapua), Charlene P.T. see Halapua, C.P.T.				
Halapua, Charlene P.T.	1988–	(Auckland) 2015–16–17	9	5
Harrison, Sarah		(Wellington) 1999	2	–
Hayes, Carol	1970–	(Southland) 1989–91–92–93	–	–
Heenan, Janet M.	1969–	(Northland) 1996–98	5	–
Heighway, Victoria L	1980–	(Auckland) 2000–01–02–03–04–05–06–07–08–09–10	32	10
Hiemer, Riki		(Wellington) 1997	2	–
Hina, Trisha R.	1977–	(Auckland) 2010	4	–
Hireme, A. Honey	1981–	(Waikato) 2014–15–16–17	18	75
Hirovanaa, Monique J.	1966–	(Auckland) 1994–95–96–97–98–99–00–01–02	24	65
Hohepa, Carla G.	1985–	(Otago) 2007–08–09–10; (Waikato) 2016–17–19	25	95
Holmes, Renee M.M.	1999–	(Waikato) 2020	–	–
Hopkins, Anna	1970–2014	(Wellington) 1991	–	–
Hull, R.M. see Mahoney, R.M.				
Huxford, Sarah		(Wellington) 1993	–	–
Inwood, Nicola A.	1970–	(Canterbury) 1989–90–91	3	–
Itunu, Aldora T.	1991–	(Auckland) 2015–16–17–18–20	20	30
Itunu, Linda F.	1984–	(Auckland) 2003–04–06–07–08–09–10–14–15–17–18	39	10

Name	B&D	Representative Team	Internationals Games	Points
Jensen, Emma M.	1977–	(Waikato) 2002–03–04; (Auckland) 2005–06–07–08–09–10–11–12–13–14–15	49	53
John, Chris		(Canterbury) 1990	–	–
Johnson, Fiona C.	1970–	(Wellington) 1990	–	–
Kahura, Dianne M.T.	1969–	(Auckland) 1998–99–00–02	12	95
Kay, Rhonda	1976–	(Waikato) 2000	1	–
Ketu, Lesley T. see Elder, L.T.				
King (nee Barclay), Fiona J.	1972–	(Otago) 1996–97–98–99–00–01–02	18	5
Kingi, Mere A.	1974–	(Auckland) 2003–04	5	10
Kiwi, Kellie H.	1972–	(Bay of Plenty) 1996–97–98	8	15
Knight, Neroli	1974–	(Wellington) 1990–91–99–00–01	4	–
Konui, Toni R.H.	1966–	(Auckland) 1998	3	–
Kupa, Mel		(Hawke's Bay) 1997	2	–
Lavea, Justine	1984–	(Auckland) 2004–05–07–09–10–11–12–13–14; (Counties Manukau) 2015	34	30
Lavea, Vaniya N.H.	1981–	(Auckland) 2003–04–07	5	–
Leiataua, Onjeurlina F.	1995–	(Auckland) 2013	1	–
Lemon, Tracey M.	1970–2012	(Auckland) 1991–94–95	2	–
Lene, Stacey O.	1980–	(Canterbury) 2003–04–05	7	35
Leti-I'iga, Ayesha A.	1999–	(Wellington) 2018–19	9	15
Levave, Sanita D.	1988–	(Wellington) 2014	5	–
Lili'i, Adrienne P.	1970–	(Auckland) 1999–02–03–04; (Waikato) 2000	12	5
Littleworth, Helen M.	1966–	(Canterbury) 1989–90–91–92–93–94; (Otago) 1995–96	8	20
Liua'ana, Rebecca	1970–	(Wellington) 1999–00–01–02	10	10
Lotui'iga, L. Brigitta	1968–	(Auckland) 1998	5	–
Love, Phillipa E.A.	1990–	(Otago) 2014; (Canterbury) 2017–18–19–20	11	5
McKay, K. Ruth	1986–	(Manawatu) 2007–08–09–10–12–13–14	25	–
McKenzie, Margaret J.	1970–	(Otago) 2000–05	5	5
McMenamin, Charmaine J.	1990–	(Auckland) 2013–16–17–18–19–20	25	20
Mahon, Helen L.	1968–	(Canterbury) 1989; (Wellington) 1991; (Waikato) 1992	3	12
Mahoney (nee Hull), Rebecca M.	1983–	(Manawatu) 2004–08; (Hawke's Bay) 2006; (Wellington) 2009–10–11	16	25
Makata, Rachel J.	1974–	(Auckland) 2006	2	5
Maliukaetau, F. Diane L.	1986–	(Auckland) 2005–06	6	5
Mallard, Beth L.	1981–	(Otago) 2006–07–08–09	8	–
Manuel, Huriana R.	1986–	(Auckland) 2005–06–07–08–09–10–14	25	70
Marino-Tauhinu, Arihiana A.H.	1992–	(Counties Manukau) 2019–20	6	–
Marsh, A. see Rule, A.				
Martin, Rochelle L.	1973–	(Wellington) 1994–95; (Auckland) 1996–97–98–99–00–02–04–05–06	32	70
Matapo, P.E.A. 'Kelani'	1983–	(Auckland) 2011	1	–
Mata'u, Aotearoa K.	1997–	(Counties Manukau) 2016–17	8	5
Mihinui, M.T. Eliza	1960–	(Auckland) 1994	–	–
Moata'ane, Kilisitina	1997–	(Otago) 2019	1	–
Moore, Aroha	1978–	(Auckland) 2004	3	–
Moors, D.B. 'Natahlia'	1995–	(Auckland) 2018–19–20	2	5
Mortimer, Stephanie A.	1981–	(Canterbury) 2003–04–05–06	11	50
Mulipola, Tala	1981–	(Auckland) 2000–01–03	7	5
Murphy, Amanda J.	1985–	(Canterbury) 2009–11	2	–

Name	B&D	Representative Team	Internationals Games	Points
Myers, H.J. see Porter, H.J.				
Natua Toka I.	1991–	(Waikato) 2015–16–17–19–20	22	25
Nelson, Aleisha P.	1990–	(Auckland) 2012–14–15–16–17–18–19–20	35	10
Nemaia, Ana		(Auckland) 1989	–	–
Nesbit, Joanne		(Canterbury) 1989	–	–
Ngan-Woo, Joanah M.F.	1995–	(Wellington) 2019	3	–
Ngata-Aerengamate, Te Kura R.	1991–	(Counties Manukau) 2014–15–16–17–18–19 (Northland) 2020	29	10
Ngatai, Melodie M.	1976–	(Auckland) 2004; (Waikato) 2005; (Hawke's Bay) 2006–11; (Canterbury) 2010–13	17	–
Nielsen, Jacinta	1972–	(Otago) 1997–98–00	7	–
O'Leary, Pauline		(Wanganui) 1993	–	–
O'Reilly, Lauren M.	1967–	(Canterbury) 1992–93–94	1	–
Paasi, Poinisitia	1970–2018	(Wellington) 2001–07	4	–
Paitai, Elsie	1963–	(Auckland) 1990–91	–	–
Palmer, Farah R.	1972–	(Otago) 1996–98–99–00; (Waikato) 1997; (Manawatu) 2001–02–03–04–05–06	35	25
Papalii, Christine	1962–	(Auckland) 1989–90–92	–	–
Parkes, Marcelle J.	1997–	(Wellington) 2018–19	5	–
Patea-Fereti, Jackie S.	1986–	(Wellington) 2012–13–14–16–18–19	18	–
Paul, Geraldine	1965–	(Bay of Plenty) 1989–91–97; (Taranaki) 1994	4	10
Paul, Tamaku	1979–	(Bay of Plenty) 2001	1	–
Penetito, Karina E. see Stowers, K.E.				
Perese, Leilani L.R.	1993–	(Counties Manukau) 2018–19	11	–
Piho, Mata	1972–	(Otago) 1998–00	3	–
Porter (nee Myers), Hannah J.	1979–	(Otago) 2000–02; (Auckland) 2003–04–05–06–08	22	169
Reader, Heidi C.	1971–	(Otago) 1993; (Waikato) 1994–96; (Bay of Plenty) 1995	3	38
Rees, Vivian L.	1971–	(Wellington) 1993–94–95	2	2
Rere (Ratu), Ericka	1963–	(Wellington) 1990–91–92; (Bay of Plenty) 1993	3	–
Reynolds, Julie	1966–	(Canterbury) 1993–94	–	–
Reynolds, Kendra L.	1993–	(Bay of Plenty) 2020	–	–
Richards, Anna M.	1964–	(Auckland) 1990–91–92–93–94–96–97–98–99–00–01–02–03–04–05–06–07–08–10	49	89
Richards, Fiona C.	1970–	(Canterbury) 1993–94–95–96; (Auckland) 1997–98–99	14	–
Richardson, Claire	1984–	(Otago) 2003–04–05–06–07–12; (Auckland) 2013–14	23	54
Rikihana-Broughton, Julie		(Wellington) 1990	–	–
Robertson, Casey J.	1981–	(Canterbury) 2002–03–04–05–06–09–10–11–12–13–14	38	10
Robins-Reti, Cheyelle R.A.	1997–	(Waikato) 2020	–	–
Robinson, Melodie C.	1973–	(Wellington) 1996–97–98–99; (Auckland) 2001–02	18	20
Robinson, Vita J.	1982–	(Auckland) 2007–09–10–11–13	14	–
Rodd, Christine A.	1959–	(Canterbury) 1990–91	2	–
Ross, L. Christine	1964–	(Mid C'bury) 1989–92–96; (Canterbury) 1990–91	5	52

Name	B&D	Representative Team	Internationals Games	Points
Rowat, Claire L.	1983–	(Wellington) 2009	–	–
Rule (nee Marsh), Amiria	1983–	(Canterbury) 2000–01–02–03–5–06–09–11–13–14	34	75
Ruscoe, Melissa J.	1976–	(Canterbury) 2004–05–06–07–08–10	22	32
Rush, Annaleah M.	1976–	(Otago) 1996–97–98–99; (Auckland) 2000–01–02	20	156
Rush, Erin	1970–	(Wellington) 2003	2	–
Saili, Alena F.	1998–	(Southland) 2018–19	5	–
Savage, Aroha	1990–	(Auckland) 2010–11–12; (Counties Manukau) 2013–14–16–17–18 (Northland) 2020	33	20
Sheck, Regina	1969–	(Auckland) 1994–96–97–98; (Waikato) 1999–00–01–02–03–04	25	25
Shelford, Exia T. see Edwards, E.T.				
Shortland, Suzanne	1974–	(Auckland) 1997–98–99–00–01–02	18	20
Simon, Kennedy W.	1996–	(Waikato) 2019–20	4	–
Simpson-Brown, Lenadeen H.	1964–	(Canterbury) 1994; (Waikato) 1995–96–97	8	15
Sio, Nina	1963–	(Auckland) 1989–91–92; (Waikato) 1994	4	–
Sione, Joan L.	1986–	(Auckland) 2005–10	6	5
Sisifa, Angelene A.F.	1989–	(Otago) 2015–16	7	–
Smith, Charmaine B.	1990–	(North Harbour) 2015–16–17; (Auckland) 2018–19	27	20
Smith, Kimberly M.	1985–	(Canterbury) 2005–06–07–08–09	11	–
Solomon, Pikihuia P.	1983–	(Otago) 2005	2	10
Steinmetz, Grace L.	1998–	(Canterbury) 2020	–	–
Stowers, Karina E. (nee Penetito) 1986–		(Auckland) 2005–09–10–11–12–13	18	–
Su'a, S.M.A. 'Nara'	1969–	(Auckland) 1996	2	5
Suasua-White, D. see White, D.M.				
Subritzky-Nafatali, Victoria S.	1991–	(Otago) 2012–14; (Counties Manukau) 2015–16–17	19	34
Sue, Kristina J.	1987–	(Manawatu) 2016–17–18	15	–
Sutorius, Aimee E.	1979–	Wellington) 2007–08–09	3	–
Tagoai, Monica F.	1998–	(Wellington) 2018	3	–
Tahu, Bella M.	1970–	(Auckland) 1996	3	–
Talawadua, Sosoli J.	1989–	(Waikato) 2016–17	8	5
Tamihana, Florence		(Wellington) 1995	1	–
Tapsell, Pia H.	1998–	(North Harbour) 2019 (Bay of Plenty) 2020	6	5
Taufateau, Doris J.T.	1987–	(Auckland) 2008–10–11	5	–
Taylor, Karen	1968–	(Bay of Plenty) 1996	2	5
Teddy, Waimania L.	1979–	(Auckland) 2005–06–07	6	–
Te Tamaki, Teresa K.	1981–	(Auckland) 2007–08–11; (Waikato) 2012–15	10	–
Tekeu, No'o		(–) 1990	–	–
Te Ohaere-Fox, Stephanie A.	1985–	(Canterbury) 2008–09–10–12–13–14; (Wasps) 2011	24	–
Thomas, Emma H.	1958–	(Bay of Plenty) 1996–97–98	9	–
Tiplady, Anika M.	1980–	(Manawatu) 2007; (Canterbury) 2009	2	–
Tiplady-Hurring, Halie A.	1986–	(Canterbury) 2008–10–14; (Otago) 2012	13	15
Tiriamai, Kimi	1964–	(Auckland) 1990–91	2	–
Tofa, L. Cristo. S.	1987–	(North Harbour) 2018 (Auckland) 2020	2	–
Tubic, Hazel S.	1990–	(Auckland) 2011–12; (Counties Manukau) 2016–17–20	11	12

Name	B&D	Representative Team	Internationals Games	Points
Va'aga, Helen	1977–	(Auckland) 2002–03–05–06	10	10
Vaeteru, Teina		(–) 1990	–	–
Vaughan, Janna M.	1988–	(Manawatu) 2015–16	6	10
Veainu, Lanulangi L.	1993–	(Counties Manukau) 2020	–	–
Waaka, Cheryl M.	1970–	(Auckland) 1997–98–00–01–02–03–04; (Northland) 1999	20	35
Waaka, Stacey J.A.K.	1995–	(Waikato) 2015–17–18	16	30
Wall, Louisa H.	1972–	(Waikato) 1994; (Auckland) 1995–96–97–98–99	15	95
Ward-Duin, Olivia Y.	1993–	(North Harbour) 2019	2	–
Waters, Tracey J.R.	1973–	(Canterbury) 1995–96–98	10	5
Wharton, Julie		(Auckland) 1990	–	–
Whata-Simpkins, Katarina R.	1990–	(Wellington) 2011	1	–
White, Davida M.	1967–	(Auckland) 1993–94–95–96–98–00	13	–
Wickliffe, Renee W.M.	1987–	(Auckland) 2009–10–11; (Counties Manukau) 2013–14–15–16–17; (Bay of Plenty) 2018–19	41	105
Wihongi, Kamila T.	1982–	(Otago) 2005	1	–
Williams, Amy L.	1986–	(Hawke's Bay) 2005–06	6	–
Williams, Tasha H.	1973–	(Manawatu) 1994	1	10
Willoughby, Shannon M.	1982–	(Otago) 2005–06	8	–
Wills, Kelsie P.	1993–	(Bay of Plenty) 2020	–	–
Wilson, Tammi	1973–	(Auckland) 1998–99–00–01–02	16	196
Wilton, Kathleen A.	1984–	(Otago) 2007–11–12–13–14	18	–
Winiata, Selica C.	1986–	(Manawatu) 2008–12–13–14–15–16–17–18–19–20	40	195
Wong, Natasha A.	1967–	(Canterbury) 1990–91–92–93–94	3	–
Wood, Rebecca J.	1987–	(North Harbour) 2017	7	–
Woodman, Portia L.	1991–	(Auckland) 2013; (Counties Manukau) 2016–17	16	110
Woodman, Sharnita K.	1986–	(Counties Manukau) 2016	2	–
Yates, Sandy	1979–	(Counties Manukau) 2001	1	–

BLACK FERNS RECORDS

NEW ZEALAND INTERNATIONAL CAPTAINS

Fiao'o Faamausili	2012–18	35
Farah Palmer	1997–2006	30
Melissa Ruscoe	2007–10	8
Lenadeen Simpson-Brown	1994–96	6
Leslie Elder	2019	5
Helen Littleworth	1991	3
Victoria Grant	2010–11	3
Rochelle Martin	2005–06	2
Victoria Heighway	2009	2
Davida White	1998	1
Anna Richards	2005	1
Casey Robertson	2011	1
Amiria Rule	2014	1
Kendra Cocksedge	2019	1

MOST APPEARANCES IN INTERNATIONALS

F.M. Faamausili	2002–18	57	K.A. Brazier	2009–19	40
K.M. Cocksedge	2007–19	53	S.C. Winiata	2008–19	40
A.M. Richards	1991–10	49	C.J. Robertson	2002–14	38
E.M. Jensen	2002–15	49	L.F. Itunu	2003–18	38
E.S. Blackwell	2011–19	43	F.R. Palmer	1996–06	35
R.W.M. Wickliffe	2009–19	41	A.P. Nelson	2012–19	35

MOST SUCCESSIVE INTERNATIONALS

K.M. Cocksedge	2011–19	45

MOST POINTS IN INTERNATIONALS

	Tries	Con	PG	DG	Total		Tries	Con	PG	DG	Total
K.M. Cocksedge	16	86	30	–	342	K.A. Brazier	11	45	15	–	190
V. Cootes	43	–	–	–	215	H.J. Porter	5	42	20	–	169
T. Wilson	21	29	11	–	196	A.M. Rush	14	34	6	–	156
S.C. Winiata	39	–	–	–	195						

MOST POINTS IN AN INTERNATIONAL

V. Cootes	v France, 1996	45	(9 tries)
P.L. Woodman	v Hong Kong, 2017	40	(8 tries)
T. Wilson	v USA, 1999	36	(6 tries, 3 conversions)
L.C. Ross	v France, 1996	34	(2 tries, 12 conversions)
K.M. Cocksedge	v Hong Kong, 2017	31	(1 try, 13 conversions)
T. Wilson	v Germany, 1998	30	(4 tries, 5 conversions)

MOST TRIES IN AN INTERNATIONAL

V. Cootes	v France, 1996	9	V. Cootes	v USA, 1998	5
P.L. Woodman	v Hong Kong, 2017	8	V. Cootes	v Germany, 2002	5
T. Wilson	v USA, 1999	6	S.C. Winiata	v Samoa, 2014	5
V. Cootes	v USA, 1996	5			

MOST PENALTY GOALS IN AN INTERNATIONAL

K.A. Brazier	v England, 2013	4	K.M. Cocksedge	v England, 2015	4

MOST CONVERSIONS IN AN INTERNATIONAL

K.M. Cocksedge	v Hong Kong, 2017	13	L.C. Ross	v Canada, 1996	9
L.C. Ross	v France, 1996	12	H.C. Reader	v USA, 1996	8

INTERNATIONAL MATCH RECORD

Year		Opponent	Venue	Result		
1991	v	Canada[1]	Glamorgan	won	24	8
	v	Wales[1]	Llanharen	won	24	6
	v	USA[1] (semi-final)	Cardiff	lost	0	7
1994	v	Australia	Sydney	won	37	0
1995	v	Australia	Auckland	won	64	0
1996	v	Australia	Sydney	won	28	5
	v	Canada	St Albert	won	88	3
	v	USA	Edmonton	won	86	8
	v	France	Edmonton	won	109	0
1997	v	England	Burnham	won	67	0
	v	Australia	Dunedin	won	40	0
1998	v	Germany[1]	Amsterdam	won	134	6
	v	Scotland[1]	Amsterdam	won	76	0
	v	Spain[1] (quarter-final)	Amsterdam	won	46	3
	v	England[1] (semi-final)	Amsterdam	won	44	11
	v	USA[1] (final)	Amsterdam	won	44	12
	v	Australia	Sydney	won	27	3
1999	v	Canada	Palmerston North	won	73	0
	v	USA	Palmerston North	won	65	5
2000	v	Canada	Winnipeg	won	41	0
	v	USA	Winnipeg	won	45	0
	v	England	Winnipeg	won	32	13
2001	v	England	Rotorua	won	15	10
	v	England	Albany	lost	17	22
2002	v	Germany[1]	Barcelona	won	117	0
	v	Australia[1]	Barcelona	won	36	3
	v	France[1] (semi-final)	Barcelona	won	30	0

Black Ferns Records

Year		Opponent	Venue	Result		
	v	England[1] (final)	Barcelona	won	19	9
2003	v	World XV	Auckland	won	37	0
	v	World XV	Whangarei	won	38	19
2004	v	Canada	Vancouver	won	32	5
	v	USA	Calgary	won	35	0
	v	England	Edmonton	won	38	0
2005	v	Scotland	Ottawa	won	30	9
	v	Canada	Ottawa	won	43	3
	v	Canada	Ottawa	won	32	5
	v	England	Auckland	won	33	8
	v	England	Hamilton	won	24	15
2006	v	Canada[1]	Edmonton	won	66	7
	v	Samoa[1]	Edmonton	won	50	0
	v	Scotland[1]	Edmonton	won	21	0
	v	France[1] (semi-final)	Edmonton	won	40	10
	v	England[1] (final)	Edmonton	won	25	17
2007	v	Australia	Wanganui	won	21	11
	v	Australia	Wellington	won	29	12
2008	v	Australia	Canberra	won	37	3
	v	Australia	Canberra	won	22	16
2009	v	England	London	won	16	3
	v	England	London	lost	3	10
2010	v	South Africa[1]	London	won	55	3
	v	Australia[1]	London	won	32	5
	v	Wales[1]	London	won	41	8
	v	France[1] (semi-final)	London	won	45	7
	v	England[1] (final)	London	won	13	10
2011	v	England	London	lost	0	10
	v	England	London	lost	7	21
	v	England	London	draw	8	8
2012	v	England	Esher	lost	13	16
	v	England	Aldershot	lost	8	17
	v	England	London	lost	23	32
2013	v	England	Auckland	won	29	10
	v	England	Hamilton	won	14	9
	v	England	Pukekohe	won	29	8
2014	v	Australia	Rotorua	won	38	3
	v	Samoa	Auckland	won	90	12
	v	Canada	Tauranga	won	16	8
	v	Canada	Whakatane	won	33	21
	v	Kazakhstan[1]	Marcoussis	won	79	5
	v	Ireland[1]	Marcoussis	lost	14	17
	v	USA[1]	Marcoussis	won	34	3
	v	Wales[1]	Paris	won	63	7
	v	USA[1]	Paris	won	55	5
2015	v	Canada	Calgary	won	40	22
	v	England	Red Deer	won	26	7
	v	USA	Edmonton	won	49	14

2016	v Australia	Auckland	won	67	3
	v Australia	Albany	won	29	3
	v England	London	won	25	20
	v Canada	Dublin	won	20	10
	v Ireland	Dublin	won	38	8
2017	v Canada	Wellington	won	28	16
	v Australia	Christchurch	won	44	17
	v England	Rotorua	lost	21	29
	v Wales[1]	Dublin	won	44	12
	v Hong Kong[1]	Dublin	won	121	0
	v Canada[1]	Dublin	won	48	5
	v USA[1] (semi-final)	Belfast	won	45	12
	v England[1] (final)	Belfast	won	41	32
2018	v Australia	Sydney	won	31	11
	v Australia	Auckland	won	45	17
	v USA	Chicago	won	67	6
	v France	Toulon	won	14	0
	v France	Grenoble	lost	27	30
2019	v Canada	San Diego	won	35	20
	v USA	San Diego	won	33	0
	v France	San Diego	lost	16	25
	v England	San Diego	won	28	13
	v Australia	Perth	won	47	10
	v Australia	Auckland	won	37	8

[1]World Cup

SUMMARY OF INTERNATIONALS

Played: 99 Points for: 3905
Won: 86 Points against: 888
Lost: 12
Drawn: 1

NEW ZEALAND BARBARIANS

The New Zealand Barbarian Rugby Club fielded its first women's team in first-class rugby with two games against the Black Ferns in November. The team proved to be competitive in both contests with some players making strong claims for Black Ferns selection in 2021. The fixtures were arranged to enable national selectors to view the leading players as the pandemic had forced cancellation of international arrangements.

NEW ZEALAND BARBARIANS, 2020

	Union	Date of Birth
Saphire Abraham	Auckland	3/7/01
Ariana Bayler	Waikato	14/12/96
Alana Bremner (capt)	Canterbury	10/2/97
Carys Dallinger	Manawatu	30/4/00
Lyric Faleafaga	Wellington	13/10/99
Morgan Henderson	Otago	25/3/98
Iritana Hohaia	Taranaki	1/3/00
Grace Houpapa-Barrett	Waikato	25/7/95
Rosie Kelly	Otago	16/1/00
Martha Lolohea	Canterbury	19/7/99
Patricia Maliepo	Auckland	13/3/03
Crystal Mayes	Manawatu	28/5/94
Kilisitina Moata'ane*	Otago	23/11/97
Natahlia Moors*	Auckland	7/12/95
Krystal Murray	Northland	16/6/93
Cindy Nelles	Canterbury	19/8/93
Joanah Ngan-Woo*	Wellington	15/12/95
Kaipo Olsen-Baker	Manawatu	7/5/02
Marcelle Parkes*	Wellington	9/9/97
Maia Roos	Auckland	27/7/01
Amy Rule	Canterbury	15/7/00
Monica Tagoai*	Wellington	17/10/98
Jay Jay Taylor	North Harbour	22/5/97
Shyanne Thompson	Counties Manukau	12/11/97
Rebecca Todd	Canterbury	14/8/91
Janna Vaughan*	Manawatu	17/7/88
Olivia Ward-Duin*	North Harbour	23.12.93

* Black Ferns
Crystal Mayes and Shyanne Thompson were brought into the squad for the second game to replace injured players Lolohea and Tagoai

Coach: Rodney Gibbs
Assistant coaches: Chad Shepherd, Whitney Hansen
Manager: La Toya Mason
Physiotherapist: Jennifer Croker
Doctor: Anika Tiplady (at Auckland), Ra Durie (at Nelson)
Strength & conditioning coach: James Young
Mental skills coach: Kylie Wilson (at Auckland), John Quinn (at Nelson)
Analyst: Daniel Cron

SAMOA v TONGA
Rugby World Cup Qualifier

The Trusts Arena, Waitakere, Auckland   November 14, 2020

Samoa won 40–0

SAMOA		TONGA
Makayla Eli	15	Meleloata Toki
Tori Iosefo	14	Taina Halasima
Josephine Falesita	13	Tiale Fa'avae
Onjeurlina Leiataua	12	Lupe Manu
Michelle Curry	11	Siutiti Maake
Aieshaleigh Smalley	10	Losaline Potaufa
Ana Afuie	9	Leilani Fuikefu
Nina Foaese	8	Emma Hopoi
Sui Pauaraisa (capt)	7	Rugby Tangulu
Olalini Tafoulua	6	Bella Cocker
Gene Solia-Gibb	5	Mafi Faukafa
Easter Savelio	4	Marissa Fale
Janet Taumoli	3	Lila Hifo
Maki Vaiouiga	2	Vainga Moimoi (capt)
Marilyn Live	1	Janie Pulu
Lulu Leuta (rep 2, 60m)	16	Sokopeti Tongotongo
Luti Sikoloni (rep 3, 50m)	17	Elisha Byrne (rep ?, ?m)
Ana Mamea (rep 6, 53m)	18	Amania Mafi (rep 8, 60m)
Joanne Seumalo (rep 11, 51m)	19	Nina Hurrell (rep 4, 47m)
Xavier Tusa (rep 4, 67m)	20	Meleane Fifita (rep 6, 69m)
Leilani Erwin (rep 14, 45m)	21	Alisi Mafi
Beryl Ena (rep 13, 60m)	22	Mele Afu (rep 10, 55m)
Jhana Magele (rep 9, 5m)	23	Lavinia Slale

Iosefo (2), Live, Leiataua, Erwin, Sikoloni   Tries
Eli (2)   Cons
Eli (2)   Pens

Kickoff: 2.05pm   **Attendance:** 3000   **Conditions:** Fine

Referee: Rebecca Mahoney
Assistant referees: Lauren Jenner, Maggie Cogger-Orr
TMO: Lee Jeffrey

Halftime: Samoa 23 – Tonga 0

Yellow cards: Hurrell (51m), Fifita (74m)
Red card: Byrne (60m)

Played as a curtain-raiser to Black Ferns v NZ Barbarians game

WOMEN'S NEW ZEALAND TRIAL
(not first-class)

North Harbour Stadium, Albany   November 7, 2020

Possibles won 28–19

POSSIBLES		PROBABLES
Selica Winiata	15	Renee Holmes
Cheyelle Robins-Reti	14	Lyric Faleafaga
Grace Brooker	13	Carla Hohepa
Kilisitina Moata'ane	12	Chelsea Alley
Janna Vaughan	11	Martha Lolohea
Hazel Tubic (rep 13, 70m)	10	Ruahei Demant
Kendra Cocksedge (capt)	9	Arihiana Marino-Tauhinu
Charmaine McMenamin	8	Aroha Savage
Kennedy Simon (rep 8, 70m)	7	Marcelle Parkes
Pia Tapsell	6	Lisa Molia
Chelsea Bremner	5	Kelsie Wills
Joanah Ngan-Woo	4	Eloise Blackwell (capt)
Amy Rule	3	Aleisha Nelson
Te Kura Ngata-Aerengamate	2	Luka Connor
Phillippa Love	1	Toka Natua
Saphire Abraham (rep 2, 40m)	16	Rebecca Todd (rep 2, 40m)
Krystal Murray (rep 1, 40m)	17	Jay Jay Taylor (rep 1, 40m)
Olivia Ward-Duin (rep 3, 47m)	18	Aldora Itunu (rep 3, 51m)
Alana Bremner (rep 6, 50m)	19	Maia Roos (rep 5, 61m)
Kendra Reynolds (rep 7, 50m)	20	Kaipo Olsen-Baker (rep 7, 51m)
Iritana Hohaia (rep 9, 60m)	21	Ari Bayler (rep 9, 40m)
Carys Dallinger (rep 10, 40m)	22	Patricia Maliepo (rep 12, 51m)
Monica Tagoai	23	Amy du Plessis (rep 13, 28m)
Rosie Kelly (rep 22, 60m)	24	Langi Veainu (rep 11, 40m)
Natahlia Moors (rep 11, 40m)	25	Grace Steinmetz (rep 14, 40m)
Grace Houpapa-Barrett (rep 16, 65m)	26	Cristo Tofa (rep 16, 61m)
Winiata, Love, Rule, Cocksedge	Tries	Connor, Molia, Maliepo
Cocksedge (4)	Cons	Demant (2)

Kickoff: 2.05pm   **Conditions:** Fine

Referee: Lauren Jenner

Halftime: Possibles 21 Probables 14

RESULTS FROM 2020 FIRST-CLASS SEASON IN NEW ZEALAND
AND TEAMS OF NEW ZEALANDERS OVERSEAS

Key:
- N   North pool Farah Palmer Cup
- S   South pool Farah Palmer Cup
- sf   semi-final
- f   final
- ST   J.J. Stewart Trophy
- *   not first-class

January

Sat/Sun	25/26	*		New Zealand WR Sevens				Hamilton

February

Sat/Sun	1/2	*		Australia WR Sevens				Sydney

September

Sat	5	N	Waikato	18	Northland	5	Hamilton
		N	Counties Manukau	89	North Harbour	3	Pukekohe
Sun	6	N	Auckland	38	Taranaki	0	Inglewood
Fri	11	N	Bay of Plenty	67	North Harbour	17	Albany
Sat	12	S	Canterbury	36	Manawatu	10	Palmerston North
		N	Waikato	76	Taranaki	14	Hamilton
		S	Wellington	62	Tasman	0	Blenheim
Sun	13	N	Auckland	29	Northland	22	Whangarei
		S	Otago	29	Hawke's Bay	20	Dunedin
Sat	19	S	Wellington	67	Hawke's Bay	17	Lower Hutt
		S, ST	Canterbury	85	Utago	10	Christchurch
		N	Taranaki	32	North Harbour	29	Inglewood
		N	Waikato	21	Bay of Plenty	10	Rotorua
Sun	20	S	Manawatu	88	Tasman	0	Palmerston North
		N	Counties Manukau	36	Auckland	22	Auckland
Fri	25	S	Manawatu	31	Wellington	28	Wellington
Sat	26	S	Otago	67	Tasman	24	Nelson
		N	Auckland	72	North Harbour	0	Albany
		N	Bay of Plenty	73	Taranaki	17	Mt Maunganui
		S	Canterbury	72	Hawke's Bay	15	Napier
Sun	27	N	Northland	32	Counties Manukau	20	Pukekohe

October

Sat	3	N	Northland	65	North Harbour	5	Whangarei
		N	Auckland	22	Bay of Plenty	19	Pakuranga
		N	Waikato	34	Counties Manukau	28	Putaruru
		S, ST	Canterbury	54	Wellington	12	Christchurch
Sun	4	S	Hawke's Bay	62	Tasman	5	Motueka
		S	Manawatu	28	Otago	14	Dunedin
Sat	10	N	Counties Manukau	17	Bay of Plenty	10	Pukekohe
		N	Waikato	62	North Harbour	0	Albany
Sun	11	N	Northland	77	Taranaki	3	Whangarei
Fri	16	S	Manawatu	29	Hawke's Bay	12	Napier

Sat	17	S, ST	Canterbury	84	Tasman	0	Christchurch
		N	Northland	32	Bay of Plenty	0	Mt Maunganui
		N	Counties Manukau	107	Taranaki	3	Inglewood
Sun	18	S	Wellington	27	Otago	24	Porirua
		N	Waikato	26	Auckland	17	Auckland
Sat	24	sf	Canterbury	36	Auckland	21	Christchurch
Sun	25	sf	Waikato	31	Manawatu	14	Hamilton
Sat	31	f	Canterbury	8	Waikato	7	Christchurch
November							
Sat	7	*	Possibles	28	Probables	19	Albany
Sat	14	RWCQ	Samoa	40	Tonga	0	Waitakere
Sat	14		New Zealand	34	NZ Barbarians	15	Waitakere
Sat	21		New Zealand	19	NZ Barbarians	17	Nelson

WOMEN'S CLUB FINALS

Results of the 2020 senior club finals. Counties Manukau and North Harbour clubs participated in the Auckland competition

Union	Winner		Runner-up	
Auckland	Ponsonby	35	Manurewa	20
Bay of Plenty	Rangiuru[1]	34	Rangataua	31
Canterbury	Canterbury University	42	Christchurch	32
Hawke's Bay	Napier Technical OB[1]	39	Hastings RS	19
Manawatu	Kia Toa[1]	39	Feilding OB Oroua	27
Northland	Te Rarawa	22	Kaikohe	19
Otago	University[2]	36	Alhambra Union	5
Taranaki	Southern	36	Clifton	10
Tasman	Waimea OB[1]	34	Wanderers	10
Waikato	Melville[2]	19	Hamilton OB	10
Wellington	Oriental Rongotai[1]		no final played	

[1] also won in 2019 [2] also won in 2018 and 2019

FARAH PALMER CUP

The pandemic forced a delay and eventual revamp of the normal competition with the premiership and championship divisions being replaced by two pools, North and South, to minimise expensive travel costs. This resulted in some high scores but the general standard lifted, assisted by the availability of Black Ferns and Black Ferns Sevens players, their schedules having been cancelled. Waikato (North) and Canterbury (South) were undefeated in pool play.

In the North pool three teams, Auckland, Northland and Counties Manukau finished the round-robin in second place, each with 21 points and the tiebreaker rules were used to decide which team advanced to the semi-final. The team with the most competition points against the other tied teams advanced. Auckland and Northland had six points, Counties Manukau had five. Auckland got six points out of their games with Counties and Northland (one against Counties and five against Northland). Northland got six points (one against Auckland and five against Counties). Counties got five points against Auckland and none against Northland. This meant it was between Auckland and Northland, and with Auckland defeating Northland in pool play, they claimed the semi-final position.

Canterbury were again undefeated, retaining the JJ Stewart Trophy and winning the Farah Palmer Cup for the fourth consecutive year. The final was a nail-biter at Rugby Park with Canterbury snatching the win over Waikato only after the fulltime siren sounded.

Final standings after round robin:

	P	W	D	L	B⁴	B⁷	Pts	T	C	PG	DG	Total	T	C	PG	DG	Total
NORTH POOL																	
Waikato	6	6	–	–	4	–	28	36*	20	5	–	237	10	9	2	–	74
Auckland	6	4	–	2	5	–	21	32	17	2	–	200	16	10	1	–	103
Northland	6	4	–	2	4	1	21	38	17	3	–	233	10	5	5	–	75
Counties Manukau	6	4	–	2	4	1	21	47	28	2	–	297	16	6	4	–	104
Bay of Plenty	6	2	–	4	2	2	12	29	14	2	–	179	20	7	4	–	126
Taranaki	6	1	–	5	1	–	5	10	5	3	–	69	66*	34	–	–	400
North Harbour	6	–	–	6	1	1	2	8	4	2	–	54	62	34	3	–	387
TOTALS								200*	105	19	0	1269	200*	105	19	0	1269
SOUTH POOL																	
Canterbury	5	5	–	–	5	–	25	52*	33	1	–	331	9	1	–	–	47
Manawatu	5	4	–	1	4	–	20	29	16	3	–	186	13*	10	1	–	90
Wellington	5	3	–	2	3	1	16	30*	19	2	–	196	19*	10	3	–	126
Otago	5	2	–	3	3	1	12	24*	11	–	–	144	25*	18	7	–	184
Hawke's Bay	5	1	–	4	1	–	5	19	8	5	–	126	34	16	–	–	202
Tasman	5	–	–	5	1	–	1	5	2	–	–	29	59	34	–	–	363
TOTALS								159*	89	11	0	1012	159*	89	11	0	1012

B⁴ *bonus points for four or more tries in a match.*   B⁷ *bonus points for loss by seven or fewer points.*

Semi-finals: Waikato 31 Manawatu 14, at Hamilton;
Canterbury 36 Auckland 21, at Christchurch

Final: Canterbury 8 Waikato 7, at Christchurch

LEADING POINTS-SCORERS

Kendra Cocksedge	Canterbury	76
Chelsea Alley	Waikato	69
Hazel Tubic	Counties Manukau	67
Selica Winiata	Manawatu	61

LEADING TRY-SCORERS

Ruby Tui	Counties Manukau	9
Portia Woodman	Northland	9
Alana Bremner	Canterbury	8
Stacey Fluhler	Waikato	8
Martha Lolohea	Canterbury	8

CAREER CHAMPIONSHIP RECORDS

Points
968	Kendra Cocksedge (Canterbury)
545	Emma Jensen (Waik/Auck/HB)
528	Selica Winiata (Manawatu)

Tries
72	Selica Winiata (Manawatu)
61	Kendra Cocksedge (Canterbury)
46	Ayesha Leti-I'iga (Wellington)
46	Fiao'o Faamausili (Auckland)

Games
125	Emma Jensen (Waik/Auck/HB)
114	Justine Lavea (Auckland/Counties Manukau)
106	Fiao'o Faamausili (Auckland)
102	Stephanie Te Ohaere-Fox (Canterbury)

GRAND FINAL RESULTS

	Winner		Runner-up		Venue
1999	Auckland	22	Wellington	0	Wellington
2000	Auckland	22	Otago	12	Auckland
2001	Auckland	28	Wellington	3	Auckland
2002	Auckland	53	Wellington	3	Auckland
2003	Auckland	35	Wellington	0	Auckland
2004	Auckland	29	Canterbury	10	Auckland
2005	Auckland	36	Canterbury	3	Auckland
2006	Wellington	11	Auckland	10	Auckland
2007	Auckland	32	Otago	27	Auckland
2008	Auckland	13	Canterbury	12	Auckland
2009	Auckland	24	Canterbury	20	Christchurch
2011	Auckland	34	Wellington	8	Hamilton
2012	Auckland	38	Canterbury	12	Christchurch
2013	Auckland	20	Canterbury	10	Wellington
2014	Auckland	28	Waikato	14	New Plymouth
2015	Auckland	39	Wellington	9	Napier
2016	Counties Manukau	41	Auckland	22	Pukekohe

	Premiership	Championship
2017	Canterbury	Bay of Plenty
2018	Canterbury	Wellington
2019	Canterbury	Otago

	Winner		Runner-up		Venue
2020	Canterbury	8	Waikato	7	Christchurch

CHAMPIONSHIP RECORDS

BY THE TEAMS

	BEST PERFORMANCE 2020	RECORD
Season Totals		
Most points	375 by Canterbury	449 by Wellington, 2018
Most tries	59 by Canterbury	69 by Wellington, 2018
Most conversions	36 by Canterbury	49 by Wellington, 2018
Most penalty goals	5 by Hawke's Bay and Waikato	14 by Otago, 2013
Most dropped goals	0	2 by Manawatu, 2002; Auckland, 2012
Match Records		
Most points	107 by Counties Manukau v Taranaki	118 by Wellington v Taranaki, 2018
Most tries	17 by Counties Manukau v Taranaki	18 by Auckland v North Harbour, 1999; by Wellington v Taranaki, 2018
Most conversions	11 by Counties Manukau v Taranaki	14 by Wellington v Taranaki, 2018
Most penalty goals	5 by Hawke's Bay v Otago	6 by Auckland v Wellington, 2001
Most dropped goals	0	1 on 10 occasions
Biggest winning margin	104 by Counties Manukau v Taranaki (107–3)	118 by Wellington v Taranaki (118–0), 2018

BY THE PLAYERS

	BEST PERFORMANCE 2020		RECORD
Season Totals			
Most points	76	Kendra Cocksedge (Canterbury)	118 Amanda Rasch (Wellington), 2018
Most tries	9	Ruby Tui (Waikato); Portia Woodman (Northland)	16 Mele Hufanga (Auckland), 2015
Most conversions	28	Hazel Tubic (Counties Manukau)	46 Amanda Rasch (Wellington), 2018
Most penalty goals	5	Chelsea Alley (Waikato); Kaitlin Bates (Hawke's Bay)	12 Chelsea Alley (Waikato), 2013
Most dropped goals	0		2 Rebecca Hull (Manawatu), 2002; Bella Milo (Auckland), 2012
Match Totals			
Most points	30	Portia Woodman (Northland) v Taranaki	45 Kelly Brazier (Otago) v Hawke's Bay, 2012
Most tries	6	Portia Woodman (Northland) v Taranaki	8 Annaleah Rush (Otago) v Hanan Shield Dist), 1999
Most conversions	11	Hazel Tubic (Counties Manukau) v Taranaki	14 Amanda Rasch (Wellington) v Taranaki, 2018
Most penalty goals	5	Kaitlin Bates (Hawke's Bay) v Otago	6 Annaleah Rush (Auckland) v Wellington, 2001
Most dropped goals	0		1 by 8 players on 10 occasions

AUCKLAND STORM

2020 Status: North Pool
NPC participation: 1999–
Coach: Richie Walker
Assistant coaches: Anna Richards, Craig Hall
Home grounds: Eden Park; Bell Park, Pakuranga (v Bay of Plenty)

RECORDS

Most appearances	106	Fiao'o Fa'amausili, 1999–2018
Most points	452	Emma Jensen, 2004–17
Most tries	46	Fiao'o Fa'amausili, 1999–2018
Most points in a season	101	Tammi Wilson, 1999;
Most tries in a season	16	Mele Hufanga, 2015
Most conversions in a season	27	Bella Milo, 2012
		Patricia Maliepo, 2019
Most penalty goals in a season	9	Emma Jensen, 2014
Most dropped goals in a season	2	Bella Milo, 2012
Most points in a match	31	Tammi Wilson v North Harbour, 1999
Most tries in a match	4	Louisa Wall v North Harbour, 1999;
		v Northland, 1999;
		Victoria Grant v Otago, 2008;
		Jade Le Pesq v Manawatu, 2012
		Mele Hufanga v Wellington, 2014;
		v Hawke's Bay, 2014;
		v Canterbury 2015;
		Natahlia Moors v Bay of Plenty, 2015
Most conversions in a match	13	Tammi Wilson v North Harbour, 1999
Most penalty goals in a match	6	Annaleah Rush v Wellington, 2001
Highest team score	116	v North Harbour, 1999
Record victory (points ahead)	116	116–0 v North Harbour, 1999
Highest score conceded	45	14–45 v Waikato, 2018;
		12–45 v Canterbury, 2019
Record defeat (points behind)	33	12–45 v Canterbury, 2019

The Storm had a disrupted preparation caused by the pandemic forcing a second lockdown in the Auckland region. This allowed the squad only five days to be together prior to the first game. Taranaki and North Harbour were comfortably defeated but there were several inconsistent efforts from a team with a fine blend of experience and youth. There were losses to Counties Manukau and Waikato in pool play, the third loss being to champions Canterbury in a semi-final, a game in which the Storm produced its best form but errors at critical times cost them dearly.

The captain Eloise Blackwell was the best forward, consistently high performer, great set piece player and very good around the field. Black Ferns Charmaine McMenamin, Aldora Itunu, Aleisha Nelson and Cristo Tofa added strength while several teenagers showed promise. Tamara Ati, aged 17, showed great physical presence off the bench, strong carries and abrasive defensively. Liana Mikaele-Tu'u (ex-Hawke's Bay), Maia Roos, Saphire Abraham and Chryss Viliko were other young forwards to appear regularly.

Theresa Fitzpatrick was a consistent high performer with great vision, high workrate and solid on defence. Patricia Maliepo continues to develop as a player of the future while Ruahei Demant was again a fine playmaker. Natahlia Moors and Princess Elliot were the regular wings. As among the forwards, some young backs made an impression. Halfback Luisa Togotogorua (aged 17) possesses a fine pass and improved with each game. Sylvia Brunt (aged 16) was a very physical player, ran good lines, was a threat on attack and solid on defence. Daynah Nankivell, Leianne Tufuga and Moana Cook were young backs also still in their teens.

After the fourth game coach Richie Walker returned to California for the birth of a child. Anna Richards and Craig Hall co-coached the team for the remainder of the season.

Higher honours went to:
New Zealand: E. Blackwell, R. Demant, A. Itunu, C. McMenamin, A. Nelson, C. Tofa
New Zealand Barbarians: S. Abraham, P. Maliepo, M. Roos
New Zealand Sevens: T. Fitzpatrick, T.B. Nathan-Wong, N.L.V. Williams

AUCKLAND REPRESENTATIVES 2020

	Club	Games for Union	Points for Union		Club	Games for Union	Points for Union
Saphire Abraham	College Rifles	14	25	Natahlia Moors	Ponsonby	27	90
Tamara Ati	College Rifles	5	0	Shannon Muru	Ponsonby	3	0
Eloise Blackwell	Ponsonby	64	70	Daynah Nankivell	Ponsonby	9	21
Sylvia Brunt	Ponsonby	5	10	Aleisha Nelson	College Rifles	75	65
Moana Cook	Ponsonby	13	0	Leilani Perese	Manurewa[1]	16	5
Rosie Cox	College Rifles	10	12	Lovely Pulotu	Marist	1	0
Ruahei Demant	College Rifles	43	169	Lydia Quedley-Tutua	Ponsonby	2	5
Princess Elliot	Ponsonby	14	40	Maia Roos	College Rifles	13	0
Theresa Fitzpatrick	Ponsonby	26	80	Ti Tauasosi	Marist	6	0
Grace Freeman	College Rifles	4	0	Vineta Teutau	Marist	1	0
Aldora Itunu	Ponsonby	46	70	Cristo Tofa	Ponsonby	16	15
Grace Kukutai	Ponsonby	3	10	Luisa Togotogorua	Marist	7	0
Tafito Lafaele	Papatoetoe	2	0	Leianne Tufuga	Marist	5	0
Shannon Leota	Ponsonby	21	25	Mele Tu'inukuafe	Ponsonby	3	0
Charmaine McMenamin	Ponsonby	60	75	Joeannah Uaseli-Purcell	Ponsonby	9	15
Patricia Maliepo	Marist	15	139	Chryss Viliko	Marist	14	0
Liana Mikaele-Tu'u	College Rifles	6	10				

1 Counties Manukau RU

INDIVIDUAL SCORING

	Tries	Con	PG	DG	Points		Tries	Con	PG	DG	Points
Maliepo	3	17	4	–	61	Tofa	2	–	–	–	10
Fitzpatrick	5	–	–	–	25	Leota	1	–	–	–	5
Abraham	3	–	–	–	15	McMenamin	1	–	–	–	5
Moors	3	–	–	–	15	Nelson	1	–	–	–	5
Blackwell	2	–	–	–	10	Quedley-Turua	1	–	–	–	5
Brunt	2	–	–	–	10	Uaseli-Purcell	1	–	–	–	5
Demant	2	–	–	–	10						
Elliot	2	–	–	–	10	**Totals**	**35**	**17**	**4**	**0**	**221**
Kukutai	2	–	–	–	10						
Mikaele-Tu'u	2	–	–	–	10	Opposition scored	22	13	1	0	139
Nankivell	2	–	–	–	10						

AUCKLAND 2020

	Taranaki	Northland	Counties Manukau	North Harbour	Bay of Plenty	Waikato	Canterbury	TOTALS
P. Maliepo	15	15	15	10	10	10	15	7
D.L. Nankivell	–	s	–	15	15	15	s	5
D.B. Moors	14	14	14	s	14	14	14	7
L.E.F. Tufuga	–	–	–	14	s	s	s	4
A-P.P. Elliot	11	11	11	–	11	11	11	6
C.G.R. Kukutai	s	–	s	11	–	–	–	3
T.M. Fitzpatrick	13	13	13	13	13	13	13	7
S.L. Brunt	12	12	12	–	–	s	12	5
L.S. Quedley-Turua	s	–	s	–	–	–	–	2
G.A. Freeman	s	–	–	–	–	–	s	3
D.R. Demant	10	10	10	12	12	12	10	7
J.N. Uaseli-Purcell	–	–	–	s	s	–	–	2
M.E. Cook	9	9	s	–	s	s	s	6
L.G. Togotogorua	s	s	9	9	9	9	9	7
L.L. Pulotu	–	–	–	s	–	–	–	1
C.J. McMenamin	8	8	8	s	8	8	8	7
S.M. Muru	7	–	7	–	–	–	s	3
S.L. Leota	s	s	s	7	7	7	7	7
R.E. Cox	–	7	–	–	–	–	–	1
L.E.T. Mikaele-Tu'u	6	6	6	8	6	6	–	7
T. Tauasosi	s	–	s	s	s	s	6	6
T.T.T.V. Ati	–	s	–	6	s	s	s	5
M.C.T. Roos	5	–	5	–	5	5	5	5
V.N. Teutau	–	5	–	–	–	–	–	1
T. Lafaele	–	–	–	5	–	–	–	1
E.S. Blackwell (capt)	4	4	4	4	4	4	4	7
A.P. Nelson	3	3	3	s	3	3	3	7
A.T. Itunu	1	s	1	3	–	s	1	6
C.Z.F. Viliko	s	1	s	1	1	1	–	6
M.L.T. Tui'nukuafe	s	–	–	–	s	–	–	2
L.L.R. Perese	–	–	–	–	–	–	s	1
L.C.S. Tofa	2	2	2	s	2	2	2	7
S.C.R. Abraham	–	s	s	2	s	s	s	6

AUCKLAND TEAM RECORD, 2020

Played 7 Won 4 Lost 3 Points for 221 Points against 139

Date	Opponent	Location	Score	Tries	Con	PG	DG	Referee
September 6	Taranaki (N)	Inglewood	38–0	Fitzpatrick (2), Tofa, Blackwell, Moors, Mikaele-Tu'u	Maliepo (4)			Brittany Andrew
September 13	Northland (N)	Whangarei	29–22	Fitzpatrick (2), Demant, Brunt	Maliepo (3)	Maliepo		Michael Winter
September 20	Counties Manukau (N)	Auckland	22–36	Moors, Tofa, Quedley-Turua, Mikaele-Tu'u	Maliepo			Michael Winter
September 26	North Harbour (N)	Albany	72–0	Nankivell (2), Kukutai (2), Abraham (2), Demant, Maliepo, McMenamin, Nelson, Leota, Uaseli-Purcell	Maliepo (6)			Lauren Jenner
October 3	Bay of Plenty (N)	Pakuranga	22–19	Elliot, Maliepo, Moors, Blackwell	Maliepo			Michael Winter
October 18	Waikato (N)	Auckland	17–26	Brunt, Maliepo	Maliepo (2)	Maliepo		Rebecca Mahoney
October 24	Canterbury (semi-final)	Christchurch	21–36	Elliot, Fitzpatrick, Abraham		Maliepo (2)		Lauren Jenner

BAY OF PLENTY VOLCANIX

2020 Status: North Pool
NPC participation: 1999–2005, 2014–
Coach: Rodney Gibbs
Assistant coaches: Brendon Phillips
Home Grounds: Blake Park, Mount Maunganui;
Rotorua International Stadium.

RECORDS

Most appearances	38	*Janina Khan, 2001–19*
Most points	96	*Sapphire Tapsell, 2016–19*
Most tries	18	*Tamaku Paul, 1999–2002*
Most points in a season	55	*Tamaku Paul, 1999*
Most tries in a season	11	*Tamaku Paul, 1999*
Most conversions in a season	12	*Puawai Hohepa, 2004*
Most penalty goals in a season	4	*Renee Wickliffe, 2018*
Most dropped goals in a season	1	*Puawai Hohepa, 2000*
Most points in a match	20	*Tamaku Paul v Counties Manukau, 1999*
		Mahina Paul v North Harbour 2020
Most tries in a match	4	*Tamaku Paul v Counties Manukau, 1999*
		Mahina Paul v North Harbour 2020
Most conversions in a match	7	*Kelly Brazier v North Harbour 2020*
Most penalty goals in a match	2	*Heidi Reader v Northland, 1999;*
		Puawai Hohepa v Waikato, 2000
		Kymbillie Raynes v North Harbour, 2016
		Renee Wickliffe v Auckland 2018
Highest team score	73	*v Taranaki, 2018*
		v Taranaki 2020
Record victory (points ahead)	73	*73–0 v Taranaki, 2018*
Highest score conceded	101	*v Auckland, 2015*
Record defeat (points behind)	101	*0–101 v Auckland, 2015*

Hopes for an improvement on a promising 2019 season diminished early in the campaign. Before the championship commenced Renee Wickliffe and Michaela Blyde were out with injury, followed by Kelly Brazier and Karli Faneva after the second game. The loss of these experienced internationals left only the captain Les Elder and Luka Connor as players of international experience. However, after appearing for North Harbour in the opening game against the Bay, Black Fern Pia Tapsell turned up during the week and joined the squad from round two.

As expected, there were big wins over North Harbour and Taranaki and creditable efforts against Waikato and Auckland. Against Counties Manukau the scores were level at 10–10 with 20 minutes remaining. Elder left the field and her absence was apparent as the team appeared to lack leadership and when the home team lost a forward, yellow-carded with 10 minutes remaining, the Volcanix had the opportunity to power over the tryline. But a series of errors and penalties had the team at the other end of the field desperately defending their line and Counties Manukau scored in the 80th minute to win the contest. It was a disappointment from which the Volcanix didn't recover and they were soundly beaten by Northland the following week.

Once Brazier departed there was no reliable goalkicker. It was a very youthful backline with newcomer Kiani Tahere showing promise with some nice incisions into the line from fullback. Mahina Paul, sister of centre Mererangi Paul, showed plenty of pace when set free out wide but that was limited in the tight games. Alena Saili had some good moments as well. Hope Parata-Kingi and 2017 Tasman rep Risi Pouri-Lane showed much promise in the key positions behind the forwards. Two girls from the Netherlands, Lisa Egberts and Esra van Ramele, will have benefited from their experiences in the squad.

Of the forwards Kelsie Wills shone in every game and deserved her Black Ferns selection. She was tremendous in taking the high ball from kickoffs and her all-round game was excellent with great defence. Les Elder led from the front and kept her team in the tight games whilst on the field. The Counties game was a perfect example of losing Elder's leadership at a crucial stage. Luka Connor and Kendra Reynolds lead the way with experience at this level. The front rowers on most occasions were sound, that being Mulu, Jacob and Walker while lock Aldridge also had some good moments.

Higher honours went to:
New Zealand: L. Connor, K. Reynolds, P. Tapsell, K. Wills
New Zealand Sevens: M.G. Blyde, K. Brazier, Mahina Paul, R.M. Tui

BAY OF PLENTY REPRESENTATIVES 2020

	Club	Games for Union	Points for Union		Club	Games for Union	Points for Union
Amanda Aldridge	Rangiuru	20	0	Mahina Paul	Rangataua	6	30
Kelly Brazier	Rangataua	2	22	Mererangi Paul	Rangataua	5	5
Luka Connor	Rangataua	37	75	Risi Pouri-Lane	Rangiuru	6	15
Natalie Delamere	Rotoiti	19	10	Kendra Reynolds	Rangiuru	37	20
Lisa Egberts	Mt Maunganui	3	0	Olivia Richardson	Rangataua	9	0
Lesley Elder	Rangataua	15	25	Alena Saili	Mt Maunganui	6	25
Karli Faneva	Mt Maunganui	8	5	Kiani Tahere	Rangataua	6	12
Tynealle Fitzgerald	Mt Maunganui	17	5	Pia Tapsell	Albany Barbarians[1]	5	5
Hope Garner	Rangataua	1	0	Ruby Tawa	Rangataua	3	0
Abbey Grainger	Mt Maunganui	4	0	Brooklyn Teki-Joyce	Rangataua	5	0
Destiny Iraia	Mt Maunganui	1	0	Esra van Ramele	Mt Maunganui	5	5
Baye Jacob	Rangiuru	30	10	Layla Te Riini	Rangiuru	5	0
Azaleyah Maaka	Rangataua	8	0	Ro Silo Togotogorua	Mt Maunganui	1	0
Sela Moata'ane	Mt Maunganui	3	0	Braxton Walker	Rangiuru	15	0
Angel Mulu	Mt Maunganui	14	15	Kura Waller	Rangataua	2	0
Hope Parata-Kingi	Rangataua	3	20	Kelsie Wills	Mt Maunganui	10	10

[1] North Harbour RU

INDIVIDUAL SCORING

	Tries	Con	PG	DG	Points		Tries	Con	PG	DG	Points
Mahina Paul	6	–	–	–	30	Faneva	1	–	–	–	5
Saili	5	–	–	–	25	Mulu	1	–	–	–	5
Brazier	–	8	2	–	22	Mererangi Paul	1	–	–	–	5
Parata-Kingi	2	5	–	–	20	Tapsell	1	–	–	–	5
Pouri-Lane	3	–	–	–	15	Van Ramele	1	–	–	–	5
Tahere	2	1	–	–	12						
Connor	2	–	–	–	10	**Totals**	29	14	2	0	179
Wills	2	–	–	–	10						
Delamere	1	–	–	–	5	Opposition scored	20	7	4	0	126
Elder	1	–	–	–	5						

BAY OF PLENTY 2020

	North Harbour	Waikato	Taranaki	Auckland	Counties Manukau	Northland	TOTALS
K.S. Tahere	15	15	15	15	15	15	**6**
O.D. Richardson	14	14	–	–	–	11	**3**
A.F. Saili	12	13	14	14	14	14	**6**
Mahina A. Paul	13	11	11	11	11	s	**6**
Mererangi K. Paul	–	s	13	13	13	13	**5**
E.F. van Ramele	s	–	s	s	s	s	**5**
A.A.M. Maaka	11	12	–	s	s	12	**5**
L.M. Te Riini	–	–	12	12	12	–	**3**
K.A. Brazier	10	10	–	–	–	–	**2**
H.R. Parata-Kingi	–	–	10	10	10	–	**3**
R.I.R. Pouri-Lane	9	9	9	9	9	10	**6**
L. Egberts	s	s	–	–	–	9	**3**
H.A.N. Garner	–	–	s	–	–	–	**1**
N. Delamere	8	8	s	8	2	s	**6**
R.E. Tawa	–	s	–	–	s	s	**3**
P.H. Tapsell	–	s	8	s	8	8	**5**
M.I.K. Waller	–	–	s	–	–	s	**2**
L-A.Te A. Elder (capt)	7	7	7	7	7	–	**5**
K.L. Reynolds	6	6	–	6	6	6	**5**
T.A. Fitzgerald	s	s	6	s	s	7	**6**
D.H.Te I. Iraia	s	–	–	–	–	–	**1**
S. Moata'ane	–	–	s	–	s	s	**3**
K.J.K. Faneva	5	5	–	–	–	–	**2**
K.P. Wills	–	–	5	5	5	5	**4**
A.V.H. Aldridge	4	4	4	4	–	4	**5**
B.M. Teki-Joyce	s	–	s	s	4	s	**5**
B.L. Jacob	3	3	3	3	3	3	**6**
A.J. Mulu	1	–	–	1	1	–	**3**
B.M.M. Walker	s	1	s	s	s	–	**5**
A.E. Grainger	s	s	1	s	–	–	**4**
R.S.V. Togotogorua	–	–	–	–	–	1	**1**
L.H.J. Connor	2	2	2	2	s	2	**6**

Reynolds was captain for final game.

BAY OF PLENTY TEAM RECORD, 2020

Played 6 Won 2 Lost 4 Points for 179 Points against 126

Date	Opponent	Location	Score	Tries	Con	PG	DG	Referee
September 11	North Harbour (N)	Albany	67–17	Mahina Paul (4), Saili, Tahere, Mulu, Elder, Connor, Faneva	Brazier (7)	Brazier		Jono Bredin
September 19	Waikato (N)	Rotorua	10–21	Mahina Paul	Brazier	Brazier		Rebecca Mahoney
September 26	Taranaki (N)	Mt Maunganui	73–17	Pouri-Lane (2), Parata-Kingi (2), Saili (2), Tapsell, Mahina Paul, Mererangi Paul, Connor, Wills, Delamere, van Ramele	Parata-Kingi (3), Tahere			Larissa Collingwood
October 3	Auckland (N)	Pakuranga	19–22	Wills, Pouri-Lane, Tahere	Parata-Kingi (2)			Michael Winter
October 10	Counties Manukau (N)	Pukekohe	10–17	Saili (2)				Maggie Cogger-Orr
October 17	Northland (N)	Mt Maunganui	0–32					Brittany Andrew

CANTERBURY

2020 Status: South Pool
NPC participation: 1999–
Coach: Blair Baxter
Assistant coaches: Whitney Hansen, Tom Christie, Melissa Ruscoe
Home Grounds: Orangetheory Stadium (v Otago, Wellington); Rugby Park

RECORDS

Most appearances	97	*Stephanie Te Ohaere-Fox, 2004–19*
Most points	968	*Kendra Cocksedge, 2007–20*
Most tries	61	*Kendra Cocksedge, 2007–20*
Most points in a season	116	*Kendra Cocksedge, 2018*
Most tries in a season	10	*Kendra Cocksedge, 2018*
Most conversions in a season	27	*Kendra Cocksedge, 2018*
		Kendra Cocksedge, 2019
Most penalty goals in a season	11	*Kendra Cocksedge, 2014*
Most dropped goals in a season	1	*Charntay Poko, 2017;*
		Kendra Cocksedge, 2019
Most points in a match	30	*Kendra Cocksedge, v Taranaki, 2013*
		v North Harbour, 2016
Most tries in a match	4	*Stephanie Mortimer v Waikato, 2004;*
		Kendra Cocksedge, v Taranaki, 2013
		v Auckland, 2018
		Martha Lolohea v Tasman 2020
Most conversions in a match	8	*Kendra Cocksedge v Hawke's Bay, 2012*
Most penalty goals in a match	5	*Kendra Cocksedge v Auckland, 2009*
		v Waikato, 2016
Highest team score	92	*v Taranaki, 2013*
Record victory (points ahead)	84	*84–0 v Tasman, 2020*
Highest score conceded	70	*v Auckland, 2015*
Record defeat (points behind)	62	*8–70 v Auckland, 2015*

Canterbury romped through the five games of the South pool section averaging 66 points per game and safely turned back three defences of the JJ Stewart Trophy. Auckland Storm were defeated in a semi-final but Canterbury could consider themselves fortunate to escape defeat by a very determined Waikato side in the final at Rugby Park. Waikato were leading 7–3 when fulltime sounded but conceded a penalty from which Canterbury hammered the line until Cindy Nelles barged over in the 82nd minute to snatch victory. It was Canterbury's fourth Farah Palmer Cup title in four years.

The core of the side returned for their third and four seasons in a row, led by influential flanker Alana Bremner, who had an outstanding season on the side of the scrum, taking over the captaincy left by Steph Te Ohaere-Fox, who added a second child to their family during the season. Lucy Anderson made a successful transition from second five-eighth to No 8. Her former position was generally filled by Olivia McGoverne moving up from fullback. Grace Steinmetz received many opportunities to impress in the 15-a-side game. Fellow outside back Martha Lolohea made a number of barnstorming runs on the wing but missed out on the opportunity to play alongside her younger sister Atlanta, who was set for her debut season, but was ruled out early in the year following a shoulder injury. Halfback Kendra Cocksedge extended her fine record, an outstanding playmaker, ever-alert to opportunities to catch the opposition off-guard.

New Coach Blair Baxter introduced five new players and four positional changes to the playing group, all of them thriving in the environment. Izzy Waterman, who seems right at home at almost any position at this level, capped off a stellar year, being named Rookie of the Year. Tighthead prop Amy Rule had a standout season and if she continues to improve in the years ahead, she's destined to have a long career in the Black jersey. Alana Bremner's younger sister Chelsea also impressed in the engine room and was once again rewarded with a chance to represent her country. Consistent performances from Pip Love saw her have her best season in the red and black jersey.

Higher honours went to:
New Zealand: C. Bremner, G. Brooker, K. Cocksedge, P. Love, G. Steinmetz
New Zealand Barbarians: A. Bremner, M. Lolohea, C. Nelles, A. Rule, R. Todd

CANTERBURY REPRESENTATIVES 2020

	Club	Games for Union	Points for Union		Club	Games for Union	Points for Union
Taylor Aldridge	Canterbury Univ	3	0	Cindy Nelles	Canterbury Univ	15	40
Lucy Anderson	Christchurch	51	110	Sophie O'Cain	HSOB	5	0
Alana Bremner	Lincoln Univ	47	75	Greer O'Rourke	Canterbury Univ	17	5
Chelsea Bremner	Lincoln Univ	31	10	Nina Poletti	Christchurch	22	15
Grace Brooker	Lincoln Univ	30	100	Georgia Ponsonby	Lincoln Univ	23	10
Kendra Cocksedge	Canterbury Univ	89	968	Nicole Purdom	Canterbury Univ	21	20
Sam Curtis	Christchurch	33	105	Amy Rule	Lincoln Univ	14	5
Te Rauoriwa Gapper	Canterbury Univ	25	35	Easter Savelio	Linwood	5	0
Catriona Greenslade	Lincoln Univ	23	10	Cassie Siataga	Linwood	29	29
Lucy Jenkins	Christchurch	30	20	Tayla Simpson	Canterbury Univ	1	0
Martha Lolohea	Christchurch	11	55	Angie Sisifa	Christchurch	14	15
Phillipa Love	Christchurch	40	60	Grace Steinmetz	Lincoln Univ	8	10
Olivia McGoverne	Canterbury Univ	42	142	Rebecca Todd	Christchurch	25	25
Amy Milnes	Christchurch	2	0	Isabella Waterman	Christchurch	4	5

INDIVIDUAL SCORING

	Tries	Con	PG	DG	Points		Tries	Con	PG	DG	Points
Cocksedge	4	25	2	–	76	Waterman	1	2	–	–	9
McGoverne	6	9	–	–	48	Penalty try	1	–	–	–	7
A. Bremner	8	–	–	–	40	C. Bremner	1	–	–	–	5
Lolohea	8	–	–	–	40	Gapper	1	–	–	–	5
Brooker	6	–	–	–	30	Greenslade	1	–	–	–	5
Nelles	6	–	–	–	30	Ponsonby	1	–	–	–	5
Curtis	3	–	–	–	15	Rule	1	–	–	–	5
Anderson	2	–	–	–	10	Todd	1	–	–	–	5
Jenkins	2	–	–	–	10						
Love	2	–	–	–	10	**Totals**	**59***	**36**	**2**	**0**	**375**
Sisifa	2	–	–	–	10						
Steinmetz	2	–	–	–	10	Opposition scored	13	2	2	0	75

* Includes one penalty try

CANTERBURY 2020

	Manawatu	Otago	Hawke's Bay	Wellington	Tasman	Auckland	Waikato	TOTALS
I.C. Waterman	s	15	15	–	s	–	–	4
G.L. Steinmetz	s	s	11	15	14	15	15	7
M.M. Lolohea	14	14	14	14	s	14	14	7
S.G.B. Curtis	11	11	s	11	11	11	11	7
G.E. Brooker	13	13	13	13	13	13	13	7
C.M.T. Siataga	12	–	s	s	12	s	–	5
O.B. McGoverne	15	12	12	12	15	12	12	7
Te R. Gapper	10	10	10	10	10	10	10	7
T.C. Simpson	–	s	–	–	–	–	–	1
K.M. Cocksedge	9	9	9	9	9	9	9	7
S.A. O'Cain	s	–	s	s	s	s	–	5
T.R. Aldridge	–	s	–	–	–	–	–	1
L.E. Anderson	8	s	8	8	–	8	8	6
A.A.F. Sisifa	s	8	s	s	8	s	s	7
G.R. O'Rourke	7	–	7	–	–	s	–	3
L.V.M. Jenkins	–	7	s	7	7	7	7	6
A.J. Bremner (capt)	6	6	6	6	6	6	6	7
N.J. Purdom	–	–	–	–	s	–	–	1
C.L. Nelles	5	5	5	5	5	5	5	7
C.J. Bremner	4	4	4	4	4	4	4	7
E.I.A. Savelio	s	s	–	s	s	s	–	5
N.J.N. Poletti	3	–	–	s	–	s	–	3
A.F. Milnes	s	–	–	–	s	–	–	2
A.M. Rule	–	3	3	3	3	3	3	6
P.E.A. Love	1	1	1	1	–	–	1	5
C.J. Greenslade	–	s	s	s	1	1	s	6
R.A. Todd	2	2	s	2	s	2	2	7
G.R.A. Ponsonby	s	s	2	s	2	s	s	7

CANTERBURY TEAM RECORD, 2020

Played 7 Won 7 Points for 375 Points against 75

Date	Opponent	Location	Score	Tries	Con	PG	DG	Referee
September 12	Manawatu (S)	Palmerston North	36–10	A. Bremner (2), Love, Steinmetz, Nelles	Cocksedge (4)	Cocksedge		Rebecca Mahoney
September 19	Otago (S, ST)	Christchurch	85–10	A. Bremner (2), Lolohea (2), Nelles, Rule, Sisifa, Gapper, penalty try, Brooker, Curtis, Anderson, Ponsonby	Cocksedge (6), McGoverne (3)			Lauren Jenner
September 26	Hawke's Bay (S)	Napier	72–15	A. Bremner (2), Lolohea (2), Brooker (2), Anderson, Cocksedge, Waterman, Steinmetz, Curtis, Greenslade	Cocksedge (4), Waterman (2)			Rebecca Mahoney
October 3	Wellington (S, ST)	Christchurch	54–12	Brooker (3), Cocksedge (2), McGoverne, Love, Nelles	Cocksedge (6), McGoverne			Lauren Jenner
October 17	Tasman (S, ST)	Christchurch	84–0	Lolohea (4), Jenkins (2), A. Bremner (2), McGoverne (2), Cocksedge, Nelles, Sisifa, Todd	McGoverne (5), Cocksedge (2)			Maggie Cogger-Orr
October 24	Auckland (semi-final)	Christchurch	36–21	McGoverne (3), C. Bremner, Curtis, Nelles	Cocksedge (3)			Lauren Jenner
October 31	Waikato (final)	Christchurch	8–7	Nelles		Cocksedge		Rebecca Mahoney

ST Stewart Trophy

COUNTIES MANUKAU HEAT

2020 Status: North Pool
NPC participation: 1999–2005, 2013–
Coach: Chad Shepherd
Assistant coaches: Suli Taufelele, Kallum Adams
Home ground: Navigation Homes Stadium

RECORDS

Most appearances	57	*Arihiana Marino-Tauhinu 2013–20*
Most points	317	*Hazel Tubic 2005–20*
Most tries	26	*Te Kura Ngata-Aerengamate, 2013–18*
Most points in a season	78	*Hazel Tubic, 2017, 2020*
Most tries in a season	10	*Renee Wickliffe, 2015*
Most conversions in a season	28	*Hazel Tubic 2017*
Most penalty goals in a season	8	*Hazel Tubic, 2013*
Most dropped goals in a season	0	
Most points in a match	27	*Hazel Tubic v Taranaki, 2013*
Most tries in a match	4	*Renee Wickliffe v Otago, 2015*
		Portia Woodman v Wellington 2016
		Waikohika Flesher v North Harbour 2020
Most conversions in a match	11	*Hazel Tubic v Taranaki, 2020*
Most penalty goals in a match	4	*Hazel Tubic v Auckland, 2013*
Highest team score	107	*v Taranaki 2020*
Record victory (points ahead)	104	*107–3 v Taranaki 2020*
Highest score conceded	65	*v Auckland B, 2005*
Record defeat (points behind)	65	*0–65 v Auckland B, 2005*

The team scored more points than any other team in the North pool, the 107 points against Taranaki inflating the total. A good win over Auckland was followed by narrow losses to Northland and Waikato. A bonus-point win over Bay of Plenty would have secured a semi-final position but an uncharacteristic performance saw Counties struggle and they only scored a converted try in the 80th minute to break a 10–10 deadlock and snatch victory. Scoring three tries, Counties needed a fourth to gain a vital bonus point.

Halfback Arihiana Marino-Tauhina was again captain, her seventh year, and she combined well with the equally experienced Hazel Tubic. Wing 'Langi' Veainu produced form which earned her Black Ferns selection. On the other wing was Black Ferns Sevens star Ruby Tui, a veteran of 39 sevens tournaments and 64 tries. Surprisingly, she had not appeared in Farah Palmer Cup competition since 2011 when with Canterbury. Her pace and strength resulted in nine tries, only fellow-sevens player Portia Woodman (Northland) scored as many. Centre Shyanne Thompson was called into the Barbarians squad.

A solid forward pack was competitive against all opposition with the only newcomer being prop Shaye Adams. Kalo Cuthers had represented Auckland in 2017. It was unfortunate for flanker 'Lisa' Molia, after being selected for the Black Ferns, to have to withdraw because of injury.

Higher honours went to:
New Zealand: A. Marino-Tauhinu, H. Tubic, L. Veainu
New Zealand Barbarians: S. Thompson

COUNTIES MANUKAU REPRESENTATIVES 2020

	Club	Games for Union	Points for Union		Club	Games for Union	Points for Union
Shaye Adams	Manurewa	4	0	Arihiana Marino-Tauhinu	Manurewa	57	230
Glory Aiono	Manurewa	18	25	Temira Mataroa	Manurewa	8	10
Ngatokotoru Arakua	Manurewa	4	5	Aotearoa Matau	Ardmore Marist	46	120
Utumalama Atonio	Ardmore Marist	11	10	Ilisapeti 'Lisa' Molia	Manurewa	10	25
Juvina Auva'a	Ardmore Marist	7	0	Yuki Ono	Ardmore Marist	15	15
Stacey Brown	Papakura	38	10	Amiria Te Iringa	Manurewa	11	5
Rebecca Burch	Ardmore Marist	10	0	Harono Te Iringa	Manurewa	24	30
Kalo Cuthers	Marist[1]	4	5	Shyanne Thompson	Ardmore Marist	13	15
Waikohika Flesher	Manurewa	17	50	Shonte To'a	Ardmore Marist	7	2
Grace Gago	Manurewa	25	35	Hazel Tubic	Manurewa	40	317
Mele Hufanga	Manurewa	6	5	Ruby Tui	Papakura	6	45
Emily Kitson	Ardmore Marist	22	42	Leititia Vaka	Ardmore Marist	10	5
Justine Lavea	Ardmore Marist	33	35	Katofoekina Veainu	Ardmore Marist	15	0
Cathy Leuta	Ardmore Marist	2	0	Lanulangi Veainu	Ardmore Marist	26	75
Larissa Lima E Silva	Ardmore Marist	25	10	Azania Watene	Ardmore Marist	30	20

1 Auckland RU

INDIVIDUAL SCORING

	Tries	Con	PG	DG	Points		Tries	Con	PG	DG	Points
Tubic	1	28	2	–	67	Arakua	1	–	–	–	5
Tui	9	–	–	–	45	Cuthers	1	–	–	–	5
Aiono	4	–	–	–	20	Hufanga	1	–	–	–	5
Flesher	4	–	–	–	20	Marino-Tauhinu	1	–	–	–	5
Gago	4	–	–	–	20	Mataroa	1	–	–	–	5
Molia	4	–	–	–	20	A. Te Iringa	1	–	–	–	5
H. Te Iringa	4	–	–	–	20	L. Veainu	1	–	–	–	5
Kitson	3	–	–	–	15						
Matau	3	–	–	–	15	**Totals**	**47**	**28**	**2**	**0**	**297**
Lima E Silva	2	–	–	–	10						
Thompson	2	–	–	–	10	Opposition scored	16	6	4	0	104

COUNTIES MANUKAU 2020

	North Harbour	Auckland	Northland	Waikato	Bay of Plenty	Taranaki	TOTALS
E.F. Kitson	15	15	–	–	15	15	4
A.O.R. Watene	s	–	s	–	–	–	2
S. To'a	–	–	15	15	–	–	2
Y. Ono	–	–	–	s	s	–	2
R.M. Tui	14	14	14	14	14	14	6
W. Flesher	11	11	–	–	–	s	3
L.L. Veainu	–	s	11	11	11	11	5
S. Thompson	13	–	–	–	13	13	3
M.M. Hufanga	12	13	13	13	12	s	6
U. Atonio	s	s	s	s	–	–	4
N. Arakua	–	12	12	12	–	12	4
H.S. Tubic	10	10	10	10	10	10	6
A.A.H. Marino-Tauhinu (capt)	9	9	9	9	9	9	6
L. Vaka	s	s	s	–	s	s	5
H. Te Iringa	8	8	8	8	8	8	6
L. Lima E Silva	7	7	7	7	7	7	6
J. Lavea	–	–	–	s	–	–	1
I.M.P. Molia	6	6	–	–	–	6	3
S.J. Brown	s	s	6	s	6	s	6
G. Aiono	s	s	s	6	s	s	6
R.M. Burch	5	5	5	5	5	5	6
A. Te Irirangi	4	4	4	4	4	4	6
T. Mataroa	–	–	–	–	s	s	2
K. Cuthers	–	3	–	s	3	3	4
A.K. Matau	3	1	1	–	–	1	4
K. Veainu	s	s	s	3	s	–	5
S. Adams	1	–	3	1	1	–	4
G.L.F. Gago	2	2	2	2	2	2	6
C. Leuta	s	–	s	–	–	–	2
J. Auva'a	–	s	s	s	s	s	5

COUNTIES MANUKAU TEAM RECORD, 2020

			Played 6	Won 4	Lost 2	Points for 297		Points against 104
Date	Opponent	Location	Score	Tries	Con	PG	DG	Referee
September 5	North Harbour (N)	Pukekohe	89–3	Flesher (4), Tui (3), Kitson (2), Tubic, Molia, H. Te Iringa, Hufanga, Gago	Tubic (8)	Tubic		Michael Winter
September 20	Auckland (N)	Auckland	36–22	Tui (2), Cuthers, Lima E Silva, Molia, H. Te Iringa	Tubic (3)			Michael Winter
September 27	Northland (N)	Pukekohe	20–32	Matau, Arakua, Aiono	Tubic	Tubic		Nick Hogan
October 3	Waikato (N)	Putaruru	28–34	H. Te Iringa, Aiono, Tui, Marino-Tauhinu	Tubic (4)			Rebecca Mahoney
October 10	Bay of Plenty (N)	Pukekohe	17–10	Kitson, Tui, Aiono	Tubic			Maggie Cogger-Orr
October 17	Taranaki (N)	Inglewood	107–3	Gago (3), Matau (2), Thompson (2), Molia (2), Tui (2), L. Veainu, H. Te Iringa, A. Te Iringa, Aiono, Lima E Silva, Mataroa	Tubic (11)			Tiana Ngawati

HAWKE'S BAY TUI

2020 Status: South Pool
NPC participation: 1999–2012, 2014–2015, 2017–
Coaches: Blair Cross, Stephen Woods
Home ground: McLean Park

RECORDS
Most appearances	75	*Chanel Atkin 2001–19*
Most points	192	*Nerina Hawkins, 1999–2004*
Most tries	21	*Deidre Hakopa, 1999–2009*
Most points in a season	61	*Nerina Hawkins, 2003*
Most tries in a season	9	*Deidre Hakopa, 2003*
Most conversions in a season	16	*Nerina Hawkins, 2003; Sylvia Bockman, 2019*
Most penalty goals in a season	8	*Nerina Hawkins, 2003*
Most dropped goals in a season	0	
Most points in a match	25	*Deidre Hakopa v Southland, 2003*
Most tries in a match	5	*Deidre Hakopa v Southland, 2003*
Most conversions in a match	7	*Nerina Hawkins v Poverty Bay, 2000*
Most penalty goals in a match	5	*Kaitlin Bates v Otago, 2020*
Highest team score	100	*v Southland, 2003*
Record victory (points ahead)	95	*100–5 v Southland, 2003*
Highest score conceded	93	*v Auckland, 2014*
Record defeat (points behind)	93	*0–93 v Auckland, 2014*

The Tui had somewhat of a mixed season. There was a big win over Tasman, a narrow defeat to Otago, and a competitive loss to Manawatu, while the one-on-one tackling and defensive line speed was exposed in the two heavy losses to Wellington and Canterbury.

In the forwards, captain and hooker Forne Burkin always gave of her best and injury ruled her out of contention for the Black Ferns trial. Lock Nina Pineaha played every minute and was a tireless worker, while in the loose forwards Niamh Jefferson was always prominent with Kathleen Brown not far behind. Nineteen-year-old prop Moomooga (Ashley) Palu was always hard to stop and scored a barnstorming try against Canterbury.

The backline suffered from a lack of possession, particularly against Wellington and Canterbury. Krysten Cottrell missed the entire club season due to knee surgery and, not surprisingly, took a while to regain confidence but improved with every outing. Debuts were given to two promising 16-year-olds Harmony Kautai and Amelia Pasikala, both still at high school, who retained their positions to the end.

Halfback Emma Jensen announced her retirement at the end of the season. The 42-year-old concluded her career having played more matches in women's first-class rugby than any other player. She first played for Hawke's Bay at the age of 15 in 1993 and on through to 1995, which were her final three years at Central HB College, before the advent of the official women's provincial championship in 1999. After representing Waikato, Auckland and the Black Ferns (three times a World Cup winner), she returned to her home province in 2018 and continued to provide grand service.

The Tui lost a lot of experience from last year's team with Hanna Brough (Waikato), Liana Mikaele-Tu'u (Auckland) elsewhere and Chanel Atkin, Te Aroha Hunt, Te Maari MacGregor and Gemma Woods all unavailable.

HAWKE'S BAY REPRESENTATIVES 2020

	Club	Games for Union	Points for Union		Club	Games for Union	Points for Union
Nicolette Adamson	Clive	4	10	Emma Jensen	Hastings R&S	19	21
Denise Aiolupotea	Napier Technical OB	4	0	Harmony Kautai	Hastings R&S	4	10
Michaela Baker	Napier Technical OB	17	35	Lara Kendrick	Napier Technical OB	6	0
Kaitlin Bates	Taradale	8	17	Amber-Jane McKenzie	Napier Technical OB	8	5
Laurae Blake	Clive	33	5	Patrice Mareikura	Napier Technical OB	2	0
Kathleen Brown	Napier Technical OB	19	40	Whitley Mareikura	Napier Technical OB	28	20
Forne Burkin	Napier Technical OB	24	25	Teagan Meyer	Napier Technical OB	9	0
Krysten Cottrell	Taradale	35	115	Moomooga Palu	Hastings R&S	9	25
Iukika Faavae	Hastings R&S	9	10	Amelia Pasikala	Hastings R&S	5	10
Hope Hakopa	Clive	11	0	Nina Pineaha	Hastings R&S	9	5
Kara Huata	Clive	9	0	Jaimee Robin (nee Edwards)	Clive	19	15
Rebekah Hurae	Clive	23	0	Jennifer Simati	Napier Technical OB	14	0
Tori Iosefo	Napier Technical OB	13	60	Cortez Te Pou	Hastings R&S	12	45
Niamh Jefferson	Clive	24	30	Shaylee Tipiwai	Clive	44	65

INDIVIDUAL SCORING

	Tries	Con	PG	DG	Points		Tries	Con	PG	DG	Points
Cottrell	1	7	–	–	19	McKenzie	1	–	–	–	5
Bates	–	1	5	–	17	W. Mareikura	1	–	–	–	5
Baker	3	–	–	–	15	Palu	1	–	–	–	5
Kautai	2	–	–	–	10	Robin	1	–	–	–	5
Pasikala	2	–	–	–	10	Tipiwai	1	–	–	–	5
Te Pou	2	–	–	–	10						
Brown	1	–	–	–	5	**Totals**	**19**	**8**	**5**	**0**	**126**
Burkin	1	–	–	–	5						
Faavae	1	–	–	–	5	Opposition scored	34	16	0	0	202
Jefferson	1	–	–	–	5						

HAWKE'S BAY 2020

	Otago	Wellington	Canterbury	Tasman	Manawatu	TOTALS
C.P. Te Pou	15	15	15	s	11	**6**
K.B. Bates	14	14	s	–	–	**3**
N.A. Adamson	–	–	14	–	s	**2**
H. Kautai	–	11	11	14	14	**4**
T.P.L.A. Iosefo	11	–	–	11	–	**2**
A. Pasikala	13	13	13	13	13	**5**
M.S.D. Baker	12	12	–	15	15	**4**
J.M. Robin	s	s	12	12	12	**5**
K.J. Cottrell	10	10	10	10	10	**5**
E.M. Jensen	9	9	9	s	9	**5**
S.T. Tipiwai	s	s	s	9	s	**5**
K.M.T. Brown	8	8	8	8	8	**5**
N.W. Jefferson	7	7	7	s	7	**5**
H.L. Hakopa	s	–	–	7	–	**2**
L.M.A. Blake	6	6	6	6	6	**5**
T.J. Meyer	–	s	s	–	s	**3**
L.S. Kendrick	5	5	s	–	–	**3**
R.K. Hurae	–	–	5	5	5	**3**
N. Pineaha	4	4	4	4	4	**5**
D. Aiolupotea	s	s	–	s	s	**4**
W.E.D.A. Mareikura	3	3	3	3	3	**5**
I. Faavae	1	1	1	s	1	**5**
P. Mareikura	s	s	–	–	–	**2**
K.T.I. Huata	s	–	s	–	–	**2**
J.L. Simati	–	s	–	1	s	**3**
M.A. Palu	–	–	s	–	s	**2**
F.K. Burkin (capt)	2	2	2	2	2	**5**
A-J. McKenzie	s	s	s	s	s	**5**

HAWKE'S BAY TEAM RECORD, 2020

Played 5   Won 1   Lost 4   Points for 126   Points against 202

Date	Opponent	Location	Score	Tries	Con	PG	DG	Referee
September 13	Otago (S)	Dunedin	20–29	Brown		Bates (5)		Maggie Cogger-Orr
September 19	Wellington (S)	Lower Hutt	17–67	Burkin, Baker, Kautai	Bates			Jono Bredin
September 26	Canterbury (S)	Napier	15–72	Faavae, Te Pou, Palu				Rebecca Mahoney
October 4	Tasman (S)	Motueka	62–5	Robin, W. Mareikura, Pasikala, Kaitai, Te Pou, Jefferson, McKenzie, Baker, Tipiwai, Cottrell	Cottrell (6)			Larissa Collingwood
October 16	Manawatu (S)	Napier	12–29	Baker, Pasikala	Cottrell			Lauren Jenner

MANAWATU CYCLONES

2020 Status: South Pool
NPC participation: 1999–
Coach: Fusi Feaunati
Assistant coach: Caleb Agnew-Jones
Home ground: Central Energy Trust Arena

MANAWATU RUGBY

RECORDS

Most appearances	87	*Selica Winiata, 2001–20*
Most points	528	*Selica Winiata, 2001–20*
Most tries	72	*Selica Winiata, 2001–20*
Most points in a season	110	*Selica Winiata, 2012*
Most tries in a season	14	*Selica Winiata, 2012*
Most conversions in a season	18	*Selica Winiata, 2020*
Most penalty goals in a season	8	*Anika Tiplady, 2004*
Most dropped goals in a season	2	*Rebecca Hull, 2002*
Most points in a match	38	*Selica Winiata v Waikato, 2012*
Most tries in a match	4	*Catherine Doyle v Poverty Bay-East Coast, 2002;*
		Selica Winiata v Waikato, 2012;
		Selica Winiata v Wellington, 2012
		Selica Winiata v Tasman, 2020
Most conversions in a match	9	*Elizabeth Goulden v Hawke's Bay, 2017*
		Selica Winiata v Tasman, 2020
Most penalty goals in a match	4	*Anika Tiplady v Bay of Plenty, 2004*
Highest team score	86	*v Hawke's Bay, 2017*
Record victory (points ahead)	88	*v Tasman 2020*
Highest score conceded	88	*88–0 v Tasman 2020*
Record defeat (points behind)	65	*5–70 v Auckland, 2011*

Winless in 2019, the Cyclones had been relegated to the Championship division but the pandemic, which forced a delay and restructure of the competition, enabled the team to again challenge themselves against the stronger teams of the South Pool.

First opponent was the formidable Canterbury side and although the champions were not threatened on the scoreboard, it was very evident from the Cyclones' performance that here was a team that showed a gutsy determination and promising prospects for the following games. Tasman were trounced by a record score before meeting Wellington Pride at Sky Stadium. Unlike many previous games against bigger, heavier, stronger opponents, the Cyclones of 2020 never wilted during the final minutes when Wellington were hammering the line. The win boosted confidence and wins followed over Otago and Hawke's Bay. Despite losing to North Pool leaders Waikato in a semi-final, the Cyclones completed a most successful season and far out-shone their Turbos brothers as Manawatu representatives in the national ratings.

Selica Winiata was again captain and from fullback was involved in many exciting moves and extended her remarkable try-scoring record to 72 from 87 appearances. Her 20 years' service to Manawatu representative teams since her debut as a 14-year-old is one of the most remarkable achievements in either women's or men's provincial first-class rugby.

Much of the season's success was due to the experience gained during the previous year by most of the squad and the availability of sevens players. Lucy Brown and Paige Lush shared the halfback position. Carys Dallinger was an astute playmaker, her season rewarded with Barbarians selection. Rebekah Tufuga and Crystal Mayes were strong midfielders with 17-year-old Kaia-

Hayes Walker-Waitoa showing promise off the bench. Janna Vaughan and Rangimarie Sturmey were regulars on the wing and a promising Kalyn Takitimu-Cook when available.

Of the forwards, none shone brighter than 18-year-old Kaipo Olsen-Baker at the back of the scrum, a talented athlete whose form was rewarded with Barbarians selection for the end-of-season fixtures against the Black Ferns. Olsen-Baker was well supported in the loose by Sam Tipene and Rhiarna Ferris. Rachel Rakatau, Kahurangi Sturmey and Ashleigh Knight were the locks. There was also experience in the front row with former Black Fern Sosoli Talawadua, current Samoan international Marilyn Live and Jayme Nuku. Two former Taranaki representatives, Alesha Williams and Caterina Poletti made appearances off the bench. Injury prevented Black Ferns Sevens captain Sarah Hirini from appearing. However, as a regular runner with water bottles, her on-field advice and encouragement during injury breaks, contributed towards the team's success.

It was Fusi Feaunati's fourth year coaching the Cyclones. During his reign he has improved the standard of play markedly, not an easy task considering unavailability of schoolgirls at certain times and selection of players for Sevens and Black Ferns duty.

Higher honours went to:

New Zealand:	S. Winiata
New Zealand Barbarians:	C. Dallinger, C. Mayes, K. Olsen-Baker, J. Vaughan
New Zealand Sevens:	S.L. Hirini

MANAWATU REPRESENTATIVES 2020

	Club	Games for Union	Points for Union		Club	Games for Union	Points for Union
Lucy Brown	Feilding OB Oroua	18	10	Layla Sae	University	9	0
Carys Dallinger	Kia Toa	15	30	Kahurangi Sturmey	University	9	5
Katelyn Donaldson	Bush	1	0	Rangimarie Sturmey	University	12	25
Rhiarna Ferris	Feilding OB Oroua	16	10	Kalyn Takitimu-Cook	Feilding OB Oroua	8	29
Vaine Greig	Feilding OB Oroua	14	25	Sosoli Talawadua	Wanganui Metro	12	10
Ashleigh Knight	Feilding OB Oroua	14	0	Ngano Tavake	University	7	0
Marilyn Live	Kia Toa	26	5	Samantha Tipene	Bush	42	30
Paige Lush	Kia Toa	5	10	Rebekah Tufuga	Kia Toa	20	15
Crystal Mayes	Linton Army	32	70	Janna Vaughan	Kia Toa	44	120
Lavenia Nauga-Grey	Wanganui Metro	3	0	Kaia Walker-Waitoa	Feilding OB Oroua	4	10
Jayme Nuku	Kia Toa	35	0	Taylor Waterson	Kia Toa	4	0
Kaipo Olsen-Baker	Feilding OB Oroua	9	0	Alesha Williams	University	3	0
Caterina Poletti	Kia Toa	2	0	Selica Winiata	Kia Toa	87	528
Rachel Rakatau	Feilding OB Oroua	12	0				

INDIVIDUAL SCORING

	Tries	Con	PG	DG	Points		Tries	Con	PG	DG	Points
Winiata	4	18	3	–	65	Ferris	1	–	–	–	5
Dallinger	5	–	–	–	25	Takitimu-Cook	1	–	–	–	5
Vaughan	5	–	–	–	25	Tipene	1	–	–	–	5
Mayes	3	–	–	–	15	Tufuga	1	–	–	–	5
R. Sturmey	3	–	–	–	15						
Lush	2	–	–	–	10	**Totals**	**31**	**18**	**3**	**0**	**200**
Talawadua	2	–	–	–	10						
Walker-Waitoa	2	–	–	–	10	Opposition scored	18*	13	1	0	121
Brown	1	–	–	–	5						

* Includes one penalty try

MANAWATU 2020

	Canterbury	Tasman	Wellington	Otago	Hawke's Bay	Waikato	TOTALS
S.C. Winiata (capt)	15	15	15	15	15	15	**6**
K. Takitimu-Cook	14	–	–	–	11	s	**3**
R.T. Sturmey	s	14	14	14	14	14	**6**
J.M. Vaughan	11	11	11	11	–	11	**5**
A.M. Williams	s	s	–	–	s	–	**3**
V.A.P. Greig	13	13	–	–	–	–	**2**
C.A.M. Mayes	12	12	13	13	13	13	**6**
R.C. Tufuga	s	s	12	12	12	12	**6**
C.N. Dallinger	10	10	10	10	10	10	**6**
K-H.I. Walker-Waitoa	–	s	–	s	s	s	**4**
L. Brown	9	9	9	9	9	9	**6**
P.T. Lush	s	s	–	s	s	s	**5**
K.T. Olsen-Baker	8	8	8	8	–	8	**5**
L.Y.J. Sae	s	s	s	–	8	s	**5**
S.J. Tipene	7	7	7	7	7	7	**6**
R.R. Ferris	6	6	6	6	s	6	**6**
T.G.M. Waterson	–	–	s	s	s	s	**4**
A.J. Knight	5	4	–	s	5	–	**4**
R.E. Rakatau	4	5	5	5	6	5	**6**
C.P.N. Poletti	s	s	–	–	–	–	**2**
K.J. Sturmey	–	–	4	4	4	4	**4**
S.J. Talawadua	3	3	3	3	3	3	**6**
M. Live	1	1	1	1	1	1	**6**
M. Tavake	s	s	s	s	s	s	**6**
L.A. Nauga-Grey	–	–	s	–	s	s	**3**
K. Donaldson	–	–	–	s	–	–	**1**
J.R. Nuku	2	2	2	2	2	2	**6**

MANAWATU TEAM RECORD, 2020

Played 6 Won 4 Lost 2 Points for 200 Points against 121

Date	Opponent	Location	Score	Tries	Con	PG	DG	Referee
September 12	Canterbury (S)	Palmerston North	10–36	Winiata, Vaughan				Rebecca Mahoney
September 20	Tasman (S)	Palmerston North	88–0	Talawadua (2), Dallinger (2), Winiata, Brown, R. Sturmey, Tipene, Vaughan, Mayes, Walker-Waitoa, Ferris, Tufuga, Lush	Winiata (9)			Nick Hogan
September 25	Wellington (S)	Wellington	31–28	Vaughan (2), Mayes, Dallinger	Winiata	Winiata (3)		Michael Winter
October 4	Otago (S)	Dunedin	28–14	Winiata, Mayes, Dallinger, Vaughan	Winiata (4)			Maggie Cogger-Orr
October 16	Hawke's Bay (S)	Napier	29–12	Winiata, R. Sturmey, Takitimu-Cook, Dallinger, Walker-Waitoa	Winiata (2)			Lauren Jenner
October 125	Waikato (semi-final)	Hamilton	14–31	Lush, R. Sturmey	Winiata (2)			Maggie Cogger-Orr

NORTH HARBOUR HIBISCUS

2020 Status: North Pool
NPC participation: 1999–2005, 2016–
Coach: Duncan McGrory
Assistant coaches: Willie Walker, Manu Colazo
Home ground: North Harbour Stadium, Albany

RECORDS

Most appearances	28	Olivia Ward-Duin 2016–20
Most points	94	Sophie Fisher, 2017–20
Most tries	10	Pia Tapsell, 2016–20
Most points in a season	52	Sophie Fisher, 2018
Most tries in a season	5	Caitlyn Cox, 2017
		Simone Small, 2019
Most conversions in a season	14	Sophie Fisher, 2018
Most penalty goals in a season	7	Rachel Howard, 2003
Most dropped goals in a season	0	
Most points in a match	24	Sophie Fisher v Taranaki, 2018
Most tries in a match	3	Simone Small v Taranaki, 2019
Most conversions in a match	7	Sophie Fisher v Taranaki, 2018
Most penalty goals in a match	3	Rachel Howard v Auckland B, 2003
Highest team score	59	v Taranaki, 2018
Record victory (points ahead)	59	59–0 v Taranaki, 2018
Highest score conceded	116	v Auckland, 1999
Record defeat (points behind)	116	0–116 v Auckland, 1999

A young team lacking experience suffered several heavy losses against the stronger unions, the only game in which Hibiscus was competitive being a three-point loss against Taranaki. The only established North Harbour players were prop Olivia Ward-Duin, hooker Amy Robertshaw and flanker Kate Williams who captained the side. Sophie Fisher made a return for the later games. Black Fern Pia Tapsell played only twice before moving to Bay of Plenty. Hayley Hutana was a valuable acquisition, the former Manawatu, Tasman and Black Ferns Sevens player, arrived as a result of an air force transfer. Auckland players from across the bridge were loaned to strengthen the squad, including locks Clementine Varea and Manutalaaho Huni, prop Finesa Makasini and threequarter Lose Mafi. Olivia Waldron had represented Otago. Dutch international Lynn Koelman came from Bay of Plenty.

Teenagers dominated the backline positions, Zakiya Kereopa, Phoenix Littin, Danielle Mellow, Hailey Beale, Latisha Trigwell-Achmad and Mollie Tagaloa. If this youth is retained their 2020 experience should be better rewarded in 2021. In the forwards, flanker 18-year-old Tenaija Fletcher started in every game. Prop Jay Jay Taylor and Ward-Duin appeared for the Barbarians.

The union again took part in the Auckland competition, fielding a team representing all North Harbour clubs and known as Albany Barbarians, The previous year a combined team, known as Bayfield, represented East Coast Bays and Glenfield clubs.

Higher honours went to:
New Zealand Barbarians: J. Taylor, O. Ward-Duin

NORTH HARBOUR REPRESENTATIVES 2020

	Club	Games for Union	Points for Union		Club	Games for Union	Points for Union
Renee Adams	Albany Barbarians	10	5	Finesa Makasini	Grammar TEC[1]	8	5
Hailey Beale	Albany Barbarians	12	0	Danielle Mellow	Albany Barbarians	5	0
Anita Berry	Albany Barbarians	9	0	Tearren Nanjan	Albany Barbarians	15	0
Roseanne Cox	College Rifles[1]	1	0	Amy Robertshaw	Albany Barbarians	21	20
Brooke Ellison	Albany Barbarians	4	0	Mikayla Robinson	Albany Barbarians	6	5
Toakase Filimoehala	Albany Barbarians	6	0	Caroline Sio	Albany Barbarians	8	0
Sophie Fisher	Albany Barbarians	22	94	Mollie Tagaloa	Albany Barbarians	5	0
Tenaija Fletcher	Albany Barbarians	12	0	Pia Tapsell	Albany Barbarians	24	50
Danjela Haigh	Albany Barbarians	8	0	Jayjay Taylor	Albany Barbarians	12	10
Manutalaaho Huni	Ponsonby[1]	6	0	Tamea Te Rauna	Albany Barbarians	5	0
Hayley Hutana	Albany Barbarians	6	14	Latisha Trigwell-Achmad	Albany Barbarians	3	0
Zakiya Kereopa	Albany Barbarians	5	10	Clementine Varea	College Rifles[1]	5	15
Lynn Koelman	Mt Maunganui[2]	5	0	Olivia Waldron	Marist[1]	3	0
Phoenix Littin	Albany Barbarians	4	0	Olivia Ward-Duin	Albany Barbarians	28	15
Lose Mafi	Marist[1]	4	0	Kate Williams	Albany Barbarians	20	5

1 Auckland RU   2 Bay of Plenty RU

INDIVIDUAL SCORING

	Tries	Con	PG	DG	Points		Tries	Con	PG	DG	Points
Varea	3	–	–	–	15	Taylor	1	–	–	–	5
Hutana	–	4	2	–	14						
Kereopa	2	–	–	–	10	**Totals**	**8**	**4**	**2**	**0**	**54**
Robertshaw	1	–	–	–	5						
Tapsell	1	–	–	–	5	Opposition scored	62	34	3	0	387

NORTH HARBOUR 2020

	Counties Manukau	Bay of Plenty	Taranaki	Auckland	Northland	Waikato	TOTALS
R.A. Adams	s	s	s	15	–	15	5
M. Tagaloa	14	14	14	14	15	–	5
L. Mafi	11	11	13	13	–	–	4
L. Trigwell-Achmad	–	–	–	11	11	11	3
Z. Kereopa	12	13	11	–	14	14	5
M.M.A. Robinson	13	12	–	–	–	–	2
D. Mellow	s	s	–	s	13	13	5
P. Littin	–	–	12	12	12	12	4
O.N. Waldron	10	10	15	–	–	–	3
H.S. Hutana	15	15	10	10	10	10	6
T. Te Rauna	9	9	–	s	s	s	5
H.D. Beale	s	s	9	9	9	9	6
P.H. Tapsell	8	8	–	–	–	–	2
T.A. Nanjan	–	s	8	s	s	s	5
K.R. Williams (capt)	7	7	7	7	7	7	6
T.V. Fletcher	6	6	6	6	6	6	6
B. Ellison	s	–	–	s	s	s	4
R.C. Sio	–	s	s	–	–	–	2
R.E. Cox	–	–	–	–	s	–	1
C. Varea	5	5	5	8	8	–	5
S.R. Fisher	–	–	s	5	5	8	4
M.H. Huni	4	4	4	4	4	5	6
A.R. Berry	–	–	–	s	s	4	3
O.Y. Ward-Duin	3	3	3	3	–	3	5
T. Filimoehala	s	s	s	s	3	s	6
J. Taylor	1	1	–	1	1	1	5
F.A. Makasini	–	–	–	–	s	s	2
A.G. Robertshaw	2	2	1	2	–	2	5
L. Koolman	s	s	2	s	2	–	5
D. Haigh	s	–	–	–	s	s	3

NORTH HARBOUR TEAM RECORD, 2020

Played 6　Lost 6　Points for 54　Points against 387

Date	Opponent	Location	Score	Tries	Con	PG	DG	Referee
September 5	Counties Manukau (N)	Pukekohe	3–89			Hutana		Michael Winter
September 11	Bay of Plenty (N)	Albany	17–67	Kereopa, Tapsell	Hutana (2)	Hutana		Jono Bredin
September 19	Taranaki (N)	Inglewood	29–32	Varea (3), Kereopa, Robertshaw	Hutana (2)			Tiana Ngawati
September 26	Auckland (N)	Albany	0–72					Lauren Jenner
October 3	Northland (N)	Whangarei	5–65	Taylor				Tiana Ngawati
October 10	Waikato (N)	Albany	0–62					Brittany Andrew

NORTHLAND KAURI

2020 Status: North Pool
NPC participation: 1999–2005, 2019–
Coach: Cheryl Smith
Assistant coaches: Susan Dawson, Murray Webb
Home ground: Semenoff Stadium

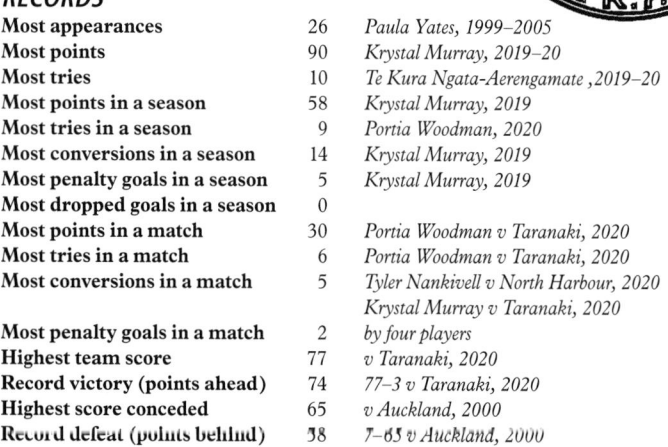

RECORDS
Most appearances	26	Paula Yates, 1999–2005
Most points	90	Krystal Murray, 2019–20
Most tries	10	Te Kura Ngata-Aerengamate, 2019–20
Most points in a season	58	Krystal Murray, 2019
Most tries in a season	9	Portia Woodman, 2020
Most conversions in a season	14	Krystal Murray, 2019
Most penalty goals in a season	5	Krystal Murray, 2019
Most dropped goals in a season	0	
Most points in a match	30	Portia Woodman v Taranaki, 2020
Most tries in a match	6	Portia Woodman v Taranaki, 2020
Most conversions in a match	5	Tyler Nankivell v North Harbour, 2020
		Krystal Murray v Taranaki, 2020
Most penalty goals in a match	2	by four players
Highest team score	77	v Taranaki, 2020
Record victory (points ahead)	74	77–3 v Taranaki, 2020
Highest score conceded	65	v Auckland, 2000
Record defeat (points behind)	58	7–65 v Auckland, 2000

Northland's promising return to the Farah Palmer Cup championship in 2019 progressed further during 2020 and the team was within one competition point of gaining a semi-final position. After losses to eventual pool toppers Waikato and Auckland at the start of the campaign, the team won their remaining four games.

Northland Kauri had the services of six current or past national representatives with the availability of sevens stars Portia Woodman and Tyla Nathan-Wong and the arrival of Aroha Savage. Their experience was welcome support to captain and hooker Te Kura Ngata-Aerengamate, prop Kamila Wihongi and first five-eighth Victoria Subritzky-Nafatali. A highlight of the season was Woodman's six tries against Taranaki. Perhaps the team's best performer was prop Krystal Murray who attracted attention with her strength in the tight and general play. Late in the year, playing for the Barbarians against the Black Ferns, she impressed as a contender for national honours in 2021.

Higher honours went to:
New Zealand: T. Ngata-Aerengamate, A. Savage
New Zealand Barbarians: K. Murray

NORTHLAND REPRESENTATIVES 2020

	Club	Games for Union	Points for Union		Club	Games for Union	Points for Union
Tui Baker	Te Rarawa	1	0	Te Kura Ngata-Aerengamate	Te Rarawa	13	50
Georgia Brierly	Otamatea	1	0	Holli O'Sullivan	City	2	0
Rangimarie Chapman-Barber	Te Rarawa	1	0	Alisha Proctor	Kaikohe	8	5
Danyel Davan	Te Rarawa	1	0	Aroha Savage	Te Rarawa	6	10
Ngawaiora Davis	Kaikohe	4	15	Victoria Subritzky-Nafatali	Te Rarawa	11	25
Leilani Erwin	Kaikohe	8	15	Janie Tairua	Kaikohe	1	0
Narissa Fale	Te Rarawa	1	0	Te Ruawai Tua	Te Rarawa	2	0
Madison Johnson	Otamatea	3	0	Louisa Tubailagi	Otamatea	2	0
Helen Kapa	Kaikohe	12	0	Stacey Tupe	Otamatea	12	15
Justice Karena	Te Rarawa	12	0	Patricia Vaka	Kaikohe	11	0
Alexandra Kingi	Te Rarawa	3	0	Manaia Webb	Kaikohe	11	0
Timara Leaf	Wahine Toa	6	21	Carly Whaikawa	City	5	0
Tui McGeorge	Wahine Toa	11	0	Kamila Wihongi	Kaikohe	13	0
Krystal Murray	Te Rarawa	13	90	Hikitia Wikaira	Kaikohe	5	0
Tyler Nankivell	Kaikohe	13	45	Portia Woodman	Kaikohe	6	45
Tyler Nathan-Wong	Te Rarawa	6	25				

INDIVIDUAL SCORING

	Tries	Con	PG	DG	Points		Tries	Con	PG	DG	Points
Woodman	9	–	–	–	45	Savage	2	–	–	–	10
Nankivell	6	5	–	–	40	Tupe	2	–	–	–	10
Murray	4	6	–	–	32	Proctor	1	–	–	–	5
Nathan-Wong	5	–	–	–	25	Subritzky-Nafatali	1	–	–	–	5
Leaf	–	6	3	–	21						
Davis	3	–	–	–	15	**Totals**	**38**	**17**	**3**	**0**	**233**
Erwin	3	–	–	–	15						
Ngata-Aerengamate	2	–	–	–	10	Opposition scored	10	5	5	0	75

NORTHLAND 2020	Waikato	Auckland	Counties Manukau	North Harbour	Taranaki	Bay of Plenty	TOTALS
S.A. Tupe	–	s	15	15	15	15	5
H. O'Sullivan	14	–	–	s	–	–	2
A. Kingi	s	14	–	–	–	s	3
L.C. Erwin	11	–	14	14	–	s	4
A.A.H. Proctor	s	s	–	–	14	14	4
L. Tubailagi	s	11	–	–	–	–	2
T.B. Nankivell	12	15	11	11	11	11	6
G. Brierly	–	–	–	s	–	–	1
D. Davan	–	–	–	–	s	–	1
P.L. Woodman	13	13	13	13	13	13	6
T.R. Leaf	–	12	12	12	12	12	5
V.S. Subritzky-Nafatali	10	10	10	10	10	10	6
M.H. Webb	9	s	–	s	s	–	4
T.B. Nathan-Wong	15	9	9	9	9	9	6
J. Tairua	–	–	–	–	s	–	1
H. Wikaira	8	s	–	8	8	8	5
A. Savage	7	8	8	7	7	7	6
M. Johnson	–	7	s	–	–	s	3
P.A. Vaka	6	s	s	s	s	4	6
T. Baker	–	6	–	–	–	–	1
N. Davis	–	–	6	6	6	6	4
C. Whaikawa	5	4	4	4	4	–	5
T.M. McGeorge	4	5	7	–	s	s	5
J. Karena	s	s	5	5	5	5	6
K.T. Wihongi	3	3	3	3	3	3	6
K.R. Murray	1	1	1	1	1	1	6
H.J. Kapa	s	s	–	s	s	s	5
Te R. Tua	–	–	s	s	–	–	2
R. Chapman-Barber	–	–	–	–	s	–	1
Te K.R. Ngata-Aerengamate (capt)	2	2	2	2	2	2	7
N. Fale	–	–	–	s	–	–	1

NORTHLAND TEAM RECORD, 2020

Played 6　　Won 4　　Lost 2　　Points for 233　　Points against 75

Date	Opponent	Location	Score	Tries	Con	PG	DG	Referee
September 5	Waikato (N)	Hamilton	5–18	Ngata-Aerengamate				Maggie Cogger-Orr
September 13	Auckland (N)	Whangarei	22–29	Subritzky-Nafatali, Nathan-Wong, Savage	Leaf (2)	Leaf		Michael Winter
September 27	Counties Manukau (N)	Pukekohe	32–20	Nankivell (4), Erwin	Leaf (2)	Leaf		Nick Hogan
October 3	North Harbour (N)	Whangarei	65–5	Woodman (2), Erwin (2), Nathan-Wong (2), Tupe (2), Murray (2), Nankivell	Nankivell (5)			Tiana Ngawati
October 11	Taranaki (N)	Whangarei	77–3	Woodman (6), Davis (3), Savage, Nankivell, Nathan-Wong, Murray	Murray (5), Leaf			Larissa Collingwood
October 17	Bay of Plenty (N)	Mt Maunganui	32–0	Proctor, Woodman, Nathan-Wong, Murray, Ngata-Aerengamate	Leaf, Murray	Leaf		Brittany Andrew

OTAGO SPIRIT

2020 Status: South Pool
NPC participation: 1999–
Coach: Scott Manson
Assistant coaches: Aimee Sutorius, Jamie Angus
Home ground: Forsyth Barr Stadium

RECORDS

Most appearances	60	*Greer Muir, 2011–19*
Most points	221	*Claire Richardson, 2002–12*
Most tries	27	*Greer Muir, 2011–19*
Most points in a season	107	*Rosie Kelly, 2019*
Most tries in a season	11	*Annaleah Rush, 1999*
Most conversions in a season	32	*Rosie Kelly, 2019*
Most penalty goals in a season	12	*Hannah Myers, 2000*
Most dropped goals in a season	0	
Most points in a match	45	*Kelly Brazier v Hawke's Bay, 2012*
Most tries in a match	8	*Annaleah Rush v Mid/South Canterbury, 1999*
Most conversions in a match	10	*Kelly Brazier v Hawke's Bay, 2012*
		Rosie Kelly v North Harbour, 2019
Most penalty goals in a match	5	*Anika Tiplady v Auckland, 2013*
Highest team score	90	*v North Harbour, 2019*
Record victory (points ahead)	90	*90–0 v North Harbour, 2019*
Highest score conceded	86	*v Auckland, 2011*
Record defeat (points behind)	81	*5–86 v Auckland, 2011*

A lack of size and strength limited Otago Spirit's successes with the only wins being over Hawke's Bay and Tasman. However, the backline was enterprising with the 2019 players again in combination from Rosie Buchanan-Brown at halfback to Hinemoa Watene at fullback. They played a skilful and expansive game with Rosie Kelly a fine playmaker and Kilisitina Moata'ane outside her. The outstanding form of centre Amy du Plessis earned her a Black Ferns shirt late in the year. On one wing, Teilah Ferguson also had a fine season. Reserve halfback, 18-year-old Maia Joseph, improved with each outing. She is a daughter of well-known coach Jamie Joseph.

The forwards were also an unchanged combination, again led by hooker Tegan Hollows between props Eilis Doyle and Isla Pringle. Behind them were locks Julia Gorinski and Kate Smith who enjoyed an outstanding year. The regular loose forwards Morgan Henderson and Bree Thomas were joined by Zoe Whatarau who returned to the side after a season's absence. Two regular loose forwards to come off the bench were teenagers Leah Miles, a Tasman representative 2018–19, and Maddie Feaunati, daughter of Isaac Feaunati, the former Wellington, Crusaders and Samoa representative

Higher honours went to:
New Zealand: A. du Plessis
New Zealand Barbarians: M. Henderson, R. Kelly, K. Moata'ane

OTAGO REPRESENTATIVES 2020

	Club	Games for Union	Points for Union
France Bloomfield	Alhambra Union	4	0
Meg Breen	University	5	20
Rosie Buchanan-Brown	Alhambra Union	17	15
Lucy Cahill	University	2	0
Jamie Church	Alhambra Union	1	0
Paige Church	Alhambra Union	17	0
Cheyenne Cunningham	Waitaki	24	50
Eilis Doyle	Alhambra Union	37	5
Amy du Plessis	Alhambra Union	15	45
Maddie Feaunati	Alhambra Union	5	0
Teilah Ferguson	Alhambra Union	12	35
Julia Gorinski	University	41	15
Morgan Henderson	Waitaki	28	20
Tegan Hollows	University	38	35
Patricia Hopcroft	University	15	15
Maia Joseph	University	5	0
Rosie Kelly	University	20	192
Leah Miles	University	5	5
Gemma Millar	Pirates	14	0
Kilisitina Moata'ane	Pirates	41	130
Isla Pringle	University	24	10
Kate Smith	University	33	5
Bree Thomas	University	12	20
Rebecca Wairau	University	2	0
Hinemoa Watene	University	10	20
Kiana Wereta	Alhambra Union	26	55
Zoe Whatarau	Alhambra Union	35	10

INDIVIDUAL SCORING

	Tries	Con	PG	DG	Points
Kelly	4	11	–	–	42
Moata'ane	4	–	–	–	20
Ferguson	3	–	–	–	15
Breen	2	–	–	–	10
du Plessis	2	–	–	–	10
Thomas	2	–	–	–	10
Watene	2	–	–	–	10
Wetera	2	–	–	–	10
Penalty try	1	–	–	–	7
Hollows	1	–	–	–	5
Miles	1	–	–	–	5
Totals	**24***	**11**	**0**	**0**	**144**
Opposition scored	25*	18	7	0	184

* Includes one penalty try

OTAGO 2020

	Hawke's Bay	Canterbury	Tasman	Manawatu	Wellington	TOTALS
H.H. Watene	15	s	15	15	–	4
F.T. Bloomfield	s	15	s	s	–	4
K.M.P.Y. Wereta	14	14	–	14	11	4
P.A. Hopcroft	s	s	–	–	–	2
M.E. Breen	–	–	14	–	14	2
J.P. Church	–	–	s	–	–	1
T.N.W. Ferguson	11	11	11	11	12	5
C.B. Cunningham	–	–	–	s	s	2
A. du Plessis	13	13	13	13	15	5
K. Moata'ane	12	12	12	12	13	5
R.C. Kelly	10	10	10	10	10	5
R.M. Buchanan-Brown	9	9	9	9	s	5
M.R. Joseph	s	s	s	s	9	5
M.A. Henderson	8	8	8	8	8	5
Z.J.T. Whatarau	7	6	7	7	7	5
L.J. Miles	s	7	s	s	s	5
B-A.J. Thomas	6	s	6	6	6	5
M.R. Feaunati	s	s	s	s	s	5
J.F. Gorinski	5	5	5	5	5	5
K.E. Smith	4	4	4	4	4	5
R.L. Wairau	–	–	–	–	s	1
E.O. Doyle	3	3	1	3	3	5
P.L.L. Church	s	s	3	s	–	4
I.R. Pringle	1	1	–	1	1	4
L.E. Cahill	s	–	s	–	–	2
G.A. Millar	2	s	s	–	s	4
T.J. Hollows (capt)	–	2	2	2	2	4

Kelly and Whatarau were co-captains for the first game

OTAGO TEAM RECORD, 2020

Played 5   Won 2   Lost 3   Points for 144   Points against 184

Date	Opponent	Location	Score	Tries	Con	PG	DG	Referee
September 13	Hawke's Bay (S)	Dunedin	29–20	Moata'ane (2), Wereta, Ferguson, Kelly	Kelly (2)			Maggie Cogger-Orr
September 19	Canterbury (S, ST)	Christchurch	10–85	Kelly, du Plessis				Lauren Jenner
September 26	Tasman (S)	Nelson	67–24	Watene (2), Moata'ane (2), Thomas (2), du Plessis, Breen, Kelly, Ferguson, Miles	Kelly (6)			Jono Bredin
October 4	Manawatu (S)	Dunedin	14–28	Hollows, Kelly	Kelly (2)			Maggie Cogger-Orr
October 18	Wellington (S)	Porirua	24–27	Breen, Ferguson, Wetera, penalty try	Kelly			Larissa Collingwood

TARANAKI WHIO

2020 Status: North Pool
NPC participation: 2000–01, 2013, 2018–
Coach: Brendan Haami
Assistant coach: Devon Berry
Home ground: TET Stadium, Inglewood

RECORDS

Most appearances	23	*Leah Barnard, 2013–20; Victoria McCullough, 2013–20*
Most points	29	*Chelsea Fowler, 2019–20*
Most tries	5	*Iritana Hohaia 2019–20*
Most points in a season	29	*Chelsea Fowler, 2019*
Most tries in a season	4	*Michaela Blyde, 2013*
Most conversions in a season	7	*Chelsea Fowler, 2019*
Most penalty goals in a season	2	*Kate Broadmore, 2013*
Most dropped goals in a season	0	
Most points in a match	12	*Gayle Broughton v North Harbour 2020*
Most tries in a match	2	*Michaela Blyde v Manawatu, 2013*
		Iritana Hohaia v Tasman, 2019
		Iritana Hohaia v North Harbour, 2020
		Paige Neilson v Bay of Plenty, 2020
Most conversions in a match	3	*Chelsea Fowler v North Harbour, 2019*
Most penalty goals in a match	1	*Five times by four players*
Highest team score	32	*v North Harbour, 2020*
Record victory (points ahead)	3	*32–29 v North Harbour, 2020*
Highest score conceded	118	*v Wellington, 2018*
Record defeat (points behind)	118	*0–118 v Wellington, 2018*

Taranaki Whio celebrated their first ever win in the championship, against North Harbour at Inglewood. The historic victory was largely due to the leadership and direction of experienced Black Ferns Sevens player Gayle Broughton who contributed 12 points in the game. The team learned much from Broughton both on and off the field. The talented and highly promising Iritana Hohaia was also very influential with her two tries. Unfortunately, she missed the last three games with injury. Broughton also missed the final two games, with the captaincy being handed to Chelsea Fowler, the Canadian whose performances will attract the interest of the Canada selectors. Her high work-rate, speed to the breakdown and solidity on defence were features of her consistent form.

Four high school players — Chloe Sampson, Danielle Muggeridge, Paige Neilson, Kelsyn McCook — each played above and beyond their age and developed with each game to become consistent performers.

Prop Jaymi Ngaia and No 8 Tiana Davison had previously represented Manawatu. Team manager La Toya Mason provided experience with her two appearances. Having represented both North Harbour and Auckland, Mason headed for England where she made 70 appearances for England until returning home and taking up the position of Taranaki union's women's high performance manager.

Higher honours went to:
New Zealand Barbarians:	I. Hohaia
New Zealand Sevens:	G. Broughton

TARANAKI REPRESENTATIVES 2020

	Club	Games for Union	Points for Union
Leah Barnard	Coastal	23	0
Gayle Broughton	Southern	4	18
Sharee Brown	Southern	17	0
Mikaylah Callaghan	Clifton	7	0
Tiana Davison	Coastal	5	5
Freedom Edmonds	Clifton	9	0
Chelsea Fowler	Clifton	12	29
Tachelle Gardiner	Southern	5	0
Bronte Gorham	Southern	1	0
Natale-Ann Haupapa	Clifton	17	0
Iritana Hohaia	Southern	9	25
Kaya-Rose Kahui	Southern	11	10
Donia King	Southern	12	0
Kelsyn McCook	Southern	5	0
Victoria McCullough	Coastal	23	0
Alicia Manuirirangi	Southern	5	0
La Toya Mason	Inglewood United	2	3
Danielle Muggeridge	Coastal	4	0
Brooke Neilson	Inglewood United	8	0
Paige Neilson	Clifton	6	15
Jaymi Ngaia	Coastal	3	0
Catherine Parkinson	Coastal	11	0
Chloe Sampson	Clifton	6	13
Jalana Smith	Coastal	14	15
Lyn Smith	Southern	4	0
Kate Thomson	Southern	4	0
Catriona Tulloch	Southern	11	0
Aliena Wallis	Clifton	3	0
Sharniqua Weston-Jacobson	Southern	5	0
Nicole Whittle	Coastal	3	0
Sarah Winter	Southern	5	0

INDIVIDUAL SCORING

	Tries	Con	PG	DG	Points
Broughton	1	5	1	–	18
P. Neilson	3	–	–	–	15
Sampson	2	–	1	–	13
Hohaia	2	–	–	–	10
Davison	1	–	–	–	5
Kahui	1	–	–	–	5
Mason	–	–	1	–	3
Totals	**10**	**5**	**3**	**0**	**69**
Opposition scored	66*	34	0	0	400

* Includes one penalty try

TARANAKI 2020

	Auckland	Waikato	North Harbour	Bay of Plenty	Northland	Counties Manukau	TOTALS
D.G. Muggeridge	15	15	12	12	–	–	4
C. Parkinson	–	–	–	15	–	–	1
S.H. Weston-Jacobson	14	14	s	14	s	–	5
B.A. Neilson	–	–	–	–	s	14	2
C.S. Sampson	11	11	14	11	15	10	6
L. Smith	s	–	–	–	–	–	1
S.J. Winter	–	–	–	–	11	s	2
P.A. Neilson	13	13	13	s	13	13	6
K-R. Kahui	12	12	11	13	14	15	6
G.P. Broughton (capt)	10	10	10	10	–	–	4
L.R. Mason	–	–	–	s	10	–	2
I. Hohaia	9	s	15	–	–	–	3
K.A. McCook	–	9	9	9	9	9	5
T.L. Davison	8	8	8	8	8	–	5
C.M. Fowler	7	7	7	7	12	12	6
A.M. Manuirirangi	s	s	–	s	7	7	5
C.A. Tulloch	6	6	6	6	6	11	6
N-A. Haupapa	s	–	s	s	s	6	5
V.L. McCullough	5	5	4	4	5	5	6
F.S. Edmonds	–	s	5	5	–	s	4
S.E. Brown	4	4	s	s	4	4	6
A.N. Wallis	s	–	–	–	s	s	3
J.R. Smith	–	s	s	–	–	–	2
K.V. Thomson	3	1	s	–	–	–	3
L. Barnard	1	3	3	3	3	3	6
T.P.G. Gardiner	–	s	1	1	s	8	5
B.A.W. Gorham	–	s	–	–	–	–	1
J.A. Ngaia	–	–	–	s	1	1	3
M.T. Callaghan	–	–	–	–	–	s	1
D.J. King	2	2	2	2	2	2	6
N.J. Whittle	–	–	–	s	s	s	3

Chelsea Fowler was captain for the final two games

TTARANAKI TEAM RECORD, 2020

Played 6 Won 1 Lost 5 Points for 69 Points against 400

Date	Opponent	Location	Score	Tries	Con	PG	DG	Referee
September 6	Auckland (N)	Inglewood	0–38					Brittany Andrew
September 12	Waikato (N)	Hamilton	14–76	P. Neilson, Sampson	Broughton (2)			Lauren Jenner
September 19	North Harbour (N)	Inglewood	32–29	Hohaia (2), Kahui, Broughton, Sampson	Broughton (2)	Broughton		Tiana Ngawati
September 26	Bay of Plenty (N)	Mt Maunganui	17–73	P. Neilson (2), Davison	Broughton			Larissa Collingwood
October 11	Northland (N)	Whangarei	3–77			Mason		Larissa Collingwood
October 17	Counties Manukau (N)	Inglewood	3–107			Sampson		Tiana Ngawati

TASMAN MAKO

2020 Status: South Pool
NPC participation: 2017–
Coach: Mel Bosman
Assistant coach: Steve Curtis
Home Grounds: Trafalgar Park, Nelson; Lansdowne Park, Blenheim; Sports Park, Motueka

RECORDS

Most appearances	24	Stephanie Mitchell, 2017–20; Tamara Silcock, 2017–20
Most points	71	Hayley Hutana, 2018–19
Most tries	7	Wairakau Greig, 2017–19
Most points in a season	45	Hayley Hutana, 2019
Most tries in a season	6	Rebecca Kersten, 2019
Most conversions in a season	9	Hayley Hutana, 2018; Hayley Hutana, 2019
Most penalty goals in a season	4	Hayley Hutana, 2019
Most dropped goals in a season	0	
Most points in a match	15	Amelia Hammett v Taranaki, 2018
Most tries in a match	3	Amelia Hammett v Taranaki, 2018
Most conversions in a match	5	Hayley Hutana v Taranaki, 2018
Most penalty goals in a match	2	Hayley Hutana v North Harbour, 2019
Highest team score	65	v Taranaki, 2018
Record victory (points ahead)	53	65–12 v Taranaki, 2018
Highest score conceded	88	v Wellington, 2018; v Manawatu 2020
Record defeat (points behind)	88	0–88 v Manawatu 2020

It was a difficult season for the Mako having lost several players, including the air force pair Hayley Hutana and Wairakau Greig who were transferred to Whenuapai in North Harbour. The change in competition format to north-south pools meant further issues for Mako, a union still in its infancy in establishing a competitive Farah Palmer Cup squad. This resulted in heavy losses to the well-established teams. Many of the regular players were in their second or third championship seasons.

Timara Silcock had moved to Canterbury but was loaned back to Tasman and was the team's best performer. She was a consistently effective flanker. Blenheim-born and Motueka-educated Elisha Godsiff, also loaned from Canterbury, was the 'rookie' of the year, a 19-year-old who gave Silcock grand support in the loose. Other teenagers to impress were versatile back Eve Findlay, lock Jess Harvie and prop Alisi Seigafo. Bethan Manners showed improvement.

Taylor Curtis, daughter of assistant coach Steve Curtis, and twin sister of Canterbury wing Sam Curtis, was loaned from Auckland

Higher honours went to:
New Zealand Sevens: R.I.R. Pouri-Lane

TASMAN REPRESENTATIVES 2020

	Club	Games for Union	Points for Union
Pallas Andrew	Waimea OB	4	0
Pippa Andrews	Moutere	16	5
Anna Bradley	Waimea OB	18	10
Michelle Curry	Wanderers	17	20
Taylor Curtis	Marist[1]	4	0
Stacey Davis	Waimea OB	9	0
Alesha Dempster	Waimea OB	8	0
Eve Findlay	Waimea OB	5	10
Amanda Fitisemanu	Riwaka	1	0
Tanita Garnet	Riwaka	1	0
Hannah Gillespie	Moutere	16	0
Elisha Godsiff	HSOB[2]	5	0
Jess Harvie	Waimea OB	6	0
Gina Healey	Wanderers	11	
Hopaea Hillman	Central	1	0
Diane Huntley	Moutere	3	0
Rebecca Kersten	Lincoln Univ[2]	8	30
Bethan Manners	Waimea OB	11	5
Stephani Mitchell	Waimea OB	24	15
Louise Nalder	Waimea OB	16	0
Meika Newman	Waimea OB	2	0
Jamie Paenga	Waimea OB	14	0
Demi Salton	Waimea OB	17	5
Anya Schultz	University[3]	9	0
Alisi Seigafo	Wanderers	4	0
Tamara Silcock	Christchurch[2]	24	10
Ariana Te Kawa-Wiremu	Waimea OB	2	0
Ashley Ulutupu	Wanderers	9	5
Sydnee Wilkins	University[4]	15	15

1 Auckland RU 2 Canterbury RU 3 Otago RU 4 Manawatu RU

INDIVIDUAL SCORING

	Tries	Con	PG	DG	Points
Mitchell	2	–	–	–	10
Andrews	1	–	–	–	5
Bradley	1	–	–	–	5
Ulutupu	1	–	–	–	5
Findlay	–	2	–	–	4
Totals	**5**	**2**	**0**	**0**	**29**
Opposition scored	59	34	0	0	363

TASMAN 2020

	Wellington	Manawatu	Otago	Hawke's Bay	Canterbury	TOTALS
E.G.S. Findlay	15	15	14	11	13	**5**
B. Manners	s	10	15	15	15	**5**
R.L. Kersten	14	–	–	–	–	**1**
T.R.B. Curtis	10	s	–	14	14	**4**
S.L. Wilkins	11	11	11	s	9	**5**
M.A. Curry	s	14	13	13	11	**5**
A.T.R.C. Te Kawa-Wiremu	–	–	s	s	–	**2**
A.J. Fitisemanu	–	–	s	–	–	**1**
A.A. Dempster	13	13	s	s	s	**5**
D.J. Salton	12	12	12	12	s	**5**
A.M. Schultz	–	s	10	10	10	**4**
J.E.S. Paenga	9	s	–	–	12	**3**
P.S. Andrews	s	9	9	9	s	**5**
L.A. Nalder	8	8	8	8	1	**6**
P.A.V. Andrew	s	s	–	s	8	**4**
T.L. Silcock	7	7	7	7	7	**5**
E.M. Godsiff	6	6	6	6	6	**5**
H.L. Hillman	–	–	s	–	–	**1**
H.E. Gillespie	5	–	5	5	s	**4**
J.M. Harvie	s	5	s	s	5	**5**
G.L. Healey	4	4	4	4	4	**5**
T.J. Garnet	–	–	–	–	s	**1**
A.M. Bradley (capt)	3	3	1	1	3	**5**
A.J. Seigafo	1	s	3	–	s	**4**
A.M. Ulutupu	s	s	s	3	–	**4**
S.L. Davis	s	1	–	s	–	**3**
D.G. Huntley	–	s	s	s	–	**3**
S.L. Mitchell	2	2	2	2	s	**5**
M.L. Newman	–	–	–	–	2	**1**

TASMAN TEAM RECORD, 2020

Played 5 Lost 5 Points for 29 Points against 363

Date	Opponent	Location	Score	Tries	Con	PG	DG	Referee
September 12	Wellington (S)	Blenheim	0–62					Brittany Andrew
September 20	Manawatu (S)	Palmerston North	0–88					Nick Hogan
September 26	Otago (S)	Nelson	24–67	Mitchell (2), Bradley, Ulutupu	Findlay (2)			Jono Bredin
October 4	Hawke's Bay (S)	Motueka	5–62	Andrews				Larissa Collingwood
October 17	Canterbury (S, ST)	Christchurch	0–84					Maggie Cogger-Orr

WAIKATO

2020 Status: North Pool
NPC participation: 1999–2005, 2012–
Coach: James Semple
Assistant coach: Cody Price
Home Grounds: Waikato University (v Northland);
FMG Stadium Waikato; Putaruru RFC

RECORDS

Most appearances	44	Victoria Edmonds, 2012–18
		Chelsea Alley, 2012–20
Most points	393	Chelsea Alley, 2012–20
Most tries	31	Stacey Fluhler 2014–20
Most points in a season	81	Chelsea Alley, 2014
Most tries in a season	11	Stacey Waaka, 2014
Most conversions in a season	21	Chelsea Alley, 2014, 2018
Most penalty goals in a season	12	Chelsea Alley, 2013
Most dropped goals in a season	1	Emma Jensen, 2000
		Chelsea Alley, 2019
Most points in a match	20	Chelsea Alley v Taranaki, 2020
Most tries in a match	3	Jordon Webber v Manawatu, 2012;
		Honey Hireme v Manawatu, 2014;
		Stacey Waaka v Canterbury, 2014;
		v Bay of Plenty, 2015
		v North Harbour, 2020
Most conversions in a match	5	Chelsea Alley v Manawatu, 2014;
		v Bay of Plenty, 2014;
		v Auckland, 2018;
		v Taranaki, 2020;
		Tenika Willison v North Harbour, 2020
Most penalty goals in a match	4	Emma Jensen v Northland, 2000
		Tenika Willison v North Harbour, 2016
Highest team score	76	v Taranaki 2020
Record victory (points ahead)	62	76–14 v Taranaki 2020;
		62–0 v North Harbour 2020
Highest score conceded	78	v Auckland, 2002
Record defeat (points behind)	78	0–78 v Auckland, 2002

Waikato were just one breakdown away from winning their first Farah Palmer Cup title. An outstanding season, the best ever, Waikato were unbeaten when meeting defending champions Canterbury at Christchurch's Rugby Park for the final. Having scored a try in the 64th minute to take a 7–3 lead, Waikato hung on until seconds before fulltime before they were penalised and lost possession. After much desperate defence as Canterbury hammered the line, the home team finally managed to crash across the line to snatch victory in the 82nd minute. It was a shattering blow for Waikato but they could reflect on a magnificent campaign.

The experienced Chelsea Alley again led the team, the backline being greatly strengthened with the availability of sevens specialists Stacey Fluhler, Cheyelle Robins-Reti and Tenika Willison. The speed and skills of Fluhler and Robins-Reti on the wings resulted in the pair contributing 14 tries, the latter winning Black Ferns selection. Fullback Renee Holmes was also outstanding and rewarded with Black Ferns selection. Halfback Ariana Bayler was a fine distributer of the ball to the quality backline. Out wide Makaia Riki-Te Kanawa appeared in every game, the majority being from the bench.

Waikato were fortunate to have the availability of 25-test veteran Carla Hohepa. The 35-year-old first represented Otago in 2006 and had returned north to her home province, but 2020 was the first year she has given Waikato a full season. Her previous appearances for Waikato were in 2012, but recent years had been spent with commitments to the Black Ferns, Black Ferns Sevens, raising a family and supporting her husband Karne Hesketh playing in Japan.

No 8 Kennedy Simon was the outstanding forward and the squad's player of the year. She was well supported by experienced flankers Emma-Lee Heta and Ashlee Gaby-Sutherland. Sina Tetet was a regular off the bench. It was a strong front row, comprising Grace Houpapa-Barrett, Toka Natua and Tanya Kalounivale, the last mentioned gaining Black Ferns honours late in the year. Eighteen-year-old Mia Anderson secured one of the lock positions, the former Northland player was the team's 'Emerging' player of the year. The other lock position was shared between Chyna Hohepa and Leomie Kloppers.

Higher honours went to:
New Zealand: Alley, R. Holmes, T. Kalounivale, T. Natua, C. Robins-Reti, K. Simon
New Zealand Barbarians: A. Bayler, G. Houpapa-Barrett
New Zealand Sevens: S. Fluhler, J.A-M.A. Hotham, S.T. Kaka, T. Willison

WAIKATO REPRESENTATIVES 2020

	Club	Games for Union	Points for Union		Club	Games for Union	Points for Union
Chelsea Alley	University	44	393	Tanya Kalounivale	Hamilton OB	21	15
Mia Anderson	Melville	8	15	Daeja-Bernice Kaponga	Putaruru	3	0
Ariana Bayler	Hamilton OB	38	47	Leomie Kloppers	Hamilton OB	18	0
Tyra Begbie	Putaruru	3	0	Stephanie Lualua	Hamilton OB	8	0
Hannah Brough	Otorohanga	8	25	Toka Natua	University	36	25
Taiari Cassidy	Otorohanga	1	0	Kiriana Nolan	Melville	5	5
Tafiau Fetalaiga	Hamilton OB	1	0	Manaia Nuku	Melville	2	5
Stacey Fluhler	Melville	26	155	Merania Paraone	Kihikihi	7	10
Ashlee Gaby-Sutherland	Melville	28	20	Makaia Riki-Te Kanawa	Hamilton OB	29	35
Emma-Lee Heta	Kihikihi	29	10	Cheyelle Robins-Reti	Melville	14	34
Sina Hetet	Otorohanga	6	0	Kennedy Simon	Hamilton OB	25	20
Renee Holmes	Hamilton OB	14	19	Kelsey Teneti	Hamilton OB	2	5
Carla Hohepa	Kihikihi	9	15	Esther Tilo-Faiaoga	Melville	16	0
Chyna Hohepa	Kihikihi	28	15	Tenika Willison	Otorohanga	18	52
Grace Houpapa-Barrett	Melville	28	35				

INDIVIDUAL SCORING

	Tries	Con	PG	DG	Points		Tries	Con	PG	DG	Points
Alley	4	17	5	–	69	Simon	2	–	–	–	10
Fluhler	8	–	–	–	40	Penalty try	1	–	–	–	7
Robins-Reti	6	–	–	–	30	Bayler	1	–	–	–	5
Anderson	3	–	–	–	15	Gaby-Sutherland	1	–	–	–	5
Houpapa-Barrett	3	–	–	–	15	Carla Hohepa	1	–	–	–	5
Willison	–	7	–	–	14	Nuku	1	–	–	–	5
Holmes	2	–	–	–	10	Teneti	1	–	–	–	5
Kalounivale	2	–	–	–	10	**Totals**	**42***	**24**	**5**	**0**	**275**
Natua	2	–	–	–	10						
Paraone	2	–	–	–	10						
Riki-Te Kanawa	2	–	–	–	10	Opposition scored	13	11	3	0	96

* Includes one penalty try

WAIKATO 2020

	Northland	Taranaki	Bay of Plenty	Counties Manukau	North Harbour	Auckland	Manawatu	Canterbury	TOTALS
R.M.M. Holmes	15	15	15	15	15	15	15	15	8
H.L. Brough	14	–	–	–	–	–	–	–	1
C.R.A. Robins-Reti	s	14	14	14	14	14	14	14	8
M.C. Nuku	11	–	–	–	s	–	–	–	2
S.J.A.K. Fluhler	–	11	11	11	13	11	11	11	7
T.K. Begbie	–	s	–	–	–	–	–	–	1
K.J. Teneti	–	–	–	–	s	–	s	–	2
M.A. Riki-Te Kanawa	13	13	s	s	11	s	s	s	8
C.G.T.O. Hohepa	–	s	13	13	–	13	13	13	6
C.H. Alley (capt)	12	12	12	12	12	12	12	12	8
K.L.A. Nolan	–	s	–	s	s	–	–	–	3
T.R. Willison	10	10	10	10	10	10	10	10	8
A.J. Bayler	9	9	9	9	9	9	9	9	8
K.W. Simon	8	8	8	7	8	8	8	8	8
E-L. Heta	7	7	7	7	s	7	7	7	8
S.T. Hetet	6	–	s	s	6	s	s	–	6
A.J. Gaby-Sutherland	s	6	6	6	8	6	6	6	8
Chyna Hohepa	5	–	–	–	5	4	4	4	5
M.T. Anderson	s	5	5	5	s	5	5	5	8
D.B. Kaponga	4	s	–	s	–	–	–	–	3
L. Kloppers	–	4	4	4	4	s	s	s	7
T.M. Cassidy	–	s	–	–	–	–	–	–	1
T.J.M. Kalounivale	3	3	–	3	–	3	3	3	6
E. Tilo-Faiaoga	s	s	3	s	3	s	s	–	7
T. Fetalaiga	–	–	s	–	–	–	–	–	1
T.I. Natua	1	1	1	1	1	1	1	1	8
S.N. Lualua	–	–	s	s	s	s	s	s	6
G. Houpapa-Barrett	2	2	2	2	s	2	2	2	8
M.M.K. Paraone	–	s	s	s	2	s	s	s	7

WAIKATO TEAM RECORD, 2020

Played 8 Won 7 Lost 1 Points for 275 Points against 96

Date	Opponent	Location	Score	Tries	Con	PG	DG	Referee
September 5	Northland (N)	Hamilton	18–5	Anderson, Alley	Alley	Alley (2)		Maggie Cogger-Orr
September 12	Taranaki (N)	Hamilton	76–14	Alley (2), Robins-Reti (2), Houpapa-Barrett (2), Fluhler, Kalounivale, Natua, penalty try, Bayler, Paraone	Alley (5), Willison (2)			Lauren Jenner
September 19	Bay of Plenty (N)	Rotorua	21–10	Robins-Reti (2), Fluhler		Alley (2)		Rebecca Mahoney
October 3	Counties Manukau (N)	Putaruru	34–28	Fluhler, Simon, Holmes, Robins-Reti, Carla Hohepa	Alley (3)	Alley		Rebecca Mahoney
October 10	North Harbour (N)	Albany	62–0	Fluhler (3), Riki-Te Kanawa (2), Paraone, Gaby-Sutherland, Houpapa-Barrett, Teneti, Nuku	Willison (5), Alley			Brittany Andrew
October 18	Auckland (N)	Auckland	26–17	Anderson (2), Holmes, Natua	Alley (3)			Rebecca Mahoney
October 25	Manawatu (semi-final)	Hamilton	31–14	Fluhler (3), Alley, Kalounivale, Robins-Reti	Alley (3)			Maggie Cogger-Orr
October 31	Canterbury (final)	Christchurch	7–8	Simon	Alley			Rebecca Mahoney

WELLINGTON PRIDE

2020 Status: South Pool
NPC participation: 1999–
Coach: Ross Bond
Assistant coaches: Aaron Jones, Brendan Reidy
Home grounds: Hutt Recreation Ground; Sky Stadium; Porirua Park

RECORDS

Most appearances	62	*Jackie Patea-Fereti, 2006–20*
Most points	235	*Ayesha Leti-I'iga, 2015–20*
Most tries	46	*Ayesha Leti-I'iga 2015–20*
Most points in a season	118	*Amanda Rasch, 2018*
Most tries in a season	12	*Ayesha Leti-I'iga, 2019*
Most conversions in a season	21	*Elizabeth Goulden, 2015*
Most penalty goals in a season	46	*Amanda Rasch, 2018*
Most dropped goals in a season	0	
Most points in a match	43	*Amanda Rasch v Taranaki, 2018*
Most tries in a match	5	*Ayesha Leti-I'iga v Manawatu, 2019*
Most conversions in a match	14	*Amanda Rasch v Taranaki, 2018*
Most penalty goals in a match	5	*Elizabeth Goulden v Taranaki, 2013*
Highest team score	118	*v Taranaki, 2018*
Record victory (points ahead)	118	*118–0 v Taranaki, 2018*
Highest score conceded	65	*v Auckland, 2012*
Record defeat (points behind)	65	*0–65 v Auckland, 2012*

Wellington Pride were again a strong and experienced team but the loss to an improving Manawatu side at Sky Stadium denied any chance of a semi-final position. Wellington hammered the Manawatu line during the final minutes but the determined Manawatu defence managed to hold out until the end and the visitors won 31–28.

Only four players were new to the Pride, reserve hooker Alia Ah Far, flanker Evelyn Tea, wing Josephine Falesita, and former Auckland and Black Ferns lock Charlene Gubb. Many of the squad had been in the side for six years or more and compiled over 25 appearances. Jackie Patea-Fereti made her debut in 2006 while Acacia Claridge-Te Iwimate and Sanita Levave made their debuts in 2008.

Wing Lyric Faleafaga, lock and captain Joanah Ngan-Woo and flanker Marcelle Parkes appeared for the Barbarians against the Black Ferns. Centre Monica Tagoai was also selected but withdrew with injury.

Oriental Rongotai were undefeated in the nine-team round-robin club championship and were awarded the championship. No final was played.

Higher honours went to:
New Zealand Barbarians: L. Faleafaga, J. Ngan-Woo, M. Parkes

WELLINGTON REPRESENTATIVES 2020

	Club	Games for Union	Points for Union		Club	Games for Union	Points for Union
Ana-Maria Afuie	Marist St Pats	17	5	Kolora Lomani	Northern United	9	35
Alia Ah Far	Paremata-Plimmerton	1	0	Fa'asua Makisi	Oriental Rongotai	44	20
Precious Auimatangi	Oriental Rongotai	8	0	Vaine Marsters	Northern United	35	35
Tyler Bentley	Hutt OB Marist	2	5	Thamsyn Newton	OB University	9	66
Acacia Claridge-Te Iwimate	Paremata-Plimmerton	55	62	Joanah Ngan-Woo	Oriental Rongotai	53	70
Georgia Daals	OB University	30	75	Marcelle Parkes	Marist St Pats	8	0
Emily Dalley	OB University	9	0	Jackie Patea-Fereti	Petone	62	85
Dhys Faleafaga	Northern United	9	35	Alicia Print	Petone	32	15
Lyric Faleafaga	Marist St Pats	5	15	Alice Soper	Petone	29	5
Josephine Falesita	Oriental Rongotai	1	0	Monica Tagoai	Marist St Pats	22	45
Nina Foaese	Northern United	16	5	Barbra Taumoli	Oriental Rongotai	10	0
Charlene Gubb	Oriental Rongotai	5	5	Janet Taumoli	Oriental Rongotai	32	15
Montana Heslop	OB University	13	5	Evelyn Tea	Oriental Rongotai	3	0
Isadora Laupola	Northern United	13	20	Sinead Toala-Ryder	Oriental Rongotai	22	30
Ayesha Leti-I'iga	Oriental Rongotai	34	230	Angelica Uila	Petone	20	40
Sanita Levave	Northern United	55	25	Rejieli Uluinayau	Oriental Rongotai	25	15
Raylene Lolo	Oriental Rongotai	24	20				

INDIVIDUAL SCORING

	Tries	Con	PG	DG	Points		Tries	Con	PG	DG	Points
Newton	3	19	2	–	59	Gubb	1	–	–	–	5
Leti-I'iga	5	–	–	–	25	Laupola	1	–	–	–	5
D. Faleafaga	4	–	–	–	20	Makisi	1	–	–	–	5
L. Faleafaga	3	–	–	–	15	Patea-Fereti	1	–	–	–	5
Lomani	2	–	–	–	10	Uila	1	–	–	–	5
Ngan-Woo	2	–	–	–	10						
Tagoai	2	–	–	–	10	**Totals**	**30***	**19**	**2**	**0**	**196**
Toala-Ryder	2	–	–	–	10						
Penalty try	1	–	–	–	7	Opposition scored	19*	10	3	0	126
Daals	1	–	–	–	5						

* Includes one penalty try

WELLINGTON 2020

	Tasman	Hawke's Bay	Manawatu	Canterbury	Otago	TOTALS
T.M.M. Newton	15	15	15	15	15	5
K.R. Lomani	14	–	–	–	14	2
L. Faleafaga	–	14	14	14	–	3
A.A. Leti-I'iga	–	11	11	11	11	4
M.F. Tagoai	13	13	13	13	13	5
E.J. Dalley	s	–	s	s	s	4
J. Falesita	–	s	–	–	–	1
F.A.R.M. Makisi	12	12	12	–	s	4
G.L. Daals	11	–	–	12	12	3
T. Bentley	s	–	–	–	–	1
M. Heslop	10	10	s	10	10	5
V.A. Marsters	–	s	10	–	–	2
A.M. Claridge-Te Iwimate	9	9	9	9	s	5
R. Uluinayau	s	–	s	–	9	3
A-M. Afuie	–	s	–	s	–	2
D.S. Faleafaga	8	8	8	–	–	3
S. Toala-Ryder	7	s	7	7	7	5
M.J. Parkes	s	7	s	s	6	5
N. Foaese	6	6	6	6	8	5
E.L. Tea	–	s	–	s	s	3
J.S. Patea-Fereti	5	–	–	–	–	1
C.P.T. Gubb	s	5	5	5	5	5
J.M.P. Ngan-Woo (capt)	4	4	4	8	4	5
S.D. Levave	–	–	s	4	–	2
J. Taumoli	3	–	–	3	–	2
I.T. Laupola	s	3	3	s	s	5
A. Uila	1	–	–	s	1	3
R. Lolo	–	1	1	1	–	3
B. Taumoli	–	s	s	–	s	3
P.S. Auimatagi	2	2	2	2	2	5
A. Soper	s	–	s	s	–	3
A. Print	–	s	–	–	s	2
A.M.M. Ah Far	–	–	–	–	s	1

Patea-Fereti was captain in first game.

WELLINGTON TEAM RECORD, 2020

				Played 5	Won 3	Lost 2	Points for 196		Points against 126
Date	Opponent	Location	Score	Tries		Con	PG	DG	Referee
September 12	Tasman (S)	Blenheim	62–0	D. Faleafaga (3), Tagoai, Patea-Fereti, Newton, Gubb, Ngan-Woo, Laupolo, Toala-Ryder		Newton (6)			Brittany Andrew
September 19	Hawke's Bay (S)	Lower Hutt	67–17	Leti-I'iga (4), L. Faleafaga (3), Newton, D. Faleafaga, Makisi, Toala-Ryder		Newton (6)			Jono Bredin
September 25	Manawatu (S)	Wellington	28–31	Newton, Leti-I'iga, penalty try, Ngan-Woo		Newton (3)			Michael Winter
October 3	Canterbury (S, ST)	Christchurch	12–54	Daals, Uila		Newton			Lauren Jenner
October 18	Otago (S)	Porirua	27–24	Lomani (2), Tagoai		Newton (3)	Newton (2)		Larissa Collingwood

WOMEN'S FIRST-CLASS STATISTICS
to January 1, 2021

100 GAMES IN FIRST-CLASS RUGBY

	Career	Games		Career	Games
Emma Jensen	1999–2020	176	Anna Richards	1990–2011	125
Fiao'o Faamausili	1999–2018	164	Casey Robertson	1999–2014	118
Justine Lavea	2001–20	152	Aleisha Nelson	2008–20	112
Kendra Cocksedge	2007–20	147	Eloise Blackwell	2009–20	110
Stephanie Te Ohaere-Fox	2003–19	128	Linda Itunu	2003–19	101
Selica Winiata	2001–20	128			

300 POINTS IN FIRST-CLASS RUGBY

	Career	Games	Tries	Con	PG	DG	Points
Kendra Cocksedge	2007–20	147	79	317	98	1	1326
Selica Winiata	2001–20	128	111	63	14	–	723
Emma Jensen	1999–20	176	12	148	81	1	602
Hannah Porter	1999–2008	59	20	115	61	–	513
Chelsea Alley	2011–20	81	28	97	44	1	469
Tammi Wilson	1998–2001	45	40	92	24	1	459
Kelly Brazier	2005–20	77	35	92	29	–	446
Hazel Tubic	2005–20	74	23	130	23	–	444
Claire Richardson	2001–14	79	36	33	25	–	321
Fiao'o Faamausili	1999–2018	164	63	–		–	315

45 TRIES IN FIRST-CLASS RUGBY

	Tries	Games		Tries	Games
Selica Winiata	111	128	Victoria Grant	51	69
Kendra Cocksedge	79	147	Renee Wickliffe	51	76
Fiao'o Faamausili	63	164	Carla Hohepa	49	56
Vanessa Cootes	54	50	Ayesha Leti-I'iga	49	49
Dianne Kahura	53	35	Louisa Wall	48	32

MOST DROPPED GOALS IN FIRST-CLASS RUGBY

	DG	Games
Rebecca Mahoney (*nee* Hull)	4	69

100 POINTS IN A SEASON

	Teams	M	Tries	Con	PG	DG	Total
Kendra Cocksedge	Canterbury/NZ, 2018	13	13	45	6	–	173
Kendra Cocksedge	Canterbury/NZ, 2017	14	11	52	4	–	171
Tammi Wilson	Auckland/NZ, 1999	10	15	34	4	–	155
Kendra Cocksedge	Canterbury/NZ, 2016	12	11	32	12	–	155
Kendra Cocksedge	Canterbury/NZ 2019	13	4	39	17	1	152
Kendra Cocksedge	Canterbury/NZ, 2014	17	5	32	16	–	137
Tammi Wilson	Auckland/NZ, 2002	11	8	20	14	1	125
Rosie Kelly	Otago/NZ Development 2019	9	9	37	1	–	122
Amanda Rasch	Wellington, 2018	8	4	46	2	–	118
Selica Winiata	Manawatu/NZ, 2012	9	15	17	2	–	115
Hannah Myers	Auckland/NZ, 2003	7	6	25	9	–	107
Hannah Myers	Auckland/NZ, 2005	12	4	27	11	–	107

MOST TRIES IN A SEASON

	Teams	Tries	Games
Dianne Kahura	Auckland/NZ, 2002	19	11
Vanessa Cootes	New Zealand, 1996	18	3
Selica Winiata	Manawatu/NZ, 2016	18	11
Mele Hufanga	Auckland 2015	16	7
Portia Woodman	New Zealand, 2017	16	8
Tammi Wilson	Auckland/NZ, 1999	15	10
Selica Winiata	Manawatu/NZ, 2012	15	9
Selica Winiata	Manawatu/NZ, 2014	15	13

MOST POINTS IN A GAME

	Match	Tries	Con	PG	DG	Points
Vanessa Cootes	New Zealand v France, 1996	9	–	–	–	45
Kelly Brazier	Otago v Hawke's Bay, 2012	5	10	–	–	45
Amanda Rasch	Wellington v Taranaki, 2018	3	14	–	–	43
Annaleah Rush	Otago v Hanan Shield Unions, 1999	8	1	–	–	42
Portia Woodman	New Zealand v Hong Kong, 2017	8	–	–	–	40
Selica Winiata	Manawatu v Waikato, 2012	4	6	2	–	38
Tammi Wilson	New Zealand v USA, 1999	6	3	–	–	36
Christine Ross	New Zealand v France, 1996	2	12	–	–	34
Kelly Brazier	Otago v Manawatu, 2009	4	7	–	–	34
Tammi Wilson	Auckland v North Harbour, 1999	1	13	–	–	31
Kendra Cocksedge	New Zealand v Hong Kong, 2017	1	13	–	–	31
Ruahei Demant	Auckland v Tasman, 2018	3	8	–	–	31
Tammi Wilson	New Zealand v Germany, 1998	4	5	–	–	30
Kendra Cocksedge	Canterbury v Taranaki, 2013	4	5	–	–	30
Kendra Cocksedge	Canterbury v North Harbour, 2016	4	5	–	–	30
Rosie Kelly	Otago v North Harbour 2019	2	10	–	–	30
Portia Woodman	Northland v Taranaki 2020	6	–	–	–	30

MOST TRIES IN A GAME

	Match	Tries
Vanessa Cootes	New Zealand v France, 1996	9
Annaleah Rush	Otago v Hanan Shield Unions, 1999	8
Portia Woodman	New Zealand v Hong Kong, 2017	8
Portia Woodman	Northland v Taranaki, 2020	6
Tammi Wilson	New Zealand v USA, 1999	6
Helen Reader	New Zealand v New South Wales, 1994	5
Vanessa Cootes	New Zealand v USA, 1996	5
Vanessa Cootes	New Zealand v USA, 1998	5
Vanessa Cootes	New Zealand v Germany, 2002	5
Deidre Hakopa	Hawke's Bay v Southland, 2003	5
Kelly Brazier	Otago v Hawke's Bay, 2012	5
Selica Winiata	New Zealand v Samoa, 2014	5
Kilisitina Moata'ane	Otago v Tasman, 2017	5
Ayesha Leti-I'iga	Wellington v Manawatu 2019	5

MOST CONVERSIONS IN A GAME

	Match	Con
Amanda Rasch	Wellington v Taranaki, 2018	14
Tammi Wilson	Auckland v North Harbour, 1999	13
Kendra Cocksedge	New Zealand v Hong Kong, 2017	13
Christine Ross	New Zealand v France, 1996	12
Hazel Tubic	Counties Manukau v Taranaki, 2020	11
Kelly Brazier	Otago v Hawke's Bay, 2012	10
Rosie Kelly	Otago v North Harbour 2019	10

MOST PENALTY GOALS IN A GAME

	Match	PG
Annaleah Rush	Auckland v Wellington, 2001	6
Kendra Cocksedge	Canterbury v Auckland, 2009	5
Elizabeth Goulden	Wellington v Taranaki, 2013	5
Kendra Cocksedge	Canterbury v Waikato, 2016	5
Kaitlin Bates	Hawke's Bay v Otago 2020	5

HIGHEST TEAM SCORES

Score	Match	Result
134	New Zealand v Germany, 1998	134-6
131	NZ Development v Papua New Guinea, 2019	131–0
121	New Zealand v Hong Kong, 2017	121-0
118	Wellington v Taranaki, 2018	118-0
117	New Zealand v Germany, 2002	117-0
116	Auckland v North Harbour, 1999	116-0
109	New Zealand v France, 1996	109-0
107	Counties Manukau v Taranaki 2020	107–3
101	Auckland v Bay of Plenty 2015	101-0
100	Hawke's Bay v Southland, 2003	100-5

WOMEN'S RUGBY REFEREES 2020
by Chris Jansen

WOMEN'S RUGBY REFEREE SQUAD 2020

	Union	Squad Debut	Tests	SR	P	HC	FPC	Sevens	Nat[1]	Prov[2]	RS[3]	Total
B.J. Andrew	Manawatu	2015	–	–	–	–	23	2	1	–	–	26
M.C. Cogger-Orr	Auckland	2017	–	–	–	–	24	2	–	–	–	26
L.J. Collingwood	Waikato	2018	–	–	–	–	9	2	–	–	–	11
E.K. Hsieh	Wellington	2019	–	–	–	–	–	4	–	–	–	4
L.M. Jenner	Counties-Manukau	2017	–	–	–	–	22	11	–	–	–	33
R.M. Mahoney	Wairarapa-Bush	2015	9	–	1	5	28	12	5	–	1	60
T.A. Ngawati	Bay of Plenty	2019	–	–	–	–	3	2	–	–	–	5
S.C. Winiata	Manawatu	2019	–	–	–	–	–	5	–	–	–	5

P   Mitre 10 Cup
HC   Heartland Championship
FPC Farah Palmer Cup
Nat1 NZR appointment — international tour, Ranfurly Shield (non-Mitre 10 Cup), national trial, and women's international.

REFEREE APPOINTMENTS 2020

Brittany Andrew

September	6	FPC	Taranaki v Auckland	Inglewood
	12	FPC	Tasman v Wellington	Blenheim
October	10	FPC	North Harbour v Waikato	Warkworth
	17	FPC	Bay of Plenty v Northland	Mt Maunganui

Maggie Cogger – Orr

September	5	FPC	Waikato v Northland	Hamilton
	13	FPC	Otago v Hawke's Bay	Dunedin
October	4	FPC	Otago v Manawatu	Dunedin
	10	FPC	Counties Manukau v Bay of Plenty	Pukekohe
	17	FPC	Canterbury v Tasman	Christchurch
	25	FPC s-f	Waikato v Manawatu	Hamilton

Larissa Collingwood

September	26	FPC	Bay of Plenty v Taranaki	Mt Maunganui
October	3	FPC	Tasman v Hawke's Bay	Motueka
	11	FPC	Northland v Taranaki	Whangarei
	17	FPC	Wellington v Otago	Porirua

Emily Hsieh

January	26/27		New Zealand World Rugby Sevens	Hamilton
February	2/3		Australia World Rugby Sevens	Sydney

Lauren Jenner

September	12	FPC	Waikato v Taranaki	Hamilton
	19	FPC	Canterbury v Otago	Christchurch
	26	FPC	North Harbour v Auckland	Albany
October	3	FPC	Canterbury v Wellington	Christchurch

		17	FPC	Hawke's Bay v Manawatu	Napier
		24	FPC s-f	Canterbury v Auckland	Christchurch

Rebecca Mahoney

	12	FPC	Manawatu v Canterbury	Palmerston North
September	19	FPC	Bay of Plenty v Waikato	Rotorua
	26	FPC	Hawke's Bay v Canterbury	Napier
October	3	FPC	Waikato v Counties Manukau	Putaruru
	18	FPC	Auckland v Waikato	Auckland
	31	FPC f	Canterbury v Waikato	Christchurch
November	14	WRWCQ	Samoa v Tonga	Auckland
	21		NZ Black Ferns v NZ Barbarians	Nelson

Tiana Ngawati

September	19	FPC	Taranaki v North Harbour	Inglewood
October	3	FPC	Northland v North Harbour	Whangarei
	17	FPC	Taranaki v Counties Manukau	Inglewood

Selica Winiata

January	26/27	New Zealand World Rugby Sevens	Hamilton
February	2/3	Australia World Rugby Sevens	Sydney

2020 INTERNATIONAL REFEREES

R.M. Mahoney   2016: Hong Kong v Japan (WRWCQ); 2018: Ireland v USA, Wales v Canada; 2019: Fiji v Hong Kong, USA v Canada, Ireland v Wales, England v France; Fiji v Samoa (WRWCQ); 2020: Samoa v Tonga (WRWCQ);

INTERNATIONAL ASSISTANT REFEREES

Maggie Cogger-Orr
November	14	WRWCQ	Samoa v Tonga	Auckland

Lee Jeffrey
November	14	WRWCQ	Samoa v Tonga (TMO)	Auckland

Lauren Jenner
November	14	WRWCQ	Samoa v Tonga	Auckland

(TMO)   Television Match Official

INTERNATIONAL REFEREES
to 1 January, 2021

Beard, J.D.L. (Counties Manukau) 2014–16	10
Inwood, N.A. (Wanganui & Canterbury) 2002–14	32
Mahoney, R.M. (Wairarapa Bush) 2016–20	9
Mellor, K.E. (North Harbour) 2006	1

TWENTY-FIVE AND MORE FIRST-CLASS MATCHES
to 1 January, 2021

N.A. Inwood (Ewins)	2000-14	86	C.F. Gurr	2011-16	37
R.M. Mahoney	2015-19	60	L.M. Jenner	2017–20	33
J.D.L. Beard	2012-16	50	B.J. Andrew	2015–20	26
L. Jeffrey	2003-16	42	M.C. Cogger-Orr	2017–20	26

MOST INTERNATIONAL APPOINTMENTS BY REFEREES
to 08 December, 2020

Clare Daniels	England	2005-13	34	Hollie Davidson	Scotland	2018-20	13
Sherry Trumbull	Canada	2009-16	33	Gabriel Lee Wing Yi	Hong Kong	2009-15	12
Nicky Inwood	New Zealand	2002-14	32	Leah Berard	USA	2013-14	11
Claire Hodnett	England	2011-17	27	Sarah Corrigan	Australia	2006-11	11
Alhambra Nievas	Spain	2014-18	22	Jess Beard	New Zealand	2014-16	10
Sara Cox	England	2014-20	21	Christine Bigaran	France	2006-14	10
Aimee Barrett-Theron	South Africa	2016-20	19	Aurelie Groizeleau	France	2018-20	10
Amy Perrett	Australia	2014-19	19	Marie Lo Matte	France	2015-18	10
Joy Neville	Ireland	2016-19	18	Kerstin Ljungdahl	Germany	2003-08	10
Dana Teagarden	USA	2006-12	16				
Joyce Henry	Canada	2006-12	14				

WOMEN'S SEVENS RUGBY

The Covid-19 pandemic forced an early conclusion to the scheduled eight tournaments for the 2019/20 HSBC Sevens Series and also the postponement of the 2020 Tokyo Olympics and the annual National Sevens.

The series commenced with a third place finish at the USA event in October 2019 followed by wins at both Dubai and South Africa in December. The Black Ferns Sevens were undefeated in the two tournaments of early 2020. When World Rugby abandoned future events and terminated the series New Zealand were declared the series winner. Stacey Fluhler, Ruby Tui and Tyla Nathan-Wong were included in the HSBC Dream Team. Fluhler, with 31 tries, was the series top try-scorer.

BLACK FERNS SEVENS 2020		New Zealand	Australia	TOTALS
Michaela Blyde	Bay of Plenty	*	*	2
Kelly Brazier	Bay of Plenty	*	*	2
Gayle Broughton	Taranaki	*	*	2
Theresa Fitzpatrick	Auckland	*	*	2
Stacey Fluhler (nee Waaka)	Waikato	*	*	2
Sarah Hirini (capt)	Manawatu	*	*	2
Jazmin Hotham	Waikato	–	s	1
Shiray Kaka	Waikato	–	*	1
Tyla Nathan-Wong	Auckland	*	*	2
Mahina Paul	Bay of Plenty	*	–	1
Risi Pouri-Lane	Tasman	*	–	1
Alena Saili	Southland	*	*	2
Ruby Tui	Bay of Plenty	*	*	2
Niall Williams	Auckland	*	*	2
Tenika Willison	Waikato	–	*	1

s reserve replacing injured Tui on second day.

Coaches: Allan Bunting and Cory Sweeney.
Assistant coach: Stu Ross.
Manager: Toni Young.
Strength & conditioning trainer: Bradley Anderson.
Video analyst: Stu Ross
Physiotherapist: Nicole Armstrong.

INDIVIDUAL SCORING

	Tries	Con	Points
Fluhler	15	–	75
Nathan-Wong	3	29	73
Blyde	10	–	50
Fitzpatrick	5	–	25
Brazier	3	–	15
Williams	3	–	15
Broughton	2	–	10
Kaka	2	–	10
Saili	2	–	10
Tui	1	–	5
Willison	–	2	4
Pouri-Lane	–	1	2
TOTALS	**46**	**32**	**294**
Opposition scored			87

Final points for 2019/20 World Rugby Sevens Series: New Zealand 96, Australia 80, Canada 80, France 70, USA 66, Russia 40, Fiji 38, England 36, Spain 28, Ireland 15, Japan 8, Brazil 6, China 4, South Africa 3. The series was held over five tournaments from October 2019 to February 2020.

Previous winners: New Zealand 2013, 2014, 2015, 2017, 2019; Australia 2016, 2018.
World Rugby Sevens Series Cup championship titles (2012 to 1 January 2021): New Zealand 26, Australia 8, Canada 4, England 2, USA 2.

NEW ZEALAND AT HSBC NEW ZEALAND SEVENS
Waikato Stadium, Hamilton   January 25/26, 2020

Date	Opponent	Result	Tries	Conversions
Jan 25	China	won 40–7	Fluhler (2), Blyde, Nathan-Wong, Fitzpatrick, Broughton	Nathan-Wong (4), Pouri-Lane
Jan 25	England	won 40–7	Blyde (4), Fluhler (2)	Nathan-Wong (5)
Jan 26	Fiji	won 38–21	Fluhler (3), Blyde (2), Saili	Nathan-Wong (4)
Jan 26	France (Cup semi-final)	won 19–7	Fitzpatrick, Fluhler, Brazier	Nathan-Wong (2)
Jan 26	Canada (Cup final)	won 24–7	Blyde (2), Williams, Fluhler	Nathan-Wong (2)

NEW ZEALAND AT HSBC AUSTRALIA SEVENS
Bankwest Stadium, Sydney   February 1/2, 2020

Date	Opponent	Result	Tries	Conversions
Feb 1	Japan	won 28–0	Fluhler, Brazier, Blyde, Tui	Nathan-Wong (4)
Feb 1	Russia	won 22–12	Kaka (2), Nathan-Wong, Fitzpatrick	Willison
Feb 2	England	won 26–12	Brazier, Williams, Fitzpatrick, Fluhler	Nathan-Wong (2), Willison
Feb 2	France (Cup semi-final)	won 24–7	Fluhler (4)	Nathan-Wong (2)
Feb 2	Canada (Cup final)	won 33–7	Nathan-Wong, Broughton, Williams, Fitzpatrick, Saili	Nathan-Wong (4)

NEW ZEALAND HSBC SEVENS
FMG Waikato Stadium, Hamilton   January 25/26, 2020

POOL

A   Fiji 26 England 19; New Zealand 40 China 7; China 17 Fiji 12;
New Zealand 40 England 7; England 31 China 0; New Zealand 38 Fiji 21.

B   USA 19 Russia 12; Australia 24 Brazil 14; USA 34 Brazil 7;
Australia 40 Russia 12; Russia 24 Brazil 14; Australia 19 USA 14;

C   France 31 Spain 7; Canada 24 Ireland 7; France 35 Ireland 7;
Canada 35 Spain 5; Spain 14 Ireland 7; Canada 21 France 19.

Play-off for 11th place   Ireland 26 Brazil 19.
Play-off for 9th place   China 31 Spain 0.
Play-off for 7th place   Russia 26 Fiji 21.
Play-off for 5th place   USA 45 England 5.
Play-off for Bronze   France 19 Australia 14

CUP CHAMPIONSHIP
Semi-finals   Canada 28 Australia 19; New Zealand 19 France 7.
Final   New Zealand 24 Canada 7.

Tournament referees: Hollie Davidson (*Scotland*), Adam Jones (*Wales*), Emily Hsieh (*New Zealand*), Tyler Miller (*Australia*), Amy Perrett (*Australia*), Selica Winiata (*New Zealand*).

SEVENS RECORDS

to January 1, 2021

BY NEW ZEALAND TEAMS

Most successive wins	50	2018-19
Most successive tournament wins	9	2018-19
Most successive appearances in finals	10	2013–15, 2018-19

Tournament records
Most points	293	Hong Kong, 2000
Most tries	47	Hong Kong, 2000
Most conversions	30	New Zealand 2001

Match records
Highest team score	83	v International Selection, Japan 2001
Record victory (points ahead)	83	83–0 v International Selection, Japan 2001
Highest score conceded	35	v Australia (final), Dubai 2013
Record defeat (points behind)	31	0–31 v Australia, Sydney 2018
Most tries	13	v International Selection, Japan 2001
Most conversions	10	v Tahiti, Fiji 2017

BY THE PLAYERS

Career records
Attended most tournaments	47	S.L. Hirini
Most points	1200	P.L. Woodman
Most tries	240	P.L. Woodman
Most conversions	507	T.B. Nathan-Wong

Tournament records
Most points	70	P.L. Woodman, USA 2015
Most tries	14	P.L. Woodman, USA 2015
Most conversions	29	A.M. Richards, New Zealand 2001

Match records
Most points	25	M. Blyde, v Samoa, Noosa 2013; P.L. Woodman v France, Brazil 2015; P.L. Woodman v USA, USA 2015; M. Blyde v England, Canada 2017; T.R. Willison v Tahiti, Fiji 2017
Most tries	5	M. Blyde, v Samoa, Noosa 2013; P.L. Woodman v France, Brazil 2015; P.L. Woodman v USA, USA 2015; M. Blyde v England, Canada 2017
Most conversions	10	T.R. Willison v Tahiti, Fiji 2017

NEW ZEALAND SEVENS REPRESENTATIVES, 2000–20

	Tournaments		Tournaments
Alley, C.H. (*Waikato*) 2014	1	Hohepa, C.H. (*Waikato*) 2012	1
Aniseko, F. (*Auckland*) 2008	1	Holden, S.E. (*Manawatu*) 2000 (*Wellington*) 2001	2
Baker, S.J. (*Wellington*) 2012 (*Manawatu*) 2013 (*Waikato*) 2016–17–18–19	21	Hotham, J.A-M.R. (*Waikato*) 2020	1
		Hurring, H.A. (*Otago*) 2013	2
Bird, O.M. (*Canterbury*) 2013	1	Hutana, H.S. (*Manawatu*) 2013	2
Blyde, M.G. (*Taranaki*) 2013–14–15–16 (*Bay of Plenty*) 2017–18–19–20	33	Itunu, L.F. (*Auckland*) 2009–12–13–14	11
		Kahura, D.M.T. (*Auckland*) 2000–01	4
Brazier, K.A. (*Otago*) 2013–14 (*Bay of Plenty*) 2015–16–17–18–19–20	36	Kaka, S.T. (nee Tane) (*Waikato*) 2013–14–15–16–18–19–20	14
Broughton, G.P. (*Taranaki*) 2014–15–16–17–18–19–20	28	Karanga, P. (*Manawatu*) 2001	1
		Kurei, N. (*Bay of Plenty*) 2000	1
Burgess, L.A. (*Taranaki*) 2012–13	2	Lavea, J. (*Auckland*) 2009	1
Cocksedge, K.M. (*Canterbury*) 2008–12–13	3	Lavea, V.N.H. (*Auckland*) 2008	1
		McAlister, K.M. (*Auckland*) 2012–13–14–15–16–17	20
Cootes, V. (*Waikato*) 2001	3		
Drummond, J.A. (*Tasman*) 2017	2	McGregor, A. (*Auckland*) 2008–09	2
Davis, M.F. (*Counties Manukau*) 2012	1	Manuel, H.R. (*Auckland*) 2008–09–12–13–14–16	16
Faleafaga, D.S. (*Wellington*) 2019	3	Mayes, C.A.M. (*Manawatu*) 2013–17	3
Ferguson, J. (*Hawke's Bay*) 2009	1	Morrow, M.L. (*Bay of Plenty*) 2014–15	3
Ferris, R.R. (*Manawatu*) 2019	2	Naoupo, T. (*Auckland*) 2001	3
Fitzpatrick, T.M. (*Auckland*) 2016–17–18–19–20	25	Nathan-Wong, T.B. (*Auckland*) 2012–13–14–15–16–17–18–19–20	44
Fluhler, , S.J.A.K. (nee Waaka) (*Waikato*) 2016–17–18–19–20	19	Ngawati, T.A. (*Auckland*) 2012	1
		Paul, M.A. (*Bay of Plenty*) 2019–20	2
Forbes, M.H. (*Tasman*) 2012	1	Paul, T. (*Bay of Plenty*) 2001	3
Gould, L. (*Canterbury*) 2000 (*Wellington*) 2001 (*Bay of Plenty*) 2012	4	Porter, H.J. (nee Myers) (*Otago*) 2000–01 (*Auckland*) 2008–09	6
Grant, K.M. (*Canterbury*) 2014	1	Pouri-Lane, R.I.R. (*Tasman*) 2018–19–20	5
Grant, V.E. (*Auckland*) 2008–09	2	Reti, T.C. (*Manawatu*) 2017	1
Greig, V.A.P. (*Manawatu*) 2013	2	Richards, A.M. (*Auckland*) 2000–01	4
Halapua, C. (*Auckland*) 2012	1	Robins-Reti, C.R.A. (*Waikato*) 2017–19	6
Hansen, S. (*Wanganui*) 2000	1	Ruscoe, M.J. (*Canterbury*) 2008	1
Harding, H.R. (*Waikato*) 2018–19	3	Rush, A.M. (*Auckland*) 2000–01	3
Hira-Herangi, A.P. (*Waikato*) 2014	1	Saili, A.F. (*Southland*) 2017–18–19–20	19
Hireme, A.H. (*Waikato*) 2013–14–15	11	Scanlan, C.R. (*Auckland*) 2014–15	3
Hirini, S.L. (nee Goss) (*Manawatu*) 2012–13–14–15–16–17–18–19–20	47	Shelford, E.T. (*Bay of Plenty*) 2001	3
		Shortland, S. (*Auckland*) 2000–01	4
Hohepa, C.G. (*Otago*) 2009 (*Waikato*) 2012–13–14–15	10	Sue, K.J. (*Manawatu*) 2013	2
		Sutorius, A.E. (*Wellington*) 2008	1

Tane, S.T. (*Waikato*) 2013–14–15–16   10
Tairakena, M.G.T. (*Waikato*) 2019   1
Tapsell, A.N.O. (*Canterbury*) 2013
  (*Bay of Plenty*) 2015   5
Te Tamaki, T.K. (*Auckland*) 2008–09   2
Te Tamaki, T.L.R. (*Waikato*)
  2016–17–18–19   17
Townsend, M.A. (*Manawatu*) 2008   1
Tubic, H.S. (*Counties Manukau*)
  2012–13–14–15–16   15
Tufuga, R. (*Manawatu*) 2016–17   3
Tui, R.M.
  (*Canterbury*) 2012–13–14–15–16–17–18–19
  (*Bay of Plenty*) 2020   39

Vaughan, J.M. (*Manawatu*) 2016   1

Webber, J.B.M. (*Waikato*) 2014–15–16   10
Whata-Simpkins, K.R. (*Wellington*)
  2014–15–16–17–18–19   20
Wickliffe, R.W.M. (*Counties Manukau*)
  2009–13–16–17   7
Wikeepa, R. (*Waikato*) 2009   1
Williams, N.L.V. (*Auckland*)
  2015–16–17–18–19–20   30
Willison, T.R. (*Waikato*)
  2016–17–18–19–20   13
Wilson, T. (*Auckland*) 2000   1
Winiata, S.C. (*Manawatu*)
  2008–09–13–14–15–16   15
Woodman, P.L. (*Auckland*)
  2012–13–14–15–
  (*Counties Manukau*) 2016–17–18   35

PLAYING RECORD OF NEW ZEALAND SEVENS TEAMS

	Tournaments			Games				Points	
	Attended	Won	Runner-up	Played	Won	Draw	Lost	For	Against
2000	1	1	–	7	7	–	–	293	20
2001	3	3	–	15	15	–	–	661	17
2008	1	–	1	6	4	–	2	174	57
2009	1	–	1	6	5	–	1	177	37
2012	2	2	–	12	10	2	–	378	69
2013	6	3	1	36	30	–	6	958	279
2014	6	5	1	37	36	–	1	1102	262
2015	6	3	–	36	30	–	6	1011	402
2016	6	1	3	36	30	–	6	915	279
2017	7	5	–	41	39	–	2	1018	251
2018	8	7	1	45	44	–	1	1432	307
2019	8	5	1	46	40	1	5	1254	430
2020	2	2	–	10	10	–	–	294	87
TOTALS	**57**	**37**	**9**	**333**	**300**	**3**	**30**	**8752**	**2497**

TOURNAMENT CAPTAINS

Sarah Hirini	2013-20	36
Huriana Manuel	2012-14	11
Anna Richards	2000-01	4
Tyla Nathan-Wong	2017, 19	4
Melissa Ruscoe	2008	1
Hannah Porter	2009	1

NATIONAL SEVENS

Anna Richards Trophy *(Player of the Tournament):*
2013	Selica Winiata (*Manawatu*)
2014	Hazel Tubic (*Counties Manukau*)
2015	Kayla McAlister (*Auckland*)
2016	Katarina Whata-Simpkins (*Wellington*)
2017	Kelly Brazier (*Bay of Plenty*)
2018	(January) Tenika Willison (*Waikato*); (December) Sarah Goss (*Manawatu*).
2019	Hazel Tubic (*Counties Manukau*).
2020	Not awarded due to Covid-19

TOURNAMENT TROPHY WINNERS

	Venue	*Cup*	*Plate*	*Bowl*
1998	Rotorua	Auckland		
1999	Palmerston North	Wellington		
2000	Palmerston North	Bay of Plenty		
2001	Palmerston North	Auckland		
2002	Palmerston North	Canterbury		
2013	Queenstown	Manawatu		
2014	Rotorua	Manawatu	Taranaki	Canterbury
2015	Rotorua	Auckland	Wellington	Otago
2016	Rotorua	Manawatu	Waikato	Tasman
2017	Rotorua	Counties Manukau	Bay of Plenty	Taranaki
2018	Rotorua (Jan)	Manawatu	Bay of Plenty	Southland
	Tauranga (Dec)	Manawatu	Canterbury	Tasman
2019	Tauranga	Counties Manukau	Manawatu	Tasman
2020	Cancelled due to Covid-19			

CHRONICLE OF EVENTS

JANUARY 2020

10 Glen Jackson announces his retirement from refereeing.

13 Last year's World Cup All Blacks report for Super Rugby training. The usual protocols apply to them this year — do not play in the pre-season matches, can only play a total of 180 minutes in the first three rounds, must have two weeks off (excluding the byes), cannot play more than six weeks in a row (byes and the two weeks off reset the count). The Collective Agreement allows for 33 players to be load managed . . . World Rugby announces six law trials will be undertaken around the world this year: (1) A 50/22 kick. If a team kicks the ball from inside their own half into touch in the opposition 22 or from inside their own 22 into touch in the opposition's half, the team that has kicked the ball out will get the throw in. (2) High tackle technique warning. Match officials and match commissioner can issue warnings to players during/after a match. If a player receives a second warning during the season the player will receive an automatic one-match suspension. (3) Reducing the tackle height to the waist. (4) An ability to review a yellow card when a player is in the sinbin for dangerous foul play to ensure it was not worthy of a red card. (5) Introduction of a free-kick/penalty infringement limit. The next offence after the limit is an automatic yellow card to the offender. (6) The awarding of a goal-line drop-out to the defending team when an attacking player is held up over the line (instead of a five-metre scrum to the attacking team) . . . Super Rugby will trial (2) High tackle technique warning.

14 NZR and their front-of-jersey sponsor AIG jointly announce that AIG will not renew their sponsorship when the current contract expires end of 2021 . . . The Halberg Awards finalists are announced. The Black Ferns Sevens are a finalist for Team of the Year.

20 SANZAAR announces that for the World Rugby trial they are undertaking, a tackle technique review officer — Glen Jackson — will oversee the trial with a particular focus on tackles made in an upright position, and no sanctions will be applied to players; the number of referees who will officiate in this year's Super Rugby competition is 12, down from the 15 used last year. The three not involved this year are New Zealanders Glen Jackson (retired) and Nick Briant, and South African Egon Seconds.

24 Italian fashion group Fashion Box S.P.A. are a new sponsor of NZR, becoming Official Formalwear Partner and Official Denimwear Partner of the All Blacks, All Blacks Sevens and Maori All Blacks in a four-year deal . . . NZR have employed independent consulting firm McKinsey and Company to review rugby in New Zealand with a goal to set up the sport for sustained success over the next decade. A Governance Group has been formed containing representatives from five provincial unions, two Super Rugby clubs and three from NZR to support the process.

25 NZR announces that plans to play the 2021 Hamilton leg of the HSBC World Rugby Sevens Series in Fiji will not now happen due to a lack of suitable infrastructure in Fiji. There is a hope it will now happen in 2023. NZR's desire is to avoid fan fatigue at Hamilton by staging there only every second year.

29 World Rugby announces the pool draw for the 2023 World Cup will be held at the end of this year using the world rankings after the matches in the November test window are completed. Twelve of the 20 teams to compete at the 2023 World Cup have already qualified — the 12 that finished in the top three positions in each of the four pools at last year's World Cup. *(See 2 October.)*

30 World Health Organisation (WHO) declares a public health emergency of international concern for a coronavirus — a pneumonia of unknown cause which presents as cold/flu-like symptoms that affects the lungs and airways — which originated in Wuhan, China last month. There are 98 cases in 18 countries outside China.

31 The China Lions are confirmed into the 2020 Global Rapid Rugby competition which began in Australia in 2018. It is outside the auspices of Rugby Australia and played with modified rugby rules. The China Lions is a joint venture between the China Rugby Football Association and the Bay of Plenty Rugby Union.

FEBRUARY

4 The 2021 women's World Cup is officially launched in Auckland with confirmation of the dates and venues. The tournament will open on Saturday, 18 September with the final on Saturday, 16 October. Waitakere Stadium and Northland Events Centre will host the pool matches and quarter-finals, while the semi-finals, bronze medal match and final will be at Eden Park. Spark Sport have been awarded the host broadcast rights.

6 Manawatu announces they are updating their name and logos by adding a macron to the u in their name, to be Manawatū. With Manawa meaning heart and tū meaning standing still, the name does not make sense in Te Reo without the macron, indicating a long vowel.

8 London *Daily Mail* reports that South Africa will leave the Rugby Championship in 2024 to join the Six Nations and create a Seven Nations championship.

9 On *Radio Sport* NZR CEO Mark Robinson outlines how both New Zealand and South Africa have signed agreements with their respective broadcasters to end of 2025 to be involved with SANZAAR.

13 Black Ferns Sevens are unsuccessful at the Halberg Awards . . . World Rugby postpones the World Series Sevens tournaments in Hong Kong and Singapore from April to October in response to the coronavirus outbreak, now officially known as Covid-19 . . . WHO reports 60,387 cases, including 1370 deaths, across 25 countries.

19 The All Blacks Sevens and Black Ferns Sevens training squads for the Olympic Games are announced. The All Blacks Sevens squad of 25 has four uncapped players and the Black Ferns Sevens squad of 22 has no uncapped players.

20 NZR announces the introduction of a national club competition for under-85 kg players to start in May.

24 Canterbury a profit of $16,203 for 2019.

28 Chiefs announce Clayton McMillan will be their coach for 2021 due to current coach Warren Gatland going to be absent coaching the British and Irish Lions in South Africa . . . The initial findings of the independent Review of Rugby in New Zealand are made to the provincial unions today in a phone hook-up. Opportunities to grow revenue and remove inefficiencies have been identified which could provide $20–30 million being reinvested per annum. Five potential areas to achieve this are: (1) High Performance Pathway, (2) Expenditure Optimisation, (3) Resourcing across Rugby, (4) Domestic Competitions, (5) Revenue Growth Opportunities. The report will not be made public. Starting next week NZR will take a roadshow to Dunedin, Christchurch, Napier, Auckland, Hamilton and Wellington to provide further detail to the provincial unions and Super Rugby clubs . . . SANZAAR announces the Sunwolves home matches against the Brumbies (8 March, Osaka) and Crusaders (14 March, Tokyo) will now be played 6 March, Brisbane and 14 March, Brisbane respectively due to Japanese Government directions concerning the Covid-19 outbreak . . . New Zealand's first case of Covid-19 is confirmed today . . . WHO reports 84,124 cases, including 2873 deaths, across 44 countries.

MARCH

3 Hawke's Bay a profit of $14,539.

9 NZR announces an All Blacks XV team has been created and will play three matches at the end of the year. It will be a second-tier national team and the intention is to play regular matches against second-tier overseas opposition.

12	The Black Ferns will play eight tests this year, including seven at home. The 2020 contracted squad is named. Five of the 31 players are new . . . Manawatu declare a loss of $28,636 . . . The Jaguares v Highlanders match at Buenos Aires on Saturday (14th) will be played behind closed doors as decreed by the Buenos Aires local government in an attempt to combat further spread of Covid-19 . . . WHO shows 130,783 confirmed cases, including 4920 deaths, across 118 countries.
14	Club rugby starts in Auckland, Counties Manukau, King Country and Tasman competitions . . . In an attempt to combat Covid-19, NZ Government announces as of 11.59 pm tomorrow night (Sunday 15th): no cruise ships will be able to dock in New Zealand until 30 June; every person arriving in New Zealand, including returning New Zealanders, must self-isolate for 14 days. The only exception is people arriving from the Pacific Islands. Cargo ships and cargo planes are allowed in. The situation will be reviewed in 16 days . . . A sixth case of Covid-19 in NZ is confirmed today . . . SANZAAR announces Super Rugby will be suspended after this weekend's matches . . . In the last three days prominent sporting events around the world like the US Masters, NBA, NHL, top football divisions in England, Germany, France, UEFA Champions League, Indian Premier League cricket, Formula One, Pro 14 and French Top 14 rugby have all been suspended or postponed . . . The Jaguares v Highlanders match scheduled for 8 pm tonight in Buenos Aires is cancelled at late notice and both teams are awarded two competition points.
16	NZ Government bans gatherings of 500 or more people in outdoor or indoor venues and advises all citizens should observe a social distance of two metres from each other. Anyone feeling unwell is to stay at home and consult their doctor . . . WHO reports 175,950 confirmed cases, including 7030 deaths, across 148 countries.
17	The Highlanders arrive home this morning from Argentina and go straight into self-isolation . . . With club competitions set to start this Saturday (21st) in most provinces, NZR advises the provincial unions that, effective immediately, all club and school rugby is postponed until Saturday, 18 April. Contact training is banned until Monday, 13 April, but non-contact training can continue . . . NZ Government announces a $12.1 billion Wage Subsidy Scheme for all businesses to end of June. Employers must demonstrate a loss of 30% revenue due to Covid-19 and retain their employees for the full 12 weeks the scheme is available for. The maximum is $585.50 gross per week per full-time employee and $350.00 gross per week per part-time employee . . . NZR CEO Mark Robinson confirms on Sky TV show *The Breakdown* they are looking at the five NZ Super Rugby teams playing a double-round competition, with the games likely to be behind closed doors. If no further rugby is played at all this year, NZR will lose out on about $120 million income.
19	NZ Government is to close its borders at 11.59 pm tonight, including from the Pacific Islands. Only NZ citizens/residents and health and humanitarian workers will be allowed in. Twenty-eight cases of Covid-19 have now been confirmed in the country, all 28 having arrived in the country from overseas. Indoor gatherings of more than 100 people are banned, but this does not apply to schools, universities, workplaces, public transport and supermarkets.
20	World Rugby cancels the World Under 20 Championship scheduled for Italy 28 June–18 July and postpones the Men's Sevens Series events in London and Paris and the Women's Sevens Series events in Langford and Paris from May to later in the year.
21	The Government announces the introduction of a four-level Covid-19 Alert system.
23	NZ Government announces it will move to Level 4 at 11.59 pm Wednesday (25th) when the country is to go into lockdown for four weeks. Schools and non-essential businesses

Chronicle of Events

are to shut. Supermarkets, pharmacies and doctors' clinics will remain open. All indoor and outdoor events are to be cancelled. The public must stay at home except for essential personal movement/essential work and stay local. People must keep two metres apart at all times outside of home including at workplaces. If people can work from home, instead of going to place of employment, they should do so . . . 36 new cases of Covid-19 are announced, which takes the total in NZ to 102, with two of the new cases suspected to be from community transmission . . . NZR announces that all rugby in the country is suspended for the foreseeable future. All teams are to cease training . . . WHO figures are 335,008 cases, including 14,653 deaths, across 186 countries.

24   North Harbour a loss of $107,222 . . . IOC announces the Olympic Games is to be postponed to 2021 due to Covid-19.

30   Radio Sport, owned by media company NZME, suddenly ceases operating at 1 pm. Falling advertising sales and the postponement/cancellation of all international and domestic sport, all due to Covid-19, is the reason . . . NZR announces that for 2020, the Heartland Championship, the Jock Hobbs Memorial Under 19 tournament and the National Sevens tournament are all cancelled. This will save NZR $20 million. The Heartland Unions themselves suggested the decision to cancel the Heartland Championship (to concentrate on club rugby) and NZR supported the suggestion. All provincial representative tournaments below Mitre 10 Cup, Heartland Championship and Farah Palmer Cup level are cancelled as well (Dev/B team, age-grade). For the time being, the Mitre 10 Cup and Farah Palmer Cup are hoped to go ahead.

APRIL

1   NZR announces emergency grants to each of the five Super Rugby clubs of $250,000 each to cover April–June, and all NZR staff, Board and All Blacks management are taking 20% pay cuts for April–June. Provincial unions will receive their full second-quarter grants in April, but they are likely to receive 15% less than previously budgeted over the rest of the year.

3   Otago a loss of $115,098, emailed to clubs.

4   WHO figures take the number of confirmed cases worldwide pass the one million mark, including 57,130 deaths.

6   Tasman a loss of $40,188, emailed to clubs . . . Five Crusaders players flout lockdown restrictions and mingle together next to Rugby Park, passing ball around while exercising. Crusaders CEO Colin Mansbridge agrees the players should not have been together and confirms they have been reprimanded.

8   Confirmed cases total in NZ passes the 1000 mark to 1009, including one death.

9   NZ Government announces, effective 11.59 pm tonight, every returning New Zealander coming into the country must go into quarantined 14-day isolation in a government-approved facility.

12   Nominations close for World Rugby elections. Current Chairman Bill Beaumont and current Vice-Chairman Agustin Pichot are standing for Chairman. Bernard Laporte is the only nomination for Vice-Chairman. There are eight nominations for the seven elected positions on the Executive Committee — Bart Campbell has been nominated by NZR. All positions are for four years.

16   NZR announces, with agreement from NZRPA, salary freezes to contracted players: 15% of monthly retainers for those paid more than $50,000 annually from 1 May, and rising to 30% from 1 September. If no further rugby is played this year, these freezes along with not having to pay assembly fees, performance incentives and promotional payments will save $25 million in expenditure by NZR . . . World Rugby announces a relief fund of US$100 million to assist national unions through the Covid-19 crisis. The money will

	be available upon appropriate criteria being met, and the package available to the Six Nations and SANZAAR unions will involve a combination of advances and loans.
17	WHO figures pass two million cases with 143,568 deaths.
21	Fiji's candidate for World Rugby's Executive Committee has his nomination withdrawn after publication of allegations against him. This means all seven remaining nominations will be declared duly elected including NZR nominee Bart Campbell.
22	NZ Government announces a move to Alert Level 3 on Monday, 27 April, 11.59 pm. Some businesses can reopen but only for staff to access, not the public, and still with physical distancing and sanitising requirements. Public can order online or by phone but are not allowed to enter the premises. Public are still required to stay at home except for essential personal movement/work and travel is restricted to region only . . . Our current confirmed cases total is 1120 including 14 deaths.
27	NZR announces it is undertaking, in conjunction with the five Super Rugby clubs, a complete review of NZ's Super Rugby model. Called *Aratipu*, the review will look at all on and off field factors in the model. All five Super Rugby licences expire at the end of this year . . . Northland RU a profit of $11,466. Annual meeting held by Zoom conference.
30	NZR AGM: All stakeholders participate via Zoom video conferencing. A $7.4 million loss is declared which was better than the budgeted $11.8 million loss forecast. Income was $187 million and reserves are now $93 million. Total player numbers last year were 159,773 (+ 2492) including 31,035 female players (+ 11%). Former All Black Ian Kirkpatrick is the new Patron, and former NZR Chairman Mike Eagle becomes a Life Member. Three changes to the Board — Bart Campbell and Jennifer Kerr are appointed by the Appointments and Recommendation Committee (replacing Peter Kean and Mark Robinson respectively — Robinson now the CEO) and in an election Bailey Mackey wins a vote over Kate Daly for Andrew Golightly's position. Chairman Brent Impey advises NZ's votes for World Rugby Chairman went to Agustin Pichot.

MAY

2	World Rugby announces Bill Beaumont has retained the role of Chairman by a vote of 28–23 and the Executive Committee is also confirmed. Voting would normally have taken place in person at the Council's AGM (12 May), but due to Covid-19 electronic voting was submitted to PwC who independently managed the election.
4	SANZAAR announces that all four countries involved in the joint venture are all committed to it to the end of 2030 and that Super Rugby in 2021 will be the 14-team competition already sold to broadcasters. This is in response to various personal opinions appearing in Australia and New Zealand media that Australia and New Zealand might be better off playing in a trans-Tasman competition instead of Super Rugby, and now is the chance to do this, which SANZAAR dismisses as 'merely speculative and have no basis to them'.
5	Ian Foster names Sam Cane as new All Blacks captain.
6	Sport NZ have created a $25 million relief package with $15 million of it being a community resilience fund so sporting clubs attached to a national sporting organisation can receive up to $1000 and regional bodies can receive up to $40,000.
7	NZ Government announces what Alert Level 2 will look like when the move is made to it. Businesses (including schools and public venues like cinemas, libraries) can reopen for staff and customers — but must ensure physical distancing and regular sanitising. Contact tracing must be implemented by the businesses — by register or QR code stickers can be provided for business entrances and an app can be downloaded by the public for scanning. Travel within NZ can resume. There is still a ban on gatherings of more than 100 people and not in more than groups of 10. Professional sports of rugby and netball

will be permissible in their controlled workplaces, but initially will happen without crowds ... NZR announces Super Rugby Aotearoa will take place between the five NZ Super Rugby teams playing each other twice, without playoffs. Two matches every weekend for 10 weeks behind closed doors. The players will need three to four weeks' training before its commencement and a start date won't be known until the Government makes the move to Level 2. The competition has the blessing of SANZAAR.

8 NZR confirms there are to be job losses among the 160 full-time positions within the organisation.

11 The Government confirms two new cases of Covid-19 today bringing the total of confirmed cases to 1151 including 21 deaths. The Government announces a move to Alert Level 2 on Wednesday 13th, 11.59 pm, but community sports (including club and school rugby) are still to remain on hold. Gatherings of more than 10 people are prohibited (a change from the 100 announced four days ago) ... NZR confirms Super Rugby Aotearoa will start on 13 June and the Mitre 10 Cup will start on 11 September (originally scheduled for a 6 August start).

12 World Rugby Council annual meeting. All countries participate by video conference. An immediate change is made to the law — a try can no longer be scored by placing the ball against the base of the padding of the goalposts which had been deemed part of the tryline. Padding on most goalposts now usually extend outside the tryline into the field of play but defenders usually have to stand on the tryline.

13 NZR announces a three-stage return of club rugby. (1) 14–25 May, Prepare to Train — clubs to put in place hygiene protocols for people, venues and facilities and contact tracing. No training to occur. (2) Prepare to Play (dates unconfirmed) — teams to begin training (including contact training) for an expected four-week period. (3) Play (date unconfirmed). The unconfirmed dates depend on when the Government lifts restrictions on mass gatherings.

14 The Government's Budget announcement includes an extension of the Wage Subsidy Scheme (see 17 March) worth $3.2 billion for another eight weeks ... 150 years of organised rugby in New Zealand is celebrated today marking the first game in this country between two club teams — Nelson Football College v Nelson College, 14 May 1870. At the gravesites of Alfred Drew (1870 Nelson FC captain), Robert Tennant (1870 Nelson FC secretary) and Charles Monro who had returned to Nelson from schooling in England in January 1870 and taught the game he had played in England to members of the Nelson FC that he had joined, there are laying of wreaths. Descendants of the three men are at each individual wreath laying as well as NZR Board member Farah Palmer and NZ Rugby Museum Chairman Clive Akers. All three grave sites are in the Manawatu province.

15 The National Secondary Schools First XV championships — top four boys, top four girls, top four co-ed — are all cancelled for 2020 ... NZR confirms the All Blacks' three home tests in July against Wales (4, 11 July) and Scotland (18 July), as well as the Black Ferns' home test against USA (18 July), are all postponed, tentatively to October.

17 The Government allocates $265 million to sport over the next four years from its Budget. $83 million is available short term for sport and recreation organisations (grassroots to elite), $104 million in medium term to national and regional organisations, and $78 million to sports groups for new technology and research.

18 Super Rugby squads return to training. The players must have their temperature taken every day and high touch areas must be regularly sanitised.

21 Sky TV announces they will enter the broadband market next year.

22 WHO figures pass five million Covid-19 cases, including 329,208 deaths.

25	Government announces that starting 12.00 midday on Friday 29th gatherings can occur for up to 100 people, but hygiene standards must be maintained and record-keeping requirements are needed should contact tracing be required. Community sports will now be able to operate.
27	Bay of Plenty a $230,828 profit. Annual meeting held by Zoom conference.
29	NZR announces the Farah Palmer Cup will start on 22 August. In a revised format the competition will be played in North Island and South Island pools instead of the Premiership and Championship divisions.
31	Counties Manukau a profit of $29,510.

JUNE

1	Queen's Birthday Honours List: Former All Blacks captain Kieran Read is an Officer of the NZ Order of Merit, and Derek Lardelli, 1988 Poverty Bay rep and composer of the All Blacks 'Kapa O Pango' haka, is a Knight Companion.
2	In Super Rugby Aotearoa: (1) Drawn matches at 80 minutes will be decided by extra-time golden point. Ten minutes of extra time will be played and a score of any kind during it will end the game immediately and win it for the scoring team. If there is no score during the 10 minutes of extra time, the game will be drawn. (2) Players who receive a red card can be replaced by another player after 20 minutes. (3) Referees will strictly enforce the breakdown and offside line to create faster attacking ball and a fairer contest.
8	Government announces the country will move to Alert Level 1 at midnight tonight. Today is the 17th consecutive day without a new case, and there are currently no active cases in the country. There is no requirement for physical distancing and no limit on group numbers. The public are to keep a record of their own movements . . . NZR announces kick-off times are changed for Super Rugby Aotearoa. Saturday matches will now be at 7.05 pm (instead of 5.05 pm) and Sunday matches will now be at 3.35 pm (instead of 3.05 pm) which will allow the away teams to arrive the day before the game instead of flying in and out on the day of the game.
9	With the Government's move to Level 1, NZR announces a start date of 20 June for playing of matches in the Community game *(see 13 May)*.
12	SANZAAR announces the impending Super Rugby Aotearoa and Super Rugby Australia competitions are not part of SANZAAR Super Rugby and are to be treated separately. The Super 15 games played in rounds 1 to 7 this year will stand in SANZAAR records, and the 2020 competition will be declared closed as having no winner.
15	A Professional Game forum comprising representatives of World Rugby, the Six Nations and SANZAAR unions, International Rugby Players Association, British and Irish Lions, England Premiership Clubs, Pro-14 Clubs, French Top14 Clubs, European Professional Club Rugby meet by teleconferencing to provide an initial platform to reform/align the northern hemisphere and southern hemisphere seasons.
16	Current Black Ferns lock Charmaine Smith announces her retirement from all rugby due to a bulging disc in her neck.
24	Crowd attendances for the first two weeks of Super Rugby Aotearoa were 105,323 for the four matches, an average of 26,330. The Blues v Hurricanes match was declared a 42,000 sellout. The average attendance for the 39 regular season games of Super Rugby in NZ in 2019 was 11,538.
25	Mitre 10 Cup draw is revised. Thursday-night matches have been removed from the schedule and there will now be three games every Sunday . . . NZR confirms a quarter of their staff (40) have been made redundant. The resumption of Super Rugby Aotearoa prevented more . . . Dan Carter's 70th test jersey sells on Trade Me for $21,300. All the proceeds will go to Carter's club Southbridge.

26 A North Island v South Island fixture is confirmed for 29 August. The criteria for determining which Island players can play for is by the province for which they first played first-class rugby.

30 World Rugby announces the 2019/20 World Rugby Sevens Series is declared closed with the unplayed tournaments now cancelled, having previously been postponed to unconfirmed dates later in the year. The All Blacks Sevens and Black Ferns Sevens are declared champions for the 2019/20 season, having led their respective points tables when the Series was brought to a halt.

JULY

1 Government announces Poverty Bay's home ground of Rugby Park will receive $8 million funding for a new grandstand to replace the John Heikell Grandstand that was closed in May last year due to earthquake concerns . . . Taranaki a $350,868 loss.

3 Beauden Barrett announces he will play for Japanese club Suntory Sungoliath next year, missing next year's Super Rugby season, but returning mid-year for the international season. This ability was negotiated in the four-year contract he signed with NZR last year . . . Super Rugby Australia competition starts in Australia with their four current Super Rugby clubs plus the return of the Western Force (privately financed) who were dropped from Super Rugby at the end of the 2017 season. Crowds are allowed but at reduced levels and spaced apart for social distancing.

15 2018 Blues rep Matt Johnson announces his retirement from rugby aged 26 after successfully undergoing open heart surgery for the third time last month, derived from contracting rheumatic fever when he was 13.

16 SANZAAR announces it favours holding the entire 2020 Rugby Championship tournament in New Zealand this year. Of the four countries involved NZ has had success in combatting Covid-19. As our borders are still closed to non-New Zealand residents/ citizens, NZ Government approval is needed for exemptions to allow the Australian, Argentinean and South African teams into the country, who will all have to serve a 14-day quarantine period upon entering. The cost of quarantining will be met by SANZAAR . . . SANZAAR also reiterates that all four countries are committed to a long-term future with SANZAAR . . . NZR Board approves the recommendations of the *Aratipu* report. The preference is for a Super Rugby Trans-Tasman competition of 8–10 teams comprising the five NZ clubs, a Pacific Islands team, and two to four Australian teams. NZR will invite submissions of interest from Australian clubs and Pacific Islands teams.

18 Rugby Australia Chairman Nick McLennan responds that no Australian teams will be appearing in a New Zealand competition and the best base for a Pacific Islands team would be Sydney rather than Auckland.

20 NZR Referees Manager Bryce Lawrence says the decision by the TMO to rule out Damian McKenzie's try in yesterday's Chiefs v Highlanders match was the result of an incorrect TMO review. Protocol is a review can only go back two phases to adjudicate on anything, but in this incident the review went back three phases. The decision to cancel the try was the correct outcome but was outside review protocol.

21 South Africa Rugby CEO Jurie Roux says there are legally binding agreements that bind all four members of the SANZAAR partnership to SANZAAR. Any breach of the joint venture by a member would make them liable for legal action and there are strong alternative options for South Africa in the northern hemisphere that can be explored if need be.

22 Wellington a profit of $109,163 for 2019.

23 The Government announces it will contribute $20 million towards the projected cost of refurbishing Taranaki's home ground of Yarrow Stadium . . . Following a meeting of the Rugby Australia Board on Monday (20th), Chairman Nick McLennan says their preferred Super Rugby model is a 10-team trans-Tasman competition containing all five Australian Super Rugby clubs.

24 The Super Rugby Aotearoa trophy is unveiled. Carved by Bill Doyle, the totara base represents an upturned waka and with a pounamu mere mounted on top.

27 Highlanders announce they will sanction seven of their squad following an evening in Queenstown on Friday night/Saturday morning which involved loud noise levels and damage to an apartment complex they were at, and the arrest of a person. No damage was inflicted by a squad member and the person arrested was not a squad member. The seven Highlanders will be sanctioned for behaving below the standards of the team.

29 World Rugby announces the first two legs of the 2020–2021 World Series Sevens: Dubai (26–28 November) and Cape Town (4–6 December) are cancelled due to Covid-19.

30 The High Performance Referee Squads are announced for both the Mitre 10 Cup and Farah Palmer Cup. Jono Bredin debuts among the 14 Mitre 10 Cup referees, and Tiana Ngawati debuts among the 10 Farah Palmer Cup referees. Tipene Cottrell and Rebecca Mahoney appear on both lists.

31 World Rugby Council meet by hook-up and confirm revised test windows for the remainder of this year. A temporary adjustment to Regulation 9 allows: In northern hemisphere from 24 October to first weekend in December the completion of the 2020 men's and women's Six Nations tournament to be followed by an eight-team tournament containing the Six Nations countries plus Japan and Fiji; in the southern hemisphere from 7 November to 12 December the Rugby Championship to be played.

AUGUST

11 After 102 days of no recorded cases of Covid-19 in NZ outside of managed isolation/quarantine, the Government announces there are four confirmed cases in the community, all in one family in Auckland. As of midday tomorrow the Auckland region from Wellsford to Pukekohe will return to Alert Level 3 and the rest of the country to Level 2, both on Friday (14th) midnight. At Level 3 Aucklanders must stay at home. Public facilities, schools, bars, restaurants, businesses must close. Key services of supermarkets, pharmacies, medical centres to remain open. Businesses deemed essential under Levels 4 and 3 last time can continue but workers to again work from home preferably. Social gatherings of more than 10 people are prohibited. Travelling into Auckland is prohibited unless you live there. Citizens in Auckland who live outside of Auckland are permitted to leave. For the rest of the country at Level 2 social distancing of two metres returns and social gatherings over 100 people are prohibited. People in Auckland are encouraged to wear masks when accessing essential services: outside of Auckland to wear masks in public if physical distancing is difficult (e.g. public transport) . . . Crusaders confirm the Super Rugby Aotearoa trophy was dropped during post-match celebrations and suffered some damage with the base chipped.

12 WHO figures pass 20 million cases worldwide, with 732,026 deaths.

14 Government announces there are now 29 cases all linked to the same outbreak and the current Alert Levels will remain in place until 11.59 pm, 26 August . . . NZR announces tomorrow's Highlanders v Hurricanes match at Dunedin will be brought forward to a 3.05 pm kick-off, from 7.05 pm, to allow the Hurricanes to fly in and out the same day. The match will be played without spectators (19,000 tickets sold) . . . All rugby activity in the North Harbour, Auckland and Counties Manukau Rugby Unions must cease until further notice . . . The Blues v Crusaders match set for Sunday at Eden Park is cancelled and both teams are awarded two points. The game was a sellout with all 43,000 tickets

sold. Rugby can continue in all other provinces but only under Alert Level 2 guidelines.
15 NZR postpones the Farah Palmer Cup, which was scheduled to start next Saturday (22nd).
18 The All Blacks selectors announce the North Island and South Island squads for the 29 August clash. The squads will assemble at Wellington next Monday (25th) with the match to be played in Wellington if not able to be played at the originally selected venue of Eden Park.
19 The Farah Palmer Cup will now start on 5 September and will still have a full schedule of matches.
21 The North Island v South Island match is postponed to 5 September at either Auckland or Wellington. The 14 players from North Harbour, Auckland and Counties Manukau involved in the match have had their exemption requests to leave Auckland on the 25th for assembly in Wellington declined by the Government.
24 Auckland will stay at Alert Level 3 until 11.59 pm on 30 August, the rest of the country remaining at Level 2. Face coverings will be compulsory for the whole country on all public transport of buses, ferries, trains and planes. The display of QR codes will be mandatory for all businesses and services for contact tracing.
30 Tomorrow Auckland can return to Level 2 with the rest of the country. Businesses can reopen and travel in and out of the region can restart, but social gatherings of more than 10 are still prohibited in Auckland, compared to 100 for the rest of the country.
31 Ticket-selling company Ticket Rocket (formerly Ticket Direct) is placed in receivership. It has left many ticket holders and organisations out of pocket including the Crusaders ($155,000) and Hurricanes ($186,000).

SEPTEMBER

1 World Rugby announces the third and fourth legs of the 2020–2021 World Series Sevens: New Zealand (Hamilton) and Australia (Sydney) scheduled for 23–24 and 30–31 January respectively are cancelled due to Covid-19. World Rugby makes available a US$2.5 million fund to help countries who have qualified for the July 2021 Tokyo Olympic Games with their preparation.
3 Highlanders announce Aaron Mauger will not be reappointed head coach now that his three-year contract is completed.
4 The country will stay at Alert Level 2 until 11.59 pm on 16 September ... NZR announces the opening round of Mitre 10 Cup next weekend will be played with limited spectators at the grounds.
6 The 35-man All Blacks squad is named.
7 Twenty-nine of the All Blacks squad are made available to play for their provinces in this weekend's opening round of the Mitre 10 Cup ... Auckland RU decides the remainder of their club competitions are abandoned, with no winners declared. No club rugby has been played since 8 August. A restart was needed on 12 September to be able to finish on the 26th but no play is possible on 12 September due to still being at Alert Level 2.
11 After a Board meeting hook-up last night, SANZAAR announces the Rugby Championship will be held in Australia, starting 7 November, due to the more favourable quarantine regulations there. Each of the three visiting countries will be able to train in their entirety from day one of the 14-day quarantine period in Australia, whereas if it was played in New Zealand the NZ Government would only allow training after individual isolation for three days, in bubbles of 15 on days four to seven, in bubbles of 25 on days eight to 14 with full squad training together on day 15. All squads will feature up to 46 players plus up to 12 management, coaches and support staff ... NZ will host Australia for two tests before the Rugby Championship.

14	Government announces the country will stay at Alert Level 2 for another seven days . . . North Harbour and Counties Manukau RU's decide the remainder of their club competitions are abandoned with no winners declared, not having played since 8 August.
15	Government announces they will relax quarantine rules to allow Australia to play two tests in New Zealand. Australia will be able to start training after three days and commence full squad training after six days . . . The two Bledisloe Cup tests are confirmed for Wellington on Sunday, 11 October and Auckland on Sunday, 18 October . . . On *The Breakdown* Mark Robinson confirms NZR received eight expressions of interest for their projected version of Super Rugby next year, including three non-New Zealand ones.
16	South Africa Rugby Union announces rugby will resume there on 26 September and their Super Rugby Unlocked competition will start on 10 October. The games will be played without crowds.
17	In the absence of test matches this year, in November the Black Ferns players will be involved in a Possibles v Probables match, and two matches against NZ Barbarians.
18	One year out from the opening of women's World Cup 2021, the Black Ferns are confirmed as playing the opening match on Eden Park.
21	Government announces Auckland region will stay at Alert Level 2 at 11.59 pm on Wednesday 23rd, but gatherings of up to 100 people can now occur. Rest of the country will move to Level 1 at 11.59 pm tonight, but people travelling on public transport, including flights in, into, out of Auckland region must wear a face covering.
22	Tyla Nathan-Wong is 2019–2020 World Rugby Sevens Series female player of the year.
24	SANZAAR releases the draw and venues for the Rugby Championship matches, to be played over six consecutive weekends from 7 November to 12 December, two matches per Saturday. This means the All Blacks will spend Christmas Day and Boxing Day in quarantine upon their return home. At the SANZAAR CEOs' meeting by hook-up on the 17th Australia and New Zealand were in favour of the competition being played over five weeks, finishing on 5 December, but unanimity was not reached by all four partners . . . NZR responds that they did not agree to the 12 December finish and will work with Rugby Australia and SANZAAR to find a solution.
25	WHO reports the total Covid-19 deaths around the world have passed one million.
26	Hawke's Bay play their match against Canterbury in one-off limited-edition jerseys. Instead of the black and white hoops, the jerseys are in a checked shirt pattern containing varying dark shades. The 23 jerseys are auctioned off on Trade Me before the match for the East Coast Rural Support Trust in aid of the Hawke's Bay farming community who are suffering drought conditions.
28	Government says the current quarantine rules for returnees of 14 days' managed isolation will not be changed for the All Blacks . . . South Africa RU Director of Rugby Rassie Erasmus says the Springboks will need at least 500 minutes of rugby to be match fit to play in the Rugby Championship, otherwise they will be very underprepared.
29	On *The Breakdown* Rugby Australia Chairman Nick McLennan says the relationship between the New Zealand and Australian Unions is 'probably at the lowest ebb it has ever been at' . . . A special meeting of the South African Rugby Union decides to enter their four Super Rugby teams into an expanded Pro-14 competition (containing teams from Ireland, Italy, Scotland, Wales) at the expense of the two current South African teams who compete in the Pro-14, the Kings and the Cheetahs who had both once competed in Super Rugby. The Springboks will continue to play in the Rugby Championship . . . World Rugby announces there will be no World Rugby Awards this year. Instead there will be a Special Edition where men and women's player-of-the decade (15s and 7s) and try-of-the-decade will be decided by public vote and a men's and women's team-of-the-decade will be decided on by a panel.

30 NZR Board decides Super Rugby Aotearoa will return next year, with a final. A combined Super Rugby competition with Australia will not happen yet because of the possibility of travel/quarantine restrictions still being in place. Of the three non-NZ applicants, none are considered ready for next year, but NZR will continue to negotiate with them for inclusion in 2022 . . . Southland a $36,000 loss for 2019.

OCTOBER

2 The third annual Red Bull Ignite Sevens will be played over 5–6 December. The All Blacks Sevens and Black Ferns Sevens players will this time feature in it alongside 60 emerging/hopeful aspirants . . . World Rugby announces the pools at the 2023 World Cup in France will now be drawn on 14 December and the world rankings as at 1 January 2020 will be used to determine them, due to Covid-19. Being ranked second, New Zealand is in Band One along with South Africa (1st), England (3rd), and Wales (4th).

5 The Government announces the Auckland region will move to Covid Alert Level 1 at 11.59 pm on Wednesday, 7th. With the whole country now at Level 1, the use of face masks on public transport/flights is no longer mandatory . . . NZR confirms the second Bledisloe Cup Test will go ahead at Eden Park, as planned, on the 18th. If the test could not have been held at Eden Park, it would have been shifted to Dunedin.

7 There are now no active community cases of Covid-19 since the 11 August outbreak. The last new case was 25 September, and a total of 179 community cases, including two deaths, were recorded since 11 August.

8 SANZAAR announces a revised draw for the Rugby Championship. The NZ v Australia clash down for 12 December has been brought forward to 31 October. This will allow the All Blacks to complete their 14-day quarantine period on return before Christmas Day. On 2 October the Australian Government announced a travel zone between New Zealand and New South Wales would be opened on the 16th for quarantine-free travel. The All Blacks and Wallabies teams will not need to go into quarantine when they enter New South Wales after the second Bledisloe Cup match on the 18th to play the Rugby Championship.

10 For North Harbour's match against Hawke's Bay today, North Harbour's principal sponsor QBE donates $2000 for every try North Harbour score to charity partner Orange Sky to mark World Homeless Day. North Harbour scores seven tries.

15 South Africa inform SANZAAR they will not be participating in the Rugby Championship, mainly due to player welfare with their players underdone in terms of match play.

16 SANZAAR announces a draw for a Tri-Nations Championship with just Argentina, Australia and NZ, which will see one game per Saturday from 31 October to 5 December . . . WHO reports the number of Covid-19 cases has passed 40 million with 1,112,524 deaths.

19 TJ Perenara announces he will exercise the sabbatical option in his NZR contract and miss Super Rugby next year to play for Japanese club NTT Docomo Red Hurricanes. He will return mid-year and be available for the All Blacks . . . The NZ Schools and NZ Barbarians Schools teams are named even though they will not play this year.

20 Highlanders announce Tony Brown will be their Head Coach for next two years . . . All Blacks squad of 36 is named for the Tri-Nations, with uncapped players George Bower and Du Plessis Kirifi also named as cover for Nepo Laulala and Ardie Savea who are currently on paternity leave.

22 Ticket-selling company Ticket Rocket is liquidated in the Dunedin High Court (*see 31 August*).

| 25 | For their home match against Southland, Tasman wear the uniform of Golden Bay-Motueka to celebrate 100 years of the formation of the Golden Bay-Motueka union. In 1969 it amalgamated with Nelson union to form Nelson Bays union which is now a sub-union of Tasman. The Golden Bay-Motueka uniform was brown and white hooped jerseys, brown shorts, brown and white hooped socks. |

NOVEMBER

3	Taranaki Regional Council announces the East Stand will now be demolished at Yarrow Stadium and rebuilt. The total cost of the refurbishment of Yarrow Stadium will be $50 million and the repair of the West Stand will hopefully allow Taranaki to return to playing their home games there next year.
4	SANZAAR confirms Argentina, Australia, New Zealand and South Africa are committed to the Rugby Championship to end of 2030. The Rugby Championship format will be restructured with all four teams playing away games on a mini-tour . . . The Halberg Foundation announces the 2021 Halberg Awards will award Decade Champions for 2010–2019 instead of awards for best performances of 2020, due to Covid-19 ruining most sporting opportunity this year, notably the Olympic Games. The best performances of 2020 will now be grouped with the best performances of 2021 for the 2022 Halberg Awards.
5	NZR CEO Mark Robinson reveals the projected loss for NZR this year will be in excess of $40 million. It is likely that Super Rugby in 2022 will be a trans-Tasman competition with five teams from both New Zealand and Australia and the possibility of Pasifika teams.
10	The Black Ferns squad of 28 is named for the two matches against the NZ Barbarians. Eloise Blackwell is the new captain and the squad contains nine uncapped players . . . The draw for 2021 Super Rugby Aotearoa is announced. The opener is on 26 February and the final will be on 8 May.
11	Rugby Australia announces the draw for 2021 Super Rugby AU. It will start on 19 February and their grand final will be on 8 May . . . NZR announces a new Strategic Advisory Group, comprising school and provincial union leaders, has been formed to work on developing and implementing a new Secondary Schools Rugby Plan. The group of nine members will be chaired by Nic Hill (Headmaster Christchurch BHS) and provide advice to NZR on retaining players and bridging the gap between school and club rugby.
12	The Maori All Blacks will play a fixture at Hamilton on 5 December against a Moana Pasifika team. Moana Pasifika Group, based in Auckland, is one of the contenders to be the sixth Super Rugby team in New Zealand . . . Kanaloa Hawaii, based in Hawaii, and another Pasifika group hoping to be the sixth Super Rugby team in New Zealand, send a letter to NZR claiming they have been treated unfairly in the process and Moana Pasifika Group is apparently NZR's preferred option even though Moana Pasifika Group has not submitted a bid in the tender process. If NZR does not address Kanaloa Hawaii's concerns within 14 days, they will take legal action.
13	NZR and Rugby Australia jointly announce a six-week Super Rugby competition for next year starting 14 May with a final on 19 June. Each NZ team will play all five Australian teams (and vice versa) . . . NZR confirms the Fiji RU and Moana Pasifika as their preferred partners to further explore the viability of Pasifika teams in Super Rugby from 2022.
16	Hawke's Bay announces free entry for their home semi-final this weekend v Taranaki . . . Government announces that from 11.59pm on the 18th face masks will need to be worn on public transport in Auckland and in and out of Auckland, and on domestic flights throughout the country . . . After their first ever loss to Argentina on the weekend, the All Blacks drop to third on the World Rankings, behind South Africa and England.

17	NZR and SANZAAR Chairman Brent Impey say he will stand down as SANZAAR Chairman on 31 December. He states it would be best for an Independent Chairman to be appointed and the current four-nations model is outdated and should increase its membership to grow the game commercially and internationally.
20	In Auckland, the Black Ferns are drawn in Pool A with Australia, Wales and a qualifier for next year's World Cup in New Zealand.
23	Auckland announces free entry for their home final this weekend.

DECEMBER

3	Super Rugby squads are named . . . World Rugby CEO Brett Gosper will leave the job in January. Chief Operating Officer Alan Gilpin will be in the role in the interim until a new appointee is found.
7	World Rugby Awards Special Edition: Richie McCaw is named men's (15s) player of the decade and Portia Woodman is women's sevens player of the decade. Six Black Ferns are named in the women's (15s) team of the decade: Eloise Blackwell, Kelly Brazier, Kendra Cocksedge, Fiao'o Faamausili, Linda Itunu and Portia Woodman. Seven All Blacks are named in the men's (15s) team of the decade: Dan Carter, Owen Franks, Richie McCaw, Ma'a Nonu, Brodie Retallick, Ben Smith and Sam Whitelock.
8	UK becomes the first country in the world to roll out a Covid-19 vaccine.
9	NZR Board meeting: Of the $5.41 million from the Government as part of the sports recovery package *(see 17 May)*, $2.4 million will be allocated to the sevens teams for next year's Olympic Games; the provincial unions will receive 10% less funding in 2021 than previously budgeted for; the Farah Palmer Cup will revert to Premiership and Championship divisions and the Heartland Championship is confirmed for next year; no decision is made on the format of the Mitre 10 Cup for next year. A proposal put to the 14 unions last month for consideration of a North Pool and South Pool, which would save NZR $700,000, needs further discussion.
10	The All Blacks will host Fiji (one test) and Italy (two) in July next year. After the Rugby Championship, they have confirmed tests against Italy, France and Ireland in November plus hopefully two more tests on that end of year tour. All games going ahead will depend on any current situation regarding Covid-19.
13	The All Blacks finish their quarantine in Auckland.
14	The schedule for Super Rugby trans-Tasman next year is released. There will be two matches on Friday nights and three matches on Saturday . . . Auckland declares an operating loss of $292,000 for 2020, but a final net profit of $48,000 from equity accounting . . . The All Blacks are drawn in Pool A with France, Italy and two qualifiers for the 2023 World Cup.
17	Government announces it has secured enough Covid-19 vaccines for the whole country from middle of next year. It will be free and optional.
20	At the ASB Rugby Awards Sam Cane wins the Kelvin R Tremain Memorial Award as NZ player-of-the-year and former All Black Sir Bryan Williams wins the Steinlager Salver for outstanding contribution to the game.
23	SANZAAR CEO Andy Marinos is appointed Rugby Australia CEO effective February.
29	WHO: Worldwide Covid-19 cases pass 80 million, with 1.77 million deaths.
31	New Year Honours List: Black Fern Kendra Cocksedge is made a Member of the MNZM; long serving Ngati Porou East Coast administrator Bill Burdett receives the Queen's Service Medal; Yoshihiro Sakata, who played for Japan in New Zealand in 1968 and for Canterbury in 1969, is made an honorary Member of the MNZM.

INTERNATIONAL RESULTS 2020

SIX-NATIONS CHAMPIONSHIP

Date	Home		Away		Location	Referee
Feb 01	Ireland	19	Scotland	12	Dublin	M Raynal (France)
Feb 01	Wales	42	Italy	0	Cardiff	L Pearce (England)
Feb 02	France	24	England	17	Paris	N Owens (Wales)
Feb 08	England	13	Scotland	6	Edinburgh	P Gauzere (France)
Feb 08	Ireland	24	Wales	14	Dublin	R Poite (France)
Feb 09	France	35	Italy	22	Paris	A Brace (Ireland)
Feb 22	France	27	Wales	23	Cardiff	M Carley (England)
Feb 22	Scotland	17	Italy	0	Rome	B O'Keeffe (NZ)
Feb 23	England	24	Ireland	12	London	J Peyper (SA)
Mar 07	England	33	Wales	30	London	B O'Keeffe (NZ)
Mar 08	Scotland	28	France	17	Edinburgh	P Williams (NZ)
Oct 24	Ireland	50	Italy	17	Dublin	M Carley (England)
Nov 01	England	34	Italy	5	Rome	P Gauzere (France)
Nov 01	Scotland	14	Wales	10	Llanelli	A Brace (Ireland)
Nov 01	France	35	Ireland	27	Paris	W Barnes (England)

FINAL TABLE

	P	W	D	L	For	Against	BP	Pts
England	5	4	0	1	121	77	2	18
France	5	4	0	1	138	117	2	18
Ireland	5	3	0	2	132	102	2	14
Scotland	5	3	0	2	77	59	2	14
Wales	5	1	0	4	119	98	4	8
Italy	5	0	0	5	44	178	0	0

International Results 2020

Date	Home		Away		Location	Referee
RUGBY CHAMPIONSHIP/TRI NATIONS						
Nov 01	New Zealand	43	Australia	5	Sydney	B O'Keeffe (NZ)
Nov 07	Australia	24	New Zealand	22	Brisbane	N Berry (Australia)
Nov 14	Argentina	25	New Zealand	15	Parramatta	A Gardner (Australia)
Nov 21	Australia	15	Argentina	15	Newcastle	P Williams (NZ)
Nov 28	New Zealand	38	Argentina	0	Newcastle	N Berry (Australia)
Dec 05	Australia	16	Argentina	16	Parramatta	A Gardner (Australia)
AUTUMN NATIONS CUP						
Nov 13	Ireland	32	Wales	9	Dublin	M Raynal (France)
Nov 14	Scotland	28	Italy	17	Florence	L Pearce (England)
Nov 14	England	40	Georgia	0	London	N Owens (Wales)
Nov 21	England	18	Ireland	7	London	P Gauzere (France)
Nov 21	Wales	18	Georgia	0	Llanelli	L Pearce (England)
Nov 22	France	22	Scotland	15	Edinburgh	W Barnes (England)
Nov 28	England	24	Wales	13	Llanelli	R Poite (France)
Nov 28	France	36	Italy	5	Paris	N Owens (Wales)
Nov 29	Ireland	23	Georgia	10	Dublin	M Raynal (France)
Dec 05	Wales	38	Italy	18	Llanelli	W Barnes (England)
Dec 05	Ireland	31	Scotland	16	Dublin	M Carley (England)
Dec 05	Fiji	38	Georgia	24	Edinburgh	M Adamson (Scotland)
Dec 06	England	22	France	19	London	A Brace (Ireland)
OTHER INTERNATIONALS						
Feb 01	Spain	31	Russia	12	Sochi	A Piardi (Italy)
Feb 01	Georgia	41	Romania	13	Tbilisi	T Foley (England)
Feb 01	Portugal	23	Belgium	17	Lisbon	S Grove-White (Scotland)
Feb 08	Portugal	22	Romania	11	Lisbon	L Cayre (France)
Feb 08	Belgium	38	Russia	12	Brussels	S Tevzadze (Georgia)
Feb 09	Georgia	23	Spain	10	Madrid	C Evans (Wales)
Feb 22	Russia	19	Portugal	18	Sochi	I Attorasagasti (Spain)
Feb 22	Romania	24	Spain	7	Bucharest	N Amashukeli (Georgia)
Feb 22	Georgia	78	Belgium	6	Tbilisi	C Serban (Romania)

Date	Home		Away		Location	Referee
Feb 29	Switzerland	33	Germany	20	Heidelberg	S Abulashvili (Georgia)
Feb 29	Netherlands	7	Poland	6	Amsterdam	K O'Brien (Germany)
Mar 07	Netherlands	36	Lithuania	17	Amsterdam	J Costa (Portugal)
Mar 07	Georgia	39	Portugal	24	Paris	B Blain (England)
Mar 07	Spain	30	Belgium	23	Brussels	S Gallagher (Ireland)
Mar 07	Russia	32	Romania	25	Krasnodar	D Jones (Wales)
Oct 11	New Zealand	16	Australia	16	Wellington	P Williams (NZ)
Oct 18	New Zealand	27	Australia	7	Auckland	A Gardner (Australia)
Oct 24	Scotland	48	Georgia	7	Edinburgh	A Ruiz (France)
Oct 24	France	38	Wales	21	Paris	K Dickson (England)
Oct 25	Chile	26	Brazil	13	Montevideo	F Mendez (Chile)
Nov 01	Spain	32	Uruguay	20	Montevideo	F Anselmi (Argentina)
Nov 06	Uruguay	19	Spain	10	Montevideo	F Anselmi (Argentina)
Nov 21	Portugal	30	Brazil	10	Lisbon	A Ionescu (Romania)
Nov 28	Portugal	33	Brazil	13	Lisbon	F Vedovelli (Italy)

THE FOREIGN LEGION
by John Lea

These New Zealand origin players were either contracted with professional overseas clubs for play in 2020/21, or commenced and completed an overseas contract during 2020 (denoted by *). Those no longer eligible for New Zealand have their country of allegiance shown in brackets.

AUSTRALIA
Super Rugby

ACT Brumbies:	Jahrome Brown, Nick Frost, Solomone Kata, Noah Lolesio (*Australia*), Peter Samu (*Australia*), Irae Simone (*Australia*), Reece Tapine, James Tucker
Melbourne Rebels:	Jermaine Ainsley* (*Australia*), Steven Misa*, Anaru Rangi *, Jordan Uelese (*Australia*)
NSW Waratahs:	Sam Caird, Tetera Faulkner (*Australia*), Lalakai Foketi, Karmichael Hunt (*Australia*), Jack Whetton
Queensland Reds:	Chris Feauai-Sautia (*Australia*), Brandon Paenga-Amosa (*Australia*), Lukhan Salakaia-Loto (*Australia*), Jack Straker*, Tuaina Tualima, Taniela Tupou (*Australia*), Suliasi Vunivalu
Western Force:	Johan Bardoul*, Pek Cowan (*Australia*), Richard Kahui, Toni Pulu (*Niue*), Henry Stowers (*Samoa*), Jeremy Thrush

ENGLAND
Aviva Premiership

Bath:	Jack Wilson (*England*)*
Bristol Bears:	John Afoa, Adrian Choat*, Jake Heenan, Nathan Hughes (*England*), James Lay* (*Samoa*), Jordan Lay* (*Samoa*), Alapati Leuia (*Samoa*), Steven Luatua, Charles Piutau, Chris Vui (*Samoa*)
Exeter Chiefs:	Tom Hendrickson
Gloucester:	Danny Drake, Willi Heinz (*England*), Josh Hohneck*, Jason Woodward (*England*)
Harlequins:	Tevita Cavubati (*Fiji*), Elia Elia (*Samoa*), Lewis Gjaltema, Paul Lasike (*USA*), Winston Stanley (*Samoa*)
Leicester Tigers:	Nemani Nadolo (*Fiji*), Jordan Taufua
London Irish:	Blair Cowan (*Scotland*), Terrence Hepetema, Sekope Kepu (*Australia*), William Lloyd, Motu Matu'u (*Samoa*), Waisake Naholo, Curtis Rona (*Australia*)
Newcastle Falcons:	Rodney Ah You (*Ireland*), John Hardie (*Scotland*), Sinoti Sinoti (*Samoa*)*, Cooper Vuna (*Australia*)
Northampton Saints:	Piers Francis (*England*), Owen Franks, Teimana Harrison (*England*), Dylan Hartley (*England*), Matt Proctor, Apisoloma Ratuniyarawa (*Fiji*), Ahsee Tuala (*Samoa*), Connor Tupai
Sale Sharks:	Bryn Evans*, Denny Solomona (*England*)
Wasps:	Malakai Fekitoa, Jimmy Gopperth, Brad Shields (*England*), Lima Sopoaga, Jeff To'omaga-Allen, Jacob Umaga
Worcester Warriors:	Ed Fidow (*Samoa*), Jono Kitto, Matt Moulds, Melani Nanai
RFU Championship	
Bedford Blues:	Grayson Hart (*Scotland*), Daniel Temm
Cornish Pirates:	Antonio Kirikiri, Fa'atiga Lemalu (*Samoa*), Shae Tucker, Marien Walker

Hartpury College:	Dan Koster
Jersey Reds:	Greg Dyer*, Samisoni Fisilau (*Tonga*), Liam Hallam-Eames*, Kurt Heatherley, Liam Howley*, Regan King, Uili Kolo'ofai (*Tonga*)
London Scottish:	Mark Bright (*England*), Chris Walker
Saracens:	Sean Maitland (*Scotland*), Mako Vunipola (*England*)

FRANCE
Top 14

Agen:	Paul Ngauamo (*Tonga*), Jordan Puletua, Jamie-Jerry Taulagi (*Samoa*), Sam Vaka
Bayonne:	Alofa Alofa (*Samoa*), Matt Graham, Census Johnston* (*Samoa*), Matt Luamanu (*Samoa*), Edwin Maka*, Jo Ravouvou, Michael Ruru, John Ulugia
Bordeaux Begles:	Ben Botica, Ben Lam, Ben Tameifuna (*Tonga*)
Brive:	So'otala Fa'aso'o, James Johnston (*Samoa*), Brandon Nansen (*Samoa*), Wesley Tapueluelu
Castres:	Paea Fa'anunu (*Tonga*), Filipo Nakosi (*Fiji*), Ma'ama Vaipulu (*Tonga*), Karena Wihongi*
Clermont:	Peter Betham, (*Australia*), Fritz Lee, Faifili Levave (*Samoa*), George Moala, Tim Nanai-Williams (*Samoa*)
La Rochelle:	Uini Atonio (*France*), Tawera Kerr-Barlow, Will Skelton (*Australia*), Teddy Stanaway, Loni Uhila, Victor Vito, Ihaia West
Lyon:	Toby Arnold, Cameron Mapusua, Temo Mayanavanua (*Fiji*), Charlie Ngatai, Alex Tulou (*Samoa*), Rudi Wulf
Montpellier:	Kahn Fotuali'i* (*Samoa*), Jarrad Hoeata^, Caleb Timu (*Australia*)
Pau:	Ziegfried Fisi'ihoi (*Tonga*), Tumua Manu, Daniel Ramsey, Dominiko Waqaniburotu (*Fiji*), Luke Whitelock
Racing 92:	Dominic Bird, Ope Peleseuma (*Samoa*), Anthony Tuitavake, Virimi Vakatawa (*France*)
Stade Francais:	Paul Alo-Emile (*Samoa*), Sione Anga'aelangi (*Tonga*), Telusa Veianu (*Tonga*)
Toulon:	Brian Alainu'ese, Bryce Heem, Liam Messam*, Nehe Milner-Skudder*, Ma'a Nonu, Duncan Paia'aua (*Australia*), Julian Savea*, Sonatane Takalua (*Tonga*), Isaia Toeava
Toulouse:	Pita Ahki, Charlie Faumuina, Jerome Kaino*, Paul Perez (*Samoa*), Joe Tekori (*Samoa*)

Second Division

Aurillac:	Jack McPhee, Adrian Smith, Leroy Van Dam
Beziers:	Elijah Niko, Jordan Puletua
Biarritz:	Johnny Dyer (*Fiji*), Tyrone Elkington-McDonald*, Adam Knight, Guy Millar, Francis Saili, Nick Smith*, Henry Speight (*Australia*), Gavin Stark
Colomiers:	Hika Elliot, Jonny Fa'amatuainu (*Tonga*), Daniel Faleafa (*Tonga*), Randall Kamea, Chris Tuatara-Morrison
Grenoble:	Leva Fifita (*Tonga*), Steven Setephano (*Cook Islands*), Taiasina Tu'ifua (*Tonga*), Edgar Tuinukuafe
Montauban:	Richard Haddon, Alex Luatua, Aviata Silago, Benson Stanley*
Nice:	Joketani Koroi

The Foreign Legion

Oyonnax:	Tony Ensor, Rory Grice, Roimata Hansell-Pune, Manu Leiataua (*Samoa*), Quentin MacDonald*, Tusi Pisi (*Samoa*), Hoani Tui, Josh Tyrell* (*Samoa*)
Perpignan:	Shahn Eru (*Cook Islands*), Piua Fa'aselele* (*Samoa*), Michael Faleafa* (*Tonga*), Siua Halanukonuka (*Tonga*), Tevita Mailau* (*Tonga*), Genesis Mamea (*Samoa*), Eric Sione*, George Tilsley, Ben Volavola (*Fiji*)
Provence:	Joe Edwards, Hikairo Forbes, Poutasi Luafutu (*Australia*), Lachie Munro, Sona Taumalolo (*Tonga*)*
Rouen-Normandie:	Carl Axtens, Matty James, Valentino Mapapalangi (*Tonga*), Anthony Perenise (*Samoa*), Belgium Tuatagaloa, Nemani Waka
Soyaux-Angouleme:	Ole Avei (*Samoa*), Sikeli Nabou (*Fiji*), Matt Vea, Jackson Willison
Stade Montois:	Siosefo Manu, Maselino Paulino (*Samoa*)
Valence-Romans	Matiaha Martin*, Peter Saili
Vannes:	Hugh Chalmers, Ambrose Curtis, Pat Leafa, Ash Moeke, Albert Vulivuli (*Fiji*)

IRELAND
Guinness Pro 14

Connacht:	Bundee Aki (*Ireland*), Jarrad Butler, Tom McCartney*, Abraham Papali'i, Dominic Robertson-McCoy
Leinster:	Michael Bent (*Ireland*), Jamison Gibson-Park (*Ireland*), James Lowe (*Ireland*)
Munster:	Tyler Bleyendaal*, Joey Carberry (*Ireland*), Rhys Marshall
Ulster:	Matt Faddes, Alby Matthewson, Sean Reidy (*Ireland*)

ITALY
Guinness Pro 14

Benetton Treviso:	Dean Budd* (*Italy*), Hame Faiva, Monty Ioane (*Italy*), Jayden Hayward (*Italy*), Nasi Manu* (*Tonga*), Iliesa Ratuva Tavuyara (*Fiji*)
Zebre:	Junior Laloifi, Josh Renton, Jimmy Tuivaiti (*Italy*)

JAPAN
Super Rugby

Sunwolves	Jarred Adams*, Leni Apisai*, Chris Eves*, Mitchell Jacobson*, Nick Mayhew*, Brendan O'Connor*, Ben Te'o (*England*)*, Tevita Tupou*

Top League

Canon Eagles:	Sef Fa'agase*, Jesse Parete
Hino Red Dolphins:	Levi Aumua, Hayden Cripps (*Japan*), Jack Debreczeni, Joel Everson*, Gillies Kaka, Nili Latu (*Tonga*), Pauliasi Manu*, Liaki Moli, Ash Parker (*Japan*), Chance Peni-Ataera, Augustine Pulu
Honda Heat:	Josh Bekhuis, Matt Duffie, Baden Kerr*, Lomano Lemeki* (*Japan*), Lelia Masaga*, David Milo*, Tetuhi Roberts, Shaun Treeby
Kobelco Steelers:	Nigel Ah Wong*, Fraser Anderson (*Tonga*), Richard Buckman, Dan Carter*, Aaron Cruden, Tom Franklin, Sefo Kautai*, Tim Lafaele (*Japan*), Ata'ata Moeakiola (*Japan*), Hayden Parker (*Japan*), Brodie Retallick*, Aidan Rodd, Ben Smith, Toni Vaihu*, Matt Vant Leven

Kubota Spears:	Ryan Crotty, Wharenui Hawera
Mitsubishi Dynaboars:	Heiden Bedwell-Curtis, Nicholas Ealey, Dan Hawkins*, Jackson Hemopo, Tevita Lepolo, Michael Little, Alaia'sa Roland, Colin Slade, Matt Vaega, James Wilson
Munakata Sanix Blues:	Mark Abbott, Jarred Adams, Siliva Ahio*, Sam Chongkit, Jason Emery, Josh Gordon*, Karne Hesketh (*Japan*), Hare Makiri, Kosei Ono (*Japan*), Dan Pryor, Dallas Tatana (*Japan*)
NEC Green Rockets:	Sam Henwood*, Jack Lam (*Samoa*), Hapakuki Moala-Liavaa*, Maritino Nemani, Tim O'Malley*, George Risale, Amanaki Savieti*, Lolagi Visinia*, Sanaila Waqa*
NTT Docomo Hurricanes:	Marty Banks, Tom Marshall, Lincoln McClutchie*, Keepa Mewett*, TJ Perenara, Liam Squire*
NTT Shining Arcs:	Brackin Karauria-Henry (*Australia*), Luteru Laulala*, Christian Leali'ifano (*Australia*), Leilua Murphy, Sekonaia Pole, Anaru Rangi (*Australia*), Fletcher Smith, Jimmy Tupou
Ricoh Black Rams:	Colin Bourke, Mike Broadhurst (*Japan*), Elliot Dixon, Ben Funnell, Damon Leasuasu, Josh Mau*, Matt McGahan, Piri Paraone, Robbie Robinson (*Japan*), Jacob Skeen, Alex Woonton* (*Cook Islands*)
Panasonic Wild Knights:	Asaeli Ai Valu (*Japan*), Michael Hobbs, Digby Ioane (*Australia*), Justin Ives (*Japan*), Chris King, Craig Millar, Hadleigh Parkes (*Wales*), Jordan Rapana*, Emerson Tamura-Paki, Tevita Tupou, Sam Whitelock*
Suntory Sun-Goliath:	Richard Judd, Joe Latta, Greg Pleasants-Tate, Jordan Smiler (*Australia*), Hendrik Tui (*Japan*), Joe Wheeler*
Toshiba Brave Lupus:	Tim Bateman, Lyndon Dunshea*, Johnny Fa'auli, Michael Leitch (*Japan*), Tom Parsons*, Jack Stratton, Seta Tamanivalu, Tom Taylor, Matt Todd
Toyota Verblitz:	Michael Allardice, Tiaan Falcon, Jamie Henry (*Japan*), Kieran Read, Charlie Lawrence, Male Sa'u (*Japan*), Shneil Singh*, Rob Thompson
Yamaha Jubilo:	Malo Tuitama

Top Challenge

Coca Cola Red Sparks:	Solomon King, Will Mangos*, Joe Tupe*, Will Tupou (Japan)
Kamaishi Seawaves:	Mike Fitzgerald*, Morgan Mitchell, Ben Nee Nee, Oliver Polson, Cody Rei*
Kintetsu Liners:	Jed Brown, Quade Cooper (Australia), Pasqualle Dunn, Semi Masirewa, Mike Stolberg, Luke Thompson (Japan)
Kyuden Voltex:	Phil Burleigh (Scotland), Tom Rowe
Toyota Industries Shuttles:	Michael Curry, Scott Fuglistaller, Jono Hickey*, Tevita Taufu'i (Tonga)

NORTH AMERICA

Major League Rugby

Austin Gilgronis:	Pele Cowley (*Samoa*), Frank Halai, Potu Leavasa* (*Samoa*), Jamie Mackintosh, Kurt Morath (*Tonga*), Isaac Ross
Dallas Jackals	Marco Fepulea'i, Tim O'Malley
Houston Sabercats:	Tim Cadwallader, Taylor Howden, Siua Maile* (*Tonga*), Moa Maliepo (*Romania*), Boyd Wiggins

New England Free Jacks:	Sam Beard, Harrison Boyle, Donald Brighouse* (*Samoa*), Naulia Dawai (*Fiji*), Tolu Fahamakioa* (*Samoa*), Brad Hemopo, Joe Johnston, Josh Larsen (*Canada*), Aleki Morris-Lome, Jack Ram (*Tonga*), Liam Steel, Beaudein Waaka
New Orleans Gold:	Tony Lamborn (*USA*)*, Kane Thompson (*Samoa*)
Old Glory DC:	Jamason Fa'anana-Schultz (*USA*), Gordon Fullerton, Callum Gibbins, Mungo Mason (*Scotland*), Apisai Naikatini (*Fiji*), Declan O'Donnell, Jason Robertson, Renata Roberts-Tenana, Mike Sosene-Feagai (*USA*), Dylan Taikato-Simpson, Danny Tusitala (*Samoa*)
Rugby Atlanta:	Bill Fukofuka, Rory Van Vugt
Rugby United New York:	Andrew Ellis, Fa'asiu Fuatai, Dan Hollinshead, Kara Pryor, Zak Taulafo (*Samoa*)
San Diego Legion:	Devereaux Ferris, Lua Li
Seattle Seawolves:	Shalom Suniula (*USA*), Brad Tucker
Toronto Arrows (*Canada*):	Tayler Adams, Richie Asiata, Sam Malcolm, Aaron McLelland*
Utah Warriors:	Arawa Elkington, Blake Hohaia, Jackson Kaka, Dwayne Polataivao (*Samoa*), Hagen Schulte (*Germany*), Kalolo Tuiloma*

ROMANIA
Continental Club Rugby League

CSM Stiinta Bucuresti:	Jason Tomane

SCOTLAND
Guinness Pro 14

Edinburgh:	Simon Berghan (*Scotland*)
Glasgow:	Corey Flynn, Nick Grigg (*Scotland*), TJ Ioane (*Samoa*), Aki Seuli, Samu Vunisa (*Italy*)

SOUTH AFRICA
Super Rugby

Bulls:	Nafi Tuitavake (*Tonga*)

SOUTH AMERICA

Corinthians (Brazil):	Josh Reeves (*Brazil*)
Olimpia Lions (Paraguay):	Matt Matich
Penarol (Uruguay):	Afa Pakalani (*Tonga*)
Selknam (Chile):	Latiume Fosita (*Tonga*), Johnny Ika (*Tonga*)

WALES
Guinness Pro 14

Cardiff Blues:	Willis Halaholo, Rey Lee-Lo (*Samoa*), Teofilo Paulo* (*Samoa*), Nick Williams*
Ospreys:	Gareth Anscombe (*Wales*), Ma'afu Fia (*Tonga*), Marty McKenzie
Llanelli Scarlets:	Kieron Fonotia* (*Samoa*), Sam Lousi (*Tonga*), Johnny McNicholl (*Wales*), Blade Thomson (*Scotland*)

OVERSEAS PLAYERS IN NEW ZEALAND FIRST-CLASS RUGBY, 2020

Compiled by John Lea

For previously capped players the most recent year and level of selection are shown.
Some players have since, or soon will, also become eligible for New Zealand.

Player	Country	Year	NZ Team in 2020
Nigel Ah Wong	Australia	Uncapped	Manawatu
Sef Fa'agase	Australia XV	2016	Otago
Kirisi Kuidrani	Australia Under 20	2011	Counties Manukau
Tyrel Lomax	Australia Under 20	2016	Tasman
Hugh Roach	Australia Under 20	2012	Crusaders
Matt Skipwith-Garland	Australia Schools	2009	Bay of Plenty
Tyler Ardron	Canada	2019	Chiefs
Jordan Olsen	Canada	2019	Northland
Alex Woonton	Cook Islands Under 20	2008	North Harbour
Alex Hodgman	Fiji Under 20	2012	Auckland
Mitieli Kaloudigebeci	Fiji	Uncapped	Buller
Tevita Nabura	Fiji Sevens	2017	Counties Manukau
Patrick Osborne	Fiji	2019	Waikato
Viliame Rarasea	Fiji Under 20	2014	Counties Manukau
Pita-Gus Sowakula	Fiji	Uncapped	Taranaki
Tuapati Taleimaitoga	Fiji	2018	Southland
Asaeli Tikoirotuma	Fiji XV	2019	North Harbour
Anton Segner	Germany Under 16	2016	Tasman
Oliver Jager	Ireland Under 18	2013	Canterbury
Conan O'Donnell	Ireland Under 20	2016	Counties Manukau
Jack Regan	Ireland	Uncapped	Otago
Stan Van Den Hoven	Netherlands	Uncapped	Bay of Plenty
Jarred Adams	Samoa Under 20	2016	Auckland
Michael Ala'alatoa	Samoa	2019	Manawatu
Donald Brighouse	Samoa	2018	Taranaki
Pele Cowley	Samoa	2019	Counties Manukau
Marco Fepulea'i	Samoa Under 20	2015	Auckland
Neria Fomai	Samoa Sevens	2018	Hawke's Bay
Kieron Fonotia	Samoa	2019	Tasman
Stacey Ili	Samoa	2018	Hawke's Bay
Josh Ioane	Samoa Under 20	2015	Otago
Luteru Laulala	Samoa Under 20	2014	Counties Manukau
James Lay	Samoa	2019	Auckland

Player	Country	Year	NZ Team in 2020
Jordan Lay	Samoa	2019	Bay of Plenty
Kane Le'aupepe	Samoa	2019	Bay of Plenty
Potu Leavasa	Samoa A	2016	Counties Manukau
Orbyn Leger	Samoa Under 20	2015	Counties Manukau
Pisi Leilua	Samoa Under 20	2015	Northland
Ray Niuia	Samoa	2019	Blues
Pepesana Patafilo	Samoa Under 20	2015	Wellington
Teofilo Paulo	Samoa	2019	Manawatu
Dwayne Polataivao	Samoa	2019	Tasman
Hisa Sasagi	Samoa	2018	Otago
Jonathan Taumateine	Samoa Under 20	2015	Counties Manukau
Tanielu Tele'a	Samoa Under 20	2017	Auckland
Chase Tiatia	Samoa Under 20	2015	Bay of Plenty
Danny Tusitala	Samoa	2019	Auckland
Hugh Blake	Scotland Sevens	2018	South China Lions
Hamilton Burr	Scotland Under 20	2016	Waikato
Ross Geldenhuys	South Africa	Uncapped	Bay of Plenty
Dylan Nel	South Africa	Uncapped	Otago
Kobus Van Wyk	South Africa Under 20	2012	Hurricanes
Tolu Fahamakioa	Tonga	2018	Waikato
Folau Fakatava	Tonga	Uncapped	Hawke's Bay
Sione Fifita	Tonga	2018	Counties Manukau
Vaea Fifita	Tonga Under 18	2010	Wellington
Latiume Fosita	Tonga	2019	Counties Manukau
Shannon Frizzell	Tonga Under 20	2014	Tasman
Kali Hala	Tonga	2019	Counties Manukau
Fine Inisi	Tonga Sevens	2019	North Harbour
Lotu Inisi	Tonga Sevens	2019	North Harbour
Zane Kapeli	Tonga	2019	Bay of Plenty
Penikolo Latu	Tonga	2019	Southland
Siua Maile	Tonga	2019	Manawatu
Nasi Manu	Tonga	2019	Otago
Fetuli Paea	Tonga	2019	Tasman
Samisoni Taukei'aho	Tonga Under 15	2013	Waikato
Tony Lamborn	United States	2019	Southland
Mike Sosene-Feagai	United States	2019	Auckland

NEW ZEALAND ORIGIN AND FIRST-CLASS PLAYERS CAPPED OVERSEAS, 2020

Provincial Union and Year indicate most recent first-class play when applicable.

Player	Country	Last Representation	Year
Jermaine Ainsley	Australia A	Otago	–
Noah Lolesio	Australia	Auckland	–
Brandon Paenga–Amosa	Australia	Auckland	–
Matthew Phillip	Australia	Southland	2016
Peter Samu	Australia	Crusaders	2018
Lukhan Salakaia-Loto	Australia	Auckland	–
Irae Simone	Australia	Auckland	–
Taniela Tupou	Australia	Auckland	–
Jordan Uelese	Australia	Wellington	–
Josh Reeves	Brazil	Canterbury	–
Willi Heinz	England	Canterbury	2015
Joe Marchant	England	Blues	2020
Mako Vunipola	England	Auckland	–
Johnny Dyer	Fiji	South Canterbury	2016
Haereiti Hetet	Fiji	Bay of Plenty	2020
Temo Mayanavanua	Fiji	Northland	2020
Nemani Nadolo	Fiji	Crusaders	2014
Peni Ravai	Fiji	Southland	2016
Samuela Tawake	Fiji	Manawatu	2020
Ben Volavola	Fiji	North Harbour	2017
Uini Atonio	France	Counties Manukau	2011
Virimi Vakatawa	France	Canterbury	–
Bundee Aki	Ireland	Counties Manukau	2014
Jamison Gibson-Park	Ireland	Taranaki	2015
James Lowe	Ireland	Tasman	2017
Dean Budd	Italy	Northland	2011
Jayden Hayward	Italy	Taranaki	2012
Monty Ioane	Italy	Bay of Plenty	2017
Jimmy Tuivaiti	Italy	North Harbour	2014
Willie Ambaka	Kenya Sevens	Manawatu	2017
Storm Carroll	Netherlands	Hawke's Bay	–

Player	Country	Last Representation	Year
Josh Gascoigne	Netherlands	Waikato	2016
Liam McBride	Netherlands	Taranaki	2015
Lucas Puts	Netherlands	Manawatu	–
Moa Mua Maliepo	Romania	Auckland	–
Thomas Alosio	Samoa Sevens	Wellington	2015
Losi Filipo	Samoa Sevens	Wellington	2019
Meli Matavao	Samoa Sevens	Otago	2018
Alamanda Motuga	Samoa Sevens	Counties Manukau	2020
Paul Scanlan	Samoa Sevens	Auckland	–
Simon Berghan	Scotland	Canterbury	–
Blair Cowan	Scotland	Wellington	–
Sean Maitland	Scotland	Canterbury	2012
Blade Thomson	Scotland	Hurricanes	2018
Brad Linklater	Spain	Auckland	–
Afa Tauli	Spain	Manawatu	–
Johnny McNicholl	Wales	Canterbury	2016
Hadleigh Parkes	Wales	Auckland	2014

ALL BLACKS TEST MATCH RECORD

to January 1, 2021

Opponents	Played	Won	Lost	Drawn	For	Against
Argentina	31	29	1	1	1203	447
Australia	170	117	45	8	3660	2417
British Isles	41	30	7	4	700	399
Canada	6	6	–	–	376	54
England	42	33	8	1	992	594
Fiji	5	5	–	–	364	50
France	61	48	12	1	1596	801
Georgia	1	1	–	–	43	10
Ireland	32	29	2	1	917	389
Italy	14	14	–	–	820	131
Japan	4	4	–	–	351	61
Namibia	2	2	–	–	129	23
Pacific Islands	1	1	–	–	41	26
Portugal	1	1	–	–	108	13
Romania	2	2	–	–	99	14
Samoa	7	7	–	–	411	72
Scotland	31	29	–	2	922	349
South Africa	99	59	36	4	2050	1577
Tonga	6	6	–	–	418	42
United States	3	3	–	–	171	15
Wales	35	32	3	–	1110	391
World XV	3	2	1	–	94	69
	597	**460**	**115**	**22**	**16,575**	**7,944**

ALL BLACKS STATISTICS
to January 1, 2021

LEADING ALL BLACKS APPEARANCES IN ALL MATCHES

R.H. McCaw	149	K.R. Tremain	86	O.M. Brown	69
C.E. Meads	133	S.S. Wilson	85	F.E. Bunce	69
K.F. Mealamu	133	B.R. Smith	85	J.T. Rokocoko	69
S.B.T. Fitzpatrick	128	I.J. Clarke	83	M.W. Shaw	69
K.J. Read	128	A.K. Hore	83	B.J. Lochore	68
S.L. Whitelock	122	J. Kaino	83	C.W. Dowd	67
T.D. Woodcock	118	S.C. McDowall	81	C.R. Jack	67
A.M. Haden	117	B.A. Retallick	81	A.D. Oliver	67
I.A. Kirkpatrick	113	J.F. Umaga	79	G.M. Somerville	67
B.G. Williams	113	G.J. Fox	78	I.J.A. Dagg	66
D.W. Carter	112	R.W. Loe	78	G.A. Knight	66
O.T. Franks	108	A.J. Williams	78	A.J. Whetton	65
I.D. Jones	105	W.J. Whineray	77	A.R. Sutherland	64
M.A. Nonu	104	W.K. Little	75	T.J. Wright	64
J.M. Muliaina	102	S.J. Cane	75	D.C. Howlett	63
B.J. Robertson	102	M.N. Jones	74	K.L. Skinner	63
G.W. Whetton	101	D.S. Coles	74	R. So'oialo	63
Z.V. Brooke	100	J.T. Lomu	73	M.R. Brewer	61
A.L. Smith	97	P.A.T. Weepu	73	M.J. Brownlie	61
J.J. Kirwan	96	W.W.V. Crockett	72	G.N.K. Mourie	61
C.G. Smith	94	A.P. Mehrtens	72	R.W. Norton	61
D.B. Clarke	89	M.G. Mexted	72	T.C. Randell	61
B.J. Barrett	89	J.W. Wilson	71	D. Young	61
J.W. Marshall	88	T.T.R. Perenara	70	C.M. Cullen	60
S.M. Going	86	R.M. Brooke	69	B.C. Thorn	60

LEADING POINTS-SCORERS IN ALL MATCHES FOR NEW ZEALAND

		Matches	Points
D.W. Carter	2003–15	112	1598
G.J. Fox	1985–93	78	1067
A.P. Mehrtens	1995–2004	72	994
D.B. Clarke	1956–64	89	781
B.J. Barrett	2012–20	84	655
W.F. McCormick	1965–71	44	453
B.G. Williams	1970–78	113	401t
C.J. Spencer	1995–2004	44	383
W.J. Wallace	1903–08	51	379
A.R. Hewson	1979–84	34	357
J.F. Karam	1972–75	42	345
A.W. Cruden	2010–17	50	322
K.J. Crowley	1983–91	35	316
J.W. Wilson	1993–2001	71	299
M.F. Nicholls	1921–30	51	284
J.J. Kirwan	1984–94	96	275
R.G. Wilson	1976–80	25	272
C.M. Cullen	1996–2002	60	266
R.M. Deans	1983–85	19	252
J.A. Gallagher	1986–89	41	251

t includes a penalty try

LEADING TRY-SCORERS IN ALL MATCHES

		Matches	Tries
J.J. Kirwan	1984–94	96	67
B.G. Williams	1970–78	113	66t
C.M. Cullen	1996–2002	60	52
I.A. Kirkpatrick	1967–77	113	50
J.W. Wilson	1993–2001	71	50
S.S. Wilson	1976–83	85	50
D.C. Howlett	2000–07	63	49
T.J. Wright	1986–92	64	49t
J. Hunter	1905–08	36	48
J.T. Rokocoko	2003–10	69	47
B.G. Fraser	1979–84	55	46
S.J. Savea	2012–17	54	46
G.B. Batty	1972–77	56	45
J.T. Lomu	1994–2002	73	43
Z.V. Brooke	1987–97	100	42
M.J. Dick	1963–70	55	42

*includes a penalty try

MOST APPEARANCES IN INTERNATIONALS

R.H. McCaw	2001–15	148	G.M. Somerville	2000–08	66
K.F. Mealamu	2002–15	132	J.J. Kirwan	1984–94	63
K.J. Read	2008–19	127	J.T. Lomu	1994–2002	63
S.L. Whitelock	2010–20	122	R.M. Brooke	1992–99	62
T.D. Woodcock	2002–15	118	D.C. Howlett	2000–07	62
D.W. Carter	2003–15	112	R. So'oialo	2002–09	62
O.T. Franks	2009–19	108	C.W. Dowd	1993–2000	60
M.A. Nonu	2003–15	103	J.W. Wilson	1993–2001	60
J.M. Muliaina	2003–11	100	A.D. Oliver	1997–2007	59
A.L. Smith	2012–20	97	B.C. Thorn	2003–11	59
C.G. Smith	2004–15	94	Z.V. Brooke	1987–97	58
S.B.T. Fitzpatrick	1986–97	92	G.W. Whetton	1981–91	58
B.J. Barrett	2012–20	88	C.M. Cullen	1996–2002	58
B.R. Smith	2009–19	84	S. Williams	2010–19	58
A.K. Hore	2002–13	83	B.T. Kelleher	1999–2007	57
J. Kaino	2004–17	81	O.M. Brown	1992–98	56
J.W. Marshall	1995–2005	81	L.R. MacDonald	2000–08	56
B.A. Retallick	2012–19	81	C.J.Taylor	2015–20	56
I.D. Jones	1990–99	79	F.E. Bunce	1992–97	55
A.J. Williams	2002–12	77	M.N. Jones	1987–98	55
J.F. Umaga	1997–2005	74	C.E. Meads	1957–71	55
S.J. Cane	2012–20	74	J.A. Kronfeld	1995–2000	54
D.S. Coles	2012–20	74	S.J. Savea	2012–17	54
W.W.V. Crockett	2009–17	71	C.S. Jane	2008–14	53
P.A.T. Weepu	2004–13	71	Q.J. Cowan	2004–11	51
A.P. Mehrtens	1995–2004	70	T.C. Randell	1997–2002	51
T.T.R. Perenara	2014–20	69	W.K. Little	1990–98	50
J.T. Rokocoko	2003–10	68	R.D. Thorne	1999–2007	50
C.R. Jack	2001–07	67	J.P.T. Moody	2014–20	50
I.J.A. Dagg	2010–17	66			

MOST POINTS FOR NEW ZEALAND IN INTERNATIONALS

	Matches	Tries	Con	PG	DG	Mark	Points
D.W. Carter	112	29	293	281	8	–	1598
A.P. Mehrtens	70	7	169	188	10	–	967
B.J. Barrett	88	36	149	55	2	–	649
G.J. Fox	46	1	118	128	7	–	645
A.W. Cruden	50	5	63	56	1	–	322
C.J. Spencer	35	14	49	41	–	–	291
D.C. Howlett	62	49	–	–	–	–	245
C.M. Cullen	58	46	3	–	–	–	236
J.W. Wilson	60	44	1	3	1	–	234
J.T. Rokocoko	68	46	–	–	–	–	230
S.J. Savea	54	46	–	–	–	–	230
D.B. Clarke	31	2	33	38	5	2	207
A.R. Hewson	19	4	22	43	4	–	201
B.R. Smith	84	39	–	–	–	–	195
J.T. Lomu	63	37	–	–	–	–	185
J.F. Umaga	74	37t	–	–	–	–	185
R. Mo'unga	22	5	58	13	-	-	180
T.E. Brown	18	5	43	20	–	–	171
J.M. Muliaina	100	34	–	–	–	–	170
M.A. Nonu	103	31	–	–	–	–	155
C.L. McAlister	30	7	26	22	–	–	153
L.R. MacDonald	56	15t	25	7	–	–	146
S.W. Sivivatu	45	29	–	–	–	–	145
J.J. Kirwan	63	351	–	–	–	–	143
R.H. McCaw	148	28t	–	–	–	–	140
I.J.A. Dagg	66	26	1	2	–	–	138
C.G. Smith	94	26	–	–	–	–	130
K.J. Read	127	26	–	–	–	–	130
R.E. Ioane	34	26	–	–	–	–	130
W.F. McCormick	16	–	23	24	1	–	121
J.W. Marshall	81	24	–	–	–	–	120
S.D. Culhane	6	1	32	15	–	–	114
A.L. Smith	97	21	1	-	.	.	107
K.J. Crowley	19	5	5	23	2	–	105
N.J. Evans	16	5	30	6	–	–	103
P.A.T. Weepu	71	7	10	16	–	–	103
J.M. Barrett	23	14	11	3	.	.	101

1 includes three tries at five points
t includes penalty try

MOST STARTS IN EACH POSITION FOR NEW ZEALAND IN INTERNATIONALS

Fullback	J.M. Muliaina	2003–11	83	No 8	K.J. Read	2009–19	118
Wing	J.T. Rokocoko	2003–10	66	Flanker	R.H. McCaw	2001–15	139
Centre	C.G. Smith	2004–15	90	Lock	S.L. Whitelock	2010–19	97
2nd five-eighth	M.A. Nonu	2003–15	81	Prop	T.D. Woodcock	2002–15	105
1st five-eighth	D.W. Carter	2004–15	94	Hooker	S.B.T. Fitzpatrick	1986–97	91
Halfback	A.L. Smith	2012–20	89	Substitute	K.F. Mealamu	2002–15	55

The player must have started the match in that position. Appearances as replacements are not included except in this case Mealamu.

MOST TRIES FOR NEW ZEALAND IN INTERNATIONALS

	Matches	Tries		Matches	Tries
D.C. Howlett	62	49	M.A. Nonu	103	31
C.M. Cullen	58	46	D.W. Carter	112	29
J.T. Rokocoko	68	46	S.W. Sivivatu	45	29
S.J. Savea	54	46	R.H. McCaw	148	28t
J.W. Wilson	60	44	C.G. Smith	94	26
B.R. Smith	85	39	I.J.A. Dagg	66	26
J.T. Lomu	63	37	K.J. Read	127	26
J.F. Umaga	74	37t	R.E. Ioane	34	26
B.J. Barrett	88	36	J.W. Marshall	81	24
J.J. Kirwan	63	35	A.L. Smith	97	21
J.M. Muliaina	100	34	F.E. Bunce	55	20

t Includes one penalty try

MOST TRIES IN AN INTERNATIONAL

M.C.G. Ellis	v Japan, 1995	6	J.W. Wilson	v Samoa, 1999	4
J.W. Wilson	v Fiji, 1997	5	J.M. Muliaina	v Canada, 2003	4
D. McGregor	v England, 1905	4	S.W. Sivivatu	v Fiji, 2005	4
C.I. Green	v Fiji, 1987	4	Z.R. Guildford	v Canada, 2011	4
J.A. Gallagher	v Fiji, 1987	4	B.J. Barrett	v Australia, 2018	4
J.J. Kirwan	v Wales, 1988	4	J.M. Barrett	v Italy, 2018	4
J.T. Lomu	v England, 1995	4	G.C. Bridge	v Tonga, 2019	4
C.M. Cullen	v Scotland, 1996	4			

MOST PENALTY GOALS IN AN INTERNATIONAL

A.P. Mehrtens	v Australia, 1999	9	D.W. Carter	v Australia, 2007	7
A.P. Mehrtens	v France, 2000	9	P.A.T. Weepu	v Argentina, 2011	7
G.J. Fox	v W Samoa, 1993	7	B.J. Barrett	v BI Lions, 2017	7
A.P. Mehrtens	v South Africa, 1999	7			

MOST CONVERSIONS IN AN INTERNATIONAL

S.D. Culhane	v Japan, 1995	20	D.W. Carter	v Canada, 2003	9
N.J. Evans	v Portugal, 2007	14	C.R. Slade	v Japan, 2011	9
T.E. Brown	v Tonga, 2000	12	G.J. Fox	v Italy, 1987	8
L.R. MacDonald	v Tonga, 2003	12	G.J. Fox	v Wales, 1988	8
T.E. Brown	v Italy, 1999	11	A.P. Mehrtens	v Italy, 2002	8
G.J. Fox	v Fiji, 1987	10	R. Mo'unga	v Canada, 2019	8
C.J. Spencer	v Argentina, 1997	10	J.M. Barrett	v Namibia, 2019	8

HIGHEST POINTS-SCORERS IN AN INTERNATIONAL

	Opponent	Tries	Con	PG	DG	Points
S.D. Culhane	Japan, 1995[1]	1	20	–	–	45
T.E. Brown	Italy, 1999	1	11	3	–	36
D.W. Carter	Lions, 2005	2	4	5	–	33
C.J. Spencer	Argentina, 1997[1]	2	10	1	–	33
A.P. Mehrtens	Ireland, 1997	1	5	6	–	33
N.J. Evans	Portugal, 2007	1	14	–	–	33
T.E. Brown	Tonga, 2000	1	12	1	–	32
M.C.G. Ellis	Japan, 1995	6	–	–	–	30
B.J. Barrett	Australia, 2018	4	5	–	–	30
T.E. Brown	Samoa, 2001	3	3	3	–	30
A.P. Mehrtens	Australia, 1999	–	1	9	–	29
A.P. Mehrtens	France, 2000	–	1	9	–	29
L.R. MacDonald	Tonga, 2003	1	12	–	–	29
D.W. Carter	Canada, 2007	3	7	–	–	29
A.P. Mehrtens	Canada, 1995[1]	1	7	3	–	28
D.W. Carter	Wales, 2010	2	4	3	–	27
A.R. Hewson	Australia, 1982	1	2	5	1	26
G.J. Fox	Fiji, 1987	–	10	2	–	26
D.W. Carter	Wales, 2005	2	5	2	–	26
D.W. Carter	England, 2006	1	3	5	–	26
T.E. Brown	Samoa, 1999[1]	–	7	4	–	26
B.J. Barrett	Wales, 2016	2	5	2	–	26
D.W. Carter	South Africa, 2006	–	2	7	–	25
G.J. Fox	Western Samoa, 1993	–	2	7	–	25
J.W. Wilson	Fiji, 1997	5	–	–	–	25
C.J. Spencer	South Africa, 1997	1	4	4	–	25
D.W. Carter	France, 2004	1	4	4	–	25
W.F. McCormick	Wales, 1969	–	3	5	1	24
B.J. Barrett	Samoa, 2017	2	7	–	–	24
D.S. McKenzie	France, 2018	2	7	–	–	24

[1] international debut

NEW ZEALAND INTERNATIONAL CAPTAINS

R.H. McCaw	2004–15	110	I.J. Clarke	1955	3
K.J. Read	2012–19	52	J. Collins	2006–07	3
S.B.T. Fitzpatrick	1992–97	51	R.R. King	1937	3
W.J. Whineray	1958–65	30	D.J. Graham	1964	3
R.D. Thorne	2002–07	23	D.S. Loveridge	1980	3
T.C. Randell	1998–2002	22	K.F. Mealamu	2008–11	3
J.F. Umaga	2004–05	21	J.M. Muliaina	2009	3
G.N.K. Mourie	1977–82	19	F.J. Oliver	1978	3
B.J. Lochore	1966–70	18	J. Richardson	1924	3
A.G. Dalton	1981–85	17	F. Roberts	1910	3
G.W. Whetton	1990–91	15	R.W. Roberts	1914	3
W.T. Shelford	1988–90	14	G.G. Aitken	1921	2
D.E. Kirk	1986–87	11	R.H. Duff	1956	2
T.J. Blackadder	2000	10	J.L. Griffiths	1936	2
A.R. Leslie	1974–76	10	A. McDonald	1913	2
A.D. Oliver	2001	10	N.A. Mitchell	1938	2
I.A. Kirkpatrick	1972–73	9	M.J. O'Leary	1913	2
S.J. Cane	2015–20	9	A.R. Reid	1957	2
C.G. Porter	1925–30	7	K.L. Skinner	1952	2
F.R. Allen	1946–49	6	J.B. Smith	1949	2
S.L. Whitelock	2017–19	6	P.B. Vincent	1956	2
R.R. Elvidge	1949–50	5	S.S. Wilson	1983	2
R. So'oialo	2008–09	5	J. Duncan	1903	1
R.C. Stuart	1953–54	5	P.W. Henderson	1995	1
M.J. Brownlie	1928	4	A.K. Hore	2011	1
D. Gallaher	1905–06	4	C.R. Laidlaw	1968	1
M.J.B. Hobbs	1985–86	4	H.T. Lilburne	1929	1
J. Hunter	1907–08	4	R.M. McKenzie	1938	1
P. Johnstone	1950–51	4	J.R. Page	1934	1
F.D. Kilby	1932–34	4	E.J. Roberts	1921	1
J.E. Manchester	1935–36	4	B.R. Smith	2017	1
J.W. Marshall	1997	4	J.C. Spencer	1905	1
C.E. Meads	1971	4	W.A. Strang	1931	1
R.W. Norton	1977	4	K.R. Tremain	1968	1
J.W. Stead	1904–08	4	L.C. Whitelock	2018	1

HIGHEST SCORES IN TEST MATCHES

Opponent	Home		Away		Opponent	Home		Away	
Argentina	93–8	(1997)	54–18	(2012)	Namibia	–	–	58–14	(2015)
Australia	51–20	(2014)	54–34	(2017)	Pacific Islands	41–26	(2004)	–	
British Isles	48–18	(2005)	–		Portugal	–	–	108–13	(2007)
Canada	79–15	(2011)	68–8	(2003)	Romania	–	–	85–8	(2007)
England	64–22	(1998)	45–29	(1995)	Samoa	101–14	(2008)	25–16	(2015)
Fiji	91–0	(2005)	–		Scotland	69–20	(2000)	51–15	(1993)
								51–22	(2012)
France	61–10	(2007)	62–13	(2015)	South Africa	57–0	(2017)	57-15	(2016)
Georgia	–	–	43–10	(2015)	Tonga	102–0	(2000)	91–7	(2003)
Ireland	66–28	(2010)	63–15	(1997)	USA	–	–	74–6	(2014)
Italy	70–6	(1987)	101–3	(1999)	Wales	55–3	(2003)	53–37	(2003)
Japan	83–7	(2011)	145–17	(1995)					

MOST POINTS BY AN ALL BLACK AGAINST AN OPPONENT

Opponent	In an International				In a Career	
Argentina	33	C.J. Spencer	1997		103	G.J. Fox
Australia	30	B.J. Barrett	2018		366	D.W. Carter
British Isles	33	D.W. Carter	2005		46	A.R. Hewson
Canada	29	D.W. Carter	2007		47	D.W. Carter
England	26	D.W. Carter	2006		178	D.W. Carter
Fiji	26	G.J. Fox	1987		29	C.M. Cullen
France	29	A.P. Mehrtens	2000		146	D.W. Carter
Georgia	15	S.J. Savea	2015		15	S.J. Savea
Ireland	33	A.P. Mehrtens	1997		81	A.P. Mehrtens
Italy	36	T.E. Brown	1999		53	D.W. Carter
Japan	45	S.D. Culhane	1995		45	S.D. Culhane
Namibia	21	J.M. Barrett	2019		21	J.M. Barrett
Pacific Islands	11	D.W. Carter	2004		11	D.W. Carter
Portugal	33	N.J. Evans	2007		33	N.J. Evans
Romania	17	N.J. Evans	2007		17	N.J. Evans
Samoa	30	T.E. Brown	2001		56	T.E. Brown
Scotland	23	A.P. Mehrtens	1995		108	A.P. Mehrtens
South Africa	25	C.J. Spencer	1997		255	D.W. Carter
	25	D.W. Carter	2006			
Tonga	32	T.E. Brown	2000		32	T.E. Brown
USA	14	J.P. Preston	1991		14	J.P. Preston
Wales	27	D.W. Carter	2010		162	D.W. Carter

PLAYING RECORDS OF NEW ZEALAND TEAMS
1884–2020

		Played	Won	Lost	Drawn	Points for	Points against
1884	in **New South Wales** and **New Zealand**	9	9	–	–	176	17
1893	in **New Zealand, New South Wales** and **Queensland**	11	10	1	–	175	48
1894	**New South Wales** in **New Zealand**	1	–	1	–	6	8
1896	**Queensland** in **New Zealand**	1	1	–	–	9	0
1897	in **New Zealand, New South Wales** and **Queensland**	11	9	2	–	238	83
1901	**New South Wales** in **New Zealand**	2	2	–	–	44	8
1903	in **Australia** and **New Zealand**	11	10	1	–	281	27
1904	**Great Britain** in **New Zealand**	1	1	–	–	9	3
1905	in **Australia** and **New Zealand**	7	4	1	2	89	30
	Australia in **New Zealand**	1	1	–	–	14	3
1905/06	in **the British Isles, France** and **North America**	35	34	1	–	976	59
1907	in **Australia**	8	6	1	1	115	53
1908	**Anglo-Welsh** in **New Zealand**	3	2	–	1	64	8
1910	in **Australia** and **New Zealand**	8	7	1	–	138	78
1913	**Australia** in **New Zealand**	4	3	1	–	79	52
	in **North America**	16	16	–	–	610	6
1914	in **Australia** and **New Zealand**	11	10	1	–	260	69
1920	in **Australia** and **New Zealand**	10	9	–	1	352	91
1921	**South Africa** and **New South Wales** in **New Zealand**	4	1	2	1	18	31
1922	in **Australia** and **New Zealand**	8	6	2	–	198	102
1923	**New South Wales** in **New Zealand**	3	3	–	–	91	26
1924/25	in **Australia, New Zealand, the British Isles, France** and **Canada**	38	36	2	–	981	180
1925	in **Australia** and **New Zealand**	8	6	2	–	132	67
	New South Wales in **New Zealand**	1	1	–	–	36	10
1926	in **Australia** and **New Zealand**	8	6	2	–	187	109
1928	in **South Africa** and **Australia**	23	17	5	1	397	153
	New South Wales in **New Zealand**	4	3	1	–	79	40
1929	in **Australia**	10	6	3	1	186	80
1930	**Great Britain** in **New Zealand**	5	4	1	–	87	40
1931	**Australia** in **New Zealand**	1	1	–	–	20	13
1932	in **Australia** and **New Zealand**	11	9	2	–	331	135
1934	in **Australia** and **New Zealand**	9	7	1	1	201	107
1935/36	in **the British Isles** and **Canada**	30	26	3	1	490	183
1936	**Australia** in **New Zealand**	3	3	–	–	65	32
1937	**South Africa** in **New Zealand**	3	1	2	–	25	37
1938	in **Australia**	9	9	–	–	279	73
1946	**Australia** in **New Zealand**	2	2	–	–	45	18
1947	in **Australia** and **New Zealand**	10	8	2	–	263	113
1949	in **South Africa**	25	14	7	4	241	157
	Australia in **New Zealand**	2	–	2	–	15	27

Playing Records of New Zealand Teams

		Played	Won	Lost	Drawn	Points for	Points against
1950	**British Isles** in **New Zealand**	4	3	–	1	34	20
1951	in **Australia** and **New Zealand**	13	13	–	–	375	86
1952	**Australia** in **New Zealand**	2	1	1	–	24	22
1953/54	in **the British Isles, France** and **North America**	36	30	4	2	598	152
1955	**Australia** in **New Zealand**	3	2	1	–	27	16
1956	**South Africa** in **New Zealand**	4	3	1	–	41	29
1957	in **Australia** and **New Zealand**	14	13	1	–	472	94
1958	**Australia** in **New Zealand**	3	2	1	–	45	17
1959	**British Isles** in **New Zealand**	4	3	1	–	57	42
1960	in **Australia** and **South Africa**	32	26	4	2	645	187
1961	**France** in **New Zealand**	3	3	–	–	50	12
1962	in **Australia**	10	9	1	–	426	49
	Australia in **New Zealand**	3	2	–	1	28	17
1963	**England** in **New Zealand**	2	2	–	–	30	17
1963/64	in **the British Isles, France** and **Canada**	36	34	1	1	613	159
1964	**Australia** in **New Zealand**	3	2	1	–	37	32
1965	**South Africa** in **New Zealand**	4	3	1	–	55	25
1966	**British Isles** in **New Zealand**	4	4	–	–	79	32
1967	**Australia** in **New Zealand**	1	1	–	–	29	9
	in **the British Isles, France** and **Canada**	17	16	–	1	370	135
1968	in **Australia** and **Fiji**	12	12	–	–	460	66
	France in **New Zealand**	3	3	–	–	40	24
1969	**Wales** in **New Zealand**	2	2	–	–	52	12
1970	in **Australia** and **South Africa**	26	23	3	–	789	234
1971	**British Isles** in **New Zealand**	4	1	2	1	42	48
1972	**Internal Tour**	9	9	–	–	355	88
	Australia in **New Zealand**	3	3	–	–	97	26
1972/73	in **the British Isles, France** and **North America**	32	25	5	2	640	266
1973	**Internal Tour** and **England** in **New Zealand**	5	2	3	–	88	83
1974	in **Australia** and **Fiji**	13	12	–	1	446	73
	in **Ireland, Wales** and **England**	8	7	–	1	127	50
1975	**Scotland** in **New Zealand**	1	1	–	–	24	–
1976	**Ireland** in **New Zealand**	1	1	–	–	11	3
	in **South Africa**	24	18	6	–	610	291
	in **Argentina** and **Uruguay**	9	9	–	–	321	72
1977	**British Isles** in **New Zealand**	4	3	1	–	54	41
	in **France** and **Italy**	9	8	1	–	216	86
1978	**Australia** in **New Zealand**	3	2	1	–	51	48
	in **the British Isles**	18	17	1	–	364	147
1979	**France** in **New Zealand**	2	1	1	–	42	33
	in **Australia**	2	1	1	–	41	15
	Argentina in **New Zealand**	2	2	–	–	33	15
1979	in **England** and **Scotland**	11	10	1	–	192	95
1980	in **Australia** and **Fiji**	16	12	3	1	507	126

		Played	Won	Lost	Drawn	Points for	Points against
	Fiji in New Zealand	1	1	–	–	33	–
	in North America and Wales	7	7	–	–	197	41
1981	Scotland in New Zealand	2	2	–	–	51	19
	South Africa in New Zealand	3	2	1	–	51	55
	in Romania and France	10	8	1	1	170	108
1982	Australia in New Zealand	3	2	1	–	72	53
1983	British Isles in New Zealand	4	4	–	–	78	26
	in Australia	1	1	–	–	18	8
	in Scotland and England	8	5	2	1	162	116
1984	France in New Zealand	2	2	–	–	41	27
	in Australia	14	13	1	–	600	117
	in Fiji	4	4	–	–	174	10
1985	England in New Zealand	2	2	–	–	60	28
	Australia in New Zealand	1	1	–	–	10	9
	in Argentina	7	6	–	1	263	87
1986	France in New Zealand	1	1	–	–	18	9
	Australia in New Zealand	3	1	2	–	34	47
	in France	8	7	1	–	218	87
1987	World Cup	6	6	–	–	298	52
	in Australia	1	1	–	–	30	16
	in Japan	5	5	–	–	408	16
1988	Wales in New Zealand	2	2	–	–	106	12
	in Australia	13	12	–	1	476	96
1989	France in New Zealand	2	2	–	–	59	37
	Argentina in New Zealand	2	2	–	–	109	21
	Australia in New Zealand	1	1	–	–	24	12
	in Canada, Wales and Ireland	14	14	–	–	454	122
1990	Scotland in New Zealand	2	2	–	–	52	34
	Australia in New Zealand	3	2	1	–	57	44
	in France	8	6	2	–	175	110
1991	in Argentina	9	9	–	–	358	80
	in Australia	1	–	1	–	12	21
	Australia in New Zealand	1	1	–	–	6	3
	World Cup	6	5	1	–	143	74
1992	Centenary matches in New Zealand	3	2	1	–	94	69
	Ireland in New Zealand	2	2	–	–	83	27
	in Australia and South Africa	16	13	3	–	567	252
1993	British Isles in New Zealand	3	2	1	–	57	51
	Australia in New Zealand	1	1	–	–	25	10
	Western Samoa in New Zealand	1	1	–	–	35	13
	in England and Scotland	13	12	1	–	386	156
1994	France in New Zealand	2	–	2	–	28	45
	South Africa in New Zealand	3	2	–	1	53	41
	in Australia	1	–	1	–	16	20
1995	Canada in New Zealand	1	1	–	–	73	7
	World Cup	6	5	1	–	327	119
	Australia in New Zealand	1	1	–	–	28	16

Playing Records of New Zealand Teams

Year		Played	Won	Lost	Drawn	Points for	Points against
	in **Australia**	1	1	–	–	34	23
	in **Italy** and **France**	8	7	1	–	339	126
1996	**Western Samoa, Scotland** in **NZ**	3	3	–	–	149	53
	Tri Nations	4	4	–	–	119	60
	in **South Africa1**	7	5	1	1	190	139
1997	**Fiji, Argentina, Australia1** in **NZ**	4	4	–	–	256	36
	Tri Nations	4	4	–	–	159	109
	in **British Isles**	9	8	–	1	395	119
1998	**England** in **New Zealand**	2	2	–	–	104	32
	Tri Nations	4	–	4	–	65	88
	in **Australia1**	1	–	1	–	14	19
1999	**Internal, Samoa, France** in **NZ**	3	3	–	–	147	31
	Tri Nations	4	3	1	–	103	61
	World Cup	6	4	2	–	255	111
2000	**Tonga, Scotland** in **New Zealand**	3	3	–	–	219	34
	Tri Nations	4	2	2	–	127	117
	in **France** and **Italy**	3	2	1	–	128	87
2001	**Samoa, Argentina, France** in **NZ**	3	3	–	–	154	37
	Tri Nations	4	2	2	–	79	70
	in **Ireland, Scotland** and **Argentina**	5	5	–	–	179	98
2002	**Italy, Ireland, Fiji** in **New Zealand**	4	4	–	–	187	42
	Tri Nations	4	3	1	–	97	65
	in **England, France** and **Wales**	3	1	1	1	91	68
2003	**England, Wales, France** in **New Zealand**	3	2	1	–	99	41
	Tri Nations	4	4	–	–	142	65
	World Cup	7	6	1	–	361	101
2004	**England, Argentina, Pacific Islands** in **New Zealand**	4	4	–	–	154	48
	Tri Nations	4	2	2	–	83	91
	in **Europe**	4	4	–	–	177	60
2005	**Fiji, Lions** in **New Zealand**	4	4	–	–	198	40
	Tri Nations	4	3	1	–	111	86
	in **Europe**	4	4	–	–	138	39
2006	**Ireland** in **New Zealand**						
	New Zealand in **Argentina**	3	3	–	–	86	59
	Tri Nations	6	5	1	–	179	112
	in **Europe**	4	4	–	–	156	44
2007	**France, Canada** in **New Zealand**	3	3	–	–	167	34
	Tri Nations	4	3	1	–	100	59
	World Cup	5	4	1	–	327	55
2008	**Ireland, England, Samoa** in **New Zealand**	4	4	–	–	203	57
	Tri Nations	6	4	2	–	152	106
	in **Hong Kong, United Kingdom** and **Ireland**	6	6	–	–	152	54
2009	**France, Italy** in **New Zealand**	3	2	1	–	63	43
	Tri Nations	6	3	3	–	141	131
	in **Japan** and **Europe**	6	5	1	–	147	80

		Played	Won	Lost	Drawn	Points for	Points against
2010	**Ireland, Wales** in **New Zealand**	3	3	–	–	137	47
	Tri Nations	6	6	–	–	184	111
	in **Hong Kong, United Kingdom** and **Ireland**	5	4	1	–	174	88
2011	**Fiji** in **New Zealand**	1	1	–	–	60	14
	Tri Nations	4	2	2	–	95	64
	World Cup	7	7	–	–	301	72
2012	**Ireland** in **New Zealand**	3	3	–	–	124	29
	Rugby Championship and **Bledisloe Cup**	7	6	–	1	195	84
	In **Europe**	4	3	1	–	147	80
2013	**France** in **New Zealand**	3	3	–	–	77	22
	Rugby Championship and **Bledisloe Cup**	7	7	–	–	243	148
	In **Japan** and **Europe**	4	4	–	–	134	69
2014	**England** in **New Zealand**	3	3	–	–	84	55
	Rugby Championship and **Bledisloe Cup**	7	5	1	1	193	119
	In **USA** and **United Kingdom**	4	4	–	–	156	59
2015	In **Samoa**, **Rugby Championship** and **Bledisloe Cup**	5	4	1	–	151	94
	World Cup	7	7	–	–	290	97
2016	**Wales** in **New Zealand**	3	3	-	-	121	49
	Rugby Championship and **Bledisloe Cup**	7	7	-	-	299	94
	In **USA, Italy, Ireland** and **France**	4	3	1	-	142	78
2017	**Samoa, Lions** in **New Zealand**	4	2	1	1	144	54
	Rugby Championship and **Bledisloe Cup**	7	6	1	–	264	142
	In **England, France, Scotland** and **Wales**	5	5	–	–	152	98
2018	**France** in **New Zealand**	3	3	–	–	127	38
	Rugby Championship and **Bledisloe Cup**	7	6	1	–	262	152
	In **Japan, England, Ireland** and **Italy**	4	3	1	–	160	65
2019	**Tonga** in New Zealand	1	1	–	–	92	7
	Rugby Championship and **Bledisloe Cup**	4	2	1	1	98	79
	World Cup	6	5	1	–	250	72
2020	**Tri-Nations and Bledisloe Cup**	6	3	2	1	161	77
	TOTALS	1,322	1,113	168	41	36,371	13,144

[1] non Tri Nations

SURVIVING NEW ZEALAND REPRESENTATIVES

(over the age of 70 years as at 31 December, 2020)

	Born	Represented New Zealand
R.A. Roper	11 August, 1923	1949–50
W.A. McCaw	26 August, 1927	1951–53–54
M.S. Cockerill	8 December, 1928	1951
L.B. Steele	19 January, 1929	1951
K.F. Meates	20 February, 1930	1952
E.S. Diack	22 July, 1930	1959
S.G. Bremner	2 August, 1930	1952–56–60
D.L. Ashby	15 February, 1931	1958
C.J. Loader	10 March, 1931	1953–54
D.N. McIntosh	1 April, 1931	1956–57
B.P.J. Molloy	12 August, 1931	1957
W.S.S. Freebairn	12 January, 1932	1953–54
I.N. MacEwan	1 May, 1934	1956–57–58–59–60–61–62
F.S. McAtamney	15 May, 1934	1956–57
W.D. Gillespie	6 August, 1934	1957–58–60
K.F. Laidlaw	9 August, 1934	1960
R.J. Boon	23 February, 1935	1960
R.J. Conway	22 April, 1935	1959–60–65
D.M. Connor	9 September, 1935	1961–62–63–64
J.R. Watt	29 December, 1935	1957–58–60–61–62
S.R. Nesbit	13 February, 1936	1960
J.F. McCullough	8 August, 1936	1959
R.W. Caulton	10 January, 1937	1959–60–61–63–64
J.N. Creighton	10 March, 1937	1962
D.W. McKay	7 August, 1937	1961–62–63
A.H. Clarke	23 February, 1938	1958–59–60
S.T. Meads	12 July, 1938	1961–62–63–64–65–66
D.H. Cameron	17 November, 1938	1960
K.A. Nelson	26 November, 1938	1962–63–64
B.A. Watt	12 March, 1939	1962–63–64
N.W. Thimbleby	19 June, 1939	1970
W.M. Birtwistle	4 July, 1939	1965–67
E.W. Kirton	29 December, 1939	1963–64–67–68–69–70
D.W. Clark	22 February, 1940	1964
A.G.T. Jennings	15 June, 1940	1967
W.J. Nathan	8 July, 1940	1962–63–64–66–67
J. Major	8 August, 1940	1963–64–67
A.J. Stewart	11 October, 1940	1963–64
M.J. Dick	3 January, 1941	1963–64–65–66–67–69–70
D.A. Arnold	10 January, 1941	1963–64
J.F. Burns	17 February, 1941	1970
R.A. Guy	6 April, 1941	1971–72
M.C. Wills	11 October, 1941	1967
T.N. Wolfe	20 October, 1941	1961–62–63–68
T.J. Morris	3 January, 1942	1972–73
P.H. Clarke	23 January, 1942	1967
R.W. Norton	30 March, 1942	1971–72–73–74–75–76–77
A.E. Smith	10 December, 1942	1967–69–70

W.L. Davis	15 December, 1942	1963–64–67–68–69–70
I.R. MacRae	6 April, 1943	1963–64–66–67–68–69–70
S.M. Going	19 August, 1943	1967–68–69–70–71–72–73–74–75–76–77
C.R. Laidlaw	16 November, 1943	1963–64–65–66–67–68–70
R.A. Urlich	8 February, 1944	1970–72–73
P.A. Johns	16 March, 1944	1968
L.A. Clark	1 May, 1944	1972–73
W.D.R. Currey	2 June, 1944	1968
A.J. Wyllie	31 August, 1944	1970–71–72–73
A.R. Leslie	10 November, 1944	1974–75–76
R.J. Barber	14 January, 1945	1974
B.D.M. Furlong	10 March, 1945	1970
A.J. Kreft	27 March, 1945	1968
K.J. Tanner	25 April, 1945	1974–75–76
M.O. Knight	20 May, 1945	1968
G.F. Kember	15 November, 1945	1967–70
G.M. Crossman	30 November, 1945	1974–76
P.C. Harris	11 January, 1946	1976
L.W. Mains	16 February, 1946	1971–76
G.S. Thorne	25 February, 1946	1967–68–69–70
B. Holmes	7 April, 1946	1970–72–73
M.W. O'Callaghan	27 April, 1946	1968
I.A. Kirkpatrick	24 May, 1946	1967–68–69–70–71–72–73–74–75–76–77
G.J. Whiting	4 June, 1946	1972–73
S.E.G. Cron	7 July, 1946	1976
P.J. Whiting	6 August, 1946	1971–72–73–74–76
A.J. Gardiner	10 December, 1946	1974
O.G. Stephens	9 January, 1947	1968
H.H. Macdonald	11 January, 1947	1972–73–74–75–76
D.J. Robertson	6 February, 1947	1974–75–76–77
M. Sayers	1 May, 1947	1972–73
O.D. Bruce	23 May, 1947	1974–76–77–78
A.M. McNaughton	5 July, 1947	1971–72
J.E. Spiers	4 August, 1947	1976–79–80–81
M.G. Duncan	8 August, 1947	1971
K.A. Eveleigh	8 November, 1947	1974–76–77
D.A. Hales	22 November, 1947	1972–73
G.D. Rowlands	10 December, 1947	1976
R.L. Stuart	9 January, 1948	1977
G.R. Skudder	10 February, 1948	1969–72–73
R.N. Lendrum	22 March, 1948	1973
J.D. Matheson	30 March, 1948	1972
I.N. Stevens	13 April, 1948	1972–73–74–76
P.H. Sloane	10 September, 1948	1973–76–79
A.I. Scown	21 October, 1948	1972–73
V.E. Stewart	28 October, 1948	1976–79
M.W.R. Jaffray	18 January, 1949	1976
W.K. Te P. Bush	24 January, 1949	1974–75–76–77–78–79
R.E. Burgess	26 March, 1949	1971–72–73

Surviving New Zealand Representatives

J.C. Ross	24 April, 1949	1981
J.K. Loveday	1 May, 1949	1978
J.S. McLachlan	23 June, 1949	1974
H.T. Joseph	25 August, 1949	1971
J.C. Ashworth	15 September, 1949	1977–78–79–80–81–82–83–84–85
L.G. Knight	24 September, 1949	1974–76–77
B.G. Ashworth	29 September, 1949	1978
K.M. Greene	31 December, 1949	1976–77
J.L. Jaffray	April 17, 1950	1972-75-76-77-78
B.McL. Gemmell	May 12, 1950	1974
J.A. Callesen	May 24, 1950	1974-75-76
E.J.T. Stokes	June 26, 1950	1976
R.G. Myers	July 6, 1950	1977-78
B.R. Johnstone	July 30, 1950	1976-77-78-79-80
K.R. Carrington	September 3, 1950	1971-72
T.W. Mitchell	September 11, 1950	1974-76
B.A. Hunter	September 16, 1950	1970-71
B.G. Williams	October 3, 1950	1970-71-72-73-74-75-76-77-78

NEW ZEALAND REPRESENTATIVES
1884–2020

Union affiliations are shown in parentheses, preceded by date of birth and, where applicable, date of death. A few of these dates have proved impossible to be traced and these are indicated with a question mark. War casualties are denoted by an asterisk. The numbers that follow each entry show the number of games played for New Zealand. These are followed in parentheses by the number of appearances in test matches, which are included in the total. Franchise team rather than Provincial teams have been used from 2013.

Name	B&D	Representative Team	Games	Tests
Abbott H.L.	1882–1971	(Taranaki) 1905–06	11	(1)
Adkins G.T.A.	1910–1976	(South Canterbury) 1935–36	10	(–)
Afeaki B.T.P.	1988–	(Chiefs) 2013	1	(1)
Afoa I.F.	1983–	(Auckland) 2005–06–08–09–10–11	38	(36)
Aitken G.G.	1898–1952	(Wellington) 1921	2	(2)
Alatini P.F.	1976–	(Otago) 1999–2001	20	(17)
Algar B.	1894–1989	(Wellington) 1920–21	6	(–)
Allan J.	1860–1934	(Otago) 1884	8	(–)
Allen F.R.	1920–2012	(Auckland) 1946–47–49	21	(6)
Allen L.	1870–1932	(Taranaki) 1896–97–1901	13	(–)
Allen M.R.	1967–	(Taranaki) 1993–95–96; (Manawatu) 1997	27	(8)
Allen N.H.	1958–1984	(Counties) 1980	9	(2)
Alley G.T.	1903–1986	(Southland) 1926; (Canterbury) 1928	19	(3)
Anderson A.	1961–	(Canterbury) 1983–84–85–87–88	25	(6)
Anderson B.L.	1960–	(Wairarapa Bush) 1986–87	3	(1)
Anderson E.J.	1931–2014	(Bay of Plenty) 1960	10	(–)
Anesi S.R.	1981–	(Waikato) 2005	1	(1)
Archer J.A.	1900–1979	(Southland) 1925	2	(–)
Archer W.R.	1930–2018	(Otago) 1955; (Southland) 1956–57	13	(4)
Argus W.G.	1921–2016	(Canterbury) 1946–47	10	(4)
Armit A.M.	1874–1899	(Otago) 1897	9	(–)
Armstrong A.L.	1878–1959	(Wairarapa) 1903	5	(–)
Arnold D.A.	1941–	(Canterbury) 1963–64	15	(4)
Arnold K.D.	1920–2006	(Waikato) 1947	8	(2)
Ashby D.L.	1931–	(Southland) 1958	1	(1)
Asher A.A.	1879–1965	(Auckland) 1903	11	(1)
Ashworth B.G.	1949–	(Auckland) 1978	7	(2)
Ashworth J.C.	1949–	(Canterbury) 1977–78–79–80–81–82–83–84; (Hawke's Bay) 1985	52	(24)
Atiga B.A.C.	1983–	(Auckland) 2003	1	(1)
Atkinson H.J.	1888–1949	(West Coast) 1913	10	(1)
Aumua A.J.	1997–	(Wellington) 2017–20	3	(1)
Avery H.E.	1885–1961	(Wellington) 1910	6	(3)
Bachop G.T.M.	1967–	(Canterbury) 1987–88–89–90–91–92–94–95	54	(31)
Bachop S.J.	1966–	(Otago) 1992–93–94	18	(5)
Badeley C.E.O.	1896–1986	(Auckland) 1920–21–24	15	(2)
Badeley V.I.R.	1898–1971	(Auckland) 1922	5	(–)
Bagley K.P.	1931–1999	(Manawatu) 1953–54	20	(–)
Baird D.L.	1894–1943	(Southland) 1920	9	(–)
Baird J.A.S.*	1893–1917	(Otago) 1913	1	(1)
Balch W.	1871–1949	(Canterbury) 1894	1	(–)
Ball N.	1908–1986	(Wellington) 1931–32–35–36	22	(5)

New Zealand Representatives 1884–2020

Name	B&D	Representative Team	Games	Tests
Barber R.J.	1945–	(Southland) 1974	6	(–)
Barrell C.K.	1967–	(Canterbury) 1996–97	4	(–)
Barrett B.J.	1991–	(Taranaki) 2012; (Hurricanes) 2013–14–15–16–17–18–19; (Blues) 2020	89	(88)
Barrett J.	1888–1971	(Auckland) 1913–14	3	(2)
Barrett J.M.	1997	(Hurricanes) 2017–18–19–20	23	(23)
Barrett S.K.	1993–	(Crusaders) 2016–17–18–19–20	42	(40)
Barry E.F.	1905–1993	(Wellington) 1932–34	10	(1)
Barry K.E.	1936–2014	(Thames Valley) 1962–63–64	23	(–)
Barry L.J.	1971–	(North Harbour) 1993–95	10	(1)
Bates S.P.	1980–	(Waikato) 2004	2	(1)
Batty G.B.	1951–	(Wellington) 1972–73–74–75; (Bay of Plenty) 1976–77	56	(15)
Batty W.	1905–1979	(Auckland) 1928–30–31	6	(4)
Bayly A.	1866–1907	(Taranaki) 1893–94–97	20	(–)
Bayly W.	1869–1950	(Taranaki) 1894	1	(–)
Beatty G.E.	1925–2004	(Taranaki) 1950	1	(1)
Bell J.R.	1900–1963	(Southland) 1923	1	(–)
Bell R.C.	1893–1960	(Otago) 1922	8	(–)
Bell R.H.	1925–2016	(Otago) 1951–52	9	(3)
Belliss E.A.	1894–1974	(Wanganui) 1920–21–22–23	20	(3)
Bennet R.	1879–1962	(Otago) 1905	1	(1)
Berghan T.	1914–1998	(Otago) 1938	6	(3)
Berry M.J.	1966–	(Wairarapa Bush) 1986; (Wellington) 1993	10	(1)
Berryman N.R.	1973–2015	(Northland) 1998	1	(1)
Best J.J.	1914–1994	(Marlborough) 1935–36	6	(–)
Bevan V.D.	1921–1996	(Wellington) 1947–49–50–53–54	25	(6)
Bird D.J.	1991–	(Crusaders) 2013–14; (Chiefs) 2017	3	(2)
Birtwistle W.M.	1939–	(Canterbury) 1965; (Waikato) 1967	12	(7)
Black J.E.	1951–	(Canterbury) 1976–77–78–79–80	26	(3)
Black N.W.	1925–2016	(Auckland) 1949	11	(1)
Black R.S.*	1893–1916	(Otago) 1914	6	(1)
Blackadder T.J.	1971–	(Canterbury) 1995–96–97–98–99–2000	25	(12)
Blair B.A.	1979–	(Canterbury) 2001–02	6	(4)
Blair J.A.	1872–1911	(Wanganui) 1897	9	(–)
Blake A.W.	1922–2010	(Wairarapa) 1949	1	(1)
Blake J.M.	1902–1988	(Hawke's Bay) 1925–26	13	(–)
Bligh S.	1887–1955	(West Coast) 1910	5	(–)
Blowers A.F.	1975–	(Auckland) 1996–97–99	18	(11)
Bloxham K.C.	1954–2000	(Otago) 1980	2	(–)
Boe J.W.	1955–	(Waikato) 1981	2	(–)
Boggs E.G.	1922–2004	(Auckland) 1946–49	9	(2)
Bond J.G.P.	1920–1999	(Canterbury) 1949	1	(1)
Boon R.J.	1935–	(Taranaki) 1960	6	(–)
Booth E.E.	1876–1935	(Otago) 1905–06–07	24	(3)
Boric A.F.	1983–	(North Harbour) 2008–09–10–11	25	(24)
Boroevich K.G.	1960–	(King Country) 1983–84; (Wellington) 1986; (North Harbour) 1988	26	(3)
Botica F.M.	1963–	(North Harbour) 1986–87–88–89	27	(7)
Botting I.J.	1922–1980	(Otago) 1949	9	(–)
Bowden N.J.G.	1926–2009	(Taranaki) 1952	1	(1)
Bowers R.G.	1932–2000	(Wellington) 1953–54	15	(2)

Name	B&D	Representative Team	Games	Tests
Bowman A.W.	1915–1992	(Hawke's Bay) 1938	6	(3)
Bradanovich N.M.	1907–1961	(Otago) 1928	2	(–)
Braddon H.Y.	1863–1955	(Otago) 1884	7	(–)
Braid D.J.	1981–	(Auckland) 2002–03–08–10	6	(6)
Braid G.J.	1960–	(Bay of Plenty) 1983–84	13	(2)
Brake L.J.	1952–	(Bay of Plenty) 1976	5	(–)
Bremner S.G.	1930–	(Auckland) 1952; (Canterbury) 1956–60	18	(2)
Brewer M.R.	1964–	(Otago) 1986–87–88–89–90–91–92; (Canterbury) 1993–94–95	61	(32)
Bridge G.C.	1995–	(Crusaders) 2018–19–20	10	(10)
Briscoe K.C.	1936–2009	(Taranaki) 1959–60–62–63–64	43	(9)
Broadhurst J.P.	1987–	(Hurricanes) 2015–1	(1)	
Brooke R.M.	1966–	(Auckland) 1992–93–94–95–96–97–98–99	69	(62)
Brooke Z.V.	1965–	(Auckland) 1987–88–89–90–91–92–93–94–95–96–97	100	(58)
Brooke-Cowden M.	1963–	(Auckland) 1986–87	6	(3)
Brooker F.J.	1876–1939	(Canterbury) 1897	4	(–)
Broomhall S.R.	1976–	(Canterbury) 2002	4	(4)
Brown C.	1887–1966	(Taranaki) 1913–20	11	(2)
Brown H.M.	1910–1965	(Auckland) 1935–36	8	(–)
Brown H.W.	1904–1973	(Taranaki) 1924–25–26	20	(–)
Brown O.M.	1967–	(Auckland) 1990–92–93–94–95–96–97–98	69	(56)
Brown R.H.	1934–2014	(Taranaki) 1955–56–57–58–59–61–62	25	(16)
Brown T.E.	1975–	(Otago) 1999–2000–01	19	(18)
Brownlie C.J.	1895–1954	(Hawke's Bay) 1924–25–26–28	31	(3)
Brownlie J.L.	1899–1972	(Hawke's Bay) 1921	1	(–)
Brownlie M.J.	1896–1957	(Hawke's Bay) 1922–23–24–25–26–28	61	(8)
Bruce J.A.	1887–1970	(Auckland) 1913–14	10	(2)
Bruce O.D.	1947–	(Canterbury) 1974–76–77–78	41	(14)
Bryers R.F.	1919–1987	(King Country) 1949	1	(1)
Buchan J.A.S.	1961–	(Canterbury) 1987	2	(–)
Budd A.	1880–1962	(South Canterbury) 1910	3	(–)
Budd T.A.	1922–1989	(Southland) 1946–49	2	(2)
Bullock-Douglas G.A.H.	1911–1958	(Wanganui) 1932–34	15	(5)
Bunce F.E.	1962–	(North Harbour) 1992–93–94–95–96–97	69	(55)
Burgess G.A.J.	1954–	(Auckland) 1980–81	2	(1)
Burgess G.F.	1883–1961	(Southland) 1905	1	(1)
Burgess R.E.	1949–	(Manawatu) 1971–72–73	30	(7)
Burgoyne M.M.	1951–2016	(North Auckland) 1979	6	(–)
Burke P.S.	1927–2017	(Taranaki) 1951–55–57	12	(3)
Burns J.F.	1941–	(Canterbury)1970	9	(–)
Burns P.J.	1881–1943	(Canterbury) 1908–10–13	9	(5)
Burrows J.T.	1904–1991	(Canterbury) 1928	9	(–)
Burry H.C.	1930–2013	(Canterbury) 1960	11	(–)
Burt J.R.	1874–1933	(Otago) 1901	1	(–)
Bush R.G.	1909–96	(Otago) 1931	1	(1)
Bush W.K. TeP.	1949–	(Canterbury) 1974–75–76–77–78–79	37	(12)
Butland H.	1872–1956	(West Coast) 1893–94	9	(–)
Butler V.C.	1907–1971	(Auckland) 1928	1	(–)
Buxton J.B.	1933–2007	(Canterbury) 1955–56	2	(2)
Cabot P.S. deQ.	1900–1998	(Otago) 1921	1	(–)
Cain M.J.	1885–1951	(Taranaki) 1913–14	24	(4)
Calcinai U.P.	1892–1963	(Wellington) 1922	5	(–)
Callesen J.A.	1950–	(Manawatu) 1974–75–76	18	(4)
Calnan J.J.	1876–1947	(Wellington) 1897	9	(–)

Name	B&D	Representative Team	Games	Tests
Cameron B.D.	1996	(Crusaders) 2018	1	(1)
Cameron D.	1887–1947	(Taranaki) 1908	3	(3)
Cameron D.H.	1938–	(Mid Canterbury) 1960	8	(–)
Cameron L.M.	1959–	(Manawatu) 1979–80–81	17	(5)
Cane S.J.	1992–	(Bay of Plenty) 2012; (Chiefs) 2013–14–15–16–17–18–19–20	75	(74)
Carleton S.R.	1904–1973	(Canterbury) 1928–29	21	(6)
Carrington K.R.	1950–	(Auckland) 1971–72	9	(3)
Carroll A.J.	1895–1974	(Manawatu) 1920–21	8	(–)
Carson W.N.*	1916–1944	(Auckland) 1938	3	(–)
Carter D.W.	1982–	(Canterbury) 2003–04–05–06–07–08–09–10–11–12; (Crusaders) 2013–14–15	112	(112)
Carter G.	1854–1922	(Auckland) 1884	7	(–)
Carter M.P.	1968–	(Auckland) 1991–97–98	10	(7)
Cartwright S.C.	1954–	(Canterbury) 1976	7	(–)
Casey S.T.	1882–1960	(Otago) 1905–06–07–08	38	(8)
Cashmore A.R.	1973	(Auckland) 1996–97	2	(2)
Catley E.H.	1915–1975	(Waikato) 1946–47–49	21	(7)
Caughey T.H.C.	1911–1993	(Auckland) 1932–34–35–36–37	39	(9)
Caulton R.W.	1937–	(Wellington) 1959–60–61–63–64	50	(16)
Cherrington N.P.	1924–1979	(North Auckland) 1950–51	7	(1)
Christian D.L.	1923–1977	(Auckland) 1949	11	(1)
Clamp M.	1961–	(Wellington) 1984–85	15	(2)
Clark D.W.	1940–	(Otago) 1964	2	(2)
Clark F.L.	1902–1972	(Canterbury) 1928	4	(–)
Clark L.A.	1944–	(Otago) 1972–73	7	(–)
Clark W.H.	1929–2010	(Wellington) 1953–54–55–56	24	(9)
Clarke A.H.	1938–	(Auckland) 1958–59–60	14	(3)
Clarke, C.D.	1999–	(Blues) 2020	5	(5)
Clarke D.B.	1933–2002	(Waikato) 1956–57–58–59–60–61–62–63–64	89	(31)
Clarke E.	1968–	(Auckland) 1992–93–98	24	(10)
Clarke I.J.	1931–1997	(Waikato) 1953–54–55–56–57–58–59–60–61–62–63–64	83	(24)
Clarke P.H.	1942–	(Marlborough) 1967	4	(–)
Clarke R.L.	1909–1972	(Taranaki) 1932	9	(2)
Cobden D.G.*	1914–1940	(Canterbury) 1937	1	(1)
Cockerill M.S.	1928–	(Taranaki) 1951	11	(3)
Cockroft E.A.P.	1890–1973	(South Canterbury) 1913–14	7	(3)
Cockroft S.G.	1864–1955	(Manawatu) 1893; (Hawke's Bay) 1894	12	(–)
Codlin B.W.	1956–	(Counties) 1980	13	(3)
Coffin P.H.	1964–	(King Country) 1996	3	(–)
Coles D.S.	1986–	(Wellington) 2012; (Hurricanes) 2013–14–15–16–17–18–19–20	74	(74)
Colling G.L.	1946–2003	(Otago) 1972–73	21	(–)
Collins A.H.	1906–1988	(Taranaki) 1932–34	15	(3)
Collins J.	1980–2015	(Wellington) 2001–03–04–05–06–07	50	(48)
Collins J.L.	1939–2007	(Poverty Bay) 1964–65	3	(3)
Collins W.R.	1910–1993	(Hawke's Bay) 1935	7	(–)
Colman J.T.H.	1887–1965	(Taranaki) 1907–08	6	(4)
Coltman L.J.	1990–	(Highlanders) 2016–18–19	8	(8)
Conn S.B.	1953–	(Auckland) 1976–80	6	(–)
Connolly L.S.	1921–2005	(Southland) 1947	5	(–)
Connor D.M.	1935–	(Auckland) 1961–62–63–64	15	(12)
Conrad W.J.M.	1925–1972	(Waikato) 1949	10	(–)

Name	B&D	Representative Team	Games	Tests
Conway R.J.	1935–	(Otago) 1959–60; (Bay of Plenty) 1965	25	(10)
Cooke A.E.	1901–1977	(Auckland) 1924–25; (Hawke's Bay) 1926; (Wairarapa) 1928; (Wellington) 1930	44	(8)
Cooke A.E.	1870–1900	(Canterbury) 1894	1	(–)
Cooke R.J.	1880–1940	(Canterbury) 1903	10	(1)
Cooksley M.S.B.	1971–	(Counties) 1992–93; (Waikato) 1994–95–97–2001	23	(11)
Cooper G.J.L.	1965–	(Auckland) 1986; (Otago) 1992	7	(7)
Cooper M.J.A.	1966–	(Hawke's Bay) 1987; (Waikato) 1992–93–94–96	26	(8)
Corbett J.	1880–1945	(West Coast) 1905	16	(–)
Corkill T.G.	1901–1966	(Hawke's Bay) 1925	4	(–)
Corner M.M.N.	1908–1992	(Auckland) 1930–31–32–34–35–36	25	(6)
Cossey R.R.	1935–1986	(Counties) 1958	1	(1)
Cottrell A.I.	1907–1988	(Canterbury) 1929–30–31–32	22	(11)
Cottrell W.D.	1943–2013	(Canterbury) 1967–68–70–71	37	(9)
Couch M.B.R.	1925–1996	(Wairarapa) 1947–49	7	(3)
Coughlan T.D.	1934–2017	(South Canterbury) 1958	1	(1)
Cowan Q.J.	1982–	(Southland) 2004–05–06–08–09–10–11	53	(51)
Creighton J.N.	1937–	(Canterbury) 1962	6	(1)
Cribb R.T.	1976–	(North Harbour) 2000–01	15	(15)
Crichton S.	1954–	(Wellington) 1983–84–85	7	(2)
Crockett W.W.V.	1983–	(Canterbury) 2009–11–12; (Crusaders) 2013–14–15–16–17	72	(71)
Cron S.E.G.	1946–	(Canterbury) 1976	6	(–)
Cross T.	1876–1930	(Canterbury) 1901; (Wellington) 1904–05	3	(2)
Crossman G.M.	1945–	(Bay of Plenty) 1974–76	19	(–)
Crotty R.J.	1988–	(Crusaders) 2013–14–15–16–18–19	48	(48)
Crowley K.J.	1961–	(Taranaki) 1983–84–85–86–87–90–91	35	(19)
Crowley P.J.B.	1923–1981	(Auckland) 1949–50	21	(6)
Cruden A.W.	1989–	(Manawatu) 2010–11–12; (Chiefs) 2013–14–16–17	50	(50)
Culhane S.D.	1968–	(Southland) 1995–96	9	(6)
Cullen C.M.	1976–	(Manawatu) 1996–97; (Wellington) 1998–99–2000–01–02	60	(58)
Cummings W.	1889–1955	(Canterbury) 1913–21	3	(2)
Cundy R.T.	1901–1955	(Wairarapa) 1929	6	(1)
Cunningham G.R.	1955–	(Auckland) 1979–80	17	(5)
Cunningham W.	1874–1927	(Auckland) 1901–05–06–07–08	39	(9)
Cupples L.F.	1898–1972	(Bay of Plenty) 1922–23–24–25	29	(2)
Currey W.D.R.	1944–	(Taranaki) 1968	7	(–)
Currie C.J.	1955–	(Canterbury) 1978	4	(2)
Cuthill J.E.	1892–1970	(Otago) 1913	16	(2)
Dagg I.J.A.	1988–	(Hawke's Bay) 2010–11–12; (Crusaders) 2013–14–15–16–17	66	(66)
Dalley W.C.	1901–1989	(Canterbury) 1924–25–26–28–29	35	(5)
Dalton A.G.	1951–	(Counties) 1977–78–79–80–81–82–83–84–85	58	(35)
Dalton D.	1913–1995	(Hawke's Bay) 1935–36–37–38	21	(9)
Dalton R.A.	1919–1997	(Wellington) 1947; (Otago) 1949	20	(2)
Dalzell G.N.	1921–1989	(Canterbury) 1953–54	22	(5)

Name	B&D	Representative Team	Games	Tests
D'Arcy A.E.	1870–1919	(Wairarapa) 1893–94	7	(–)
Davie M.G.	1955–	(Canterbury) 1983	5	(1)
Davies W.A.	1939–2008	(Auckland) 1960; (Otago) 1962	17	(3)
Davis C.S.	1975–	(Manawatu) 1996	2	(–)
Davis K.	1930–2019	(Auckland) 1952–53–54–55–58	25	(10)
Davis L.J.	1943–2008	(Canterbury) 1976–77	16	(3)
Davis W.L.	1942–	(Hawke's Bay) 1963–64–67–68–69–70	53	(11)
Davy E.	1850–1935	(Wellington) 1884	3	(–)
Deans I.B.	1960–2019	(Canterbury) 1987–88–89	23	(10)
Deans R.G.	1884–1908	(Canterbury) 1905–06–08	24	(5)
Deans R.M.	1959–	(Canterbury) 1983–84–85	19	(5)
Delamore G.W.	1920–2008	(Wellington) 1949	9	(1)
Delany M.P.	1982–	(Bay of Plenty) 2009	2	(1)
de Malmanche A.P.	1984–	(Waikato) 2009–10	5	(5)
Dermody C.	1980–	(Southland) 2006	3	(3)
Devine S.J.	1976–	(Auckland) 2002–03	10	(10)
Dewar H.*	1883–1915	(Taranaki) 1913	16	(2)
Diack E.S.	1930–	(Otago) 1959	1	(1)
Dick J.	1912–2002	(Auckland) 1937–38	5	(3)
Dick M.J.	1941–	(Auckland) 1963–64–65–66–67–69–70	55	(15)
Dickinson G.R.	1903–1978	(Otago) 1922	5	(–)
Dickson D.McK.	1900–1978	(Otago) 1925	7	(–)
Dixon E.C.	1989–	(Highlanders) 2016	3	(3)
Dixon M.J.	1929–2004	(Canterbury) 1953–54–56–57	28	(10)
Dobson R.L.	1923–1994	(Auckland) 1949	1	(1)
Dodd E.H.*	1880–1918	(Wellington) 1901–05	3	(1)
Donald A.J.	1957–	(Wanganui) 1981–83–84	20	(7)
Donald J.G.	1898–1981	(Wairarapa) 1920–21–22–25	22	(2)
Donald Q.	1900–1965	(Wairarapa) 1923–24–25	23	(4)
Donald S.R.	1983–	(Waikato) 2008–09–10–11	25	(23)
Donaldson M.W.	1955–	(Manawatu) 1977–78–79–80–81	35	(13)
Donnelly T.J.S.	1981–	(Otago) 2009–10	15	(15)
Dougan J.P.	1946–2006	(Wellington) 1972–73	12	(2)
Douglas J.B.	1890–1964	(Otago) 1913	9	(–)
Dowd C.W.	1969–	(Auckland) 1993–94–95–96–97–98–99–2000	67	(60)
Dowd G.W.	1963–	(North Harbour) 1992	8	(1)
Downing A.J.*	1886–1915	(Auckland) 1913–14	26	(5)
Drake J.A.	1959–2008	(Auckland) 1985–86–87	12	(8)
Drake W.A.	1879–1941	(Canterbury) 1901	1	(–)
Drummond M.D.	1994–	(Crusaders) 2017–18	2	(1)
Duff R.H.	1925–2006	(Canterbury) 1951–52–55–56	18	(11)
Duffie M.D.	1990	(Blues) 2017	2	(–)
Duggan R.J.L.	1972–	(Waikato) 1999	1	(1)
Dumbell J.T.	1859–1936	(Wellington) 1884	5	(–)
Duncan J.	1869–1953	(Otago) 1897–1901–03	10	(1)
Duncan M.G.	1947–	(Hawke's Bay) 1971	2	(2)
Duncan W.D.	1892–1961	(Otago) 1920–21	11	(3)
Dunn E.J.	1955–	(North Auckland) 1978–79–81	20	(2)
Dunn I.T.W.	1960–	(North Auckland) 1983–84	13	(3)
Dunn J.M.	1918–2003	(Auckland) 1946	1	(1)
Earl A.T.	1961–	(Canterbury) 1986–87–88–89–91–92	45	(14)
Eastgate B.P.	1927–2007	(Canterbury) 1952–53–54	17	(3)
Eaton J.J.	1982–	(Taranaki) 2005–06–08–09	17	(15)
Eckhold A.G.	1885–1931	(Otago) 1907	3	(–)

Name	B&D	Representative Team	Games	Tests
Eliason I.M.	1945–2019	(Taranaki) 1972–73	19	(–)
Elliot H.T.P.	1986–	(Hawke's Bay) 2008–10,12; (Chiefs) 2015	5	(4)
Elliott K.G.	1922–2006	(Wellington) 1946	2	(2)
Ellis A.M.	1984–	(Canterbury) 2006–07–08–09–10–11; (Crusaders) 2015	28	(28)
Ellis M.C.G.	1971–	(Otago) 1992–93–95	21	(8)
Ellison T.E.	1983–	(Wellington) 2009; (Otago) 2012	5	(4)
Ellison T.R.	1867–1904	(Wellington) 1893	7	(–)
Elsom A.E.G.	1925–2010	(Canterbury) 1952–53–54–55	22	(6)
Elvidge R.R.	1923–2019	(Otago) 1946–49–50	19	(9)
Elvy W.L.	1901–1977	(Canterbury) 1925–26	12	(–)
Ennor, B.M.	1997–	(Crusaders) 2019	1	(1)
Erceg C.P.	1928–2019	(Auckland) 1951–52	9	(4)
Evans B.R.	1984–	(Hawke's Bay) 2009	2	(2)
Evans C.E.	1896–1975	(Canterbury) 1921	1	(–)
Evans D.A.	1886–1940	(Hawke's Bay) 1910	4	(1)
Evans G.O.	1991–	(Hurricanes) 2018	1	(1)
Evans N.J.	1980–	(North Harbour) 2004; (Otago) 2005–06–07	16	(16)
Eveleigh K.A.	1947–	(Manawatu) 1974–76–77	30	(4)
Fanning A.H.N.	1890–1963	(Canterbury) 1913	1	(1)
Fanning B.J.	1874–1946	(Canterbury) 1903–04	9	(2)
Farrell C.P.	1956–	(Auckland) 1977	2	(2)
Faumuina C.C.	1986–	(Auckland) 2012; (Blues) 2013–14–15–16–17	50	(50)
Fawcett C.L.	1954–	(Auckland) 1976	13	(2)
Fea W.R.	1898–1988	(Otago) 1921	1	(1)
Feek G.E.	1975–	(Canterbury) 1999–2000–01	10	(10)
Fekitoa M.F.	1992–	(Highlanders) 2014–15–16–17	24	(24)
Fifita V.T.L.	1992–	(Hurricanes) 2017–18–19	12	(11)
Filipo R.A.	1979–	(Wellington) 2007–08	5	(4)
Finlay B.E.L.	1927–1982	(Manawatu) 1959	1	(1)
Finlay J.	1916–2001	(Manawatu) 1946	1	(1)
Finlay M.C.	1963–	(Manawatu) 1984	2	(–)
Finlayson I.	1899–1980	(North Auckland) 1925–26–28–30	36	(6)
Fisher T.	1891–1968	(Buller) 1914	5	(–)
Fitzgerald C.J.	1899–1961	(Marlborough) 1922	5	(–)
Fitzgerald J.T.	1928–1993	(Wellington) 1952–53–54	17	(1)
Fitzpatrick B.B.J.	1931–2006	(Poverty Bay) 1951; (Wellington) 1953–54	22	(3)
Fitzpatrick S.B.T.	1963–	(Auckland) 1986–87–88–89–90–91–92–93–94–95–96–97	128	(92)
Flavell T.V.	1976–	(North Harbour) 2000–01; (Auckland) 2006–07	22	(22)
Fleming J.K.	1953–	(Wellington) 1978–79–80	35	(5)
Fletcher C.J.C.	1894–1973	(North Auckland) 1921	2	(1)
Flynn C.R.	1981–	(Canterbury) 2003–04–08–09–10–11	17	(15)
Fogarty R.	1891–1980	(Taranaki) 1921	2	(2)
Ford B.R.	1951–	(Marlborough) 1977–78–79	20	(4)
Ford W.A.	1895–1959	(Canterbury) 1921–22–23	9	(–)
Forster S.T.	1969–	(Otago) 1993–94–95	12	(6)
Fox G.J.	1962–	(Auckland) 1984–85–86–87–88–89–90–91–92–93	78	(46)
Francis A.R.H.	1882–1957	(Auckland) 1905–07–08–10	18	(10)

Name	B&D	Representative Team	Games	Tests
Francis W.C.	1894–1981	(Wellington) 1913–14	12	(5)
Franks B.J.	1984–	(Tasman) 2008–10–11–12; (Hurricanes) 2013–14–15	48	(47)
Franks O.T.	1987–	(Canterbury) 2009–10–11–12; (Crusaders) 2013–14–15–16–17–18–19	108	(108)
Fraser B.G.	1953–	(Wellington) 1979–80–81–82–83–84	55	(23)
Frazer H.F.	1915–2003	(Hawke's Bay) 1946–47–49	15	(5)
Freebairn W.S.S.	1932–	(Manawatu) 1953–54	14	(–)
Freitas D.F.E.	1901–1968	(West Coast) 1928	4	(–)
Frizell S.M.	1994–	(Highlanders) 2018–19–20	13	(13)
Fromont R.T.	1969–	(Auckland) 1993–95	10	(–)
Frost H.	1869–1954	(Canterbury) 1896	1	(–)
Fryer F.C.	1886–1958	(Canterbury) 1907–08	9	(4)
Fuller W.B.	1883–1957	(Canterbury) 1910	6	(2)
Furlong B.D.M.	1945–	(Hawke's Bay) 1970	11	(1)
Gage D.R.	1868–1916	(Wellington) 1893–96	8	(–)
Gallagher J.A.	1964–	(Wellington) 1986–87–88–89	41	(18)
Gallaher D.*	1873–1917	(Auckland) 1903–04–05–06	36	(6)
Gard P.C.	1947–1990	(North Otago) 1971–72	7	(1)
Gardiner A.J.	1946–2021	(Taranaki) 1974	11	(1)
Gardner J.H.	1870–1909	(South Canterbury) 1893	4	(–)
Gatland W.D.	1963–	(Waikato) 1988–89–90–91	17	(–)
Gear H.E.	1984–	(Wellington) 2008–10–11–12	15	(14)
Gear R.L.	1978–	(North Harbour) 2004; (Nelson Bays) 2005; (Tasman) 2006; (Canterbury) 2007	20	(19)
Geddes J.H.	1907–1990	(Southland) 1929	6	(1)
Geddes W.McK.	1893–1950	(Auckland) 1913	1	(1)
Gemmell B.McL.	1950–	(Auckland) 1974	6	(2)
Gemmell S.W.	1896–1970	(Hawke's Bay) 1923	1	(–)
George V.L.	1908–1996	(Southland) 1938	7	(3)
Gibbes J.B.	1977–	(Waikato) 2004–05	8	(8)
Gibson D.P.E.	1975–	(Canterbury) 1999–2000–02	19	(19)
Gilbert G.D.M.	1911–2002	(West Coast) 1935–36	27	(4)
Gillespie C.T.	1883–1964	(Wellington) 1913	1	(1)
Gillespie W.D.	1934–	(Otago) 1957–58–60	23	(1)
Gillett G.A.	1877–1956	(Canterbury) 1905–06; (Auckland) 1907–08	38	(8)
Gillies C.C.	1912–1996	(Otago) 1936	2	(1)
Gilray C.M.	1885–1974	(Otago) 1905	1	(1)
Given F.J.	1876–1921	(Otago) 1903	9	(–)
Glasgow F.T.	1880–1939	(Taranaki) 1905–06; (Southland) 1908	35	(6)
Glenn W.S.	1877–1953	(Taranaki) 1904–05–06	19	(2)
Glennie E.	1870–1908	(Canterbury) 1897	6	(–)
Goddard J.W.	1920–1996	(South Canterbury) 1949	8	(–)
Goddard M.P.	1921–1974	(South Canterbury) 1946–47–49	20	(5)
Going K.T.	1942–2008	(North Auckland) 1974	3	(–)
Going S.M.	1943–	(North Auckland) 1967–68–69–70–71–72–73–74–75–76–77	86	(29)
Goldsmith J.A.	1969–	(Waikato) 1988	8	(–)
Good A.	1867–1938	(Taranaki) 1893	4	(–)
Good H.M.	1871–1941	(Taranaki) 1894	1	(–)
Goodhue E.J.	1995–	(Crusaders) 2017–18–19–20	19	(18)
Gordon S.B.	1967–	(Waikato) 1989–90–91–93	19	(2)
Gordon W.R.	1965–	(Waikato) 1990	3	(–)

Name	B&D	Representative Team	Games	Tests
Grace, C.J.	1999–	(Crusaders) 2020	1	(1)
Graham D.J.	1935–2017	(Canterbury) 1958–60–61–62–63–64	53	(22)
Graham J.B.	1884–1941	(Otago) 1913–14	19	(3)
Graham M.G.	1931–2015	(New South Wales) 1960	1	(–)
Graham W.G.	1957–	(Otago) 1978–79	8	(1)
Granger K.W.	1951–	(Manawatu) 1976	6	(–)
Grant L.A.	1923–2002	(South Canterbury) 1947–49–51	23	(4)
Gray G.D.	1880–1961	(Canterbury) 1908–13	14	(3)
Gray K.F.	1938–1992	(Wellington) 1963–64–65–66–67–68–69	50	(24)
Gray R.	1870–1951	(Wairarapa) 1893	2	(–)
Gray W.N.	1932–1993	(Bay of Plenty) 1955–56–57	11	(6)
Green C.I.	1961–	(Canterbury) 1983–84–85–86–87	39	(20)
Greene K.M.	1949–	(Waikato) 1976–77	8	(–)
Grenside B.A.	1899–1989	(Hawke's Bay) 1928–29	21	(6)
Griffiths J.L.	1912–2001	(Wellington) 1934–35–36–38	30	(7)
Gudsell K.E.	1924–2007	(Wanganui) 1949	6	(–)
Guildford Z.R.	1989–	(Hawke's Bay) 2009–10–11–12	10	(10)
Guy R.A.	1941–	(North Auckland) 1971–72	9	(4)
Haden A.M.	1950–2020	(Auckland) 1972–73–76–77–78–79–80–81–82–83–84–85	117	(41)
Hadley S.	1904–1970	(Auckland) 1928	11	(4)
Hadley W.E.	1910–1992	(Auckland) 1934–35–36	25	(8)
Haig J.S.	1924–1996	(Otago) 1946	2	(2)
Haig L.S.	1922–1992	(Otago) 1950–51–53–54	29	(9)
Halai F.	1988–	(Blues) 2013	1	(1)
Hales D.A.	1947–	(Canterbury) 1972–73	27	(4)
Hames K.S.	1988–	(Chiefs) 2016–17	10	(9)
Hamilton D.C.	1883–1925	(Southland) 1908	1	(1)
Hamilton S.E.	1980–	(Canterbury) 2006	2	(2)
Hammett M.G.	1972–	(Canterbury) 1999–2000–01–02–03	30	(29)
Hammond I.A.	1925–1998	(Marlborough) 1951–52	8	(1)
Handcock R.A.	1874–1956	(Auckland) 1897	8	(–)
Hardcastle W.R.	1874–1944	(Wellington) 1897	7	(–)
Harding S.	1980–	(Otago) 2002	1	(1)
Harper E.T.*	1877–1918	(Canterbury) 1904–05–06	11	(2)
Harper G.	1867–1937	(Nelson) 1893	3	(–)
Harris J.H.*	1903–1944	(Canterbury) 1925	8	(–)
Harris N.P.	1992–	(Chiefs) 2014–16–17–18	22	(20)
Harris P.C.	1946–	(Manawatu) 1976	4	(1)
Harris W.A.	1876–1950	(Otago) 1897	9	(–)
Hart A.H.	1897–1965	(Taranaki) 1924–25	17	(1)
Hart G.F.*	1909–1944	(Canterbury) 1930–31–32–34–35–36	35	(11)
Harvey B.A.	1959–	(Wairarapa Bush) 1986	1	(1)
Harvey I.H.	1903–1966	(Wairarapa) 1924–25–26–28	18	(1)
Harvey L.R.	1919–1993	(Otago) 1949–50	22	(8)
Harvey P.	1880–1949	(Canterbury) 1904	1	(1)
Hasell E.W.	1889–1966	(Canterbury) 1913–20	7	(2)
Havili D.K.	1994–	(Crusaders) 2017	5	(3)
Hay-MacKenzie W.E.	1874–1946	(Auckland) 1901	2	(–)
Hayman C.J.	1979–	(Otago) 2001–02–04–05–06–07	46	(45)
Hayward H.O.	1883–1970	(Auckland) 1908	1	(1)
Hazlett E.J.	1938–2014	(Southland) 1966–67	12	(6)
Hazlett W.E.	1905–1978	(Southland) 1926–28–30	26	(8)
Heeps T.R.	1938–2002	(Wellington) 1962	10	(5)

Name	B&D	Representative Team	Games	Tests
Heke W.R. (played as W. Rika)	1894–1989	(North Auckland) 1929	6	(3)
Helmore G.H.N.	1862–1922	(Canterbury) 1884	7	(–)
Hemara B.S.	1957–	(Manawatu) 1985	3	(–)
Hemi R.C.	1933–2000	(Waikato) 1953–54–55–56–57–59–60	46	(16)
Hemopo J.N.	1993–	(Highlanders) 2018–19	5	(5)
Henderson P.	1926–2014	(Wanganui) 1949–50	19	(7)
Henderson P.W.	1964–	(Otago) 1989–90–91; (Southland) 1992–93–95	25	(7)
Hendrie J.M.	1951–	(Western Australia) 1970	1	(–)
Herewini M.A.	1940–2014	(Auckland) 1962–63–64–65–66–67	32	(10)
Herrold M.	1869–1949	(Auckland) 1893	2	(–)
Hewett D.N.	1971–	(Canterbury) 2001–02–03	24	(22)
Hewett J.A.	1968–	(Auckland) 1991	1	(1)
Hewitt N.J.	1968–	(Hawke's Bay) 1993; (Southland) 1995–96–97–98	23	(9)
Hewson A.R.	1954–	(Wellington) 1979–81–82–83–84	34	(19)
Hickey P.H.	1899–1942	(Taranaki) 1922	2	(–)
Higginson G.	1954–	(Canterbury) 1980–81; (Hawke's Bay) 1982–83	20	(6)
Hill D.W.	1978–	(Waikato) 2001–06	3	(1)
Hill S.F.	1927–2019	(Canterbury) 1955–56–57–58–59	19	(11)
Hines G.R.	1960–	(Waikato) 1980	12	(1)
Hobbs F.G.	1920–1985	(Canterbury) 1947	6	(–)
Hobbs M.J.B.	1960–2012	(Canterbury) 1983–84–85–86	39	(21)
Hodgman, A.T.O.A.	1993–	(Blues) 2020	4	(4)
Hoeata J.M.R.A.	1982–	(Taranaki) 2011	3	(3)
Hoeft C.H.	1974–	(Otago) 1998–99–2000–01–03	31	(30)
Hogan J.	1881–1945	(Wanganui) 1907	2	(–)
Holah M.R.	1976–	(Waikato) 2001–02–03–04–05–06	39	(36)
Holden A.W.	1907–1970	(Otago) 1928	3	(–)
Holder E.C.	1908–1974	(Buller) 1932–34	10	(1)
Holmes B.	1946–	(North Auckland) 1970–72–73	31	(–)
Hook L.S.	1905–1979	(Auckland) 1928–29	12	(3)
Hooper J.A.	1913–1976	(Canterbury) 1937–38	7	(3)
Hopa A.R.	1971–1998	(Waikato) 1997	4	(–)
Hopkinson A.E.	1941–1999	(Canterbury) 1967–68–69–70	35	(9)
Hore A.K.	1978–	(Taranaki) 2002–04–05–06–07–08–09–10–11–12; (Highlanders) 2013	83	(83)
Hore J.	1907–1979 (Otago)	1928–30–32–34–35–36	45	(10)
Horsley R.H.	1932–2007	(Wellington) 1960; (Manawatu) 1963	31	(3)
Hotop J.	1929–2015	(Canterbury) 1952–55	3	(3)
Howarth S.P.	1968–	(Auckland) 1993–94	10	(4)
Howden J.	1900–1978	(Southland) 1928	1	(–)
Howlett D.C.	1978–	(Auckland) 2000–01–02–03–04–05–06–07	63	(62)
Hughes A.M.	1924–2005	(Auckland) 1947–49–50	7	(6)
Hughes D.J.	1869–1951	(Taranaki) 1894	1	(–)
Hughes E.	1881–1928	(Southland) 1907–08; (Wellington) 1921	9	(6)
Hullena L.C.	1965–	(Wellington) 1990–91	9	(–)
Humphreys G.W.	1870–1933	(Canterbury) 1894	1	(–)
Humphries A.L.	1874–1953	(Taranaki) 1897–1901–03	15	(–)
Hunt D.	1995–	(Highlanders) 2017–18	2	(1)
Hunter B.A.	1950–	(Otago) 1970–71	10	(3)

Name	B&D	Representative Team	Games	Tests
Hunter J.	1879–1962	(Taranaki) 1905–06–07–08	36	(11)
Hurst I.A.	1951–	(Canterbury) 1972–73–74	32	(5)
Ieremia A.	1970–	(Wellington) 1994–95–96–97–99–2000	40	(30)
Ifwersen K.D.	1893–1967	(Auckland) 1921	1	(1)
Innes C.R.	1969–	(Auckland) 1989–90–91	30	(17)
Innes G.D.	1910–1992	(Canterbury) 1932	7	(1)
Ioane A.L.	1995–	(Blues) 2017–20	3	(2)
Ioane, J.	1995–	(Highlanders) 2019	1	(1)
Ioane R.E.	1997–	(Blues) 2016–17–18–19–20	34	(34)
Irvine I.B.	1929–2013	(North Auckland) 1952	1	(1)
Irvine J.G.	1888–1939	(Otago) 1914	10	(3)
Irvine W.R.	1898–1952	(Hawke's Bay) 1923–24–25–26; (Wairarapa) 1930	41	(5)
Irwin M.W.	1935–2018	(Otago) 1955–56–58–59–60	25	(7)
Ivimey F.E.B.	1880–1961	(Otago) 1910	1	(–)
Jack C.R.	1978–	(Canterbury) 2001–02–03–04–05; (Tasman) 2006–07	68	(67)
Jackson E.S.	1914–1975	(Hawke's Bay) 1936–37–38	11	(6)
Jacob H.	1894–1955	(Horowhenua) 1920	8	(–)
Jacob J.P. LeG.	1877–1909	(Southland) 1901	2	(–)
Jacobson, L.B.	1997–	(Chiefs) 2019	2	(2)
Jaffray J.L.	1950–	(Otago) 1972–75–76–77–78; (South Canterbury) 1979	23	(7)
Jaffray M.W.R.	1949–	(Otago) 1976	4	(–)
Jane C.S.	1983–	(Wellington) 2008–09–10–11–12; (Hurricanes) 2013–14	55	(53)
Jarden R.A.	1929–1977	(Wellington) 1951–52–53–54–55–56	37	(16)
Jefferd A.C.R.	1953–	(East Coast) 1980–81	5	(3)
Jennings A.G.T.	1940–	(Bay of Plenty) 1967	6	(–)
Jervis F.M.	1870–1952	(Auckland) 1893	10	(–)
Jessep E.M.	1904–1983	(Wellington) 1931–32	8	(2)
Johns P.A.	1944–	(Wanganui) 1968	6	(–)
Johnson L.M.	1897–1983	(Wellington) 1925–28–30	25	(4)
Johnston D.	1903–1938	(Taranaki) 1925	2	(–)
Johnston W.	1881–1951	(Otago) 1905–07	27	(3)
Johnstone B.R.	1950–	(Auckland) 1976–77–78–79–80	45	(13)
Johnstone C.R.	1980–	(Canterbury) 2005	3	(3)
Johnstone P.	1922–1997	(Otago) 1949–50–51	26	(9)
Jones I.D.	1967–	(North Auckland) 1989–90–91–92–93; (North Harbour) 1994–95–96–97–98–99	105	(79)
Jones M.G.	1942–1975	(North Auckland) 1973	5	(1)
Jones M.N.	1965–	(Auckland) 1987–88–89–90–91–92–93–94–95–96–97–98	74	(55)
Jones P.F.H.	1932–1994	(North Auckland) 1953–54–55–56–58–59–60	37	(11)
Jordan, W.T.	1998–	(Crusaders) 2020	2	(2)
Joseph H.T.	1949–	(Canterbury) 1971	2	(2)
Joseph J.W.	1969–	(Otago) 1992–93–94–95	30	(20)
Kahui R.D.	1985–	(Waikato) 2008–10–11	18	(17)
Kaino J.	1983–	(Auckland) 2004–06–08–09–10–11; (Blues) 2014–15–16–17	83	(81)
Kane G.N.	1952–	(Waikato) 1974	7	(–)
Karam J.F.	1951–	(Wellington) 1972–73–74; (Horowhenua) 1975	42	(10)

New Zealand Representatives 1884–2020

Name	B&D	Representative Team	Games	Tests
Katene T.	1929–1992	(Wellington) 1955	1	(1)
Keane K.J.	1953–	(Canterbury) 1979	6	(–)
Kearney J.C.	1920–1998	(Otago) 1947–49	22	(4)
Kelleher B.T.	1976–	(Otago) 1999–2000–01–02–03–04; (Waikato) 2004–05–06–07	58	(57)
Kelly J.W.	1926–2002	(Auckland) 1949–53–54	16	(2)
Kember G.F.	1945–	(Wellington) 1967–70	19	(1)
Kenny D.J.	1961–	(Otago) 1986	3	(–)
Kerr A.	1871–1936	(Canterbury) 1896	1	(–)
Kerr-Barlow T.N.J.	1990–	(Waikato) 2012; (Chiefs) 2013–14–15–16–17	29	(27)
Ketels R.C.	1954–	(Counties) 1979–80–81	16	(5)
Kiernan H.A.D.	1876–1947	(Auckland) 1903	8	(1)
Kilby F.D.	1906–1985	(Wellington) 1928–32–34	18	(4)
Killeen B.A.	1911–1993	(Auckland) 1936	2	(1)
King R.M.	1980–	(Waikato) 2002	1	(1)
King R.R.	1909–1988	(West Coast) 1934–35–36–37–38	42	(13)
Kingstone C.N.	1895–1960	(Taranaki) 1921	3	(3)
Kirk D.E.	1961–	(Otago) 1983–84; (Auckland) 1985–86–87	34	(17)
Kirkpatrick A.	1898–1971	(Hawke's Bay) 1925–26	12	(–)
Kirkpatrick I.A.	1946–	(Canterbury) 1967–68–69; (Poverty Bay) 1970–71–72–73–74–75–76–77	113	(39)
Kirton E.W.	1939–	(Otago) 1963–64–67–68–69–70	49	(13)
Kirwan J.J.	1964–	(Auckland) 1984–85–86–87–88–89–90–91–92–93–94	96	(63)
Kivell A.L.	1897–1988	(Taranaki) 1929	5	(2)
Knight A.	1906–1990	(Auckland) 1926–28–34	14	(1)
Knight G.A.	1951–	(Manawatu) 1977–78–79–80–81–82–83–84–85–86	66	(36)
Knight L.A.G.	1901–1973	(Auckland) 1925	5	(–)
Knight L.G.	1949–	(Auckland) 1974; (Poverty Bay) 1976–77	35	(6)
Knight M.O.	1945–	(Counties) 1968	8	(–)
Koteka T.T.	1956–	(Waikato) 1981–82	6	(2)
Kreft A.J.	1945–	(Otago) 1968	4	(1)
Kronfeld J.A.	1971–	(Otago) 1995–96–97–98–99–2000	56	(54)
Kururangi R.	1957–	(Counties) 1978	8	(–)
Laidlaw C.R.	1943–	(Otago) 1963–64–65–66–67; (Canterbury) 1968 (Otago) 1970	57	(20)
Laidlaw K.F.	1934–	(Southland) 1960	17	(3)
Lam P.R.	1968–	(Auckland) 1992	1	(–)
Lambert K.K.	1952–	(Manawatu) 1972–73–74–76–77	40	(11)
Lambie J.T.	1870–1905	(Taranaki) 1893–94	12	(–)
Lambourn A.	1910–1999	(Wellington) 1934–35–36–37–38	40	(10)
Larsen B.P.	1969–	(North Harbour) 1992–93–94–95–96	40	(17)
Latimer T.D.	1986–	(Bay of Plenty) 2009	6	(5)
Laulala C.D.E.	1982–	(Canterbury) 2004–06	3	(2)
Laulala N.E.	1991–	(Crusaders) 2015–17–18 (Chiefs) 2019–20	29	(29)
Laumape K.H.	1993–	(Hurricanes) 2017–18–19–20	17	(15)
Lauaki S.T.	1981–2017	(Waikato) 2005–07–08	17	(17)
Law A.D.	1904–1961	(Manawatu) 1925	4	(–)
Lawson G.P.	1899–1985	(South Canterbury) 1925	2	(–)
Lecky J.G.	1863–1917	(Auckland) 1884	7	(–)
Lee D.D.	1976–	(Otago) 2002	2	(2)
Leeson J.	1909–1960	(Waikato) 1934	5	(–)
LeLievre J.M.	1933–2016	(Canterbury) 1962–63–64	25	(1)

Name	B&D	Representative Team	Games	Tests
Lendrum R.N.	1948–	(Counties) 1973	3	(1)
Leonard B.G.	1985–	(Waikato) 2007–09	14	(13)
Leslie A.R.	1944–	(Wellington) 1974–75–76	34	(10)
Levien H.J.	1935–2008	(Otago) 1957	8	(–)
Leys E.T.	1907–1989	(Wellington) 1929	5	(1)
Lienert-Brown A.R.	1995–	(Chiefs) 2016–17–18–19–20	50	(49)
Lilburne H.T.	1908–1976	(Canterbury) 1928–29–30; (Wellington) 1931–32–34	40	(10)
Lindsay D.F.	1906–1978	(Otago) 1928	14	(3)
Lindsay W.G.	1879–1965	(Southland) 1914	4	(–)
Lineen T.R.	1936–2020	(Auckland) 1957–58–59–60	35	(12)
Lister T.N.	1943–2017	(South Canterbury) 1968–69–70–71	26	(8)
Little P.F.	1934–1993	(Auckland) 1961–62–63–64	29	(10)
Little W.K.	1969–	(North Harbour) 1989–90–91–92–93–94–95–96–97–98	75	(50)
Loader C.J.	1931–	(Wellington) 1953–54	16	(4)
Lochore B.J.	1940–2019	(Wairarapa) 1963–64–65–66–67–68–69–70; (Wairarapa Bush) 1971	68	(25)
Lockington T.M.	1913–2001	(Auckland) 1936	1	(–)
Loe R.W.	1960–	(Waikato) 1986–87–88–89–90–91–92; (Canterbury) 1994–95	78	(49)
Lomas A.R.	1894–1975	(Auckland) 1925–26	15	(–)
Lomax T.S.	1996–	(Highlanders) 2018 (Hurricanes) 2020	6	(6)
Lomu J.T.	1975–2015	(Counties Manukau) 1994–95–96–97–98–99; (Wellington) 2000–01–02	73	(63)
Long A.T.	1879–1960	(Auckland) 1903	10	(1)
Loveday J.N.	1949–	(Manawatu) 1978	7	(–)
Loveridge D.S.	1952–	(Taranaki) 1978–79–80–81–82–83–85	54	(24)
Loveridge G.	1890–1970	(Taranaki) 1913–14	11	(–)
Lowen K.R.	1976–	(Waikato) 2002	1	(1)
Luatua D.S.	1991	(Blues) 2013–14–16	15	(15)
Lucas F.W.	1902–1957	(Auckland) 1923–24–25–28–30	41	(7)
Lunn W.A.	1926–1996	(Otago) 1949	2	(2)
Lynch T.W.	1892–1950	(South Canterbury) 1913–14	23	(4)
Lynch T.W.	1927–2006	(Canterbury) 1951	10	(3)
Maber G.	1869–1894	(Wellington) 1894	1	(–)
McAlister C.L.	1983–	(North Harbour) 2005–06–07–09	31	(30)
McAtamney F.S.	1934–	(Otago) 1956–57	9	(1)
McCahill B.J.	1964–	(Auckland) 1987–88–89–90–91	32	(10)
McCarthy P.	1893–1976	(Canterbury) 1923	1	(–)
McCashin T.M.	1944–2017	(Wellington) 1968	7	(–)
McCaw R.H.	1980–	(Canterbury) 2001–02–03–04–05–06–07–08–09–10–11–12; (Crusaders) 2013–14–15	149	(148)
McCaw W.A.	1927–	(Southland) 1951–53–54	32	(5)
McCleary B.V.	1897–1978	(Canterbury) 1924–25	12	(–)
McClymont W.G.	1905–1970	(Otago) 1928	3	(–)
McCool M.J.	1951–2020	(Wairarapa Bush) 1979	2	(1)
McCormick A.G.	1899–1969	(Canterbury) 1925	1	(–)
McCormick J.	1923–2006	(Hawke's Bay) 1947	3	(–)
McCormick W.F.	1939–2018	(Canterbury) 1965–67–68–69–70–71	44	(16)
McCullough J.F.	1936–	(Taranaki) 1959	3	(3)
McDonald A.	1883–1967	(Otago) 1905–06–07–08–13	41	(8)
Macdonald A.J.	1981–	(Auckland) 2005	2	(2)

Name	B&D	Representative Team	Games	Tests
Macdonald H.H.	1947–	(Canterbury) 1972–73–74; (North Auckland) 1975–76	48	(12)
MacDonald L.R.	1977–	(Canterbury) 2000–01–02–03–05–06–07–08	56	(56)
McDonnell P.	1874–1950	(Wanganui) 1896	1	(–)
McDonnell J.M.	1973–	(Otago) 2002	8	(8)
McDowall S.C.	1961–	(Auckland) 1985–86–87–88; (Bay of Plenty) 1989; (Auckland) 1989–90–91–92	81	(46)
McEldowney J.T.	1947–2012	(Taranaki) 1976–77	10	(2)
MacEwan I.N.	1934–	(Wellington) 1956–57–58–59–60–61–62	52	(20)
McGahan P.W.	1964–	(North Harbour) 1990–91	6	(–)
McGrattan B.	1959–	(Wellington) 1983–84–85–86	23	(6)
McGregor A.A.	1953–	(Southland) 1978	3	(–)
McGregor A.J.	1889–1963	(Auckland) 1913	11	(2)
McGregor D.	1881–1947	(Canterbury) 1903; (Wellington) 1904–05–06	31	(4)
McGregor N.P.	1901–1973	(Canterbury) 1924–25–28	27	(2)
McGregor R.W.	1874–1925	(Auckland) 1901–03–04	10	(2)
McHugh M.J.	1917–2010	(Auckland) 1946–49	14	(3)
MacIntosh C.N.	1869–1918	(South Canterbury) 1893	4	(–)
McIntosh D.N.	1931–	(Wellington) 1956–57	13	(4)
McKay D.W.	1937–	(Auckland) 1961–62–63	12	(5)
Mackay J.D.	1905–1985	(Wellington) 1928	2	(–)
McKechnie B.J.	1953–	(Southland) 1977–78–79–81	26	(10)
McKellar G.F.	1884–1960	(Wellington) 1910	5	(3)
McKenzie D.S.	1995–	(Chiefs) 2016–17–18–20	27	(27)
MacKenzie R.H.	1869–1940	(Auckland) 1893	2	(–)
MacKenzie R.H.C.	1904–1993	(Wellington) 1928	2	(–)
McKenzie R.J.	1892–1968	(Wellington) 1913; (Auckland) 1914	20	(4)
MacKenzie R.M.	1909–2000	(Manawatu) 1934–35–36–37–38	35	(9)
McKenzie W.	1871–1943	(Wairarapa) 1893; (Wellington) 1894–96–97	20	(–)
Mackintosh J.L.	1985–	(Southland) 2008	2	(1)
Mackrell W.H.C.	1881–1917	(Auckland) 1905–06	7	(1)
Macky J.V.	1887–1951	(Auckland) 1913	1	(1)
McLachlan J.S.	1949–	(Auckland) 1974	8	(1)
McLaren H.C.	1926–1992	(Waikato) 1952	1	(1)
McLean A.L.	1898–1964	(Bay of Plenty) 1921–23	3	(2)
McLean C.	1892–1965	(Buller) 1920	5	(–)
McLean H.F.	1907–1997	(Wellington) 1930–32; (Auckland) 1934–35–36	29	(9)
McLean J.K.	1923–2005	(King Country) 1947; (Auckland) 1949	5	(2)
McLean R.J.	1960–	(Wairarapa Bush) 1987	2	(–)
McLeod B.E.	1940–1996	(Counties) 1964–65–66–67–68–69–70	46	(24)
McLeod S.J.	1973–	(Waikato) 1996–97–98	17	(10)
McMeeking D.T.M.	1896–1976	(Otago) 1923	2	(–)
McMinn A.F.	1880–1919	(Wairarapa) 1903; (Manawatu) 1905	10	(2)
McMinn F.A.	1874–1947	(Manawatu) 1904	1	(1)
McMullen R.F.	1933–2004	(Auckland) 1957–58–59–60	29	(11)
McNab J.A.	1895–1979	(Hawke's Bay) 1925	1	(–)
McNab J.R.	1924–2009	(Otago) 1949–50	17	(6)
McNaughton A.M.	1947–	(Bay of Plenty) 1971–72	9	(3)
McNeece J.*	1885–1917	(Southland) 1913–14	11	(5)

Name	B&D	Representative Team	Games	Tests
McNicol A.L.R.	1944–2017	(Wanganui) 1973	5	(–)
McPhail B.E.	1937–2020	(Canterbury) 1959	2	(2)
MacPherson D.G.	1882–1956	(Otago) 1905	1	(1)
Macpherson G.	1962–	(Otago) 1986	1	(1)
MacRae I.R.	1943–	(Hawke's Bay) 1963–64–66–67–68–69–70	45	(17)
McRae J.A.	1914–1977	(Southland) 1946	2	(2)
McRobie N.	1873–1929	(Southland) 1896	1	(–)
McWilliams R.G.	1901–1984	(Auckland) 1928–29–30	27	(10)
Maguire J.R.	1886–1966	(Auckland) 1910	6	(3)
Mahoney A.	1908–1979	(Bush) 1929–34–35–36	26	(4)
Mains L.W.	1946–	(Otago) 1971–76	15	(4)
Major J.	1940–	(Taranaki) 1963–64–67	24	(1)
Maka I.	1975–	(Otago) 1998	4	(4)
Maling T.S.	1975–	(Otago) 2001–02–04	13	(11)
Manchester J.E.	1908–1983	(Canterbury) 1932–34–35–36	36	(9)
Mannix S.J.	1971–	(Wellington) 1990–91–94	9	(1)
Markham P.F.	1891–1953	(Wellington) 1921	1	(–)
Marshall J.W.	1973–	(Canterbury) 1995–96–97–98–99–2000–01–02–03–04–05	88	(81)
Masaga L.T.C.	1986–	(Counties Manukau) 2009	1	(1)
Masoe M.C.	1979–	(Taranaki) 2005; (Wellington) 2006–07	20	(20)
Mason D.F.	1923–1981	(Wellington) 1947	6	(1)
Masters F.H.	1893–1980	(Taranaki) 1922	4	(–)
Masters R.R.	1900–1967	(Canterbury) 1923–24–25	31	(4)
Mataira H.K.	1910–1979	(Hawke's Bay) 1934	5	(1)
Matheson J.D.	1948–	(Otago) 1972	13	(5)
Mathewson A.S.	1985–	(Wellington) 2008–10	5	(4)
Mathieson R.G.	1899–1966	(Otago) 1922	4	(–)
Matson J.T.F.	1973	(Canterbury) 1995–96	5	(–)
Mattson H.A.	1900–1980	(Auckland) 1925	6	(–)
Mauger A.J.D.	1980–	(Canterbury) 2001–02–03–04–05–06–07	46	(45)
Mauger N.K.	1978–	(Canterbury) 2001	2	(–)
Max D.S.	1906–1972	(Nelson) 1931–32–34	8	(3)
Maxwell N.M.C.	1976–	(Canterbury) 1999–2000–01–02–04	36	(36)
Mayerhofler M.A.	1972–	(Canterbury) 1998	6	(6)
Meads C.E.	1936–2017	(King Country) 1957–58–59–60–61–62–63–64–65–66–67–68–69–70–71	133	(55)
Meads S.T.	1938–	(King Country) 1961–62–63–64–65–66	30	(15)
Mealamu K.F.	1979–	(Auckland) 2002–03–04–05–06–07–08–09–10–11–12; (Blues) 2013–14–15	133	(132)
Meates K.F.	1930–	(Canterbury) 1952	2	(2)
Meates W.A.	1923–2003	(Otago) 1949–50	20	(7)
Meeuws K.J.	1974–	(Otago) 1998–99–2000–01–02–04; (Auckland) 2003	45	(42)
Mehrtens A.P.	1973–	(Canterbury) 1995–96–97–98–99–2000–01–02–04	72	(70)
Mehrtens G.M.	1907–1954	(Canterbury) 1928	3	(–)
Messam L.J.	1984–	(Waikato) 2008–09–10–11–12; (Chiefs) 2013–14–15	45	(43)
Metcalfe T.C.	1909–1969	(Southland) 1931–32	7	(2)
Mexted G.G.	1927–2009	(Wellington) 1950–51	5	(1)
Mexted M.G.	1953–	(Wellington) 1979–80–81–82–83–84–85	72	(34)
Mika B.M.	1981–	(Auckland) 2002	3	(3)
Mika D.G.	1972–2018	(Auckland) 1999	8	(7)
Mill J.J.	1899–1950	(Hawke's Bay) 1923–24–25–26; (Wairarapa) 1930	33	(4)

New Zealand Representatives 1884–2020

Name	B&D	Representative Team	Games	Tests
Miller P.C.	1975–	(Otago) 2001	2	(–)
Miller T.J.	1974–	(Waikato) 1997	4	(–)
Milliken H.M.	1914–1993	(Canterbury) 1938	7	(3)
Mills H.P.	1873–1905	(Taranaki) 1897	8	(–)
Mills J.G.	1960–	(Auckland) 1984	2	(–)
Millton E.B.	1861–1942	(Canterbury) 1884	7	(–)
Millton W.V.	1858–1887	(Canterbury) 1884	8	(–)
Milner H.P.	1946–1996	(Wanganui) 1970	16	(1)
Milner-Skudder N.R.	1990–	(Hurricanes) 2015,17–18	13	(13)
Mitchell J.E.P.	1964–	(Waikato) 1993	6	(–)
Mitchell N.A.	1913–1981	(Southland) 1935–36–37; (Otago) 1938	32	(8)
Mitchell T.W.	1950–	(Canterbury) 1974–76	17	(1)
Mitchell W.J.	1890–1959	(Canterbury) 1910	5	(2)
Mitchinson F.E.	1884–1978	(Wellington) 1907–08–10–13	31	(11)
Moala G.	1990	(Blues) 2015–16	4	(4)
Moffitt J.E.	1889–1964	(Wellington) 1920–21	12	(3)
Moli A.	1995–	(Chiefs) 2017–19	5	(4)
Molloy B.P.J.	1931–	(Canterbury) 1957	5	(–)
Moody J.P.T.	1988–	(Crusaders) 2014–15–16–17–18–19–20	50	(50)
Moore G.J.T.	1923–1991	(Otago) 1949	1	(1)
Moreton R.C.	1942–2016	(Canterbury) 1962–64–65	12	(7)
Morgan H.D.	1902–1969	(Otago) 1923	1	(–)
Morgan J.E.	1945–2002	(North Auckland) 1974–76	22	(5)
Morris T.J.	1942–	(Nelson Bays) 1972–73	23	(3)
Morrison T.C.	1913–1985	(South Canterbury) 1938	5	(3)
Morrison T.G.	1951–	(Otago) 1973	5	(1)
Morrissey B.L.	1952–	(Waikato) 1981	3	(–)
Morrissey P.J.	1939–2013	(Canterbury) 1962	3	(3)
Mourie G.N.K.	1952–	(Taranaki) 1976–77–78–79–80–81–82	61	(21)
Mo'unga R.	1994–	(Crusaders) 2017–18–19–20	23	(22)
Mowlem J.	1870–1951	(Manawatu) 1893	4	(–)
Muliaina J.M.	1980–	(Auckland) 2003–04–05; (Waikato) 2006–07–08–09–10–11	102	(100)
Muller B.L.	1942–2019	(Taranaki) 1967–68–69–70–71	35	(14)
Mumm W.J.	1922–1993	(Buller) 1949	1	(1)
Munro H.G.	1896–1974	(Otago) 1924–25	9	(–)
Murdoch K.	1943–2018	(Otago) 1970–72	27	(3)
Murdoch P.H.	1941–1995	(Auckland) 1964–65	5	(5)
Murray F.S.M.	1871–1952	(Auckland) 1893–97	20	(–)
Murray H.V.	1888–1971	(Canterbury) 1913–14	22	(4)
Murray P.C.	1884–1968	(Wanganui) 1908	1	(1)
Myers R.G.	1950–	(Waikato) 1977–78	5	(1)
Mynott H.J.	1876–1924	(Taranaki) 1905–06–07–10	39	(8)
Naholo W.R.	1991	(Highlanders) 2015–16–17–18	27	(26)
Nathan W.J.	1940–	(Auckland) 1962–63–64–66–67	37	(14)
Nelson K.A.	1938–	(Otago) 1962–63–64	18	(2)
Nepia G.	1905–1986	(Hawke's Bay) 1924–25; (East Coast) 1929–30	46	(9)
Nesbit S.R.	1936–	(Auckland) 1960	13	(2)
Neville W.R.	1954–	(North Auckland) 1981	4	(–)
Newby C.A.	1979–	(North Harbour) 2004–06	3	(3)
Newton F.	1881–1955	(Canterbury) 1905–06	19	(3)
Ngatai C.J.	1990–	(Chiefs) 2015	1	(1)
Nicholls H.E.	1900–1978	(Wellington) 1921–22–23	7	(1)

Name	B&D	Representative Team	Games	Tests
Nicholls H.G.	1897–1977	(Wellington) 1923	1	(–)
Nicholls M.F.	1901–1972	(Wellington) 1921–22–24–25–26–28–30	51	(10)
Nicholson G.W.	1878–1968	(Auckland) 1903–04–05–06–07	39	(4)
Nonu M.A.	1982–	(Wellington) 2003–04–05–06–07–08–09–10–11–12; (Highlanders) 2013; (Blues) 2014; (Hurricanes) 2015	104	(103)
Norton R.W.	1942–	(Canterbury) 1971–72–73–74–75–76–77	61	(27)
O'Brien A.J.	1897–1969	(Auckland) 1922	3	(–)
O'Brien J.	1871–1946	(Wellington) 1901	1	(–)
O'Brien J.G.	1889–1958	(Auckland) 1914–20	12	(1)
O'Callaghan M.W.	1946–	(Manawatu) 1968	3	(3)
O'Callaghan T.R.	1925–2004	(Wellington) 1949	1	(1)
O'Connor T.B.	1860–1936	(Auckland) 1884	7	(–)
O'Dea R.J.	1930–1986	(Thames Valley) 1953–54	5	(–)
O'Donnell D.H.	1921–1992	(Wellington) 1949	1	(1)
O'Donnell J.M.	1860–1942	(Otago) 1884	7	(–)
O'Dowda B.C.	1874–1954	(Taranaki) 1901	2	(–)
O'Halloran J.D.	1972–	(Wellington) 2000	1	(1)
O'Leary M.J.	1883–1963	(Auckland) 1910–13	8	(4)
O'Neill K.J.	1982–	(Waikato) 2008	1	(1)
Old G.H.	1956–	(Manawatu) 1980–81–82–83	17	(3)
Oliphant R.	1870–1956	(Wellington) 1893; (Auckland) 1896	3	(–)
Oliver A.D.	1975–	(Otago) 1996–97–98–99–2000–01–03–04–05–06–07	67	(59)
Oliver C.J.	1905–1977	(Canterbury) 1928–29–34–35–36	33	(7)
Oliver D.J.	1907–1990	(Wellington) 1930	3	(2)
Oliver D.O.	1930–1997	(Otago) 1953–54	20	(2)
Oliver F.J.	1948–2014	(Southland) 1976–77; (Otago) 1978–79; (Manawatu) 1980–81	43	(17)
Orchard S.A.	1875–1947	(Canterbury) 1896–97	8	(–)
Ormond J.	1891–1970	(Hawke's Bay) 1923	1	(–)
Orr R.W.	1923–2011	(Otago) 1949	1	(1)
Osborne G.M.	1971–	(North Harbour) 1995–96–97–99	29	(19)
Osborne W.M.	1955–	(Wanganui) 1975–76–77–78–80–82	48	(16)
O'Sullivan J.M.	1883–1960	(Taranaki) 1905–07	29	(5)
O'Sullivan T.P.A.	1936–1997	(Taranaki) 1960–61–62	16	(4)
Paewai L.	1906–1970	(Hawke's Bay) 1923–24	8	(–)
Page J.R.	1908–1985	(Wellington) 1931–32–34–35	18	(6)
Page M.L.	1902–1987	(Canterbury) 1928	1	(–)
Palmer B.P.	1901–1932	(Auckland) 1928–29–32	18	(3)
Papali'i D.R.	1997	(Blues) 2018–19–20	4	(4)
Parker J.H.	1897–1980	(Canterbury) 1924–25	21	(3)
Parkhill A.A.	1912–1986	(Otago) 1937–38	10	(6)
Parkinson R.M.	1948–2009	(Poverty Bay) 1972–73	20	(7)
Parsons J.W.	1986–	(Blues) 2014–16	2	(2)
Paterson A.M.	1885–1933	(Otago) 1908–10	9	(5)
Paton H.	1881–1964	(Otago) 1907–10	8	(2)
Pauling T.G.	1873–1927	(Wellington) 1896–97	9	(–)
Pene A.R.B.	1967–	(Otago) 1992–93–94	26	(15)
Pepper C.S.*	1911–1943	(Auckland) 1935–36	17	(–)
Perenara T.T.R.	1992–	(Hurricanes) 2014–15–16–17–18–19–20	70	(69)
Perry A.	1899–1977	(Otago) 1923	1	(–)
Perry R.G.	1953–	(Mid Canterbury) 1980	1	(–)

Name	B&D	Representative Team	Games	Tests
Perry T.G.	1988–	(Crusaders) 2017–18	8	(6)
Petersen L.C.	1897–1961	(Canterbury) 1921–22–23	8	(–)
Phillips W.J.	1914–1982	(King Country) 1937–38	7	(3)
Philpott S.	1965–	(Canterbury) 1988–90–91	14	(2)
Pickering E.A.R.	1936–2016	(Waikato) 1957–58–59–60	21	(3)
Pierce M.J.	1957–	(Wellington) 1984–85–86–87–88–89–90	54	(26)
Piutau S.T.	1991–	(Blues) 2013–14–15	17	(17)
Pokere S.T.	1958–	(Southland) 1981–82–83; (Auckland) 1984–85	39	(18)
Pollock H.R.	1909–1984	(Wellington) 1932–36	8	(5)
Porteous H.G.	1875–1951	(Otago) 1903	3	(–)
Porter C.G.	1899–1976	(Wellington) 1923–24–25–26–27–28–29–30	41	(7)
Potaka W.P.	ca 1903–1967	(Wanganui) 1923	2	(–)
Preston J.P.	1967–	(Canterbury) 1991–92; (Wellington) 1993–96–97	27	(10)
Pringle A.	1899–1973	(Wellington) 1923	1	(–)
Pringle W.P.	1869–1945	(Wellington) 1893	5	(–)
Procter A.C.	1906–1989	(Otago) 1932	4	(1)
Proctor M.P.	1992–	(Hurricanes) 2018	1	(1)
Pulu A.W.	1990–	(Chiefs) 2014	2	(2)
Purdue C.A.	1874–1941	(Southland) 1901–05	3	(1)
Purdue E.	1879–1939	(Southland) 1905	1	(1)
Purdue G.B.	1909–1981	(Southland) 1931–32	7	(4)
Purvis G.H.	1960–	(Waikato) 1989–90–91–92–93	28	(2)
Purvis N.A.	1953–2008	(Otago) 1976	12	(1)
Quaid C.E.	1908–1984	(Otago) 1938	4	(2)
Ralph C.S.	1977–	(Auckland) 1998; (Canterbury) 2001–02–03	16	(14)
Ranby R.M.	1977–	(Waikato) 2001	1	(1)
Randell T.C.	1974–	(Otago) 1995–96–97–98–99–2000–01–02	61	(51)
Randle R.Q.	1974–	(Waikato) 2001	2	(–)
Ranger R.M.N.	1986–	(Northland) 2010; (Blues) 2013	6	(6)
Rangi R.E.	1941–1988	(Auckland) 1964–65–66	10	(10)
Rankin J.G.	1914–1989	(Canterbury) 1936–37	4	(3)
Rawlinson G.P.	1978–	(North Harbour) 2006–07	4	(4)
Read K.J.	1985–	(Canterbury) 2008–09–10–11–12; (Crusaders) 2013–14–15–16–17–18–19	128	(127)
Reece, S.L.	1997–	(Crusaders) 2019–20	8	(8)
Reedy W.J.	1880–1939	(Wellington) 1908	2	(2)
Reid A.R.	1929–1994	(Waikato) 1951–52–56–57	17	(5)
Reid H.R.	1958–	(Bay of Plenty) 1980–81–83–84–85–86	40	(9)
Reid K.H.	1904–1972	(Wairarapa) 1929	5	(2)
Reid S.T.	1912–2003	(Hawke's Bay) 1935–36–37	27	(9)
Reihana B.T.	1976–	(Waikato) 2000	2	(2)
Reside W.B.	1905–1985	(Wairarapa) 1929	6	(1)
Retallick B.A.	1991–	(Hawke's Bay/Bay of Plenty) 2012; (Chiefs) 2013–14–15–16–17–18–19	81	(81)
Rhind P.K.	1915–1996	(Canterbury) 1946	2	(2)
Richardson J.	1899–1994	(Otago) 1921–22; (Southland) 1923–24–25	42	(7)
Rickit H.A.	1951–	(Waikato) 1981	2	(2)
Ridge M.J.	1969–	(Auckland) 1989	6	(–)
Ridland A.J.*	1882–1918	(Southland) 1910	6	(3)

Name	B&D	Representative Team	Games	Tests
Riechelmann C.C.	1972–	(Auckland) 1997	10	(6)
Righton L.S.	1898–1972	(Auckland) 1923–25	9	(–)
Roberts E.J.	1891–1972	(Wellington) 1913–14–20–21	26	(5)
Roberts F.	1882–1956	(Wellington) 1905–06–07–08–10	52	(12)
Roberts H.	1862–1949	(Wellington) 1884	7	(–)
Roberts R.W.	1889–1973	(Taranaki) 1913–14	23	(5)
Roberts W.	1871–1937	(Wellington) 1896–97	8	(–)
Robertson B.J.	1952–	(Counties) 1972–73–74–76–77–78–79–80–81	102	(34)
Robertson D.J.	1947–	(Otago) 1974–75–76–77	30	(10)
Robertson G.S.	1859–1920	(Otago) 1884	8	(–)
Robertson S.M.	1974–	(Canterbury) 1998–99–2000–01–02	23	(23)
Robilliard A.C.C.	1903–1990	(Canterbury) 1924–25–26–28	27	(4)
Robins B.G.	1958–	(Taranaki) 1985	4	(–)
Robinson A.G.	1956–	(North Auckland) 1983	4	(–)
Robinson C.E.	1927–1983	(Southland) 1951–52	11	(5)
Robinson J.T.	1906–1968	(Canterbury) 1928	3	(–)
Robinson K.J.	1976–	(Waikato) 2002–04–06–07	12	(12)
Robinson M.D.	1975–	(North Harbour) 1997–98–2001	8	(3)
Robinson M.P.	1974–	(Canterbury) 2000–02	9	(9)
Rokocoko J.T.	1983–	(Auckland) 2003–04–05–06–07–08–09–10	69	(68)
Rollerson D.L.	1953–2017	(Manawatu) 1976–80–81	24	(8)
Romano L.	1986–	(Canterbury) 2012; (Crusaders) 2013–14–15–16–17	32	(31)
Roper R.A.	1923–	(Taranaki) 1949–50	5	(5)
Ross I.B.	1984–	(Canterbury) 2009	8	(8)
Ross J.C.	1949–	(Mid Canterbury) 1981	5	(–)
Rowlands G.D.	1947–	(Bay of Plenty) 1976	4	(–)
Rowley H.C.B.	1924–1956	(Wanganui) 1949	1	(1)
Rush E.J.	1965–	(North Harbour) 1992–93–95–96	29	(9)
Rush X.J.	1977–	(Auckland) 1998–2004	8	(8)
Rushbrook C.A.	1907–1987	(Wellington) 1928	10	(–)
Rutledge L.M.	1952–	(Southland) 1978–79–80	31	(13)
Ryan E.	1891–1965	(Wellington) 1921	1	(–)
Ryan J.	1887–1957	(Wellington) 1910–14	15	(4)
Ryan J.A.C.	1983–	(Otago) 2005–06	9	(9)
Ryan P.J.	1950–1985	(Hawke's Bay) 1976	5	(–)
Ryan T.	1863–1927	(Auckland) 1884	9	(-)
Sadler B.S.	1914–2007	(Wellington) 1935–36	19	(5)
Saili F.	1991–	(Blues) 2013	2	(2)
Salmon J.L.B.	1959–	(Wellington) 1980–81	7	(3)
Sapsford H.P.	1949–2009	(Otago) 1976	7	(–)
Savage L.T.	1928–2013	(Canterbury) 1949	12	(3)
Savea A.S.	1993–	(Hurricanes) 2016–17–18–19–20	51	(49)
Savea S.J.	1990–	(Wellington) 2012; (Hurricanes) 2013–14–15–16–17	54	(54)
Saxton C.K.	1913–2001	(South Canterbury) 1938	7	(3)
Sayers M.	1947–	(Wellington) 1972–73	15	(–)
Schuler K.J.	1967–	(Manawatu) 1989–90; (North Harbour) 1992–95	13	(4)
Schuster N.J.	1964–	(Wellington) 1987–88–89	26	(10)
Schwalger J.E.	1983–	(Wellington) 2007–08	2	(2)
Scott R.W.H.	1921–2012	(Auckland) 1946–47–49–50–53–54	52	(17)
Scott S.J.	1955–1994	(Canterbury) 1980	4	(–)
Scown A.I.	1948–	(Taranaki) 1972–73	17	(5)
Scrimshaw G.	1902–1971	(Canterbury) 1928	11	(1)

Name	B&D	Representative Team	Games	Tests
Seear G.A.	1952–2018	(Otago) 1976–77–78–79	34	(12)
Seeling C.E.	1883–1956	(Auckland) 1904–05–06–07–08	39	(11)
Sellars G.M.V.*	1886–1917	(Auckland) 1913	15	(2)
Senio K.	1978–	(Bay of Plenty) 2005	1	(1)
Seymour D.J.	1967–	(Canterbury) 1992	3	(–)
Shannon H.G.	1869–1912	(Manawatu) 1893	6	(–)
Shaw M.W.	1956–	(Manawatu) 1980–81–82–83–84–85; (Hawke's Bay) 1986	69	(30)
Shearer J.D.	1896–1963	(Wellington) 1920	5	(–)
Shearer S.D.	1890–1973	(Wellington) 1921–22	8	(–)
Sheen T.R.	1905–1979	(Auckland) 1926–28	8	(–)
Shelford F.N.K.	1955–	(Bay of Plenty) 1981–84–85; (Hawke's Bay) 1983	22	(4)
Shelford W.T.	1957–	(North Harbour) 1985–86–87–88–89–90	48	(22)
Sherlock K.	1961–	(Auckland) 1985	3	(–)
Siddells S.K.	1897–1979	(Wellington) 1921	1	(1)
Simon H.J.	1911–1979	(Otago) 1937	3	(3)
Simonsson P.L.J.	1967–	(Wellington) 1987	2	(–)
Simpson J.G.	1922–2010	(Auckland) 1947–49–50	30	(9)
Simpson V.L.J.	1960–	(Canterbury) 1985	4	(2)
Sims G.S.	1951–	(Otago) 1972	1	(1)
Sinclair R.G.B.	1896–1932	(Otago) 1923	2	(–)
Sivivatu S.W.	1982–	(Waikato) 2005–06–07–08–09–11	46	(45)
Skeen J.R.	1928–2001	(Auckland) 1952	1	(1)
Skinner K.L.	1927–2014	(Otago) 1949–50–51–52–53–54; (Counties) 1956	63	(20)
Skudder G.R.	1948–	(Waikato) 1969–72–73	14	(1)
Slade C.R.	1987–	(Canterbury) 2010–11; (Highlanders) 2013; (Crusaders) 2014–15	21	(21)
Slater G.L.	1971–	(Taranaki) 1997–2000	6	(3)
Sloane P.H.	1948–	(North Auckland) 1973–76–79	16	(1)
Smith A.E.	1942–	(Taranaki) 1967–69–70	18	(3)
Smith A.L.	1998–	(Manawatu) 2012; (Highlanders) 2013–14–15–16–17–18–19–20	97	(97)
Smith B.R.	1986–	(Otago) 2009–11–12; (Highlanders) 2013–14–15–16–17–18–19	85	(84)
Smith B.W.	1959–	(Waikato) 1983–84	10	(3)
Smith C.G.	1981–	(Wellington) 2004–05–06–07–08–09–10–11–12; (Hurricanes) 2013–14–15	94	(94)
Smith C.H.	1909–1976	(Otago) 1934	2	(–)
Smith G.W.	1874–1954	(Auckland) 1897–1901–05	39	(2)
Smith I.S.T.	1941–2017	(Otago) 1963–64; (North Otago) 1965–66	24	(9)
Smith J.B.	1922–1974	(North Auckland) 1946–47–49	9	(4)
Smith P.	1924–1954	(North Auckland) 1947	3	(–)
Smith R.M.	1929–2002	(Canterbury) 1955	1	(1)
Smith W.E.	1881–1945	(Nelson) 1905	1	(1)
Smith W.R.	1957–	(Canterbury) 1980–82–83–84–85	35	(17)
Smyth B.F.	1891–1972	(Canterbury) 1922	3	(–)
Snodgrass W.F.	1898–1976	(Nelson) 1923–28	3	(–)
Snow E.M.	1898–1974	(Nelson) 1928–29	16	(3)
Solomon D.	1913–1997	(Auckland) 1935–36	8	(–)
Solomon F.	1906–1991	(Auckland) 1931–32	9	(3)
Somerville G.M.	1977–	(Canterbury) 2000–01–02–03–04–05–06–07–08	67	(66)
Sonntag W.T.C.	1894–1988	(Otago) 1929	8	(3)
So'oialo, R.	1979–	(Wellington) 2002–03–04–05–06–07–08–09	63	(62)

Name	B&D	Representative Team	Games	Tests
Soper A.J.	1936–2020	(Southland) 1957	8	(–)
Sopoaga L.Z.	1991–	(Highlanders) 2015–16–17	18	(16)
Sotutu, H.C.R.	1998–	(Blues) 2020	5	(5)
Souter R.	1905–1976	(Otago) 1929	4	(–)
Speight C.R.B.	1870–1935	(Auckland) 1893	7	(–)
Speight M.W.	1962–	(North Auckland) 1986	5	(1)
Spencer C.J.	1975–	(Auckland) 1995–96–97–98–2000–02–03–04	44	(35)
Spencer G.	1878–1950	(Wellington) 1907	5	(–)
Spencer J.C.	1880–1936	(Wellington) 1903–05–07	6	(2)
Spiers J.E.	1947–	(Counties) 1976–79–80–81	28	(5)
Spillane A.P.	1888–1974	(South Canterbury) 1913	2	(2)
Squire L.I.J.	1991–	(Highlanders) 2016–17–18	24	(23)
Stalker J.	1881–1931	(Otago) 1903	6	(–)
Stanley B.J.	1984–	(Auckland) 2010	3	(3)
Stanley J.C.	1975–	(Auckland) 1997	3	(–)
Stanley J.T.	1957–	(Auckland) 1986–87–88–89–90–91	49	(27)
Stapleton E.T.	1930–2005	(New South Wales) 1960	1	(–)
Stead J.W.	1877–1958	(Southland) 1903–04–05–06–08	42	(7)
Steel A.G.	1941–2018	(Canterbury) 1966–67–68	23	(9)
Steel J.	1898–1941	(West Coast) 1920–21–22–23–24–25	38	(6)
Steele L.B.	1929–	(Wellington) 1951	9	(3)
Steere E.R.G.	1908–1967	(Hawke's Bay) 1928–29–30–31–32	21	(6)
Steinmetz P.C.	1977–	(Wellington) 2002	1	(1)
Stensness L.	1970–	(Auckland) 1993–97	14	(8)
Stephens O.G.	1947–	(Wellington) 1968	1	(1)
Stevens I.N.	1948–	(Wellington) 1972–73–74–76	33	(3)
Stevenson D.R.L.	1903–1962	(Otago) 1926	4	(–)
Stewart A.J.	1940–	(Canterbury) 1963; (South Canterbury) 1964	26	(8)
Stewart D.T.	1872–1931	(South Canterbury) 1894	1	(–)
Stewart E.B.	1901–1979	(Otago) 1923	1	(–)
Stewart J.D.	1889–1973	(Auckland) 1913	2	(2)
Stewart K.W.	1953–	(Southland) 1972–73–74–75–76–79–81	55	(13)
Stewart R.T.	1904–1982	(South Canterbury) 1923–24–25–26–28; (Canterbury) 1930	39	(5)
Stewart V.E.	1948–	(Canterbury) 1976–79	12	(–)
Stohr L.	1889–1973	(Taranaki) 1910–13	15	(3)
Stokes E.J.T.	1950–	(Bay of Plenty) 1976	5	(–)
Stone A.M.	1960–	(Waikato) 1981–83–84; (Bay of Plenty) 1986	23	(9)
Storey P.W.	1897–1975	(South Canterbury) 1920–21	12	(2)
Strachan A.D.	1966–	(Auckland) 1992; (North Harbour) 1993–95	17	(11)
Strahan S.C.	1944–2019	(Manawatu) 1967–68–70–72–73	45	(17)
Strang W.A.	1906–1989	(South Canterbury) 1928–30–31	17	(5)
Stringfellow J.C.	1905–1959	(Wairarapa) 1929	7	(2)
Stuart A.J.	1858–1923	(Wellington) 1893	7	(–)
Stuart K.C.	1928–2005	(Canterbury) 1955	1	(1)
Stuart R.C.	1920–2005	(Canterbury) 1949–53–54	27	(7)
Stuart R.L.	1948–	(Hawke's Bay) 1977	6	(1)
Sullivan J.L.	1915–1990	(Taranaki) 1936–37–38	9	(6)
Surman J.F.	1866–1925	(Auckland) 1896	1	(–)
Surridge S.D.	1970–	(Canterbury) 1997	3	(–)
Sutherland A.R.	1944–2020	(Marlborough) 1968–70–71–72–73–76	64	(10)
Svenson K.S.	1898–1955	(Buller) 1922; (Wellington) 1924–25–26	34	(4)

Name	B&D	Representative Team	Games	Tests
Swain J.P.	1902–1960	(Hawke's Bay) 1928	16	(4)
Swindley J.T.	1876–1918	(Wellington) 1894	1	(–)
Ta'avao–Matau A.W.F.	1990	(Chiefs) 2018–19	14	(14)
Tahuriorangi T.T.H.	1995	(Chiefs) 2018	3	(3)
Taiaroa J.G.	1862–1907	(Otago) 1884	9	(–)
Taituha P.	1901–1958	(Wanganui) 1923	2	(–)
Tamanivalu S.	1992–	(Chiefs) 2016–17	5	(3)
Tanner J.M.	1927–2020	(Auckland) 1950–51–53–54	24	(5)
Tanner K.J.	1945–	(Canterbury) 1974–75–76	27	(7)
Taumoepeau S.	1979–	(Auckland) 2004–05	4	(3)
Taylor C.J.	1991–	(Crusaders) 2015–16–17–18–19–20	56	(56)
Taylor G.L.	1970–	(North Auckland) 1992–96	6	(1)
Taylor H.M.	1889–1955	(Canterbury) 1913–14	23	(5)
Taylor J.M.	1913–1979	(Otago) 1937–38	9	(6)
Taylor K.J.	1957–	(Hawke's Bay) 1980	1	(–)
Taylor M.B.	1956–	(Waikato) 1976–79–80	30	(7)
Taylor N.M.	1951–	(Bay of Plenty) 1976–77–78; (Hawke's Bay) 1982	27	(9)
Taylor R.*	1889–1917	(Taranaki) 1913	2	(2)
Taylor T.J.	1989–	(Crusaders) 2013	3	(3)
Taylor W.T.	1960–	(Canterbury) 1983–84–85–86–87–88	40	(24)
Tetzlaff P.L.	1920–2009	(Auckland) 1947	7	(2)
Thimbleby N.W.	1939–	(Hawke's Bay) 1970	13	(1)
Thomas B.T.	1937–2018	(Auckland) 1962; (Wellington) 1964	4	(4)
Thomas L.A.	1897–1971	(Wellington) 1925	3	(–)
Thompson B.A.	1947–2006	(Canterbury) 1979	8	(–)
Thomson A.J.	1982–	(Otago) 2008–09–10–11–12	31	(29)
Thomson H.D.	1881–1939	(Wanganui) 1905–06; (Wellington) 1908	15	(1)
Thorn B.C.	1975–	(Canterbury) 2003–09–10–11; (Tasman) 2008	60	(59)
Thorne G.S.	1946–	(Auckland) 1967–68–69–70	39	(10)
Thorne R.D.	1975–	(Canterbury) 1999–2000–01–02–03–04–06–07	51	(50)
Thornton N.H.	1918–1998	(Auckland) 1947–49	19	(3)
Thrush J.I.	1985–	(Hurricanes) 2013–14–15	12	(12)
Tialata N.S.	1982–	(Wellington) 2005–06–07–08–09–10	44	(43)
Tiatia F.I.	1971–	(Wellington) 2000	2	(2)
Tilyard F.J.	1896–1954	(Wellington) 1923	1	(–)
Tilyard J.T.	1889–1966	(Wellington) 1913–20	10	(1)
Timu J.K.R.	1969–	(Otago) 1989–90–91–92–93–94	50	(26)
Tindill E.W.T.	1910–2010	(Wellington) 1935–36–38	17	(1)
Tiopira H.	1871–1930	(Hawke's Bay) 1893	8	(–)
Todd M.B.	1988–	(Crusaders) 2013,15–16–17–18–19	25	(25)
Toeava I.	1986–	(Auckland) 2005–06–07–08–09–10–11	37	(36)
Tonu'u O.F.J.	1970–	(Auckland) 1996–97–98	8	(5)
To'omaga–Allen J.L.	1990–	(Hurricanes) 2013–17	3	(1)
Townsend L.J.	1934–2020	(Otago) 1955	2	(2)
Tregaskis C.D.	1965–	(Wellington) 1991	4	(–)
Tremain K.R.	1938–1992	(Canterbury) 1959; (Auckland) 1960; (Canterbury) 1961; (Hawke's Bay) 1962–63–64–65–66–67–68	86	(38)
Trevathan D.	1912–1986	(Otago) 1937	3	(3)

Name	B&D	Representative Team	Games	Tests
Tuck J.M.	1907–1967	(Waikato) 1929	6	(3)
Tuiali'i M.M.	1981–	(Auckland) 2004–05–06	10	(9)
Tuigamala V.L.	1969–	(Auckland) 1989–90–91–92–93	39	(19)
Tu'inukuafe G.Z.K.	1993	(Chiefs) 2018 (Blues) 2020	17	(17)
Tuipulotu P.T.	1993–	(Blues) 2014–16–17–18–19–20	37	(35)
Tuitavake A.S.M.	1982–	(North Harbour) 2008	7	(6)
Tuitupou S.	1982–	(Auckland) 2004–06	9	(9)
Tunnicliff R.G.	1894–1973	(Buller) 1923	1	(–)
Turnbull J.S.	1898–1947	(Otago) 1921	1	(–)
Turner R.S.	1968–	(North Harbour) 1992	2	(2)
Turtill H.S.*	1880–1918	(Canterbury) 1905	1	(1)
Tu'ungafasi A.O.H.M.	1992–	(Blues) 2016–17–18–19–20	41	(39)
Twigden T.M.	1952–	(Auckland) 1979–80	15	(2)
Tyler G.A.	1879–1942	(Auckland) 1903–04–05–06	36	(7)
Udy D.K.	1874–1935	(Wairarapa) 1901–03	9	(1)
Udy H.	1860–1933	(Wellington) 1884	8	(–)
Umaga J.F.	1973–	(Wellington) 1997–99–2000–01–02–03–04–05	79	(74)
Umaga-Jensen, P.I.J.	1997–	(Hurricanes) 2020	1	(1)
Urbahn R.J.	1934–1984	(Taranaki) 1959–60	15	(3)
Urlich R.A.	1944–	(Auckland) 1970–72–73	35	(2)
Uttley I.N.	1941–2015	(Wellington) 1963	2	(2)
Vaa'i, T.P.O.	2000–	(Chiefs) 2020	4	(4)
Valli G.T.	1954–	(Southland) 1980	1	(–)
Vanisi O.K.	1972–	(Wellington) 1999	1	(–)
Vidiri J.	1973–	(Counties Manukau) 1998	2	(2)
Vincent P.B.	1926–1983	(Canterbury) 1956	2	(2)
Vito V.V.J.	1987–	(Wellington) 2010–11–12; (Hurricanes) 2013–14–15	33	(33)
Vodanovich I.M.H.	1930–1995	(Wellington) 1955	3	(3)
Vorrath F.H.	1908–1972	(Otago) 1935–36	12	(–)
Waldrom S.L.	1980–	(Taranaki) 2008	1	(–)
Wallace W.J.	1878–1972	(Wellington) 1903–04–05–06–07–08	51	(11)
Waller D.A.G.	1974–	(Wellington) 2001	3	(1)
Walsh P.T.	1936–2007	(Counties) 1955–56–57–58–59–63–64	27	(13)
Walter J.	1904–1966	(Taranaki) 1925	7	(–)
Warbrick J.A.	1862–1903	(Auckland) 1884	7	(–)
Ward E.P.	1899–1958	(Taranaki) 1928	10	(–)
Ward F.G.	1900–1990	(Otago) 1921	1	(–)
Ward R.H.	1915–2000	(Southland) 1936–37	4	(3)
Waterman A.C.	1903–1997	(North Auckland) 1929	7	(2)
Watkins E.L.	1880–1949	(Wellington) 1905	1	(1)
Watson J.D.	1872–1958	(Taranaki) 1896	1	(–)
Watson W.D.	1869–1953	(Wairarapa) 1893–96	3	(–)
Watt B.A.	1939–	(Canterbury) 1962–63–64	29	(8)
Watt J.M.	1914–1988	(Otago) 1936	2	(2)
Watt J.R.	1935–	(Southland) 1957; (Wellington) 1958–60–61–62	42	(9)
Watts M.G.	1955–	(Taranaki) 1979–80	13	(5)
Webb D.S.	1934–1987	(North Auckland) 1959	1	(1)
Webb P.P.	1854–1920	(Wellington) 1884	8	(–)
Weber B.M.	1991–	(Chiefs) 2015–19–20	7	(7)
Webster T.R.D.	1920–1972	(Southland) 1947	4	(–)

Name	B&D	Representative Team	Games	Tests
Weepu P.A.T.	1983–	(Wellington) 2004–05–06–07–08–09–10–11–12; (Blues) 2013	73	(71)
Wells J.	1908–1994	(Wellington) 1936	3	(2)
Wells W.J.G.	1867–1911	(Taranaki) 1897	7	(–)
Wesney A.W.*	1915–1941	(Southland) 1938	3	(–)
West A.H.	1893–1934	(Taranaki) 1920–21–23–24–25	24	(2)
Weston L.H.	1892–1963	(Auckland) 1914	1	(–)
Whetton A.J.	1959–	(Auckland) 1984–85–86–87–88–89–90–91	65	(35)
Whetton G.W.	1959–	(Auckland) 1981–82–83–84–85–86–87–88–89–90–91	101	(58)
Whineray W.J.	1935–2012	(Canterbury) 1957; (Waikato) 1958; (Auckland) 1959–60–61–62–63–64–65	77	(32)
White A.	1894–1968	(Southland) 1921–22–23–24–25	38	(4)
White H.L.	1929–2016	(Auckland) 1953–54–55	16	(4)
White R.A.	1925–2012	(Poverty Bay) 1949–50–51–52–53–54–55–56	55	(23)
White R.M.	1917–1980	(Wellington) 1946–47	10	(4)
Whitelock G.B.	1986–	(Canterbury) 2009	1	(1)
Whitelock L.C.	1991–	(Crusaders) 2013–17–18	8	(7)
Whitelock S.L.	1988–	(Canterbury) 2010–11–12; (Crusaders) 2013–14–15–16 –17–18–19–20	122	(122)
Whiting G.J.	1946–	(King Country) 1972–73	31	(6)
Whiting P.J.	1946–	(Auckland) 1971–72–73–74–76	56	(20)
Wickes C.D.	1962–	(Manawatu) 1980	1	(–)
Wightman D.R.	1929–2012	(Auckland) 1951	4	(–)
Williams A.J.	1981–	(Auckland) 2002–03–04–05–06–07–08–11–12	78	(77)
Williams A.L.	1898–1972	(Otago) 1922–23	9	(–)
Williams B.G.	1950–	(Auckland) 1970–71–72–73–74–75–76–77–78	113	(38)
Williams C.W.	1916–1998	(Canterbury) 1938	4	(–)
Williams G.C.	1945–2018	(Wellington) 1967–68	18	(5)
Williams P.	1884–1976	(Otago) 1913	9	(1)
Williams R.N.	1909–2001	(Hawke's Bay) 1932	1	(–)
Williams R.O.	1963–	(North Harbour) 1988–89	10	(–)
Williams S.	1985–	(Canterbury) 2010–1–12; (Chiefs) 2014–15; (Blues) 2017–18–19	58	(58)
Williment M.	1940–1994	(Wellington) 1964–65–66–67	9	(9)
Willis R.K.	1975–	(Waikato) 1998–99–2002	12	(12)
Willis T.E.	1979–	(Otago) 2001–02	7	(5)
Willocks C.	1919–1991	(Otago) 1946–47–49	22	(5)
Willoughby S. de L.P.	1904–1985	(Wairarapa) 1928	4	(–)
Wills M.C.	1941–	(Taranaki) 1967	5	(–)
Wilson A.	1874–1932	(Auckland) 1897	8	(–)
Wilson A.L.	1927–2009	(Southland) 1951	7	(–)
Wilson B.W.	1956–	(Otago) 1977–78–79	12	(8)
Wilson D.D.	1931–2019	(Canterbury) 1953–54	14	(2)
Wilson F.R.*	1885–1916	(Auckland) 1910	2	(–)
Wilson H.B.	1957–	(Counties) 1983	3	(–)
Wilson H.C.	1868–1945	(Wellington) 1893	7	(–)
Wilson H.W.	1924–2004	(Otago) 1949–50–51	13	(5)
Wilson J.W.	1973–	(Otago) 1993–94–95–96–97–98–99–2001	71	(60)
Wilson N.A.	1886–1953	(Wellington) 1908–10–13–14	21	(10)
Wilson N.L.	1922–2001	(Otago) 1949–51	20	(3)
Wilson R.G.	1953–	(Canterbury) 1976–78–79–80	25	(2)
Wilson R.J.	1861–1944	(Canterbury) 1884	6	(–)
Wilson S.S.	1954–	(Wellington) 1976–77–78–79–80–81–82–83	85	(34)
Wilson V.W.	1899–1978	(Auckland) 1920	7	(–)

Name	B&D	Representative Team	Games	Tests
Wise G.D.	1904–1971	(Otago) 1925	7	(–)
Witcombe D.J.C.	1978–	(Auckland) 2005	5	(5)
Wolfe T.N.	1941–	(Wellington) 1961–62; (Taranaki) 1963–68	14	(6)
Wood M.E.	1876–1956	(Wellington) 1901; (Canterbury) 1903; (Auckland) 1904	12	(2)
Woodcock T.D.	1981–	(North Harbour) 2002–04–05–06–07–08–09–10–11–12; (Highlanders) 2013; (Blues) 2014–15	118	(118)
Woodman F.A.	1958–	(North Auckland) 1980–81	14	(3)
Woodman T.B.K.	1960–	(North Auckland) 1984	6	(–)
Woods C.A.	1929–	(Southland) 1953–54	14	(–)
Wright A.H.	1914–1990	(Wellington) 1938	4	(–)
Wright D.H.	1902–1966	(Auckland) 1925	7	(–)
Wright T.J.	1963–	(Auckland) 1986–87–88–89–90–91–92	64	(30)
Wright W.A.	1905–1971	(Auckland) 1926	1	(–)
Wrigley E.	1886–1958	(Wairarapa) 1905	1	(1)
Wulf R.N.	1984–	(North Harbour) 2008	4	(4)
Wylie J.T.	1887–1956	(Auckland) 1913	12	(2)
Wyllie A.J.	1944–	(Canterbury) 1970–71–72–73	40	(11)
Wyllie T.	1954–	(Wellington) 1980	1	(–)
Wynyard J.G.*	1914–1942	(Waikato) 1935–36–38	13	(–)
Wynyard W.T.	1867–1938	(Wellington) 1893	7	(–)
Yates V.M.	1939–2008	(North Auckland) 1961–62	9	(3)
Young D.	1930–2020	(Canterbury) 1956–57–58–60–61–62–63–64	61	(22)
Young F.B.	1874–1946	(Wellington) 1896	1	(–)

NZR ANNUAL AWARDS

Since 1994 the NZRU has hosted, at the end of each year, an annual awards function to honour players, personalities and teams. With the exception of the Tom French Cup all trophies were new. The Tom French Cup had been presented in 1949 by Mr J. Morris of Sydney, following the New Zealand Maori tour of Australia, in honour of the team's coach Mr T.A. French. The trophy has been awarded to the outstanding Maori player each season.

PLAYER OF THE YEAR
Kelvin Tremain Memorial Trophy

1994	Zinzan Brooke (*Auckland*)
1995	Jonah Lomu (*Counties*)
1996	Sean Fitzpatrick (*Auckland*)
1997	Jeff Wilson (*Otago*)
1998	Josh Kronfeld (*Otago*)
1999	Andrew Mehrtens (*Canterbury*)
2000	Tana Umaga (*Wellington*)
2001	Todd Blackadder (*Canterbury*)
2002	Chris Jack (*Canterbury*)
2003	Richard McCaw (*Canterbury*)
2004	Daniel Carter (*Canterbury*)
2005	Daniel Carter (*Canterbury*)
2006	Richard McCaw (*Canterbury*)
2007	Daniel Braid (*Auckland*)
2008	Andrew Hore (*Taranaki*)
2009	Richard McCaw (*Canterbury*)
2010	Kieran Read (*Canterbury*)
2011	Jerome Kaino (*Auckland*)
2012	Richie McCaw (*Canterbury*)
2013	Kieran Read (*Canterbury*)
2014	Brodie Retallick (*Waikato*)
2015	Ma'a Nonu (*Wellington*)
2016	Beauden Barrett (*Taranaki*)
2017	Samuel Whitelock (*Canterbury*)
2018	Kendra Cocksedge (*Canterbury*)
2019	Ardie Savea (*Wellington*)
2020	Sam Cane (*Chiefs*)

ALL BLACKS PLAYER OF THE YEAR

2019	Ardie Savea (*Hurricanes*)
2020	Sam Cane (*Chiefs*)

SUPER RUGBY PLAYER OF THE YEAR

1996	Joeli Vidiri (*Blues*)
1997	Christian Cullen (*Hurricanes*)
1998	Andrew Mehrtens (*Crusaders*)
1999	Byron Kelleher (*Highlanders*)
2000	Scott Robertson (*Crusaders*)
2001	Deon Muir (*Chiefs*)
2002	Chris Jack (*Crusaders*)
2003	Carlos Spencer (*Blues*)
2004	Daniel Carter (*Crusaders*)
2005	Rico Gear (*Crusaders*)
2006	Daniel Carter (*Crusaders*)
2007	James Cowan (*Highlanders*)
2008	Andrew Hore (*Hurricanes*)
2009	Mils Muliaina (*Chiefs*)
2010	Alby Mathewson (*Blues*)
2011	Wyatt Crockett (*Crusaders*)
2012	Conrad Smith (*Hurricanes*)
2013	Ben Smith (*Highlanders*)
2014	Jerome Kaino (*Blues*)
2015	Lima Sopoaga (*Highlanders*)
2016	Beauden Barrett (*Hurricanes*)
2017	Samuel Whitelock (*Crusaders*)
2018	Richie Mo'unga (*Crusaders*)
2019	Ardie Savea (*Hurricanes*)
2020	Richie Mo'unga (*Crusaders*)

TEAM OF THE YEAR

2000	New Zealand Under 21
2001	Canterbury
2002	New Zealand Sevens
2003	All Blacks
2004	Canterbury
2005	All Blacks
2006	All Blacks
2007	Auckland
2008	All Blacks
2009	Canterbury
2010	Black Ferns
2011	All Blacks
2012	All Blacks
2013	All Blacks
2014	All Blacks
2015	All Blacks
2016	All Blacks
2017	Black Ferns

NEW ZEALAND TEAM OF THE YEAR

2018	Black Ferns Sevens
2019	Black Ferns Sevens
2020	Black Ferns Sevens

NATIONAL TEAM OF THE YEAR

2018	Crusaders
2019	Crusaders
2020	Tasman

PREMIER DIVISION PLAYER OF THE YEAR
Duane Monkley Medal from 2017

2006	Richard Kahui (*Waikato*)
2007	Isa Nacewa (*Auckland*)
2008	Jamie Mackintosh (*Southland*)
2009	Mike Delany (*Bay of Plenty*)
2010	Robbie Fruean (*Canterbury*)
2011	Aaron Cruden (*Manawatu*)
2012	Robbie Fruean (*Canterbury*)
2013	Andy Ellis (*Canterbury*)
2014	Seta Tamanivalu (*Taranaki*)
2015	George Moala (*Auckland*)
2016	Jordie Barrett (*Canterbury*)
2017	Jack Goodhue (*Northland*)
2018	Luke Romano (*Canterbury*)
2019	Chase Tiatia (*Bay of Plenty*)
2020	Folau Fakatava (*Hawke's Bay*)

HEARTLAND CHAMPIONSHIP PLAYER OF THE YEAR

2006	Scott Leighton (*Poverty Bay*)
2007	Ross Hay (*North Otago*)
2008	Cameron Crowley (*Wanganui*)
2009	Asaeli Tikoirotuma (*Wanganui*)
2010	Peter Rowe (*Wanganui*)
2011	Jon Smyth (*Wanganui*)
2012	Peter Rowe (*Wanganui*)
2013	Jon Dampney (*Mid Canterbury*)
2014	James Lash (*Buller*)
2015	Lindsay Horrocks (*Wanganui*)
2016	Te Rangatira Waitokia (*Wanganui*)
2017	Scott Cameron (*Horowhenua Kapiti*)
2018	Brett Ranga (*Thames Valley*)
2019	Josh Clark (*North Otago*)
2020	Not awarded

MAORI PLAYER OF THE YEAR
Tom French Cup

1949	Johnny Smith (*North Auckland*)
1950	Manahi Paewai (*North Auckland*)
1951	Percy Erceg (*Auckland*)
1952	Keith Davis (*Auckland*)
1953	Keith Davis (*Auckland*)
1954	Keith Davis (*Auckland*)
1955	Pat Walsh (*South Auckland*)
1956	Bill Gray (*Bay of Plenty*)
1957	Muru Walters (*North Auckland*)
1958	Pat Walsh (*Counties*)
1959	Bill Wordley (*King Country*)
1960	Mac Herewini (*Auckland*)
1961	Victor Yates (*North Auckland*)
1962	Waka Nathan (*Auckland*)
1963	Mac Herewini (*Auckland*)
1964	Ron Rangi (*Auckland*)
1965	Ron Rangi (*Auckland*)
1966	Waka Nathan (*Auckland*)
1967	Sid Going (*North Auckland*)
1968	Sid Going (*North Auckland*)
1969	Sid Going (*North Auckland*)
1970	Sid Going (*North Auckland*)
1971	Sid Going (*North Auckland*)
1972	Sid Going (*North Auckland*)
1973	Tane Norton (*Canterbury*)
1974	Tane Norton (*Canterbury*)
1975	Bill Bush (*Canterbury*)
1976	Kent Lambert (*Manawatu*)
1977	Bill Osborne (*Wanganui*)
1978	Eddie Dunn (*North Auckland*)
1979	Vance Stewart (*Canterbury*)
1980	Hika Reid (*Bay of Plenty*)
1981	Frank Shelford (*Bay of Plenty*)
1982	Steven Pokere (*Southland*)
1983	Hika Reid (*Bay of Plenty*)
1984	Michael Clamp (*Wellington*)
1985	Wayne Shelford (*North Harbour*)
1986	Frano Botica (*North Harbour*)
1987	Wayne Shelford (*North Harbour*)
1988	Wayne Shelford (*North Harbour*)
1989	Wayne Shelford (*North Harbour*)
1990	Steve McDowell (*Auckland*)
1991	John Timu (*Otago*)
1992	Zinzan Brooke (*Auckland*)
1993	Arran Pene (*Otago*)
1994	Zinzan Brooke (*Auckland*)
1995	Robin Brooke (*Auckland*)
1996	Errol Brain (*Counties Manukau*)
1997	Mark Mayerhofler (*Canterbury*)
1998	Tony Brown (*Otago*)
1999	Norman Maxwell (*Canterbury*)

2000	Daryl Gibson (*Canterbury*)
2001	Caleb Ralph (*Canterbury*)
2002	Carlos Spencer (*Auckland*)
2003	Carlos Spencer (*Auckland*)
2004	Carl Hayman (*Otago*)
2005	Rico Gear (*Nelson Bays*)
2006	Carl Hayman (*Otago*)
2007	Daniel Braid (*Auckland*)
2008	Piri Weepu (*Wellington*)
2009	Zac Guildford (*Hawke's Bay*)
2010	Hosea Gear (*Wellington*)
2011	Piri Weepu (*Wellington*)
2012	Liam Messam (*Waikato*)
2013	Liam Messam (*Waikato*)
2014	Aaron Smith (*Manawatu*)
2015	Nehe Milner-Skudder (*Manawatu*)
2016	Dane Coles (*Wellington*)
2017	Rieko Ioane (*Auckland*)
2018	Codie Taylor (*Canterbury*)
2019	Sarah Hirini (*Manawatu*)
2020	Ash Dixon (*Hawke's Bay*)

NZ RUGBY PLAYERS' ASSN KIRK AWARD

2016	Justin Collins (*Northland*)
2017	DJ Forbes (*Counties Manukau*)
2018	Fiao'o Faamausili (*Auckland*)
	Keven Mealamu (*Auckland*)
2019	Josh Blackie, Seilala Mapusua & Hale T-Pole
2020	Andy Ellis (*Canterbury*)

AGE GRADE PLAYER OF THE YEAR

1994	Taine Randell (*Otago*)
1995	Anton Oliver (*Otago*)
1996	Andrew Blowers (*Auckland*)
1997	Norman Maxwell (*Northland*)
1998	Doug Howlett (*Auckland*)
1999	Samiu Vahafolau (*Auckland*)
2000	Ben Blair (*Canterbury*)
2001	Under 21
	Richard McCaw (*Canterbury*)
	Under 19
	Sam Tuitupou (*Auckland*)
2002	Luke McAlister (*North Harbour*)
2003	Ben Atiga (*Auckland*)
2004	Jerome Kaino (*Auckland*)
2005	Isaia Toeava (*Auckland*)
2006	Michael Paterson (*Canterbury*)
2007	Zac Guildford (*Hawke's Bay*)
2008	Zac Guildford (*Hawke's Bay*)
2009	Aaron Cruden (*Manawatu*)

2010	Liaki Moli (*Auckland*)
2011	Sam Cane (*Bay of Plenty*)
2012	Jason Emery (*Manawatu*)
2013	Ardie Savea (*Wellington*)
2014	Damian McKenzie (*Waikato*)
2015	Akira Ioane (*Auckland*)
2016	Jordie Barrett (*Canterbury*)
2017	Asafo Aumua (*Wellington*)
2018	Tom Christie *(Canterbury)*
2019	Fletcher Newell *(Canterbury)*
2020	Not awarded

SEVENS PLAYER OF THE YEAR
Richard Crawshaw Memorial Trophy from 1998

1994	Eric Rush (*North Harbour*)
1995	Jonah Lomu (*Counties*)
1996	Christian Cullen (*Manawatu*)
1997	Caleb Ralph (*Bay of Plenty*)
1998	Rico Gear (*Auckland*)
1999	Orene Ai'i (*Auckland*)
2000	Karl Te Nana (*North Harbour*)
2001	Karl Te Nana (*North Harbour*)
2002	Chris Masoe (*Taranaki*)
2003	Eric Rush (*North Harbour*)
2004	Liam Messam (*Waikato*)
2005	Amasio Valence (*Hawke's Bay*)
2006	Tafai Ioasa (*Hawke's Bay*)
2007	D.J. Forbes (*Auckland*)
2008	D.J. Forbes (*Counties Manukau*)
2009	Zar Lawrence (*Bay of Plenty*)
2010	Kurt Baker (*Taranaki*)
2011	Tim Mikkelson (*Waikato*)
2012	Tomasi Cama (*Manawatu*)
2013	Kurt Baker (*Taranaki*)
2014	DJ Forbes (*Counties Manukau*)
2015	Scott Curry (*Bay of Plenty*)
2016	Rieko Ioane (*Auckland*)
2017	DJ Forbes (*Counties Manukau*)
2018	Scott Curry (*Bay of Plenty*)
2019	Tone Ng Shiu *(Tasman)*
2020	Scott Curry *(Bay of Plenty)*

WOMEN'S PLAYER OF THE YEAR

1994	Anna Richards (*Auckland*)
1995	Rochelle Martin (*Wellington*)
1996	Vanessa Cootes (*Waikato*)
1997	Louisa Wall (*Auckland*)
1998	Farah Palmer (*Otago*)
1999	Suzanne Shortland (*Auckland*)
2000	Fiona King (*Otago*)
2001	Annaleah Rush (*Auckland*)

2002	Monique Hirovanaa (*Auckland*)	2010	Gordon Tietjens
2003	Monalisa Codling (*Auckland*)		(*New Zealand Sevens*)
2004	Stephanie Mortimer (*Canterbury*)	2011	Graham Henry (*All Blacks*)
2005	Melissa Ruscoe (*Canterbury*)	2012	Steve Hansen (*All Blacks*)
2006	Amiria Marsh (*Canterbury*)	2013	Steve Hansen (*All Blacks*)
2007	Victoria Heighway (*Auckland*)	2014	Steve Hansen (*All Blacks*)
2008	Victoria Grant (*Auckland*)	2015	Steve Hansen (*All Blacks*)
2009	Victoria Heighway (*Auckland*)	2016	Steve Hansen (*All Blacks*)
2010	Carla Hohepa (*Otago*)	2017	Glenn Moore (*Black Ferns*)
2011	Fiao'o Faamausili (*Auckland*)		
2012	Rawinia Everitt (*Auckland*)		
2013	Kelly Brazier (*Otago*)		

NEW ZEALAND COACH OF THE YEAR

2014	Rawinia Everitt (*Counties Manukau*)
2015	Kendra Cocksedge (*Canterbury*)
2016	Selica Winiata (*Manawatu*)
2017	Sarah Goss (*Manawatu*)
2018	Kendra Cocksedge (*Canterbury*)

2018	Clark Laidlaw (*All Blacks Sevens*)
2019	Corey Sweeney & Allan Bunting (*Black Ferns Sevens*)
2020	Corey Sweeney & Allan Bunting (*Black Ferns Sevens*)

BLACK FERNS PLAYER OF THE YEAR

2019	Charmaine McMenamin (*Auckland*)
2020	Chelsea Alley (*Waikato*)

NATIONAL COACH OF THE YEAR

2018	Alama Ieremia (*Auckland*)
2019	Scott Robertson (*Crusaders*)
2020	Scott Robertson (*Crusaders*)

FARAH PALMER CUP PLAYER OF THE YEAR
Fiao'o Faamausili Medal

2017	Hazel Tubic (*Counties Manukau*)
2018	Kendra Cocksedge (*Canterbury*)
2019	Chelsea Bremner (*Canterbury*)
2020	Kendra Cocksedge (*Canterbury*)

REFEREE OF THE YEAR

1994	Colin Hawke (*South Canterbury*)
1995	Paddy O'Brien (*Southland*)
1996	Paddy O'Brien (*Southland*)
1997	Steve Walsh jnr (*North Harbour*)*
1998	Paddy O'Brien (*Southland*)
1999	Colin Hawke (*South Canterbury*)
2000	Colin Hawke (*South Canterbury*)
2001	Kelvin Deaker (*Hawke's Bay*)
2002	Paddy O'Brien (*Southland*)
2003	Paddy O'Brien (*Southland*)
2004	Paddy O'Brien (*Southland*)
2005	Paul Honiss (*Waikato*)
2006	Paul Honiss (*Waikato*)
2007	Steve Walsh (*North Harbour*)
2008	Bryce Lawrence (*Bay of Plenty*)
2009	Bryce Lawrence (*Bay of Plenty*)
2010	Bryce Lawrence (*Bay of Plenty*)
2011	Bryce Lawrence (*Bay of Plenty*)
2012	Glen Jackson (*Bay of Plenty*)
2013	Chris Pollock (*Hawke's Bay*)
2014	Glen Jackson (*Bay of Plenty*)
2015	Glen Jackson (*Bay of Plenty*)
2016	Glen Jackson (*Bay of Plenty*)
2017	Ben O'Keeffe (*Wellington*)
2018	Glen Jackson (*Bay of Plenty*)
2019	Paul Williams (*Taranaki*)
2020	Paul Williams (*Taranaki*)

WOMEN'S SEVENS PLAYER OF THE YEAR

2013	Portia Woodman (*Auckland*)
2014	Sarah Goss (*Manawatu*)
2015	Tyla Nathan-Wong (*Auckland*)
2016	Sarah Goss (*Manawatu*)
2017	Ruby Tui (*Canterbury*)
2018	Michaela Blyde (*Bay of Plenty*)
2019	Tyla Nathan-Wong (*Auckland*)
2020	Stacey Fluhler (*Waikato*)

COACH OF THE YEAR

1994	Brad Meurant (*North Harbour*)
1995	Graham Henry (*Auckland*)
1996	John Hart (*All Blacks*)
2001	Colin Cooper (*New Zealand Under 21*)
2002	Robbie Deans (*Crusaders*)
2003	Wayne Pivac (*Auckland*)
2004	Vern Cotter (*Bay of Plenty*)
2005	Graham Henry (*All Blacks*)
2006	Graham Henry (*All Blacks*)
2007	Peter Russell (*Hawke's Bay*)
2008	Graham Henry (*All Blacks*)
2009	Dave Rennie (*New Zealand Under 20*)

* for the Outstanding Referee Performance (Canterbury v Auckland round robin match)

STEINLAGER SALVER
For outstanding service to rugby

1999	Colin Meads
2000	Zinzan Brooke*
2001	Sir Terry McLean
2002	Fred Allen
2003	Sir Brian Lochore
2004	Peter Bush
2005	Richie Guy
2006	Stan Hill
2007	Ron Don
2008	Tane Norton
2009	John Graham
2010	Keith Quinn
2011	Jock Hobbs
2012	Ray Harper
2013	Graham Mourie
2014	Dick Littlejohn
2015	Mike Eagle
2016	Gavin Service
2017	Wayne Smith
2018	Waka Nathan
2019	Steve Tew
2020	Sir Bryan Williams

* celebrating 25 years of the NPC

SKY FANS TRY OF THE YEAR

2013	Selica Winiata (*Black Ferns*)
2014	Malakai Fekitoa (*Highlanders*)
2015	Samu Kubunavanua (*Wanganui*)
2016	Isaiah Punivai (*Christ's College*)
2017	Portia Woodman (*Black Ferns*)
2018	Chris Hala'ufia (*St Peter's College*)
2019	TJ Perenara *(All Blacks)*
2020	Jack Jones *(Christ's College)*

VOLUNTEER OF THE YEAR
**Charles Monro Memorial Trophy
from 2009**

2002	John George (*Taranaki*)
2003	Ru Rangi (*Wellington*)
2004	Adelle Wakely (*Hawke's Bay*)
2005	Daphne Boden (*Hawke's Bay*)
2006	Jason Martin (*Otago*)
2007	Robbie Ball (*Northland*)
2008	Ken Swain (*Horowhenua Kapiti*)
2009	Blair Crawford (*Otago*)
2010	Hilton Williams (*Horowhenua Kapiti*)
2011	Andy MacDonald (*Canterbury*)
2012	Ray Watson (*Bay of Plenty*)
2013	Rob Jones (*Manawatu*)
2014	Dean File (*Horowhenua Kapiti*)
2015	Tania Karaitiana and Vio Ugone (*Wellington*)
2016	Gary Donovan (*Auckland*)
2017	Sid Tatana (*Wairarapa Bush*)
2018	Irene Eruera-Taiapa (*Horowhenua Kapiti*)
2019	Ian Spraggon *(Bay of Plenty)*
2020	Jane Chamberlain *(Horowhenua Kapiti)*

OBITUARIES

NEW ZEALAND REPRESENTATIVES

Andrew Maxwell Haden *(Auckland)*, born at Whanganui on 26 September 1950, was one of the rugby giants of his generation. He also gave great value to the game, although administrators may have held dissenting opinions about that. One thing Haden never forgot was that the game was all about the players. He respected, and was respected by, his rivals and teammates.

He was one of the first to storm the bastion of amateurism and make some headway. Previously dissidents had simply been ignored; Haden was too big to be ignored, and he wouldn't go away. His career ended just before the first World Cup was played; it was a tournament he had been a vocal proponent of, and he was delighted to see it finally coming to fruition. Professionalism, which he knew was inevitable 20 years before it happened, was also too late to directly benefit the man who once listed his occupation as 'Itinerant Rugby Player' and ambition as 'Becoming rugby's first millionaire' — but that's not to say he didn't cash in on his rugby fame.

Haden arrived in Auckland in 1971 and had an unusual introduction to Ponsonby, then a tough inner-city neighbourhood. During his first training run his car was broken into, and a variety of items removed. When he mentioned the fact at the next run, and suggested he might look elsewhere, he was advised to 'wait and see what happens'. The missing items magically reappeared before he was done; the pragmatic Haden never afterwards locked his car and began what was a fruitful 16-year playing career with the club.

In 1972 Haden won selection for the New Zealand Juniors tour of Australia, dominated the lineouts in Auckland's successful Ranfurly Shield challenge at Whangarei, and was chosen as one of many young players for the 1972–73 All Blacks tour of Great Britain. While never threatening a test place, he learned a lot on that tour which stood him in good stead later. In late 1974, disillusioned by the attitude he found in Auckland officialdom, he took a sabbatical in Europe. As part of his preparation for this sojourn, he and Trecha brought their wedding forward and the couple left for what proved to be 18 months away.

By 1976, when he returned to try to win a place in the All Blacks team for South Africa, he was a different proposition to the slightly callow youth of 1974. Now harder, physically and mentally, he was the outstanding lock at the trials (after coming into the early match as a replacement) but wasn't chosen for the tour, a move seen by some as punishment for his time away, and for refusing to toe the line. Haden showed just what the All Blacks were missing with a dominant domestic season, was a shoo-in to be named Player of the Year, and was certain to be chosen for the tour of Argentina undertaken by a new team — none of the South African tourists were eligible for selection. He became one of the most influential players and, with Peter Whiting retiring, was the obvious choice for test selection in 1977.

That marked the start of Haden's years of dominance.

He was a significant performer in every home test series until 1985 and often one of the most influential players. He contributed mightily on tour, frequently playing midweekers as well as big games, and on eight occasions leading the All Blacks. His contribution to the 1978 Grand Slam tour went way beyond his flailing exit from a late lineout against Wales, although that is the one thing that lives in most memories. Ironically the subsequently goaled penalty was for a separate offence; referee Roger Quittenton didn't see Haden's theatrical dive at all.

His contributions to wins over the 1981 Springboks and 1983 Lions were huge, and long before he retired he was part of the furniture — only noticed when he was missing for any reason. For most of his test career there wasn't a lock in the world that could touch him. His star was fading when he was a lead organiser for the 1986 Cavaliers tour, an excursion that was not a highlight. His last great playing moment was captaining Auckland to Ranfurly Shield success in the epic

1985 match at Lancaster Park.

Multilingual after his years in Europe, Haden was the most important All Black on his two tours of France, often defusing situations that could have got out of hand. An ideal sergeant-major rather than an officer, he also negotiated the 'Lurks and Perks' which were shared equally among the team members — a state of affairs that contributed much to team bonding. His presence on tour often saved the NZRFU a lot of heartache.

He was one of a small handful to play 100 matches for his club (the total is around 200), his province (157) and his country (117). Coincidentally, he was only a week older than great friend Sir Bryan Williams, who achieved the same feat with almost identical numbers for the same teams.

Once, in response to an inaccurate story that he was transferring to East Coast Bays, he said: 'There are two types of rugby player in Auckland: those who play for Ponsonby and those who wish they did.' Haden played in seven Gallaher Shield triumphs — the last two players before him to win seven titles were Edwardian stars Bubs Tyler and George Nicholson — and made many other contributions to the club over 50 years.

Haden was to be nominated for life membership of the Ponsonby club in 2020; the process was under way when he died on 29 July after a lengthy battle with cancer. The nomination was allowed to stand and was passed at the AGM, with daughter Laura accepting the medallion and speaking on Andy's behalf. *(Contributed by Paul Neazor)*

Andy Haden's first-class record:

For	Matches	Tries	Points
Auckland (Ponsonby) 1971(2), 1972(8), 1973(13), 1974(3), 1976(14), 1977(10), 1978(7), 1979(14), 1980(9), 1981(10), 1982(11), 1983(15), 1984(17), 1985(13), 1986(11)	157	12	48
Auckland Colts 1971	1	–	0
Auckland B 1974	1	–	0
Auckland Invitation XV 1974	1	–	0
Wasps Club 1976	1	–	0
Barbarians Club 1977(3), 1981, 1984(3), 1985(2)	9	–	0
Kaponga Invitation XV 1982	1	–	0
Poneke International XV 1983	1	–	0
S.S. Wilson's Invitation XV 1984	1	1	4
Condors XV 1985	1	–	0
World XVs 1977(2), 1979(5), 1981, 1982, 1983, 1986	11	2	8
New Zealand Juniors (Under 23) 1972	8	1	4
North Island 1973, 1976, 1979, 1980, 1981, 1982, 1983, 1984	8	1	4
New Zealand Trials 1972, 1973, 1974(2), 1976, 1977, 1979, 1981, 1982, 1983	10	–	0
NEW ZEALAND 1972(16), 1973(2), 1976(8), 1977(13), 1978(16), 1979(13), 1980(20), 1981(13), 1982(3), 1983(5), 1984(4), 1985(4)	117	8	32
TOTALS	**328**	**25**	**100**

At Auckland, 29 July 2020, aged 69.

Terence Raymond Lineen *(Auckland)*, by today's standards, had a brief rugby career at the highest level, just managing slightly more than 100 first-class games and retiring after a serious shoulder injury at just 24. But he will be always remembered as one of the most gifted attacking midfield backs of his generation and inevitably there will be wonder what he might have achieved had he played in later years as a professional or at a time when there was more emphasis on enterprising back play. For Lineen played his rugby from the mid-1950s until 1960 when in New Zealand 10-man rugby was in vogue and when talents like Lineen's were often stifled.

Yet Lineen, a tall, strong-running midfield back, usually at second five-eighths, achieved much: 12 tests and 35 All Blacks games and tours to Australia in 1957, to Japan in 1958 with the national under-23 side and to South Africa in 1960 and an Auckland Ranfurly Shield win in 1959.

A product of a celebrated rugby nursery, Auckland's Sacred Heart College, Lineen excelled in schoolboy rugby. He was soon in some strong Marist club sides which often could boast of a backline which as well as Lineen contained other All Blacks like Keith Davis, Des Connor, Steve Nesbit and Paul Little.

Lineen was only 18 when played three times for Auckland B in 1954 and in 1955, having played only four first-class games, he was suddenly called into the North side for the inter-island match. While the North won the match many of the leading critics of the day, notably Terry McLean, believed that Lineen's promotion had been premature and he needed more time to develop. He did not play in any of the 1956 national trials but appeared for Auckland against the touring Springboks and in a Barbarians festival match at the tour's end in which many of the South Africans played.

Lineen's impressive performance won him a place for the 1957 All Blacks tour of Australia, along with his Auckland midfield partner Frank McMullen. Both played in the two tests against the Wallabies and for the next few seasons remained automatic All Blacks selections. Lineen played all three tests against the Wallabies in 1958 and in all four tests against the touring British and Irish Lions in 1959. With his thrustful running Lineen was one of the few All Blacks backs who was compared favourably with their Lions counterparts.

Lineen continued to star in South Africa in 1960 and with 10 tries was the team's leading try-scorer, which he had also been with the under 23s in Japan in 1958. But towards the end of the tour he injured the shoulder which was to bring an early end to his career and which meant he had to miss the fourth test. His absence drastically reduced the All Blacks' hopes of at least squaring the series.

Lineen's early retirement meant he took no part in the momentous Auckland Ranfurly Shield era of 1960–63 and prevented him forming a substantial midfield partnership with his club-mate and close friend, Paul Little. With Lineen and McMullen both retired, Little from 1961 soon became the Auckland and All Blacks' midfield mainstay. But curiously, though friends since primary school, Lineen and Little only played twice together at representative level. One of those games was the successful 1959 shield challenge against Southland when each scored a try and club-mate Nesbit scored the other.

Lineen's son, Sean, also a midfield back, played 64 games for Counties 1983–88 and in 29 tests for Scotland, including being in the 1990 Grand Slam-winning team. He qualified for Scotland because of his Scottish-born maternal grandmother. *(Contributed by Lindsay Knight)*

Terry Lineen's first-class record:

For	Matches	Tries	Con	Points
Auckland (Marist) 1955(13), 1956(13), 1957(12), 1958(8), 1959(11)	57	23	1	71
Auckland B 1954(3), 1955	4	2	–	6
Auckland XV 1955	1	–	–	0
Spartans Club 1955	1	1	–	3
New Zealand Juniors Trial 1957	1	1	–	3
New Zealand Juniors (Under 23) 1958	9	10	–	30
North Island 1955, 1958, 1959	3	1	–	3
New Zealand Trials 1957(2), 1958, 1959(2), 1960	6	3	–	9
White XV 1957	1	2	1	8
New Zealand XV 1958	1	-	–	0
NEW ZEALAND 1957(10), 1958(3), 1959(4), 1960(18)	35	16	–	48
TOTALS	**119**	**59**	**2**	**181**

At Auckland, 17 February 2020, aged 84.

Michael John McCool *(Hawke's Bay and Wairarapa Bush)* was an experienced lock in his eighth season of representative rugby when the national selectors took an interest in him in 1979. The selectors ventured to Masterton to watch Wairarapa Bush play Wellington and were impressed with the lineout work of the 27-year-old who outshone his opponent, All Black John Fleming. His performance earned him his first national trial during which he marked Frank Oliver and stood his ground against the All Black. Haden and Oliver were chosen for the two tests against France, but Oliver became injured and could not make the trip to Australia for the one-off test. McCool was selected and partnered Fleming in the warm-up game against Queensland B at Brisbane. McCool was then chosen ahead of Fleming to partner Haden in the test at Sydney. The All Blacks lost 12–6 and with it the Bledisloe Cup.

McCool became a casualty of the loss. All Blacks who played in the tests against France were ineligible for the two 'tests' against Argentina who arrived in the country. With Haden and Oliver out of consideration, McCool was a likely choice, but the selectors chose Vance Stewart to partner Fleming and the Wairarapa farmer was never again given a trial.

Born at Hastings and educated at Kereru School and St Patrick's College, Silverstream, Mike McCool entered the Hawke's Bay team as a 20-year-old in 1972 and became a regular lock through until 1978, appearing in 76 games. Apart from being a member of the NZ Juniors team in 1974, he was not considered for higher honours, being regarded as a solid and reliable lock who gave his best in every game. At 1.93 m and 108 kg he was respected for his excellent skills in winning lineout ball and also his strength in scrums.

McCool moved south to farm in the rugged and remote Puketoi district, east of Pahiatua. He played for the local United club, based at Pongaroa, the club being in the diminishing Puketoi sub-union. Although not playing in the Wairarapa Bush senior club competition, McCool was chosen for Wairarapa Bush's first representative game, against Wellington. Knowing the national selectors were attending, he wanted to impress and chose to drive down to Masterton the day before the game so that he could be fully rested and prepared for the game. His decision paid off as he gave an outstanding lineout performance, the selectors took note and, two months later, he was an All Black.

Wairarapa Bush had a disappointing season in 1979. The second division side, apart from the early-season 16–16 draw with Wellington, won only one championship game. The *Almanack* commented on McCool's season: 'after playing a dominant role in the earlier games he faded later'.

McCool played a further four seasons for Wairarapa Bush, finishing in 1983 after 50 games. New coach Brian Lochore took charge in 1980 and guided the union to win the second division in 1981 and a return to the first division for 1982. Lane Penn commenced his four years' tenure as coach in 1983, McCool's final year. McCool had played a prominent role in lifting the small union to first-division status, a position Wairarapa Bush was able to hold until the end of 1987 when relegated back down.

Mike McCool later moved to Auckland and died suddenly while working on one of the many lifestyle blocks he was maintaining.

Mike McCool's first-class record:

For	Matches	Tries	Points
Hawke's Bay (Hastings Celtic) 1972(13), 1973(12), 1974(14), 1975, 1986(8), 1977(14), 1978(14)	76	–	0
Wairarapa Bush (Pongaroa United) 1979(11), 1980(12), 1981(13), 1982(4), 1983(10)	50	1	4
Saracens Club 1978	1	–	0
BJ Lochore's Invitation XV 1981	1	–	0
New Zealand Marist 1976	1	–	0
New Zealand Juniors (Under 23) 1974	6	–	0
New Zealand Trial 1979	1	–	0
NEW ZEALAND 1979	2	–	0
TOTALS	**138**	**1**	**4**

At Auckland, 23 June 2020, aged 68.

Bruce Eric McPhail *(Mid Canterbury, Canterbury and Nelson)* played on the wing in two tests against the 1959 British Isles, both being as a late replacement. During training in Dunedin in preparation for the first test, Tuppy Diack was forced to withdraw and McPhail was rushed into the team. Two months later, when the team assembled in Auckland for the fourth test, Frank McMullen withdrew and McPhail, in Palmerston North attending a course at Massey Agricultural College, was summoned north to replace McMullen. In both tests McPhail was given very few opportunities to exhibit his speed while his defence was tested and exposed, the Lions very classy outside backs dominating. At Auckland, neither McPhail nor his fellow-wing Ralph Caulton received the ball through the backline, one match review saying the pair 'could both have joined the spectators without anyone being the wiser'. While the All Blacks won the first test 18–17, thanks to Don Clarke's six penalty goals, the Lions were deserving winners at Eden Park 9–6.

Born and educated in Ashburton, Bruce McPhail entered first-class rugby as a 19-year-old for Mid Canterbury in 1956. Moving to Canterbury the next year, he gained selection for South Island in 1958, but it was the 1959 season in which he attracted much attention, scoring three tries in each of two trial games. South Island selection followed and, five weeks later, he was called into the All Blacks at Dunedin.

McPhail was at Lancaster Park on the day of the third test, appearing for Canterbury against

NZ Services in the curtain-raiser, and the wing scored a record seven tries in the game. In Canterbury's next game he scored a further four against Buller. McPhail finished the 1959 season as the highest try-scorer in the country with 20 tries from his 13 games.

A work transfer to Nelson in 1960 saw his opportunities restricted in a team which had few successes. Although he played two further games for South Island and appeared in national trials, he was never again considered for the All Blacks. When the 1961 a French team visited Nelson, McPhail scored both tries for the combined team in the 29-11 loss. In 1962 Nelson enjoyed a better year with six wins from 10 games and McPhail being the country's top try-scorer with 14, which included two in the South Island trial. In the season opener he scored five tries against Golden Bay-Motueka, then another four tries against the same team late in the season. The *Almanack* commented: 'McPhail was in outstanding form on the wing and gained 12 tries for his Union; some of them brilliant efforts.'

It appeared McPhail enjoyed playing against Golden Bay-Motueka, as in the seven times the two unions met 1961-62-63 he scored on each occasion and totalled 15 tries.

Having retired, Bruce McPhail turned to coaching lower grade teams of his Nelson College Old Boys club during 1964-65 and in 1966 was assistant coach to Ron Horsley of the Nelson rep team. Returning to his home town, he was a referee in Mid Canterbury 1972-76. He was an enthusiast of veteran athletics and took part in several World Masters Games during the 1980s and 90s.

A son, Graham, was also a successful athletic sprinter and represented both Mid Canterbury and West Coast at rugby.

Bruce McPhail's first-class record:

For	Matches	Tries	Con	Points
Mid Canterbury (HSOB) 1956	6	1	–	3
Canterbury (Christchurch) 1957(5), 1958(11), 1959(8)	24	23	–	69
Nelson (Nelson College OB) 1960(8), 1961(7), 1962(10), 1963(10)	35	27	4	89
Marlborough, Nelson, Golden Bay-Motueka 1961	1	2	–	6
South Island 1958, 1959, 1960, 1961	4	1	–	3
New Zealand Trials 1958, 1959(2), 1960(2), 1961(2), 1962	8	12	–	36
Rest of New Zealand 1960	1	–	–	0
NEW ZEALAND 1959	2	–	–	0
TOTALS	***81***	***66***	***4***	***206***

At Hamilton, 21 July 2020, aged 83.

Alistair John Soper *(Southland)* was among the many fine loose forwards produced over many years from Southland. A No. 8 in the old corner-flagging style, he came into Southland sides just as two All Blacks from the 1950s, Bill McCaw and Eddie Robinson, were ending their careers. In turn, in maintaining the standard, Soper, always known by the nickname 'Ack', preceded others from the province who became All Blacks in Kenny Stewart, Leicester Rutledge and Paul Henderson.

He also had a special place in New Zealand rugby history as captain of the first national age-group side, the JJ Stewart-coached under 21s which he led on a tour of Ceylon (now Sri Lanka) in 1955. He was chosen for the captaincy ahead of two players who would become legends, Wilson Whineray and Colin Meads. Soper, by contrast, achieved a little less fame, for despite a long and notable career he was an All Black only on the 1957 tour of Australia when he was still not quite 21. He appeared in eight of the matches, but in neither of the test matches, and so remained forever in the ranks of uncapped All Blacks.

Soper made the second of his tours as an age-group player when he was one of 14 players who were or were to become All Blacks in the under-23 junior side which toured Japan in early 1958. Whineray and Meads were both in this side too, only on this occasion Whineray, rather than Soper, was captain.

Soper remained for the rest of his career on the fringes of national selection, making the third of his South Island appearances in 1959 and playing the last of his nine All Black trials in 1965. But a recall to All Blacks status eluded him. Instead, he had to be content with a worthy record with Southland, for which he had first played as an 18-year-old in 1954, only a year or so out of Waitaki Boys High School.

When he retired after the 1966 season, he had become a Southland centurion and had shared in some of the province's most celebrated triumphs, including wins over the 1958 Wallabies and 1966 British and Irish Lions and in the 1959 Ranfurly Shield victory over Taranaki.

Soper came from a prominent rugby family, especially in rural Southland. His father, Clarrie, was a Southland representative in the 1930s and like his son was in a winning Ranfurly Shield side. And both were presidents of the Southland union, Clarrie in 1975 and Alistair in 1985.
(Contributed by Lindsay Knight)

'Ack' Soper's first-class record:

For	Matches	Tries	Con	PG	Points
Southland (Country Pirates) 1954(2), 1955, 1956(7), 1957(10), 1958(9), 1959(13), 1961(11), 1962(10), 1963(11), 1964(9), 1965(14), 1966(6)	103	17	1	1	56
Centurions Club 1958	1	–	–	–	0
South Island Colts 1955	1	–	–	–	0
New Zealand Colts 1955	7	2	–	–	6
New Zealand Juniors Trial 1957	1	2	–	–	6
New Zealand Juniors 1958	8	3	–	–	9
South Island 1956, 1957, 1959	3	–	–	–	0
New Zealand Trials 1956, 1957(2), 1958, 1959(2), 1960, 1963, 1965	9	1	–	–	3
Black XV 1957	1	–	–	–	0
New Zealand XV 1956	1	1	–	–	3
NEW ZEALAND 1957	8	1	–	–	3
TOTALS	**143**	**27**	**1**	**1**	**86**

At Invercargill, 16 June 2020, aged 83.

Alan Richard Sutherland *(Marlborough)* was a leading loose-tight forward, mainly as a No. 8, in New Zealand rugby for the best part of a decade in the 1960s and 70s. He became a worthy All Black, playing in 64 games between 1968 and 1976, and might well have been acclaimed among the greats, but for injuries and for a time being out of favour for reasons not entirely related to ability. Of his 64 All Blacks appearances only 10 were in tests. He also competed for a regular All Blacks position in an era when there was an abundance of accomplished players of his type. His early career coincided with Brian Lochore in his prime and among his contemporaries were Ian Kirkpatrick, Alex Wyllie and Tom Lister.

Sutherland was only 18 when he first played representative rugby for Marlborough in 1962, following his elder brother Ramon, into the side. The brothers were of a similar physique at around 1.90 m and 100 kg and with a raw-boned ruggedness derived from a tough working life as farming contractors and summers spent rowing. While Alan became an All Black, Ray received little national recognition. But he, too, achieved iconic status with Marlborough, playing a record 177 games for the union, many as captain, including the celebrated wins over the 1968 French touring team and the 1973 Ranfurly Shield win over Canterbury.

Alan also became a Marlborough centurion and featured in those historic wins and with Lochore, from Wairarapa, and the Meads brothers, from King Country, offered a reminder that once great players could become All Blacks directly from smaller unions.

Sutherland had a flair for scoring tries and remains with Kel Tremain, Kirkpatrick and Zinzan Brooke as the only New Zealand forwards to have more than 100 first-class tries. In 1966 he scored 12 tries in representative matches and that season played in the national under-23 side against the touring Lions. He was in the South Island side for the first time in 1967 and an All Blacks trialist, narrowly missing selection for the tour of Britain and France.

However, he was chosen the following year for the tour of Australia, and while impressing failed to win a test spot and, indeed, played many of his matches as a lock. In Australia he revealed another talent as a goal-kicker and in one match he scored 27 points, 21 of them from his boot.

Sutherland finally was capped in two tests in South Africa in 1970, but again as a lock and not in his preferred No. 8 position. With Lochore retired, Sutherland appeared to have his chance to become the established All Blacks No. 8, but after playing in the first test against the 1971 Lions he suffered a broken leg.

He enjoyed his only prolonged All Blacks tenure in 1972, making that year's internal tour, all three tests against Australia, scoring a try in each, and appearing in four of the five internationals on the 1972–73 tour of Britain and France. But when JJ Stewart became All Black coach in 1973 it seemed his international days were over and it was not until the 1976 tour of South Africa, following a fine display in the 1975 inter-island match, that he was recalled. On his second tour of South Africa, he failed to displace the captain Andy Leslie as the test No. 8 and was affected by a knee injury. His one consolation was to captain the tourists in five of the midweek matches.

Sutherland played in an era when little attention was paid to sevens rugby. But he was a fine sevens player, leading Marlborough to considerable provincial success and representing New Zealand at the 1973 Melrose tournament. Sutherland returned to southern Africa in the late 1970s, coaching and playing in what is now Zimbabwe and then in Natal. He married a former Miss South Africa and became a successful breeder of thoroughbred horses. *(Contributed by Lindsay Knight)*

Alan Sutherland's first-class record:

For	Matches	Tries	Con	PG	Points
Marlborough (Awatere) 1962(7), 1964(7) (Opawa) 1965(10), 1966(11), 1967(11), 1968(7), 1969(4), 1970(3), 1971(2), 1972(9), 1973(14), 1974(7), 1975(13), 1976(4)	109	60	3	5	225
Marlborough, Nelson, Golden Bay-Motueka 1965(2), 1966(2)	4	2	–	–	6
Marlborough-Nelson Bays 1971	1	1	–	–	3
Centurions Club 1970, 1972	2	3	–	–	11
I.A. Kirkpatrick's XV 1973	1	–	–	–	0
Evergreens Club 1974	1	–	–	–	0
Wasps Club 1974, 1975	2	1	–	–	4

D.A. Hales Invitation XV 1976	1	–	–	–	0
President's Overseas XV (in Scotland) 1973	2	1	3	–	10
World XV (in South Africa) 1977	3	1	–	–	4
New Zealand Juniors 1966	2	–	–	–	0
South Island 1967, 1968, 1972, 1973, 1975	5	–	–	–	0
New Zealand Trials 1965, 1966, 1967(2), 1968, 1969, 1970(2), 1971(2), 1972, 1973, 1974, 1976	14	2	–	–	7
NEW ZEALAND 1968(8), 1970(15), 1971, 1972(29), 1976(11)	64	32	16	3	155
TOTALS	**211**	**103**	**22**	**8**	**425**

At Mooi River, KwaZulu-Natal, 4 May 2020, aged 76.

John Maurice Tanner *(Otago and Auckland)* belonged to that group of mainly young backs who in the 1950s, while thrilled with their elevation to national ranks, must have regarded some of the then All Blacks selection processes as something of a lottery. Tanner's sporadic tenure in the All Blacks in 1950–54 was a typical example of the lack of consistency and planning in the selection policies of that time.

Tanner played 24 games in all for the All Blacks, but only once on New Zealand soil, his debut in the fourth test at Eden Park of the 1950 series against the touring British and Irish Lions. All of his other appearances came on the 1951 tour of Australia and the 1953–54 tour of Britain and France.

Tall and strongly built at 1.81 m and about 82 kg, Tanner was mainly a midfield back, either at centre or second five-eighths, but with his good turn of speed he was frequently placed, especially by Auckland, on the wing.

After schooling at Auckland Grammar, Tanner shifted to Dunedin to study dentistry and in 1947, when only 20 years old, he gained a place in the Otago representative side which had a vintage season defending the Ranfurly Shield. He played eight games, partnering Ron Elvidge in the midfield, including an epic win over his home province, Auckland. He also played that year for South in the inter-island match, but he had a disrupted 1948 season because of an injury in one of the early trials to pick the 1949 All Blacks team to tour South Africa.

In 1949 he began to practise dentistry back in his home city and it was as an Auckland representative that he received a surprise call-up to replace at second-five the injured Elvidge for the final test against the Lions. He also played for the North in the 1950 inter-island match, putting him in an elite group who have played for each island.

Tanner was a backline star along with Ron Jarden on the 1951 New Zealand Universities tour of Australia and soon after both joined the All Blacks for their tour of that country. Tanner was made the vice-captain and led the All Blacks in two of the midweek games. He also was at centre, with Tom Lynch at second-five, for all three of the tests against the Wallabies, scoring a try in the final test.

But the presumption after the senior role he had enjoyed on the 1951 tour that this would lead to a lengthy run in international rugby did not eventuate. He was overlooked for both 1952 tests against the Wallabies and for other national selections.

He was recalled for the 1953–54 tour of Britain and France, but that was somewhat surprising as he had only appeared in one of the early trials. He played at centre in only the international against Wales but was sparingly used in subsequent matches, making only 14 appearances in all, several of which were on the wing.

Tanner continued playing for Auckland up until the 1957 season, making 58 appearances for the union, but by then he had slipped down the national pecking order. There was, however, one more personal triumph awaiting Tanner. Despite being 29 and having long since graduated from Otago University, he played in the NZ Universities side which in 1956 beat the touring Springboks, scoring a crucial late try from a spectacular interception.

Tanner's elder brother, Murray, played as fullback for Auckland B and NZU. *(Contributed by Lindsay Knight)*

John Tanner's first-class record:

For	Matches	Tries	DG	Points
Otago (University) 1947	8	4	–	12
Auckland (University) 1949(7), 1950(6), 1951(5), 1952(13), 1953(4), 1954(10), 1955(8), 1956(4), 1957	58	15	1	48
Auckland B 1949, 1951	2	1	–	3
Auckland XV 1955	1	–	–	0
Olympians Club 1951	1	2	–	6
Barbarians Club 1954, 1955	2	1	–	3
Spartans Club 1954, 1955	2	1	–	3
South Island Universities 1947, 1948	2	1	–	3
North Island Universities 1950, 1953, 1956	3	2	–	6
New Zealand Universities 1948, 1949(3), 1950, 1951(2), 1953, 1954, 1956(3)	12	6	–	18
South Island 1947	1	–	–	0
North Island 1950	1	–	–	0
New Zealand Trials 1948, 1953	2	–	–	0
New Zealand XV 1954	1	–	–	0
NEW ZEALAND 1950, 1951(9), 1953(14)	24	11	–	33
TOTALS	*120*	*44*	*1*	*135*

At Auckland, 5 October 2020, aged 93.

Lindsay James Townsend *(Otago and North Auckland)* was one of the many fine halfbacks who in the 1950s enjoyed only sporadic international careers because of the inconsistent national selection policies which applied for most of the decade. Townsend was only 21 when he played in the first and third tests of the 1955 series against the touring Wallabies, having been earmarked from the 1954 season as an exceptional prospect.

Townsend first played for Otago in 1953, aged 19, and the following year made a big impact. He impressed so much for South Island in the inter-island match that he was chosen for the Rest which in 1954 played a special match against the 1953–54 All Blacks touring team and then for the New Zealand XV against NZ Maori. He duly gained his test caps for the Australian series, making his debut in the 16–8 win in the first test at Athletic Park and after making way for Keith Davis for the second test at Carisbrook returned for the final test at Eden Park. But he and his inside back partner, Canterbury's John Hotop, failed to combine and an unhappy All Blacks side lost 8–3. Townsend and Hotop were among the scapegoats, neither playing for the All Blacks again.

In Townsend's case, in view of the promise he had shown especially in 1954 and his youth, it seemed rather a waste. He did appear in the inter-island match of 1956 and in trials but was overlooked for the test series against the Springboks. He reappeared in only preliminary trials in each of the 1957-58-59 seasons and was never again a serious All Blacks contender, even though for first Otago and then North Auckland he was regularly among the country's best provincial performers.

Townsend played the last of his 35 games for Otago in 1957, then from 1958 to 1963 played 45 games for North Auckland, including its wins over the 1958 Wallabies and the 1961 French tourists.

Both as a player and coach he was involved in several Ranfurly Shield triumphs and dramas. He was Otago's halfback in the celebrated 9-all draw with Canterbury in 1954, then played in Otago's 1957 win over Wellington. In 1960 he missed North Auckland's shield win over Auckland because of injury but recovered for the return shield match which Auckland won. In 1976-79 he was North Auckland's selector coach and was in charge of the side which beat Manawatu for the shield in 1978 and then for its 1979 defences.

This shield reign, however, was marred by controversy when North Auckland in 1978 refused challenges, ironically for Townsend, from two unions with whom he had close ties, Otago and Southland.

His father, Lyall, played for both those unions in the 1920s and two cousins, Graham and Warren Townsend, played for Southland and Otago respectively, as well as the South Island. One of his daughters, Fleur, was a nationally ranked squash player. *(Contributed by Lindsay Knight)*

Lindsay Townsend's first-class record:

For	Matches	Tries	DG	Points
Otago (University) 1953(7) (Southern) 1954(3), 1955(7), 1956(7), 1957(11)	35	2	–	6
North Auckland (Kamo) 1958(10), 1959(9), 1960(3), 1961(9), 1962(5), 1963(9)	45	7	1	24
South Island Universities 1953	1	–	–	0
South Island 1954, 1955, 1956	3	–	–	0
New Zealand Trials 1956, 1957, 1958, 1959	4	1	–	3
Rest of New Zealand 1954, 1955	2	1	–	3
New Zealand XV 1954, 1955	2	–	–	0
NEW ZEALAND 1955	2	–	–	0
TOTALS	**94**	**11**	**1**	**36**

At Whangarei, 2 June 2020, aged 86.

Dennis Young *(Canterbury)* was one of New Zealand's leading hookers over a long period in the 1950s and 60s and a graphic illustration of how much the role has changed in the modern era. Young was an old-school exponent of the hooking art. This did not require hookers throwing to lineouts, and rather than acting as a fourth loose forward hookers in Young's era were more involved with the tight. And their primary asset was as swift strikers of scrum ball. Like one of his illustrious predecessors from the 1940s, Has Catley, Young excelled in this aspect of the game.

Like some, but not all, of his hooker contemporaries Young was not a big man. He was no more than 1.73 m, but had a nuggety, square build which enabled him to withstand any disruptive attempts from bigger front-row players. Though never as accomplished in the open as one of his main rivals for an All Blacks position, Waikato's Ron Hemi, Young did have a measure of athleticism derived from his youthful interest in tap dancing and a background in field athletics.

Young was only 18 when he made his first-class debut for a Canterbury XV and it was two years later when he began his 14-season tenure in the Canterbury representative side. When he finished after the 1963 season he had played 137 games for the union, including notable triumphs like successful Ranfurly Shield challenges in 1950 and 1953 and wins over the 1956 Springboks and 1959 Lions.

He made the first of his inter-island appearances in 1951 and was in the 1953 trials to pick the All Blacks team to tour Britain and France. But he did take some time to establish himself at national level and it was not until he was in his seventh representative season that he made his All Blacks debut, replacing Hemi for the second test against the 1956 Springboks. Hemi returned for the final two tests and generally was the first choice for the next few seasons, though with Hemi unavailable Young did play all three tests against the 1958 touring Wallabies.

In 1960 Hemi and Young were both chosen for the tour of South Africa, but an early injury ruled Hemi out of all the tests and at the age of 30 Young finally became the All Blacks' first-choice hooker. He remained so for the next three seasons, having an especially fine tour of Britain and France in 1963–64 when as the team's oldest player he won the affectionate nickname of 'Dad'. He retired at the tour's end and with 22 tests was at that time the All Blacks' most-capped hooker, even if his tally seems insignificant compared to the numbers compiled by his successors in the professional era.

A bubbly personality, Young, without the aid of a 'ghost', wrote a column for the *Sunday Times* in the late 1960s to mid-70s. He played an active role in the Cantabrians and Canterbury Supporters clubs and was Canterbury union president in 2003–04. He was also an early supporter of Pacific Island rugby, and he acted as a mentor to the Tongan team which toured New Zealand in 1969.

A cabinetmaker by trade, Young became a high school woodwork teacher and then ran a successful Christchurch travel company. *(Contributed by Lindsay Knight)*

Dennis Young's first-class record:

For	Matches	Tries	Con	Points
Canterbury (Technical COB) 1950(19), 1951 (14), 1952(13), 1953(11), 1954(12), 1955(14), 1956(6), 1957(10), 1958(12), 1959(9) (TCOB-Shirley) 1960(2), 1961(7) (Shirley) 1962(10), 1963(7)	137	5	–	15
Canterbury XV 1948	1	–	–	0
Canterbury B 1961	1	–	–	0
Centurions Club 1961	1	–	–	0
Barbarians Club 1964	1	–	–	0
South Island Colts 1951	1	–	–	0
South Island 1951, 1955, 1956, 1957, 1958, 1959, 1961, 1962, 1963	9	1	–	3
New Zealand Trials 1951(2), 1953(2), 1956, 1957(2), 1958, 1959, 1960(3), 1961(2), 1962(2), 1963(4)	20	2	–	6
South Island XV 1956	1	–	–	0
White XV 1957	1	–	–	0
Rest of New Zealand 1956	1	–	–	0
New Zealand XV 1956	1	–	–	0
NEW ZEALAND 1956, 1957(8), 1958(3), 1960(17), 1961(3), 1962(7), 1963(22)	61	1	3	9
TOTALS	*236*	*9*	*3*	*33*

At Christchurch, 21 June 2020, aged 90.

PROVINCIAL REPRESENTATIVES

Desmond Walter Bergman *(West Coast)* made his debut in 1957 but did not establish a regular place as a prop until 1959. He played a total of 24 games including all 19 fixtures of the 1960 and 1961 seasons. At Rotorua, 21 February 2020, aged 81.

Moray Vivian Bevan *(Wellington and Hawke's Bay)* played a total of 97 first-class games 1952–61 with 27 being for Wellington A 1954–60 and 17 for Wellington XVs. In 1961 he played once for Hawke's Bay. A loose forward, he was a regular in NZ Maori teams from 1954 to 1960 playing 31 games, and included tours to Fiji (1954), Australia (1958) and captain to Tonga and Samoa (1960). At Wellington, 4 November 2020, aged 86.

Robert Maxwell 'Bob' Blakeman *(Thames Valley)* appeared in 26 games 1958–67 playing at lock. A son, Neil, made one appearance for the union in 1987. At Thames, 2 October 2020, aged 83.

Gavin Paul Booth *(Otago)* played 63 games for his union 1963–68, commencing at prop until moving to hooker in 1966, and represented South Island in 1967. At Dunedin, 30 December 2019, aged 80.

Butler Brown *(Tai Rawhiti)* was a 19-year-old hooker from Bay of Plenty when making his sole first-class appearance, for Tai Rawhiti in the 1957 Prince of Wales Cup fixture against Te Waipounamu at Gisborne. At Whakatane, 22 November 2019, aged 81.

Russell Peter Bayliss Burman *(Waikato)* scored one try during his nine games on the wing in 1979. At Pukeatua, 12 December 2020, aged 61.

John Lindsay Carter *(Auckland)* made one appearance for Auckland A, against Waikato in 1960, the halfback scoring a try. He also made four first-class appearances for Auckland B 1960, 66–67. In later years he served on the Auckland union management committee during 1980s/90s and was team manager for a period. Sons John and Mark also represented Auckland, Mark being an All Black. At Auckland, 20 April 2020, aged 81.

Cyril Henry Chamberlain *(Golden Bay-Motueka)* was a wing, appearing in 11 games 1961–62. At Hastings, 21 January 2020, aged 87.

Francis John 'Frank' Colthurst *(Auckland, Thames Valley and North Auckland)* enjoyed a career of 137 first-class games from 1959 until 1971 followed by one more appearance, off the bench, in 1976 when he was assistant coach for North Auckland. After 49 games for Auckland 1959–64 he moved to Thames Valley where he played a further 27 games 1965–67 and, finally, to North Auckland for 44 games 1968–71, with one final outing in 1976. For many years he was regarded as one of the best hookers in the country, with North Island honours in 1964 and 1965 and regular appearances in national trials, but he never gained All Blacks selection. He was considered a favourite for the 1963/64 tour to UK and to South Africa in 1970, but the nearest he got was as a reserve for the first test against 1965 Springboks. He later coached North Auckland 1980–82. At Whangarei, 10 March 2020, aged 81.

Barry Michael Delahunty *(Bay of Plenty)* was a flanker in three games during 1970. At Tauranga, 22 May 2020, aged 71.

Obituaries

Ian Lawrence Drummond *(Golden Bay-Motueka)* was a flanker making one appearance in 1959 and a second in 1962. At Nelson, 20 May 2020, aged 84.

Graham Neil 'Jock' Edwards *(Nelson Bays)* was one of four fullbacks used during 1975, playing in five games, one being as a replacement. He also kicked two conversions and four penalty goals. Better known as a popular cricketer, he represented Central Districts and played eight tests and six ODIs for New Zealand. At Nelson, 6 April 2020, aged 64.

Greg Ambrose Fraser *(West Coast)* was a lock in two games during 1986. At Wellington, 21 June 2020, aged 69.

Frank Alexander Geddes *(NZ Services)* served in the navy 1942–46 and played one game for NZ Services in 1943, against Public Schools Wanderers, at Sudbury in Suffolk, England. At Whangarei, 18 November 2020, aged 100.

Simon James Gibson *(Nelson)* played four games as a loose forward in 1965. At Auckland, 22 July 2020, aged 81.

Donald James Gordon *(Wanganui, Auckland, Thames Valley and Hawke's Bay)* played a total of 30 first-class games, firstly for Wanganui with two games in 1953 followed by a solitary appearance for Auckland the next year. Thirteen games for Thames Valley 1955–56 and 10 for Hawke's Bay 1959–60 rounded off his provincial career. He played as a loose forward. Gordon became a most successful breeder of thoroughbreds in Hawke's Bay. At Hastings, 2 December 2020, aged 87.

Maurice Patrick Greene *(Waikato)* made two appearances in 1953, firstly at five-eighth for Waikato B then, later in the season, one appearance for the A team as a wing. At Hamilton, 27 April 2020, aged 87.

Francis William 'Bill' Hale *(Counties)* was a forward in the first two games played by the new union, South Auckland Counties, in 1955. At Pukekohe, 22 February 2020, aged 90.

Kit Archer Halford *(Hawke's Bay B)* played five first-class games for Hawke's Bay B during 1966–68. Sons Greg and Simon later represented the union. At Hastings, 15 April 2020, aged 76.

Peter Ross Hall *(Auckland)* played 32 games, as a loose forward, during 1952–57. He also made eight appearances for Auckland B in games given first-class status. He was the Otahuhu club delegate on the Auckland union management committee 1965–95 and was given life membership of the union in 1995. At Auckland, 10 February 2020, aged 92.

David Mark Halligan *(Otago and Auckland)* was one of several players chosen for the All Blacks but who never played. Selected at fullback to play the first test against Scotland in 1981, Halligan was forced to withdraw with injury on the day before the test. In 1982 he was a reserve in three tests against Australia but never took the field. His career commenced when a law student in Dunedin in 1979, making his debut for Otago, and representing NZ Colts and NZ Universities. In 1980 and 1982 he was in the NZ Juniors team and represented South Island in 1981. After 43 games for Otago, he moved to Auckland in 1983; unfortunately a bout of glandular fever affected his form and he made only three appearances for Auckland. Halligan was a highly promising natural talent, either at fullback or first five-eighth, but frequent injuries and then illness resulted in him departing the first-class scene at the age of 23. He scored 398 points in his career of 72 games. At Mount Maunganui, 14 September 2020, aged 61.

Richard Andrew 'Dick' Hodges *(Manawatu)* was a loose forward in 17 games 1961–62 and was in the NZ Universities team which toured California and British Columbia early in 1962. On tour the Massey Agricultural College student was rested for only one of the 10 games. At Cambridge, 3 September 2020, aged 79.

Peter Noel Hope *(Wellington and Marlborough)* was a reserve hooker for Marlborough when a Wellington XV played at Blenheim on 4 June 1951. Wellington, having flown over Cook Strait in a DC-3 on the morning of the game, taking only two reserves due to the limited number of seats, had used both reserves and when a third player was forced to leave the field Hope was asked to assist and he duly went on to play against his own union. The next month Hope made his debut for Marlborough, again as a replacement, but it wasn't until 1954, with three appearances, that he was in the run-on fifteen. His fifth, and final, game was in 1959. He became a successful owner and trainer of standardbred horses. At Blenheim, 13 November 2020, aged 89.

Richard 'Dick' Hurn *(Manawatu and Wanganui)* played the first of his 23 games for Manawatu in 1951, the 20-year-old lock also appearing for North Island in a Colts inter-island game. He later moved to prop and represented Wanganui in 32 games 1956–59. At Palmerston North, 17 May 2020, aged 89.

David Johnston *(Otago)* played 34 games for his union 1956–60. A lock forward, he toured Japan with NZ Juniors in 1958. He served on Otago RU board 1984–2004, deputy chairman 1991–98. President NZRFU 1998. At Mosgiel, 6 September 2020, aged 85.

Richard Harold 'Dick' Jones *(Poverty Bay)* was a flanker appearing in 17 games 1955–59. At Gisborne, 25 May 2020, aged 89.

Robert Henry 'Bob' Jones *(Bush, Wanganui and Taranaki)* moved about with railways work commencing with one appearance for Bush when aged 18 followed by an appearance for Wanganui in 1953 and, lastly, six appearances on the wing for Taranaki in 1954. At Timaru, 11 November 2019, aged 87.

Trevor Stanley Jones *(Marlborough)* played three games in the forwards during 1957. At Te Kuiti, 12 March 2020, aged 86.

Basil Tuhaka 'Cappy' Kapua *(Bay of Plenty)* was a three-quarter, appearing in 19 games 1950–55. At Mount Maunganui, 30 June 2020, aged 92.

Henare Kingi 'Henry' Lardelli *(Poverty Bay)* played 17 games as a flanker 1957–62. At Gisborne, 3 May 2020, aged 85.

Arnold Lindsay *(Wellington)* was a flanker appearing in eight games 1948–49; he also made four first-class appearances for Wellington B. At Wellington, 13 May 2020, aged 92.

Mervyn James Little *(Golden Bay-Motueka and Nelson Bays)* was aged 16 when making his debut at centre for Golden Bay-Motueka in 1962. Moving into the forwards, he returned to the team in 1964 and played a further 11 games until 1968. Following his union's amalgamation, he played 13 games for Nelson Bays 1970–71. At Nelson, 9 June 2020, aged 74.

Obituaries

William John 'Bill' McAuley *(Otago)* was a three-quarter, playing 15 games 1958–59 and a further 15 during 1962–63. He scored 10 tries and received a national trial in 1959. At Dunedin, 6 September 2020, aged 81.

Alan John 'Scorch' McEnaney *(West Coast)* was the top try-scorer on the 1955 NZ Colts tour to Ceylon (now Sri Lanka) with seven tries in six games. However, the wing's career for his union was brief, one game in 1955, six the following year and one in 1957. He also played for the combined West Coast-Buller team in 1956 against NZ Maori and the Springboks. At Greymouth, 23 June 2020, aged 84.

William Archibald George 'Bill' McGavock *(Hawke's Bay)* played at five-eighth in the first of his union's two games of 1944. At Havelock North, 20 August 2020, aged 94.

Andrew John Mackie *(Taranaki)* was a regular lock in Taranaki teams 1955–63 including the Ranfurly Shield era of 1957–59. He played a total of 85 games. At New Plymouth, 19 May 2020, aged 88.

Alan Malcolm McLaren *(Manawatu and South Canterbury)* made 28 appearances for Manawatu 1970–73 before moving to Twizel where he played 72 games in succession for South Canterbury 1974–78. A second five-eighth, his 104 first-class games included appearances for Manawatu-Horowhenua against the 1971 British Lions and for Hanan Shield Unions against the 1977 Lions. At Nelson, 25 December 2020, aged 72.

Noel McQueen *(Manawatu)* was a loose forward, making two appearances in 1955 and a further one in 1959. At Palmerston North, 13 October 2020, aged 89.

John Hoani 'Big John' Manuel *(East Coast)* played 38 games 1961–68 as a loose forward or at lock. He was later president of his union 2006–09 and made a life member. In recent years he was seen at home games at Whakarua Park riding his white horse Tore with mane, tail and fetlocks painted in sky-blue colours. At Rangitukia, 29 June 2020, aged 78.

Henry Maurice Rangi Maxwell *(Poverty Bay and Counties)* was a solid prop playing a total of 135 first-class games. He first appeared for his home union Poverty Bay 1980–81 with 13 games before moving to Counties where he played 106 games 1982–93. National honours were gained with NZ Colts (1981), NZ Juniors (1982), NZ Maori (1986) and NZ Divisional (1993). At Gisborne, 10 May 2020, aged 59.

Wilfred Jack Moffat *(Manawatu)* played six games in 1956 as a loose forward. At Palmerston North, 25 November 2020, aged 90.

Robert Clement 'Bob' O'Dowda *(Taranaki)* played four games 1961–62 but didn't reappear until 1968 when he played 20 games through until 1970. He played either at five-eighth or fullback. His brother Barry, father Clement and grandfather Barney (All Black in 1901) also represented Taranaki. At New Plymouth, 29 October 2020, aged 79.

William Ross Parkes *(Otago)* was a dental student in Dunedin and was a flanker in four of Otago's games of 1957 and a further six appearances in 1961. He was later an orthodontist in Timaru. At Dunedin, 11 September 2020, aged 84.

Raymond Stanley Parr *(King Country)* and Colin Meads made their debuts for King Country together, against Counties in 1955. Within two weeks of their first-class debuts both were chosen for national teams, Parr for NZ Maori and Meads for NZ Colts. Playing either at prop or No. 8, Ray Parr was a member of the respected King Country forward pack during the Meads era, Parr retiring in 1966 when aged 36, having accumulated 62 appearances for the union. He was co-selector for Wanganui 1970–72. At Whanganui, 15 July 2020, aged 89.

Lelea 'Lea' Potaufa *(Taranaki)* made only one appearance, against Argentina in 1997, the wing celebrating with a try. At Helensville, 28 February 2020, aged 43.

Stephen Sapich *(Auckland)* was a forward, playing five games during 1962 and three the next year. At Auckland, 16 September 2020.

Gordon Harold Scholes *(Horowhenua)* played 42 games for his union 1952–59, the lock having brothers Mervyn and Trevor also appear for Horowhenua. Another brother, Ewen, represented Bay of Plenty. At Ohauiti, 30 September 2020, aged 88.

Ted Skipper *(Taranaki)* was a midfield back appearing in 17 games 1953–54. He also played for Tai Hauaru in 1954. At New Plymouth, 11 March 2020, aged 87.

Alan Henry Ayson 'Arnie' Smith *(Mid Canterbury)* had a distinguished career for his union, first as a wing then settling in at fullback. He became the first to play a century of games in succession for a first-class team. From 1957 through to 1967 he played 101 games without a break. He scored 598 points (a record which still stands) in his total of 109 games for Mid Canterbury. At Ashburton, 26 September 2020, aged 83.

Colin Rex Smith *(Taranaki)* made just one appearance, at fullback against Auckland, in 1956. At New Plymouth, 18 September 2020, aged 86.

Trevor Walter Smith *(Waikato)* was a five-eighth, playing 16 games for his union between 1954 and 1956. At Auckland, 30 September 2020, aged 88.

Nathan Lawrence Strongman *(Bay of Plenty)* was a Hamilton-based midfield back from Fraser Tech club loaned to Bay of Plenty, playing 40 games during the years 1997–98–99 and 2003. At Hamilton, 26 November 2020, aged 49.

Rewi Tereanuku 'Tere' Tapsell *(Bay of Plenty)* made one appearance, in 1958, against North Auckland. At Maketu, 24 February 2020, aged 87.

Peter Ambrose Teen *(West Coast)* played on the wing in 48 games 1972–79, scoring 20 tries. He was also in the combined West Coast-Buller side which met the British Isles in 1977. At Hokitika, 16 January 2020, aged 67. His brother Tim died three months later.

Timothy Patrick Teen *(West Coast)* played 16 games during 1967–68, 71–72, 74–75. During his later years he was joined by his brother Peter in five games. At Christchurch, 12 April 2020, aged 70. Peter had died three months earlier.

Henry David 'Harry' Tibble *(Bay of Plenty, Waikato, Marlborough and Horowhenua)* made brief appearances for four unions commencing with one for Bay of Plenty in 1953. Four games for Waikato during 1955, 10 games for Marlborough during 1957–58 and, finally, one appearance for Horowhenua in 1961. At Masterton, 3 April 2020, aged 88. His brother Tui died a few weeks earlier.

Tuherirangi 'Tui' Tibble *(Bay of Plenty)* made six appearances during 1956–57 and had a NZ Maori trial in 1958. At Ruatoria, 19 February 2020, aged 85. His brother Harry died a few weeks later.

William Haddon Vernon *(Auckland and Canterbury)* was a versatile back, appearing as a five-eighth or three-quarter in 27 games for Auckland 1949–53 and two games for Canterbury in 1955, also making first-class appearances for both unions' B teams. He played in All Blacks trials in 1951 and 1953. At Papakura, 12 May 2020, aged 89.

Warren David 'Oscar' Voss *(Wellington)* was a flanker who scored two tries in a first-class game for Wellington Colts in 1971, then making four first-class appearances for Wellington B during 1972–73. At Wellington, 24 August 2020, aged 72.

Craig William Walters *(Taranaki)* made only one appearance, in 1964 against Counties, playing at second five-eighth between All Blacks Ross Brown and Neil Wolfe. At Otaki, 25 December 2020, aged 75.

Philip Cecil Watson *(Golden Bay-Motueka)* was hooker in four games during 1954. At Lower Hutt, 18 March 2020, aged 88.

Parekura Billy-Louise Dinsdale Whareaorere *(Bay of Plenty Volcanix)* made three appearances, as a 17-year-old, for the Bay of Plenty women's team during 2016. She died suddenly at Te Araroa, 1 January 2020, aged 20.

Graham Trevor Wiig *(Hawke's Bay)* made his debut in 1968 but didn't break into the Ranfurly Shield side until late 1969 when he played in the successful defence against Taranaki and then the following week when the shield was lost to Canterbury. A prop forward, he played 69 games to the end of 1977. Missing the 1975–76 seasons, he returned for a further 12 games in 1977. A keen sailor, he was a national champion in the Flying Fifteen class in 1984. At Tauranga, 7/8 March 2020, aged 71.

Alfred Thomas Williams *(Wanganui)* played 13 games 1954–56, the wing scoring three tries. At Whanganui, 1 May 2020, aged 89.

FIRST-CLASS REFEREES

Murray Edgar Dombroski *(Taranaki)* controlled 37 games between 1973 and 1990, his final appointment being Taranaki v Fiji in 1990. At Inglewood, 22 May 2020, aged 78.

Peter Fahey Gaines *(Wellington)* in 1968 had his sole first-class appointment when he refereed Wellington B v Bush at Athletic Park. At New Plymouth, 26 November 2019, aged 86.

Peter Murray Hankins *(Wanganui)* had 22 appointments between 1969 and 1986, two being at the national sevens of 1979 and 1982. He was later a life member of Wanganui RRA. At Whanganui, 10 May 2020, aged 83.

Francis 'Frank' Hubbard *(Thames Valley)* controlled 17 first-class games 1959–71, only two not being Thames Valley home games. At Te Aroha, 28 March 2020, aged 90.

ADMINISTRATORS

Jim Blair was the former Scottish professional soccer player who became a major influence on the way New Zealand rugby players trained in the early 1980s, firstly with the Alex Wyllie-coached Canterbury teams and then the John Hart-coached Auckland teams. Blair, a physical education lecturer at the North Shore Training College, introduced grid-type exercises to training sessions and streamlined those sessions with his fitness programmes. He was associated with the 1987 All Blacks World Cup side and worked with other New Zealand sporting teams, including America's Cup yachting crews. At Gold Coast, Queensland, July 2020, aged 85.

Merlin Dale Shannon was a member of the NZRFU council from 1986 to 1995. He served on the Manawatu RU management committee 1965-66, 68-95 and was made a life member in 1989. He was union president 1996-99. During the period the national sevens tournaments were hosted by Manawatu, from 1982 to 1996, he was chairman of the organising committee. At Feilding, 30 October 2020, aged 89.

George Dreadon Simpkin was an innovative coach for Waikato representative sides 1976-84, taking his side to a Ranfurly Shield win over Auckland in 1980 and then holding it for much of 1981. Before taking Waikato, he had been a successful coach of Matamata College first XVs, producing several All Blacks. Because of injuries he played no first-class rugby, but at Whangarei Boys High he was a promising first five-eighths who played first XV rugby 1958-60. He had a season of senior club rugby in Canterbury for the Belfast club in 1965, kicking eight dropped goals in a season, which was then the record for a Canterbury club season. Simpkin, a physical education teacher, later coached overseas in Fiji, Hong Kong, China and Sri Lanka. At Matamata, 7 May 2020, aged 76. *(Contributed by Lindsay Knight)*

Edward James Tonks was an effective, pragmatic chairman of the old New Zealand union board in 1990-95 when the game was going through a challenging period as it moved towards professionalism from a strict interpretation of amateurism. The owner of a successful exporting company, Eddie Tonks combined considerable business expertise with a strong rugby background. A product of Wellington's Onslow club, he played as a midfield back in its senior side and then became involved in many executive roles before being made a life member. He served many years on the Wellington union management committee, as deputy chairman for more than a decade, and joined the NZRFU council in 1986. One of his early roles at national level was to ensure, along with other unpaid councillors and key provincial administrators, that after some initial difficulties the 1987 World Cup was a success. He succeeded Russ Thomas as chairman in 1990, joining two other Onslow club members, Cuth Hogg and Tom Morrison, in that role. His term as chairman was not without controversy, mainly over the All Blacks' coaching post with Tonks perceived as a supporter of John Hart ahead of Alex Wyllie and Laurie Mains. But despite these pressures as well as a demanding business and a busy life he always presented an affable image. Tonks made a surprise departure from the council in 1995, becoming a life member of the national union in 2004. At Wellington, 18 October 2020, aged 85. *(Contributed by Lindsay Knight)*

AMENDMENTS

to 2020 edition

Page 55	Individual Scoring. Vaa'i and Klein also scored one try each.
Page 75	May 17. Jaguares 28 Hurricanes 20.
Page 96	Crusaders v Hurricanes. Semi-final was played on June 29.
Page 153	v Buller. N. Hogan, not Morgan, was the referee.
Page 162	v Hawke's Bay. Add penalty goals to Malcolm and Black.
	v Counties Manukau. Delete penalty goal credited to Malcolm.
Page 179	Debreczeni's totals should be 2 tries, 21 con, 12 pg, 88 pts. Team totals 29t, 22con, 12pg, 225pts.
Page 181	v Tasman. Debreczeni 2pg, not 2 con.
Page 184	Opposition scoring totals should be 54* tries, 43con, 16pg
Page 185	v Nth Otago. Koroi should be 15, Nareki 11; v Bay of Plenty Sasagi 3, Seiuli 1; v Taranaki Morris-Lome 13, Tomkinson 12.
Page 186	v Thames Valley. Referee N. Webster, not Watson.
Page 209	v Auckland. Blackadder scored 2 tries. S. Havili did not score.
Page 212	Dan Pearce, not Peace.
Page 214	v Otago. Referee was N. Webster, not Watson.
Page 227	v East Coast. Tutauha was a sub, did not start.
Page 241	Yvette Corlett was made a Dame posthumously.
Page 243	Most consecutive losses. Taranaki should read 1993-94-96, not 1994-95-96.
Page 247	Debreczeni's scoring should be 4 tries, 34 con, 14 pg, 130 points.
Page 254	Bredin. Did not do Buller v East Coast. Replace with South Canterbury v North Otago, at Timaru.
Page 255	Doleman. Delete USA World Rugby Sevens at Las Vegas.
Page 256	Fraser. Delete Rebels v Bulls and Blues v Bulls
	Griffiths. Replace South Canterbury v North Otago with Buller v East Coast at Westport.
Page 257	Jackson. Add August 10 USA v Japan and Suva.
Page 260	Williams. Three games were omitted:
	July 20 — South Africa v Australia at Johannesburg
	August 31 — NZ Heartland v Samoa at Auckland
	September 7 — Australia v Samoa at Sydney
Page 336	v Wellington. Nelles scored two tries.
	v Waikato. S. Curtis scored two tries.
Page 345	v Tasman. Cottrell did not kick two penalties.
Page 365	v Tasman. Williams also scored a try.
Page 377	v Bay of Plenty. Score should read 32-29.
Page 383	M. Dalley did not referee FPC fixture Hawke's Bay v Taranaki

JOURNALISTS

Phillip Laurence Campbell was a prominent rugby reporter in the 1970s commencing as a journalist in Blenheim. He received a national journalism award in 1973 for his coverage for Wellington's *Dominion* of Marlborough's Ranfurly Shield win over Canterbury. He was on the staff of Tauranga-based *Rugby Review* 1978–79 and later a community journalist in Rotorua. In 2013 he received the Queen's Service Medal (QSM) for services to journalism and the community. At Hamilton, 25 March 2020, aged 72.

Paul Dobson *(South Africa)* was for many years a correspondent to *Rugby News* and played a prominent role in South African rugby as a referee, historian and journalist. A schoolteacher by profession, he was on the staff for 29 years of Cape Town's exclusive private school, Diocesan (Bishops) College. Among his publications was a biography on his close friend, Dr Danie Craven, and a comprehensive, authoritative history of South African rugby which was published in 1989. A long-time referee, he served a lengthy term as chairman of the Western Province Referees Society. His son, John, in 2020 was the Stormers Super Rugby coach. At Cape Town, 20 July 2020, aged 84.

Graeme William Jenkins was a journalist with NZPA from 1954 and covered several rugby tours including the 1958 NZ Under-23 team to Japan, 1956 Springboks, 1959 British Isles and tours to South Africa in 1960 and Britain in 1967. He also covered Olympic and Commonwealth Games events from 1952 to 1978. He was later editor and general manager of the NZ Press Association. At Waikanae, 27 May 2020, aged 91.